RETREAT FROM
RECONSTRUCTION

RETREAT FROM RECONSTRUCTION 1869–1879

WILLIAM GILLETTE

Louisiana State University Press

BATON ROUGE AND LONDON

Design: Dwight Agner
Typeface: VIP Aster
Composition: Graphic Composition, Inc.
Printing: Thomson-Shore, Inc.
Binding: John H. Dekker and Sons, Inc.

LIBRARY OF CONGRESS CATALOGING IN PUBLICATION DATA

Gillette, William.
    Retreat from Reconstruction, 1869–1879.

    Bibliography: p.
    Includes index.
    1. Reconstruction. 2. United States—Politics and
government—1865–1877. I. Title.
E668.G45   973.8'2   79–12450
ISBN 0–8071–0569–4

For Elisa

CONTENTS

PREFACE

ALTHOUGH historians have written a great deal about reconstruction, they have attempted surprisingly little intensive analysis of reconstruction politics during the 1870s. To be sure, in the last two decades a number of excellent studies have concentrated on Andrew Johnson's presidency, and others have dealt with various states during reconstruction. Few, however, are concerned exclusively with the administration of Ulysses S. Grant, and still fewer of these are of much worth. None at all concentrates on national reconstruction between 1869 and 1879. Of the larger works, only Allan Nevins' *Hamilton Fish* and William B. Hesseltine's *Ulysses S. Grant* are still valuable.[1] Both were published in the 1930s, when comparatively limited research resources were available; both place inordinate emphasis on motives of economic gain and give no interpretation of the racial dimension of politics; and, on certain matters, both take the southern view of reconstruction at face value. The two works are nevertheless comprehensive, surveying all domestic events and diplomatic developments during Grant's tenure. Understandably they cannot cover all the complex developments of reconstruction politics.

To fill the gap, I have undertaken a detailed assessment of national reconstruction during the 1870s. My hope is that with the benefit of a variety of historical sources and the assistance of modern photoduplication, I have succeeded in deepening the understanding of a crucial and controversial period in American history.

Retreat from Reconstruction treats the politics of reconstruction directly before, during, and directly after the administration of President Ulysses S. Grant. The purpose of the book is to analyze the nature of the reconstruction program and the reasons for its having ended. Working from frequently incomplete evidence, I have tried to trace how policy was made and by whom, as well as how it was administered, in order to explain the gap between what had been intended and proclaimed and what had in fact been accomplished or left undone.

This study is concerned primarily with the course of reconstruction as national policy, rather than with the individual southern states and their internal political fortunes. It does, however, interweave local and national developments in following the course of federal policy and the process of administration. It is not a study of the history of the Negro, of the Democratic or Republican parties, or of the abolitionists, although all are considered when relevant. Nor is it primarily concerned with nonpolitical developments, even though racial attitudes as well as social, economic, intellectual, and educational influences are treated as they bear on the politics of reconstruction. This study is not a history of public opinion, of Congress, or of the Supreme Court, though all are touched on at various points. *Retreat from Reconstruction* does assess presidential, and to a lesser extent, congressional purposes, policies, and performance in achieving reconstruction; the book also delineates the declining support for—and retreat from—postwar reform as shown by events in the South as well as by political developments in the North during the 1870s.

One must keep in mind that the fate of reconstruction was by no means decided by events in the South alone. No matter how important southern white recalcitrance and resistance happened to be, the national government's will and ability to carry out reconstruction depended ultimately on popular support and partisan interest in the North. The disintegration of reconstruction and the accompanying disillusionment went hand in hand. Moreover, the reconstruction effort was not confined to the southern states, for the elimination of legal caste and the enfranchisement of blacks were also undertaken in the northern states.

The retreat had several causes: the waning of popular support and the waxing of conservative sentiment; the increasing desire for reconciliation on the part of northerners despite terrorism and repression in the South; the gradual reduction of federal troops in the South, accompanied by the collapse of federal election enforcement; the resurgence of racism in political campaigning, which speeded up the displacement of Republican governments in the South by Democratic ones and helped bring about conservative victories in the North; the restriction on federal action imposed by judicial decision; and finally, the initiation of a conservative southern policy by design and by default in 1875. To coherently present the diverging strands of this story, it is organized into a series of interpretative essays on the following topics: popular reaction to black suffrage in the North between 1867 and 1870, federal election enforcement, the presidential election of 1872, President Grant's southern policy, the congressional elections of 1874, battles in 1875 over civil rights and disorder in the South, the presidential campaign and electoral dispute of 1876–1877, and President Rutherford B. Hayes's southern policy.

The question of the failure or the success of reconstruction has often provoked extreme judgments. The Bourbon school, notably historians William A. Dunning and James Ford Rhodes, whose point of view was predominant at the turn of the century, viewed reconstruction as a mistake—a misconceived enterprise that came to a swift and unlamented close.[2] Those historians magnified the flaws and closed their eyes to the solid achievements of reconstruction. More recently, however, the pendulum has swung in the other direction, so that some historians, in revising the earlier Dunning interpretation, have magnified the successes of reconstruction and have minimized its weaknesses and shortcomings. One reason for this unwarranted optimism is the fact that these historians have focused their attention primarily upon the birth and growth of reconstruction during the administration of Andrew Johnson, rather than on its development, decline, and demise during the administration of Ulysses S. Grant. They have thus emphasized the brief period of political victory and legislative success rather than the longer period of legislative fumbling, administrative failure, and popular retreat.

If reconstruction ever had a chance, it was during Grant's administration, when the Republicans controlled—in fact, not just in form—both the presidency and Congress for the first time during the postwar period. Therefore, only then were the combined powers of both the legislative and executive branches ready to be harnessed together; moreover, only then were both the validity and the legality of congressional reconstruction established and accepted. Since this opportunity for reconstruction came during the 1870s, those years, and not the earlier ones, provided the truer test of its potential and performance. Those were the shaping years, both for subsequent southern and national history and for the history of American race relations right down into the twentieth century.

As for the question of why reconstruction failed, some historians who have concentrated on the 1860s have argued that if the integration of the Negro into American life ever had a chance of success, it was subverted by President Andrew Johnson, who had delayed the experiment for so long that the golden moment passed. Such an observation perhaps misconstrues the aim of reconstruction, which was not racial integration in itself. It also identifies the success of reconstruction exclusively with the success of the radical faction and its measures. And although the ways and means of moderate Republicans often differed from those of the radicals, these moderates were also very much interested in the success of reconstruction. Such a point of view, in addition, oversimplifies the postwar political situation by placing all blame for obstructing congressional reconstruction on one man, Andrew Johnson, who was hardly its only obstacle; moreover, the view also assumes that southern whites played a passive role, which they seldom did. This outlook thus assumes a large degree of political freedom and flexibility in inaugurating sweeping reforms, which did not exist at the end of the war, for neither the means nor a consensus were then at hand; and this same observation can be made about the 1880s.

As a more general explanation for the failure of reconstruction, the absence of a strong, firm, and complete commitment is often given. But problems arise as to what the nature of that commitment was, what precise form it took, and who in fact made it. Indeed, it is not altogether fair to place the responsibility on the majority for the failure to carry a particular course of action undertaken only by a minority. Nor does the explanation cast light on precisely *how* and *why* reconstruction failed. And some historians now brush aside the failure of that commitment—whatever and whoever's it was—with the explanation that no electorate or party can sustain indefinitely an overriding commitment. This is frequently true, but the results of a particular course cannot be so readily waved away.

Yet another argument sometimes advanced to explain reconstruction's failure views it as inevitable and caused entirely by the existence of the unmitigated racism that dominated nineteenth-century America. Such a monolithic explanation is too simplistic, however, placing inordinate emphasis on feelings and beliefs rather than on actions and behavior. Attitude is not always expressed through action; both are capable of change in form and degree, so that such a deterministic and mechanistic view of racism not only obscures the shading and denies the variety and ambiguity of racist notions and norms, but belittles the complexities of the historical evidence. Clearly, if racism had in fact completely dominated the political actions of the national government, the Republican party, and the northerners, no effort to achieve racial progress could or would have been undertaken in the first place, nor would it have advanced in a limited way in certain spheres of public law and action. Despite deep-seated racism in both the South and the North, there was change. It was hardly the millennium, and it was followed by dark, bitter days; but at least reconstruction was undertaken and did battle for a time with the forces of racism and reaction.

What, then, *was* reconstruction? It was essentially a postwar political and constitutional settlement—the peace treaty ending the Civil War—the terms of which would define and consolidate the gains of the victor over the vanquished. Although support and strategies for a concrete plan for reconstruction varied, the goal remained constant—to lodge national political power permanently in the North within the national Republican party and to republicanize the South.

Regarding the primacy of political goals, some observers have pointed out that without social reconstruction of the South, any sort of reconstruction was destined to fail because economic and social power must precede political power in order to secure and preserve

xiii

it. Yet the immigrant experience suggests that the acquisition of political power afforded by the democratic process often can precede or parallel such progress by augmenting economic independence, social stability, and educational advancement. Although recognizing the limits of political power, one need not dismiss the political intent or potential out of hand. Also, it must be pointed out that the federal program to reconstruct the polity of the South and the nation was not intended to revolutionize either the southern society or its economy, for this was not favored by either the government or the vast majority of the people. Even if the blacks had become landowners, they would not have escaped the poverty and indebtedness that plagued the cotton economy nor would they have avoided the decline and disappearance of the family farm in the South. As historian David M. Potter observed in his *Division and the Stresses of Reunion*: "These evils caused hundreds of thousands of landowning farmers, both white and Negro, to lose their farms between 1880 and 1940 and to fall into a condition of tenancy and sharecropping. The trend was continuous throughout the South. There is no reason to suppose that the recipients of forty acres and a mule would have escaped this inexorable process."[3]

The need today is not to dwell upon what concerned the Dunningites, or to walk along the narrow, well-worn path to reunion, or to discover the blueprints for the ideal reconstruction, or to skirt its shortcomings. The need is rather to assess the purposes and policies of reconstruction as they were undertaken. What must be confronted and analyzed are the flaws and failures of reconstruction. A fascinating story of unsuspected paradox, unexplained defeat, and unexplored tragedy remains to be told.

The notes to this book constitute a guide to the variety of sources consulted, but for the sake of brevity, I have chosen merely a representative selection and have greatly compressed both primary and secondary accounts. Secondary works that have not proved useful in the writing of a particular passage are not cited in the notes but are frequently mentioned or assessed in the bibliographical essay.

RETREAT FROM
RECONSTRUCTION

1
REVEILLE FOR RECONSTRUCTION

1867–1870

APPOMATTOX signified much but settled little. The war had reduced the South to rubble and ashes, had destroyed the old regime and discredited its ways, but the martial triumph had succeeded only in preventing disunion. Defeat on the battlefield had also meant the death of slavery, but what would become of the freedmen who found themselves in a condition of uncertain emancipation? The war had decided vital matters with negative decisions: secession and slavery were closed questions but victory was posing new ones. How the North would impose a peace and maintain it, as well as how victor and vanquished would deal with each other in a reunified nation, were to vex that nation and plague its politics. Experiences in other countries might be repeated: the turmoil of the transition from civil war to domestic peace, and from slavery to freedom, could well bring further disorder and disorientation. The governance of the southern states and their place in a restored Union, the loyalty of the southern whites, and the status of the freedmen raised difficult questions.

The war had also shifted the balance of power between parties and among sections and interests. The Republican party ruled the nation; yet with the prospect that the southern states would eventually return to Congress and the possibility that the formerly dominant Democratic party might regroup its national conservative coalition, people were already wondering how long the Republicans could retain control of the Executive Mansion and Congress. Determining what policy ought to be applied to the South and whether

Congress or the president ought to apply that policy added to the political uncertainty. Central to political control was the question of suffrage: Who should vote? Only loyal whites? Only the loyal, both white and black? Or only whites, both loyal and disloyal? Since decisions as to the composition of the electorate could determine power and office, the establishment of and control over suffrage requirements became a leading issue.

Victory imposed new burdens and unanticipated responsibilities on the North, for some of the results of the Civil War had little to do with its origins. The war had, in fact, freed the slave, although that had not been its initial or central purpose. At the start, most northerners were opposed not to slavery as an institution but to its expansion westward; they had wished to contain, not to abolish, slavery. Some northerners opposed the class of slaveowners—the plantation oligarchy, which they regarded as having caused the war and as exercising an inordinate and injurious influence upon the South—and they also wanted to end southern Democratic hegemony in Washington. The North, then, had fought to save the Union, not to save souls, white or black. To be sure, the nationalist objective had its humanitarian rationale and, in its fervor, released idealistic energies, but the northern wartime sentiment, "God and Our Country," was patriotic, little more. President Abraham Lincoln, in his letter to New York *Tribune* editor Horace Greeley, had written in 1862: "My paramount object in this struggle *is* to save the Union, and is *not* either to save or to destroy slavery. If I could save the Union without freeing *any* slave I would do it, and if I could save it by freeing *all* slaves I would do it; and if I could save it by freeing some and leaving others alone I would also do that."[1] To achieve his goal, Lincoln, the flexible craftsman, used whatever means he believed would secure it. The purpose of the war would not extend a hair's breadth beyond preservation of the Union and maintenance of the government; there were to be no political, economic, or social changes beyond what the needs of war dictated.

But when the war went badly and wore on interminably, more was needed to win than had been intended or foreseen. It was the "terrible Educator *War*" that finally brought Lincoln and the North to regard emancipation as a war measure necessary to weaken the

Confederacy by fostering white demoralization and black defection and by depleting southern farms of their labor force, as well as to strengthen the Union by influencing European opinion and recruiting blacks into the Federal army. As *Harper's Weekly* observed, the "rebellion struck at the government to save slavery; the government abolished slavery to save the Union."[2]

When the war was over, its searing memory remained very much alive. Beneath the surface rhetoric of peace, magnanimity, and forbearance flowed a strong undercurrent of wartime emotions. Even during the long and bloody struggle General William T. Sherman had written as he marched through Georgia: "how mad, how senseless in the People of Carolina and Georgia to arouse the *Demon Spirit* 'War' in our Land."[3] Such a vengeful spirit did not quickly fade out with peace; the most powerful political force in the postwar decade throughout the North continued to be war-born hatred of rebellion and rebels, especially their leaders. The cold, implacable side of this hatred was rooted in the harsh realities of destruction and turmoil, the death of kin and comrades on the battlefield, the suffering and sacrifice of military duty or wartime imprisonment, and the shock of Lincoln's murder. Such hatred had a hysterical side as well, feeding on nightmarish fantasies of rebel resurgence and the return to slavery, Confederate purpose and determination unchanged. Fantasy generated overreaction: isolated incidents became widespread conspiracy, rumor became fact, suspicion was substituted for judgment. "Bourbon" or "conservative" replaced the wartime "Confederate" or "copperhead" as terms of opprobrium. The widespread conviction in the North was tacit but clear and compelling: the South deserved to be punished and needed to be reformed because it had mounted an unjustified rebellion, had started a devastating war, and was obliged to take the consequences. Thus the war would not be truly over until the rebels had ceased being rebellious. On the other hand, there was the determination to achieve freedom for the blacks and a confidence, forged by the war, in a triumphant nationalism that would convert past disloyalty into genuine reunion. Inevitably, all such negative and positive feelings in the North would affect any peace settlement for the reconstruction of the South and the reestablishment of the Union.

3

In the first steps toward the reconstitution of the nation, begun in 1865, President Andrew Johnson, a prewar southern Democrat but a wartime unionist from Tennessee, stubbornly and incautiously pursued his own appeasement policy of an extensive, premature pardoning of the rebels, entrusting the restoration of the southern states to conservative sympathizers and, during 1866, vetoing congressional plans for a peacetime Freedmen's Bureau as well as civil rights legislation. An infuriated Congress overrode his vetoes of both bills.[4] Under his presidential plan the former Confederate states would be quickly restored to the Union after they had legally abolished slavery and had repudiated their state war debts. By thus seeking restoration of the Union without reform and reconstruction, Johnson aroused the fury of much of the North, where many were understandably worried that the president, out of misplaced leniency, would resurrect the Old South and precipitate further head-on collisions with Congress.

Then, when the white southerners in late 1865 elected former Confederate leaders and officers to their state legislatures and to Congress, when these legislatures enacted vagrant laws and black codes which confined freedmen to virtual peonage by restriction of ownership, work, and movement, and which limited their rights in court and contract, and made them second-class citizens, when southern legislators defiantly refused to repeal legislation governing slavery and secession, when race riots resulted in the massacres of blacks in the South, most northerners saw such occurrences as a refusal to lower the Confederate flag. Many northern Republicans began to fear that with dissension in the North and disorder in the South the southern and northern Democrats would regain control of Congress, recapture the presidency, and then undermine the results of the war and kill the proposed reforms of the peace.

Galvanized into action by Johnson's abrasive style and alarming policy—which seemed to reward rebels and discredit loyalists and to make disaffection virtually respectable in the South—and faced with the clear-cut choice of restoration on his terms or its own, Congress asserted itself by framing the Fourteenth Amendment on June 16, 1866. The Fourteenth Amendment was an essentially moderate measure devised as a compromise between the two major Republican factions. In order to please the moderates, the former Confederates were spared disfranchisement; yet to soothe the radicals, the former rebels who previously had held federal office were disqualified from holding public office unless they received a congressional pardon. The moderates were satisfied because the Negroes were not enfranchised in the South, whereas the radicals were mollified by a representation provision, which allowed southerners to exclude Negroes from voting at the risk of losing seats in the House of Representatives. Either way, the Republicans would gain—by a reduction in the number of southern, presumably Democratic, congressmen, accompanied by a loss of presidential electoral votes, or by the addition of black, presumably Republican, voters. By mandating certain federal civil rights in the amendment, Congress negated the black codes enacted by southern state legislatures. Disqualifying former rebels would furthermore prevent their election to Congress. Thus the amendment dealt effectively with the pressing political questions of early reconstruction.

In the fall congressional elections of 1866 the pending amendment became the central campaign issue. During that canvass the Republicans were prudent, keeping many extreme radicals in the background. In contrast, President Johnson vigorously stumped in his own defense and in behalf of his own policy and of a new party that he proposed. His speechmaking tour during the election became a parade of blunders. Making one *faux pas* after another in his choice of both issues and words, he was heckled and lost his temper, with the result that his intended party came to nought.[5] He was thoroughly repudiated by the Republican landslide, and northerners' prevailing distrust of the South was confirmed. As a man from New Jersey summed it up: "the recent election proves that the 'my policy' of president Johnson is not supported by the people." Nonetheless, in his December message to Congress following the election, Johnson continued to insist that his proposals provided the only solution, prompting New Jersey Republican Senator Frederick T. Frelinghuysen to remark that the "President has not learned that the people have spoken."[6]

Congress thus wrested control over reconstruction policy from the executive branch. Then, when the southern legislatures still refused to ratify the Fourteenth Amendment, Congress decided that more stringent requirements were necessary and, entirely bypassing the presidential plan for reconstruction, enacted on March 2, 1867, the First Reconstruction Act, which largely superseded the still pending Fourteenth Amendment. This act imposed temporary army occupation in the South, partially restricted voting and officeholding to loyal unionists, opened voting to Negroes, and required ratification of the Fourteenth Amendment (which was secured on July 28, 1868). The result assured Republican majorities and regimes, for a while at least, through the proscription of some white Democrats and the enfranchisement of black Republicans.

That reconstruction took a different course from the one set by Johnsonian conservatives was due more to war-born sectional animosity and to anger over restoration gone awry than to reformist zeal for a radical reconstruction. It was an unexpected boon for both the congressional approach to reconstruction and Republican success; in the words of the New York *Herald*, it was "a windfall, a godsend. He [Johnson] gave them Johnson to fight instead of fighting among themselves." Once again, as during the war, it was essentially political necessity and expediency that redirected southern policy. The majority of northerners had not enthusiastically embraced emancipation before, nor did they embrace enfranchisement now, but they were convinced that southern black enfranchisement could prevent a conservative comeback and would keep the Republicans in power throughout the South and in Washington. The security of the nation and the safety of the Negro were thus linked with the survival and supremacy of the party. But it was the issue of union that would win votes, not that of Negro suffrage, for as New Yorker John Binny advised his fellow Republicans, the party "cannot carry the elections on the universal negro suffrage issue, as there is much prejudice still in the Northern States." This approach had been recommended earlier by radical Republican Henry Winter Davis, who had suggested that it was unwise for abolitionists to talk of justice and humanity to the Negro as if these were decisive considerations. It was a question not of justice "but of political dynamics. It is a question of power, not of right"—a question of self-preservation, not of morals.[7]

The northerners' well-grounded distrust of the southerners for a time simply outweighed their prejudice against blacks. Ill will in the North toward the Negro, which was widespread before the war, had not changed. Manifested in varying degrees by different groups, Negrophobia had been expressed brutally during the war, for slavery was sectional but racism was national. In July, 1863, the year of the proclamation of emancipation, whites in the New York City draft riots had smashed the heads of black babies against fire hydrants in a barbaric orgy. During the postwar years the northern antipathy toward the Negroes, which was clearly evidenced by many Democrats and to a lesser degree by many Republicans as well, remained much the same, though not on the same wartime scale of violence.

Despite northern racism, the Republican party recognized southern black suffrage as the only counterpoise to Democratic resurgence in the South. "Negro suffrage is the hinge of the whole Republican policy," declared the Democratic New York *World*; "it is what they most value in the Reconstruction laws; it is the vital breath of the party."[8] Yet the unpopularity of black suffrage hinted at a tenuous support for the entire program of reconstruction. Republican triumphs in late 1866 and early 1867 were to prove temporary. Almost immediately, there were unmistakable signs that northerners were disenchanted with blacks casting ballots, for by the fall of 1867 the first steps taken in congressional reconstruction were already causing political difficulties for the Republicans.

Nor did the imposition of Negro voting in the South by any means assure Negro enfranchisement in the North; indeed, the issue was almost always opposed in northern state referendums and generally evaded by northern Republicans. The partisan Democratic New York *World* asked: "How can you blame the South for hesitating when you hesitate? . . . the party is forcing on the South a measure too odious to be tolerated at home."[9] Despite the fact that the issue was volatile, Republican radicals wished to rectify the existing double standard and pushed to the fore their program of universal manhood suffrage on grounds of principle.

The test for northern support of Negro enfranchisement took place in the state election of Ohio, where radical Republicans were influential. Radicals hoped that a referendum to amend the state constitution in the fall of 1867 would decide the question in their favor and start a stampede toward black enfranchisement throughout the rest of the North. Many other Ohio Republicans, however, entered the campaign reluctantly and chose to sidestep the controversial question. The state Republican chairman observed privately that the party was "stuck" with it as an election issue. As outgoing Republican governor Jacob D. Cox confidentially described his platform strategy: "I keep clear of the suffrage question, except to say that *if* we are determined to adhere to our policy of forcing negro suffrage on the South, common consistency demands that we should not shrink from it in Ohio." One southern Ohioan was worried about strong local prejudice against conferring suffrage on the Negro, but he endorsed the measure because it was a matter of justice and he also wanted "to get the nigger out of politics if possible."[10]

During the Ohio canvass Republican Burke A. Hinsdale observed that "both sides are making their strongest appeal to prejudice—the one harping on the 'nigger' and the other harping on the 'copperhead.'" According to the former Democratic president, James Buchanan, the secret of Democratic success was "opposition to Negro suffrage in the South, as well as in the North. . . . Abandon this, and we are gone."[11] It became standard political fare for each party to pander to a particular phobia—Republicans to the distrust of the South and the danger of reaction, and Democrats to hatred of the black race and the danger of radicalism. For every wave of the "bloody shirt of rebellion" by Republicans, Democrats answered with a shriek of "white man's country." Each side avoided divisive issues: the Republicans tried to dodge northern Negrophobia, and the Democrats evaded talk about the war and its results. To politicians it was simply shrewd politicking to tap the emotional undercurrent and release pent-up anxieties, which might stir voters up enough to bring them to the polls.

In Ohio, as elsewhere, the much exploited issue plumbed the depths of northern racial antipathy. As the campaign progressed, it became evident that the suffrage issue was doing harm to the Republican campaign; and to make matters worse, the proposed state constitutional amendment angered many whites with a clause that would disfranchise whites who had been rebels, draft dodgers, or deserters during the war. Adding to Republican woes in the Ohio campaign, a month before the October election the party suffered a big loss in their bastion, Maine—a setback that hurt badly "in the pinch of our suffrage fight," according to the Republican gubernatorial candidate Rutherford B. Hayes.[12]

In the end, Ohio voters overwhelmingly rejected Negro suffrage. Indeed the opposition was so strong that it helped cause the Republican loss of both houses of the legislature and thus the federal senatorship. Only by a narrow margin did the Republicans retain the governorship.[13] Added to the Ohio setback were defeats in other states in which the issue of Negro suffrage had figured prominently (Pennsylvania, New York, and New Jersey). All factions recognized that a conservative reaction in the North had set in before reconstruction was barely underway. As the radical *Independent* observed: "Negro Suffrage, as a political issue, never before was put so squarely to certain portions of the Northern people as during the late campaigns. The result shows that the Negro is still an unpopular man. . . . in the estimation of nearly all the Democratic, and of nearly half the Republican party." Senator Frelinghuysen commented: "The people have said that they are not ready for colored suffrage."[14]

At the end of 1867 the Republicans' political future looked gloomy, and some radicals confessed that the defeat was a disaster. Clearly, they had gone too far too fast and had overreached the limits of northern sentiment: most northern whites simply refused to accept blacks as political equals. The moderate Republicans had allowed the radicals to take the lead in the fall elections by default, and the radicals, by making Negro suffrage the prominent party issue in the North, had appeared so extreme and doctrinaire that many northern voters were disturbed. To many moderate observers, the radicals had talked too much about suffrage rights and logical sequences to people who cared little about rights and did not know what a logical sequence was. Other critics claimed that the radicals displayed a foolhardy reliance upon goodness of principle to carry the day and, to their detriment, injected puritanism into politics by espousing a moral issue with crusading and uncompromising zeal. Moreover, the radicals' penchant for restricting nominations to those holding similar views and tailoring platforms to their own opinions did not help carry the moderate Republican vote. To Governor Cox and many

9

other disenchanted Republicans, defeat was certain unless Negro suffrage for the North was dropped.[15]

Democratic and conservative journalists even contended that 1867 marked the end of reconstruction. As the radical Republicans had liberally interpreted their victory against Andrew Johnson and for the Fourteenth Amendment in 1866 as an advance endorsement of the First Reconstruction Act, the Democrats read the defeat of Negro suffrage in the North in 1867 as a repudiation of southern reconstruction and demanded that the reconstruction acts be repealed. The New York *Herald* considered the revolution of 1866 to have been ended by the counterrevolution of 1867 and concluded that already the "republican element of the country [was] tired and disgusted with the radical programme" because the prospect of "Southern negro political supremacy and . . . a negro balance of power in our national affairs, have startled the public mind of the North."[16]

Moderate Republicans also counseled retreat from the advanced positions of reconstruction. The New York *Times*, for example, argued that the Republicans in Congress had committed the party to a principle that Republican voters did not hold and suggested that qualified Negro suffrage for the South, with property and education restrictions, be substituted for unrestricted Negro suffrage. In the newspaper's opinion, "too much relative importance, in national legislation, has been given to the negro," and the defeats were a warning to Republicans to be "wiser, more discreet, less arbitrary and extreme in their measures, less arrogant and overbearing in their tone. If the lesson is heeded all these mistakes can be corrected—all these losses can be retrieved." The *Nation* characterized 1867 as a "year of disenchantment" in which a number of illusions were shattered by the election returns. It was critical of the congressmen who pursued their own wishes regardless of public sentiment. To "reconstruct in the right way," the journal advised, and to secure support required more patience, persuasion, and moderation. The radicals stuck by their guns, repeating that the Republican party could not betray blacks, must stand fast by its allies, and ought not compromise its principles.[17]

The popular current against their party convinced many Republican moderates that the party must drop the Negro—at least temporarily—to save itself, which meant postponing manhood suffrage for blacks in the North. New Yorker John Binny wrote that the greatest danger to reconstruction was premature action. He advised the congressional party to "carry the majority of the loyal people of the North along with you in your measures of reconstruction; otherwise you will make the cone rest on its apex instead of on its base."[18] Moreover, the people and the politicians wanted a leader and, above all, a winner; as a Philadelphian pungently remarked: "Great Victories are preferred to long speeches and long letters."[19] And one Ohioan advised that Congress must be " 'wise as serpents' as well as 'harmless as doves' or the de'ill will be to pay."[20]

Ignoring moderate calls for circumspection, however, the radicals pushed for the impeachment of President Johnson during the spring of 1868 despite the waning popular fervor against him and despite the fact that he was by now merely serving out the remaining year of his term in political isolation. If impeachment should succeed, Johnson would automatically be replaced in the presidential succession by the Senate president pro tempore, Benjamin F. Wade, an extreme radical Republican and, indeed to some, a wild, reckless man.

Why the radical leaders went ahead with impeachment when the popular tide of anti-Johnson feeling had already ebbed, when the legal foundation for their action was shaky, when the chances of victory seemed uncertain, and when the consequences of failure would be grim, remains something of a mystery. Perhaps they wanted, as a party measure, control over presidential patronage. Possibly the radical faction wanted greater influence within the Republican party, in order to dictate nominations and the platform. Clearly, the radicals wished to gain complete control of reconstruction policy by preventing Johnson from frustrating the congressional reconstruction program and by wresting from him authority over the army, which was governing the military districts of the South. Perhaps, too, passions were responsible: some congressmen simply wanted revenge for Johnson's numerous provocations, whereas others needed release from the severe frustration of their chronic conflict with him and the executive branch. Or it may be that political desperation was the motive—fear that the 1867 fall electoral reverses in the North might

11

be repeated in 1868. And this, combined with the likelihood of the Democrats' success in disfranchising blacks and thus stealing the election in the South, might result in the Republicans' loss of their two-thirds majority or even their control of Congress or the presidency. Some radical Republicans may have been convinced, therefore, that they had to take advantage of their present opportunity to seize power and to impose their reconstruction regimen.

In any event, Johnson had strong conservative and significant bipartisan support at the bar and in the Senate jury, and he cleverly delayed the proceedings and allowed congressional reconstruction to proceed. The attempt to convict Johnson fizzled by May. Impeachment, a reckless gamble, had further decreased the radicals' waning influence and compounded the existing hostility toward them. Scorning political limits, constitutional bounds, and moderate public opinion, the radicals had undercut their influence.

After the widely criticized impeachment, however, the Republicans were fortunate in that presidential politics took the spotlight. The nomination of General Ulysses S. Grant, with his popular appeal as a war hero and his apolitical background, proved irresistible and turned out to be unanimous, and the popular Speaker of the House of Representatives, Schuyler Colfax, received second place on the ticket. Grant's letter of acceptance struck the keynote of the campaign: "Let us have peace." "It was spoken in a way and came from a source which gave it peculiar strength and significance," wrote Maine Republican James G. Blaine, for Grant had expressed the fondest hopes of the American people.[21] Indeed, many believed that he had condensed his political program into a single sentence. Peace, prosperity, and progress became the Republican campaign themes.

Grant was born in 1822 in an Ohio village located on the Ohio River, right on the border between the free North and the slaveholding South. His youth had revealed no traces of extraordinary talents. Although an undistinguished graduate of West Point, he had displayed bravery in action during the Mexican War, but afterward, exiled to Pacific Coast outposts, he had become bored and lonely and resigned from the army in 1854. In the next six years he had failed in farming, collecting rents, and clerking in a customhouse. Finally, gaining security as a storekeeper in the family leather goods store at

Galena, in northwestern Illinois, he seemed a certified failure before having reached the age of forty. All this changed when the Civil War broke out. In the eight meteoric years to come, he was magically transformed from a clerk to a general to a war hero to a presidential candidate.

Although the party platform on which Grant ran was forthright in endorsing the congressional plan of reconstruction, the plank concerning Negro suffrage was equivocal, leaving it to the northern states to decide for themselves, while simultaneously endorsing black voting as necessary for the southern states. The New York *Herald* noted that the platform had several faces to suit the various visions of long-sighted, short-sighted, and double-sighted people. "Like an old campaigner," the newspaper declared, "the Convention moves with a bold step where the ground is firm, but treads cautiously and gingerly over the boggy places." The Republicans entered the campaign unburdened by what would have been a major liability in the North—endorsement of black suffrage there.[22]

Although the Democrats needed to turn the divisions and recent mistakes of the Republicans to their own advantage, they were still suffering from their self-inflicted wounds of the past: fratricide before the war, obstruction during the war, and resistance to its result. Stumbling over the inevitable and squabbling over the irrelevant, they made defeat a habit. The Republicans, who were still relying upon the Democrats to blunder, were not disappointed. Former rebel soldiers and statesmen were on conspicuous display at the Democratic convention in New York City. The unrepentant, states'-rightist, black-baiting speeches seemed more reminiscent of a southern conclave than of a political convention held in the North by a party intent on winning back war Democrats and recruiting conservative Republicans. The platform denounced the reconstruction acts as unconstitutional, revolutionary, and void and demanded immediate restoration of the southern states to civil government. It repudiated Negro supremacy and espoused white amnesty. But the suffrage plank merely endorsed exclusive state control over voting matters and ignored the question of Negro voting. Indeed, the only explicit Democratic pledge for future action was to reduce the size of the army and to abolish the Freedmen's Bureau. In an effort to lure midwesterners, the platform endorsed payment of the national debt in greenbacks.

During a contentious stalemate, the Democrats first rejected Ohioan George H. Pendleton as being too strong on currency inflation and too weak on the war and reconstruction, and then fellow Ohioan Chief Justice Salmon P. Chase as being too sympathetic toward Republican reconstruction and Negro suffrage. Finally, the convention broke the deadlock and nominated for the presidency the cautious and colorless conservative Horatio Seymour, former governor of New York, wartime critic of Lincoln, and hard-money man. Then the delegates impetuously chose for vice-president the South's candidate, Francis P. Blair, Jr., of Missouri, a former Union general who now talked like a Confederate chief. The Democratic *Leslie's Newspaper* termed the ticket a "good man out of the past . . . with an unpopular man out of the present." In fact, the convention had been abrasive in tone, intolerant in feeling, imprudent in its reconstruction plank, contradictory in its economic policy, and impolitic in its nominations. The party thus guaranteed that it would be unsatisfactory to the moderate conservative voter, would alienate unionist Democrats, and would antagonize Republicans. Preferring to ride their own hobby horse, the ultras in control of the convention had sacrificed the party's opportunity for a comeback by failing to head the ticket with a war Democrat.[23]

In the course of the campaign Blair not only spoke and drank to excess but made speeches and wrote letters that further damaged the party's prospects. He characterized reconstruction as a military despotism, and Grant as a potential military dictator. He asserted that Seymour as president could treat congressional legislation as void, abolish existing Republican state governments, and restore the previous conservative ones. Blair declared that the "white race is the only race in the world that has shown itself capable" of self-government. He warned that the Negroes' rape of government would inevitably lead to their rape of southern white women. He said that Republicans, themselves now treasonous, had made "copperheadism" respectable. His speechmaking was about as serious a fiasco as Andrew Johnson's had been two years earlier. The effect was summed up by the New York *World* as "disastrous." The damage was so great that Seymour attempted to lower the pitch of the canvass, playing down reconstruction, muting racist themes, and emphasizing economics. A very worried Seymour undertook a western speechmaking tour in the fall to counteract his running mate's bluster and bravado.[24]

Voters had reason to doubt whether the smiling Seymour would be an improvement over the growling Johnson. It looked as if a Seymour presidency, either obstructing reconstruction or scrapping it completely, might have a tiresome similarity to Johnson's. Republicans promised that a Republican executive would put an end to divided, discordant government and claimed that Grant had a steely purpose and a managerial ability that Seymour lacked.[25] In contrast to Grant's heroic performance, Seymour's conduct during the war seemed questionable. His campaign was neither aided by the intemperate remarks of southern Democrats, who declared that his election would surely help the South, nor was it enhanced by the widespread political terrorism against blacks in Georgia, Louisiana, and South Carolina. A Georgia Republican advised the national campaign manager to "give the rebels rope enough to hang themselves." Developments in the South, predicted a North Carolina Democrat, "will produce great excitement at the North and will help Grant." Summing up the significance of the Democratic campaign, Ohio Republican Senator John Sherman wrote that if the Democrats had acted sensibly at their convention and during their campaign, Republicans would have been in danger of defeat. "It is the rebel element that now serves us by preventing divisions among us."[26] Clearly, many Democrats recognized this. There were urgent pleas from party men to replace the old-fashioned Seymour or foolish Blair or both and produce a new ticket, but it was too late: the Democrats had thrown away the election.[27]

One extreme conservative from North Carolina claimed that Blair's campaign "was the main cause of our defeat, North and South. The fear of another war frightened thousands of our ignorant, timid people and kept them from the polls. The enthusiasm of the New York Convention far outran its better judgment. They sacrificed the real men of the party, because neither had the magnanimity to yield and join his rival: rather than do this they united on men who

ism. Republican politicians were frightened by portents of their waning power and, in desperation, were willing to run limited risks and promote political reform in order to maintain power. Abolitionist Wendell Phillips, recognizing that impartial justice alone would never be sufficient, wrote in May, 1868, that Negroes would not obtain suffrage in the North until reluctant Republican politicians were willing to "sell their prejudices for success"—until they were moved by interest and not ideology, by fear and not daydreams. Clearly, both practical radicals and pragmatic moderates, understanding that few institutions or human arrangements could remain viable and stable unless some men had a vested interest in their survival and stability, acted accordingly and made possible what they considered necessary.[32]

Thus, during early 1869 the Republicans in the lame-duck Congress pressed for a constitutional amendment to secure impartial manhood suffrage in every state, therefore avoiding further popular rejection in state referendums. They opted for the usual, but more indirect, method of having Republican state legislatures that were still in session ratify the amendment. Thus they avoided the risk of possible rejection by special conventions.

The amendment finally passed Congress in February, 1869, after a number of compromises. To secure enough moderate votes, the sponsors had to omit a clause that would have outlawed property qualifications and literacy tests. Such a clause was dispensable because the tests would affect more Negroes in the South than in the North, and because the proponents of the amendment were intent primarily upon securing the northern Negro voter for the Republican party. For the same reasons, they omitted any provision for Negro officeholding. A provision for federal authority over voter qualifications was defeated, and so the potential for evasion in the southern and border states was left wide open.

The legislative history of the Fifteenth Amendment indicated no triumph of radical idealism, but served to demonstrate its failure— a fact underscored by the fury and frustration of that band of radicals who had favored idealistic and uncompromising reforms. A moderate measure, the amendment had the support of those who understood the limits of party power and who had practical goals in mind; they took into account the possible difficulties of ratification. Time was short, the pressures were great, and the options were limited.

The primary objective—the enfranchisement of the blacks in the northern and border states—was clearly understood, stated, and believed by the politicians, the press, and the people. As the abolitionist organ, the *National Anti-Slavery Standard*, declared, "evenly as parties are now divided in the North, it needs but the final ratification of the pending Fifteenth Amendment, to assure . . . the balance of power in national affairs." The black newspaper, the Washington *New National Era*, predicted the same for the border states. Indeed, most newspapers both in the North and in the South during 1869 and 1870 unequivocally, incontrovertibly, and repeatedly spoke of the Republican objective of ensuring party hegemony by means of the Fifteenth Amendment. Moreover, congressmen and state legislators, in arguing for passage and ratification, referred again and again to the partisan need for those votes. The southern Negro, already a voter, was not irrelevant—an important secondary purpose of the amendment was to assure the continuance of Negro suffrage in the South by putting it in a virtually unrepealable amendment to the federal Constitution. Still, the anticipated importance of the black electorate in the North and in the borderland was clearly the overriding concern.[33]

To be sure, the political motives of many Republican politicians were not incompatible with a sincere moral concern. The idealistic motive reinforced the pragmatic one. Happily, there was no conflict at the outset between the ideal and the practical or between the interests of the black electorate and those of the Republican party.[34] A radical congressman, William D. Kelley, declared, "party expediency and exact justice coincide for once." A Negro clergyman from Pittsburgh observed that "the Republican Party had done the negro good but they were doing themselves good at the same time." Indeed, the amendment as framed was both bold and prudent: bold in enfranchising Negroes despite concerted opposition and in ordering change by establishing constitutional guidelines; prudent in adapting methods to circumstances so that the amendment would not only pass Congress but be ratified by the states.[35] With the Fifteenth

Amendment sent to the state legislatures for action, the desk was finally cleared for the adjournment of the Fortieth Congress and the inauguration of the new president on March 4, 1869.

A sense of anticipation and of a new beginning animated Washington on the eve of the inauguration as every train swelled the throngs of well-wishers who came from all over the country to celebrate the occasion. Bewildered visitors new to the city wandered in search of lodgings and paid dearly for cots hastily erected in billiard rooms and hotel hallways. Long into the night, parades and bands filled the streets.

On inauguration day threatening skies and mud-filled roads failed to discourage onlookers who jammed the route from the Executive Mansion to the Capitol. People stood on house tops, crowded into balconies, perched on tree limbs, and clung to lamp posts to catch a glimpse of the great general. Enthusiasm was more evident than organization, however, for upon entering the Senate chamber, Grant glanced hesitantly at one chair, then at another, uncertain which was his. Proceeding from the Senate to the inauguration platform outside the Capitol, the entourage nearly overwhelmed the president-elect in the scramble for good places on the platform, which bore an unfortunate resemblance to a scaffold. After Grant had taken the oath of office, wild cheers joined the artillery salutes, engine bells, and brass bands. His inaugural, delivered in his characteristic low murmur, was punctuated by the clanging of bells and the banging of brass. Few were able to hear the address, but they did not miss much: written by Grant himself, it was a string of platitudes that deserved praise only for its brevity. "The responsibilities of the position I feel, but accept them without fear," the president declared, and he went on to repeat the standard affirmations of the Republican party. "Grant's great diffidence almost overwhelmed him," one observer noted. "No one could have believed that the shrinking, unpretentious man stammering through the well-prepared address had commanded thousands of men and conquered as many more."[36]

The evening inaugural ball, in the newly completed Treasury Building, next door to the White House, was intended to be a lavish affair. By eight o'clock all was in readiness. Gas jets brilliantly illuminated the walks and building; lights arranged across the portico blazed with the word *peace*. Festooned and garlanded ballrooms on four separate stories were linked by a telegraphic system to synchronize the dance program. And, below, tables that could seat nine hundred groaned under a vast array of delicacies.

Soon wave after wave of carriages brought the prospective merrymakers. Since twice as many people were admitted as the building could accommodate, the stairways and rooms became so crowded it was almost impossible to move. The stifling heat and pervasive odor of perspiration compelled some to depart early. They were the fortunate ones. Those who stayed could hardly breathe as dancers raised clouds of marble dust left over from the recently completed construction. Some guests fainted. The dining room was so jammed that most could not even get near the tables and left hungry. Some bribed stewards for a chance to eat. Some hungry people broke down doors and burst into the kitchen in search of food, only to be repulsed by an indignant cook who threw dirty, wet dishcloths at them. In the milling throng, finery became streaked with chocolate, and the trains of gowns were rent from the waist by careless male feet. The improvised cloakrooms were a scene of indescribable confusion. The best coats and hats were stolen early in the evening. The rest of them were piled on the floor for their owners to find, so that many swearing men and weeping women, hatless and coatless, left the building "vowing dire vengeance on the 'getters up of the swindle.'" Those women who were too cold and timid to leave and contend with the biting early morning wind were still crouched in corners or on window ledges at daylight. Unable to find transportation, many guests were forced to walk miles to their lodgings. The event, a New York *Times* correspondent remarked, was "too much of a success to be really a good thing."[37]

If the inaugural ball was something less than a successful debut for the new administration, the cabinet appointments were even less promising. The mediocrity of many of the choices reflected Grant's desire to reward his personal friends. Disappointment was heightened because expectations regarding the new presidency had been so great. Grant seemed to have forgotten his military maxim of the right man in the right place. Democrats sneered. Some Republicans, however, regarded the cabinet as a refreshing sign of a desirable change from the undue influence of rings and cliques.[38]

The country as a whole remained resolutely confident that Grant would yet realize his expressed wish: "Let us have peace." The war hero was perhaps the physician who could heal the wounds still festering from the war. Even the South was surprisingly moderate and benign in its acceptance of the new president. Grant had treated General Robert E. Lee with dignity and respect; perhaps he would treat the South with fairness and magnanimity. The often partisan New York *World* itself grudgingly acknowledged that Grant would be a tolerably satisfactory president. Indeed, each party and every section looked forward to the *pax Grantis*—a new epoch in which peace, prosperity, and sectional harmony would prevail.[39]

Many were confident that the controversy over reconstruction would subside once the suffrage amendment had been adopted. Although the struggle over ratification lasted only thirteen months, it was hard going and the outcome was uncertain until the very end. The fight was especially close in the Middle Atlantic states and in Indiana and Ohio, where the parties were competitive and a black electorate had the potential for deciding victory or defeat. In the Democratic border states and on the Pacific Coast, where racial feeling ran high, the Republicans feared that pushing the amendment would lose them votes and so they refrained from working hard in those regions. The amendment had the backing of the Grant administration, with its rich patronage. Those Republican politicians who held or aspired to hold national office added the weight of their influence. As one Ohioan advised, "By hook or by crook you must get the 15th amendment through or we are gone up."[40]

The Fifteenth Amendment became law on March 30, 1870. Republican euphoria followed the hard battle for ratification. Grant, in his message to Congress, wrote that the amendment "completes the greatest civil change and constitutes the most important event that has occurred since the nation came into life." Blacks everywhere celebrated, and their outstanding leader, Frederick Douglass, announced that now they would "breathe a new atmosphere, have a new earth beneath, and a new sky above." In Washington a hundred guns boomed forth for "the greater revolution than that of 1776."

Throngs crowded the parade route along which white and black men marched shoulder to shoulder, bearing aloft torches and banners with such messages as "The Nation's second birth" and "the fifteenth amendment, Unce Sam's bleaching powder." Sympathetic prominent citizens lighted up their homes with candles and lanterns. At the White House, President Grant came out to greet the gathering and reiterated his confidence that the newly given ballot would be wisely used.[41]

Blacks regarded the Fifteenth Amendment as political salvation, as a solemn written guarantee that would never be abridged. They now felt secure, protected by both the vote and the "long strong arm of the Government." For abolitionists, ratification was the dream finally realized. Wendell Phillips announced it as the real birthday of the nation, because now the Declaration of Independence applied to all. The determined Negro, with his use of the ballot, could right the social injustice in the South in a single generation, for "a man with a ballot in his hand is the master of the situation. He defines all his other rights. What is not already given him, he takes. . . . The Ballot is opportunity, education, fair play, right to office, and elbow-room." Implicit in this idealist's faith was the widely held view of the ballot as a panacea and, indeed, as redemption.[42]

Many northern Democrats, although hardly jubilant, were surprisingly acquiescent once ratification was a fact. To be sure, some of them continued their familiar refrain of states' rights denied and raised the specter of black control and race war. Many others, however, were more philosophical, regarding black suffrage as an irrevocable fact which at last closed a chapter on a great national issue and would finally end the tiresome domination of national politics by the Negro question. Some northern Democrats gave veiled hints to their southern fellow partisans that intransigence would be pointless, for the amendment was virtually unrepealable and would certainly be enforced.[43]

The Fifteenth Amendment was a climax of the work the Republicans had done for the Negro. Believing they had reached that summit, they thought it appropriate to stop and take a rest. On record were three amendments to the Constitution: the Thirteenth, which secured freedom; the Fourteenth, which guaranteed civil equality;

23

and the Fifteenth, which presumably granted suffrage. The Negro was now a man, a citizen, and a voter. He could take care of himself. There need be no more talk of Washington giving him land or racially integrated schools. Putting the burden on him, the Republican New York *Tribune* advised: "Neither Constitutions nor good-will can permanently secure Freedom to those who neglect to make themselves worthy of it." Antislavery societies throughout the country disbanded, now confident that they could fairly leave their "client to the broad influences of civilization and country," because "no power ever permanently wronged a voting class without its own consent."[44]

To many nineteenth-century Americans, equality before the law was deemed sufficient. In the people's enthusiasm over the great constitutional achievements, in their reliance on the law to solve all problems, and in their impatience to be done with the difficult work of reconstruction, very few of them realized that the translation of law into reality was a task not yet entirely achieved.[45]

2

BULLETS AND BALLOTS

Enforcing the Right to Vote

Now that eligible Negroes everywhere could vote, the Republicans had a better than even chance in close contests in the North, as well as a greater possibility of maintaining their threatened regimes or recapturing control in the border and southern states. But many whites in the South had already demonstrated their determination and ability to disfranchise blacks by various means. Thus everything turned upon the exercise of the right to vote, for the effectiveness of the ballot depended on its maintenance and its use, which in turn depended upon federal enforcement.

President Grant made sweeping declarations of federal support to ensure that Negroes could vote freely, and Congress passed many acts that spelled out in detail the powers and responsibilities of the federal government in enforcing the Fifteenth Amendment. The Enforcement Act of May 31, 1870, banned the use of force, bribery, or any intimidation that interfered with the right to vote because of race. This prohibition affected every local and state election and applied to any officials who might refuse to receive honest votes or who might be tempted to count dishonest ones. It prohibited disguised groups from going upon the public highways or upon the premises of another with intent to injure or intimidate citizens. The federal courts would hear cases arising under the law, and federal officials and troops could supervise elections and make arrests.

25

The Enforcement Act of July 14, 1870, strengthened the first by providing enforcement machinery for congressional elections, though only in cities of at least twenty thousand. Special deputy marshals were to police elections, with power to make arrests without warrants. The Enforcement Act of February 28, 1871, not only amplified the earlier law by spelling out the duties of enforcement officers and by defining crimes in more detail, but also required written ballots in congressional elections. This act provided that in cities with populations of at least twenty thousand, a federal judge of the circuit court, upon request, could appoint two election supervisors in each precinct. They were to stand guard at the ballot box, challenge doubtful voters, and count all ballots. To oversee the entire enforcement operation in each judicial district in the circuit, a federal commissioner could be appointed to serve as chief supervisor.

Aimed expressly at terrorist organizations, the Enforcement Act of April 20, 1871, or the Ku Klux Klan Act, outlawed, in effect, the Klan and similar groups that conspired to deprive citizens of their civil and political rights by interfering with trials or voting. The law provided for severe measures, including presidential authorization of martial law and suspension of habeas corpus. Finally, the Enforcement Act of June 10, 1872, which was inserted in the sundry Civil Appropriations Act, enlarged election supervision to cover rural areas, but denied supervisors the power of arrest or interference. The law thus reduced them to powerless poll watchers, quite unlike their counterparts in large cities.[1]

Such sweeping legislation immediately became a passionate political issue. The Democrats argued that enforcement was unnecessary and unconstitutional. They either denied the existence of the Ku Klux Klan or contended that its purpose was distorted, its influence and atrocities magnified, and its causes misunderstood. Their press played down Klan incidents, explaining them away as the inventions of the Republicans "to hide Radical rottenness behind a cloud of Ku-Klux," and as merely trumped-up excuses for persecuting Democrats. When confronted with specific Klan disorders, they rationalized them as the inevitable result of Republican rule in the South and claimed that if corrupt carpetbaggers and impudent blacks trampled upon the rights and liberties of whites, then the upright men of the South had the right and the duty to resist such oppression. It was no coincidence, the Democrats insisted, that the worst Klan violence occurred under the most entrenched and corrupt regimes.[2]

The Democrats also contended that the reconstruction amendments in no way sanctioned such sweeping and stringent legislation as the election enforcement acts. Ohio Senator Allen G. Thurman, for one, declared that the Fifteenth Amendment only prohibited official state disfranchisement. By trying to go beyond state action, the Democratic argument ran, the Republican Congress was destroying the essence of the federal system itself, for the states had a constitutional right to regulate their own suffrage. Typical of Democratic rhetoric was Kentucky Representative William E. Arthur's statement that "under the pretext of protecting the people, the people [were] being enslaved; under the pretext of establishing order, liberty [was] being overthrown"; and under the pretext of banning racial discrimination, the white race was being discriminated against. Summing up the Democratic view, Gideon Welles of Connecticut pronounced: "We are embarked in a centralism—a dreary voyage."[3]

The Republicans countered that the pretexts given for opposition to enforcement came with particular ill grace from the Democrats, who were merely trying to prevent the establishment of order in the South, since it would not serve their interests. The country could not afford to indulge in legal hairsplitting while citizens were being denied their liberties and their lives. Under the mandate of the Fifteenth Amendment, the federal government could and must redress wrongs. To do less would make the amendment and the Constitution dead letters.[4]

Authorized by unprecedented statutory powers during peacetime and supported by federal troops, attorneys, marshals, and supervisors, the attorney general of the United States undertook to enforce the new election laws. In the process, the will and skill of President Grant's government was to be tested.

The most immediate challenge to federal officials was mob violence, which threatened not only the integrity of the democratic process, but the order of society itself, as the Ku Klux Klan, the Knights of the White Camellia, and similar organizations attempted to take

27

away the vote from their recently enfranchised political opponents. Such terrorism was more extensive and more effective than has been commonly believed. Hatred of the federal government, "carpetbag control," and Negro suffrage fed southern whites' fears and frustrations, causing the restless and the reckless to vent their rage. An absence of massive violence existed only in states where such violence served no political purpose. Virginia, for example, having fallen to conservative control as early as 1869, suffered no very serious disturbances, though it did experience election irregularities. Terrorist activities centered in places where chances of a Democratic comeback were best. Intending first to undermine Republican power and then to regain supremacy at the polls for white Democrats, bands of masked men, often disguised in peaked hoods and flowing robes, frequently emboldened by liquor and wild talk, rode off into the woods to whip some Negroes and to murder others.

Such mass lawlessness was always festering just below the surface, ready to erupt where passions and prejudices ran high, and where cutthroats, war veterans, and young swaggering firebrands, eager for a fight and for a chance to prove their manhood by "shooting a nigger," were in ample supply. Violence and rowdyism, of course, were not unusual in the South, where settlement of differences with guns was a tradition. But secret political societies of armed and disguised members bent on a disciplined and systematic campaign of terror against another race were ominously new. The organized savagery of the Klan and the Knights, in the words of one Georgia Republican, was the "darkest blot on Southern character." During the Klan trials, Judge Hugh L. Bond observed: "I would not believe had I not seen it that the beast was so close under the skin of men."[15]

The Klan was first organized in 1866 in southern Tennessee, at Pulaski, as a social club of former Confederates. It did not become an important political force until 1867, when it mounted a three-year counterattack to end Republican control. By 1870, with the election of a Democratic governor, John C. Brown, himself a former Klan member, and with Democratic control of the legislature assured, the Klan had achieved its main object in Tennessee. Without competition from the Republicans, however, the Democrats reverted to squabbling among themselves. As a result, in 1872 they lost badly to the Republicans, who had again become a serious political force, thanks in part to the black voter and white independents. The Republicans, having secured control of the state legislature, repealed the Democratic-sponsored poll-tax requirement for voting, and so they could expect a still larger Negro vote in future.

The 1874 state and congressional elections would decide the question of Republican resurgence. That campaign in Tennessee was the most heated and bloody since secession. "I had been quite hopeful that a better state of feeling was growing and that we had done with Ku Klux murderers," a federal marshal observed during the campaign. "Unfortunately I have been disappointed."[6] In the Gibson County election in early August, the Democrats "had a mob at every poll and created a perfect reign of terror. Intimidation, violence, repeating, the delay and preventing of the colored citizens from voting was the order of the day." In a fair vote, another federal marshal estimated, the Republicans should have carried the county by roughly two thousand votes. Instead, the Democrats won by double that figure.[7]

One night in August, following the local election, a group of Negroes returned fire when shot at by a band of masked men. The next day state authorities arrested and jailed sixteen blacks, including two preachers, who were taken bodily from their church pulpits. Later a band of about a hundred armed and disguised men surrounded the jail, forced the sheriff to give them the prisoners, took them to a nearby riverbank, and riddled them with bullets, killing five and severely wounding the rest. The uproar following the murders forced the Democratic governor's hand. He offered a reward of five hundred dollars and earnest words against such wrongdoing, but his high-sounding message meant little when state authorities dragged their feet about prosecution and the governor himself protested to President Grant against any federal interference.

Finally, federal authorities took action, arresting and trying fifty-three defendants. Not one of them was convicted. Black witnesses understandably had hesitated to tell the court what they had seen, for fear of becoming the next victims. "They are ignorant and afraid and easily become confused," the federal attorney reported to Washington, "and in this case were confronted not only by the very men who had attempted to murder them, but the sheriff of Gibson County or his deputy [who] came into open court and demanded of the court in their presence these witnesses to be taken to that county and tried for a trumped up charge of felony now pending there against them and these witnesses thereupon became so terrified that some of them in tears and piteous tones besought the court to allow them to be excused from testifying."[8]

Such conditions were duplicated elsewhere with similar results. It was difficult to obtain blacks as jurors or witnesses. A federal attorney in Mississippi explained: "I cannot get witnesses as all feel it is sure death to testify before the grand jury." Juries composed of conservative whites usually refused to indict or to convict. Fear pervaded the countryside, yet only hard facts mattered in the courtroom. Everything the blacks had to leave unsaid—the indignities they endured, the terrors they suffered—went unnoticed and unpunished. The story was to become familiar: endemic violence was accompanied by Democratic landslides.[9]

Southern whites, high and low, either actively resisted reconstruction or passively sat by. In Kentucky, state legislators were prepared to "move heaven and earth" to save from punishment a young member of the prominent Crittenden family. "When you strike a Crittenden," one observer declared, "you strike the State of Kentucky and his friends will never consent to have justice meted out to him." In Mississippi, it was reported, "Public opinion of course sets with 'our boys,'" and so whites in the county "will go to any extreme to get them clear. Money seems like water for 'our boys' that have been kidnapped by the Yankees." In Texas, a federal judge summed up the depressing truth: "I am fully convinced that a large majority of the white population in this state would not be convinced that any man had violated . . . the enforcement acts by any testimony." Since most white southerners regarded federal prosecution as northern persecution, they were resourceful and persistent in helping to corroborate the alibis for defendants, such as illnesses and visits to relatives. Even most Democrats of law-abiding inclinations were "awed into silence by the many who give loose reins to passions of hate and violence." Prominent Confederate leaders who had been proscribed from holding public office, General Sherman observed, "now sit with their hands in their pockets and say that their kuklux outrages are none of their business."[10]

Operating in such unfriendly territory, federal officials single-handedly had often to fight not only terrorism and hostility but also sabotage. Federal marshals and attorneys were compelled to look over their shoulders; and some were indicted in state courts for assault to kill, for assault and battery, and for carrying concealed weapons. Prisoners escaped from jail by the "connivance, if not by the direct assistance of the State authorities." Too often the federal government seemed unprepared to cope with the situation. "If it is the policy of the administration to act," a federal marshal in Kentucky declared, "I beg that such action will be taken as will be swift and certain." The federal authorities, however, could not provide the force and personnel to make this possible.[11]

Lack of money was one stumbling block. Two million dollars was the total amount allotted each year for the expenses of federal courts and marshals throughout the nation—a sum that could hardly keep the bureaucracy efficiently operating, much less support an ambitious and energetic program of enforcement. Federal attorneys were often obliged to spend their own money on a case. But there still was not enough money to hire detectives to investigate, buy tips, break alibis, or provide transportation for witnesses. "If it be true that black men are kept from the polls by intimidation, we ought to see that going to the polls is made as safe as going to church," the *Nation* observed; "but to pass bills providing for this, without voting the men or the money to execute them, is a wretched mockery, of which the country and the blacks have had enough." Yet, despite the increase of federal prosecutions in the South, there was no corresponding increase in appropriations. In communications to and from the Department of Justice the refrain was always the same: complaints from federal officials in southern districts that their efforts were hamstrung by lack of money, and answers, even rebukes, from Washington that stringent economy must be maintained. As a result, the program went on being underfunded and after 1873 it slowly languished.[12]

Another difficulty was the caliber of many federal officials. Some

31

were ignorant of the law or did not know how to frame indictments. And although low salaries and political patronage were somewhat responsible for lack of quality, there were more serious problems, such as working in a hostile environment. As one federal commissioner stated, "we have too many weak and temporizing U.S. Attorneys and U.S. Marshals in the South," and "*timidity* is the bane of Southern Republican officials. They are so peaceable that they submit to wrong, some wink at it, to pacify their own every day life with the enemy. Some hesitate to do their duty by reason of the influence of democratic kinsmen and friendly disposed neighbors."[13]

Even though manpower was rarely sufficient, occasionally an overreaction provided too much help for a certain locality. One federal official, deluged with more subordinates than he could use and manage, pleaded: "For heaven's sake entreat him [the attorney general] to send me no more assistance. We are literally falling over one another as it is; and I fear if any more are appointed it will require . . . the General of the armies to command the squad." It was common practice to pay fees rather than salaries to marshals for legal paperwork, so that each one would be interested in doing as much business as possible, securing warrants and initiating cases with or without securing convictions. Occasionally officials with political grudges were overzealous, and there were some cases of corruption. But sheer ignorance and lethargy were more common faults.[14]

Compounding these difficulties, the numerous organizational snarls, excusable at the start of the program, were never remedied. For one thing, there were not enough judges and judicial districts. Interminable delay resulted from abbreviated and erratic court sessions, crowded dockets, and drawn-out trials of a handful of accused, while hundreds of other indicted offenders remained untried. The overburdened judicial system broke down in several districts in South Carolina, North Carolina, Mississippi, and elsewhere. The jails were not large enough to hold prisoners, nor was there enough clerical help. Although the government was enmeshed in red tape, the chief clerk of the Justice Department employed only four copy clerks, and the head of the department had no idea how many deputy marshals had supervised polls in any one presidential election. Furthermore, there was internal conflict and inefficiency within the Department of Justice, as well as a lack of coordination between it and the War Department. The administrative apparatus of the Department of Justice, the court system, and the military establishment were comparable to a dinosaur—slow, cumbersome, and monumental in inefficiency.[15]

Nor was there much help from the federal judges themselves. Despite notable exceptions, such as Judge Bond, southern judges, who had often been appointed by previous administrations with divergent political sympathies, did their best to undermine enforcement. Sometimes they did so through deliberate sabotage and active connivance; more frequently they relied on indirection and narrow interpretation, especially when ambiguous wording of the acts provided the opportunity for a judge to construe them according to his predilection. Federal attorneys complained of federal judges putting Democratic constructions on the laws, thus virtually destroying them. In many districts "the judiciary succumbs to the pressure of a local sentiment," Attorney General Amos T. Akerman noted. Federal enforcement was so decentralized and so divergent that Washington often was not in control. Indeed, in several southern and border states the actual administration of federal law served parochial partisan interests.[16]

Prominent national attorneys such as Reverdy Johnson and Henry Stanbery, both Democrats, in arguing the South Carolina case in 1871 took the position that the enforcement acts were unconstitutional. So did Alexander H. Stephens and Linton Stephens in Georgia. In the early skirmishing over a Louisiana case, Associate Justice Joseph P. Bradley, a New Jersey Republican, declared in 1874 that the power of Congress to prohibit certain actions of state officials did not apply to the actions of ordinary citizens. With all these much publicized legal opinions, chances of an adverse decision by the Supreme Court seemed more than likely, and this was clearly an encouragement to political terrorists. One federal attorney in Alabama declared: "If it could once be known and felt, that the enforcement law . . . was the settled law and policy of the Government," then the Klan would be broken up, "but as long as a hope is entertained of an entire change of this policy, we may look for a continuation of these K K intimidations and outrages." Finally, after several years, the Su-

33

preme Court in 1876 struck down indispensable provisions of the enforcement acts. Well before that time, however, confusion and uncertainty had progressively paralyzed the enforcement machinery.[17]

The enforcement acts were, in fact, vulnerable to judicial scrutiny. Often the hastily planned and framed statutes were so worded that effective administration could not be provided and the legal limits were uncertain. The legislators had not appreciated the immensity of the racial problem or properly assessed the strength of southern white disaffection, and consequently they had not provided adequate means for dealing with either of those difficulties. At the same time, Congress perhaps had in several respects exceeded the prevailing constitutional norms by circumscribing state authority.

Thus election enforcement remained a constitutional halfway house, for federal law did not displace state election law, yet in some instances it superseded it. Wide discretion was left not only to the state legislators, who wrote the letter of election regulation, but also to the local registrars, who supplied the proscriptive spirit in qualifying voters. National control of all elections, not merely those for Congress, was thought to be out of the question. Thus federal election enforcement went too far in one sense and not far enough in another. Finally, the wide-ranging and vague statutory language gave the courts too much latitude or quite simply left crucial matters up in the air; for Congress did not make it altogether clear under what circumstances federal jurisdiction applied to private individuals. Nor did the laws explicitly indicate where the lines of state and federal authority diverged and where they intersected or coincided.[18]

The failure of army support added to the difficulties of enforcement. Although white southerners complained of bayonets doing judicial duty, the standard urgent request of federal enforcement officials was something like this: "We have 50 U.S. soldiers here but we need 500." With the slashing of army appropriations, consequent troop reductions, and the reassignment of available soldiers to duty in the West, there were not enough troops in the South to serve as a deterrent to crime.[19] Those in the region were often stationed in the wrong place at crucial times; and often the troops lacked the proper authority to take necessary action. Guidelines for use of troops were vague; permissions sometimes became impossible to secure in times of emergency, and there were delays between calls for soldiers to control violence and their arrival. Often, too, when haste was essential there were nothing but slow-moving infantry outfits available rather than the fast-moving cavalry, which was reserved for the Indian wars. There was also some reluctance on the part of the army to become another police force or to get involved in politics. One army man in North Carolina complained of "this most disagreeable duty" of "being used in dirty work" for political purposes. As General Sherman wrote, "we subject our soldiers to dangers worse than an ordinary battle."[20]

The actual number of troops in each state was generally negligible; only twice did it, in a given southern state, exceed a thousand. Outside of Texas, where regional garrisons were mainly preoccupied with patrolling the frontier, there were only six thousand troops in the South in 1869, or roughly half of the total in 1868. After the number of troops was further reduced by two thousand in 1870 and by another thousand in 1872, the total remained roughly stationary at thirty-four hundred. By October 1876, there were about three thousand troops left in the South, one half of the number in 1869, whereas in the nation as a whole the total had been reduced by only one fourth. In response to a rise in violence during the congressional campaigns of 1874, the number of garrisons were ordered to be increased by a third in the South; but since the number of soldiers actually stationed in the region was not increased, the existing allotment of troops was spread even thinner.[21]

The truth was stark: there simply was no federal force large enough to give heart to black Republicans or to bridle southern white violence. As one federal authority in Mississippi declared: "a little 'Color-line' of blue had a wonderful influence upon these people." But there were just enough troops to antagonize southern whites and add to their sense of common grievance. When the troops were removed from a particular locality, the conditions of the blacks there worsened, as federal retreat emboldened many whites to increase or renew their defiance and persecution. A deputy marshal in Louisiana, where there was a strong but short-lived show of federal force, observed that "our operations here which for the time have upset all the calculations of the whites leaguers will only add increased revenge when we retire." The solution seemed to him self-evident: "If the President intends to make good the assertion that any citizen shall be as safe in any part of Louisiana as in Massachusetts, he will have to order a company of troops to remain here permanently." Even more pointed was one Georgian's claim that "If the friends of the National Government cannot be protected in their constitutional rights in this State, by the strong arm of the Government, we had best, and must give up."[22]

That was precisely what did happen, and it was exemplified by the federal posture in the Carolinas between 1872 and 1874. At issue was the question of whether to continue the vigorous federal prosecution of the Klan in those states, particularly at election time. The United States attorney for South Carolina realized that since the deep-seated feelings of many whites might well be channeled into another sort of Klan organization in the future, the present prosecutions had to be handled judiciously, but firmly. The instigators of the worst crimes had to be tried and punished in order to persuade them and others to give up terrorism as a political tool. Otherwise, the perpetrators would "construe their immunity from prosecution and punishment into license to do the like again when it pleases them."[23]

Despite this warning from an officer in the field, the Grant administration decided to rely upon the good faith of the enemy. Attorney General George H. Williams ordered the suspension of prosecution in South Carolina and North Carolina in the spring of 1873, hoping that this friendly overture from Washington would persuade Klansmen to reform. Williams expected that the effect would be "to produce obedience to the law, and quiet and peace among the people." President Grant pardoned Klansmen sentenced for atrocities. By the spring of 1874 Williams declared that the objective of enforcement had been achieved and that there were good reasons for hoping that disorder would not return: "at all events, it affords the Government pleasure to make an experiment based upon these views."[24]

Such hasty leniency was typical of the government's failure to follow through or to take a consistent, clear stand. There was little interest in federal enforcement "except when an election was pending," as Senator Carl Schurz noted. Thus, in September, 1874, just before the important congressional elections, Attorney General Williams instructed federal attorneys and marshals to "proceed with all possible energy and dispatch to detect, expose, arrest, and punish the perpetrators of these crimes . . . you are to spare no effort or necessary expense." Then, after the elections, in late November, 1874, he dispatched a brisk communication to federal marshals, stressing the need for "proper care and economy." By December he was most concerned about avoiding unnecessary prosecutions, "which are not only an annoyance and an irritation to the people, but are a matter of great expense to the United States."[25]

Intermittent and insufficient action made a mockery of the earlier predictions that President Grant would execute the enforcement acts relentlessly and consistently. The plight of many blacks resembled that of the group in Trousdale County, Tennessee, who wrote to Grant during the bloody month of August, 1874. They gave details about the murder of a local teacher and the intimidation of other blacks by night riders and begged for assistance: "we want the promise of the U.S. protection Mr. President—not only the promise but—we want the aid Truly, and if you will not help us, send us the army and Say that you will help us; be as good as your word." The paradox, then, was real: armed with the ballot to make them more secure in their freedom, many blacks found that the privilege in fact jeopardized their lives or their livelihood.[26]

Grant received criticism from prominent Republicans in the North. The *National Anti-Slavery Standard* constantly nagged at him to make good his promises to southern blacks. Senator Charles Sumner in March, 1871, asserted on the Senate floor that if Grant had been as zealous for the protection of southern Republicans as he had been for the annexation of Santo Domingo, "our Southern Ku Klux would have existed in name only." That same year the Springfield *Republican* complained that the "attempt to cure the ku klux evil from Washington has, so far, been an entire and lamentable failure." By September, 1875, even the Washington *National Republican*, which loyally supported the administration, had termed the reconstruction amendments "dead letters."[27]

What the southern Democrats could not accomplish by means of the rifle, the whip, the rope, the torch, and the knife, they attempted by means of fraud, threat, bribery, or trickery. In several contests the Democratic ballot was headed with a lithograph of President Grant to lure illiterate Negro voters. Sometimes the Democrats warned blacks not to vote Republican or they would lose their jobs or be moved off their farms. Such threats could be "very simple and quiet, yet very effective," commented *Harper's Weekly*. "Every employer and every country neighborhood understands that." If Negroes could not be scared away from the polls or fooled into voting Democratic, they were paid to stay at home on election day, or they were plied with liquor and then persuaded to vote Democratic. Republican ballots were lost, burned, buried, or disregarded. Democratic ballots were cast or counted more than once. Cheating, then, became well organized and widespread, and Democratic victories were manufactured with efficiency and ingenuity.[28]

Blacks were disfranchised by means of redistricting, changing polling places, or other devices. In Georgia, all precincts were abolished in one county so that nine thousand voters would have to vote in a single crowded place in Savannah. Some Kentucky cities eliminated Negro neighborhoods as voting districts. Frankfort, Kentucky, authorities made Negroes wait at the polls all day and then closed the polls before the Negroes had a chance to vote. In West Virginia and other states, judicial, legislative, and congressional districts were gerrymandered so that black voting was neutralized. In North Carolina and Virginia, local offices were made appointive rather than elective, and black political influence was thus reduced. Elsewhere Negroes were kept from voting by such measures as a poll tax in Tennessee, an education tax in Georgia, and a county tax in Delaware.[29]

In Delaware, in particular, the ingenuity of the Democrats matched their desperation. If, in 1870, the eligible blacks were to vote in full force, the Republicans would surely carry the federal and state tickets. So Democratic officials refused to let Negroes pay their county poll or property taxes and thus qualify as voters. Those who succeeded in registering faced challenges at the polls from Democratic election officials, and in many places Democratic rowdies swarmed around the polls crying "down with the nigger" or "clean 'em out." Riots erupted in Wilmington's sixth ward on election eve and day.

Downstate, at Broad Creek, a drunken mob prevented Negroes from voting, while at Smyrna a crowd shoved them away from the Republican window. In Odessa, the polling place for St. George's Hundred, in populous New Castle County, a crowd cursed, knocked down, and beat black voters, driving them from the polls. In both Smyrna and Odessa, federal deputy marshals also had to flee. The federal attorney in Delaware telegraphed President Grant to send in the marines, but no help arrived.[30]

The Republican defeat in Delaware was complete and there was no doubt about what had happened. The Wilmington *Commercial* observed: "Republicans have lost New Castle county, and the Democrats secure control of the Levy Court [which functioned as the voting registrar], solely on account of the terrorism and intimidation used against the colored people in St. Georges Hundred." The Republicans had optimistically counted on forty-five hundred Negro voters throughout the state, but very few were allowed to vote on election day. Without their black support, the Republicans had been robbed of victory.[31]

Infuriated, the Republicans sought federal assistance in enforcing the Negro's right to the franchise. Their motives were a mixture of impartial justice and partisan expediency. At stake, though the estimate was low, were "from one thousand to fifteen hundred colored citizens," reported the federal attorney in Delaware, who added that "partisan interest felt in the case was intense." Washington responded with additional money for extra expenses and personnel.[32]

Federal prosecution began in 1872 and concentrated upon New Castle County. The tax collector for the western district of Wilmington, Archibald Given, was tried in federal court under the second section of the Enforcement Act of May 31, 1870, which required officials to qualify any voter impartially. Federal counsel showed that tax collector Given had gone out of his way to prevent five Negroes from qualifying to vote—by being absent from his office, by refusing payment of the tax on the street, by failing to provide tax bills, by entering the names of five blacks in his "can't find" list, then changing them to his "left the State" list, and by preventing inspection of his records by Republican officials. He was found guilty of submitting false returns and was fined two thousand dollars, barely escaping imprisonment. Federal Judge Edward G. Bradford ruled that the tax collector was, by his duties, an election official and not merely a revenue officer and that he was subject to federal as well as state authority. The federal attorney exulted: "No event had happened in the history of the State, which will go so far to secure to its citizens pure and free elections."[33]

The timing of the case was important. The initial decision against the Democratic registrars was made in October, 1872, just before the presidential election. Republicans now insisted, as Delaware's Democratic Senator Eli Saulsbury complained, that "any person not on the assessment rolls offering to pay to a collector a tax thereby becomes entitled to vote if otherwise qualified. And that the Election Officers are bound to receive and count the vote of such person offering to vote under such circumstances." The practical effect, continued Saulsbury, would be "to intimidate some from opposing the right of such persons to vote and will possibly induce Inspectors and Judges of elections to receive the votes of negroes not on the Assessment lists."[34]

The Democrats' doubts about maintaining their hold on the ballot box were borne out by the 1872 election returns. Indeed, the Republicans did so well in New Castle County that they won the state for their presidential and congressional candidates and gained eight seats in the legislature. Although there were Democratic defections from an unpopular presidential candidate and platform, the increase in the black electorate proved decisive, especially where federal election supervisors were stationed at the polls. The Republican *Commercial* regarded the election as a vindication of Republican principles and a rebuke to political trickery, its editor predicting that with a full assessment and full vote, the Republicans had forged a new majority party in Delaware.[35]

Republican hopes were short-lived. Delaware Democrats regrouped and gambled on a daring strategy. Capitalizing on their solid control of the state government, they determined to change the law in order to keep blacks away from the polls. At the request of the governor, and on a strictly partisan vote, the Democrats, in April, 1873, rammed through the legislature a delinquent tax law. This kept the payment of county property taxes as a prerequisite for voting. It also provided that people who were not taxed for property (mostly propertyless blacks) must pay their individual tax or poll tax to the collector each year. If they failed to do so, the collector had the option of returning them as delinquents to the county commissioners, who were to drop the names of such persons from the tax assessment list. Once off the list, it took monumental perseverance and almost two years to get back on. Few succeeded.

In administering the law, the Democratic officials in Delaware dropped black Republican delinquents just before election day, but continued to carry white Democratic delinquents. Democrats who wanted to register slipped in the back door of the city hall and were easily qualified, whereas blacks stood in long lines in front and, once inside, had great difficulty getting properly registered. When the Negroes appeared before them, Democratic qualifying officials performed their duties in a state of perpetual absentmindedness, consistently mispelling names, omitting initials, or recording incorrect addresses—all errors that rendered the registration null and void. Often the officials played hide-and-seek with prospective black voters; once a group of Negroes followed their tax collector to Philadelphia and forced their money on him at gunpoint after knocking down his hotel room door. By relieving all qualifying officials of their legal responsibilities but not their real power, the Democrats continued to disfranchise in large numbers with impunity so long as they maintained county control. Such officials were thereby spared the fate of Archibald Given.[36]

States throughout the South were to copy the innovations the border states had introduced. Border conservatives, not having experienced federal reconstruction, felt secure enough to blaze the trail. Tennessee produced the Klan in 1866, introduced a discriminatory poll tax in 1870, and legalized racial segregation in 1881. West Virginia not only pioneered with the "separate but equal" formula but began the exclusion of blacks from jury service. Kentucky contributed in 1870 the use of antiblack gerrymandering, the postponement of elections, and the extension of terms of office for incumbents. Maryland in 1870 enacted a property qualification and protracted registration in such a way that an old suffrage law, which restricted voting to whites, remained in effect. And Delaware began the disfranchising county tax in 1873 and authorized segregation in 1875.

As the Democratic New York *World* pointed out, blacks could easily be excluded from voting by the simple legal expedient of state statutes requiring property and educational qualifications. In that way the Democrats could "accomplish *nearly* all they desire without raising any question under the XIVth or the XVth amendment." Such advice was well heeded: the uses of fraud and the abuses of law were as varied as the methods of force, and all too often complaints and charges against both were filed and forgotten.[37]

Although the northern Republicans continued to proclaim the sanctity of the ballot, the federal government did little to ensure it. "It is always well to *insist* on the right, but it is better to *enforce* the right," a Virginia Republican admonished. Instead, "our northern friends had abandoned us to the tender mercies of the Ku Klux and 'Bulldozers.' " Summing up the situation, a former South Carolina Republican who had returned to the North wrote: "Reconstruction was and is a political mistake, not because of any defect in principles enunciated, but because it is *not enforced.*"[38]

THE POLITICS OF ENFORCEMENT

The record of federal election enforcement was pitiable indeed; the few minor successes in South Carolina in 1872, in North Carolina in 1871 and 1873, and in Mississippi in 1872 and 1873, were limited both in length of time and in effect, and subsequently turmoil became as endemic as in those places where little or no enforcement had been attempted. Only 34 percent of the cases tried under the enforcement laws in the South between 1870 and 1877 resulted in conviction, and a mere 6 percent of them in the border states. Out of 4,187 enforcement cases in the entire country, only 1,246 resulted in convictions. Although widespread political disorder continued during reconstruction in most of the South, there were but two convictions under the enforcement acts in chaotic Louisiana, a mere ten in Alabama, four in Georgia, one in Texas, and none in Arkansas. Indeed, there was scarcely any federal enforcement at all except in three southern states, and that only between 1871 and 1873.[39]

Consequently, political violence flourished unabated, and elec-

CRIMINAL PROSECUTIONS UNDER ENFORCEMENT ACTS, 1870–1877
BY SECTION AND BY YEAR

	South	Border	North	National
Total Convictions	1,143	38	65	1,246
Total Dismissals	2,241	601	99	2,941
Total Actions	3,384	639	164	4,187
Average % of Conviction	34%	6%	40%	30%

By year, percentage of
convictions, and
representation of C/D
(ratio of convictions to
dismissals)

(Dismissal includes both
acquittal and nolle)

Year	South		Border		North		National	Total	
1870	0%	0/16	61%	17/11	100%	15/0	32/27	or 59 cases	54%
1871	57%	108/82	11%	9/72	41%	11/16	128/170	298	43%
1872	74%	448/155	1%	2/224	22%	6/21	456/400	856	53%
1873	41%	466/683	1%	1/122	6%	2/30	469/835	1,304	36%
1874	11%	97/793	1%	1/66	33%	4/8	102/867	969	11%
1875	7%	16/205	15%	2/11	0%	0/0	18/216	234	8%
1876	2%	2/106	0%	0/40	100%	1/0	3/146	149	2%
1877	5%	6/127	10%	6/55	65%	26/14	38/196	234	16%

Sections are identified as follows: Solid South (Alabama, Arkansas, Florida, Georgia, Louisiana, Mississippi, North Carolina, South Carolina, Texas, Virginia); border states (Delaware, Kentucky, Maryland, Missouri, Tennessee, West Virginia); North (remaining states of the Union) which were listed in the reports of the attorney general under enforcement actions as: California, Connecticut, Indiana, Kansas, Michigan, New Jersey, New York, Ohio, Pennsylvania, Rhode Island, and Idaho Territory. *House Executive Documents*, 41st Cong., 3rd Sess., No. 90; 43rd Cong., 1st Sess., No. 6; 2nd Sess., No. 20; 45th Cong., 2nd Sess., No. 7; and *Senate Executive Documents*, 42nd Cong., 3rd Sess., No. 32.

toral fraud was commonplace, sophisticated, and highly successful. Even after the Klan and the Knights had disbanded, their political purpose and terrorist tactics survived and became even more effective in such new, more highly disciplined organizations as the rifle clubs and Red Shirts of South Carolina, the White Liners of Mississippi, the White Man's Party in Alabama, and the White Leaguers of Louisiana. These organizations also employed the less direct but very

CRIMINAL PROSECUTIONS UNDER ENFORCEMENT ACTS IN SOUTHERN STATES 1870–1877
(ratio of convictions to dismissals and conviction rate by year and by state)

States	1870	1871	1872	1873	1874	1875	1876	1877	State Totals
Mississippi	n/a	n/a	356/134 73%	184/84 69%	57/63 48%	6/181 3%	0/4 0%	0/6 0%	603/472 or 1,075 cases 56%
N. Carolina	n/a	49/16 75%	1/2 33%	263/40 87%	35/146 19%	0/2 0%	1/2 33%	1/1 50%	350/209 or 559 cases 63%
S. Carolina	n/a	54/58 48%	86/10 90%	14/540 3%	0/555 0%	6/3 67%	0/1 0%	2/56 3%	162/1,223 or 1,385 cases 12%
Alabama		n/a	5/7 42%	0/3 0%	1/1 50%	2/10 17%	1/73 1%	1/30 3%	10/124 or 134 cases 7%
Florida		1/3 25%	n/a	1/6 14%	4/13 24%	1/0 100%	0/5 0%	0/7 0%	7/34 or 41 cases 17%
Virginia		4/4 50%	n/a	0/4 0%	0/2 0%	0/2 0%	0/3 0%	n/a	4/15 or 19 cases 21%
Georgia		n/a	n/a	4/3 57%	0/7 0%	0/4 0%	0/14 0%	0/25 0%	4/53 or 57 cases 7%
Louisiana		0/1 0%	n/a	0/1 0%	n/a	n/a		2/0 100%	2/2 or 4 cases 50%
Texas		n/a	n/a	0/2 0%	0/6 0%	1/2 33%	0/4 0%	0/2 0%	1/16 or 17 cases 6%
Arkansas	0/16 0%	n/a	0/2 0%	n/a	n/a	0/1 0%	n/a	n/a	0/19 or 19 cases 0%
Yearly Totals	0/16 0% (16)	108/82 57% (190)	448/155 74% (603)	466/683 41% (1,149)	97/793 11% (890)	16/205 7% (221)	2/106 2% (108)	6/127 5% (133)	

useful weapons of social ostracism and economic pressure, which had the added advantage of not arousing the North. Indeed, political violence and disturbance were so persistent, so widespread, and so formidable as to constitute civil disobedience and guerrilla warfare.

Blame for the federal government's failure to enforce the right to vote is, we have been told by some historians, to be placed on the Grant administration or on unfriendly judges. Certainly the executive branch since 1870 had exhibited a singular lack of administrative energy and leadership. Yet any criticism that virtually ignores the congressmen who had initiated the policy, drafted the law, and authorized the funds, cannot be entirely fair. After all, both suspension of prosecution and the policy of clemency, as well as the cutback in funds, had actually begun in 1873; this was much earlier than the judicial decisions of 1876, which circumscribed the reach of federal election enforcement. In fact, enforcement had collapsed by 1874, well before the adverse decisions of the Supreme Court were handed down and before the Democratic House of Representatives began to reduce appropriations even more.

Why, then, had the effort to enforce the Fifteenth Amendment been so badly planned, so inadequately executed, and so feebly supported? Perhaps, as often happens with American lawmakers, Republican congressmen had fallen victim to their own hopes by quickly passing a law and expecting it would somehow enforce itself. Although it had been evident that without appropriate legislation and effective execution the Fifteenth Amendment would amount to little or nothing in the South and the borderland, certain ends had been encouraged without marshaling the necessary means. Moreover, not needing to amend the Constitution or to override a presidential veto by a margin of two thirds, the Republicans in Congress had required no more than a simple majority to pass such bills as the enforcement acts. Without the requirement of fashioning a compromise and securing broad support, the caution, self-restraint, and circumspection that had gone into framing the Fifteenth Amendment were not as evident in the enactment of the enforcement laws.

In the process, the experience of the immediate past seemed to have been forgotten. After all, the Fifteenth Amendment had been but a modest step forward, yet it had barely survived congressional infighting. Ratification by the state legislatures had provoked a great deal of opposition and had required extraordinary exertions. Although the legislative history of the Fifteenth Amendment was rather inconclusive when it came to conveying the scope of the enforcement powers allowed to Congress, it was clear by what Congress had voted down that the framers had intended to deal not with the whole problem of election regulations but only with the most serious offenses, and that they were more concerned about the North than the South. Few congressmen had suggested that under the reach of the amendment Congress establish comprehensive voter qualifications and thereby assault the foundations of electoral federalism. Instead, congressmen in fashioning the Fifteenth Amendment had put through the limited reform of banning racial tests in voting without eliminating all barriers, such as the poll tax and literacy requirements. So when Congress subsequently enacted five sweeping enforcement acts, there was bound to be stiff resistance.

The laws had been passed partly in response to the sense of outrage Klan violence had aroused in Congress and throughout the North. The enforcement legislation had also been spurred on by its obvious political value. Republican congressmen saw federal law as a means of reversing the drift back to Democratic control, which was taking place throughout much of the South and the borderland. Then, too, the Klan issue was useful in keeping the faction-ridden Republican party together. In private, prominent Republicans admitted as much. Ohio Governor Rutherford B. Hayes, for one, wrote to Senator John Sherman: "I thank you for your speech on the Ku Klux outrages. It will do us great good. You have hit the nail on the head. Nothing unites and harmonises the Republican party like the conviction that Democratic victories strengthen the reactionary and brutal tendencies of the late rebel States. It is altogether the most effective thing that has lately been done." Similarly, outgoing Attorney General Akerman stated in late 1871 that "such atrocities as Ku Klux fire up Congress and the North." To be sure, party interest was synonymous with national interest. As former Republican chairman Edwin D. Morgan wrote to Senator Sherman: the enforcement bill "is of great importance to the party and to all who want justice at the ballot box." Clearly, justice and self-interest, moral outrage and political self-preservation coincided, but it is instructive to note which came first for Morgan.[40]

Congressional hearings on the Klan also served Republican interests. Such investigations, wrote Attorney General Akerman, would "horrify the North. . . . all that is necessary to hold the majority of the northern voters to the Republican cause, is to show them how active and cruel the Confederate temper still is in the South." Public statements by the president regarding the Klan were also "politically beneficial," as George S. Boutwell, secretary of the treasury, told a meeting of the cabinet early in the presidential reelection year. Certain congressmen also showed unwonted zeal toward the subject when they thought it would promote their reelection. According to the Ohio Congressman James A. Garfield, "I have never been more disgusted with Sherman than during this short session. He is very conservative for 5 years and then fiercely radical for one. This is his radical year which always comes just before the Senatorial Election. No man in the Senate has talked with so much fierceness as Sherman. He seems to have been striving to make himself appear much more zealous than the rest of us. . . . His conduct deceives nobody here, but it may at home." Thus, although congressmen supported the enforcement laws out of equalitarian convictions and humanitarian concern, many of them also hoped to reap a rich harvest from the Klan issue, and still others went along, supporting such measures for fear of being considered too conservative.[41]

The Democrats were quick to decry the Republicans' motives, denouncing those efforts that fanned the embers of sectional hate and the fear of conspiracy in order to stoke the political fires. Indiana Congressman Daniel W. Voorhees remonstrated: "It is a strong diet on which feed the prejudices and antipathies of the northern people." The New York *World* contended that the Republican purpose was to resuscitate the agitation of the southern question because it had been dying out, and with that "sinking tide sink the fortunes and hopes of the Republican party." Once again Republican leaders "want a 'bloody shirt' to be borne aloft in the electioneering processions." The *World* claimed that this partisan strategy had been the real impetus behind passage of the enforcement acts, for they were strong enough to provoke Democratic resistance, which in turn had rekindled Republican enthusiasm. The Democratic newspaper further maintained that the statutes could never be enforced in places where public opinion was opposed to Negro voting; and in states where opinion sanctioned black voting, there would be no need for federal enforcement. The *World* therefore warned Democrats not to fall into the trap by providing pretexts for federal regulation and military intervention: "The Democratic party has nothing to gain—it is only the Republican party that can gain—by a revival of the negro agitation."[42]

The fact of Klan terrorism *was* indisputable; nevertheless, any pretense of extending the suffrage and then not effectively enforcing it was a dangerous policy. What if people began to suspect that the "blood and murder cry was used as convenient partisan stage-thunder merely to catch votes"? asked Senator Schurz. Would they begin to question whether the hue and cry over murdered blacks was raised just before elections merely to keep Republicans in power? And what would happen when the country grew weary of the cry of Ku Klux outrages, when constant repetition of the story would exhaust the indignation of the North, and when recurrences of such events necessarily had a lesser effect on the northerners?[43]

The Republicans also wanted to increase their strength in the North by other means. The first phase of their northern strategy had been clear earlier on, when northern and border Negroes were enfranchised by the ratification of the Fifteenth Amendment for the primary purpose of adding to Republican voter rolls, in hopes of capturing northern and border swing states. The second phase was to enact enforcement laws so as to reduce or limit the northern Democratic city vote by eliminating Democratic fraud and thus carrying marginal states in presidential elections. The Republicans wanted New York state in particular, which, as they believed with good reason, had been stolen from Grant in 1868 by irregularities committed by Tammany Hall.

This second phase, federal regulation in northern cities, was evident in the early enforcement acts as well as in the Enforcement Act of February 28, 1871. Since real power under enforcement was granted only to election supervisors in cities with a population of twenty thousand, and since all but five of those sixty-eight cities were in the northern and border states, the political intent and the practical effects were obvious. Congress, while framing the various acts, intensively investigated the electoral problem in northern cities, discussed the importance of northern elections, and then legislated a solution by regulating elections and registration there. The cabinet also became involved, with New York City central to its discussion. President Grant consulted with John I. Davenport, the federal election supervisor in the city, and diverted secret service funds allocated for the investigation of the Klan in the South to a federal registration of voters in New York City.[44]

Moreover, the bulk of enforcement expenditures had been made in the North, not the South. Monies had been concentrated in eight northern (especially northeastern) cities and disbursed more heavily in presidential elections than in off-year congressional races. Indeed, half of the total expenditures between 1871 and 1894 for federal election officers had gone to New York state, and a quarter of the national outlay to New York City alone. For the same reason, the number of deputy marshals employed in the North had been vastly greater than in the South. In contrast, federal election officials serving in rural areas had not received any compensation and had lacked the power to arrest. Republicans had pressed for federal election supervision in northern cities that frequently went Democratic, but not in northern rural Republican areas. There had been a higher rate of convictions in the North as well. Federal troops had been moved into New York and Philadelphia and into such border cities as Baltimore and Wilmington, Delaware, to back the enforcement effort. Because the margins of victory of presidential, congressional, and state elections had frequently been narrow during the period between 1870 and 1894, and the control of Congress had remained precarious, federal election enforcement in the North often had meant the difference between victory and defeat for the Republicans. Moreover, by tightening registration as well as by reforming naturalization, the Democrats' strength, swelled by the influx of immigrants to northern cities, could be lessened.[45]

To be sure, the Negro voter in the southern states had not been an irrelevant consideration. As Illinois Senator Lyman Trumbull put it, the Klan bill had been designed "for political purposes to enable

49

them [the Republicans] to carry the South." Indeed, the Republican program had been built on the assumption that if the southern black electorate were properly organized and adequately protected, Republicans could retain several southern and border states, possibly even a majority of them. Not only had Attorney General Akerman repeatedly made the point in letters to his fellow Georgians, but other southern Republicans had also stressed, in urgent appeals, the intimate and indispensable relationship between federal enforcement and their party's political fortunes. The chairman of the Alabama Republican committee had opposed the dismissal of the federal attorney, because "his removal will be death to the Republican party here." Of course, Washington had maintained that enforcement was to be strictly impartial—that there would be no double standards dependent upon political allegiance when it came to punishing violators of the law. However, that did not mean nonpartisan employment of enforcement officials. On the contrary, no Democratic attorneys had been hired as special counsel; only Republican lawyers had been considered. Attorney General Akerman summed up the situation when he wrote that Republican employees "are more likely to have their hearts in the work." Thus, by enforcement, Republicans had reasoned, the party could be saved and its partisans protected.[46]

Another related motive for legislating enforcement was the cover it might provide for federal intervention in shoring up Republican regimes that were in trouble in the Deep South. If federal activity and military intervention were needed to prevent the Democrats from securing control of state governments, enforcement could supply the pretext and rationale for a military presence; also, with the power provided by the enforcement acts, martial law could be instituted, if it were deemed necessary, for political purposes. Obviously, such powers had been merely potential, but looking toward the future, they were nonetheless important. On several grounds, then, federal enforcement had been necessarily partisan in character. In the words of one official, it had meant nothing less than "our political salvation."[47]

The overall ineffectiveness of the program in the South and the borderland, however, raises the fundamental question of the regional

50

primacy of Republican motivation and the priority of the federal enforcement effort. Federal election enforcement for the South had too often been more like a campaign document than a genuine effort, more a salvage operation than a permanent reform. Often, winning elections in the North had seemed to matter more than suppressing violence in the South. The northern strategy had relied, on the one hand, upon the political dividend that had accrued from pressing the Klan issue and, on the other, upon the elimination of election irregularities in northern cities; both attention and appropriations had been concentrated on those twin efforts to keep the North as the Republican bastion. The legislative record of enforcement, then, was replete with paradox: the most far-reaching reconstruction measures of a national political character had been undertaken precisely when support for reconstruction was on the wane; the federal government had undertaken these bold innovative programs at a time when Republicans were losing their power and purpose. The grandiose objectives and the endless statutes filled with interminable sentences, along with the poor record of actual enforcement, suggested even then, during the early 1870s, the decline and decay of reconstruction.

The extraordinary circumstances of the birth and life of the enforcement acts reflected intense partisan interest at every stage. Both parties had wanted to create campaign issues that supported or opposed enforcement legislation, as well as to encourage or to obstruct the federal effort to correct voter registration in northern cities; both parties had also wrestled with the subject of federal election enforcement at each session of Congress as a test of strength and an exercise in partisan jockeying. In 1872 Republican Senator Cornelius Cole of California had declared, with regard to the pending enforcement bill: "The Democrats are determined not to let the amendment pass and we cannot let the bill pass without it now."[48] To bring those party measures into existence, the Republicans had relentlessly pushed them through Congress in all-night sessions which had been kept going by policemen rounding up congressmen for quorums. Often, such measures had been adopted in the last days of lame-duck sessions by strict party votes. Complex bills had not been printed, and debate had been restricted; as a result, members sometimes hadn't known precisely what they were voting on. And the final enforcement act had become law as a rider to an appropriation act. Describing the fight over the Klan Act, moderate Republican Congressman Garfield wrote: "when I was in the midst of the Ku-Klux fight, I found a kind of party terrorism pervading, and oppressing, the minds of our best men here, on the question." When Garfield denounced such pressures and obstructed extreme proposals, he was accused of lacking backbone.[49] The Democrats had responded in kind to Republican initiatives by mustering all their members to prevent passage of the various enforcement bills by means of filibusters and crippling amendments.

Less than a year after enforcement had been in operation, however, doubts about the program had increased among Republican congressmen. By April, 1871, some of them had strongly believed that the policy was misguided in some aspects and potentially mischievous in others. Garfield, who had earlier been concerned about the need for, but proper limitation of, such laws, became even more dubious: "I have never suffered more perplexity of mind, on any matter of legislation, than on that we are now attempting, concerning the Ku Klux. We are working on the very verge of the Constitution, and many of our members are breaking over the lines, and, it seems to me, exposing us, to the double danger, of having our work overthrown by the Supreme Court and of giving the Democrats new material for injuring us, on the stump." He had believed that certain powers and functions of state government were then threatened by the pending bill, which not merely limited state jurisdiction but superseded it. Congress, he had contended, lacked the authority to deal with individuals; congressional legislation could not bear directly upon citizens, for there was no clear grant of power to legislate for the protection of life and liberty within the states. Garfield had also objected to the provision of martial law: legislators could not provide by law for the suspension of all law when there was no war. Martial law was, by definition and by need, that which was declared by a general in time of war, not by Congress in time of peace. Moreover, during suspension of the writ of habeas corpus, there had been no safeguards for citizens, no limit to time in prison, nothing but the will of the commander who ordered arrests. Garfield had declared that the federal government was not the police and could not act as such.[50]

Similarly, Republican Congressman Samuel Shellabarger of Ohio wrote that he did not wish to push federal authority any further into "doubtful latitudes" unless he was absolutely required to. The moderate Illinois Representative John F. Farnsworth had agreed, declaring that during reconstruction Congress had acted out of necessity, but the steps it had taken could no longer be defended or bear the test of constitutional review: "We passed laws . . . and the country knows it, which we did not like to let go to the Supreme Court for adjudication. And I am telling no tales out of school." But the war had then been over for five years, and the time to overstep constitutional bounds had passed: "We have reconstructed, and reconstructed, and we are asked to reconstruct again. . . . we are governing the South too much." Michigan moderate Republican Congressman Austin Blair had concluded that there was no point in piling "statute upon statute to sleep in your books unused. . . . it is not law that is wanted in the South; it is the execution of the laws." Following Garfield's lead, the House of Representatives, now wary of extreme enforcement measures, had balked at more stringent proposals during 1871 and 1872.[51]

The furious fight between the more radical Senate and the more moderate House had underlined the growing unpopularity of such sweeping legislation in Congress and the country, a trend reflected in the greatly increased strength of Democratic representatives following the 1870 elections. To many Americans, what the Constitution appeared only to allow now mattered more, especially when the people were increasingly clear about what they did not want. The leader of the Republican turnabout as to enforcement was the New York *Evening Post*, which had launched an editorial offensive against the Klan Act. The *Post* contended that the law was a constitutional sham, combining bad law with poor politics; it would bring the Republican party into disrepute: "If the law-makers turn law-breakers, if the guardians of the Constitution tear it in pieces" when it suited their interests, "what remains but endless and yearly increasing disorder?" Since it had been impossible and, more importantly, undesirable to put a corporal's guard at every door, the *Post* had recommended that the solution was to have as little federal interference as possible.[52] Similarly, the *Nation*, which had previously supported election enforcement, had been disturbed by the faith in force as a means of solving problems, a solution that could only result in increasing reliance upon a policy of coercion. Once ideals took the place of respect for law and the forms of law, once the law was either broken or bruised, then "we have sown the seeds of anarchy, because one man's ideal is as good as another's," leading to one party's trying to substitute its ideal for the other's.[53]

Nonetheless many Republicans had recognized that reconstruction in large measure depended on the success of election enforcement. Postmaster General Marshall Jewell wrote: "if we cannot protect them [the black voters in the South] we shall lose most of the fruits of this tremendous war." And in the words of North Carolina Republican Senator John Pool: "Upon that ground the Republican party must stand in carrying into effect the reconstruction policy, or the whole fabric of reconstruction, with all the principles connected with it, amounts to nothing at all; and in the end, it will topple and fall unless it can be enforced by the appropriate legislation."[54]

Yet the federal program to prosecute and punish perpetrators of force and fraud in southern elections had not accomplished much that was substantial or enduring. With election enforcement often characterized by pious platitudes and undercut by penny-pinching; governed by episodic expedients and often overseen by mediocre administrators; lacking central control and local coordination; plagued by delay and timidity and undermined by premature suspension and pardoning; beset by an unwieldy, inefficient court system and ravaged by an understaffed, underfinanced prosecution—moreover, with the magnitude of the enforcement problem being greater than the scope of the federal remedy, with unenforceable law being abandoned in the face of unyielding opposition, and with state statutes legalizing noncompliance and federal courts often rationalizing local practice—the law of enforcement was no law at all.

Under a covering fire for each advance, the federal campaign of enforcement had moved forward by inches, then backward by miles. The problem of the Klans, the Knights, the White Liners and the White Leaguers in the South had been real, but the Grant administration and the Republican Congress had frequently used the issue for partisan effect, mounting a vigorous propaganda barrage in the North. The federal government had never mobilized a sustained campaign of effective suppression of political terrorism throughout the South. There had been brave talk but timid action.[55] Enforcement had thus generated the highest hopes, the deepest hates, and the bitterest disappointments.

3
DOUBLE LIABILITY

The Presidential Campaign of 1872

AMERICANS had expected greatness from Grant as president because they had found greatness in him as a general. But the hero's halo, burnished by Vicksburg and Appomattox, had faded fast through four years in the Executive Mansion. In contrast to his wartime determination and resourcefulness, as president he often appeared to lack leadership and vigor. His appointments, with but few exceptions, were nondescript; tested incompetence was frequently rewarded, whereas excellence brought suspicion and often dismissal. Scandal began to reach many people associated with Grant by ties of friendship, favor, or family; the administration was reeling from charges of corruption, cronyism, and absenteeism.

Nor did Grant's policies enjoy success. The enactment of a new tariff in 1870 alienated reformers.The plan to annex Santo Domingo during 1870 was ill-conceived—the nation had enough problems without annexing more territory. Also, Grant disappointed many southerners in their hope that reconstruction would cease. Overall, he frequently mismanaged or simply neglected politics,[1] with the significant exceptions of his role in helping secure ratification of the Fifteenth Amendment and his administration's success in negotiating war claims with Britain. By 1872 a number of Republicans lacked confidence in the president.

The problem was not just Grant's presidency but also the limits and liabilities of the Republican party, as well as its change in character. By 1872, the party had come of age with a transformed identity. The organization was an entrenched institution which had developed a life and a purpose, a truth and a ritual of its own. Vested interests, patronage, and preservation of power now were of prime importance. By the 1870s the party was full of ambitions, jealousies, suspicions, hostilities, and all the factional squabbling that attend the success of a party long in control. Also, as the sense of common danger engendered by the war evaporated—that which had brought the party's leaders together—the old war feeling began to subside, although it could still be revitalized by the Democrats' intransigence and southern violence. Wartime idealism was beginning to wear thin, especially as the old ranks of Republican leaders and supporters were being decimated by death. New issues demanded attention. Moreover, the new Republicans in Congress and the cabinet were more pragmatic and opportunistic than their predecessors; though still repeating the old slogans and supporting the old causes, the new recruits employed such causes more as a means than as an end. Still, the issues of the war and reconstruction remained vital to the party. And with no alternative to Grant's renomination, his re-election was regarded as essential to continuing control of the federal government. Thus he was swiftly renominated in early June.

The Democrats, for their part, faced the presidential election with uncertainty. Although the Democracy continued to show itself remarkably resilient in its ability to survive as a party, despite a succession of national defeats, there was a huge gap between survival and success. The party continued to be a large minority, but it nonetheless remained discordant and unconfident. To be sure, it had made gains[2] in the congressional elections of 1870, but these had been followed during 1871 by the sensational scandal of the Tweed Ring in New York City and the setbacks in state elections. Then, in the New England state elections during the spring of 1872, the Democrats again fared badly.[3] Numerous divisions between conservatives and moderates continued to plague the party. The northern wing was still deeply divided between peace and war Democrats, and as a whole, they disagreed over reform, economic policy, and even tactics. This was reminiscent of the past—of 1864, for example, when they had nominated a war Democrat for president on a peace platform, and of 1868, when they had nominated a hard-money man on a soft-money platform.

Each faction was suspicious of the other and made political differences into personal enmities. The ultra conservatives, who tended to be doctrinaire, rigid, and intense, regarded the moderates as opportunistic weaklings, ready to sell out the principles of the party for the sake of momentary success. The pragmatic moderates were equally impatient with the conservatives' reliance on unpopular and unsuccessful political strategies. The Democratic Louisville *Courier-Journal*, noting the tendency of the conservatives to engage in foolish and damaging debates and to harp on questions about which the North no longer cared, dismissed the group as "dry bones and dead languages." The moderates, on the other hand, wished to escape recurrent failure by making changes in order to attract new adherents and to regain earlier supporters. Therefore, party members suggested a number of simple but superficial solutions designed to hoist the party out of its rut: reorganize the party structure, change its name to "Liberal," "Conservative," "Liberal Democracy," or "National Democracy," and revamp the image of the party by proclaiming new slogans or new departures. But the difficulty remained of how to form and hold together a coalition of racist reactionaries, reformist moderates, and disenchanted Republicans.[4]

Even more challenging was the job of harmonizing the conflicting interests of the northern and southern wings of the party—a problem exacerbated by parochial southern Democrats who repeatedly placed their sectional interests above those of the nation or the needs of the national party. The Louisville *Courier-Journal* observed that the "South is drifting out of reach and control, its sole care being to save itself" by getting, somehow or anyhow, attached to the side or faction that advanced southern interests. For their part, moderate party members in the North viewed the southern wing as something of an albatross, slowing down even the modest changes that some in the northern contingent were ready to accept. Congressman Michael C. Kerr of Indiana, for example, noted the negative, narrowly sectional posture of the southern congressmen, their refusal to exercise restraint or to accept the postwar situation and to obey the reconstruction amendments, or to work for future reform and amelioration of conditions in the South. Southerners simply expected, as the price of support, much more from the national Democratic party than most northerners were willing to give.[5]

Another, and truly fundamental, problem for the Democrats was their lack of credibility in the North. Not only had they compromised themselves during the war, but later they had also proved to be ambiguous about reconstruction. Although some of them preached equality before the law, few sincerely wanted it or thought it should be achieved. Although the Democrats at their national convention in 1872 were to endorse equal rights in principle, state Democratic conventions subsequently denounced those rights in fact. The Democrats might embrace the new constitutional amendments in word, but their hostility to the purpose of those amendments, their resistance to enforcement, and their agitation for repeal still remained dominant, though often dormant, in the party. Vague pronouncements advocating home rule were also unclear. Was it simply the Democrats' desire to have local governance of purely local affairs? Or was it a euphemistic term for a harsh dose of states' rights and racial segregation in order to "put the nigger where he belongs"?

Indeed, the entire Democratic record on reconstruction appeared very chameleon-like, for the party often took its prevailing hue from the surrounding environment as constituency needs and moods shifted. Reluctant acceptance or empty espousal of black rights and interests alternated with cold indifference or open opposition. Sometimes the Democrats made disarming appeals in fitful efforts to recruit black voters. More often, they attempted to reduce the number of votes cast by blacks or curried favor with the whites by ferocious black-baiting. But despite changing rhetoric and recruitment efforts, the party's behavior remained on the whole unfriendly to the Negro and to reconstruction. Southern Democrats neither encouraged peace nor discouraged disorder, and both northern and southern Democrats stressed the fallibility of universal suffrage and tried at every opportunity to undercut federal enforcement.

Indicative of the party's problem was the ineffectuality of the Democratic contingent in Congress. Democrat Richard Vaux, a former mayor of Philadelphia, complained that only the Democrats in

Congress were forced to fight on a battlefield chosen by the enemy: "We always wait till they [the Republicans] act, and then pick up the odds and ends and so are [put on] the defensive from the start." He condemned the sluggishness of the Democratic congressmen, who, he wrote, had brains but no guts: "the democracy in Congress deserve defeat for they have no claim to victory while they act as they do."[6]

Clearly, both in Congress and in the country a new approach was needed by the Democrats. Some sort of coalition, combining defectors from the Republican party (the so-called "Liberal Republicans") and the Democrats came to be a subject for discussion among many Democratic and Liberal politicians and editors. After all, such a coalition had paid off handsomely since 1868 in several states below the Mason-Dixon line, notably in such border states as Missouri and in the upper South, particularly in Virginia.[7] The pivot on which such a coalition might turn was amnesty, which would serve both as the purpose and the method by which to unite Liberals and Democrats in their bid for power. Both groups advocated complete amnesty for those former Confederates who had been prevented from voting and holding any office, a stand grounded both in conviction and a desire for crucial votes. Supporters of amnesty argued that it was time to declare the war completely over and to treat the rebellion as an error rather than as a crime. To do less would further embitter the disaffected and, by fostering martyrdom, encourage them to make terrorist mischief. Besides, proscription, they contended, had left the South bereft of able and intelligent leadership, for many of its influential and experienced men were barred from holding office. Furthermore, the proscribed had no interest in maintaining order and could not be expected to give wholehearted support to the public authority that labeled them political outlaws. The peace offering of amnesty, they maintained, would lead to harmony and stability.[8]

Such arguments in favor of amnesty struck many Republicans as naive, with enemies being transformed into friends overnight and the southern Democrats' efforts to disfranchise blacks stopping short once amnesty was presented as a peace offering. The further premise that the nation could be completely reunited and genuinely reconciled only if southern white Democrats had a free hand was ominous.

If the South could be ruled only by the proscribed, then reconstruction was a confessed failure.[9]

But amnesty as well as a mutual interest in forming a political partnership remained common concerns of the Democrats and the Liberals, despite mutual distrust on both sides. Many Democrats believed that an alliance with former Republicans would be dishonorable, even treasonable. Many Democrats also worried that the Liberals were more interested in advancing their pet reforms than in gaining power. The Liberals, in turn, wondered whether a coalition with the Democrats would be profitable in the North, where voters identified the Democracy with the South and distrusted both. Many Liberals feared, moreover, that the Democrats were more interested in power than in reform. However, the advocates of such an alliance papered over all the suspicions and differences by brandishing ideas of reform and reconciliation, without being definite about which reforms they had in mind or whose reconciliation was intended. Regarding coalition as a panacea and cooperation and coordination as automatic, these advocates concentrated more on the anticipated benefits of an alliance than on its price. Under such conditions it was doubtful that the projected bipartisan coalition between former slaveholders and old freesoilers, states' rightists and nationalists, would be real and effective. Indeed, circumstances suggested that it might be a coalition in name only.[10]

An additional problem was the nature of the Liberal Republican movement itself, for the Liberals lacked cohesion, common experience, organization, and the leadership necessary to develop an internal consensus and to sustain a successful party campaign. Having been formed between 1870 and 1872 as an opposition to various policies and patronage decisions of the administration, the Liberals were more united in their opposition to Grantism than unified on a program or as a party. In fact, the Liberal ranks were so diverse that there was a real danger of disintegration. Each constituent group, inflationists and deflationists, revenue reformers and free traders, civil service reformers and politicians hungry for patronage, seemed more interested in having their own way than in having a party at all.[11] Then, too, what of the limitations of the Liberals as politicians? In organizing their new party, instead of beginning at the grass roots by building a party with a wide appeal and giving the people what they wanted, they tried to start with the top, envisioning a party of like-minded men who imposed their own policies and lectured the people about what was good for them. The Liberals, then, with their evident distaste for politicking and organizing, seemed merely to dabble in politics; although they created a political party, they in fact distrusted parties. How such a group could be effective and persuasive when its members so mistrusted not only one another but the electorate as well raised the question of whether the Liberal movement itself was a misalliance, not a party.[12]

When in early May, 1872, the Liberal Republicans nominated New York *Tribune* editor Horace Greeley, the political situation suddenly changed, and the options for both Liberals and Democrats were drastically narrowed. The Liberal delegates, after floundering about in indecision and division, had finally and spontaneously chosen a candidate.[13] But Greeley was hardly an appropriate or sensible choice. Since he was not an ardent champion of such Liberal views as civil service reform or tariff reduction, his selection could only, and did, result in splitting the ranks of the reformers.[14] Moreover, Greeley's age, sixty-two, was another liability, not to mention his eccentric appearance and style—a big round face and bald head, neck whiskers, drooping eyeglasses, a crumpled white coat, slouched figure, tall white hat, squeaky voice, and illegible handwriting. Nor did his personality help: he was impulsive, vain, vindictive, and, yet again, eccentric in his views. At various times he had flirted with such unpopular causes as utopian socialism, spiritualism, vegetarianism, and prohibition, and during the war he had alternated between heedless radicalism and mindless pacifism. Diplomat Charles Francis Adams believed that Greeley's bizarre nomination would divert attention from the limits and liabilities of the Grant administration and was thus "a great escape" for the Republicans, for "success with such a candidate is out of the question."[15]

To those who favored coalition with the Liberals, Greeley's nomination came as a shock. Instead of choosing a potential ally in a conservative Republican, the Liberals had selected an implacable enemy in an old radical Republican—"the most conspicuous and heated opponent of the Democratic party that could be found in the whole country," thundered the New York *World*. It was Greeley who had once said: all Democrats might not be rascals but all rascals were Democrats. One of them wrote that "Greeley has spit and stomped upon every principle of Democracy during his entire life." And the Pittsburgh *Post* put the matter bluntly: "If the managers of the liberal movement ever expected to enlist the support of the democratic party, they could not have adopted a plan better calculated to make it impossible."[16]

Similarly, California's Senator Eugene Casserly in June found congressional Democrats dismayed by the choice, for "Greeley's show of strength in the Republican party thus far has greatly disappointed us," although "his chief strength is in our party, where it manifests itself by tearing us to pieces." Warning of potential Democratic defection, Casserly continued: "when a great party goes so far out of its way for a candidate for the Presidency as to nominate a man like Greeley, it is not on party affinities, traditions or convictions you can rely for success." He noted that without sufficient Republican support and without substantial, united, enthusiastic Democratic support, Greeley would prove a disastrous choice for the Democracy. Concerned that Greeley's nomination, despite the Democrats' reservations, was already a foregone conclusion, the Democratic presidential nominee of 1864, George B. McClellan, remarked: "the absurd part of the whole thing seems to be the utter impossibility of finding any one who wants to see Greeley President—yet they all go for him because everybody else wants him." Congressman Kerr was also deeply troubled: "When I reflect upon this Greeley movement, I am utterly unable to analyze it. It is a most stupendous and illogical blunder. But it has won the popular fervor. It sweeps the country. It will possess Baltimore [Democratic convention] on the 9th prox. It is inevitable. But what then? Will it be victory? I fear not. And if it is, will it be useful victory? Very doubtful. To me in every respect, it is the bitterest pill of my whole political life."[17]

But other Democrats thought that there was little prospect of doing better and a far greater possibility of doing worse. The Louisville *Courier-Journal* tried to persuade Democrats that Greeley would provide an honest and frugal administration, civil supremacy and state autonomy, constitutional governance and sectional reconciliation. A number of southerners expressed similar ideas; earlier, newspaperman Littleton D. Q. Washington had observed that it was idle for the Democratic party to fight the Fourteenth and Fifteenth amendments: *"to do so is to throw away the election. If we got power we can neutralize the mischief in them."* By May, 1872, Washington noted that the Liberals previously had been more interested in reform than in reconciliation, but that had changed because the Liberals were now embracing and emphasizing reconciliation with the South in their state platforms and in the national campaign. Moreover, he believed that Greeley would "be open to us [the South] and our views . . . liberal and kindly toward us. . . . If *we* elect him, he will be our President." Even Democratic Pennsylvania diehard Jeremiah S. Black, a former attorney general in James Buchanan's administration and still prominent in the party, pointed out that it was a question of choosing between Grant and Greeley: "even if we find no *good* in either of them, we must take that one who shall appear to be least bad." Finding Greeley less objectionable, Black considered his faults to lie mainly in his abrasive manner. Furthermore, though he had been with the radical abolitionists before the war, he had not always been one of them. And even if Greeley could not get rid of the "tyranny of the fourteenth and fifteenth Amendments," at least he could execute them mercifully. Thus, the wicked Republicans had to be replaced at all costs.[18]

Also trying to make the best of what he termed the Liberals' "blunder," the chairman of the Democratic national committee, August Belmont, wrote that the party must endorse Greeley in order to beat Grant, for "any thing is better than the present state of affairs in Washington." Nominating a former Republican, moreover, might divide Republicans. Furthermore, the Democrats were genuinely at a loss for a nominee, and Greeley's advocates were more active and enthusiastic for him than his opponents were united against him and for someone else. Many influential Democratic leaders, state conventions (notably the Indiana meeting in mid-June, which had been expected to oppose Greeley and insist upon a separate nomination, but did neither), and delegates to the national convention thus concluded that the real option was between possible victory with Greeley and certain defeat without him.[19] So in early July at the convention, the

Democrats swallowed their many doubts about Greeley, with the "outs" scrambling to get in. Desperation whetted by hope had prevailed. The Democrats also adopted the Liberal platform word for word, accepting reconstruction as well as Liberal reform, at least on paper.[20]

During the campaign the well-organized Republicans[21] relied upon the northern fears of the Democracy. Stressing Greeley's unfitness, they predicted that, if elected, he would be the Democrats' stalking-horse and would allow southerners to undermine the results of the war and reconstruction. Greeley's election meant change, they emphasized, and change meant uncertainty and trouble.[22] For his part, President Grant did not actively campaign in deference to custom as well as for fear of blundering. But although he did not make many speeches, he was not averse to newspaper reporters doing that for him. For example, he deftly slipped into an interview the embarrassing fact that the idealistic Senator Sumner, who supported Greeley, had not always been quite the champion of the Negro that he was supposed to be, given the fact that he had dodged the final vote when Congress passed the Fifteenth Amendment in 1869.[23] Grant also remained in close touch with the political situation—that is, with discussions of political prospects during several meetings of the cabinet. And he shrewdly employed federal patronage and party subsidy to win the support of certain politicians and newspaper editors. Given his political offensive in the spring, his party's platform promises in the summer, and his party's concerted campaigning in the fall, Grant showed that he was a resourceful and persistent politician intent upon being reelected.[24]

The Republican barrage put Greeley and the coalition on the defensive. Greeley himself denied that he would be a tool of the Democrats or support any prosouthern moves in the future. In spite of his checkered past of contradictions and fads, his supporters declared that their candidate was a new man and would prove, as president, wiser than his words. Once elected, the Liberals predicted, he would rise to the challenge, prove susceptible to sound Liberal influences, and be guided in the right direction by a wise cabinet, which would in itself guarantee a safe administration. However, in the same breath they argued that Greeley was too much of a political maverick to be led by the Democrats or indeed by any party or group. In any case, only his presidency could bring lasting peace and stability. The disorders in the South would cease and reconstruction be secure only if his policy of amnesty was put into effect. On the other hand, undercutting their own reasoning, the Liberals persisted in believing that he really couldn't do very much. After all, it was the business of Congress to make the laws, not the president's, and with the Senate likely to remain Republican, all of Greeley's recommendations and appointments would be thoroughly scrutinized. Such arguments in his defense were bizarre: elect a chief executive for what he could not do, save him from himself by means of the Congress and the cabinet checkmating him, maintain reconstruction by electing one of its present critics, and create a new Greeley without destroying the old one. Some supporters, however, emphasized that it was the cause, not the candidate, that counted. According to one of them, "there is not much good expected of Greeley and but little harm. That his term will be a sort of bridge over which we can go into the promised land of reform."[25]

Greeley, for his part, wanted to follow Grant's example and remain silent. But some of his Liberal advisers, chafing at their candidate's inactivity, arranged a stumping tour through New England in August. Its results should have been a warning, for Greeley rambled on from topic to topic, uttering inanities and making a bad impression.[26] Then, concerned about the outcome of critical congressional and state elections on October 8 in Pennsylvania, Ohio, and Indiana, along with their effect on the presidential race, pressured by the Democratic national committee to give impetus to a flagging campaign, and unable to resist the temptation to talk—Greeley went west. Between September 17 and 29, 1872, he delivered almost two hundred speeches in New Jersey, Pennsylvania, Ohio, Indiana, and Kentucky, making as many as twenty-two in a single day. He stressed his chief issue—reconciliation between the sections—which, he promised, would usher in a new dawn.[27]

Historians have praised Greeley's speeches for their statesmanlike magnanimity and conciliatory spirit; yet they could hardly have been called politically astute. A concerned supporter cautioned Greeley not to reopen volatile political questions, for "in silence there is safety." Greeley's managers recognized the danger of extemporaneous speeches, and Greeley himself wrote that he wished to avoid making blunders. However, he did not succeed.[28]

At Pittsburgh, on September 19, Greeley denounced the recent soldiers' convention there as having the "single purpose of rekindling the bitterness and hatred, the animosities and antipathies, the fears and exultations of civil war. . . . for the sake of partisan advantage." Whatever the truth of this charge, the speech was an insult to Union veterans, and the New York *Evening Post* likened it to trampling on the wreaths at soldiers' graves. And Greeley did not stop there. Speaking of the war itself, he even reopened the secession question, declaring that he would abide by a peaceful separation of the Union if that were the verdict of southerners in a free and fair referendum. Separation, he said, was preferable to war. After causing an uproar, being quoted extensively and severely criticized, he had to clarify his inflammatory remarks several times.[29]

The Pittsburgh speech was quite enough to strike down a candidate, but there was more to come. At Louisville, on September 21, Greeley characterized Negroes as ignorant, deceived, and misguided because they either misunderstood or misrepresented him. As a result, he said, "they are steeled against us. They will not hear us; they don't believe us." If Greeley intended to lure the black voter, he went about it in a curious way. After the speech, when a Negro delegation visited him, he told them he was no special friend of any race.[30] Subsequently, at Jeffersonville, Indiana, on September 23, Greeley announced: "I was, in the days of slavery, an enemy of slavery, because I thought slavery inconsistent with the rights, the dignity, the highest well-being of free labor. That might have been a mistake." In truth, it was his speechmaking tour that was a mistake. Greeley was aiming an inappropriate message at the wrong targets in unsuitable places; he was also unsettling matters that had supposedly been settled by the war. Increasingly, he had to spend time replying, as he said, to "one or two of the million calumnies which have been aimed at me." To be sure, there were huge crowds to greet him, but they often included, in addition to his enthusiastic supporters, a good number of the merely curious. Americans, according to the Washington *National Republican*, like shows. But the reception was not always friendly: veterans hooted, hissed, and jeered at him, and a rock was thrown through his train window in Ohio. As a newspaper in Washington, the *New National Era*, summed up the tour: "we are heartily glad to see Mr. Greeley on the stump, bent, as it were, on giving the final blow to his rapidly waning chances."[31]

A number of other observers also suggested that Greeley in his western swing had indeed dealt himself a death blow. An Ohio Republican wrote on September 26, "Our folks are making it dreadful warm for Horace in Ohio and now I see that overwhelmed with his blunders and mistakes, they have switched him off," adding: "I am very glad they did not do it before he had done us a power of good." He also alluded to the Indiana junket: "The faithful abasement of Horace in Indiana before the rebel Democracy has filled many who otherwise would have supported him with sullenness and disgust; and they say if that is the way he eats dirt, that they'll be damned if they support him." Another Ohioan, former governor Hayes, observed on September 22 that "Greeley's foolish speeches must surely weaken him, and destroy what chances he had," and he noted further on September 29, at the end of the tour, that Greeley's tour had been "an advantage" to the Republicans. Similarly, Ohio Republican Congressman Garfield wrote the following entry in his diary on September 27: "Greeley's recent career of speaking . . . has been I think unwise on his part. It has helped us. Grant's 'silence' even though it be enforced 'is golden' in comparison with Greeley's garrulity." On October 11, after the state election, Garfield added: "I think Mr. Greeley has been a positive element of weakness. . . . His speeches in his own behalf hurt him seriously."[32]

The New York *Times* editorial, assaulting Greeley's southern strategy, was partisan but acute, describing it as designed "to appeal insidiously to the passions and prejudices of the South, while pretending to be anxious to heal them—to rekindle animosities while talking sweetly about burying them." The newspaper considered the strategy both deceptive and dangerous: "Can any people be mad enough to intrust their destinies to a man who goes about talking in this incendiary fashion? He is like a man who walks into a powder magazine with a lighted torch, saying 'I know the powder will not go off.'" The less partisan *Atlantic Monthly* agreed, reasoning that Greeley did not talk like a president and was not fit to be one, a conclusion shared by the New York *Evening Post*, which also criticized Greeley for ignoring the reform agenda of the Liberals. The Democratic Chicago *Times* used stronger language, terming Greeley a "political quack" and characterizing his effusive speeches as a "whining appeal for sympathy." In contrast, Grant now appeared positively desirable: "The chooser of the minor evil may almost exult in the man [Grant] who is to save us from such a President as we are threatened with in Mr. Greeley," claimed the *Atlantic Monthly*. And Garfield remarked that Greeley's nomination "makes the candidacy of Grant tolerable and respectable."[33]

The disastrous tour highlighted Greeley's defective strategy of trying to win by ingratiating himself with the South. In his attempt to please the southerners, he offended and frightened a great many northerners who interpreted his appeal as capitulation to southern demands. As a Virginian viewed the matter, the "North does not respond to and is not ready to accept Mr. Greeley's *idea* of amnesty and reconciliation. The Grant men have successfully worked the hatred opinions of the Civil War. . . . It is obvious to me that the Northern people will vote *against* anybody *we* [southerners] vote *for*."[34]

The approach was premature. To be sure, the war was over, but it had ended barely seven years before, and its wounds still hurt and haunted the people; its fruits were not to be questioned. A clerk in the White House confessed: "I cannot get over a distrust I have had always of the southern states. I never did believe any of them could be made Republican and kept so. The moment the curb is loosened they go back where they have always been." The majority of northerners were not about to clasp hands and blindly rush into the arms of the former rebels, especially when they were convinced that reconciliation might well bring about a Democratic restoration. The South in fact had shown no haste to shake hands across the bloody chasm, so why should the North?[35]

Actually, Greeley was asking the impossible of northerners: to conciliate the ultra southerners by letting them have their own way, to remove the supposed enemies of the spirit of amnesty—the Republicans—and to replace them with the unappeasable Bourbon Democrats, who would undoubtedly subvert reconstruction. The Liberals, in the opinion of the New York *Evening Post*, talked sentimentally, even hypocritically, about reconciliation, but did not make clear who was to be reconciled and to what. When Greeley returned to New York, he had succeeded only in convincing Republicans that they should be resigned to Grant. Once again, for most northern voters, there was sectional safety in Republican stability.[36]

Greeley's western tour was reminiscent of President Andrew Johnson's swing around the circle in the 1866 election—as awkward, as desperate, and as ineffective. Indeed, they rivaled each other in their obtuseness with regard to dominant northern public opinion, and both speechmaking expeditions helped greatly to wreck the two candidates' political ambitions. Greeley, like Johnson, was his own worst enemy. His parade of blunders out west, in stressing reconciliation over reform, suggested that his political judgment was unsound, his speech rather loose, his leadership unsafe, his past and recent record overwhelmingly damaging.[37]

Greeley had wanted to run for president in the worst way, and indeed he did—in the worst way possible. In the November election he lost every state except six in the South.[38] To reform-minded *Nation* editor Edwin L. Godkin the election meant, among other things, "contempt for Greeley."[39] Dissatisfied Republicans failed to defect in large numbers, and many disgruntled Democrats refused to vote. The whole character of the campaign was borne out by the patterns of voting and nonvoting: Greeley succeeded in nothing but in uniting the Republicans and in dividing the Democrats. Massive Democratic abstention in the North indicated that the region had rejected Greeley on the fitness issue, for it was not merely the bigoted and Bourbon elements that had refused to vote for him. Other candidates would doubtless have appealed more to dissatisfied Republicans and would have kept the loyalty of staunch Democrats. But only Greeley could have done so poorly with both. Thus the notion that a qualified Democratic candidate could not have improved upon Greeley's record does not take into account the poor Democratic turnout and the fact that Greeley ran behind other Liberal contenders virtually everywhere, except by a razor-thin margin in New Jersey, whose entire electoral vote nonetheless was won by a Republican presidential candidate for the first time. The Liberal following was small and the coalition was weak, but Greeley was even weaker, for he won fewer electoral votes (20) and a lower proportion of the popular vote (3 percent) than Seymour had in 1868 without the benefit of a coalition. In fact, Greeley was one of the historic presidential losers, receiving the lowest electoral total for any major party candidate between 1864 and 1932, and the lowest percentage of the popular vote between 1860 and 1892 (43 percent).[40]

General George G. Meade believed that "the botching of the Cincinnati Convention [of the Liberals] and the fears of Greeley have combined with the distrust of the Southern influence to throw into the Grant party—hundreds of thousands who would have voted against him, if the opposition had set up . . . a good ticket." In sum, the incidents, outcomes, and consequences of the election of 1872 were negative. A party and a president remained in power as a result of the dual liability of the opposition—the Democrats' disgust with Greeley's lack of qualifications for the presidency and the Republicans' distrust of the implications of Democratic control of the nation. Thus Greeley's nomination and southern strategy had dashed all hopes of victory and had sealed the fate of the Liberal party, which had not only been defeated but was to disappear. Clearly, the Democracy was decimated; its championship of premature reconciliation in 1872 had proved as catastrophic as its championship of premature counterrevolution in 1868.[41]

The course of the campaign also had implications for the future of reconstruction. Even though Greeley's argument for reconciliation on his own terms was thoroughly repudiated by the Republican press, the debate had succeeded in articulating and advertising the idea of reconciliation, which in time was to become more pronounced in the editorial columns of Republican organs. Following the election, the Washington *National Republican*, for example, sometimes sounded like a Liberal newspaper in its discussions of reunion and reconciliation. Even the radical Chicago *Inter-Ocean* talked of true reconciliation. Some Republican editors began to praise timid enforcement as discretion and forbearance and to oppose any new enforcement laws; greater reliance started to be placed upon moral suasion rather than on legal coercion. Increasing stress was being given to reconciliation between the sections rather than between the races. It was also suggestive that in the course of the 1872 campaign the Republican editorial writers, more than ever before, had rationalized reconstruction in defensive, negative, and narrowly sectional terms. To be sure, reconstruction had still been proclaimed as the North's bulwark against the onslaughts of an aggressive South, but reconstruction rarely had been praised as desirable, right, successful, and necessary in itself. And during the campaign, too, the subject of reconstruction had been relegated to secondary importance in Republican editorials; the earlier wartime arguments about northern self-interest in preventing national Democratic control had been primary. To be sure, such developments had not begun in 1872, but the Liberal-Democratic offensive and the Republican defense had accelerated the northern disengagement from reconstruction in the South. Finally, the Republican Congress, in order to blunt the Liberal-Democratic offensive, had granted amnesty to roughly twenty thousand former Confederates, and their opportunity to hold public office surely would further erode reconstruction. That action was far more significant for the future of the South than all the war talk of the Republican politicians on the stump in the North.[42]

Many Republican newspapers overconfidently assumed, however, that Greeley's decisive defeat would make southerners give up their opposition to reconstruction. Now having no chance to overthrow emancipation, enfranchisement, and civil equality, the South, predicted the New York *Times*, would have to abandon all reckless schemes to subvert reconstruction. Its success, many assumed, was assured by the landslide victory and the huge Republican majorities in Congress.[43] But this argument overlooked the fate of reconstruction during the first administration under Grant's leadership—a record that suggested pessimism, not optimism, with regard to the future. There was a measure of irony, then, in the fact that Grant's overwhelming victory and the party's retention of Congress had prevented a repudiation of reconstruction, but had not reinvigorated it.

Jubilant over his electoral triumph, President Grant had the highest hopes and the noblest of desires. Traveling to the funeral of Horace Greeley, who had died a broken man only a few weeks after the election, the president talked enthusiastically of the grand opportunity to make a great name for himself and to do great good for the country. But the bubble burst almost immediately. Corruption in Congress, which the New York *Sun* had first disclosed in the course of the presidential campaign during September, 1872, now became credible as the damning evidence mounted. Soon it was irrefutable that the outgoing vice-president, Schuyler Colfax, and perhaps the incoming vice-president, Henry Wilson, as well as eight prominent congressmen, many of whom were serving as chairmen of important committees, had accepted stock in a construction company, the Credit Mobilier, organized by promoters of the Union Pacific Railway, in return for anticipated political influence benefiting the railroad. By early 1873, as Congress proceeded to investigate and to censure, the Credit Mobilier was on everyone's lips, ruining the reputation of many Republican leaders in Congress and placing the party in disrepute.[44]

Grant's second inauguration on March 4, 1873, added an unpromising note. The day dawned cold and bitter. An icy piercing wind swirled funnels of dust through the streets, tearing off the flags and buntings that decorated Washington's buildings. The procession up Pennsylvania Avenue was a dismal display: two marching regiments did not arrive until after the ceremonies; the thin parade grew scraggly as frostbitten cadets from West Point and Annapolis dropped out of line from the cold, fatal pneumonia later claiming several of them; and little drummer boys, tears frozen on their faces, marched bravely before empty reviewing stands. With everyone trembling and shivering, the inaugural ceremony was brief. Indeed, the wind almost swept away the text of Grant's address. Balancing a call for reconciliation with the need for further reconstruction, Grant pledged to restore good feeling between the North and the South, claiming with more faith than facts that the former Confederate states were "now happily rehabilitated." He was vague in his endorsement of civil rights legislation for blacks. Grant, however, tempered his proposal for this legislation with the revealing aside: "social equality is not a subject to be legislated upon, nor shall I ask that anything be done to advance the social status of the colored man, except to give him a fair chance to develop what there is good in him."[45]

The president and his wife had wished for inaugural pomp and splendor on a grand scale. To accommodate them, contributions were levied on Republican officeholders, and tickets were sold at a high price. A mammoth wooden building was erected especially for the crowning event of the day, the inaugural ball. The hall itself was so large that all six thousand public employees in the capital could be fitted snugly inside the gigantic ballroom.

The fact that Negroes had been invited to it caused a stir and provoked comment: race relations in the southern-style Washington society had not caught up with Republican politics. Prominent members of the Washington social elite boycotted the ball because blacks attended it. Many who went were taken aback to see white midshipmen dancing with the wives of colored congressmen. As the racist New York *World* observed: "They [the blacks] are here in gorgeous array, with glares of defiance in their faces or expressions of excessive patronage." In the crowd, commented the Springfield *Republican*, "a perfectly white man was sandwiched between two colored women. This caused general remark and irritation." Other newspapers also expressed disapproval at the presence of blacks, indicating that there remained a gaping chasm between equalitarian rhetoric and everyday reality.[46]

As night approached, the weather grew colder and colder, but the inaugural program ground inexorably on. No one had anticipated a drop in temperature to four degrees above zero, and there were no heaters in the huge, flimsily constructed building. Icy winds swept through the hall and the elegantly clad guests, determined to show their finery, shivered miserably. The less vain chose to cover their expensive gowns and suits, dancing like polar bears in furs and heavy overcoats. The feast in the banquet hall congealed; the ice cream became inedible solid chunks, and the coffee froze to a soft mush. The musicians were unable to play their instruments, for the valves had frozen. Several hundred yellow canaries, which had been purchased to provide a pleasing twitter between the dances, were soon stiff little corpses. On the dance floor, a woman with a bronchial condition suddenly collapsed and died. Both the cold and the unexpected death cut short the ceremonies; everyone rushed to get a carriage, and there was great confusion inside and out. All the festivities ended abruptly as the guests left Washington as fast as the trains could carry them. Thus the second administration began its long agony. According to the Chicago *Times*, the weather "only typified the chilly indifference with which the nation greeted" Grant's second term. The biased observer concluded that most Americans knew that it promised no great good to the nation and hoped it threatened no serious evil.[47]

4

FEDERAL POWER TESTED

Grant's Early Southern Policy in Five States

DURING Grant's second term the relationship between his administration and the southern Republican state governments became a major problem that generated much criticism. To be sure, during his first term the national government played a major role in the affairs of southern governments, but it did not involve itself as frequently, as controversially, or with such untoward results as after 1872. The interaction between these southern regimes and Washington during the eight years developed into what became President Grant's southern policy. In the process, presidential purposes, federal influence, northern interests, and southern Republican survival were to be tested.

Some historians and journalists have argued that Grant and his government did not in fact have a southern policy—a question that depends largely on what is construed as policy: administrative management by the executive, discernible patterns of federal action, or a settled course toward specific objectives? In fact, the first two interpretations are more or less appropriate; the third also applies with certain qualifications; for Grant's was an intentional course, though sometimes inconsistent, contradictory, or inconstant, reflecting usually tacit priorities, and revealing definite purposes which, however, varied as to time and place. Further interpretative problems are raised by the term "policy." It is true that Grant pledged only to execute the laws and enforce court decisions, promising to follow the lead of Congress by carrying out, instead of inaugurating, policy regarding the South. It has therefore been suggested that one should concentrate on the events of the Grant administration rather than on the actions of the president himself, since Grant personally took no part in the shaping of events. A partisan advocate of that view, the New York *World*, in 1871 described President Grant in the councils of state as "a dummy, possessing neither ideas nor information."[1]

Yet Grant most definitely did put his personal stamp of approval or disapproval on a number of federal actions that vitally affected, at one time or another, each of the southern states. Indeed, by his orders and decisions, by taking action or permitting inaction, Grant often decided the outcome of southern events, for he was president in fact as well as in name. He had the greatest power, and it was he who usually defined the larger outlines of policy by expressing a clearcut choice and by showing his hand when he attained a specific result. Thus his policy can be inferred from his acts and from those of his subordinates.[2]

True, Grant's policy was neither preconceived nor consistent; his invocation "Let Us Have Peace" was a campaign slogan, not a presidential program. But seldom does any new president have a program mapped out in advance, ready to be put into effect regardless of changing circumstances. Moreover, the actions and proclamations prompted by events did not originate solely with Grant himself, for the details of policy were affected by subordinates and advisers in Washington whose position and power changed, as well as by loyal deputies and free agents in the South. Like all presidents, Grant was neither omnipotent nor omniscient, nor did he work in a political vacuum, for policy was mutated as it encountered obstacles and opposition. His policy, then, was usually decisive and controlling, but his actual influence varied.[3]

Like federal election enforcement, Grant's southern policy involved the national government in southern state and local affairs. Although enforcement was meant to protect Republican voters, especially Negroes, in their right to vote, thereby promoting Republicanism, southern policy was intended to maintain and strengthen the Republican regimes themselves. Although related, enforcement and southern policy differed in a number of ways. Enforcement was concerned with the actions of individuals under federal law, whereas southern policy was concerned with the relations between state and federal governments and the political control of a southern state. Accordingly, enforcement efforts were meant to cope with limited and contained outbreaks—curbing a riot or controlling organized political violence directed against persons and property of the opposition, when it was confined to a particular locality or district. Southern policy, on the other hand, had to contend with general uprisings that were intended to cripple or overthrow state governments.

Moreover, and unlike enforcement, the struggles to fashion and execute a southern policy were rarely fought in federal courts but rather within the offices of the White House and the governors' mansions, as well as in the chambers of Congress and the statehouses. At issue was the sanctioned use of federal force and the exercise of national authority to ensure the security and legality as well as the stability and loyalty of state regimes. The legal grounds on which federal intervention rested also often differed. Enforcement was based on the Fourteenth and Fifteenth amendments, as well as on recent legislation to define and enforce civil equality under these amendments; federal intervention with state governments was justified by the fourth or guarantee article of the Constitution, which authorizes suppression of internal violence and guarantees a republican form of government to every state. However, the demarcation and interpretation of this previously little-used section of the Constitution remained unclear and were the subject of changing construction and ceaseless controversy. Fighting to gain power under unprecedented postwar conditions, each side and faction attempted to ensnare the opposition in a web of constitutional theory; the ensuing debate amply demonstrated that legal logic can obediently serve political expediency.

Thus, acting without clear legal precedent and always facing charges of political opportunism, the government in Washington grappled with two recurring problems in the execution of southern policy. One was the question of when federal intervention was necessary and justifiable in order to suppress insurrectionary violence against a state government or to stop widespread sabotage of the election process; the other was what initiatives Washington ought to take to settle disputed elections or to recognize one of the rival authorities (two contesting governors, for example, or two disputing legislatures)—problems that had resulted from political crises or manipulated elections. When action was taken, it took various forms: a presidential decision, proclamation, or message, a judgment on the part of the attorney general, execution of a court order by the Department of Justice or by a communication from the secretary of war, or a resolution by Congress. Most important among these initiatives from Washington was recognition of the winner of an election by a presidential decision to provide, withhold, or withdraw support. President Grant could make or unseat a governor or a senator, thus sometimes assuring that such governments would consist of administration governors and senators. The ultimate weapon for enforcing the federal will in the South was the use of troops—that is, threatening to deploy them, merely mobilizing them, or employing them in some concerted action.

The next four chapters will attempt to explain the patterns of Grant's policy toward the South during his presidency and to speculate on why policy was adopted and how it changed. Above all, it needs to be kept in mind that Grant's motives were mixed and obscure, for he was not given to explaining the thoughts behind his actions or the premises behind his conclusions. Political motivation clearly accounts, in part, for Grant's responses to southern problems. He had two political purposes that did not always coincide: his desire for reelection in 1872 and his wish to aid his party. Aware of the political realities, he recognized the obvious advantage of appealing to the dominant constituency within a state. Thus, in southern states with a majority of white voters and where the Republican party was relatively weak, it was logical to attempt to develop a largely white (and therefore moderate) Republican party. By allowing native Republicans to share influence with native Democrats, Grant initially thought it might be possible to shape a political coalition with cooperating conservatives. On the other hand, in states where blacks were numerous and Republican governments reasonably certain of reelection so long as the blacks continued to vote, it was sensible to uphold these governments, should they need assistance from Washington.[4]

Both these considerations gave rise to certain tendencies in Grant's policies, especially at the beginning of his administration. A conciliatory posture, including patronage and amnesty, was tried in a number of border states, especially Virginia. Elsewhere, where there was a black-based Republican party, Grant tended to uphold such regimes with proscriptive policies. This was often his strategy for the Deep South, particularly the Gulf Coast states of Louisiana and sometimes, until 1875, Mississippi, but also at the start for Georgia and, intermittently, Alabama.

However, these overarching, political purposes did not influence Grant's decisions, for, except in the case of a few states, his plans were seldom fully formed and lacked both specific long-term goals and sustained programs to achieve them. For one thing, other political considerations impinged upon them. His actions in the South—particularly his use of the army to support Republican regimes—had immediate and frequently damaging repercussions in the North, thus eroding Republican support there. In addition to constant changes in public opinion, there were conflicting political forces within Grant's own cabinet, party, and the Congress. Moreover, the nature of the crises in the South varied enormously—from the acute to the chronic, and from the major to the ephemeral. In turn, responses from Washington ranged from the limited to the comprehensive, and from the direct to the indirect, depending upon the disposition to intervene, the actual opportunity to intervene, and the level of intervention, once it was undertaken.

Then, too, Grant's temperamental predilections imposed numerous restraints on many underlying political considerations. For one thing, his reactions to situations in the South were sometimes influenced by the people involved: friends would receive aid, which in some cases was unwarranted, whereas those he disliked or was indifferent to could not expect as much. Also, he displayed a tendency to oscillate from one extreme to another according to a momentary preference. Although he frequently chose a passive, temporizing stance, it was clear that some whim, some caprice, or merely impatience on his part could result in impulsive action.

Faced with occasionally unpalatable alternatives and unpredictable outcomes and forced to act in explosive emergencies (for southern crises seemed to burgeon overnight), President Grant had to

make rapid and important decisions as to whether to render or refuse federal aid in the South. The end result was a curious, often
contradictory record of bits and pieces, parts of a political puzzle
that was termed a southern policy, or more precisely, a series of half-
policies—separate yet successive steps in pursuit of often divergent
objectives. The southern situation posed difficulties that were intri-
cate, intractable, and seemingly interminable. In coping with them,
the government's actions illustrated the diverse priorities of the Republican party, the difficulties of the Grant presidency, and the erratic course of retreat from reconstruction.

Upon becoming president, Grant first had to formulate a policy that
would provide for the return of the last southern states to the Union.
When he assumed office in 1869, Virginia, Mississippi, and Texas
were still not represented in Congress. To be sure, the earlier requirements had already been defined in the reconstruction acts of 1867
and 1868. But the states would have to satisfy those broad, general
requirements as specifically defined by the new president, who would
arrange for the elections and devise the procedures, as well as settle
all intervening disputes at his own discretion. For the first time since
the war, true Republicans in fact controlled both the executive and
legislative branches, and the president was the potential master in
making regimes and maintaining them.

Virginia became the test case. Beginning on a magnanimous note
in the spirit of his "Let Us Have Peace" campaign motto, which had
captivated the country, President Grant agreed to strike the bargain
that was being pressed by Virginia moderates. If substantial dis-
qualification of former Confederates in voting and holding office
could be avoided, then in return the state would accept Negro suffrage. Accordingly, Grant recommended on April 7, 1869, a referendum on the state constitution, with the likelihood of a separate vote
on disfranchisement. This would enable Virginians to ratify the new
constitution, meet the requirements of reconstruction, and gain
readmission to Congress, but to vote down sweeping proscription. In
point of fact, the disaffected could vote in their own amnesty. Congress on April 10 entrusted the administration to Grant instead of to
the military commanders, as had been done previously, and left to

him the ticklish decisions about which referendums and what voter requirements ought to be employed.[5]

To radicals in the state, Grant's proposal was a stab in the back. One of them observed that reconstruction ought only be entrusted to its friends, which meant preventing its enemies, Virginia's conservative voters, from governing whether by voting or by holding office. Wholesale proscription, the radicals argued, would only come about if it were imposed as the price of readmission. Virginia moderates and conservatives disagreed, believing that Grant had saved them from much mischief, for the president had blocked a harsher policy and had given a new cue to Congress.[6]

On July 6, 1869, with the conservatives acquiescing and the Republicans divided, Virginia's voters rejected the extremes of Democratic reaction and Republican radicalism, endorsing the constitution and rejecting proscription. The conservatives' jubilant chairman sent Grant a telegram congratulating him on the success of his policy in Virginia, while bitter radicals blamed their defeat squarely on Grant's plan of submitting the disfranchisement clause to a separate vote, in direct opposition to the opinion of the rank and file of the Virginia Republican party. An abolitionist newspaper denounced what it incorrectly regarded as Grant's "do-nothing policy—this no-policy, in fact," considering his policy subversive in its humoring of enemies and snubbing of friends. One Virginia radical announced that his party was "destroyed here, and no power can resurrect it."[7]

Northerners disagreed sharply about the meaning of the election, with Republican journals proclaiming victory and Democratic organs reading Republican defeat.[8] The difference of editorial opinion reflected the political flux within Virginia as well as some uncertainty as to the possible course of southern policy that the Grant administration might have set. To be sure, moderate Republicans had selected and helped elect a governor, Gilbert C. Walker, who was in fact a nominal Republican, the so-called "True Republican" candidate, although formerly a northern Democrat and destined in the future to represent Virginia as a Democratic congressman. A moderate in politics, if no friend of equal education for the races, Walker was nonetheless a Republican pledged to support the administration. Moreover, the election did not bring about a counterrevolution, since the voters approved both a reconstruction constitution and black suffrage.

More importantly, however, the legislature did fall under conservative control. Indeed, the election had curious results—an on-the-surface Republican victory won, in part, by the enemies of Republicanism, as well as potential difficulties for that party in Virginia, with the whites voting for Walker, and the blacks for the defeated radical Republican slate. The conservative (or so-called Liberal) Republicans and the moderate conservatives had shown themselves to be shrewd and resourceful in fashioning an effective coalition, selecting acceptable candidates, assiduously cultivating influence in Washington, and pretending to serve national Republican party interests. Thus they captured control of their state, proclaiming that they were either Grant Republicans or Grant conservatives. One conservative declared about priorities: "If Grant and Co. are timorous about what we mean as to Federal politics, this should be put at rest instantly. The White people of Virginia don't care a cuss about Federal Politics! about Senatorships, or anything else at *Washington*. We want peace at Home"—which meant conservative power at home. Anticipating Virginia's readmission to the Union and to Congress, a conservative Richmond editor predicted: "'Just wait till we are safe in Congress. I tell you Virginia is Democratic for all time to come.'" [9]

During the campaign the future conservative governor James L. Kemper requested funds to be used in "securing or in at least silencing a considerable number of negroes." For the blacks, the election results were a disturbing omen; according to one Virginia conservative, the legislative majority was so large that it proved "the real lessons of the fight . . . giving him [the Negro] a most affecting proof of the power of the Virginia home-folks, and the true capacity of the Carpetbaggers to run the political machine." And indeed, the conservatives would henceforth be in charge of Virginia politics by having cleverly turned reconstruction to their advantage. [10]

Soon after their victory at the polls, Grant with some hestitation further assisted Virginia moderates and conservatives by preventing a radical counterattack designed to overturn the results of the election. Overruling his army commander in Virginia, the president in September ordered Attorney General E. Rockwood Hoar to allow the newly elected Virginia legislature to convene for a restricted session without taking the required test oath. This action prompted one Virginian to observe: "our anticipated embarrassments have been removed by the *virtuous* opinion of a *Hoar*." The military authority also validated the result of the election, and thus the newly elected state administration was installed. The radicals within Grant's own cabinet criticized the election result but were unable to persuade Grant to reverse them or to prevent the meeting of the conservative controlled legislature.[11]

For his conciliatory role, Grant was hailed by moderates as the architect of a new era of good feeling and sectional reconciliation. But the United States Senate's interminable delay and deliberate sabotage when it came to completing the state's readmission did postpone Grant's shortcut; yet though new, if unenforceable, conditions imposed by congressional radicals on voting and officeholding rights, as well as on equal education for blacks, tarnished the generosity of Grant's policy, they did not overturn conservative control in Richmond. Exploding with impatience over all the congressional stalling, the New York *Times* believed it was now too late to talk of magnanimity, because such a policy, to be efficacious, had to be "prompt and hearty—just the opposite of the captious and haggling and dilatory methods" of congressional radicals, who seemed bent on keeping old wounds open until doomsday. However, finally, if grudgingly, Congress did sanction the state constitution and election. On January 26, 1870, a now somewhat disgruntled Virginia returned to the Union. Moderates throughout the country were disgusted by the timing, but their policy, in substance if not in spirit, had prevailed. The radicals, despite their glee over having saved face by succeeding in mandating conditions of readmission, had no cause for celebration, for they had failed to repudiate the result of the election or to prevent the readmission of Virginia to representation in Congress.[12]

Grant's new departure, however, came at a high price. The "True Republicans" of 1869 did not remain so in fact or in name, becoming conservative in both. And by 1873 the honeymoon between them and the Grant administration was over. Grant now supported for governor a regular Republican candidate who tried to reconcile the seemingly irreconcilable races, while the conservatives launched outright their own party, which relied upon racist issues and promised to uphold the "white man's rule." This appeal to race prejudice was reportedly fortified by the intimidation of Republicans and the stealing of votes. The conservatives easily won the governorship in November, 1873. Party lines, which had earlier and temporarily broken down, were now redrawn. Ironically, during the heated and sometimes hysterical campaign, the conservatives' headquarters continued to prominently display a portrait of their former ally, Grant.[13]

His attitude of propitiation in Virginia[14] in 1869 suggests that Grant, early in his presidency, had already sensed that Republicans in many southern states either did not or would not in the future hold the balance of political power. Yet his favoring of Virginia conservatives and moderates did seem to pay off in the short run, for he carried Virginia in the 1872 presidential race, partly because of the goodwill of some Grant conservatives and also because of the ill will of a number of conservatives toward Greeley.[15]

Both his desire to fashion a balanced and moderate presidential performance with an eye to future electoral possibilities, and his sporadic interest in responding to the dominant northern sentiment, which increasingly reflected the wish for peace, quiet, and the ordinary operation of the government, comprised one strand of Grant's southern policy. Although observers had regarded his early Virginia policy as shrewd and judicious, the apparent benefits were ephemeral. The supposed victory in 1869 and the short-term gain in 1872 were subsequently offset by decisive defeats. Grant's policy of generosity, which amounted to appeasement, succeeded only too well in disarming and destroying the Republican party in Virginia, which, along with its candidates, was obviously paralyzed by 1873. By not allowing the radicals time to exploit their opportunity of temporarily proscribing the conservatives and by not providing the protection, patronage, and leadership that is indispensable to building a party, Grant sold out the radicals and, with them, the blacks, who lost many of their rights in the scramble.

If Grant tempered his generosity with calculation and moderation in Virginia, he combined realism and radical politics in Georgia—a policy dictated by the intolerable conditions of Georgia's politics, which virtually required federal intervention. When the Democrats expelled black members from the legislature in September, 1868, and then carried the state for Democrat Seymour at knife point in the presidential election in November, heedless Georgia Democrats unleashed a storm and thereby punished only themselves. In March, 1869, the Republicans counterattacked. By way of a controlled revolt, an unholy alliance of reactionary Democrats who opposed black suffrage on racist principles, and of radical Republicans who desired a return to military government in the hope of regaining control of the legislature by readmitting the black legislators who had earlier been expelled, defeated the ratification of the pending Fifteenth Amendment in order to obtain federal intervention.[16]

The battle then shifted to Washington. Congress fumbled about with the question before adjournment, but was so divided that a decision was postponed. Although Congress refused to count the state's electoral vote and the Senate refused to seat its conservative members, the status of Georgia was nevertheless not settled, because the Senate and its judiciary committee were deadlocked on the question. There was some doubt about whether Georgia was in or out of the Union, and Grant, like Congress, took no decisive action. This inaction and confusion, which lasted for nine months, merely encouraged the unrepentant southern reactionaries in their boldness. The delay also complicated the legal question: if Georgia were a state, Congress could take action only in the cause of maintaining a republican form of government; if it were still a military district, Congress had more freedom of action and could set new conditions of readmission.

By December, 1869, action could no longer be postponed, because chances for ratification of the Fifteenth Amendment appeared bleak. Many of the Republicans who wanted and needed ratification had no qualms about forcing Georgia to ratify in return for attaining unquestioned status as a state. The northerners generally agreed that white Georgians had asked for trouble in 1868. Since then there had been plenty of time for them to have had second thoughts and to have undertaken remedial action. But despite a state court ruling in the interim which endorsed the right of Negroes to hold office in the legislature, Georgia Democrats had refused to allow blacks to return to the statehouse. And that flagrant refusal to set their own house in order antagonized not only the North but also the outraged supporters of reconstruction. Since moral suasion had not worked, Congress, according to the radicals, would probably not be averse to a little gentle compulsion.[17]

On December 6, 1869, Grant finally broke the impasse. Anxious for the Fifteenth Amendment to be ratified, the president, in a message to Congress, recommended that Georgia be required to do her homework on reconstruction over again, proposing that the state be temporarily returned to military rule so that her legislature could be revamped to include black legislators. The Republican press was certainly right when it pointed to the hypocrisy of Georgia conservatives, who, under the banner of universal rights, had previously demanded their own, but cynically denied the exercise of the same rights to blacks.[18] Moreover, Georgia would be a good example for the public—an unmistakable warning to white southerners that they had better behave. Also, a new and radical reconstruction of Georgia would soothe those radicals in Congress and the cabinet who had been previously disenchanted with Grant's moderate policy in dictating the readmission of Virginia; the lenient requirements set for Virginia would thus be counterbalanced by the stringent conditions imposed on Georgia. But even Grant's radical strategy in Georgia was never so extreme as to reinstate wholesale military occupation or guarantee that Republican Governor Rufus B. Bullock would have perpetual power.

Although Grant's magnanimity was then loudly touted by the moderates, during the first year of his administration he had actually followed both a soft and a hard line in his southern policy. He had pleased the moderates within and outside the South by his conciliation in Virginia, at the same time satisfying radicals everywhere by having rebuked the reactionary Georgians. Grant also apparently hoped to reinvigorate the Republican party in the South by building upon the most available and stable foundations—Virginia, which had a white voter majority, and Georgia, which had black voter strength. He even pleased his party by espousing the ratification of the Fifteenth Amendment. The result of his early policy, then, was a deft balancing between the radical and moderate factions of the Republican party and a shrewd response to northern public opinion, which expressed alternately a wish to complete reconstruction and a desire to punish the Democrats for their repression in the South.

Congress, for its part, quickly complied on December 22, 1869, by adding the stringent requirement that Georgia had also to ratify the Fifteenth Amendment.[19] As a result, the state again became a military district, and the army briefly assumed authority and attempted to determine who would be members of the legislature. After a period during which army officers evaded responsibility and avoided decisions, the army district commander, General Alfred H. Terry, with the support of the Grant administration and the radical Republican faction in Atlanta, proceeded to revamp the state legislature. During the furious fight that ensued, Terry wrote: "the pressure upon me . . . is very great and I would not again go through with a job of this kind even if it would make me a Marshal of France." By January, 1870, control of the Georgia legislature shifted from the Democrats to the Republicans, with the conservatives ousted and the blacks reseated. The Fifteenth Amendment, previously rejected, was swiftly approved in February. Congress, however, because of indecision and interminable debates (which the newspapers scornfully termed "Georgia Hash") delayed Georgia's readmission to the Union until July 15, 1870. Clearly, Congress was still deeply divided on what would be a proper and advantageous settlement for that state. One major cause of disagreement was the question of whether, or when, new legislative elections were to be held there. Some radical Republicans, notably Congressman Benjamin F. Butler, favored postponing the elections to give the party time to gather strength to resist the Democrats in order to hold the state, whereas the moderate Republicans believed that any delay was wrong in principle and could only injure the party's prospects in Georgia and elsewhere.[20]

Meanwhile, Georgia radicals were back in the saddle, and the reconstructors were riding hard. Radical Governor Bullock quickly made enemies in Atlanta and Washington because of his legislative purge, his abrasive personality, and his questionable tactics. Caught between Bullock's opponents and proponents during 1870, Grant tried to duck the crossfire of the factional fighting. But it was soon obvious that he and the Republican Congress were only fair-weather friends when it came to the Georgia radicals. While they and their allies in Washington were trying to postpone the elections, extend terms of office, and prolong tenure by various maneuvers in Congress and in the legislature in order to improve their chances of holding the state, neither Grant nor Congress provided any leadership or active support for Bullock and his Republican faction. Indeed, what the president created was confusion, and he lowered morale by first leaning one way and then the other. At first, he seemed to favor holding legislative elections, a stand that was hardly helpful to Georgia Republicans; but he then apparently qualified his attitude by backing a proposal to provide three days for the voting, to enable the state's Republicans to collect a large vote. When finally Congress, in July, 1870, became weary of the imbroglio and of responding to the manifest impatience in the North, which had had its fill of chaos in Georgia, it demanded that the state hold regular legislative elections in December. About a month later, Georgia Republicans agreed to go along with that; yet when the state party tried to mount a campaign, the national party refused to supply funds. Still, the election in mid-December provided a solution, however unpalatable, to the myriad problems of Georgia Republicans, for the Democrats captured the legislature. Subsequently, in various disputed elections for Congress, the Republican Senate refused to seat holdover Republican senators from the state, and by February, 1871, the Republican Congress had seated Georgia Democrats in both chambers.[21]

Despite those reversals, the Georgia Republicans nonetheless hoped to salvage something from the pending gubernatorial dilemma. Faced with imminent impeachment by the new Democratic legislature, Governor Bullock hastily resigned in October, 1871, whereupon the legislature demanded an immediate election instead of retaining the acting Republican governor, Benjamin Conley, until the next scheduled election. Conley in November, 1871, pleaded for help from Grant in order to block the special election for governor, warning that "upon the maintenance of the position I have taken, depends the salvation of the republican party in Georgia." He pointedly added that "it rests with you to determine whether the enemies of the administration and of the government in this State shall be allowed . . . to crush out the last vestige of republican government in Georgia." During a cabinet meeting in December, 1871, Grant replied that he could have nothing to do with so speculative a case: it was up to the state to settle it, and if any question happened to come before the federal government, it would then be time enough to deal with it. Attorney General Amos T. Akerman of Georgia, who had replaced Hoar in July, 1870, and was intimately involved with state developments, advised his fellow citizens to hold the election and select for the governorship a nominee who was a "decided Republican. We shall never bring the people of Georgia to our principles by appearing to be ashamed of them." But despite this encouragement, the party defaulted, for it could not induce a Republican to run as its candidate. Thus, with no opposition whatever, a Democrat won the special election for governor in mid-December, 1871, and took office the following January. And with the Democrats already in control of the legislature, the question of credentials and of federal intervention would not be raised.[22]

From these developments in Georgia, it became clear that there was considerable tension and ill will between the northern and southern wings of the party. The northern Republicans generally agreed that their Georgia colleagues were as reckless and irresponsible in their management of affairs as the southern Democrats were in their campaign of intimidation. As for the southern Republicans, they had grown disenchanted because of Washington's refusal to help. Akerman, however, claimed that the problem was not confined to his state, noting that Congress and northern Republicans were usually unwilling to help southern Republicans "in a matter that is directly political."[23]

The upshot of the political problems in Georgia was a funeral, with the bungling Republicans, in both Atlanta and Washington, virtually burying their party, first by ineffective intervention and inconstant support, then by inaction, timidity, and withdrawal. After Georgia had played its vital role in securing ratification of the Fifteenth Amendment, the administration no longer showed any overwhelming interest in keeping the state Republican. It was a sad end to such a bold beginning.

Another emergency, this time in North Carolina, added yet another dimension to Grant's southern policy. By early 1870, Republican Governor William W. Holden was in serious trouble. With the results of the approaching legislative election dependent upon the turnout of voters, Holden, confronted with intimidation and the killing of blacks, feared a Democratic victory. The control of the legislature was at stake, and since tangible results were more important than scrupulous means, the governor answered illegal violence in kind, by meting out extralegal justice. According to the Holden organ, the Raleigh *Standard*: "If the Ku Klux and their friends want war they can have it! The die is cast."[24]

Declaring two Piedmont counties (one, Caswell, with a small black majority, and the other, Alamance, with a large white majority) in a state of insurrection during 1870, Holden sent a state military expedition in July to quash it. However, the militia proceeded to act imprudently: the orders were broad and vague; men were thrown in jail under military arrest without charge and without trial, and some prisoners were mistreated.[25]

During the crisis the North Carolina Republicans were confident of President Grant's and the United States Army's assistance if local efforts failed. Holden asked for federal troops three times during 1870—in March and May, before a state force was activated, and then again in July.[26] In reply, Grant gave Holden his wholehearted approval to undertake a state expedition and promised military aid if local authorities were unable to suppress the insurrection; he also pledged complete support provided by the full power of the federal government at his command. Although Grant did dispatch six companies to the state capital, Raleigh, they stayed in barracks; only a handful of troops were actually sent to the two troubled counties nearby, where they were held in readiness for action. Washington also provided the state militia with ammunition, clothing, and equipment. Yet Grant did not clearly authorize the use of federal troops either to provide Holden with a substitute for a state military expedition or, later, to help him in his undertaking. Instead, there was a vague order to preserve the peace, but no specific positive instructions to cope with contingencies. Indeed, the army specifically ordered the commanding officer at Raleigh not to use federal troops as a police force but to remain subordinate to civil authority.[27]

Then when Holden, who lacked the authority to suspend the writ of habeas corpus, refused to recognize the writ issued by state judges for the release of prisoners, a federal judge intervened on behalf of the prisoners with a federal court order. Holden would not comply, refusing to provide evidence and demanding that the military trials be continued. Hoping for presidential support of his stand, he protested to Grant in August against federal judicial interference. Meanwhile, adding to the conflict between state and federal authority and to the suspicion that existed between the state militia and the army, a drunken army man was mistakenly shot by a state militiaman. Acting for Grant, Attorney General Akerman firmly advised that the state authorities yield to the federal judge.[28]

That rejection from Washington had been preceded by defeat in North Carolina when the Democrats captured the legislature on August 4, 1870. With the state militia on patrol, Alamance and Caswell counties had gone Republican, but Democratic victories elsewhere in the state were what had decided the election. Both the state expedition and Governor Holden had been repudiated, and the new legislature, after ousting some Republican legislators, irregularly impeached and convicted Holden during March, 1871. Thus North Carolina quickly and unexpectedly succumbed to Democratic influence. The Raleigh *Standard* intoned the eulogy: "the work of reconstruction took years to effect and is obliterated in a second." The previous failure of the Republican state government to curb the terrorists, the unexpected federal court intervention in the state prosecution, the defeats in the legislative elections, and the impeachment and conviction of Holden strongly suggested that his military expedition had been as unwise in execution as it was unanticipated in outcome. Indeed, the combination of Holden's foolishness and Grant's indifference proved devastating.[29]

Northern opinion diverged sharply over the developments, but pointed to further deterioration of popular support for reconstruction. The Republican newspapers generally condemned Democratic terrorism and endorsed Holden's state action, contending that lawlessness must be met with force. Yet support was mixed with criticism and reservations. The Springfield *Republican* questioned Holden's motives, commenting that his lack of vigor against the guerillas had emboldened them to act with impunity for several years; then his more recent and surprising initiative, which had been accomplished just before election day, left one with the "not unreasonable suspicion that he was using the militia to control the election," according to the Cincinnati *Commercial*. Newspapers in general believed Holden had done more harm than good to the Republican cause. In fact, their unfriendly tone had prompted the Democratic Raleigh *Sentinel* to gloat even before the election that reconstruction's days were numbered. With the crushing defeat of the Republicans at the polls, the North's leading newspapers argued that the results showed Holden's high-handed measures and his resort to brute force to be ultimately futile; his eagerness to secure victory had boomeranged and reinforced white opposition. It was obvious, declared the Republican New York *Times*, that in the future more consideration should be given to the white population of the South and less to the black voter there; issues must be addressed to the interests of the "whole people, without regard to color." Otherwise, the party would be defeated in every southern state. Surveying the domains of the southern Republicans and the southern Democrats, northerners were beginning to mutter curses on both houses.[30]

During his impeachment trial Holden had gone to Washington with the great expectation of obtaining federal action on his behalf. Upon meeting Grant, he had noted that "there was no mistaking the cordial grasp of his hand" and had written to his wife that Grant told him federal cavalry was being dispatched to North Carolina, concluding that the president was "thoroughly with us."[31] Holden did not have all that faith in Congress, but he was still hopeful: "The impression here is that *at last* Congress will do its duty." He had written to his wife for help in prolonging the trial by all means possible, hoping for a presidential move or congressional action at the new session. However, Grant had again done nothing: he had neither intervened nor assuaged defeat with an immediate federal appointment. Exiled from North Carolina because he feared imprisonment and largely ignored in Washington, Holden had grown angry and despairing. Later, meeting Grant after his conviction, Holden had found him friendly, but surprised to discover that he was still in Washington. "I told him if I returned home I might return to 'bonds and imprisonment.' He replied, 'that is very hard.'" Frustrated in his expectations, Holden had attacked his supposed allies as cautious and cold-blooded. Realizing that there was to be no help for his cause from the administration, he had lashed out: "This city is selfishness, not to say wickedness, impersonated. Our members of Congress amount to little."[32]

In turn, both sides had heaped scorn upon Holden when he was removed from office in 1871. Zebulon B. Vance, the Confederate governor and future Democratic governor, had written that the trial was the "longest hunt after the poorest hide." Staunch Carolinian Republican Albion W. Tourgée had claimed that Holden was "at every stage, if possible, a more egregious ass than his bitterest enemy ever wished or thought him." However, it had been one observer's belief that the Republican politicians had deserted Holden by treating the impeachment trial "merely as an expedient to be applied to party advantage. But this sting has been . . . extracted by the defection of some of his own political friends—for how can a party complain when its own members voted for the deposition?"—a reference to the embarrassing fact that some Republicans had voted for impeachment, having publicly disowned their own leader in disgust.[33]

President Grant, who had evidently regarded Holden as a bungler and seemed to have given him just enough rope to hang himself, had weaseled out of his promises of support and abandoned Holden and his party to their fate. Yet foresight and prompt action could have prevented the poorly executed state military operation, and a judicious placement of federal troops and officials to oversee the approaching elections in the crucial sections might well have averted much trouble and avoided the betrayal of Republican interest.

Having received no sympathy and no help, Holden defended his record of having attempted to suppress the Klan, adding: "No doubt mistakes were made, but the object was good, and was pursued unflinching[ly] and boldly."[34] The time for confession and second thoughts had just begun, since any opportunity for a federal rescue of the Republicans in North Carolina had probably passed.

In Alabama, the Democrats had developed strength more quickly than in many other southern states,[35] which raised serious questions for Grant at the beginning of his first term. The Democrats had narrowly captured the governorship in early November, 1870, and the Republicans had disputed the results on the grounds that campaign violence and electoral fraud had secured the victory. In the scramble for office, both sides had committed irregularities, the opportunity for which had been created by the divided control of the legislature, with a Republican upper chamber (consisting of holdovers not elected in November) and a newly elected Democratic lower chamber. Incumbent Republican Governor William H. Smith, charging intimidation and fraud, claimed the election, and the Republican chamber agreed. With this support, Smith not only refused to recognize the Democratic victor, Robert B. Lindsay, but obtained a state court injunction restraining the legislature from counting the vote for governor. On the evening of November 26 Governor Smith requested the post commander at Montgomery, Captain W. F. Drum, to provide United States troops to prevent rioting and to keep peace in the city. On the advice of a colonel, Drum complied. The local sheriff assumed control of his "possee" and directed that the soldiers be placed so as to block entry to the governor's office.[36]

For a month Alabama had rival governors, until the Republican incumbent, Smith, with great bipartisan pressure in the state and elsewhere about to overwhelm him, and with a court proceeding about to take a menacing turn, stepped down on December 9. During the litigation, Smith had become turncoat, denouncing the black electorate in an attempt to woo the Democrats, while the Republicans in different factions had jockeyed for the senatorship. The Democratic Mobile *Register* termed the crisis an "audacious farce" made possible only by what another paper termed the "odious interference" of Washington.[37]

Nor was the northern press impressed by Smith's tactics: "served him right" was the typical response to his final surrender. The Cincinnati *Commercial* reasoned that if Smith, with control of the state government and with federal troops at his call, could not maintain order at the polls, he had only "his own lack of executive energy and foresight" to thank for his overthrow—the same type of criticism as that leveled at North Carolina Governor Holden. Although the New York *Evening Post* admitted the possibility of trickery on the part of the Democrats, it advised that the proper remedy was not to over-turn this election but to right any wrongs during the next. Otherwise, every defeated candidate in every contest could charge fraud, and the courts, rather than the electorate, would decide elections.[38]

The Grant administration had officially disavowed any intention to intervene, after having done so, and had withdrawn federal troops from around the statehouse at the end of November, at which time they were replaced by a civil posse. At Grant's direction, the adjutant general had informed Democrat Lindsay that "U.S. troops will not be used to obstruct any legal decision of the questions." Shortly thereafter, on December 9, 1870, lacking either federal or state sup-port, Smith had resigned. Reflecting the administration's new mood favoring noninterference, the Washington *National Republican* had indicated displeasure with the army's earlier role and declared that the federal government was not going to take sides in a strictly local quarrel: no troops had been or were about to be dispatched to Ala-bama; the mission of the army was to preserve the peace only if civil authority could not, and the guard provided Governor Smith inside the statehouse had not been authorized by either the president or the military commander and was in fact a mistake of the local officer in charge: "the responsibility . . . falls upon one who had no right to meddle in the least." Clearly, the administration organ had wanted to wash its hands of Smith and to escape responsibility for the pre-vious occupation of the statehouse. But an army report had noted that compliance with the governor's requisition was "in accordance with existing orders and the usage of the [War] Department." Al-though the administration might have disclaimed responsibility and the army high command might have been unhappy with the local army action, the fact remained that previous orders had been so broad and so vague in their granting of authority that army com-manders in Alabama had felt justified in supplying troops in re-sponse to requests from both state and federal officials.[39]

Two years later, as a result of factional squabbling and sectional divisions, the Democrats lost the governorship in November, 1872; moreover, another controversy arose over control of the legislature and, with it, the choice of the federal senatorship. Although the elec-tion results indicated that the Democrats had captured both chambers, the Republicans disputed the honesty of the returns. Some Democratic legislators were charged with election violations and jailed by federal officials in Alabama until Washington stepped in and ordered their release. With this plan foiled, Alabama Republicans decided to organize their own legislature, camping in the federal courthouse while the Democrats occupied the statehouse. When conflict appeared imminent, and at the request of state Republicans, federal troops were stationed near the capitol as a buffer between the rival legislatures. Adding a curious note to the chaotic situation, the new Republican governor, David P. Lewis, who had been declared elected by the Democratic legislature at the statehouse, recognized the Republican bolters at the courthouse as the legitimate legislature. Thus, in accepting the governorship, Lewis had repudiated those who had given it to him.[40]

The anarchy in Alabama continued from November, 1872, to February, 1873, with double legislatures in session, causing the Chicago *Times* to offer a flippant solution: since Connecticut had two capitals (Hartford and New Haven) and only one legislature, and Alabama two legislatures and only one capital, the former ought to send down a capital, or the latter send up a legislature. But the proadministration New York *Times* was not amused, viewing the Alabama imbroglio as yet another instance of "scandalous quarrels for power, where each party relies on technical advantages."[41]

In the interim, rival delegations rushed to Washington to represent the claims of each legislature, both sides appealing to President Grant for recognition and support. Grant first declined to take any action, and Attorney General George H. Williams, who had replaced the ousted Akerman in January, 1872, refused to give the Alabamians an opinion. However, when collision between state and federal forces in Montgomery became likely, Grant stepped in to settle the matter. In a cabinet meeting on December 10, 1872, Williams expressed confidence that an accommodation between the contenders was possible and received carte blanche to arrange a settlement. Buttressed with the potential use of federal troops, Williams could now force the will of Washington upon Montgomery. He proposed that the rival legislatures be dissolved and a new legislature organize itself, with the contested seats to be filled by action of the respective branches. Underneath the legal veneer, the implication was clear: Washington would recognize the irregular legislature of the Republicans, unless the Democrats surrendered control of the regular legislature by expelling enough Democrats to ensure Republican control of the lower chamber. The so-called compromise was in fact a *diktat*. The Mobile *Register* characterized Attorney General Williams' proposals as "absolute dictation in terms of pretended compromise." But the Democrats, recognizing that they had no alternative in the face of determined and overwhelming federal force, complied, and the Republicans, using sharp tactics, including the expulsion of one conservative senator, soon seized control of the upper chamber as well.[42]

Actually, it was a heavy-handed solution, for the administration had preserved party control of the state government and had ensured the election of a Republican to the United States Senate at the price of reversing the results of a state election by, in effect, determining the organization and composition of the legislature and the qualifications of its membership. The New York *Herald* denounced Attorney General Williams as a pretender to the role of peacemaker while in fact acting the bully in the interest of the Republicans. Yet what was striking about this episode of federal involvement was the northerners' general acceptance of the *fait accompli*: many of them may have blushed at the methods, but they were willing to pay the price of federal paternalism in order to avoid chaos in yet another state. A desire for order was paramount, regardless of the means and possible consequences. Order could be secured by sustaining one regime through the use of presidential power and patronage; likewise, peace could be restored by the withdrawal of presidential support and allowing a regime to fall. Many northerners were, in the end, less concerned about which method was used so long as the tiresome southern turmoil abated.[43]

This extraordinary effort during 1872 to maintain control in Alabama turned out to be in vain: two years later, despite the presence of federal troops in some counties, the Democrats captured both the governorship and the legislature, after a bitter and occasionally uproarious campaign. Despite a request for federal intervention, President Grant took no action in early 1875, nor did the final session of the last Republican Congress during reconstruction. Reconstruction was over and done with in Alabama, the state having been a victim not only of factionalism as well as the disparate interests and divergent aims of both state and national Republicans, but also of the Grant government's contradictory mixture of incautious and unprecedented manipulation combined with the neglect that was more customary and, in the end, more decisive.[44]

While anarchy in Alabama was troubling the administration, problems in Texas also demanded its attention.[45] The deep-seated division there between moderate and radical Republicans was played out in Washington during 1869, each faction vying for Grant's recognition and patronage. The moderates supported amnesty, whereas the radicals opted for proscription, opposing the proposed state constitution for a time because it failed to disfranchise former Confederates. However, the radicals soon recognized the futility of their opposition to the new constitution and moved in a moderate direction during June, 1869, endorsing the constitution. The moderates, despite signs of their waning influence, still received federal patronage at the beginning of Grant's administration and appeared to have the ear of the president and his general in Texas, Joseph J. Reynolds.

The radical contingent, however, was encouraged when Congress approved a proscription list endorsed by Texas radicals rather than the one proposed by the moderates and was further strengthened when the Republican national committee in early July recognized the radical faction as the Republican party of Texas. And although Grant, on July 15, 1869, rejected the radicals' former demand for a new draft of the state constitution, he did meet one of their requests by postponing, as in Mississippi, the constitutional referendum from July until late November, thus giving them valuable time to organize their forces as well as to avoid the possibility of the Texas and Mississippi referendums becoming a damaging issue in the early November elections. At the same time, he soothed congressional radicals, who were dismayed by the recent election results in Virginia.[46]

The Texas radicals used their time to good advantage. General Reynolds, the military commander, possibly hoping for military or, more probably, political advancement, changed his tune and favored the radicals instead of the uncooperative moderates, who, he complained to Grant, were not good Republicans because they were appeasing the Democrats. With Reynolds, who had been Grant's friend since their cadet days at West Point, exerting influence on behalf of the radicals, along with pressure from that contingent within the cabinet and Congress, the president in September wholeheartedly sided with the radical faction, ordering Reynolds to proceed on their terms. Voter registration, officeholder eligibility, and federal patronage were given over to them; many moderates found themselves dismissed from state and federal office; and not only were a few conservatives disfranchised on election day in November, 1869, but the election returns in some counties were thrown out altogether.[47]

As a result, the radicals won the election and the governorship. But the decisive cause for the moderates' defeat was doubtless not any rigging of the election but the disaffection of white conservatives. According to an army man stationed in Galveston, the moderate candidate was defeated not by the votes of his enemies but by the neglect of his supposed friends, since the conservatives had refused to back him because he was both a unionist and a Republican. The army officer observed that the election in the city and county had been "perfectly fair and *yet* only *two thirds* of the registered vote was polled." With the conservatives divided over how to oppose the Republicans and dismayed with the available candidates, they were no match for the black and white radicals who had voted en masse.[48]

The conservatives' apathy changed abruptly, however, once they experienced radical Republican rule after the state was readmitted to the Union in March, 1870. The downfall of the Texas Republicans began with the congressional elections in October, 1870, and the legislative elections in November, 1872. In spite of the Republican maneuvers of postponing legislative elections, locating polling places only at inaccessible county seats, sometimes manipulating the state police, and declaring martial law, the Democrats were victorious in both elections. Observers noted that what had happened to the Republicans in Texas was very liable to happen elsewhere and warned that the party had no more states to spare. The Grant organ, the Washington *National Republican*, however, blamed not Republican mismanagement but Democratic election fraud for all the trouble in Texas and commented: "It is high time the Federal laws were being made a reality in the South, and that the Federal Government should step in and not allow a loyal Governor and the heroic party at his back to fight this battle against treason single-handed." The reaction of the same newspaper two years later was altogether different: instead of praising the Republican governor, it denounced his blunders and indicted both branches of the Republican party in Texas. Actually, the Grant administration had good reasons for its exasperation. Not only had party fortunes under Governor Edmund J. Davis gone from bad to worse, but irrepressible factionalism and squabbling over patronage took their toll when Greeley carried the state in 1872.[49]

In the fiercely contested gubernatorial election on December 2, 1873, the Democrats won overwhelmingly, but the Republicans nonetheless made an attempt to keep the governor's chair on a flimsy pretext. Discovering legal flaws after the defeat, the Republicans claimed that the election should have been held for four days as prescribed by the state constitution, instead of on a single day under the new election law. The Republican-dominated state supreme court in January, 1874, seized on this technical point, issuing a decision declaring unconstitutional the law under which the election was conducted, thus nullifying both the election and an approved constitutional amendment that had ended the tenure of supreme court judges. Simultaneously, Grant was implored repeatedly to block the Democratic takeover by dispatching troops to enforce the court order and maintain the Republicans in power.[50]

But having burned his fingers earlier in other states when he had discarded elections by enforcing dubious court orders, Grant did not want another political hot potato in his still sensitive hands. Fearing political repercussions from the Texas affair during the 1874 northern congressional election, and recognizing the flimsiness of the Republican case, he refused to order army intervention and advised prudence. Attorney General Williams' counsel was the type of conciliation that bordered on negotiatory timidity, for he suggested that the Republicans bargain with a weak hand: "I can only appeal to the parties to peaceably adjust their difficulties if possible. Cannot someone negotiate a settlement? I have no power to interfere with force nor have you [a federal official in Texas] any duty to perform . . . except to use your moral influence for peace."[51]

101

Ignoring his plea, armed Republicans in Austin occupied the basement of the capitol, refusing to surrender the governor's office to the newly elected Democrat. But armed Democrats outsmarted them by scaling a ladder during the night so that they might sit in the legislative chambers above, in order to substantiate by physical possession their rightful claim to seats in the legislature. Each side then tried to organize a legislature without a quorum. When the Democratic winner was inaugurated, Republicans aimed a cannon at the second floor where the Democratic legislature was in session, and violence appeared imminent. However, caution prevailed when it became absolutely clear that Grant would do nothing to save the state Republicans. By January, 1874, his cold neutrality with regard to Texas was clear and unswerving. Grant pungently reminded the Texas Republicans that since they had approved the election law, had campaigned under it, and had questioned its validity only after they had lost the election, they would now have to abide by the results and peacefully capitulate. That final dispatch broke the back of the Republican resistance. However furious they were at being let down, the Texas Republicans surrendered the statehouse, though not without making it necessary to use an ax to force open the door of the governor's office so that its new occupant might enter.[52]

Weary of disputes elsewhere and everywhere, both Republican and Democratic observers in the North commended Grant for doing nothing in Texas and were in hopes that he was now abandoning coercion and embracing conciliation. To northerners of all political persuasions, the previous Republican methods in Texas appeared to have been not only too blatant and too high-handed, but the plays had been used too late in the game. The New York *Herald* reflected the northern consensus: if the people would not stand by the results of a clear judgment at the polls, if that judgment was to be set aside on some flimsy pretext by politicians grasping for a chance to stay in power; then popular government itself was nothing but a sham.[53]

Despite Grant's hope of building Republican power in the South by satisfying differing constituencies with varying tactics, all five states had succumbed to conservative control of their legislatures by 1874, and most of them even earlier. To be sure, some of the temporary tactics that had been designed to help out friends, to prevent blood-shed, to secure short-term stability, to help with the ratification of the Fifteenth Amendment, and to advance Grant's interests at the next presidential election had paid off for a short time: Grant carried most of the states in 1872, and conservative resurgence was delayed by over a year in Georgia and by two in Alabama. In other words, Grant's performance was at best a resourceful holding action.

What proved to be more significant than his temporary tactical triumphs were his lasting strategic failures. Despite all Grant's efforts to appease conservative white constituencies by fashioning a moderate policy, as in Virginia, conservatives readily and quickly took over and proceeded on their own terms. Elsewhere, the opposite tack yielded the same results. For example, despite all his efforts to enlist black and radical Republican support, initially in Georgia and intermittently in Alabama, the Republican parties and regimes in those states went under all the same. The middle courses of combin-ing moderate and radical stances in some measure or alternating between the two proved disappointing as well. Thus, Republicanism, no matter what the prescription, fared no better than it did when the particular policy was clearer in outline and had a definite goal. The ultimate results in every case amounted to drifting, delay, and some-times deception, all caused by long-term neglect.

Even when, early on, Grant had demonstrated a vigorous and de-cisive policy, he had not maintained it. His strong-handed policy in Georgia in 1869 and Alabama in 1872 had been short-lived, for bold activist intervention in both states had been followed by noninvolve-ment. The dominant pattern was in effect presidential withdrawal: Grant had backed down in Virginia in 1869, then again in Georgia and North Carolina during 1870 and 1871, and he completely with-drew from Texas in 1874 and from Alabama between 1873 and 1875. As a result, that string of little defeats formed a fabric of larger failure.

5

THE LONGEST BATTLE

Intervention in Louisiana

THE REPUBLICANS were more successful in keeping control of Louisiana than in the five states just treated, but at great cost. Party feeling ran high in that state too, often overflowing with the same destructive force as the Mississippi River, internal strife being swelled by outside interference. Thus Louisiana became one of the main arenas in the battle over reconstruction and the test of Grant's southern policy.

Not the most populous of southern states, and with a negligible electoral total in comparison with many northern states, Louisiana was, on the whole, not critically important in presidential elections. But it possessed a magnet that no other southern state could match—New Orleans, with its great and disproportionate concentration of Louisiana's population, wealth, power, and influence. Consequently, the city was resented by the people and the politicians in the rural areas of the state. In particular, New Orleans had a huge customhouse controlled by patronage; and with significant unemployment, especially after 1873, the customhouse became an obsession of state politics. Moreover, the customs collector of the port, James F. Casey, was the husband of the favorite sister of Julia D. Grant, the First Lady.

The makeup of the state population intensified those political pressures. Blacks were slightly more numerous than whites, constituting 50.1 percent of the population; they also constituted a numerical majority in over half of the state's counties or parishes (thirty-six out of fifty-eight, or 62 percent), including the parishes along the Mississippi, the Red River, and the delta surrounding New Orleans. Moreover, with so many white Republicans having defected by 1869, the rank and file of the Louisiana Republican party was overwhelmingly black. In particular, the black and mulatto population of New Orleans, which was more educated, articulate, and politically more active and organized than the rural blacks, further reinforced the dominant role of New Orleans in state politics. As a result, the black voter was more influential in local politics and within the state Republican party than in any other Gulf state, so that the state party sometimes championed racial integration, a stance that infuriated conservative whites and added virulent racial conflict to endemic strife. Given the precarious balance between parties, factions, and sections, as well as a deep-seated racial antagonism, political turmoil in the state was increasingly exacerbated.[1]

Although Grant's tactics in coping with the recurrent problems in Louisiana varied, as did their effectiveness, he generally supported in one way or another the radical Republican faction of the state party. The sole exception to that policy was made in January, 1872, when federal troops blocked the takeover of the statehouse by the radical forces because of Grant's fear that such a takeover would precipitate a fusion of Democrats and Liberal Republicans, possibly bringing them to victory in the state's presidential election in November. Otherwise, he endorsed the regular Republicans—which in Louisiana meant the radical Republicans under the direction of the customhouse crew—for both personal and political reasons. For one thing, he was trying to help out his brother-in-law and his cronies in the state by allowing them the freedom to grab power and patronage. For another, since Grant wanted to create a viable Republican party in Louisiana, he really had no choice but to sustain the more radical wing of the party. However, he did so somewhat sporadically and lackadaisically between emergencies, thus creating problems for himself, his party, and his allies in Louisiana. Radical Republicans, for their part, availed themselves of—indeed, abused—federal hospitality. As in other southern states, federal force and facilities were appropriated for the factional needs and advantage of the state party's local leaders, but in no other state was it done so consistently and so brazenly.[2]

The story of Grant's actions in Louisiana is important, since it most clearly delineates the intermittent character of his performance with regard to his southern policy in general. The events as a whole show how the power of the Republican party gradually diminished in one state in the Deep South despite lavish, albeit erratic, federal patronage and support. Moreover, the developments there highlight the role of the army as a force in an unstable political situation. Finally, the story plainly indicates both how Grant's policy and how southern reconstruction were viewed by southerners and northerners.

The first Louisiana crisis to trouble President Grant began in August, 1871, with a fight for power between the statehouse and the customhouse, in which state officials and federal officeholders clashed over civil rights, party control, federal patronage, and succession to the governorship and senatorships. The customhouse wing—consisting of the federal customs collector James F. Casey, the federal marshal Stephen B. Packard, the postmaster Charles W. Lowell, and United States Senator William Pitt Kellogg—was an ally of Grant and his administration, whereas Republican Governor Henry C. Warmoth headed the opposing and increasingly conservative faction, which sometimes aligned itself with the Democrats. Conflicting ambitions erupted in a quarrel over the federal senatorship, which Casey desired and in which he was supported by the Grants. Governor Warmoth, whom Grant disliked personally, had used his influence in the state legislature to prevent Casey's election to the Senate earlier, in January, 1871, and had his own man chosen instead. During the summer the struggle for power intensified as both sides scrambled for control of the party machinery that could determine the future nomination of a governor and the validation of his election.

Hoping to dominate the Republican state convention, which was to elect the party central committee in August, each faction tried to organize ward and county clubs to select delegates in order to carry the convention; and since both sides employed dubious tactics, over half the delegates of each faction were contested by the other. In addition, the location of the convention, New Orleans, was disputed. The Warmoth wing wanted to meet in the statehouse, where its police were in control, whereas the customhouse faction pressed for a meeting in the federal customhouse, where United States troops protected federal property and so at the same time could be employed to control the convention.[3]

During the campaign, Washington was besieged with requests from the customhouse faction for deputy marshals and troops on the grounds that their constitutional rights were being violated by New Orleans street gangs, while the metropolitan police, under the control of the Warmoth faction, stood idly by and did nothing to protect anti-Warmoth Republicans. On August 3, 1871, federal officials at the customhouse received carte blanche from Grant to settle the problem. Two days later, however, Attorney General Akerman informed Grant that there were no legal grounds on which he could intervene. Yet Akerman gave Marshal Packard freedom of action: if there were conspiracies, they were to be prosecuted, and "if you need help in executing process, employ as many deputies as are necessary, at expense of United States." But Akerman warned him that no assistance "in fact or appearance," was to be given to either of the factions.[4]

On August 9, the Republican meeting was held in the customhouse: 150 soldiers with loaded muskets and two Gatling guns stood guard, while deputy marshals denied opponents admission to the meeting and thousands of people milled around outside. The federal army was thus used to control a state party convention. Excluded from it, the Warmoth faction went elsewhere and organized its own, and the rival conventions simultaneously elected rival state Republican committees, which in turn created rival parties. The Republican rupture was clear, and endemic conflict ensued. By their overzealous housecleaning, federal officials in New Orleans had made matters worse than before and, in the process of purging the party, had defiled not only themselves but Grant. Interviewed by a New York *Herald* reporter, Grant appeared perplexed and declared that "the muddle down there is almost beyond my fathoming." Most northern newspapers, however, both Republican and Democratic, were able to fathom the muddle perfectly well and condemned the improper use of a federal building as the meeting place for a state party, as well as the employment of federal troops to control the customhouse convention. Since federal officials, who commanded all the machinery of the United States government in Louisiana, had misused their power, the press suggested that Grant fire both Collector Casey and Marshal Packard. But Grant disclaimed all responsibility for the whole affair and neither rebuked nor removed Casey; what he did, in fact, was to reappoint him.[5]

Subsequently, during January, 1872, Casey and his men tried to gain undisputed sway by ousting their enemies, Governor Warmoth and his lieutenant governor, and replacing them with friends. To do this they needed to gain control of the legislature, which they partly succeeded in doing, during the legislative session in January, by temporarily securing control of the state house of representatives after arresting and expelling their enemies; however, they still didn't have enough votes to capture the senate. The customhouse men stalled for time, preventing a quorum in the senate by providing shelter, champagne, and cigars to fourteen friendly senators for five days aboard a federal revenue cutter that cruised up and down the Mississippi, keeping the senators out of reach of state authority and thus avoiding being served a writ requiring their attendance. But when a public outcry arose against the federal government actively aiding one side in a local political dispute, their plan backfired.[6]

Consequently, there was a stalemate, which resulted in the creation of rival legislatures: Governor Warmoth's faction held the statehouse with the support of local police, who were fortified by state militia, and the customhouse faction withdrew to a barroom of the Gem Saloon, guarded by federal employees from the customhouse. Each side claimed, quite rightly, that the other was conspiring to gain control of the legislature. Meanwhile the legal situation became so chaotic as to be comic; the flurry of arrests, writs, attachments, and counterattachments reached such a point that no member of either legislature dared to emerge during its sessions lest the sergeant at arms of its rival capture him. One Warmoth legislator was dragged from his bed in the middle of the night; another was killed in a street scuffle. The Warmoth forces finally succeeded in seizing the Gem Saloon without much of a fight, but the opposition merely met elsewhere. Then the customhouse faction tried to seize the state-house, guarded by Warmoth's forces, but failed. So with Warmoth's men holding onto the capitol, they finally achieved a quorum in the senate on January 15 by threatening to expel any absentees and by bribing their former enemies. On January 24, 1872, the customhouse faction, having decided that their cause was futile, rejoined the regular session, and the two legislatures were reduced to one. Warmoth then secured the election of his own man as lieutenant governor.[7]

Amid all that confusion, President Grant had sent orders that the army was not to interfere, and so the troops generally stayed in their New Orleans barracks. Although ostensibly neutral, the Grant government had in fact helped by noninterference to sustain the Warmoth government, to the astonishment of the customhouse faction. Further support for Warmoth again came in the guise of noninterference when Washington had warned its officials on the scene not to abuse federal authority by assisting either faction in the controversy and had ordered an end to federal hospitality aboard the cutter on January 6, 1872. The army had then stood by, neither preventing Warmoth's takeover of the Gem Saloon on January 10, nor helping the customhouse crew to recover it. Furthermore, the army had refused to oust Warmoth's guards from inside the statehouse. Then, in a sudden switch from his posture of neutrality, Grant had ordered his army commander on the scene to prevent the customhouse mob from seizing the statehouse on January 22.[8]

The end result was that there had been no violence, as threatened, but the army had virtually kept the Warmoth forces in political control as the established government, since possession virtually guaranteed title. And all the while, Grant had covered his tracks with a smokescreen by requesting Congress to investigate and take action. He had written: the "condition of affairs there [Louisiana] is as bad as possible . . . but I have not been able to see any justification for executive interference." Apparently, Grant had wanted to avoid further antagonizing Governor Warmoth, whose control of the electoral machinery might later prove critical; probably, he also had wanted to prevent the formation of a conservative coalition in Louisiana be-

tween the Democrats and the Liberal Republicans, who had influence in the Warmoth faction. Presumably Grant had believed such
an alliance would have been encouraged if he had helped sabotage
the Warmoth victory, thus endangering his chances of carrying the
state in the presidential election ten months hence. Faced with a
choice between what was good for the Republican party in Louisiana
and what was good for himself, Grant had opted for self-preservation. However, his tactics didn't succeed, for Warmoth was to join
the Liberal Republican movement and help form a coalition of the
state's Liberals and Democrats; and Congress was subsequently to
throw out all that state's electoral votes on grounds of irregularity.[9]

The congressional decision was based on a host of illegalities and
irregularities in both the Louisiana campaign and election. During
the 1872 gubernatorial campaign the conservative coalition nominated Democrat John McEnery for governor. The regular Republicans, or customhouse group, endorsed Senator Kellogg for governor.
And from that camp James Casey still hoped for the senatorship.

Election day was deceptively quiet, given the amount of cheating
by both parties. The returns indicated a conservative victory, and
when they were disputed, another crisis burgeoned. Unlike most
states, Louisiana had a board of returning officers, or a state canvassing board, which was both judge and jury, entrusted with the
duty of counting the vote and declaring the results of the election. It
was the key to power, since the board, with its extraordinary authority as absolute arbiter, could decide victory on the grounds of
fictitious and fabricated returns, regardless of the actual results.
After outgoing Governor Warmoth had replaced men on the board,
packing it with conservatives, the board declared conservative candidate McEnery governor, gave the legislature to the conservatives,
and reported a popular margin of 8,000 votes. Not to be outdone, the
Republicans created their own board and claimed that their party
had won the election. Not in possession of a single official election
return and relying instead on newspaper reports, whose figures for
the rural parishes the Republicans freely adjusted, they declared
their candidate, Kellogg, as lawful governor and claimed control of
the legislature, certifying that their party had received a statewide
majority of 18,000 votes. Each rival board then tried to undo the

other and enforce its own decision; the doubles match was about to be played yet again.

The Republicans, who relied initially on a friendly state judge and then a sympathetic federal court, declared a violation of the federal election enforcement law because 10,000 blacks had allegedly been denied the ballot on election day. The conservatives, of course, preferred the dispute to remain in state courts, where the judges were more favorable to their side; they also created a new returning board to reaffirm their claim. The tangle that ensued virtually paralyzed public authority and snarled the judicial process with lawsuits and injunctions. Finally, federal circuit court Judge Edward H. Durell, stretching his power and straining the law, recognized the Republican board as the only legitimate one, handing the Republicans the governorship and the legislature. Durell proclaimed the conservative board nonexistent and high-handedly swept away all the proceedings in the state courts. His judgment was based on the simple but dubious legal logic that certain witnesses had sworn they would have voted for Kellogg if they had been allowed to; therefore Kellogg was necessarily elected.[10]

Late at night on December 5, 1872, Durell issued an order from his home for Marshal Packard to take possession of the statehouse and to admit only authorized members of the Kellogg legislature— those who had been certified by the Republican board. Just previous to this order, and anticipating—indeed, paving the way for—the court order, Grant ordered Attorney General Williams on December 3 to authorize use of federal forces to enforce all federal court orders, even though at the time there was no disturbance and no threat of any. Not coincidentally, the army arrived in New Orleans on December 5. At 2:00 A.M. on December 6, about one hundred federal troops and marshals swiftly and silently seized the statehouse. Guarded by armed troops and a cannon in front of the capitol, the Kellogg legislature convened. First it impeached Governor Warmoth and put acting lieutenant governor Pinckney B. S. Pinchback in his place until Kellogg was proclaimed winner of the election and the lawful governor; it then reorganized or abolished state courts to meet customhouse specifications. The legislature also requested continued federal protection because of threatened violence and asked for explicit recognition by Washington as the legitimate state government. All requests were met. The conservatives, however, did not give up and persisted in maintaining a rival legislature which met at various hideaways around the city.[11]

Grant, who denounced the Louisiana affair as a "miserable scramble" for the spoils of office, again declared his determination that Washington would give no help to either side. But in point of fact, he quickly took sweeping action by backing Durell's decision while the dispute over offices was still pending in the state courts. Promising to be impartial and not to interfere, Grant promptly proclaimed his partisanship and swiftly intervened. In December, with the presidential election out of the way, he again embraced his friends from the customhouse whom he had snubbed in January: he put down the conservatives, and he set up a new regime by granting it recognition on December 12. Grant had saved Louisiana for his party, but at the price of bringing it to the verge of anarchy. By having invoked federal authority in civil law and having employed federal force in state politics, he had mounted a successful coup d'etat.[12]

The strength of the alliance between Washington and the state regime was soon tested when, on December 13 and 14, 1872, the state militia, then occupying the state arsenal, mutinied against the Kellogg forces. However, when Grant authorized the army to back the pro-Kellogg group, the state militia laid down their arms and surrendered their armory. Yet another test of Grant's resolve was his refusal of the rival conservative legislature's appeal to intervene on behalf of McEnery.[13]

The reaction in the North to such maneuvers was overwhelmingly critical. Newspapers and officials publicly condemned Grant's partisanship and deplored the subordination of civil rule to military fiat. Observers wondered whether the cure of autocracy was worse than the disease of anarchy; the New York *Herald*, for example, believed that the Grant government was keeping its factional friend in power "regardless of the will of the people, the right of local self-government, or the forms of State law," causing the ballot to become a farce and the Constitution nothing more than waste paper. Disenchanted, Jacob D. Cox, the former secretary of the interior who had resigned in 1870, wrote that were such interference permanently established, it would be the "end of all State existence worth the name."[14]

A month later, in January, 1873, with the impending meeting of the rival legislatures and the forthcoming inauguration of the rival governors, Grant's position again became critical for Louisiana. Grant pledged that the army would maintain order and that there would be no overthrow of the Kellogg government, which he recognized and supported. But then, in this latest political crisis, he proceeded to undercut his own and Kellogg's position by forbidding any use of the army to disperse the rival forces, informing his secretary of war, on January 5, that the army was "not to be drawn into taking any side should there be a conflict in the organization of a state government"— a curiously timid position, given the fact that both the army and the federal authorities had, a month earlier, been ordered by the president to take sides and decide the issue. Probably reacting to the furor in the nation over his previous actions in New Orleans, Grant ordered that the conservatives be allowed to organize—in effect, condoning two governors and two legislatures. Thus the Kellogg regime was installed in the statehouse, while, at the same time, the McEnery regime arranged its own inauguration, swore in its legislature elsewhere, and set up its own shop. This decision not to disperse the conservatives prolonged the political crisis, for allowing the opposition to organize not only gave it life and hope but strengthened its political position; indeed, its very existence perpetuated a semblance of legality and served as a rallying point for the enemies of the Kellogg government to dispute its authority.[15]

At that point, Grant seemed unwilling to deliver the coup de grace. The fact of putting troopers in the statehouse had helped his friends but had not got rid of their enemies; trying to keep peace had in no way eliminated the causes of unrest; and enabling one party to gain power over the other was no assurance that it would stay in power. Grant had poured a bit of water on the fire, but had permitted others to fan the flames; and in accepting two separate governments, he had spread the chaos and encouraged more bloodshed. Clearly, a show of power had been in order, and Grant ought to have exercised it decisively and continuously.

Then, in an effort to divest himself of responsibility for federal action or to defuse an explosive situation by delay, Grant made a gesture to include Congress. In February, 1873, he presented Congress in the last hours of its final session with a limited choice: either Congress solve the puzzle of Louisiana or Grant would continue recognizing Kellogg. Congress, close to adjournment, fumbled with the problem, disagreed sharply, and decided not to interfere, thereby upholding Grant, Durell, and Kellogg. But although they declined to repudiate the Kellogg regime, Senate Republicans expressed their own doubts as to its legitimacy by not seating that faction's senator and by criticizing Judge Durell's decision. There was talk in Congress of making Durell a scapegoat by impeaching him and thus relieving the administration of responsibility, but again nothing was done. And though a new election for governor was suggested, nothing came of it. Cox complained that Congress chose the worst possible alternative: "Of course a Republican Congress that will admit that Kellogg's government is not the de jure government and yet keeps it in power, is responsible for this; for it gives the Southern whites a confession that they are under a usurpation, to justify them in rebellion, and then sends the black troops of the usurper to force them into subjection. Could the Devil himself contrive it better?"[16]

The northern press was divided over Congress' inaction. The Springfield *Republican*, for example, believed that Congress had better ignore the political situation if the state authorities could not unravel it, rather than risk federal interference. Other newspapers grasped at straws to settle the dispute, but none of them were in agreement. The fact of being one step removed from the heat of battle did not result in objectivity. Solutions were as unavailing as inclinations to compromise.[17]

Meanwhile, each of the rival regimes in Louisiana tried to establish its power as the government de facto, by attempting to assert authority over court sessions, collection of taxes, and control of the militia and the police. McEnery's forces, refusing to fade away, varied the monotony of jurisdictional resistance by occasional threats or skirmishes with the enemy. In March, 1873, federal troops once again intervened; while an armed mob of conservatives, about five hundred strong, were attacking a New Orleans police station on March 5, the army, acting under presidential orders, arrived at the scene. Without firing a shot, the mob dispersed. During that crisis Governor Kellogg telegraphed Marshal Packard, who was in Washington: "Had I better not move on Odd-Fellow's Hall [the meeting place of the McEnery legislature]. See President." Next day the Kellogg police seized and occupied the conservative legislative hall, thus preventing sessions there, and arrested several members. In this operation the army, by indirection, backed up the police action by refusing to undo any act of the Kellogg government, thus preventing the recapture of the hall by McEnery's supporters. In the precarious position of having been ordered to uphold the Kellogg regime and also instructed to allow the McEnery regime to function without molestation, army commander William H. Emory, acting for Washington, maintained Kellogg's fait accompli.[18]

As unrest spread from the capital to the countryside, violence erupted in the parishes in the form of sickening slaughters between the races. The worst of them took place in April, 1873, at Colfax, on the Red River in the northern part of the state. Grant Parish, named after the president, was a black-belt county created as an advantage to the Republicans and had a Negro majority; at its county seat, Colfax, named after Grant's first vice-president, a heated dispute broke out over who had won the 1872 county election. The blacks, representing the Kellogg forces, seized the courthouse in late March and, barricading themselves inside, held it for several weeks. Then on April 13 about 200 whites of the McEnery faction, with the help of a cannon, surrounded and attacked the courthouse, which was being defended by about 150 blacks. After heavy fighting a truce was declared, but shortly afterward it was broken by both sides. Adding atrocity to political violence, the whites set fire to the courthouse. Some blacks were burned alive; others were shot as they ran from the flaming building. The wounded were bayoneted where they lay or ridden down in the fields. The prisoners never even reached the jail, for their drunken guards opened fire on them during the night. Their bodies were mutilated, abdomens ripped open and brains blown out. Since the families of the slain were too terrified to claim the bodies, their remains were thrown into the river. About 71 blacks and 2 whites died. Thus McEnery's forces were temporarily triumphant until federal troops arrived and restored order. Many northern newspapers obtusely placed the blame for the savage Colfax massacre not on the Louisiana whites, who had committed it, but on the Louisiana blacks, who, they thought, had created the crisis by occupying the courthouse, as well as on Grant and Kellogg, who had set up the regime in the first place.[19]

The rival governments again collided at St. Martinsville over collection of taxes. With the army's support, the Kellogg government won another victory in early May. In addition to such pitched battles within the state, there was an attempt to assassinate Governor Kellogg. The explosive situation required decisive action to end the anarchy, for Grant had allowed affairs to drift from bad to worse. Governor Kellogg, hoping to put down the opposition once and for all, requested carte blanche to send federal troops into any part of the state to suppress disturbances and asked Grant to bolster the authority of his government. Finally, in a proclamation of May 22, 1873, Grant belatedly complied, authorizing further help from the army and ordering the McEnery forces to disperse. With this unequivocal show of support, matters generally quieted down in the parishes, although the volcano went on smouldering.[20]

Clearly, Grant had already gone too far in assisting Kellogg to withdraw his support, but he had delayed too long in eliminating the challenge to constituted authority. If his delay had been dictated by a fear that Congress might tie his hands and forbid, in advance, any sort of presidential intervention, he could nonetheless have taken definitive action three months earlier in March when Congress had adjourned. If his delay was caused by some hope that the McEnery regime would die a natural death, subsequent events had proved him wrong. "All we ask," Kellogg wrote, "is that our friends in Congress stand by us in our difficult and onerous task. . . . Early and prompt action in our case will save this state to the republican party to whom it rightfully belongs, for all time to come."[21]

Early in 1874 the major participants cast about for some solution to the problem of the legality and validity of the state government before the fall elections, for instability not only was a hazard to the state Republican party, but also created great embarrassment for the national party. Grant, for his part, suggested sending a special message to Congress on Louisiana, but since it was repetitious and proposed nothing new, it was strongly opposed by the cabinet and, finally, the proposal was scrapped. Although, according to widespread rumors, Grant wanted to wash his hands of what he reportedly referred to as the Louisiana "monstrosities," by holding a new election for governor, he eventually lost his enthusiasm for that idea. With the Kellogg regime trying to scuttle any plan for holding another election, which it might easily lose, lobbyist and prominent Republican William E. Chandler advised Grant to make no change, for it would be "fatal" and would result in the defeat of the Republicans because of the Democrats' well-known inclination to intimidation and trickery. "Rather than desert Governor Kellogg now," he concluded, "it would have been better to have abandoned him a year and half ago, before the long and arduous conflict." Since the customhouse Republicans had backed Grant in the presidential election, they were "now entitled to the same consideration and firmness." When the idea of a new senatorial election was also dropped, Grant's initiative came to nought in an agonizing anticlimax. Given the depth of his involvement, it would have been too awkward, too late, and too cowardly to retreat gracefully at that point.[22]

Meanwhile, the Kellogg forces, recognizing their tenuous position at home, tried to procure Congress' favor toward, and legal recognition of, their regime by seating their candidate in the United States Senate, but his credentials for admission were not accepted. Thus Louisiana, although fully represented in the House of Representatives, continued to be represented by only one senator. In July, in preparation for the fall legislative elections, the Kellogg government decided to mount an offensive at home by enacting a law that gave the governor the power to appoint all election registrars, who, in turn, had the authority to add or to eliminate voters. Kellogg's men also seized arms that were bound for the opposition. Given the likelihood of a rigged election, the Democrats became desperate. Because most federal troops had been withdrawn in early summer, except for a small garrison in New Orleans, there was a power vacuum in the state, and the Democrats thus decided to act boldly. With McEnery away in Mississippi, the head of the conservative forces, David B. Penn, a former Confederate colonel, assumed the leadership and formed an alliance with the White Leagues, which were paramilitary cadres formed during 1874.

Instead of relying on secrecy like the Knights and the Klan, the White Leagues—doubtless emboldened by federal inaction in nearby states and encouraged by the recent collapse of Republican regimes in Texas and Arkansas—resorted to direct and open action on a platform of white supremacy, with the specific political objective of restoring the government to the whites. In late August six Republican officials were murdered in Coushatta on the Red River. Then, in New Orleans, on September 14 and 15, 1874, the McEnery forces, consisting of about eight thousand men, mounted a coup d'etat by seizing city hall, the statehouse, the arsenals, and the police stations, and by cutting the wires of the fire alarm and the police telegraph system. At the same time, the White Leaguers barricaded the streets in Parisian fashion, and the city quickly came under their control. Stunned and overwhelmed by the sudden uprising, the Kellogg forces offered little resistance; but even so, thirty-two persons were killed and seventy-nine wounded.[23]

The ease, speed, and completeness with which the Kellogg regime was overthrown cast great doubts on its stability and popular support, while this new episode added to Grant's embarrassing predicament. Only the federal customhouse, where three hundred troops were quartered and where panicky Governor Kellogg and his state officials took refuge, was not under rebel control. During the crisis Kellogg had proved that he was neither capable nor courageous, for, as many observed, he had been vanquished almost instantaneously. The overthrow startled the country. Writing with a light touch during the three-day governorship, the New Orleans *Times* noted that five men had served as acting governor of Louisiana (the latest being Penn, who now proclaimed himself acting governor in McEnery's absence): "it's not our fault that we haven't had more. Times are hard, and we can't afford as much style as Costa Rica." A few Democratic journals justified the revolution, arguing that the McEnery-Penn contingent had quite rightly sought redress with muskets because they hadn't been given a fair chance with the ballot. But the northern newspapers generally spoke out firmly against the action. The Cincinnati *Commercial*, for example, stated that Kellogg's administration, however worthless, corrupt, and initially usurping, had to be reinstated at any cost, because the "bayonet is not to supersede the ballot-box in redressing grievances and changing administrations." If the uprising were not suppressed, remarked the New York *Times*, it would be like a "torch flung into a powder magazine" all over the South.[24]

Both Penn and Kellogg put pressure on the president either to sustain or to subvert the new Democratic regime in New Orleans. The crisis had its usual reception in Washington—consternation, followed by confusion when the New Orleans telegraph system went dead. However, news did slowly trickle into Washington and communication was restored the next day. After Grant consulted with Attorney General Williams, he quickly decided to issue a proclamation on September 15, ordering the revolutionary McEnery forces to disperse within five days. As for the cabinet itself, it had neither been consulted nor informed and did not learn of the proclamation until it came out in the evening newspapers. Grant was about to leave for the New Jersey shore when some members of the cabinet persuaded him to stay in the capital and call a cabinet meeting for the next day to discuss the situation and to plan policy.[25]

At that meeting, on September 16, Grant suggested convening Congress for a special session, but the cabinet vetoed the idea, since the congressional election in the fall was both so near and so uncertain, and if there were any fumbling, it would only make the dangerous campaign issue more explosive. When Grant then suggested that he issue a proclamation declaring his intention not to convene Congress, he was again opposed by the cabinet, for in that case he would have no alternative should another emergency arise. Although both Grant and the cabinet denounced Governor Kellogg for his ineptitude and desertion, there appeared no easy way to get rid of him. Protracted and often heated discussions during several meetings of the cabinet disclosed great differences over the proper course to take in Louisiana, with proposals that ranged all the way from accepting the revolutionary regime to deposing it, and from holding a new election to installing a military government. Clearly, any course had its risks. Doing nothing was an admission of past errors and might lead Democrats in other southern states to conduct similar revolu-

119

tions; holding a new election might encourage lawlessness and suggest a way to undermine other such Republican regimes; and imposing a military government would undoubtedly outrage most of the nation. Finally, the cabinet decided to put down the rebellion and to reinstate the Kellogg government.[26]

At first, President Grant had planned to do no more than issue his original proclamation, but he then strengthened his position by instructing his general not to recognize the insurgent government under any circumstances and by ordering the dispatch of five thousand troops and three gunboats to New Orleans. The insurgency quickly collapsed. Relinquishing their positions, arms, and offices, Penn's forces disbanded on September 17. Penn's bravado, due to the mistaken belief that Grant would not interfere, and fortified by revolutionary rhetoric and hot tempers, was transformed overnight into meek surrender. The Kellogg regime was restored as suddenly as it had been overthrown. However not all the Democrats concurred: in the rural parishes political fires continued to smoulder in the form of fresh outbreaks of terrorism.[27]

The crisis and its aftermath brought home to the administration and to the country the precarious nature of the situation in Louisiana and Kellogg's utter dependence upon Washington in preventing another coup. Reports received in Washington left no room for doubt. In one communication the White House was informed that Kellogg's government "can only stand at present by support of U.S. troops"; also, it was powerless to suppress any of the insurgents' meetings and drills. General Emory advised that a sufficient display of force was essential in order to thoroughly quell the Democrats' disorder and, anticipating serious trouble should the Democrats lose the upcoming November legislative elections, urged that federal troops not be withdrawn until after the legislature met in January. But once again the Grant administration chose to deal with the deteriorating situation from a position of weakness and reduced the federal force before election day; for though Grant was concerned about order, he did not act on that concern; and after the election he ordered on November 17, 1874, that the troops be withdrawn from the statehouse, thus foreclosing the option of being in the best location to take action quickly and firmly in the event of an emergency. When Governor Kellogg informed the president in early December that White Leaguers intended to mount a future attack on the statehouse, he replied: "It is exceedingly unpalatable to use troops in anticipation of danger." Thus, although forewarned, especially if the trouble were to come from inside, not outside, the statehouse, the administration refused to take the necessary precautions.[28]

Louisiana settled down again, just simmering on until on November 2, 1874, the dishonest election for the state legislature sparked off another controversy. As the returning board canvassed and compiled the vote, uncertainty and suspicion grew. Flushed with their easy show of strength and their temporary victory in September, yet aware of the determination and force of the federal government, the Democrats subsequently employed covert fraud and overt intimidation in their strong efforts to dismantle the Kellogg regime. Yet that regime itself, despite the control of the returning board, showed signs of recurrent insecurity. Its returning board, after having conducted a dilatory investigation of purported fraud for almost two months, "manipulated the returns for weeks and weeks, until," in Senator Carl Schurz's words, "by hook or crook, that conservative majority was transformed into a republican one." The Springfield *Republican*'s view was that despite the fact of Democratic intimidation in the election, the honesty of the Republican board members' purposes, the accuracy of their arithmetic, and the validity of their conclusions were not to be trusted. The crucial question was the logic of the board's assumption that every Negro in Louisiana who did not vote the Republican ticket must have been intimidated. Most observers agreed that such a contention was difficult, if not impossible, to prove and were appalled by the cynical juggling of votes. The Louisville *Courier-Journal* angrily denounced the decision as the "bastard offspring of a political rape," noting that Republican claims would not have been made if the board had not received fresh assurances from Washington that its decision would be upheld by Grant at any price.[29]

By late December the board, despite wholesale manipulation, decided that there was a tie in the lower house of the legislature, with five contests yet to be decided by that chamber. The Democrats immediately claimed eighty seats instead of the fifty-three granted them by the board. Therefore party feeling was whipped up to a frenzy, and there was excited talk about the Democrats intending to lynch the members of the returning board.

The position taken by the administration was ambivalent in word but not in deed. On December 7, 1874, Grant made a major statement of policy to the public in his eloquent annual message to Congress. He expressed his distaste for any new federal action in the South and was obliquely critical of several of its Republican regimes. The implication seemed to be that those regimes, while under some sort of assumed but undefined federal protection, had better behave prudently. Grant alluded to the increasing unpopularity of federal intervention, which was repugnant to the public who had to endure it, to the military who had to enforce it, and to the president who had to order it. He observed that whether or not intervention was authorized by law, it was universally and roundly condemned. Grant expressed the hope that eventually, when the Republicans had ceased to "magnify wrongs and outrages" and when the Democrats had ceased to "belittle them or justify them," then executive action in the South would become unnecessary. Although mildly chastising his southern allies, he at the same time placed the responsibility for interference squarely on the shoulders of the white southern Democrats, promising that only when peace prevailed and when blacks were treated fairly as citizens and voters, would executive action in local southern affairs come to an end.[30]

Once again, as in 1872 and 1873, he not only asked Congress to resolve Louisiana's difficulties and relieve him of that responsibility, but he also ordered troops to suppress any revolutionary violence in the state. On December 24, anticipating trouble when the new legislature met in early January, he authorized General Philip H. Sheridan to investigate the situation in New Orleans and to assume command there if necessary. The New York *Herald* predicted that Sheridan's presence meant stern and swift repression if trouble broke out, and the Louisville *Courier-Journal* regarded it as a declaration of war. On December 29, when the cabinet discussed Louisiana, Grant suggested that should there be violence, the state might be placed under martial law, although Attorney General Williams questioned the legal authority of such action on the part of the federal government. In any event, troops were stationed near but not inside the statehouse.[31]

The seething cauldron boiled over during the meeting of the legislature on January 4, 1875. Kidnapping three Republican legislators and seizing the speaker's rostrum, the anti-Kellogg forces illegally and forcibly organized the lower chamber, elected their candidate speaker, and confirmed the election of five Democrats whose elections had been contested, thus assuring a Democratic majority. The Kellogg forces had been caught off guard by that unexpected and audacious coup. To break a quorum, the Republicans darted out of the chamber. There was scuffling at the doors. The Republican members were hauled out into the lobbies by the Republican police, but the Democratic doormen, trying to keep a quorum, pulled them back into the chamber. Thus by dragging five unwilling Republicans back and blocking the doors, the quorum was saved. At the request of the Democrats, Colonel Philippe R. de Trobriand appeared on the scene in civilian clothes and attempted to calm down the Republicans, who were causing an uproar in the corridors. Although the crowd dispersed, it returned in two hours. This time, on the request of Governor Kellogg and fortified both by the instructions of General Sheridan, who said "do not hesitate a moment," and by General Emory's "do it discreetly," Trobriand, now in uniform, returned with federal troops. They marched into the legislative chamber and ejected the five Democratic members previously not recognized by the Republican returning board. Trobriand had temporarily assumed the duties of a sergeant at arms, for his forces did not assist the state forces but, rather, replaced them. So with the expulsion of the Democrats, the Republicans were able to seat their five legislators, choose their own speaker, and resume control of the chamber and thus of the legislature. In protest, the Democrats walked out.[32]

This grave situation was exacerbated by General Sheridan's off-the-cuff remarks. To begin with, he telegraphed Washington that the situation was fraught with danger and that he was assuming army command of the two thousand troops in the city. He assured the Department of War that the "Dog [the White League terrorist group] is dead," and in subsequent reports defended the army operation in the statehouse as preventing bloodshed and preserving peace. He requested that the ringleaders of the powerful White Leagues be tried by military tribunal and be punished for fomenting disorder; for only in this way would the "banditti" be exterminated. Suggesting that several southern states required the same type of military control and requesting this authority by mere presidential proclamation, Sheridan sounded like Napoleon and proposed to act as proconsul. Moreover, he brusquely dismissed all critics of his tactics as merely "manufacturing sensational protests for northern political consumption."[33]

Secretary of War William W. Belknap further inflamed the public when on January 6, in two dispatches, he replied that the "President and all of us have full confidence and thoroughly approve your course," characterizing it as wise and judicious. The purge, along with the well-publicized telegrams, infuriated a majority of people North and South and crystallized public feeling more than any other event of reconstruction. It became the most explosive issue of Grant's presidency, and one on which there was a widespread consensus that Washington had gone too far, indicated by the flurry of states' rights resolutions that were adopted in the first fifteen days of January, 1875—more, one observer noted, than had been issued in the preceding fifteen years.[34]

There were, to be sure, loyal backers of Sheridan, many of whom were former soldiers; one of them wrote: "The only brother I had was shot through the heart by a Southern sharp-shooter and the sons of b—— shall not vaunt their treason again if my life can help check them." Some of them suggested that perhaps the war had ended too soon or at least the North had relaxed its grip too soon, and it was now time to finish the job. Prominent abolitionist Wendell Phillips confidently advised: "The firm decisive hour will scatter the whole conspiracy." A federal district attorney in Kentucky wrote that it was not a crime to make a mistake by suggesting a wrong remedy (in creating military courts) for the greater evil of lawlessness. Some Republicans, and some state legislatures which they controlled, declared that it was not only the right but the duty of the federal government to suppress the White Leaguers and their activities. Characteristic of the supporters' arguments were those of the St.

Paul *Press*, which pointed out the hypocrisy of the Democrats, who affected mock indignation when the strong arm of force was used, yet whose resort to violence made peaceful methods impossible. The Chicago *Inter-Ocean*, a bellwether radical newspaper, also condemned the double standard of those northern Republicans who regarded the butchery of blacks in the South with stolid indifference but were roused to indignation by General Sheridan, who called things by their right names. Defending the role of the army as the ally not of tyranny but of liberty, the paper pointed out that the military action did not deprive the people of the ballot but, rather, tried to make good their enfranchisement. However, if the government and the people were unwilling to use the army for this purpose, it claimed, then there was little hope for reconstruction. Nevertheless, there was a disturbing undercurrent in its defense of Sheridan's statements: "one clear-cut, ringing, decisive sentence, having the clank of a saber and the ring of the carbine behind it, is worth whole volumes of argument and entreaty."[35]

But denunciation, not defense, was the dominant response, reflecting outrage over use of the army, pent up frustration with regard to the southern problem, and a profound reaction against reconstruction. The affair also whipped up a whirlwind of wrath against Grant. One Republican described it as a "foul disgrace perpetrated by our presidential horse-jockey." Even the vice-president, Henry Wilson, termed Grant the millstone around the neck of the Republican party, given the unpopularity of his Louisiana policy and the recent election defeats in the North. As for Sheridan, he took a drubbing as well. One Connecticut clergyman, incensed at Sheridan's demand for congressional action to suit his idea of expediency, declared: "Now is the time for honest Republicans to denounce dishonest ones." Another New Englander wondered how Sheridan could ever have sent such dispatches about banditti and how the administration could ever have approved and published them. Many others agreed with that Yankee's view that both the general and the president were bent on self-destruction: "I cannot account for it in any way except in the fact that suicide is sometimes epidemic."[36]

People also feared for the future of constitutional limits and safeguards. Prominent attorney William M. Evarts, for example, terming

125

the event a "high-handed act of military subversion of civil government," launched a political thunderbolt: Could such a military maneuver as had occurred in Louisiana change a future majority in the electoral college and steal the presidency? Recent events, according to Evarts, suggested a growing disposition of those in power to veto the popular will by tearing up the Constitution and local election returns. Similarly, the disenchanted Charles Francis Adams pondered the meaning of this "momentous catastrophe" and wondered whether the whole federal system was going over the precipice, taking freedom along with it. Indeed, the prerequisites for federal intervention—actual violence, followed by efforts of the state militia to keep the peace, a request for aid from the governor, and a presidential proclamation—all were lacking. There simply was no justification for the army action, admitted the old abolitionist *Independent*. Another Republican journal, *Harper's Weekly*, observed that "liberty is secure only under the forms of law, and that when the form is destroyed or disregarded, liberty itself is mortally wounded" and claimed that given the recent constitutional amendments as the sheet anchor of the Negro's welfare, the Republicans could not violate one part of the Constitution with the intention of helping the blacks, yet condemn the Democrats for violating another part for the purpose of harming the blacks.[37]

The Democrats, of course, were quick to capitalize on the issue of Louisiana. "Without waiting for the facts or permitting this feeling [of indignation] to subside, they [Democrats] at once sought to commit leading republicans to an unqualified condemnation of the Administration. In this they were only too successful," said a New York Republican, referring to public protests in New York City, Cincinnati, and elsewhere, in which prominent Republicans participated. The Democratic press enjoyed a heyday. The headlines of the New York *World* screamed "Tyranny!," "A Sovereign State Murdered," and "The Strangled State." Some newspapers called for Grant's impeachment, others for his censure by a joint resolution of Congress; still others advocated a change in the laws governing presidential authority to employ the army; others believed that a new state election ought to be held. The Democratic New Orleans *Daily Picayune* termed the legislative expulsion the final outrage, characterizing it as the most violent, illegal, and shameless act in the history of any free government. It noted that there was a prevailing monotony in the chronicle of "Kelloggdom," associated as it was with federal bayonets through every phase of its existence: "brought forth by bayonets, nursed by bayonets, pricked into animation and infused with life by bayonets, it now finds itself unable to perform the most ordinary functions without their aid."[38]

In Washington congressional moderates reacted with shock and anxiety. The Speaker of the House of Representatives, James G. Blaine, was privately appalled at the Louisiana mess. Representative Henry L. Dawes of Massachusetts bemoaned the administration's "stupidity and blindness." They and other Republicans were amazed by Sheridan's audacity and feared that the army, on Grant's order, would again violate the Constitution in another state by marching into the legislature and throwing out the opposition. They admitted being confused as to how to respond to the present situation and to uneasiness about their party's future. Congressman Garfield, for one, regarded the expulsion as the darkest day for his party since the war, remarking that it was as if all the gods had conspired to destroy the Republican party. He feared that the army's having taken action now forced Congress to choose "between a reckless and careless set of scamps (*i.e.*, Kellogg and his set), on the one hand, and the armed-negro hating band of murderers on the other."[39]

However, private dissatisfaction among Republican politicians was one thing, public protest, another. Moderate Congressman Dawes noted that although few Republicans in Congress approved of the recent events in New Orleans, so far no Republican congressmen had broken rank. Even reports of congressional sentiment were contradictory. Republican Representative Lorenzo Danford of Ohio, for example, reported that a majority in the Republican caucus on January 9 "was largely in sympathy with Sheridan but as a matter of precaution resolved to go slow for the present." Given the division in Republican ranks and the explosiveness of the crisis, caution seemed the best course to follow. Republicans in Congress stalled for time, delaying discussion as long as possible until the president sent in his message, at which point they could present a united front.[40]

But the Democrats gave them no respite and exploited their own opportunity to the full. Richard Vaux suggested the Democrats' strategy: "By all means keep our friends *quiet* in the South. Don't let them *do* anything which will give Grant any opportunity to excite the people *here*. . . . The New York [protest] meeting will give a tone to public opinion, and we ought to *ride on it*. The effort of Grant and his *infamous tools* will be to change the current of opinion by all sorts of lies. Take a look out for his message and *strike at it* boldly. . . . *Keep Grant on the Defensive*! . . . He [Sheridan] and Grant must be kept together in this infamy," and every attempt to "fire the northern heart" must be countered. The Democratic governors or legislators of thirteen states lodged protests.[41]

On January 5, 8, 11, and 12 the cabinet wrestled with the question. In contrast to his position in late December, Attorney General Williams now argued for an aggressive policy: he wanted to fight it out to the end, justifying the army's role as merely a posse called in to maintain peace. Secretary of War Belknap, who had been impulsive and indiscreet in his communications with Sheridan, first defended his telegrams, then backed down, claiming that he had not intended to imply that all the cabinet members approved of Sheridan's actions. Secretary of State Hamilton Fish, joined by Secretary of the Treasury Benjamin H. Bristow and Postmaster General Marshall Jewell, led the cabinet opposition to the handling of Louisiana. Fish stated not only that the army action had been an unwarranted invasion of the independence and integrity of a state legislature, but that he regarded Belknap's endorsement as irresponsible. He argued further that the situation was made infinitely worse by Sheridan's foolish statements that all Louisianians were bandits and by his illegal proposal for military trials. In conclusion, Fish advised the cabinet to disclaim all responsibility for the affair and to denounce the army operation.

At first Grant was adamant and angry. He endorsed Williams' defense of the army as a posse, refused to criticize its action or Sheridan's conduct, and was determined that under no circumstances would he apologize for anything that had been said or done. However, as the discussion wore on, he seemed taken aback by the excited and concerned reactions of some of the cabinet members, who tried to impress upon him the emotional explosiveness, the political repercussions, and the constitutional implications of the situation, as well as the necessity to keep the military subordinate to civil authority. The result was that Grant's certainty as to the proper course of action was shaken. Nevertheless, in spite of a deeply divided cabinet and strong pressure from Congress and the press, a judicious compromise was worked out in the form of the January 13 presidential message to the Senate. In substance, rather than a stubborn defense, it almost amounted to an apology. The cabinet members suggested two major lines of argument as a rationalization of the administration's position. Secretary of the Navy George M. Robeson advised that the message begin with a rundown of recent events to show conclusively that White Leaguers had conducted a systematic campaign of terror and trickery for several years in Louisiana and, quite recently, inside its statehouse, and that therefore troops, at the request of the governor, were properly and lawfully present in both the state and the statehouse. Thus the message shifted the blame to the White Leaguers and the responsibility for all decisions from Washington to New Orleans.

Fish and Robeson recommended that the administration dissociate itself from the army's action without, however, denouncing it or encouraging the White Leaguers and declare that it was triggered off not by President Grant but by Governor Kellogg and the army officers who had been on the scene and had bungled matters. On the other hand, the action taken could be rationalized, on the grounds of necessity, for there had indeed been an emergency at the statehouse. When bloodshed had seemed almost inevitable, the army officers had erroneously but understandably followed the governor's order to eject the five contestants from the chamber; and the military—who, after all, were not lawyers but soldiers—had, under the circumstances, made the mistake of overstepping their authority. By showing that Grant on December 9 had restricted the scope of army operations by excluding any army interference in state politics and that the White House had not authorized the contestants' expulsion, and by pointing out that the Constitution forbade the military to become involved in civil affairs in general or in the political organization of the legislature in particular, the administration would be spared both embarrassment and responsibility.

According to the message, the administration would no longer approve of the operation or justify it legally, but assured the Senate that no Democrat would be returned to the statehouse, nor would Republican control of the legislature be overturned. Therefore, despite the action that had been taken, it would not constitute a precedent and any repetition of it would be prevented. The last point made was once again to hand the whole matter over to Congress for possible investigation. The final draft of the message, then, was an artful dodge, but one that made considerable sense—submitting the legal principle to constitutional criticism in exchange for political support in the North, without surrendering power in New Orleans.[42]

As a result, the conciliatory message of January 13 prevented any further outbursts of indignation from the nation and provoked a reaction unfavorable to Louisiana Democrats. Also, Sheridan's subsequent reports provided a different view of the army's actual role, for Louisiana Democrats had asked for federal intervention in the first place by requesting the army to establish order in the statehouse. Trobriand had, after all, given equal time to both sides, entering the statehouse first on behalf of the Democrats and later on behalf of the Republicans. The Chicago *Times* observed that Grant had backed down a bit so that the Republicans could be induced to back him up. After the message had been delivered, Wisconsin Senator Timothy O. Howe noted that the "Republican party has been scared to death. But the color is coming back. It shall be all right as soon as their teeth stop chattering."[43]

The Republicans were beginning to forgive Grant because of his virtual admission of error, and their residual distrust of all things Democratic began to reassert itself as it had so often done in the past. Many of them now regarded Louisiana Democrats as the instigators of the crisis because of their attempt to forcibly and illegally organize the legislature. Moreover, the Democratic press had overplayed its hand; by attempting to whitewash the White Leaguers, it had in the end merely aroused bad feeling with regard to all southern Democrats. According to a Massachusetts politician, the recent events in Louisiana had succeeded in drawing Republican lines closer together than they had been for several years, with the result that the Democrats, who had earlier launched a spirited offensive, were again forced to be on the defensive. Taking a longer view, Garfield observed: "I have for some time had the impression that there is a general apathy among the people concerning the War and the Negro. The public seems to have tired of the subject and all appeals to do justice to the Negro seem to be set down to the credit of partisan prejudice. Perhaps the affairs in Louisiana will raise the right feeling on this question."[44]

Given Grant's request to the lawmakers for a solution, Congress wrestled with the Louisiana problems once again. Several solutions were proposed and then rejected. Holding a new election under federal supervision might well have provoked further disorder and risked a defeat for the Republicans. Imposing a military regime might have generated further controversy over the role of the army and have raised the question of the legality of creating a military territory. Installing a provisional government would prolong the agony because of uncertainty. However, the course of debate indicated that Congress, as usual, was more concerned with political window dressing than with practical solutions.

Each chamber subsequently took a different course of action. In late March, 1875, the Senate quite simply approved what Grant had done—that is, having protected the Republican government against insurrection, merely declaring that Kellogg was in fact governor and supporting Grant's recent move to maintain him. Although Grant and Kellogg had wanted a stronger and broader resolution—one to the effect that Kellogg was governor in law as well as in fact and that Grant's entire policy in the past had been valid—the Senate would agree only to a very watered-down version of it. Democratic Senator Allen Thurman characterized the Senate's endorsement as the palest whitewash, which wouldn't cover up anything or remove one spot from the record. In another test of strength the Senate again refused to seat the Louisiana mulatto senator-elect Pinchback, who had been chosen by the Kellogg legislature—a refusal that was far more telling than the Senate's opinion with regard to the validity of his election, the legality of the legislature itself, Governor Kellogg's authority, and the fact that Pinchback was not white. (Pinchback never took his seat in the Senate, having been finally refused in March, 1876.)

The House of Representatives similarly showed itself to be independent of the administration by seating the Democratic representative at large, who was opposed to Kellogg, as a member of the Louisiana delegation.[45]

As for the broader issue of the legislative dispute, the House, in an unusual departure from its previous state of indecision, began to evolve a settlement. After hearing contradictory reports by various subcommittees, and after many false starts and evasive shifts by the principals, a compromise was painfully worked out by William A. Wheeler, the moderate Republican representative from upstate New York. In early March, following a bitter struggle and acrimonious debate, the House endorsed the Wheeler compromise, a plan for Louisiana that was meant to achieve stability and to bring federal intervention there to an end. The plan, roughly, was to restore the status quo of the time directly before the army had expelled the Democratic legislators. The arbiters recommended that eleven Democratic state legislators in the lower chamber, who had not been certified by the Kellogg returning board, be seated, making the lower chamber of the legislature Democratic, but leaving the senate largely Republican. In short, the very men who had been expelled from the legislature by the army would be reinstated by Congress. A majority of the congressmen also recommended that Kellogg be recognized as the de facto governor and that his tenure no longer be disputed by the Democrats. By April 17 the compromise was effected and was met with general praise and a fervent hope for a lasting settlement.[46]

However, the spirit, if not the terms, were violated within three days, when the Democrats, in hopes of getting a majority of the legislature on a joint ballot in order to elect the United States senator, unseated four more Republican legislators on April 20, 1875. Later the agreement was completely repudiated when the Democrats tried unsuccessfully to impeach Governor Kellogg during February and March, 1876. Given the intensity of the struggle for power in Louisiana, any bargain was necessarily elusive and, as it turned out, delusive. Violations of the compromise during 1875 were glossed over by northern Republican newspapers in a desperate search for tranquillity and an escape from reconstruction. Even Wheeler philosophically observed that northerners mistakenly expected too much from the South; it was high time that the North understood how unwise the previous southern policy had been in trying to promote peace with the sword. Indeed, the northern Republicans were learning in earnest how to retreat.[47]

A close look at Grant's behavior toward Louisiana shows that his actions were affected by both political considerations and cronyism, as well his personal penchant for fluctuating between active and passive stances. Between August, 1871, and January, 1872, he was relatively passive and ineffectual. At first, he gave a free hand to the unreliable customhouse crew, who took foolish risks. Instead of serving the president as his agents, many of those federal officials became principals in Louisiana politics, and buccaneers and blind partisans at that. Since Grant appeared unwilling or unable to restrain their abuses and seemed loath to dismiss his federal and state protégés, he was held responsible for them and thereby incurred heavy political liabilities. Then, in a sudden reversal in January, 1872, and with considerations of the presidential election uppermost in his mind, Grant took firm control: he denied protection to his allies and formed a temporary alliance of convenience with their enemies. However, somewhat less than a year later, with the election out of the way, he resumed support of the customhouse circle and in December, 1872, recognized the Kellogg government, thereafter supporting this faction during its chronic crises.

When Grant realized that having recognized the Kellogg regime, he had also to maintain it, he provided the necessary assistance. He had federal troops stationed at the entrance to the statehouse in December, 1872, to seat a Republican majority in the legislature. On the other hand, in January, 1875, he had them march into the chamber to oust a Democratic majority. He also provided federal force to suppress uprisings in New Orleans and the various disturbances in the rural parishes. Thus, in coping with the supreme challenges, Grant's responses were swift and sure, and his patronage was certain and comprehensive. However, on other occasions during 1873 and 1874, when the emergencies had passed but conditions were still threatening and Kellogg's power unsure, Grant withdrew some army units, which helped to precipitate several political crises and race riots.

Of course, Grant had only himself to blame for all those constant problems, for at the beginning of his second term it was he who had taken the initiative, recognizing Kellogg as governor on his own authority. He probably had no other choice if he was to save the state for the Republicans at the time. He then endorsed the fiasco in January, 1875, apparently not realizing the enormity and the implications of General Sheridan's actions and statements until deluged by adverse public opinion and confronted with horrified members of the cabinet and Congress. Actually, and paradoxically, Grant had intervened both too little and too much.

Was Louisiana worth the investment of presidential involvement and military intervention? Certainly not, judging from the electoral advantage Grant derived from it, for he never received the state's electoral vote (although Hayes did in 1876–1877, when it proved to be critical). From Congress' viewpoint, the Republicans were helped in only a minor way by controlling the state's delegation until 1875. Grant's brother-in-law, Casey, never made it to the Senate, so that Grant's efforts on his behalf came to nought. In the state, the Republicans controlled both the governorship and the legislature until 1875, but their control was marginal and precarious, and its cost to the national party was considerable. Federal intervention was extremely damaging, with Louisiana plaguing both the president and his party and causing grave mistakes, which were followed by bitter censure. Grant found it difficult and dangerous either to get rid of Kellogg or to keep him, and with Congress, for the most part, proving incapable of taking action or making decisions, its share of the responsibility naturally fell on Grant's shoulders. Moreover, the unceasing upheavals in Louisiana caused a loss of confidence in Grant's southern policy in general, contributing to the defeat of northern Republicans in 1874. The national party was quite simply dragged down by the burden of Louisiana.

Clearly, in retrospect, Grant's initial recognition of Kellogg was a serious miscalculation. Lacking both ability and authority, the Kellogg government had not been able to maintain itself and had gone to pieces every time the army marched around the corner back to the barracks. The real governor—that is, the person with enough power to compel obedience and to guarantee a semblance of order—had been the general in the saddle or the man in the White House. Grant had thus staked a great deal on shaky ground by identifying the national party exclusively with the customhouse clique, which had required periodic federal intervention and had then produced even more trouble. One step had led inexorably to another, and each step, though ostensibly designed to cure, had made every bad situation that much worse. There was a familiar pattern to the dreary developments in Louisiana: electoral shortcuts with attendant anarchy, followed by mob terror and disorder, temporarily arrested by army occupation and presidential fiat.

The results were pernicious. Obsessed out of fear or hope with the possibility of outside interference, neither side had been willing to put its own house in order and come to terms with its enemies. Federal intervention and Grant's practically unconditional, if erratic, support had allowed Louisiana Republicans to become increasingly irresponsible and intransigent; it had enabled the Kellogg crew to abuse Grant's confidence and to exploit the federal apparatus in order to enjoy the fruits of power and had permitted them to treat the electorate, who cast meaningless ballots, with contempt. At the same time, intermittent federal intervention, along with numerous indecisive intervals, had encouraged the Louisiana Democrats' obstinancy in steadfastly refusing to recognize Kellogg; they had yielded and scattered only when faced with federal authority and force, but had quickly reformed their ranks for the numerous skirmishes between showdowns.

Consequently, instead of bringing about resolution and stability, federal intervention had institutionalized instability and increased the bad feelings between the parties. The state had never had the opportunity to show that it could govern itself, having been not only awed by the presence of federal soldiers and White League terrorists, but distracted by the intrigues of federal officials and local politicians. Washington's intervention had fostered recklessness, as each side had disregarded local opinion with impunity in their heedless pursuit of power, and it had also generated a strong distaste for reconstruction even among its friends. As a result, Louisiana had become the most persistent problem in Grant's southern policy, and the legislative expulsion in January, 1875, had provoked his most damaging domestic crisis, which had deleterious effects on his presidency, on his party, and on reconstruction.

6

POLITICS OR WAR?

The Federal Response to Arkansas and Mississippi

ARKANSAS was another state in which postwar politics were infected with endemic political instability. Indeed, a federal marshal working there did not exaggerate when he reported to Washington: "We are peculiarly situated in this State as to politics, very little difference here in a political campaign and war." At times, the happenings in Arkansas somewhat resembled a comic opera scenario, the various Republican and Democratic factions frantically using each other in strange and constantly shifting alliances. But however burlesque the events were, in fact they were too bloody to be really comical.[1]

In early 1871 the initial skirmish had to do with the gubernatorial succession, a no-holds-barred contest between feuding Republican factions. Grant, during the crisis in February, informed his secretary of war that the situation was "not well enough understood to justify" presidential recognition of the governor, so that federal troops were not to aid either faction but merely to preserve order if a riot took place. Within three months of pandemonium—that is, between January and March—the outgoing Republican governor, Powell Clayton, was elected to the United States Senate; then, farcically impeached as governor though denied a trial, he was again elected senator and was finally replaced by a new governor, one of his own men. One Arkansan informed the White House that Clayton's election to the Senate was a triumph for the administration and predicted that Grant would surely win the state's electoral votes in 1872 if federal help were forthcoming: "Clayton will work with the President if he gets half a chance! . . . I am on the look out for General Grant." And Orville E. Babcock, Grant's influential personal secretary, cryptically hinted at reciprocity when he replied: "I think Clayton will have no trouble."[2]

Subsequently, any doubts about the administration's position were dispelled when the Clayton faction received federal patronage and when Clayton himself represented Arkansas on the Republican national committee during 1872. Under the circumstances, the political situation simmered down for a while, with Clayton working for state control and Grant interested in support for his own renomination and reelection. When November came, however, the withholding of votes (altogether in three counties and partially in those scattered precincts that favored opponent Joseph Brooks for governor) became a national scandal. Arkansas' electoral votes, flagrantly manipulated for Grant by Clayton's clique, were thrown out by a Republican Congress. The Democrats and the dissident Republicans, who had become allies in support of Brooks, the Liberal candidate, promised there would be a revolution but were restrained by the presence of federal troops in Little Rock. Thereupon the politicos reverted to hard bargaining behind the scenes, with the result that Clayton's man, Elisha Baxter, who was running for governor on the Grant ticket, was fraudulently counted in, whereas Brooks was fraudulently counted out.[3]

During 1873 and 1874, however, Governor Baxter showed disquieting signs of independence by enthusiastically adopting a compromise policy—far too enthusiastically, in the eyes of the regular Republicans. He surprised the Democrats by being more accommodating than they had expected, assuaging them at the price of alienating the Republicans over issues of patronage, finance, registration of voters, and revision of the constitution. The Clayton forces watched helplessly as their own governor vetoed their measures; a man who had been their tool had turned traitor and, even worse, with the clear possibility of a fair election in the future, a Democratic victory was likely. When, in March, 1874, Baxter refused to sign railroad subsidy bonds which were worth two million dollars and would have been advantageous to a number of influential Republicans, it was the last straw. During a dizzying game of musical chairs, some fast footwork was done by Clayton, Senator Stephen W. Dorsey, and their Republican cohorts, who joined forces with their former enemy Joseph Brooks, while the Democrats and the dissident Republicans deserted Brooks and embraced Baxter. In other words, the Clayton faction now wanted to put Brooks—the very man they had cheated out of election—into the governor's chair, whereas the Democrats, in an equally abrupt turnaround, now regarded Baxter as their patron saint and endeavored to keep him in power.

Governor Baxter, expecting trouble, reorganized the militia and fortified himself in the statehouse. And the judges in federal and state courts began jumping on or off the political merry-go-round. In 1873 they had ruled out the replacement of Governor Baxter because of a lack of jurisdiction over the question; but a year later, in 1874, a state lower court was employed irregularly in a legal shortcut to oust Baxter and install Brooks by order of a circuit judge. In sum, the political situation was completely reversed: Baxter, who had been counted in by electoral fraud in 1872, was ousted from office and replaced during 1874 by Brooks, who was put into office by judicial irregularities. Finally, on April 15, 1874, Brooks seized the local armory and the statehouse and was sworn in as governor.[4]

The coup had been successful, but Arkansas was on the verge of civil war. Throughout the state, gangs of lawless men, many of whom were not responsible to any faction, roamed the countryside. Property was seized, trains were stopped, a steamboat loaded with arms was captured, arbitrary arrests were made, and about twenty or thirty men were killed in several clashes between the forces of Brooks and Baxter. In Little Rock, angry, armed, drunken mobs, dignified as "militia," formed behind each contender and paraded down the streets, refusing to obey the local police, starting fights, and firing shots that killed and injured enemies and bystanders alike, while officers from the opposite camp were busy recruiting soldiers in the ranks of the rival army. As neither side had uniforms and both were trigger-happy, each occasionally fired at its own men by mistake. Terrified horses, just as out of control as the politicians, ran up and down the streets. Brooks's men barricaded themselves in and around the statehouse with two cannon ready on the capitol lawn. Baxter's forces built fortifications three hundred yards away, installed cannon aimed at the statehouse, and made a nearby hotel their headquarters. Troops of each faction milled about at opposite ends of that street, taunting each other until tempers reached a breaking point, whereupon both Brooks, the usurper de facto, and Baxter, the usurper de jure, appealed to the president for military protection and official recognition.[5]

Grant's position now became critical, for both sides were depending upon him to decide which man was governor. At the start of the crisis Grant had sided with the Republican Senators Clayton and Dorsey, who had reportedly set up the coup with Brooks earlier in March. In keeping with his previous announcements regarding the state, Grant declared that Washington would not interfere in the political controversy but would prevent bloodshed. Therefore, in order to keep the rival forces apart, he saw to it that troops and artillery were placed on the street between the two. In point of fact, he was using the army to maintain the status quo, enabling the insurgent Brooks to hold onto the statehouse and preventing Baxter's militia from regaining occupancy of it as well as of the governor's office. The army was also put in control of the state arms stored in the federal armory, and it occupied the telegraph office, which earlier had been held by Baxter's forces. The federal government, then, under the semblance of armed neutrality, had in fact provided both actual and potential armed protection for Brooks so that he might retain his hold on the capitol, and with it, his position as governor de facto. Indeed, Baxter declared that his chances had been destoryed by the army. Meanwhile, Brooks was putting pressure on the courts to make his government de jure. And Washington again showed its obvious partiality for Brooks when, during a cabinet meeting at which the state's problem was to be discussed, Baxter's represenative, Congressman William W. Wilshire, was not included, but the two Arkansas senators of Brooks's faction were. As in Louisiana, cronyism combined with Republicanism was thus far characteristic of Grant's support.[6]

The administration's stand was reflected in the Washington *National Republican*. Having taken pains to discover some sort of legal justification for Brooks's position, it noted that his case had at least a "semblance of legal or judicial authority which almost, but not entirely, removes from it the stain of revolution or insurrection"—at best a rather damaging admission. The newspaper was on firmer ground when it moved on from the swamp of legality into politics, observing that Brooks was a good Republican who would, as governor, restore complete party control to the state government and seeing Baxter now the enemy, who had "sold himself out to the Ku-Klux Democracy." The Republican New York *Times* agreed that Baxter had become the willing and wicked tool of the Democrats, but maintained that that was no reason to alter his legal status; if he had been the lawful governor before his apostasy, as the Republicans had agreed earlier on, he remained the lawful governor. A mere semblance of legality did not convince the *Times*: since the state supreme court had previously refused to intervene, how could an inferior state court, without jurisdiction, overrule a decision of the highest court of the state? As for the Democratic New York *Sun*, it went straight to the heart of the matter: "There is a good deal said in the newspapers about Grant's 'neutrality' in this matter, which consists in using United States troops to prevent Baxter from maintaining the authority of the [governor's] office." And the Louisville *Courier-Journal* made the damaging comparison that in Louisiana Grant had ordered his troops to support a bogus governor who had not been recognized, whereas in Arkansas not only had he refused to order troops to support a legal governor who had been recognized, but he had directed those troops in such a way as to prevent the established governor from discharging his duties.[7]

On the other hand, a number of northern Republicans were openly thankful that Grant had at least limited disturbances and that he had not openly intervened, as he had brazenly done in Louisiana. This reaction suggested yet again that the northerners often cared very little about the means used to achieve an end, or about who was governor, if only order were restored. In the words of the New York *Herald*: "We have closed the [Civil] War, but we have not made a peace."[8]

Baxter, despite his unpromising position, continued to bluff and bluster around, still threatening to stage a coup, and he did not disband his militia. So, in a way, the stalemate continued. But the administration acted more cautiously, no doubt because of the coming 1874 election for the control of Congress. The pro-Brooks senators, who had previously attended cabinet meetings, were now conspicuously absent.[9] This official hands-off attitude changed, however, when the anarchy continued unabated, with scattered outbreaks of violence. Attorney General Williams made every effort to negotiate a settlement; Grant, for his part, wrote on April 22 that he would now accept any compromise and any means that would end the impasse. Nevertheless, both sides hardened their positions. Then on April 30, when there was serious violence near Pine Bluff, Washington became anxious to solve the problem before the situation got further out of hand. Meanwhile, the northern newspapers now were convinced that the presence of the federal government could only prolong the stalemate. Seeing that Baxter was not going to quietly fade away, such newspapers began to emphasize his rightful and legal claims. Given that the present federal stand was unsatisfactory and that overt intervention on Brooks's behalf was likely to weaken the northern Republicans' chances for election to Congress, the only viable alternative was to recognize the lawfully elected Baxter.[10]

Having received reports of increasing unrest from Arkansas, the cabinet on May 5 decisively changed its posture. According to the attorney general, there was no possible doubt that Baxter was legally entitled to the governorship, that the legislature had recognized him, that no one could question or change the electoral count or the previous decision of the legislature, and that the source of all the trouble had been Baxter's refusal to sign the coveted railroad bonds. Thus, backed by Grant, who agreed, the attorney general put an end to the administration's support of Brooks. Meanwhile, maneuvers in the Arkansas camps continued. There were further outbreaks of violence on May 7, when a half-dozen men were killed in a bloody battle over a steamboat, and on May 9, when another skirmish took place in Little Rock because of rumors to the effect that the Baxter faction planned to shell the statehouse. Both sides received reinforcements and worked feverishly to build barricades. The Baxter group, which had originally been made up exclusively of whites, began to recruit blacks in order to make a favorable impression on Washington. Although roughly equal in size at the beginning, the Baxter group soon outnumbered the Brooks group two to one. By May 9, another and greater confrontation seemed imminent. The attorney general's reaction was to alternately threaten and cajole representatives of both sides so that they would accept a compromise under which the legislature, which appeared to favor Baxter, would decide the governorship. Further, he wanted a mutual demobilization and a legislative investigation of Brooks's charge of a fraudulent electoral count.[11]

In Arkansas, Williams' strategy was interpreted as an indication of the president's weakness and uncertainty. Hoping to gain an advantage, both Baxter and Brooks backed and filled. The former, assisted by talented legal and political advisers, at first shrewdly refused the attorney general's May 9 suggestions. And then, on May 11, Baxter accepted a watered-down version which omitted the legislative investigation that was to analyze the 1872 election returns (which were likely to be damaging to Baxter) and demanded that Brooks evacuate the statehouse, though not necessarily implying that it would be occupied by Baxter. The idea of making the statehouse neutral and allowing the legislature to meet there seemed to strike a reasonable compromise. However, it in fact favored Baxter, because were Brooks to have evacuated the capitol, it would have critically undermined his bargaining power while allowing the legislature, which supported Baxter, to decide the governorship. Brooks at first claimed that he wanted only the courts to rule on the governorship, but then suggested that a congressional committee do so. In any case, realizing that the attorney general's terms were tantamount to surrender, he not only declined to accept them but refused to evacuate the statehouse or to recognize the legality of any forthcoming state legislative decision.[12]

As time went on, Brooks became increasingly uncooperative, even impudent. He went so far as to send an insulting telegram to President Grant on May 11 in which he lectured his erstwhile patron on his duties, charging him with the responsibility for the deaths of Arkansas blacks, suggesting that he stop shilly-shallying, and practically challenging him to recognize Baxter. Thereupon a presidential clerk informed the attorney general to be prepared to issue a proclamation. The following day, during a meeting of the cabinet, Grant pressed for getting rid of Brooks as quickly as possible, but action was delayed until the state legislature convened and officially requested Grant's intervention to counter statewide violence and to clear out the statehouse.[13]

The country was "sick and tired of the miserable wrangle," an editorial declared in the Washington *National Republican*. Similarly, Attorney General Williams delivered an opinion on May 15, 1874, which sidestepped the question of the 1872 election returns, scrapped the investigation of that election, and merely stated that since the legislature had declared Baxter the legal governor, he was. Then Grant officially recognized him, ordered everyone around the statehouse to disperse, and authorized the army to enforce obedience. While the Baxter supporters were celebrating in the streets of Little Rock, Brooks and his followers at first received the report with disbelief. A newspaperman broke the news to the federal army commander, who was the last to hear of Grant's decision. Brooks, enraged but helpless, surrendered the statehouse on May 19, 1874, thus ending the so-called Brooks-Baxter war, to the great relief of the nation.[14]

Doubtless, the presence of the army had increased the president's influence as well as the bargaining strength of his negotiator, Williams. Moreover, before the final settlement, the federal display of strength had limited, although not altogether prevented, bloodshed in Little Rock. Nevertheless, the number of troops was not large enough to preserve peace throughout the state, and their very presence implied an overall purpose and an operational plan, neither of which were provided by the president. Had Grant done swiftly in April what he finally did in May—that is, crush Brooks's coup at its very inception by recognizing Baxter—he would have obviated the need for violence. After all, no important developments or new evidence had been brought to light in the interim. Instead, by siding first with Brooks in April and then dropping him in May, Grant had allowed a local quarrel to grow into a small-scale civil war. To be sure, his delaying tactics had, in a sense, been helpful to Grant, for the anarchy in Arkansas had so exasperated the northerners that they finally called for federal intervention, having initially opposed it. In the end, they applauded Grant's belated recognition of Baxter, having earlier praised his supposed neutrality; in short, they had demanded in Arkansas what they had previously condemned in Louisiana. But the price of all the violence and disorder in Arkansas had been high. Grant, rather than having led and formed public opinion, had falteringly picked his way in its wake.

To sum up, Grant in Arkansas had employed shrewd short-run tactics combined with clever rationalization when he backed Brooks without having seemed to. But since he had given little evidence of any determination when he encountered considerable opposition, his tactics were shown to be meaningless. Thus, instead of settling the conflict with the deployment of troops around the statehouse, he had actually protracted it; instead of suppressing insurrection, he had in fact helped to maintain it; and instead of restoring order, he had allowed disorder to flourish, since the established state government was prevented from suppressing a rebellion. The presence of the army had made it impossible for Grant not to decide who the legal governor was; yet he had kept everything in limbo by making no definitive decision and treating Baxter for a month as if he were not the governor. All the trouble could have been averted had Grant, for example, sent a personal representative, such as General Sherman, the head of the army, to Little Rock to negotiate and enforce a political settlement. At the very least, he might have used his influence to press the state legislature into securing a quorum earlier, thus settling the dispute. But Grant, who had encouraged the hopes of the Arkansas Republicans, shattered them with a blow from which the state party was not to recover.

During the months following the spring conflict, the Arkansas Democrats mounted an attack to wipe out all vestiges of Republican power. They already had control of the legislature. Then came a massive purge of the state officials and judges who had supported Brooks. More importantly, the Democrats rammed through a new state constitution that curtailed the powers of the governor, required the election rather than the governor's appointment of judges, revamped apportionment, and vacated all elective offices by eliminating tenure. On October 13, 1874, the Democrats decisively captured the governorship, replacing their sometime ally Baxter with a full-fledged Democrat, Augustus H. Garland, and firmly restored the Democrats to power. Thus another state was lost to the Republicans, and by immense majorities.[15]

After that election, the Arkansas Republicans nevertheless attempted a counterattack on several fronts. Anxious to get the president to intervene, they questioned the validity of the new state constitution and the legality of the gubernatorial election. They claimed the governorship, contending that since the old constitution was still in force, the gubernatorial term did not end until 1877. The former lieutenant governor, Republican Volney V. Smith, who had been officially elected in 1872 along with Baxter, requested that Grant recognize him as the lawful governor and provide him with armed protection; there was even wild talk of setting up a government in exile, placed appropriately at Pine Bluff. Coincidentally, an on-the-spot congressional investigation had been underway since July and was expected to justify federal intervention. Grant and the cabinet deemed that silence was the best response, more especially since the Democrats jokingly remarked that the new Republican contender's following was too small to start even a second class riot. Indeed, Smith was, for the most part, not considered in Washington as having any legal standing or popular following.[16]

But the critical question remained—that of the legitimacy of the new Arkansas state constitution. Of the reconstructed states, Arkansas was the first to abrogate her progressive constitution—a warning that Republican reconstruction could be undermined in every other southern state, once the legislature had a conservative majority. In this way the Democrats could repudiate the congressional conditions of readmission, which were the legal backbone of reconstruction, and ensure full Democratic restoration by changing voter qualifications and election regulations. Democrats throughout the South, especially in North Carolina and Mississippi, who were anxious to rid themselves of reconstruction constitutions, viewed Arkansas as a test case that would indicate the strength of the administration's commitment to reconstruction and a Republican South. If the federal government acquiesced in amended or new state constitutions, the balance of power throughout the South could well shift. The Washington *National Republican* termed the actions of the Arkansas constitutional convention as "adoption of peaceable methods, by which the people have since then in reality revolutionized the State government."[17]

Since the Republicans were to lose control of Congress in March, 1875, and thus also the opportunity to influence events in the South, timing was critical. The question of the validity of the Arkansas state constitution was raised in cabinet meetings during November, 1874. After much discussion, Grant and the cabinet decided to postpone any action, awaiting the report of the congressional committee investigating Arkansas.[18]

For two months the issue hung in the balance. There were conflicting reports about what the committee, chaired by the administration's stalwart and bitter partisan Representative Luke P. Poland, a lame duck from Vermont, would recommend, and that tug of war created great anxiety among Arkansas Democrats, for their political fortunes were at stake. Meanwhile, Governor Garland moved in several directions to head off federal intervention. He promised Grant that he would break up any terrorist organization in the state and punish all offenders. He also warned Democratic Congressman Alexander H. Stephens that "to turn us back here will be to remit us to chaos—There will be nothing but anarchy here, and Mexico will be a paradise compared with it." The Arkansas Republicans, along with former District of Columbia boss Alexander R. Shepherd, a friend of Arkansas Senator Dorsey and Grant's secretary Babcock, coaxed and bullied Grant to influence the committee and succeeded in getting him to try. Finally, on February 6, 1875, resisting pressure from the administration, the Poland committee, to the dismay of the Clayton-Dorsey clique, announced its view that the new Democratic regime of Governor Garland held power lawfully and that there was no ground for federal intervention; the political and constitutional changes in Arkansas had been made regularly and peacefully and, therefore, could not be undone.[19]

Of course, Poland's report merely provoked the Arkansan Republicans into intensifying their pressure on the president to try to salvage Arkansas for their party, and it paid off. But Grant, under the cover of neutrality, was after all, merely repeating his earlier support of Brooks during April, 1874. With power slipping out of the Republicans' hands and with the likelihood of a dangerous precedent being established in the form of a conservative state constitution, at the eleventh hour Grant decided that something had to be done, especially since it meant doing a good turn for friends. Also, he was most probably piqued that Poland's committee had repudiated his suggestions. Without consulting the cabinet, he held a conclave with Clayton and his cohorts in the Capitol, and on February 8, 1875, in his message to Congress, Grant flatly rejected the recommendation of the Poland committee not to intervene in Arkansas, thus reversing his earlier course, that of having forsaken Brooks in May, 1874.[20]

Grant found both the election of the Garland government and the ratification of the Democratic-sponsored constitution invalid and believed that Governor Garland should be turned out of office and replaced by Brooks, the legally elected executive, thus sweeping away both Garland and his predecessor Baxter. Moreover, he warned that if Congress did not take immediate positive action to settle the Arkansas question, it would encourage other southern states to change their constitutions and subvert reconstruction. To avoid this, he threatened to depose Garland and install Brooks on his own authority. Indeed, his message read more like an order than a recommendation, for the wording implied that Grant intended to interfere in any case, and only wanted Congress to give him an excuse for doing so.[21]

The press was genuinely appalled by the presidential message. And, since it came so soon after the army's expulsion of legislators in Louisiana in January, editorial writers wondered whether it was yet another indication of a new southern policy of intervention. The Democratic Richmond *Dispatch* denounced Grant as a Janus with one peace face and one war face, who displayed them in turn, according to his capricious whim. Reflecting independent opinion, the New York *Herald* declared not only that Grant must have lost both his memory and his common sense but also called his southern policy a stupendous mistake and his administration a political failure. The Springfield *Republican* warned that the federal government could no longer trespass upon local jurisdiction by marching into a state, tearing up its constitution, and treating it as a province. Like most newspapers of all political persuasions, the formerly radical *Independent* was also extremely critical of Grant, urging Congress to disregard his message and leave Arkansas alone, in hopes that another southern fiasco could be avoided. Several members of the cabinet were privately dismayed. In Secretary of State Fish's view, Grant's message was a "grievous error," and the constitutional precedent, dangerous. John Marshall Harlan, a staunch Kentucky Republican, advised that Grant's astonishing proposal had to be killed before adjournment, for if Congress kept silent, the president would take such action as he deemed proper, with mischief sure to follow. However, the radical Chicago *Inter-Ocean* delivered a minority opinion: Arkansas' new constitution may have been adopted peacefully but its consummation represented a political revolution nonetheless, and Congress ought not set the precedent of recognizing a revolution of any sort.[22]

The showdown came in the House of Representatives on March 2, 1875, just two days before the Republican-controlled Congress was to expire. On the first and test vote to adopt the administration position recognizing Brooks as governor, the motion was decisively defeated, 152 to 79. The result was a complete surprise to the administration, which had been confident that Congress would vote to sustain Brooks and to support Grant's recommendation. Similarly, those Republicans who opposed the president's plan had expected that a sufficient number of weak-kneed party members could be whipped into line by the administration. But many House Republicans were dismayed by Grant's intentions, and probably some of them had been influenced at the last minute by the forceful speech of Representative Poland in his closing argument on behalf of his committee's conclusions. Next came the motion to kill Poland's resolution that the federal government ought not intervene in Arkansas, which was defeated, 194 to 147, thus keeping the proposal on the floor. Then the Poland resolution (the majority report) was adopted, 150 to 81. A slim Republican majority had voted, along with the Democrats, to oppose federal interference. In effect, they had cast a vote of no confidence in Grant's proposed policy for Arkansas.[23]

The Senate then concurred by refusing to pass its own resolution endorsing federal intervention. Congressional rulings were at least keeping the southern scoreboard even: Arkansas continued to be Democratic, whereas Louisiana remained Republican, giving the impression that Congress had struck a rough bargain, trading Arkansas for Louisiana. In any event, the Democratic victory in Arkansas was now irreversible, for the new Democratic House of Representatives in Washington could wreck any future action attempted by the Republicans in the Senate.[24]

Even more significant to the Republicans than the loss of a state was the repudiation of Grant's Arkansas policy by those congressional moderates who had become disenchanted with his southern policy in general. When the House endorsed the Poland committee's resolution, Grant lost face and reconstruction was shunted aside. As for Poland, there were rumors that he was punished for his independence by losing an appointment to a federal judgeship. So Grant was left no choice but to reverse his stand yet again, and on March 11 he recognized the Garland government. The Louisville *Courier-Journal* interpreted Congress' Arkansas resolution, in opposition to Grant, as a "slap in the face; it was the plucking of his beard." Similarly, the New York *Herald* termed the House vote a decisive and humiliating defeat. And Congressman Garfield considered the vote on Arkansas a check on presidential intervention in the South as well as something of a public veto of further federal involvement in election enforcement in the region. The forces of the administration, for their part, condemned the cowardice of the House resolution and predicted widespread disorder in the South.[25]

Meanwhile, in Arkansas, Governor Garland proclaimed a day of thanksgiving for the escape from Republicanism, remarking that the state had been sustained by the "true conservative Republican sentiment in the North." As for Joseph Brooks, Grant rewarded him with the postmastership of Little Rock, as William Holden had been appointed to oversee the mail in Raleigh. The New York *Herald* observed that from the executive chamber to the local post office did not seem a very laudable transfer, but at least Grant had got rid of another white elephant on very reasonable terms.[26]

Although Grant dispensed patronage deftly in this case, he had been less successful with his Arkansas policy. Any charitable doubt about it was dispelled when he reopened the question in 1875—an about-face that lacked credibility and was badly timed. He had waited almost a year, until the Garland government was well established and had adopted a new constitution; then he proposed to revive a dead regime by retrieving a discarded constitution and reinstating a man he had publicly repudiated; furthermore, he had seriously proposed this new approach with three weeks left in the lame-duck session of the Republican Congress. It had been too late for Grant to save Brooks, but not too late to do damage to himself. Perhaps, though, Grant had reckoned that something had to be done to counter the Democratic constitutional revolution before the new Democratic House convened; thus he had fought a daring but foolish last-minute battle and had lost. In any event, his policy in Arkansas was a series of stops and starts and turnabouts which further discredited reconstruction.

In Mississippi, the enormity and extent of the use of force and fraud by white Democrats by 1874 had become a national scandal. The major crisis began in the midst of the Vicksburg municipal election campaign in the summer. Republican Governor Adelbert Ames requested federal troops to be stationed in Vicksburg, where the Democrats were arming themselves and threatening violence. President Grant refused, claiming lack of jurisdiction, his usual rationalization when he chose not to help. Governor Ames attributed that refusal to Grant's desire for a third term, believing it was part of an appeasement policy of nonintervention designed to court southern Democrats. Although his idea of a third-term scheme proved irrelevant, Ames predicted quite rightly that if Grant continued in his refusal to dispatch federal troops, "Republicanism must go down in the South."[27]

The city election took place in August, and by intimidating the blacks as well as manipulating the votes, the Democrats, all of whose candidates were white, defeated the Republican incumbents. Their victory marked the turning point in state politics, with a local government displaced by sanctioned violence and racist appeal; indeed, it was the beginning of widespread racial conflict for political gain.[28]

That conservative triumph in a city with a black majority of hundreds emboldened the white Democrats to try for a greater prize—control of the county, which had a black majority of thousands. Consequently, another serious flare-up took place in volatile Vicksburg the following December. While incompetent Republican officials, who had already been indicted for corruption and forgery by a Republican grand jury, fought hard to hold onto their power and tenure, the records relevant to the pending case, being in the custody of the accused officials, mysteriously disappeared. Also, the tax rate and county spending were criticized. Then the black sheriff, who was also the tax collector, was forced to resign, but he later repudiated his resignation and attempted to regain office. His attempt—with the verbal encouragement of Governor Ames and with the direct assistance of blacks from the countryside who marched into the city—provoked a fiery dispute between the races. Each side grew more headstrong and hysterical. Recognizing their inadequate strength, the blacks finally decided to withdraw from the city. But wild mobs of whites, who roamed Vicksburg and the countryside spoiling for a fight, declared war, leading to riots on or after December 7, 1874, in which about three hundred blacks and two whites were slaughtered.[26]

Governor Ames quite rightly linked the December riots to the violence in August, affirming that the Vicksburg Democrats did not want any legal or legislative remedy for their political problems but were determined to foment a war of races, for political purposes. In December, he finally proclaimed a state of insurrection and called a special session of the legislature, which in turn authorized a request for federal troops in Vicksburg. After a second request from Ames, the troops arrived belatedly, in mid-January, 1875, occupying the courthouse, forcing out the newly elected Democratic sheriff, and replacing him with a Republican. Under army control, Vicksburg calmed down temporarily, but the Republicans were still in fear of future violence from the Democrats.[30]

Despite well verified published reports of violence against Republicans and Negroes during the previous summer of 1874, the northern press, in large part, had agreed with Grant that it did not warrant federal intervention. The Republican Chicago *Tribune* observed that southern Republicans still had the mistaken notion that a patriarchy existed in the nation, with governors running to the president like bawling children to a father asking him to protect them from all mischief-making and every bully. Yet according to the Republican New York *Evening Post*, no cure for Mississippi or for the South in general could come from the outside; it had to come from the southerners themselves and their own governing bodies: "No political quack medicines, such as federal interference or military protection or Congressional investigation, will do any real good, because the moment these temporary appliances are removed the evils will break out more violently and virulently than before." However, the independent-minded New York *Herald*, although it had often been critical of federal intervention in the past, suggested that dismissing every appeal to the president to maintain order as merely an electioneering trick was a dangerous assumption. It was high time, thought the *Herald*, that the South adjusted to the emancipation and enfranchisement of the Negro: "nothing could be more wanton and unnecessary than the war now waged upon the blacks of Mississippi by the whites." Similarly, the Washington *National Republican* viewed Mississippi as symptomatic of both northern and southern attitudes; in other words, the Mississippi whites, emboldened by their recent electoral success, were encouraged by the northern press in their belief that the "Northern people have lost all interest in the welfare of colored Southern Republicans."[31]

As more complete information and gruesome details issued from Mississippi, many northerners, repelled by the tales of horror and bloodshed in Vicksburg, were roused from their indifference and, by midwinter, roundly condemned the terrorism. They nonetheless were highly critical of both the political and the legal precedents set by the president and the army, along with Governor Ames, when they had settled the local election dispute in January, 1875, by deciding who was sheriff of Warren County (Vicksburg). Even the *Independent* agreed with the general opposition to federal intervention in a local quarrel, especially when there had been no insurrection involved; in its view, the Ames regime had confessed its "utter and absolute imbecility" in requesting federal help without first mobilizing its own supporters. And according to the New York *Times*, the removal of the Democratic sheriff by the army was as ill-judged and irregular as the earlier ejection, by mob terrorism, of his Republican predecessor.[32]

The Democrats, however, learned a valuable lesson from the Vicksburg eruptions: they had succeeded in capturing city hall by the covert means of election trickery but had failed to secure the county courthouse by overt mob action. Control of all of Mississippi was their goal; all they needed was to evolve an appropriate strategy.

One tactic was suggested by the Meridian *Mercury*: "The negroes are our enemies . . . we must accept them as our enemies, and beat them as enemies." Thus, heartened by the developments during the summer and the national Democratic victories in the fall (which they interpreted as the North's repudiation of reconstruction) as well as by recent elections in nearby Louisiana and Alabama, yet sobered by their miscalculations that winter, the Mississippi Democrats prepared for a showdown in 1875.[33]

The whites' indignation against the so-called "black reconstruction," spawned by rumors both spontaneous and calculated, bordered on mass psychosis. Many whites were out for blood but realized that in order to secure the state they had to avoid upsetting the North and disputing national authority, for it was essential that federal intervention be prevented. The state's envoy in the capital, Democratic Congressman Lucius Q. C. Lamar, remained in Washington during the Christmas recess to monitor developments and to defend Vicksburg's interests. In late December, 1874, he wrote: "The wolf (at the White House) is panting for the blood of our people. Oh that the 4th of March [1875, when the Republican Congress would expire] were here so that the Democracy could stand in the popular branch [House of Representatives] between him and his victories."[34]

Seeing the mounting determination of the Democrats, Governor Ames grew increasingly uneasy. He had confided to his wife in October, 1874, that the Republican disasters in the midwestern elections and the "gradual and seemingly certain falling away of Republican states in the South makes us all a little gloomy and full of forbodings of a like fate." In early 1875 he had warned that the "old rebel is ripe for anything. . . . The whole question south is that of the personal liberty and security of the negro"; the "freedom of a race is at stake." Late in the year, as the Democrats became increasingly organized, he prophesied the "intimidation and murdering of the poor negroes. If they [the Democrats] extend their savage policy in Vicksburg we can not predict the results." Expressing at once a wish and a doubt, he concluded: "We do hope the North will stand true to the rights of the colored men."[35]

In autumn, 1875, the Democrats began what amounted to a revolu-

153

tion, rather than a campaign, under the seemingly innocuous term "Mississippi Plan" or "straight-out policy." Although they framed a state party platform that endorsed civil and political equality, it was partly manufactured for northern consumption. For local consumption, in their stump speeches, they preached the principle of caste and sanctioned those tactics of terror that were appropriate to each locality. White Democrats in every county conducted their own campaigns in their own ways, but the intent was always the same—to win—peacefully if possible, by force if necessary. As the campaign developed, Mississippi newspapers sparked their editorial comments with incendiary appeals to white supremacy. The whites organized private military outfits, and the formula "vote blacks down or knock them down" became increasingly popular.[36]

The Democrats' plan was to foment just enough terror in the strong Republican counties to demoralize and defeat the black Republicans, but not enough to provoke any federal reaction. To avoid army interference, orders were given to the White Liners' troops to avoid battle after the initial skirmishes in early September, but then to open fire just before the election—that is, when it was too late for Washington to have time to send forces in to establish order and to police the voting. Clearly, it required skillful timing to frighten the blacks out of registering in September and to prevent those who had from voting in November. Thus while appearing friendly to the North and pleasantly pronouncing high-sounding principles, Mississippi Democrats were carrying out a program of persecution and terror at home. In some counties, however, the conservatives tried to reassure and recruit the blacks.[37]

With the color line savagely drawn, some white Republicans followed the lead of the White Liners out of racial prejudice. Others were cowed into following it because they feared physical intimidation, economic pressure, or social ostracism. And not only were the Negroes generally unarmed, unprepared, and afraid, but even worse, the state government was by then nearly paralyzed and incapable of maintaining order or protecting its citizens. No statewide militia existed, and efforts to form one were hampered not only by the legislature, which, with considerable strength from the conservative wing, dragged its feet and held tightly onto the purse strings, but also by the fact that disaffected whites and terrified blacks generally refused to enlist. Finally, the legislature authorized and appropriated funds for two regiments, but Ames did little or nothing to organize the units, apparently out of fear that it would enrage the whites and cause even more violence. The last hope for the Republicans in the election appeared to be the use of United States troops to stop the intimidation of black Republican voters. However, the state's inaction did nothing to inspire northern support, for the northerners had concluded that if Mississippi Republicans didn't try to help themselves, they had no reason to expect outside assistance.[38]

Throughout September the situation deteriorated, with disorder in Yazoo, Warren, and Hinds counties. In Hinds, just outside of Jackson, on September 4, a few young drunken whites fired into a large gathering at a Republican barbecue in Clinton, killing four black women and children and scattering the terrified crowd. The blacks struck back, catching two of the white culprits and hacking them to death. In swift and indiscriminate retribution, a group of whites formed an impromptu posse, rounded up about thirty blacks, and slaughtered them. Although northerners were accustomed to the idea of the South being characterisitically lawless and violent, their press did mention the exceptionally brutal butchery at Clinton. The New York *Herald*, for example, noted that the whites in Mississippi actually tolerated such attacks. Nevertheless, the organ of the administration, the Washington *National Republican*, remarked on the relative lack of indignation in the North toward these recent events in Mississippi. And, in fact, as a leading Republican paper in the South, the Greensboro *New North State*, declared, there was little use in even calling attention to those outrages, for almost no one seemed to care.[39]

On September 8 Governor Ames asked Grant for federal assistance to suppress any such subsequent attacks. But both his views and his request were undercut by factional rivals, opposition leaders, and some federal officials in Mississippi, who notified Washington that federal intervention was unwise and unnecessary, given the fact that peace generally prevailed and that such disturbances were rare. The administration, however, was well apprised of the true situation by reports from a number of federal officials that were clear and definite as to the scope and extent of terrorism in the state. For example, the federal attorney at Jackson reported that state authorities were in fact powerless and the situation grave, since it was the "intention of the Democracy to carry this state by intimidation and violence"; such riots and bloodshed as the Clinton incident would be repeated if the Republicans tried to hold meetings, and measures ought to be taken to guarantee peace and order until the elections were over. "Nothing short of military protection will enable the Republicans to enjoy a free ballot in Mississippi this year," the federal attorney continued, urging that the protection "should be full and unequivocal"; lukewarm support and half-way measures would only jeopardize the lives of citizens. Other federal officials in the state similarly maintained that there was only one solution to the reign of terror: to move the army into Mississippi en masse, quickly and decisively. And officials in the Department of Justice were clearly informed by Mississippi Republicans of the reign of terror in the state.[40]

Since Grant was vacationing on the New Jersey shore, Attorney General Edwards Pierrepont, who had replaced Williams on May 15, 1875, was in operational control. Pierrepont, a war Democrat who later became a staunch Republican and had strongly supported Grant's election in 1868 and 1872, took a very narrow view of federal powers of intervention. He pressed Governor Ames for clear evidence of an insurrection that the state government was unable to suppress, strongly hinting that he thought Ames was making a fool of himself in asking for assistance, as well as implying that he was not much of a governor if he could not suppress the disturbances. Indeed, Pierrepont's words indicated that he was not preparing to move into Mississippi. Ames, who mistakenly avoided the attorney general's question, did not furnish the required facts, but went on insisting that he was powerless to protect the blacks or to enforce the law.[41]

Meanwhile, Grant remained on vacation; when he was informed, however, his initial response to the crisis was firm: through the adjutant general he authorized army assistance to suppress any uncontrollable insurrection. The message read: "Be ready to furnish aid, forthwith, to Governor of Mississippi in case further orders are sent you to assist in preserving order in that State." But the orders from the president never came. Two days later, having received Pierrepont's own message—"the war in Mississippi over"—the president hesitated. His confidential reply to the attorney general on September 13, 1875, was laced through with contradictions and indecision. Admitting that he was "somewhat perplexed to know what directions to give in the matter," he observed that the "whole public are tired out with these annual, autumnal outbreaks in the South, and there is so much unwholesome lying done by the press and people in regard to the cause and extent of these breaches of the peace that the great majority are ready now to condemn any interference on the part of the Government." Yet despite his obvious exasperation with the interminable southern fracas, Grant reluctantly endorsed an active federal role and continued to favor army intervention: "I do not see how we are to evade the call of the Governor, if made strictly within the Constitution and Acts of Congress." The constitutional provision to uphold the republican form of government against domestic violence must be exercised, he wrote, or it would become a dead letter by sheer default under a "well meaning but timid executive." The decision as to whether and when to send federal troops must not be left to the opposition press, he added and concluded, with some reservations, that he would sign a proclamation and then intervene.[42]

But the final decision was very different indeed. There was to be no federal intervention, because Pierrepont quite simply seized the initiative and took charge. Grant's statement of the thirteenth was selectively quoted in Pierrepont's letter of September 14 to Governor Ames, which was released to the press. Taking advantage of Grant's fatal ambiguity, which could be selectively used to support quite different courses of action, Pierrepont proceeded to impose his own will and to block federal intervention. Quoting from Grant's letter but out of context, he eliminated the president's appraisal of the situation, made his original intention misleading, narrowed his interpretation of the reach of federal authority, and related nothing but the idea of pressing the Ames government to take defensive action on its own. President Grant, apparently willing for his attorney general to make the decision, shunned further responsibility and acquiesced.[43]

Pierrepont added material of his own to the selected portions of

Grant's letter and declared that the federal government would intervene only if it became absolutely necessary to prevent large-scale disorder and to put down a rebellion against the state government itself. Yet in point of fact, disorder was rampant, the democratic process was a mockery, and virtual insurrection existed throughout the state. Rigidly orthodox, he suggested that the problem was wholly an internal matter and would have to be handled accordingly by the governor, who was to take "all lawful means and all needed measures to preserve the peace by the forces in your own State." The trouble was that no such required force existed, as Pierrepont well knew. Besides, the small appropriation for militia could not easily be spent because of the Democrats' legal maneuvers. Also ignored was the fact that the whites had stolen arms from the state armory and from a wharf at Vicksburg, thus making it impossible to furnish arms to any enlarged militia until new equipment was received. And although Pierrrepont suggested that the legislature be convened, the Democrats could and had absented themselves to prevent a quorum in the state senate. Then came the usual northern call for heroism, for self-defense and self-reliance: the black Republicans had to manfully defend themselves if attacked, for only then would they command the respect and forbearance of their enemies and deserve the support of their friends. But the blacks, unarmed and unorganized, and with no help whatever from militia or the army, faced the obvious possibility of being slaughtered.[44]

Pierrepont had, of course, ignored the hard facts of the relationships between white violence and electoral victory and had instead delivered a hollow pep talk. And Grant's willingness to go along was probably due to Pierrepont's persuasiveness, though perhaps the pending elections in the North had counted as well. For although Grant had intervened in Louisiana in January, 1875, when no critical election was pending elsewhere, he failed to move during the fall of 1875, when the gubernatorial campaign was at its height in Ohio. The Ohio contest was crucial: failure to carry the state, with its lucrative patronage in 1875, could well have meant losing it in 1876 and, with it, the presidency. The Democrats had been holding the statehouse there since 1872; indeed, Republican Hayes was to win the governorship in the October, 1875, election by a slim margin—

less than 3,000 votes. As Governor Ames of Mississippi wrote afterward: "I was sacrificed last fall that Mr. Hayes might be made
Gov[ernor] of Ohio."[45]

According to black Mississippi Congressman John R. Lynch, Grant
told him in November, 1875, that pressure had been exerted by a
delegation of Ohio politicians not to intervene in Mississippi in order
to win in Ohio; and Grant possibly concluded that whereas the Mississippi election was lost in any case, the Ohio gubernatorial campaign might be lost as well if the federal government intervened in
Mississippi. The danger was recognized at the time and appeared
compelling when the Republicans made a poor showing in Maine in
September. One Mississippian noted that the "interest of the Party
in other Sections would have been jeopardized by such an act" as
federal military intervention in Mississippi, and a dispatch in the
New York *Tribune* stated that the "interest shown in Washington in
the result of the election in Ohio tomorrow surpasses anything of the
kind since 1872. Almost nothing else is talked about." In short, the
northern strategy to save Ohio fitted Pierrepont's disposition toward
nonintervention. And that priority, combined with growing Republican conservatism, brought the administration's full retreat from
Mississippi. Fashioning a southern policy had become increasingly
difficult: federal intervention in the South was dangerous for party
interests in the North; yet doing nothing at all was clearly suicidal
for party interests in the South.[46]

The decision not to intervene was widely applauded, with few dissenters. Either deluded, or simply ready to desert, most northerners
agreed that there was no disturbance of any consequence in Mississippi. The Republican New York *Times* found nonintervention judicious and sound, combining good law with common sense. The New
York *Tribune* observed that the nation had a new attorney general in
office, and thus there was a new southern policy of nonintervention.
Grant's refusal to help Ames, remarked the New York *Herald*, would
be the surely well-deserved undoing of the governor, who had waved
the bloody shirt too often. The *Independent* described Pierrepont's
opinion as "unquestionably right," because Mississippians should
govern themselves; indeed, they were doing so. Even the Republican
Greensboro *New North State*, though critical of Pierrepont's lack of

understanding when it came to the difficulties faced by southern Republicans, meekly conceded that his solution was doubtless the only one. Most newspapers seemed to agree that reconstruction had to be replaced by reconciliation. Nonintervention was commendable because, now that the blacks had been granted freedom and the franchise, they could not, according to the Chicago *Tribune*, be furnished with bodyguards; they had to act like men, not sheep, and show they were worthy of freedom.[47]

Not everyone, however, shared the conventional wisdom that the task of reconstruction was completed and that federal responsibility had been met. The Washington *National Republican*, breaking openly with the administration for a few days during the crisis in September, observed that it was the Republican party that had undertaken reforms in the first place and, in the process, had aroused many southern whites to bitter hatred against the blacks; yet the same party "now abandons them poor, weak, ignorant and defenseless to the relentless vengeance of enemies. . . . It is but 'the beginning of the end,' for with the mangled remains of these victims of false promises will be fragments of a broken Constitution and violated law, and . . . 'free suffrage,' will be buried with them." Thus the party that had fathered reconstruction was now cooperating in strangling it. Similarly, the Washington *Chronicle* criticized Grant for his procrastination in the Mississippi affair and hoped that he would act as decisively in dealing with the enemies of the Union as had President Andrew Jackson with South Carolina in 1832–1833. Some Republicans, then, were clearly upset; but the reaction of their colleagues in Mississippi was pathetic, reflecting the vain hope of the dying. On the other hand, the Republican Jackson *Times* preferred to interpret Grant's refusal to intervene not as a rejection of their cause but only as a temporary delay in furnishing federal support, awaiting Governor Ames's try at taking action.[48]

Although Ames's position seemed hopeless after the rebuff in September from Washington, he continued in his efforts, however hesitantly and belatedly, despite Democratic obstruction within the state. At Jackson he drew together a small force of black militiamen, ignoring protest from the whites. But then, after antagonizing them by recruiting blacks, he did not, with one exception, mobilize that unit for concerted action. Also, he requested Grant to provide special detectives to investigate and penetrate the organization of the White Liners. Grant lamely agreed with the request, provided that funds were available. Ames also pressed Pierrepont to ensure adequate election inspection by using federal officials and troops and to replace an uncooperative federal attorney and marshal.[49]

Although apparently none of these requests was met, Pierrepont did have his agent George K. Chase fashion a compromise to avoid large-scale bloodshed—a compromise that was subsequently agreed to by both the chairman of the state Democratic party and Governor Ames on October 15. Clearly, Ames had become demoralized as a result of the pressure from the Democrats and the lack of help from the Grant government. Thus he subsequently agreed in October that two activated companies of state militia be demobilized and disarmed and that no new units be organized; therefore those blacks who turned in their weapons were denied any means of self-defense, although the whites still had their arms. The Democrats, in return, pledged to end their terrorist campaign and to conduct a peaceful, fair election. It was a bad bargain: it not only destroyed any strength the Republicans might have had in the state in exchange for mere verbal promises that would surely be methodically disregarded, but it discouraged the likelihood of federal intervention by giving the impression that the problem had been ameliorated. Therefore, Ames, by placing unwarranted trust in the promises of his bitter enemies and by taking into his confidence Pierrepont's agent, Chase, won neither the respect of his opponents nor the allegiance of his allies. Indeed, Ames himself had perhaps unwittingly discouraged the very help he had been seeking by writing to President Grant in late September, "Your letter and Atty. General Pierrepont's have produced marked improvement in the condition of affairs here. The white liners, whose only policy is intimidation, are themselves somewhat intimidated."[50]

However, despite his acceptance of this compromise and his soothing letter to the president, behind the scenes through intermediaries in Washington, Ames continued to press for the control and use of army units in the state. In response, he received a spate of double-talk about disposition of army units. At first, Grant and Pierrepont, who had backed the peace agreement with the Democrats, promised that troops would be sent if the Democrats broke their agreement. But the troops were stationed too far away to be ready for an emergency. At the last minute, just before the election, Washington did authorize troops to be ordered into action by Governor Ames, but only to suppress disorder, not to prevent it or to police the polling places to ensure a fair election. Indeed, the insubstantial substance of the instructions—preserve order if possible—was an indication of both pessimism and fatalism.[51]

As election day drew near, violence and intimidation reached epidemic proportions in another reign of terror. The whites, with guns in their hands and murder in their hearts, were intent on control. Most Republican meetings were broken up or canceled, out of fear. Republican nominations were often not made, the candidates didn't campaign, and some Republican nominees and officials even fled their homes. One Republican from Yazoo County described the peace agreement "as a mockery and a snare," for conditions were even worse than before the compromise. Repeating rifles were distributed to whites throughout the state. Some blacks were hanged. Economic coercion was added to physical intimidation as the whites refused to lease land, give jobs, or provide credit to blacks. Whole counties were virtually under military siege; the Democrats wore red shirts, symbolizing bloodshed; in some towns, graves were dug for those Negroes who might vote Republican. As a clear warning, whites shot guns into the air on the night before the election, and cannon, manned by uniformed volunteers, were stationed in front of polling places on election day. Many blacks, fearing for their lives, did not dare to vote, and most of those who tried either did not receive ballots or were driven from the polls; ballot boxes were seized and stuffed. The Democrats had realized their rallying cry and either had voted the blacks down or had knocked them down.[52]

The work had been well done: election day, November 2, 1875, in many counties was funereally quiet; it was the passivity of surrender. So complete and thorough was the rout that the Democrats won every county but two with their state ticket, won all but twelve with their county tickets, captured both chambers of the legislature, and carried two thirds of the congressional districts. The record of black voting illustrated just how successful the campaign had been: in Yazoo County, for example, where formerly there had been a black majority of two thousand, only 7 Republican votes were cast in 1875. There was no reason to suppose that within a few years the blacks had moved away or had changed their politics en masse; deliberate and wholesale intimidation and violence had won the election for the Democrats. A Mississippian wrote that the "recent *So Called* Election" was a sad commentary upon the franchise: "Without cause, or provocation, Republicans [were] driven from the polls. Maltreated and murdered, death threatened if these wrongs were reported or acted upon. All for want of Federal protection."[53]

With the Democrats having captured both chambers of the legislature and threatening to impeach Ames, he resigned on March 29, 1876, and was replaced by a Democrat. Mississippi now had the freedom to construct a closed society of caste and one-party politics, for the White Liners had succeeded in making the state a hell first and Democratic forever after. Very early on, Ames had foreseen the Republican fate in what he correctly predicted would become a race war. After the murders in early September, he had remarked that the "'white liners' have gained their point—they have by killing and wounding so intimidated the poor Negroes that they can . . . prevail over them at the election." By October he had thought the odds were against a fair election and believed the contest would prove fatal to the party. He had predicted that election day "may find our voters fleeing before rebel bullets rather than balloting for their rights." In mid-October he proclaimed: "Yes, a *revolution* has taken place—by force of arms—and a race are disfranchised—they are to be returned to a condition of serfdom—an era of second slavery."[54]

Dependent upon the North, Ames had become increasingly disillusioned with it. At first, he had thought northerners were merely ignorant or obtuse about conditions in Mississippi: "What I regret more than everything else is that the North can not and will not understand the rebellious and barbarous spirit which prevails among the whites here." To be sure, Ames had realized that his call for federal troops was dangerous and controversial, especially coming in the midst of a difficult campaign in a crucial northern state. As he had put it at the time, it was like an "exploding shell in the political canvass at the North." But when his call was refused, he had bitterly denounced what he regarded as inappropriate priorities: "When the liberties of the people were in jeopardy the nation abandoned us for political reasons."[55]

Ames had also recognized that there were larger ramifications to federal intervention. He had believed, with considerable justification, that his call for troops had been identified with those of other Republican regimes: the "sins and iniquities of Republican rule in South Carolina, Louisiana, and other Southern states are weighed against me in judgment of the country." Above all, he had been concerned that reconstruction itself was in jeopardy because of the prejudice and apathy of northerners. "I am fighting for the Negro; and to the whole country a white man is better than a 'Nigger.' " Inveighing against the "selfish, cold blooded spirit" of the administration, he later declared that the "nation should have acted [by intervening in Mississippi] but *it* was *tired* of the annual autumnal outbreaks in the South'—see Grant's and Pierrepont's letter to me. The political death of the Negro will forever release the nation from the weariness from such 'political outbreaks.' "[56]

During 1875 Grant had talked of his earnest sympathies with the blacks of Mississippi; he had also warned that it would be "no child's play" were the army sent to the state. In fact, the Grant government played games with people's lives and liberties, as well as with the peace of the state, for resistance by White Liner Mississippians had brought not federal mobilization but full retreat in September, 1875. Bold when he should have been cautious, Grant, with regard to an earlier local difficulty in Vicksburg, had sent troops in too late, in January, after the violence had already subsided. Then he had annoyed much of the country by ousting the ostensibly elected Democratic county officials and reinstating the Republican incumbents. During the fall, however, he had been timid when he should have been bold, failing to suppress a statewide counterrevolution that became a bloody tragedy, evidenced by the black bodies that were strewn about the Mississippi countryside. The tragedy also was apparent in the fear that gripped officials and voters in the state, in the arrogance and freedom of action of the White Liners, and in hope turned to dismay; Mississippi Republicans were left scattered, demoralized, and powerless. As one of them phrased it, the "architects of our ruin will leave the State like rats leave a sinking ship."[57]

Thus Grant's so-called "healing influence" of nonintervention brought about a decisive retreat from reconstruction. He himself admitted as much to Congressman Lynch after the election: "What you have just passed through in the State of Mississippi is only the beginning of what is sure to follow."[58]

7

A STUDY IN INCONGRUITIES

Grant's Southern Policy and Performance

GRANT had assumed office on a great wave of public confidence, initially armed not only with immense potential power and influence in the South, but with control of the Republican Congress. Nonetheless, during his administration the southern states, one by one, had slipped from the Republicans' grasp. By November, 1870, the legislatures of four southern states (Virginia, Tennessee, North Carolina, and Georgia), along with the rest of the border states (now joined by West Virginia and Missouri), were again under Democratic control. By November, 1874, four more states (Texas, Arkansas, Alabama, and Florida) had drifted back toward the Democracy. Thus, the Republicans had already lost roughly three quarters of the southern state legislatures. And the election of 1874 marked the end of complete Republican power in six Confederate states and underscored the continuing erosion of effective federal authority throughout the South. Grant had failed in his attempts at reconciliation in Virginia (1869), in his retreat early on in North Carolina (1870) and then tragically in Mississippi (1875), his juggling about in Arkansas (between 1874 and 1875), his temporary show of determination in Texas, Georgia, and Alabama, and his intermittent displays of force in Louisiana.

Grant's course in the South was, according to the New Orleans *Daily Picayune*, an "incomprehensible muddle and mystery, a parable that cannot be understood, a riddle that defies all guesswork." In fact, Grant's southern policy was a study in incongruity: a curious, confusing, changeable mix of boldness and timidity, decision and indecision, activity and passivity, as he shifted between reinforcement and retrenchment, coercion and conciliation.[1] Its underlying intention was to promote the fortunes of both President Grant and the Republican party through the process of reconstruction and also to carry on the business of government by maintaining order and guaranteeing republican rule.

Those aims were often in conflict, for the struggle for supremacy and the desire for stability seemed sometimes to be mutually exclusive. Also the hopes for a lasting reform in the South were not easily reconciled with the demands for reconciliation between the sections of the nation. Indeed, contradictions and inconsistences abounded in the administration's actions. For example, the Grant government occasionally permitted the two extremes, arbitrary rule and unchecked anarchy, to prevail in the South; Grant himself abided by certain court decisions and disregarded others; some Republicans received carte blanche and a great deal of assistance, whereas others, both worthy and unworthy, were ignored. Moreover, political considerations frequently determined President Grant's position at a particular juncture. For instance, during the winter of 1869–1870, when Georgia's vote was needed for ratification of the Fifteenth Amendment, Grant initially acted vigorously in that state. Yet, in hopes of gaining electoral votes for his reelection, he sometimes pursued a conciliatory policy in other southern states, notably in Virginia, which had a majority of white voters and strong support from the conservatives. That desire to be reelected probably also motivated him to desert, momentarily, in January, 1872, his favored clique in Louisiana. On the whole, during the first two years of his first administration, President Grant had tried to balance the political forces and factions in the various states in his own and in partisan interests.

However, even before 1872, Grant's impatience with the southern situation increased as reconstruction steadily deteriorated. He thus allowed various Republican regimes to crumble, for when it was expedient Grant was quick to fall back on the limitations of presidential power and duty. Because of such tendencies as well as because of these governors' own inadequacies, Holden in North Carolina had gone down during the summer of 1870 and Bullock had lost power in Georgia during 1871. After Grant's reelection, the hold of the various remaining southern Republican regimes became even more precarious and northern public opinion grew increasingly unfavorable to federal intervention in the South, so that political considerations and calculations became ever more difficult to reconcile. Texas was lost to the Republicans in early 1874; Brooks's regime in Arkansas collapsed in the spring of that year, and then, partly because of the gubernatorial election in Ohio during September, 1875, Grant declined to interfere in beleaguered Mississippi.

Still, he did on several occasions and for various reasons challenge the comeback of the Democrats in the South. His administration vigorously, albeit briefly, suppressed the Democrats' terrorism by enforcing federal election laws, notably in the Carolinas during 1871–1872. He also secured control of the legislature in Alabama during late 1872; he took the initiative in Arkansas between 1874 and 1875 in order to overturn its conservative regimes; and he maintained control of the Louisiana legislature between 1872 and 1875. But to ensure that the rest of the southern states remain Republican often required using the military on questionable pretexts, which merely led to the loss of Republican support in the North. Taken as a whole, whether the Grant government opted for nonintervention—being lenient with conservative opponents and neglecting southern Republicans—or whether it chose to intervene, protecting the Republicans in a heavy-handed way, the administration finally came up empty-handed, its sudden, strong initiatives frequently alternating with just as sudden about-faces in the end.

But however important the political considerations, they were not always Grant's only motives, nor in some cases were they the overriding ones. Cronyism sometimes played a part, most notably in Louisiana, where Grant generally supported the customhouse clique. Thus he promoted dubious causes, such as advancing the political career of his brother-in-law Casey in New Orleans or aiding friends in Little Rock or rescuing a ring in Vicksburg, even though such factions used, rather than served, the party. In fact, Grant's objectives were often unclear: Was he protecting a state from political instability and election irregularities or saving his party or a faction of it from defeat? For such different objectives were separated by a thin line when republicanism and Republicanism were frequently synonymous in the administration's view.

Then, too, Grant's own preference for a passive rather than an active presidency—a tendency which, of course, he was quite willing to abandon when it suited him—and his strain of capriciousness also impinged on considerations of policy. Moreover, his seemingly personal annoyance with the ineptitude of certain southern Republican leaders who were not his friends or close associates added to his unwillingness to employ federal intervention in their behalf. Thus, by choosing benign neglect, which at the time was called "masterly inactivity," he allowed friendly regimes to crumble, even in states where the past support for, and the latent strength of, Republicanism were considerable. Veteran abolitionist James Redpath, who was involved in the congressional investigation of the Mississippi election of 1875, did not exaggerate when he aptly noted in August, 1876, that such "masterly inactivity means dastardly surrender."[2]

That combination of activity and neglect, of Grant's overreacting and underreacting when it came to his southern policy, mirrored the pattern of his administration's election enforcement efforts. The suppression of the Klan in upland South Carolina in 1871, for example, was analogous to the expulsion of the Louisiana legislators in January, 1875. Both spasmodic efforts came to nought in the long run. Terrorism continued in South Carolina, with the Red Shirts replacing the Klan, and Congress reseated the Democratic legislators who had been ejected by the army in New Orleans. Erratic federal enforcement, then, paralleled the president's intermittent intervention, and both were ineffective and inconclusive.

In Grant's defense, the enormous difficulties he faced must be reckoned with. Obviously, the challenges in the South were formidable and the conditions turbulent. And with the situation in each state varying and frequently changing, the lines of presidential authority and federal responsibility were unclear. Also, the challengers were both resourceful and ruthless. As the Mobile *Register* ominously counseled: "When the knife is used for political reform it should cut deep and clean to the roots of all political tumors."[3] Grant, to be sure, had no illusions about his enemies or, for that matter, his allies in the South. With Republican factions often fighting for power and patronage, and at the same time nursing grievances and plotting revenge, with black voters understandably fearful in the face of awesome intimidation, with white Republicans growing uneasy in their alliance with the blacks, and with frequently ineffectual Republicans in the governors' mansions, the future of the southern party did not appear altogether promising.

Nevertheless, disorder in the South demanded immediate decision. The president, being the first to formulate policy and to take action, had to act in effect as a chief legislator who shaped the law and as a chief justice who interpreted it. He had to be able to second-guess both the Congress and the Supreme Court so that later both would support his actions and endorse his judgments. But the political and constitutional task was simply too much for him. It was also too much for his string of generally mediocre attorneys general. They frequently read bad law, made snap judgments on the least satisfactory of legal grounds, and created dangerous precedents, their construction of the Constitution being too often intellectually arbitrary and weak. Similarly, their public policy vacillated between being too broad-gauged and too narrow. Indeed, the attorneys general and the president revised their judgments and reversed their public stands so often that proclamations of policy lost their force and credibility. Such inconsistency led to uncertainty and further instability, since the grounds for federal intervention were so vague, the various situations so abnormal, and the possibilities for discretionary power so vast that they burdened federal officials with unprecedented responsibility. When the administration decided similar controversies in quite different ways, it merely provoked more quarrels by making all things seem possible to the unscrupulous politicians of every faction and party in the South.

The federal government found itself established in various locations in the South which federal power alone could maintain. At the end of Grant's administration a string of federal forts still existed throughout the South, but as no more than isolated and beleaguered islands. The American flag still flew over the forts, but they were besieged on all sides, not by a rival army but by something more effective—an entrenched, armed, determined political opposition, civilian in appearance yet paramilitary in nature. The federal forts served both as a beacon of hope to local Republicans and as a rallying cry for the counterrevolutionaries who put pressure on the government to withdraw the remaining army units. But formidible as the fortresses might appear from the outside, they were in fact hollow shells. The complement of soldiers had decreased to a mere handful of men pulling garrison duty and rarely venturing outside. The edifices were jerry-built and rested on the frailest of foundations. They were but fortresses of failure.

That distressing situation pointed up both the uses and the limitations of coercion. Overwhelming federal force was necessary to enforce law and to command obedience. Yet such force as could only be supplied by the army was often not immediately available in a particular location, nor was it generally available throughout the South. Thus the presence of the military was visible enough to provoke local Democrats, but not strong or sustained enough to protect loyal citizens and officials. Clearly, the use of force in the South during the 1870s had inherent drawbacks, since military resolution of political problems rarely provided a permanent solution. Military rule was at best an armed truce that taught men to have more respect for physical force than for the rule of law. Moreover, when the army was employed intermittently and indecisively—which was the overall pattern of southern intervention—political difficulties were merely postponed for a brief time. Invariably, the unstable conditions recurred, and often the temporary show of federal military strength served only to foment new and frequently more serious disturbances, thus demanding yet another army operation.

Then, too, when the army was periodically employed, as in Louisiana, every call for troops was regarded as a confession of weakness. Indeed, repeated reliance upon federal force for political survival only served to isolate Republican regimes that could neither govern nor win on their own. Such dependence merely showed that in the long run coercion could not replace a sanctioned consensus. During the 1870s Grant's army occasionally overreacted out of a mistaken sense of duty—an error that only made matters worse. "Fitful interference of military force," as Senator Schurz phrased it, did nothing but accelerate the pace of retreat from reconstruction. In a nation that demanded civilian control and majority rule and distrusted peacetime armies and military occupation as unnecessary and undemocratic, the use of force was self-defeating. The army commander himself, General Sherman, concluded that it was wrong to bolster weak and unpopular state governments with United States troops, as had been done in Louisiana during January, 1875. He predicted that "outside help sooner or later must cease, for our army is ridiculously small, in case of actual collision. It is only the Memory of our War Power that operates on the Rebel Element now. They [the southern Democrats] have the votes, the will, and *will* in the End prevail. Delay only gives them sympathy Elsewhere."[4]

Because of this disturbing cycle, in which episodic local disorder and temporary federal suppression were repeated over and again, with Washington failing to dispatch troops in time of desperate need, as in Mississippi during September, 1875, whatever credibility the army and the federal government retained was destroyed. Grant, with all his power to command, could not be depended upon; the position from which he would not retreat continued to be an enigma. To southern Republicans the bitter experience of falling victim to timidity, severity, or a baffling mixture of both, weakened their confidence in him and, in time, brought his administration into open contempt.

Grant came to the presidency pledging peace, but at the end of his second term, his southern policy had brought neither true peace for the nation, nor secure power for his party, nor popularity for his administration. The southern Republican regimes had never been much strengthened or protected or, for the most part, even maintained; nor had they had help in becoming effective and self-reliant. Rather, Grant had weakened any appeal they might have had, further divided their leaders, promoted discord, and dissipated federal influence. Such actions won the Grant government few friends and created many enemies. After the state election of 1875, a Mississippi Republican wrote that the Grant administration could no longer afford to use the army to establish order during a southern election because "Republicanism at the South *stinks* in the nostrils of the nation . . . . are you Grant not to some extent responsible for the odor?"[5]

Administrative inadequacy accounted in part for these failures, for there was no coherent organization to help the president plan an effective policy. No federal official stood daily watch, giving the southern problem his direct, detailed supervision or continuous, comprehensive review, which would have provided the necessary unity of purpose, uniformity of administration, and possibilities for sure and swift methods of execution. If the attorney general or the secretary of war was sometimes sarcastically referred to as "the Secretary of State for Southern Affairs," both the title and the role were largely fictitious. Moreover, there was a growing isolation and fragmentation within the cabinet: Secretary of the Interior Cox, for example, complained that "my own Department keeps me busy enough, but one can't help feeling that we ought to have a common policy on which the administration should be a unit and not drift into a bureaucracy in which each Department minds only its own business, as we are doing."[6] Thus the administration of reconstruction foundered for lack of systematic attention and continual direction.

Although Congress was frequently asked by the president, local politicians, the press, and the people for solutions to southern crises, it provided little help.[7] During the 1870s Congress was often hampered by disagreement and indecision regarding reconstruction and was consequently plagued by procrastination and paralysis, notably in its dealings with Louisiana from 1872 to 1875. Congress during Grant's tenure was in fact less attentive and effective than has been realized. Seldom did it initate southern policy, except during the late winter of 1875 when it successfully put pressure on the president to back down and to compromise in Louisiana and rejected Grant's newly proposed intervention in Arkansas. The legislative branch, even more than the executive, gave itself to empty talk and evasive inaction.

Clearly, one of the main reasons for the foibles and flaws in the administration's policy toward the South was due to Grant himself. The paradoxes within his policy as well as within his personality were rich and varied. Although he apparently did not believe in an activist presidency, he frequently behaved as if he did. He professed to be opposed to military intervention and political meddling, yet at times he intervened more bluntly and arbitrarily than any peacetime president before or since. For all his military attitudes, which he still cherished, he nevertheless in several instances stood idly by while his allies were crushed and innocent blacks were systematically slaughtered for want of federal troops and protective interference. Grant did show soldierly courage when he acted directly and forcefully, but he showed none in his devastating displays of irresolution and inaction. Although he was elected in part because of his presumed impartiality, he more often than not thought, talked, and acted like an intense factionalist engaged in favoritism, rewarding unreliable friends, punishing honest critics, and stubbornly protecting a discredited regime or an old cohort in trouble.

Most commentators then and since have dismissed his failings with the oversimplified view that a great soldier often proves to be a poor politician.[8] But, in fact, Grant was not generally obtuse about, or ineffectual in, politics. He possessed an instinct for self-preservation; he not only recognized and respected power but had an intuitive feel about where it could be found, and he showed an ability to change as influence, problems, and public opinion changed. Such sensitivity had helped him to advance his career. His wartime rise to the top army commands, then his election and reelection to the presidency, revealed talent and resourcefulness during turbulent times when the more politically naive went under in the struggle for power in Washington.[9] Thus in politics as well as in the role of president, Grant was neither ignorant about, nor unsuccessful in, gaining and maintaining personal power. His reelection strategy of efficiently rewarding his supporters and effectively punishing his enemies by isolating them within his party, while neutralizing and then destroying his Liberal-Democratic opponents, was masterful. Also, he could be shrewd and penetrating both in his political judgment and his behavior, as his often trenchant letters and several decisive acts amply prove. Neither before nor during his presidency could Grant be dismissed as a "political ignoramus," though many people believed he was.[10]

Part of the confusion in assessing his performance may have been caused by a failure to distinguish between his quadrennial success in presidential politics in general and the serious limitations of his southern policy, which failed to achieve any of his stated and tacit objectives. That, however, ought not obscure his several successful if temporary maneuvers in the southern states. Grant was, in fact, more active, stronger, firmer, and far better at getting his own way when faced with problems, at least in the short-run, than has been generally realized. In handling a southern crisis, once the matter reached his desk (with certain significant exceptions during 1875, when, in the late winter, he was rebuffed by Congress over Louisiana and Arkansas, and when, in the fall, he did not intervene in Mississippi), President Grant was often in operational command and frequently in personal control. Indeed, he made the critical decisions and was often successful in his tactical skirmishing, if not in his shifting strategies. In many cases, he chose his options with an eye to enhancing his power and position and achieving his immediate, limited, and varying objectives. Such was the case, for example, in Louisiana, when he brought about several faits accomplis by first using force and then rationalizing or denying it, though not reversing the results; similarly, during the spring of 1874 he waited for the public, which had been previously hostile to intervention in Arkansas, finally to clamor for presidential action in order to end the chaos so that he could act without provoking the usual barrage of criticism. Nevertheless, he was sooner or later defeated almost everywhere, since the more important strategic triumphs seemed beyond his reach.

It was all very ironical: Grant's political strengths and weaknesses were precisely the opposite of his military strengths and weaknesses. During the Civil War, General Grant had been a supreme strategist, not a splendid tactician, whereas those talents were reversed when he became president. Unlike General Lee, who could win the battles and yet lose the war because he did not understand the nature of the conflict and the changed requirements of modern warfare, General Grant understood both, fully realized the potential of the North, and knew how the rebellion could be crushed by battering down the Confederacy, which he did, relentlessly and resourcefully. In contrast, President Grant, in the way he handled reconstruction, displayed the tactical resilience of the politician, but as a statesman he had no coherent, long-term policy. His temporary forays against his southern white opponents didn't deter them for long in attempting to get northerners fed up with the relentless struggle over reconstruction. Swiftly alternating his decisions in the treatment of southern crises did not, in the end, either unbalance or confuse southern resistance, but it certainly did both those things to his own columns of support in the North and the South. Lacking an overall strategy for the South, Grant failed to come up with a workable set of priorities for his numerous and often conflicting aims or a method to deal with recurring problems in any systematic way.

Obviously, all the Republican regimes were not identical, nor did they have the same chances of survival or deserve the same type of support. Some were assets, others burdens. A few were relatively strong and stable; the majority were weak and chronically unstable. Some were well governed and benevolent; others were maladministered and corrupt. Each state and each crisis had to be treated separately, but, at the same time, regarded as part of a whole. The establishment of presidential priorities, a skillful dispensing of federal patronage, proper timing, the concentration of resources, and giving continuous patient attention to certain states, notably to North Carolina and certainly to Mississippi, might have yielded dividends. Clearly, Grant did not intervene enough in Mississippi and in some other states. If he had, some of these regimes might have been saved and the existence of others prolonged. Grant brought to the numerous crises neither enduring resolve nor settled purpose but instead demonstrated temporary expedients. What Grant's *ad hoc* approach produced was only half a policy—a piecemeal and patchwork policy— which included means without ultimate ends in view and occasionally ends without sufficient means. There were also times when Grant should have been pliant but was rigid, though more frequently he was pliant when he should have been firm. At the very least, reconstruction should have been maintained in part by negotiation, in part by force and fear, in part by influence.

The task was indeed formidable, and few could have achieved it. Yet in addition to Grant's other weaknesses, he persisted in keeping his own counsel. Some observers mistook his silence for wisdom, likening him to the Sphinx. Possibly he misled himself, for, as the New York *Herald* put it: the "praise of his reticence may have given him the notion that wisdom consisted in holding one's tongue." Others claimed, superficially, that Grant's reticence was understandable: he simply had nothing to say. Still others more accurately observed that it was merely his way of doing things. According to Grant himself, he tended to prefer a defense that gained time to an offense that wasted it: "I never get excited, and I have made it a rule through life never to borrow trouble or anticipate it. I wait until it reaches me, and then I am prepared to meet it." So his noncommital, uninvolved attitude on many occasions was an indication that he had not yet formed any plan of action. In the short run, his silence helped him pick up support from opposing sides, but it eventually undermined his political influence and executive authority, for he was not always candid about his stands or persuasive about his actions, with either the politicians or the public. Moreover, his tendency to keep his ideas to himself meant that he often avoided essential discussions of problems. Of course, there were exceptions to this characteristic silence. President Grant could be decisive and direct in his proclamations and his state papers, and he could be equally persuasive in a set interview, an inspired report, or an informal chat with a caller.[11] But too often his silence caused unnecessary confusion and difficulties.

Moreover, like so many of his military counterparts who had been voted into the Executive Mansion because of their fame as military men, Grant, for all his political talents, remained a soldier at heart. Despite having enough political sense to further his own fortunes, he seldom acted on the principle that power must expand or contract, that it must be active and successful or it will decline and then vanish. Essentially, he could not decide whether to be a caretaker or a catalyst, and so he alternated, playing each role in turn. He also lacked the experience, training, and innate aptitude necessary for the delicate art of statesmanship. As a former general occasionally oversensitive to the charge of Caesarism, he at times refrained from using his legitimate authority. On the other hand, as a former soldier he seemed to equate law with force. When roused to fury or acting from frustrated impatience, he sometimes impulsively cut the knots of southern politics with the sword of army intervention.

Another of Grant's problems was his frequent irritability in response to criticism, perhaps as a reaction to his prewar years of poverty and failure, as well as to the justified adulation he had later been accustomed to receiving as the great war hero. He often refused to learn from his critics; as he himself wrote, "I pay no attention to them [the Democratic and independent press] and would not know what they say only that there are always *friends* to tell you everything that is disagreeable."[12]

Grant also had trouble using his time efficiently and employing his advisers effectively. Meetings of the cabinet were often consumed in lengthy discussions of such trivia as minor patronage; Secretary of State Fish, for example, continually complained of the "absence of serious consultation" on great questions of policy, and he was by no means alone in criticizing the way in which the cabinet conducted its business. Grant's executive appointments, a test of political judgment, were usually made without proper consultation, political consideration, or care for functional fitness. With but few exceptions, he insisted upon placing small men in high places, appointing nonpolitical nobodies to the cabinet. One man from Connecticut attributed this to a latent sense of inferiority that led Grant to refuse anyone in the cabinet who might "overtop his small stature."[13]

Mediocrity and just plain incapability were often attributes of the federal bureaucracy as well. As that same man from Connecticut remarked: "To my mind we never had so low a *personel* in our government as under and with Grant,"[14] who chose mainly military men instead of seasoned politicians for service at the White House and sometimes put blind trust in opportunistic cronies. The same may be said of his controversial appointments in the South, which showed a marked failure to distinguish between sometime friends and lasting interests.

Since the military profession had imbued Grant with the notion that the commander's arbitrary and unadvised will is unquestionable, he sometimes, in civil affairs, assumed that his will had the viceregal force of law, that he could govern by decree and impose consent. Moreover, he also tended to believe that it was the primary duty of all his subordinates—including cabinet members—to carry out his orders as glorified clerks. In addition, President Grant sometimes regarded as impertinent and insubordinate the talented, gritty officials in his administration who spoke their minds, raising troublesome questions and unpleasant issues that he did not wish to hear. And such strong members of the cabinet as Hoar, Cox, Bristow, and Jewell seldom lasted very long.[15]

President Grant took a similar attitude toward congressmen, rarely seeking out their views unless they were among his group of intimates. Gratuitous advice he frequently ignored. Preferring a fait accompli, he often consulted or informed congressmen only after he had taken action. Unversed in the mechanics and dynamics of Capitol Hill, he did not concern himself enough with consulting, compromising, or sometimes just placating members of Congress. Thus he frequently ruffled politicians' feelings and often failed to secure their cooperation or confidence. In turn, many Republican congressmen regarded him as inaccessible and secretive, which is why he seldom succeeded in having much influence over Congress. He consequently had less chance of helping devise a durable means to achieve long-range political ends.[16]

To be sure, it was because of the American people's political illusions that Grant had been catapulted into the White House. Had the country wanted an experienced politician, a tested statesman, or an acknowledged social reformer, the people would not have elected Grant. Is it altogether fair, then, to reproach Grant for not being what he never was and never promised to be? When he was elected, the people knew almost nothing about his intentions, but they put their hopes in him—for the wrong reasons. Weary of all the postwar strain and political wrangling, Americans wanted to escape from politics. Therefore Grant was elected as the antidote to politicians and as the war hero who would win the peace, suppress disorder in the South, banish trouble everywhere, and bring an end to extremism. However, the electorate had misjudged the problems at hand. They had chosen a great soldier at a time when a master politician was needed. Although they wouldn't have thought of waging war without trained generals, many voters virtually stigmatized politicians for engaging in the business of holding public office, managing civil affairs, and being versed in political warfare, because, in a state of wishful anticipation, they ignored the fact that war brought inevitable dislocation, that peace, especially after a civil war, would not come easily, and that victory would impose great responsibilities.

The result was necessarily disillusionment. Having clearly deceived themselves, the American people proceeded to condemn Grant because he did not measure up to their false hopes. Effusively praised at the beginning of his presidency by friends who likened him to Caesar, he was soon castigated precisely because the likeness was true. Many voters whom Grant had disappointed came to the conclusion that the country had had enough of military presidents who had been elected not because they were fit for office but as a sentimental reward for past services, or because the politicians who supported them could cynically exploit them.[17]

However, Grant was not the only obstacle to the success of the government's southern policy. Another was the change in both the attitude and actions of northern Republicans toward their southern counterparts. As early as 1871 the moderate Republican New York *Times*, discussing reconstruction, noted that the "mere mention of it is almost nauseating." And as time went on, the northerners, growing more and more disenchanted with the purported dishonesty and the conspicuous disorder, began to identify such developments exclusively with Republican rule in the South. Despite their claims of serving the country or saving the blacks, southern Republicans seemed interested only in power for themselves.[18]

Southern epithets—carpetbag, scalawag, black rule—became popular northern stereotypes, due in part to the publication of unfavorable reports by such respected and widely read northern journalists as James S. Pike and Charles Nordhoff. Although these reports were distorted and exaggerated, as was the biased coverage by many northern newspapers, they were increasingly thought to be true during the 1870s. And although the label *carpetbagger* was used indiscriminately, with no regard to the behavior or competence of individuals, there was just enough truth in the accusations of corruption, mismanagement, and mediocrity in general to justify the term to intelligent northerners at the time and to lend credence to the conservatives' criticism. In December, 1874, Postmaster General Jewell commented: "One of the greatest drawbacks we have is the character" of the southern Republican officeholders, "for we have not among them one really first class man." In response to both the northerners and the conservatives, a Virginia Republican bitterly complained that the southern Democrats had by every conceivable means blackened the character of southern Republicans "until you and the North regarded us—Republicans—of the South as the worst class of people on this Continent."[19]

More importantly, even to strongly partisan northern Republicans, the recurring disturbances in the South and the continuous need for federal intervention to rescue Republican regimes were proof that the regimes had fundamental weaknesses. It was generally true that they owed their existence to a narrow base of popular support, that they frequently lacked leadership, and that they were plagued almost everywhere with acrimonious and divisive factions which proliferated like southern mosquitoes. Mississippi Governor Ames had been dismayed to see southern Republicans cutting each others' throats with "strifes, envies, jealousies, animosities existing in our own ranks."[20]

Southern Republicanism was further weakened by differences and disagreements between southern white natives and northern white immigrants, as well as between white and black Republicans.[21] Therefore, dissatisfied with the party and faced with hostility and even some violence on the part of white Democrats, the white Republicans defected in growing numbers. Although, in the words of a federal customhouse official in Savannah, many of them realized that "a white Republican party must be built up on issues above the race question, that is so powerful a lever in the hands of Democrats," southern whites defected not only in the upper South but overwhelmingly in the Deep South. By 1875 the party consisted almost exclusively of blacks, making it the perfect target for racist Democrats, who could now strike simultaneously at the black man and at what remained of the Republican party's power.[22]

Despite the precarious position of southern Republicanism, its ranks had already been condemned by the northerners because of their incessant calling for help; in fact, they were considered malingerers who tried to get Uncle Sam to do their work for them. Thus, faced with the violence and counterinsurgency of the Democrats, as

181

well as with their own inexperience and, occasionally, incompetence, the southern Republicans, despairing and helpless, became according to a North Carolina Republican, Tourgée, "the worst frightened men you ever saw—actually scared out of their wits."[23]

To the southern white demand that the South be let alone, most northerners were to agree or to acquiesce. The Washington correspondent of the abolitionist *Independent* had declared in 1870 that the Republicans of the South—black and white—had to handle their problems on their own. Four years later, in January, 1874, President Grant said the same thing publicly: "I begin to think that it is time for the republican party to unload. There has been too much dead weight carried by it . . . . all the disaffection in the Gulf States [has been imposed] on the administration. I am tired of this nonsense. Let Louisiana take care of herself, as Texas will have to do. I don't want any quarrel about Mississippi State matters to be referred to me. This nursing of monstrosities has nearly exhausted the life of the party. I am done with them, and they will have to take care of themselves." Commenting on Grant's remarks, the New York *Herald* noted that the phrase "nursing monstrosities" described "accurately the general activity of the republican party. If that party addresses itself to the subject of reconstruction it solves no vexed problem, pacifies no excitement, lays the foundation of no useful progress; it only nurses some monstrosity conceived by profligate wretches eager to utilize for their own advantage public misfortune or national ruin." The newspaper's solution was simple and urgent: "Reconstruction, the carpet-baggers, the usurpation of power supported by troops— all this is dead weight, a millstone, that if not speedily disengaged will carry republicanism to the bottom."[24]

Reconstruction itself was beginning to fare badly because of its allies as well as its enemies. Washington and northern Republicans had certainly never done enough to help their "feeble friends" in the South, as one northern Republican termed them. Instead of having nurtured the southern party in its infancy, Washington had often starved it by withholding support for party organization and campaigns and by not subsidizing local Republican newspapers. Moreover, northern Republicans had seldom contributed to the coffers of the southern party or dispatched speakers to that region. They never understood the problems of their southern partisans, who had "endured more, dared more, and risked more" for reconstruction than anyone else and yet had received more abuse than sympathy from the North.[25] Characteristic of southerners' efforts to prod the national party into action was a communication to President Grant from the party's central committee in Virginia, to the effect that although "the very existence" of the party in that state was endangered, administration officials had proved indifferent to its welfare and often more friendly, responsive, and useful to its opponents. According to southern Republicans, their wing was in a disorganized state because of the "utter waste of the government patronage as a political engine"; administration appointments in the South, they complained, had actually converted federal patronage into an "engine of defeat" and a "means of destruction to the party by the government in the hour of its death struggle."[26] Alabama Republican Senator George E. Spencer, who also complained about the appointments, was met by "procrastinating promises which is Administration fashion for polite refusal." By February, 1877, an employee of the Savannah customhouse very rightly observed: "I never knew the [Republican] National Committee to do anything sensible for the South[ern wing] and would not expect anything so unlikely now."[27]

The truth of the matter was that the entire southern wing had always been treated as a subservient appendage to be controlled and used in the interest of maintaining the power of the national party, which was automatically identified with the national interest. According to the former attorney general, Amos Akerman of Georgia, the southern Republican party would become neither a durable majority nor an effective opposition "unless it can be divested of its colonial character, and can take root in the soil"; he considered that "at the North we are regarded as a subordinate portion of this Republican party, entitled to no effective voice in its counsels." Similarly, deposed North Carolina governor Holden pointed out the fundamental shift in power: the "South is a sort of plantation. It ruled the North forty years and now the North is ruling. This explains all." Retrospectively, in 1879, Tourgée wrote in his novel, *A Fool's Errand*, that northern Republicans had regarded southern party members "as mere instruments in their hands,—to be worked as puppets, but to be blamed as men, for the results of their acts."[28] Of course, some southern Republicans had behaved badly in office and had disgraced a good cause, but that by no means invalidated the cause. Nevertheless, the southern party was slowly but surely dying, with its lifeline to the North cut by a negative attitude, inadequate aid, bad appointments, and, above all, ineffective support in the form of federal enforcement and presidential intervention.

By 1874–1875 there was growing recognition that Grant's southern policy was neither sound nor successful. In December, 1874, just before the fiasco in New Orleans, the editor of the Springfield *Republican* wrote what other papers continued to confirm: "manipulation of the southern states from Washington had been a failure. Perhaps it would have been, even if it had not been so grossly abused; but the abuses have insured its failure, and insured, also, the disgust of the North, and the certainty that, either by this administration or the next, the opposite policy [of noninterference] will be tried." In most quarters throughout the North there was the conviction that the time had come when both the states and races of the South "must be left to work out their own peace and salvation," as journalist Samuel Bowles phrased it. Although opposing such a trend, the radical Chicago *Inter-Ocean* during January, 1875, acknowledged the existence of an "overwhelming public sentiment *at the North* adverse to the protection of life at the South by the use of the Federal authority."[29]

Clearly, that willingness on the part of the northern people and the federal government to abandon the federal role as the protector of reconstruction rights and the guarantor of popular rule in the South was the ultimate indictment against the party's and the government's record of attempting to fulfill those objectives for a decade. During the tumultuous postwar period, when chronic instability was the order of the day, the paramount need was for a government that wielded power firmly so as to keep society intact and maintain order. To govern, public authority needed to win the respect and support of the people and, with concerted energy, to work its will. When an end was required, the leader had to fashion a means and then persevere in it, bending men to his purpose by vigorous initiative, skillful influence, and masterful policy.

In the last analysis, President Grant had not been the man to meet the numerous and varied postwar challenges that required joining bureaucratic expertise and military muscle to political judgment. Whether he had intervened too much or not enough is only part of the issue; the other consideration is, when he did intervene, how effectively did he do it and to what purpose? Grant had wished to keep the South Republican, but he failed for want of any concerted strategy, of any sustained energy in building up enough presidential and partisan power to enforce reconstruction, and of any vital interests beyond momentary objectives—political or personal. The southern situation thus became increasingly unmanageable; reconstruction disintegrated; and the authority of Washington, the integrity of the states, and probity of the elections were compromised.

Henry Adams recommended that a ship of state have a strong captain in command: "He must have a helm to grasp, a course to steer, a port to seek; he must sooner or later be convinced that a perpetual calm is as little to his purpose as a perpetual hurricane, and that without headway the ship can arrive nowhere."[30] Had Grant provided an effective policy, clear direction, and strong leadership, he might have achieved a great deal; but he could do little without them. It would have been in the greatest interest of the nation that the South be governed in compliance with the reconstruction amendments—self-governed if possible; well-governed, with luck; but it had, at the very least, to be governed.

RACISM AND RECONSTRUCTION

Congress and the Country Debate Equality After 1872

THE INITIAL problems of the second Grant administration were compounded by economic dissension and political difficulty. The Coinage Act of 1873 omitted the silver dollar from coinage and began a protracted battle between silvercrat inflationists and goldbug contractionists. Hard on the heels of the Credit Mobilier scandal, Congress, in 1873, enacted a law that raised federal salaries, retroactively, for two years. Although it was in large measure repealed by January, 1874, the law nevertheless had increased public indignation. In September, 1873, the banking firm of Jay Cooke collapsed, triggering off the longest depression of the century, which lasted until 1879 and added to the woes of existing rural depression, with bank and business failures, substantial unemployment, and strikes that led to bloodshed. The severity of the depression was expressed in prices and wages: the price of wheat fell from two dollars to fifty cents a bushel, and wages were cut in half.[1]

Off-year elections in 1873 gave voters an opportunity to vent their misgivings about the Republicans' bad management. Although during that year state elections in Connecticut, Ohio, New York, and Wisconsin were influenced by the prohibition issue and local matters, Republican voters in those states expressed their lack of confidence in their party by staying at home or voting Democratic. The election results also indicated that the Democratic party, despite its drubbing in 1872, was beginning to revive due in part to its effective exploitation of racial issues, as in the Virginia campaign of 1873.

Indeed, by late that year the Democrats had regained control of the legislature in Arkansas and recaptured both the governorships and the legislatures in Texas and Virginia.[2]

By 1874 a number of Republicans were seriously concerned about the coming elections. Congressman Dawes wrote from Washington, "Things are drifting sadly here. Nobody, except those who feed at the crib, seems to have the slightest desire to maintain the supremacy of the party, and everybody is finding fault with the administration except those who bask in its sunshine." Grant increased this dissatisfaction when he gave the impression of mishandling his most important appointment—the selection of a new chief justice to the Supreme Court. To replace Salmon P. Chase, who had died in May, 1873, Grant first selected an undistinguished lawyer but an outstanding machine politician, New York Republican Senator Roscoe Conkling, who forestalled a political storm by declining the honor. Then Grant presented his second choice, Attorney General Williams, a reliable Republican but at best a second-rate lawyer. One lawyer, informed that there was talk in Congress of abolishing the office of chief justice, commented: "Yes, I observe so. The confirmation of Mr. Williams will do it effectually." Under the pressure of Congress' opposition as well as widespread disapproval in newspaper editorials, Grant finally withdrew Williams' nomination. His third choice, Caleb Cushing, a first-class attorney and personal friend, but an old man and an old-fashioned conservative who had ostensibly converted to Republicanism, also encountered opposition, so that Grant was forced to withdraw his name as well. For although Cushing was a thoroughbred, his nomination was indeed preposterous; as the New York *Tribune* noted, he was "an unsafe man to whom to intrust the decision of numberless important questions arising out of the war and the constitutional guarantees resulting from it."[3]

Grant's nominations suggested that he was perhaps more interested in making a choice than in making a great one, for he seemed indifferent to the implications of the appointment, not realizing that selecting mediocrities or an antebellum conservative was no way to maintain reconstruction by means of the Court. Grant finally nominated, as his fourth choice, Morrison R. Waite, a respectable but in no way exceptional attorney who was regarded as lacking not only national experience and reputation but also any comprehensive understanding of postwar problems. However, Waite was to prove far more impressive during his tenure as chief justice than his reputation and last-choice selection suggested.

Surveying Republican fortunes in an editorial, "The Turning-Point," in January, 1874, the Springfield *Republican* remarked that Grant's inappropriate nominations as well as their prompt withdrawals had crystallized "a vast quantity of vague doubt and anxiety and distrust . . . a vague inkling . . . that things were going wrong . . . that the party was getting into a pretty bad way." The equally critical Cincinnati *Commercial*, which had also once been a Liberal Republican newspaper, noted Grant's loss of power over Congress and his loss of popularity with the people, and Georgia Democrat Alexander H. Stephens predicted a "bust up" between Grant and his party sooner or later.[4]

Recognizing the administration's waning influence, its mouthpiece, the Washington *National Republican*, observed that "the negro question, with all its complications, and the reconstruction of the Southern States, with all its interminable embroilments, have lost much of the power which they once wielded to rally the voters of the North to support of the party." Such questions, it believed, should be subordinated to the needs of the present. As for the maintenance of reconstruction, the editorial significantly remarked that the "impression prevails very generally . . . that having set the machine in motion it will now run itself."[5]

Disinterest was compounded by the death, on March 10, 1874, of Senator Charles Sumner, the great advocate of equal rights for blacks. His death was considered by many as the passing of one of the last of the old prophets of reform, who had left no successor; people seemed to be in mourning as much for a lost idealistic fervor and the passing of postwar good intentions as for Sumner himself. Idealism, which in some measure had inspired Republican reformism, seemed to some observers to have vanished along with him. Moreover, his passing completed the changing of the guard in the Senate and set in bold relief the contrast between the party's past and present, for Sumner's integrity was markedly at variance with the sordid scandals of the spoilsmen. Indeed, that once influential radical had for several years not only been estranged from his party but powerless, and as the New York *Evening Post* observed: "The moment any party identifies itself with its office-holders, and not with the great political inspirations which gave it birth, it has reached its climax, and its hours are numbered."[6]

During the spring of 1874 a number of Republicans began to fear the fruits of the congressional elections. According to one Yankee, the Republicans in Washington were rapidly assuming a "bad odor" in Vermont and elsewhere. Singling out the liability of federal intervention in Louisiana, Elihu B. Washburne wrote: "I fear we will lose the next House. That Louisiana business is very unfortunate. . . . The sooner the whole gang [the Kellogg government] is thrown overboard the better." And a Democrat, Richard Vaux, went so far as to predict that his party's success required only an aggressive, sustained assault on the administration.[7]

The New Hampshire election of March 10 confirmed the Republicans' pessimism, with the Democrats narrowly capturing both the governorship and the legislature. Even staunch Republican George Templeton Strong wrote afterward that the Republicans were "losing ground, I fear. We are dissatisfied with many things—with corruption, extravagance, and Ben Butlerism at Washington—with the currency, the tariff." Since the New Hampshire campaign was complicated by local and personal, as well as national, issues and characterized by an absence of clear-cut party choices, the result, especially with the returns so closely divided, was not a thorough rebuff. Still, for the first time in twenty years the Democrats had gained complete control of that state's government.[8]

Connecticut followed New Hampshire's lead on April 7, 1874. Despite the fact that Connecticut Republicans assumed a reformist posture and adopted a plank obliquely critical of President Grant's intervention in the South, the Democrats, by stressing the issues of dishonesty, depression, and federal interference in the South, recruited disaffected voters. As a result, the Democrats not only won the governorship, but, for the first time in twenty-two years, also captured both branches of the legislature and a Senate seat in Washington to boot. The Republican defeat was so complete and so stunning as to constitute an open and unmistakable rebuke.[9]

In reply to the partisan Republican newspapers' dismissal of their second spring reversal as merely the product of local side issues, the New York *Tribune* drew an analogy between the current political situation and that of the 1854 election, when the Democrats had lost control of the national House of Representatives, and the Republicans had mushroomed overnight into a powerful party. The *Tribune* went on to remind the Republicans that the Democrats then had failed to discern "the indications of a political revolution which was destined very shortly to banish it from place and power" and warned that "now, as then, the element of weakness is concealed under this apparent strength. . . . the leaders of the party in power will make the mistake of a political lifetime if they allow themselves to be deceived." Similarly, the Springfield *Republican* noted that the handwriting was on the wall with "this quiet but significant political stampede."[10]

Directly afterward, in April, President Grant succeeded in somewhat shoring up the sagging prestige of the party by vetoing an inflationist bill, drawing praise from the eastern and urban deflationists and provoking the indignation of the western and southern rural inflationists. The Republicans were deeply divided on this issue, over which even the Democrats were by no means united. However, many people thought that Grant's financial stand, bolstered by the appointment in May of a new secretary of the treasury, the highly regarded Benjamin H. Bristow, would increase the Republicans' chances in the upcoming congressional contests. Party manager William E. Chandler, for one, was confident: "Up to the time of the President's veto we were drifting helplessly on a lee shore; and were tolerably sure to lose the next House. . . . Now the President's veto has changed all that." And the Republican *Harper's Weekly* expressed its hope that the party would "spring to its feet with the old light in its eyes and the old faith in its heart."[11]

If economic dislocation and administrative mismanagement caused the party in power considerable trouble during the congressional campaign, the issue of civil rights, brought to the fore again at this time, posed the greatest challenge of all. Long pending in Congress was a bill designed not only to establish the equality of the races, with a more comprehensive definition of civil rights for Negro Americans, but also to enforce those rights by imposing heavy penalties for noncompliance.

Certainly the country as a whole had no friendly feelings toward such a legal measure, for most white Americans believed unquestioningly in white supremacy. "The white man—the man of the superior race—will always have the ascendancy," was the succinct comment of the New York *Herald*. To be sure, attitudes varied both in the South and in the North, ranging from venomous racism to philanthropic concern with paternalistic overtones. The latter, however, was often more an acceptance of the white man's burden than an endorsement of egalitarianism, and when racial inferiority was not emphasized, so-called racial peculiarity was. In fact, the majority regarded America as a white man's country, with a government and a society run by and for the benefit of the whites. They excluded the blacks by denying them power, wealth, and position, and mistreated them by perpetrating racial violence, riots, and lynchings. Fear was rampant as well. *"Negrophobia,"* remarked the Reverend Samuel T. Spear in the *Independent*, "is a prevalent characteristic of the white American mind." Also stressing the innate inequality between the races, Gideon Welles wrote: "Thank God slavery is abolished, but the Negro is not, and never can be the equal of the White. He is of an inferior race and must always remain so." Indeed, the abolitionists' assertion that the black man was simply a "white man in ebony" had few adherents and now was questioned even by disillusioned reformers. Thus, given such apparently ineradicable prejudice, what law could change human nature and the feeling of social incompatibility that separated the two races?[12]

Solutions to the racial question varied. Prejudice ruled out intermarriage. A few believed that the only practical alternatives were extermination or subjugation, and that if ever it came to a war of races, the "extermination of the negro is as sure as that of the red Man." Yet, to most people, genocide was unthinkable. To others, the sole solution was colonization; however the mass deportation of blacks to Latin America or Africa was more extensively debated than actually undertaken. Many whites thought longingly of acquiring Santo Domingo in order to relieve racial tensions at home by establishing a segregated outpost where black Americans could prosper on their own; but emigration on so large a scale was too difficult and too expensive. On the other hand, the fairminded recognized that America was as much the home of the black man as of the white man. One speculation was shared by both blacks and whites—that of a black exodus to those southern states with existing black majorities, or even to a new federal territory or state reserved as a black enclave. Yet although there was some migration of blacks in search of land or jobs, most Negroes remained where they had always lived, and most northerners were thankful that it was generally not in the North.[13]

Although racist attitudes were widespread, the practice of racism was more flagrant in the South. To embittered southern whites, the freedmen represented an impudent personal insult added to the ignominy of defeat. The whites regarded reconstruction as having turned their world upside down, with the bottom rung now on top, the former slave now master. One southerner, writing just after the war had ended, vented her hatred of both southern blacks and northern whites, denouncing the Yankees, who "hug and kiss the niggers, promenade the streets with them, and carry the black babies in their arms. Ain't this enough to make a Christian curse. I wish that in ten years that there would not be a white man [left] in Yankee land," adding, "I wish they [the blacks] were all married to Yankees." A Georgia newspaper believed that all efforts to "raise the negro to the station and dignity of the Southern white race, are as silly and futile as the attempt of Xerxes to bind the ocean with an iron chain." Even a few isolated attempts at integrating public accommodations met with white intransigence and noncompliance; "as blacks are now, their society would be degrading," claimed a white woman from North Carolina.[14]

If mixing the races as equals was anathema to the majority of white southerners, so was limited equality in voting, for they regarded black enfrachisement as northern vindictiveness intended to humiliate and to enfeeble the South. The general view of southern Democrats, as paraphrased by the Springfield *Republican*, stigmatized the black man as "unfit for the suffrage as a child, and . . . disastrous consequences [were] certain to flow from his admission to a share in the work of government. He *was* a child to all practical intents and purposes. . . . to give him the ballot was to put an edged tool in his hands with which to hurt himself and his neighbors. It was at once a folly and a cruelty to thus spoil a good laborer in making [him] an utterly incompetent and preposterous citizen." As a southern Democrat corroborated in 1872: "Every day gives fresh proof of the terrible permanent evil inflicted on us by the 13th. Amendment and what a dangerous element the negro vote will ever be. One moment's relaxation of party discipline will cause us to be overwhelmed by the black tide."[15]

White southerners found black enfranchisement bad enough, but they considered black officeholding unbearable. The appointment of a Negro as the postmaster of Little Rock was regarded as "an expression of contempt—a slap in the face of the State—an unprovoked and unfeeling insult." But they consoled themselves with the idea that "this unnatural condition of affairs may be produced for awhile by bayonets and bribes but it cannot last. The Almighty never intended the white man to be in subjection to the African and he never will be." They believed that time was on their side and that natural talent would win out, ensuring that the blacks would settle down in their natural lower positions in society.[16]

Although white northerners had generally accepted the political equality of the blacks by 1874, they had the same social prejudices and practiced similar racial discrimination, and the patterns it took on both sides of the Mason-Dixon line were of an infinite variety, complexity, and ambiguity. On the whole, Negroes in the North were shunned and separated—in other words, treated like lepers. And northern whites often had less contact with them than southern whites, for racial segregation in housing, recreation, education, and employment was deeply rooted. The Negro men, for example, were generally restricted to such menial jobs as porters, night-workers, painters, and cooks, having lost their former positions as coachmen, barbers, and waiters to Irish and German immigrants. Furthermore, the practice of excluding blacks from first-class hotel dining rooms and from choice seats in first-class theatres and opera houses was as general a phenomenon in the North as in the South. In New York City, for example, wealthy blacks were refused admission to the Grand Opera House. In Philadelphia, during a Republican party convention in 1872, influential blacks were highly visible in the convention hall and hotel lobbies but conspicuously absent from the dining rooms. Indeed, discrimination ranged from overt exclusion to subtle pressure. Even those who professed their love for Negroes were more in favor of elevating the race than being in proximity with it.[17]

Nevertheless, integration was sporadically successful in the North during the postwar years. The blacks organized, and they managed to end segregation in streetcars in Philadelphia, Washington, San Francisco, Cincinnati, and New York City. In some places trains and steamboats also made no distinction. In the District of Columbia the municipal government enacted a local civil rights law. And three states (Massachusetts, New York, and Kansas) passed similar anti-discrimination provisions.

Schools, however, were another matter. For example, though public schools were open to both white and black children in New England and parts of the Midwest by state law, the law was seldom enforced; in addition, separate schools were not abolished and new ones were established. In fact, attempts elsewhere at racial mixing in the schools met with rare approval and even less success. Half of the southern states, virtually all of the border states, as well as Pennsylvania, Ohio, and Indiana, had statutes requiring racial segregation in the schools. In many other states explicit provision was made for voluntary segregation, and in some areas the entire question was left to the local education officials.

The evidence suggests that the custom of maintaining racial segregation in the schools was more prevalent in 1874 than the laws indicated (notably in New Jersey and Illinois, but in other states as well), that strict and explicit racial separation tended to be more widespread in states controlled by the Democrats, and that separate schools existed virtually everywhere the blacks were numerous, including the lower northern states of New York, New Jersey, Pennsylvania, Ohio, Indiana, Illinois, and Kansas. An exception to this general pattern occurred in a few southern states that were still controlled by the Republicans (Louisiana and South Carolina, for example), where at least an attempt was made at desegregating the schools, though without any lasting success. The admission of blacks to the University of South Carolina caused an exodus of most of the white students and relatively few of them returned. At Louisiana State University the administration took the lead, foregoing state subsidies that required integration; attempts to integrate the rural parish schools also failed. Desegregation was only achieved in New Orleans, in about one third of the public schools. The city was a somewhat atypical southern community, more cosmopolitan and racially mixed than most; the black population was relatively small (one fourth) and spread evenly throughout the city. But even there only 9 percent of the black children were involved, and integration lasted for only seven years—years marked by intermittent racial tension, during which progress was undercut by extensive white student boycotts and the growth of private segregated schools for whites. So despite the possibilities, the experiment did not survive the demise of political reconstruction.[18]

Unfortunately, the Grant administration itself shared the entrenched northern racist attitudes. Correspondence issuing from the government, as well as the private letters of officials, generally emphasized race when referring to individual blacks. And not only did the officials frequently use the term *nigger*, but they consistently denied blacks jobs in the federal government. When New Jersey Negro William E. Walker in 1871 complained about that fact, Attorney General Akerman brusquely explained that it was due solely to the blacks' lack of education, though there were numerous government jobs that did not require extensive education or experience. When Walker also objected to their virtual exclusion from service on federal juries and warned that the blacks might not continue to vote Republican unless that particular form of discrimination was ended, Akerman cavalierly replied that jury duty was generally regarded as a bane, not a benefit, and if the black citizens of New Jersey should desert the Republican party because a federal marshal had failed to select some of them as jurors, "it would be an instance of political ingratitude which would justify all that their enemies have said against them. . . . I cannot believe that they [New Jersey blacks] are capable of such meanness!"[19]

When on another occasion four years later, a group of blacks in Louisville, Kentucky, not only made known their dissatisfaction for similar reasons but threatened to defect, Secretary of the Treasury Bristow replied that many white Republicans were now of the opinion that the party had already done enough for blacks and advised them to "accept with gratitude the great results that have been accomplished for them by the courage and heroic efforts of the Republican party, and to wait with patience future developments."[20] Of course, whenever the blacks in order to advance their rights and interests acted politically independent, such departures—unlike white factions and their bargaining—were regarded as sinister designs to form a "black man's party." Indeed, the Washington *National Republican*, in August, 1873, denounced the local Equal Rights League for trying to "make of Washington a sort of Hayti, where black men alone shall rule." Implicit was the assumption among many whites that equality for Negroes meant inevitable black supremacy, under which the ignorant would rule the intelligent.[21]

Clearly, the government's and the country's racism was manifestly illogical: if the blacks did not assert their rights, they were dismissed as hopelessly backward; if they made demands, they were decried as clamoring demagogues. The ultimate example of such rampant hypocrisy came when the whites denounced the blacks as inferior, but refused to allow them to prove otherwise. The whites deplored the illiteracy of the blacks, yet would not open their school doors to them; they scorned the blacks as indolent, but denied them employment; they characterized the blacks as dependent, yet refused to hand any responsibility over to them; they denounced the clannishness of the blacks, but systematically excluded them from their own society and organizations. In short, double-talk, double standards, and double-dealing were what kept the blacks down, while the whites, imbued with the deterministic notions of pseudoscientific racialism and social Darwinism, sneeringly offered the menial occupations, poverty, and poor health of Negroes as proof of their innate inferiority. As one black New Yorker commented: "Bind a man hand and foot and bid him help himself; strike him and taunt him with cowardice for nonresistance, and you have a picture of our condition. With prejudice hanging over us like a cloud, please inform us how we are to surmount it." Slavery was dead, yes, but its spiritual legacy lived on.[22]

Legislation to break down the traditional separation of the races had been argued since emancipation. Although the Civil Rights Act of 1866, as well as the three amendments to the Constitution and the election enforcement acts, had laid the groundwork for citizen and voter rights, these laws had done little or nothing to change the fact of segregation. Arguments about the intentions, methods, and effects of proposed legislation for civil rights reflected the racial problems involved in reconstruction and raised the question of the government's capacity to regulate race relations. The debate was of less importance when the Democrats, playing on prejudice for political profit, voiced their strident and ritualized opposition to civil rights.[23] Still, during the seventies they did change their tone and emphasis depending on the constituency.

Sounder barometers of racial feeling were the honest doubts and deep misgivings voiced by many Republicans when it came to pending legislation that was meant to put the blacks on an equal footing with the whites. Despite the waning influence of the radical Republican reformers in the 1870s, there was still a vocal and articulate group calling for supplementary legislation to provide fuller equality for the blacks. Protesting the limited access allowed to Negroes, the well known black leader Frederick Douglass stated that the people of his race were now free citizens and should therefore, in law and in fact, have the full possibilities of any other citizen. That long-time champion of civil rights Senator Charles Sumner had contended all along that equality was the law of the land; racial segregation violated that law, and therefore segregation must be swept away with one bold and unequivocal act of Congress. The latest in a long series of civil rights bills—that is, the pending Senate version of April 29, 1874 (the legacy of Sumner and the work of New Jersey Senator Frederick T. Frelinghuysen)—required equal access to accommodations in private railroads, steamboats, stagecoaches, streetcars, restaurants, hotels, and theatres, as well as equal entry into public schools, institutions, land-grant colleges, and cemeteries, plus the right to serve on juries. On the other hand, the bill did not include equal access to saloons, barbershops, bathhouses, and churches. Supporters of the bill claimed that since the Fourteenth Amendment bestowed equality on all men, then laws had to be passed to ensure its practical application in social as well as in political matters. Furthermore, noted *Harper's Weekly*, enactment and enforcement of such laws would change people's actions and therefore their attitudes.[24]

Many people, however, rejected any sort of legislation granting civil rights on theoretical, constitutional, or practical grounds. Some of those who had previously recognized legal equality as necessary and even desirable, now parted company with the equalitarians. To them legal rights and social privileges had nothing to do with each other. Legal and political rights, such as voting, were public in nature and therefore to be regulated by the government; access to public accommodations was purely social and to be governed by the customs of society. The black citizen, like all citizens, had to achieve social status and opportunity for himself. Legislating such matters, these opponents argued, would merely encourage the blacks' dependency on federal power, which was regarded as especially pernicious by the majority of Americans, who favored laissez-faire. Another argument was that the civil rights legislation under consideration constituted not equal opportunity but special privilege: the blacks would benefit under the proposed legislation, but those whites who suffered because of ethnic discrimination would not. A different double standard would be created: the blacks would have the option of mixing in theatres or of not mixing, whereas the whites, preferring the exclusive company of their own race, would no longer be guaranteed it in public places. Therefore injustice would remain and offend a larger element of society. A number of other whites, although abhorring laws of racial exclusion, maintained that the absence of discriminatory legislation presumed equal opportunity and that equality required only the abolition of legal segregation, not the elimination of segregation in fact.[25]

The debate also raised doubts about the constitutionality of civil rights legislation. Some proponents of it contended that the pending measure was supported by the Fourteenth Amendment, by plenary powers in the Constitution, and even by the authority of the Declaration of Independence and natural law. Their opponents argued that the federal government had no authority to regulate the exclusive and proper concerns of state governments. The control of such public institutions as schools, established under state laws and supported by state and local taxes, was the legal prerogative of the states alone. Surely the Supreme Court would strike down any federal civil rights law that included regulation of local schools. Moreover, the Fourteenth Amendment contained prohibitions only against the action of states, not of individuals who might exclude blacks from equal access. In addition, Congress could not assume the power to break the private contract of common carriers in order to allow access to everyone. Given the Supreme Court's interpretation of the Fourteenth Amendment in 1873, it was, in large part, believed that the Court would sooner or later declare the civil rights measure unconstitutional on several grounds. If the Republicans, acting with good intentions, stretched and strained the reconstruction amendments to cover matters that were never meant to be included, what, asked the New York *Times*, would prevent the Democrats, should they gain power, from manipulating the Constitution so as to narrow the reach, nullify the intent, and destroy the effect of the reconstruction amendments?[26]

There was also the counterargument that such a law was quite unworkable. As the Republican Baltimore *American* remarked: "where the local sentiment is hostile to a statute it becomes inoperative and void." In the face of the overwhelming opposition to equality, getting recalcitrant individuals to adhere to the law would have required an army of officials. In fact, some people were convinced that attempts to enforce social legislation might well impede rather than promote social progress. The *Nation*, for example, which had formerly championed political equality for blacks, now warned that it was the moral sense of the community, not the federal marshal, that ought to decide where blacks could be admitted. Otherwise, the "surest way of hardening a social prejudice is to levy penalties for the display of it in matters which the community does not believe to be in the domain of law." The journal advised waiting for a change in mores; respect and regard could not be achieved by act of Congress. Similarly, the New York *Times* warned that the more the politicians assailed prejudice, the more virulent it would become: "you try to stamp it out, and it burns more mischievously than before."

Moreover, the federal government and courts could not prosecute large numbers of violators. Time and events would operate more effectually than law against discrimination, counseled the paper: "give him [the Negro] fair play, and do not make too much fuss about him."[27]

Further complicating the complex debate, some opponents did not reject the proposed law out of hand, but grudgingly accepted certain clauses of the bill and objected to others. Then there were those who advocated an end to segregation in transportation by common carriers and in lodgings run by licensed innkeepers, but who objected to a law that required equal accommodation in restaurants, theatres, schools, and graveyards. The New York *Herald*, for example, considered it a luxury, not an indispensable requirement, that blacks be received as guests in aristocratic hotels or exclusive resorts, or sit at tables in an inn, or occupy choice boxes in theatres. Religiously inclined Americans were particularly upset about the provision for equal access to cemeteries. The *Nation* suggested that it was wicked for deceased relatives and friends to be interned alongside Negroes "for the resurrection in their company. Graveyards are no places for the service of writs, and the denizens of tombs do not care a rush for disabilities based on race, color, or previous condition of servitude."[28]

However objectionable the other clauses might have seemed, to most of the opponents the prohibition of racial segregation in the schools was anathema and soon became the focus of debate. Moderate white southerners joined the conservatives in the view that if separate schools for the races were eliminated by the federal government, public education in the South would cease; for southern whites would surely abolish public schools rather than integrate, and wealthy whites would send their children to private schools. Several border and southern state school superintendents agreed that many communities were "not yet prepared for so long a step forward." The Chicago *Tribune* believed that southern blacks had everything to lose and nothing whatever to gain by insisting on mixed schools since the probable result would be the schools' demise and the end of their only hope of acquiring any sort of education. The Democrats, of course, leapt on the proposal, pandering to the hysterical fears provoked by the possible cultural, social, and sexual consequences of racially mixed schools. Hoping to mitigate their attacks, the Washington *National Republican* called the Democratic charges a false alarm, yet at the same time denounced school amalgamation as an obnoxious policy, both impossible and undesirable.[29]

There was even a group of blacks who expressed reservations about racial mixing in the schools. But, then, there was no unanimity among Negroes about civil rights legislation in general. A sizable majority of them did make it clear through the resolutions and petitions of Negro organizations, as well as in speeches and statements by prominent black spokesmen, that they favored—indeed some insisted upon—civil rights legislation. Others, however, either harbored reservations or went so far as to oppose the pending measure outright. What the Negroes disagreed about was not only whether integration or independence ought be the objective, but also whether their energy ought to be concentrated on achieving status before the law or on improving welfare among their population. Although they were fully aware that freedom and justice were entirely on the side of civil rights, at the same time many of them realized how great the problems were of applying the principle of equality in an inhospitable, often openly hostile, environment.[30]

If congressmen had any illusions about the opinion of the country on civil rights, they had only to read the newspapers, which generally were either critical or condemnatory. Even radical Republican papers, although staunchly endorsing Senator Frelinghuysen's bill in principle, were sometimes ambivalent. The Chicago *Inter-Ocean* claimed that "no man of the Republican party has ever contended for the enforcement of social equality of the blacks and whites, for that is a question which every man regulates for himself," maintaining, as did *Harper's Weekly*, that in a certain sense civil rights was academic because the black man disliked going where he was not wanted as much as the white man disliked seeing him there. In addition, *Harper's Weekly*, after arguing eloquently for the cause of civil rights, admitted that the goal of perfect equality might well be a "sentimental mistake," although laudable and worthy of being tried. Other supporters, such as the Boston *Journal*, were relatively negative about the bill: if it served no need, then even if it were passed it would do no harm; and if it did no good for the blacks, it would necessarily do no harm to the whites.[31]

While the country was debating, so was Congress. To many congressmen it was a wearisome rerun, for they had wrestled with Senator Sumner's civil rights legislation on numerous occasions after he had first introduced it in 1867 and again in 1870. Since then, every time the measure had been considered it had been defeated either by the Democrats through filibuster and sabotage, or by the Republicans, who sidetracked it on the floor or in committee. Indeed, the tortuous legislative history of civil rights shows the issue to have been so controversial that it was handled like "deadly poison" by both parties.[32]

Yet despite the measure's continuing unpopularity and perennial failure, there was a new feeling on the Republican side of the aisle during spring, 1874, that a supplementary bill mandating civil rights ought to be passed. That impetus came from several sources. One minor faction working for its passage consisted of a group of equalitarian idealists who wished to honor the late Senator Sumner by enacting a civil rights bill as a fitting memorial. However, that small a group had no control over Congress, as the future debate and votes were to reveal. On the other hand, though the bill was unpopular with many congressmen, it had of late become a favored project in some congressional circles. Apparently a number of those who had joined the bandwagon did so in the hope that somehow the pending bill might reunite an increasingly divided party by raising aloft its somewhat tattered equalitarian standard during the congressional campaign. Therefore certain Republican congressmen displayed more zeal than they apparently felt, extolling the bill in public declarations, while voicing misgivings about it in private conversation and correspondence.[33]

An even more important influence in bringing up the question before the Senate yet again was the strong and sustained pressure that many black voters brought to bear on the party. Black newspapers, such as the Washington *New National Era* and the San Francisco *Elevator*, argued that if the party was not true to its principles, it could not expect the Negro to be true to the party. One member of a prominent Philadelphia black family added that if the bill failed, then the Republicans had failed the blacks, who thereafter would not be bound by any loyalty or gratitude to support the party ticket. The New York *Tribune* noted that many Negroes were so earnest and insistent in demanding passage that Republicans could not risk incurring their hostility or the loss of their votes. Those considerations were what most especially compelled the Republican congressmen to do, or seem to do, something to ensure continued Negro support for the party in the upcoming congressional election.[34]

But the timing was important. If civil rights legislation were to be enacted as a party necessity, many politicians and observers believed it would be best to get the potentially unpopular measure out of the way before it could become a liability in the congressional canvass. Yet others were not sure of what effect the measure might have on the elections and thus remained uneasy and uncertain both about what tactics to use and what the right timing might be. Still others wished to take action on civil rights so that they could get on with what they regarded as more pressing business. The Washington *National Republican*, for instance, observed that since the civil rights bill was the only purely political legislation pending, the sooner it was disposed of the sooner the "real, vital questions before Congress [could] be taken up."[35]

Nevertheless, the Senate moved slowly. First there was delay in committee, then disagreement in the party caucus as to the features of the bill. Finally, there was a long and repetitious debate on the floor. Although every aspect of the measure had been exhaustively discussed many times before, and though there was little hope of changing anyone's mind, certain senators nevertheless aired their views at length, prompting observers to remark that they were merely trying to create a righteous image of themselves in the eyes of their constituents. Also indicative of ambivalence among the Republicans was their reluctance to hold night sessions—and they had the numbers to impose them—in order to reach a vote. As the debate dragged on toward the close of the spring session and as the start of campaigns in those southern and border states that held August elections grew near, some Republicans started to grow increasingly uneasy. Fearing that the debate would be used against the party in those campaigns, they would have preferred to stop all discussion and delay a vote until after the elections, when the final session of the Forty-third Congress would meet in December.

As for the debate itself, the provision covering schools ("All persons . . . shall be entitled to full and equal enjoyment . . . of common schools and public institutions of learning . . . supported, in whole or in part, by public taxation") became the major battleground in discussion. The Democrats, although opposed to the entire measure, concentrated their fire on that particular clause. In reply, the Republican senators, both northern and southern, who were nervous about it, made compromising statements which raised doubts about whether they truly desired prohibition of racial segregation in the schools.[36] Even the sponsor and framer of the pending measure, Senator Frelinghuysen, declared that "when in a school district there are two schools, and the white children choose to go to one and the colored to the other, there is nothing in this bill that prevents their doing so." Likewise, Republican Senators Timothy O. Howe of Wisconsin, Daniel D. Pratt of Indiana, as well as Henry R. Pease and James L. Alcorn of Mississippi, argued that the school clause could be construed to allow blacks equal facilities in separate schools, so long as such an arrangement was voluntary rather than compulsory—an assumption that seemed to be tacitly understood in discussions of the Senate Republican caucus. By implying that the provision allowed equivalent schools and not necessarily mixed schools, many Republican proponents of the bill gave the impression that they had no expectation of any substantial achievement of school desegregation.[37]

While the debate was going on, the senators narrowly defeated an amendment providing for separate but equal schools, though many of them had, by implication, argued for voluntary segregation. They also decisively rejected an amendment to exempt schools entirely from the measure. Republican senators, it seemed, were attempting to please all groups by endorsing educational equality in principle and through statutes to satisfy the blacks, while, to placate the whites, they were pointing out the narrow reach of the law and suggesting possibilities of circumventing it. Such hedging strongly suggested that what was purported to be a testimonial to Sumner in fact bordered on a travesty.

As for the passage of the bill, the division among the Republicans was reflected in their absences, their abstentions, and the outright opposition of three of their number. Nevertheless, a determined group in the party, a majority of whom were not up for reelection, persisted and finally succeeded in outmaneuvering the Democratic filibuster. Although lacking a majority of the whole body, the Senate—by finally imposing night sessions, managing to maintain a quorum, and fortifying themselves with liquor, cigars, and catnaps—did, to the surprise of many observers, pass a strong civil rights measure on May 22, 1874, which was similar to Sumner's version but excluded churches. The timing and circumstances would suggest that the only reason enough votes were secured was because a number of Republicans, although dubious about the proposal, supported it because they were convinced it would never pass in the House of Representatives. There, they assumed, it would languish and die because of a lack of time, procedural delays, a Democratic filibuster, and, in the end, insufficient Republican support, which, after all, was precisely what had happened in 1872 and 1873, when the Senate had passed similar bills that had gone down to defeat in the House.[38]

Actually, a large part of the legislative history of civil rights reminded the Democratic Chicago *Times* and the Republican New York *Times* of a game of congressional football in which the measure was kicked from one chamber to the other, its supporters reluctant to see it become law, but equally reluctant to assume responsibility for its defeat. The question had become one that the bipartisan opponents of the civil rights bill termed a pious fraud. There never had been a measure, declared the New York *Times*, concerning which there had been so little sincerity, either in the arguments advanced or in the stands assumed by partisans and demagogues.[39]

As many senators had realized, the considerations that had prompted the passage of the Frelinghuysen bill in the more radical Senate were not as powerful in the House of Representatives, in which all of the members were up for reelection. Despite a Republican majority of two thirds in the House (regained in the 1872 landslide), there was little indication of strong support for the Senate bill. Some Republicans had already perceived that a political disaster might result, for repercussions, especially in the South, had followed directly after the bill's passage in the Senate. For example, contracts for building schools and hiring teachers had been canceled in many places in the South and in the border states. As an uncle of the federal commissioner of education reported: "You have no idea of the amount of prejudice created here against the public school system by the Civil Rights Bill. It is very strong and I fear the result." Further, the parliamentary status of the proposed legislation was perilous: awaiting action on the Speaker's table, the only way it could be taken up, debated, and voted upon was by suspending the rules—a step requiring a two-thirds vote—and it all had to be accomplished in the few weeks remaining before adjournment. Although time was short, what action there was in the House proved to be desultory, and the floor managers of the bill were not vigorous in organizing support for the measure.[40]

With some northern Republicans not voting, and just enough southern and border Republicans, along with a few from the North, opposing the motion to consider the measure, the Senate bill never even reached the floor of the House, despite several votes to suspend the rules. The vote on May 25 was close and the motion failed, only 6 votes short of the required two thirds. It was rumored that had there been any prospect of obtaining the necessary votes, a number of additional Republicans would have voted against it. Thereafter, on subsequent occasions before adjournment in June, the same motion failed by larger margins.[41]

It was most especially the southern and border Republican delegations that were responsible for the decrease in support. Facing reelection with uncertainty, they considered themselves vulnerable on the school issue and were unwilling to risk defeat in defense of what they regarded as empty idealism. Thus, either out of principle or because of politics, they voted against taking up the bill in hopes that their recorded disapproval or lack of comment would improve their chances. Moreover, in fear of political reprisals, representatives from particularly insecure districts tended to oppose the bill outright. But the opposition was not altogether confined to the South and the borderland, as the stunning defeat on June 8 seemed to indicate, for a number of northern Republican representatives found it prudent to be absent at the time. During the debate Wisconsin Democratic Representative Charles A. Eldredge had made the point that the civil rights bill had been buried half a dozen times during that session and was beyond the power of resurrection; then, turning to face the Republican side, he concluded: "it is the deadest corpse you ever saw and you are all glad of it." Thus the measure finally fell victim to both its declared enemies and its supposed friends.[42]

Many Republicans were relieved that the bill had been defeated in the House, although most of them had not dared to oppose it openly. Some of them had wanted the House's inaction to be blamed on the Democrats so that they, the Republicans, could take credit for support of the bill; in that way, the black electorate wouldn't blame them for the measure's failure to pass. At the same time they hoped that since the bill had been defeated, the white voters wouldn't disapprove of them. Otherwise, according to predictions in the press, passage would have so alienated southern white Republicans that no Republican candidate for Congress would have been elected from any white-belt district in the South.[43]

Faced with this predicament, House Republicans and some senators sought survival in a quiet burial of the bill. North Carolinians predicted that if the civil rights bill were to become law, "our party is doomed to defeat in our Elections," for "clamor . . . will know no bounds." Fear of defeat because of the civil rights issue also plagued northern Republicans. Indeed, it was reported that leading northern Republican congressmen were anxious that the bill be "consigned to the tombs of the Capulets."[44] One observer reported that Speaker Blaine was "very uneasy" for fear it would pass the House and therefore advised Democrats to be in their seats ready for roll calls that would defeat the measure. The report concluded that there was "no vitality in the desire even among the Republicans that it should pass."[45] As for floor leader Benjamin F. Butler, who in the past had zealously advanced radical measures, he was criticized by proponents of the bill for his apathy and negligence in his management of it, prompting the New York *Tribune* to remark that its failure was "skillfully effected by sharp parliamentary maneuvering."[46]

During the congressional wrangling over civil rights, President Grant's position had become increasingly important and, as in regard to so many matters, doubtful. To be sure, in 1873 Grant had twice recommended that Congress pass some sort of civil rights legislation, but his qualified recommendation sounded pro forma, and to many it lacked conviction and resolution, for he publicly opposed legislating social equality and privately made unenthusiastic remarks about it. By spring, 1874, given the precarious fate of the bill, the president was in a crucial position to influence Congress. But Grant had appeared to be indifferent to the measure, or at least unhappy with the Senate version of it and, specifically, with the school provision. All that was rumor, however, so that whether he would have vetoed the bill had it been enacted remains an open question, although certain members of Congress had apparently thought he would have. For example, one observer, while the bill was pending in the House, claimed Grant had told a friend that if the lower chamber passed the measure, he would indeed veto it. There were also persistent reports in the newspapers to the effect that Grant would not sign any bill mandating mixed schools, and later in September it had been reported that he had said so himself. Of course, after the congressional election on November 3, he openly acknowledged his hostility to the Senate version of the bill. It was conceivable that he had opposed it because of his evident distaste for mixed schools, but also because, as a result of his opposition, southern Republican congressmen who had also opposed it but had not voted against it for fear of angering southern black voters, would have been saved. In any event, the expectation that Grant would have vetoed the measure, combined with rumors that he had been using pressure to get it scuttled in the House, had indeed influenced the opposition.[47]

Yet another influence during the congressional struggle had been the editorial views of most Republican journals, which had shown no great enthusiasm for civil rights legislation in general and had been particularly hostile toward the Senate bill. The moderate New York *Times* had claimed that enough had already been done for the Negro, and that should the bill pass, it would be due more to some romantic gesture than to any deep conviction. The Philadelphia *Inquirer*, agreeing, had noted that there were already several civil rights provisions on the books, which only required enforcement, and that passage of this bill would merely lead to the demand for another. The idea that the bill was necessary to complete the agenda of reconstruction also came under attack by the *Times*, which stated that the original policy implied "nothing more than the political enfranchisement of the blacks. . . . It was no part of the Republican purpose to force mixed schools upon the people. . . . The great question is whether such a law as this is necessary to protect the blacks in any of their material rights. . . . If it [the bill] is accepted as a Republican measure, the party is sure to suffer from it." As for the Chicago *Tribune*, its view had been that the bill had welded the whites of the South into a unit against the party. Those comments in the northern press had not gone unnoticed in the South. The Columbus, Georgia *Enquirer*, for example, had seen them as "only the whispering breezes of a storm that is arising"—a widespread revulsion toward all of reconstruction accelerated by the attempt to legislate civil rights.[48]

Certain papers in the North of course had disagreed. For example, the Springfield *Republican*, which had taken issue with the argument of the New York *Times*, contended that the pending civil rights bill was in the direct line of the Republican party's logic: "it is the capstone . . . of the reconstruction edifice. All the previous enactments lead up to it, all the solemn . . . expostulations of the canvass of 1872 point to it, the party is fully committed to it by its declarations not less than by its record." Therefore, according to *Harper's Weekly*, the Republicans could not reject civil rights, for that would be tantamount to a confession that they did not trust their own principles and policy.[49]

Civil rights had for years been essentially an academic question evaded by most Republican politicians, who wished not to be embroiled in such a controversy. But once civil rights seemed less Sumner's pet idea brought up yet again for debate, and more of an immediate threat to segregationist custom and ingrained prejudice, there was no way to avoid it as a fierce election issue. Had the Senate not passed the bill, there would have been no controversy; without the inclusion of the mixed-school clause, there would have been no central rallying point for the Democrats to seize upon. If idealism had been the reason for its passage in the Senate, that idealism had been perverse in nature and fraught with mischief, for the senators had done their counterparts in the lower chamber no good and had handicapped those fellow partisans throughout the country who were about to enter a campaign at a time when their party's future did not seem promising. After all, the voters' reaction to the question of civil rights would surely depend in part on what they thought would be the fate of the bill. The bill was still on the House calendar awaiting action; the prevailing popular view and the predictions in some newspapers held that the measure would probably be enacted when the lame-duck session of the Republican-controlled Congress met in December, after the Republicans had faced the electorate and therefore had less to lose. So far from stifling civil rights as an issue, inaction in the House had only increased its importance in the campaign.

Up to then federal reconstruction had been primarily civil and political, its legislation dealing mainly with citizenship and suffrage. Now one chamber of Congress had attempted to broaden the scope of federal law to include matters that affected social relations between the races. Yet there were extensive laws relating to citizens' rights; all that was needed was a way to enforce them. The right of blacks to vote, for example, although guaranteed by the Constitution, was nonetheless still denied them in many localities in 1874. Despite the obvious task at hand, the Senate, with its bill, had proposed to greatly enlarge the work of the government at the very time when the machinery of federal election enforcement was breaking down. Many Americans recognized that civil rights, however desirable, were of secondary importance compared to maintaining black suffrage; as the Washington *New National Era* noted, "even the Civil Rights Bill dwindles into insignificance." Waning Republican power, as reflected in the spring elections, suggested to former Connecticut senator Truman Smith that even a discussion of the measure was the "height of imprudence"; the time was not propitious for such a "hazardous experiment." Conservative currents were too strong, the demagogues too numerous, and the elections too near.[50]

BLACK AND WHITE

Civil Rights and Counterrevolution

THE 1874 canvass opened with unusual excitement for an off-year election, with the Democrats hoping to press their advantage should the freshet of the spring state elections become a torrent by the fall. Some predicted that the congressional election might well prove to be the most interesting and perhaps the most important in two decades. To be sure, the Republicans' control of the United States Senate was thought to be secure; in the House of Representatives, however, despite a healthy margin of 195 Republicans to 88 Democrats, there existed the remote possibility that the latter might well gain 59 seats and obtain an absolute majority. In the *Independent*'s view, the congressional election might be the most severe struggle the Republican party had yet faced, and the outcome might be a forecast of presidential results in the 1876 election.[1]

The Republican leaders faced the campaign with dismay, for the faithful seemed on the verge of breaking ranks. For the first time, loyal radical Republican cartoonist Thomas Nast of *Harper's Weekly*, who had formerly defended Grant and the party on every issue, declared war on the administration by portraying the president staggering under a mountainous burden of political disasters. Nast also showed his disapproval of the blacks in the South Carolina legislature by depicting legislators quarreling under a banner that proclaimed: "Let Us Have Peace." The New York *Times*, heretofore reliably Republican, began to repudiate the Republican rings and regimes, both northern and southern, and frequently gave editorial space to Republican misgovernance in the South and to its misgivings about the pending civil rights legislation. Even the Washington *National Republican* wrote either apologetically or defensively about Republican rule in the South. Meanwhile, all the party organs tried to gain adherents in order to guard against the supreme danger—the Democrats' recapturing of the House of Representatives.[2]

In July, 1874, the keynote of the congressional campaign was made clear in an address issued by the Republican congressional committee. As usual, the party requested continued support to secure what had already been gained by Republican rule and warned the electorate not to be tricked into giving power over to the wicked Democrats, who would bring certain disaster to the nation. The author of the address admitted that the Republican party was not without its shortcomings, but guaranteed that it would mend its ways were it given a chance to continue in power. He also denounced the Democrats' record, especially their discreditable activities during the 1850s, but, of course, made no mention of the current Republican record, emphasizing economic improvements and, more especially, national transportation.[3]

In the address, the issue of reconstruction was played down. To be sure, conventional obeisance was made to that yet unfinished task, but the siren song had become decidedly muted. Although three sentences obliquely referred to the Fourteenth Amendment, whose enforcement was indirectly endorsed, the only civil right specifically singled out was the "common law rights of locomotion." Racial integration of schools was ignored and there was no explicit reference to the civil rights bill enacted by the Senate. Thus the campaign call could hardly have been construed as a strong endorsement of the pending measure, and no pledge to renew enforcement of the Fifteenth Amendment was included. Nor was Grant's southern policy endorsed; indeed, comments on the administration's record as a whole were conspicuously absent. In short, Grant was then apparently regarded more as a liability than as an asset to those Republicans running for Congress. And in striving for a broad-based appeal to the electorate, the party quite simply made the policy of deviation from reconstruction a fact.[4]

Since the campaign took place during a severe depression, and one marked by widespread unemployment, it would have been expected that such matters should predominate. In fact, economic issues were discussed at length during the campaign. However, despite the Republicans' inclination toward deflationary monetary policies and the Democrats' toward inflationary ones, both parties actually were divided internally, with both views represented in each party. In fact, the tendency to adopt inflationary or deflationary solutions to pressing economic problems was more influenced by sectional needs than by other considerations. Both parties in many states were often in agreement on the financial issues in their platforms, since they both wished to represent the popular view of their constituencies. But in states where economic concerns were not clear-cut, such questions were often studiously avoided in both parties' conventions and the candidates frequently underplayed them. Then, too, as the campaign progressed, economic issues attracted less and less interest and even started to bore voters in many localities. In fact, the inflationists' more extravagant proposals were highly criticized, and after Grant's veto of the currency bill in late April, their program was virtually useless since there was no immediate prospect of inflation.[5]

Another question that provoked exhaustive discussion but fizzled out by the end of the campaign in most states was whether Grant would run for a third term. Many newspapers claimed that he was planning to and overplayed even the slightest evidence to that effect.[6] And although doubts about his intentions did outweigh all speculations,[7] even the members of the cabinet were unable to distinguish between speculation and fact. Secretary of State Fish suspected that Grant did harbor ambitions toward a third term, but was convinced that any attempts in that direction would be unsuccessful. Postmaster General Jewell, who doubted that the president truly wanted to go for another term, was troubled by the atmosphere of feverish speculation: "I am of opinion that there is nothing in it, and that Grant does not want it; and yet, as he does not say so . . . it is impossible to tell what may not eventuate from all this talk." Grant could have scotched the rumor at any time with a public denial, but characteristically, he remained silent.[8]

Coupled with widespread opposition to a third term for Grant was a general demand for honesty in government. When the Democrats guaranteed it, the Republicans countered that, judging from the past, including Boss Tweed's operation and other well-oiled machines, the Democrats would bring the same shady methods to national politics, were they given the opportunity. The Republicans also maintained that it was they who had rooted out corruption and that it would not recur. Since many voters were incensed about the scandals in high places that had been uncovered during the two previous years, the issue of honesty remained a difficult one to sidestep. As a result, some Republican campaigners tried to disengage themselves from the calumny surrounding the national party. The Republican New York gubernatorial candidate, John A. Dix, for example, wrote that though Grant's intentions were honest and laudable, they had been ill served by a faulty, and even weak, administration.[9]

Yet the question of reconstruction, despite the Republicans' efforts to muffle any debate on it, was a hardy perennial issue and soon loomed large in the campaign. The Democrats, as in every contest since the war, denounced federal interference with the state governments of the South and espoused home rule. And the Chicago *Times* gratuitously advised the Republicans to save the South and themselves by dismantling reconstruction, for it was destroying the party.[10]

Although there was nothing novel in the Democrats' approach, by 1874 the Republicans were beginning to sense that in this issue lay their vulnerability. Their state party platforms were defensive, often apologetic, and sometimes openly critical of reconstruction. In the Michigan platform, for instance, it was pointed out that Negroes had out of ignorance sometimes blundered in their freedom, but their errors were excused as the inevitable legacy of slavery. Similarly, the Kansas convention resolved that the powers of the federal government in the wartime and postwar crises had been stretched to an "unhealthy extent" and should "now be restored to their normal action." Even Indiana Senator Oliver P. Morton, a staunch supporter of reconstruction, no longer termed it a positive good but rather a necessary evil resulting from the rebellion; he went so far as to acknowledge that the blacks as a group were not very well qualified to govern. The New York Republicans stated openly that certain evils did exist; indeed, the temporary chairman of their state convention, Theodore M. Pomeroy, declared that he took "no pride or pleasure" in the carpetbaggers and did not "believe in lying, and giving stale and stolid excuses about reconstruction." Senator Roscoe Conkling granted that "ignorant men, weak men, venal men have seized the opportunity to work their way into places of trust and power. Bad legislation, excessive taxation, unwise and profligate administration, with their trains of evil have ensued." As for New York congressional candidate Isaac H. Bailey, his view was that the so-called carpetbaggers had brought misfortune upon the blacks of the South and disgrace upon the Republican party, which, he believed, had to rid itself of all responsibility for the rascals.[11]

The extent of a possible change of policy toward reconstruction was foreshadowed in a spring commencement address at Yale University given by Edwards Pierrepont, who shortly was to be appointed attorney general. He characterized the congressional approach as unsound idealism, attacking the notion that the majority ought to rule the southern state governments even if it were the most ignorant portion of the population and claiming that good government was impossible through universal suffrage. After all, he argued, no one ever employed a stupid lawyer to try an important case or an ignorant mariner to sail a valuable ship. Yet he believed that was what the reconstructed states were doing when they allowed blacks to elect and staff Republican regimes. Thus "politicians hastened to reconstruct the South upon theories crude, ill considered, and impossible of success." As a result, Pierrepont strongly believed that the southern Negro, by misusing the ballot and abusing power, had become a source of weakness to the party.[12]

His speech prompted the partisan New York *World* to quip: "Negro suffrage was sweet enough in the Republican mouth, but it is bitter, alas! in the Republican belly." Such disenchantment as Pierrepont's caused the New York *Times* to remark that the "condition of the South is one of the great coming questions of the day—we say a 'coming' question, because we shall have to deal with it under a totally new phase." Indeed, some Republicans now argued that if the freedmen could not handle freedom themselves, it was beyond the duty, authority, and ability of the federal government to save them. Yet another party stalwart, Massachusetts Congressman George F. Hoar, declared that one of the greatest errors ever committed was having given universal suffrage to the blacks without also imposing universal education.[13]

Although reconstruction was still a daily topic in northern Republican newspapers, many editorial writers now expressed either visionary hopes and empty feelings or fatalistic despair and profound pessimism, in contrast to the certitude and faith that had earlier characterized their writings. They now pleaded for a type of reconstruction that would be genuine, or lasting, but they neglected to define those terms. Moreover, they construed reconstruction to mean not so much a well-defined national policy, with specific ends and means, as the "southern problem" or the "southern question"—as an irritating difficulty in a distant place, defying solution. Instead of calls for rededication, which had been frequent in the past, they demanded retrenchment. Many Republican journalists had come to believe that the noble experiment had lasted long enough.[14]

There remained, however, a minority of radical Republicans who vigorously rebutted that stance. According to them, reconstruction itself was sound, and its difficulties were caused merely by postwar dislocation and were exacerbated by the Democrats. They admitted, of course, that great confusion, a good deal of misgovernment, and a fair amount of injustice had damaged reconstruction, but argued that any other course of action would have led to more permanent impairment. As *Harper's Weekly* pointed out, "This is the very time to insist that the policy which has been adopted shall not be abandoned." The radicals, who were in agreement about creating and maintaining a Republican South, differed in evaluating the current status of southern and border blacks. Some of them claimed that the Negroes had achieved their civil and political rights, maintaining them was all that was necessary. Certain others declared that the blacks were fast losing their rights because of the successful machinations of their enemies, whereas still others were of the opinion that the promised guarantees had never been realized. According to the Newark *Advertiser*, "there is *not* yet impartial suffrage in the South. Caste is not conquered. The amended Constitution is not accepted as law. The rights of the freedmen are not secured."[15]

Putting the third-term issue aside as a lot of fuss over little or nothing, rejecting the financial issue as hopelessly obscure, and sensing that the question of dishonesty had not—at least early in the campaign—developed a visible cutting edge, the Republicans had, by partially passing the civil rights bill in May, unintentionally made that incendiary question of racial equality the great national issue of the congressional elections. And drawn into it was the entire question of reconstruction. As a result, in most congressional districts the election of 1874 constituted no more than a referendum on existing or proposed reconstruction at a time when both were under attack from many sides.

The Democrats made the most of what the Atlanta *Constitution* termed the "delectable" issue of forcing social equality upon the country and making the black man the equal of the white. The issue of civil rights was depicted as the imminent prospect of racial equality by coercion—a scheme of the national government's to introduce the "nigger into our tea and coffee," as Kentucky editor Henry Watterson phrased it. Opponents plumbed the depths of racial fears with strident emotional appeals, such as the following, from a Democratic Kentucky newspaper:

The graveyards you have selected, beautified, and adorned as a resting-place of those you have loved must be desecrated to satisfy the spite of those liberty lovers, and choice places given to the negro, even if it should require the exhuming of friends long buried. You must divide your pew in church, even if your wife and child are forced to sit on the floor, and no complaint must be made should Sambo besmear the carpet you have placed there with juice of tobacco. Your children at school must sit on the back seats and in the cold, whilst the negro's children sit near the stove and on the front seats, and enjoy in every instance the money you toil for, whilst Sambo is sleeping and stealing. Or, as the darky explained to his less posted brother: "We's gwine to ride free on de railroads, smoke in de ladies' car, and put our feet on the percushions of the seats whenever we damn please. We's gwine to be allowed to stop at de hotels, an set at de head of de table, and hab de biggest slice ob de chickens, and lay around in de parlors and spit on de carpets, and make de white trash hustle themselves and wait on us without grumblin'. We's gwine to be allowed to go to de white schools and set upon the platform with de teacher. We's gwine to be buried in italic coffins on top of de white folks, and Gabriel shall call: 'All ob you colored gemmen rise furst.'"[16]

However, the issue was not strictly partisan. Appalachian whites in western Maryland, West Virginia, eastern Kentucky, and east Tennessee, who had been unionists during the war and strong Republicans afterward, were now infuriated by the civil rights bill. Emancipation had been a bitter pill, declared a Maryland Republican politician, but loyal whites had swallowed it without any fuss; enfranchisement of blacks was a "horrible bolus" (a large pill for animals), yet Republican whites along the border had gulped it down. "But now the party comes at them with the Civil Rights bill—and they'll see . . . the whole Radical party cremated before they submit to any such indignity." A similarly truculent Republican newspaper in Huntsville, Alabama, declared that if the pending Senate civil rights measure "embodies the principles of the republican party then count us out." Indeed, throughout the South and the borderland, the bill was a subject of constant conversation and often as great an object of bitter opposition among Republicans as among Democrats. In the opinion of a Baltimore correspondent, whites of both parties simply refused to be taken in by the "tinsel tattle of Radical orators, by appeals to the Declaration of Independence, and all that muck-mammocky rot about liberty and equality and 'the philosophy of first principles'; in which the Senators indulged."[17]

After touring the South during the summer, correspondent Horace V. Redfield predicted a Republican downfall in that region in the November election, noting that in Alabama twelve thousand whites, mainly in the northern area, held the margin of control and that the agitation over civil rights was effectively alienating those whites who normally voted Republican. With the color line drawn "snappishly tight," it appeared inevitable that the Democrats would annihilate the Republican party in states where whites constituted a majority of the voters. Except for Louisiana, Mississippi, and South Carolina—all states with black voter majorities—Redfield was certain that the issue of civil rights would cause the South to be irretrievably lost to the Republican party.[18]

The Republicans' concern about the groundswell of opposition to the civil rights bill was reflected in the resolutions of state party conventions. Only in six Republican state platforms was it implied, in some fashion, that the pending bill would be endorsed, whereas only four (Louisiana, Arkansas, South Carolina, and Nebraska) en-

dorsed it explicitly. In twelve states the Republicans dodged the issue, and in three (Delaware, Tennessee, and Alabama) the state parties
strongly opposed any new measure. The Democrats, of course, unequivocally opposed civil rights in twelve state platforms and avoided
mention of the question in thirteen others. Thus they were generally
as cautious and evasive as the Republicans, probably in an effort to
dissociate their party from any racist reputation and to make it more
palatable to dissatisfied black and white Republicans. Head-on con-
frontations between Republicans who favored civil rights in their
state platforms and Democrats who vehemently opposed them took
place in only three states—closely contested Pennsylvania, Ohio, and
Louisiana.[19]

Although party platforms, which were designed for public proclamation to an audience with a variety of political beliefs, were not
unimportant in revealing the general views of a state party, they
naturally tended to be circumspect. Campaign rallies, however, where
stumpers forsook discretion and played on emotions, were more accurate indicators of precisely what moved the voters. In Wilmington,
Delaware, for example, a Democratic speaker was warmly applauded when he declared that the Constitution would be rewritten
in the spirit of "not we the people, but 'We the White Men.'" And at
many Democratic meetings it was the civil rights issue that provided
the political fireworks. However, Republican campaigners greatly
differed in their response to the question: not many of them used
overt appeals to racial antagonism, and only a few chose to support
the pending bill boldly and unequivocally. Virginia Republican Representative William H. H. Stowell, for example, who was running in
a district where blacks were numerous, was the only Republican
campaigner in the state to do so. Most Republicans seeking election
tried to circumvent the issue in one way or another. They would, for
example, champion civil equality but not social equality, stress the
principle of equal rights but not the Senate civil rights bill, endorse
the measure but claim that its provision for school integration did
not mean what it seemed to, embrace equalitarianism but not explicitly mention blacks, or accept equal rights in theory but not press
for equal opportunity in officeholding or in the schoolhouse.[20]

Further complicating intraparty differences, the various levels within the Republican organization in the same state sometimes took contradictory views. In New Jersey, for instance, the state convention evaded the issue of civil rights in its platform, but a resolution of one congressional district convention supported it; in turn, that district's own congressional candidate declared in the campaign that he had voted against the civil rights bill because it might be harmful rather than helpful to blacks. Depending on the constituency or on a campaigner's personal conviction, many candidates, to use their own expression, spit upon the party platform. However, Democratic candidates, recognizing their best issue since the war, generally opposed the measure aggressively and resourcefully, characterizing it variously as an insult to the South, as a shame to the North, and, above all, as a dangerous assault against the traditional and desirable separation of the races.[21]

During the summer the controversy over civil rights burgeoned in the Tennessee and North Carolina campaigns. Two years before, in Tennessee, the Democrats, weakened by factionalism, had lost seven of their ten congressional seats; now the state party was again united and determined to retrieve lost fortunes in the August elections for county offices, and in the November elections for Congress and the governorship. While the civil rights bill was hanging in abeyance in Washington, it became the controlling issue in Tennessee. One writer from Memphis claimed that the large margin by which the measure went through the Senate in Washington had "excited considerable anxiety in the public mind"; and a federal marshal reported that the Democrats were presenting the "Civil Rights Bill . . . as the great issue and the white people were lashed into a frenzy"[22]

Restiveness in the Republican stronghold of east Tennessee soon turned into open revolt. Some newspapers contended that the pending bill was about to wipe out Republicanism in the region; others believed that discussion of the measure in itself had already destroyed the party there. What had particularly stirred white Republicans to mutiny was the provision for integrated schools. Urging defection, the Memphis *Appeal* raised the Democratic battle cry: "The black flag of mixed schools, negro equality, is already fluttering in the breeze. . . . Up then with the banner of the white man! . . . since the issue has at last been forced upon you, let every true man with a white skin rally to his color." In response to this intense opposition, the leaders of the state Republican party and their newspapers either rejected the pending bill outright or else strongly objected to the school provision. Republican Senator William G. Brownlow, who was openly hostile to the measure, summed up the general feeling of the mountain men when he claimed that white Republican voters of east Tennessee had resolved to get along without the Republican party and the colored votes, sooner than submit to the abominations of mixing the races in the schools.[23]

In the midst of a vociferous state campaign, county elections on August 6 brought out a heavy vote and excited general interest outside Tennessee. Although the elections were for relatively unimportant offices, the canvass turned upon national political issues, particularly civil rights; this early election was thus looked to as an indicator for November elections in that and other states. The outcome was auspicious for the Democracy, which made great gains, carrying every county in the state except three. There were unexpectedly large Democratic majorities in western and middle Tennessee, where the Republicans were defeated in two of their urban strongholds, Memphis and Nashville. Most important, sweeping majorities for the Democratic ticket grabbed the Republican heartland of east Tennessee; even Knox County (Knoxville), the home territory of incumbents Senator Brownlow and Representative Horace Maynard, went Democratic. Simultaneously, in neighboring Kentucky the Democrats also made unprecedented gains.[24]

"Civil rights did it," read the terse telegram from Tennessee. Characteristic of the observations of most newspapers in the nation, the Louisville *Courier-Journal* announced: "the civil rights bill has played smash with the Republican party in Tennessee." According to Senator Brownlow, the sole issue in the election had been the pending measure, which had doomed the Republican party in the state and in the South, and he believed it would take a generation to recover from the disaster. Similarly, a Kentucky Republican noted how his state party was "hopelessly demoralized. The Civil Rights Bill has played havoc."[25]

In North Carolina, too, the August elections revolved principally

221

around the civil rights issue. And, again, the rest of the nation followed the events most attentively to see what effect the Senate bill would have. The Democrats' war cry everywhere was "Down with Civil Rights!" Democratic campaigners blamed their Republican opponents for passage of the bill in the Senate and, preying on current fears, claimed that any reelected Republicans would help pass the measure in the House of Representatives. Republicans in the state tried to dodge the issue, because endorsement of the Senate bill would drive away the white Republicans of the Piedmont and mountain areas, whereas repudiation of it might cause black voters in coastal counties to defect or abstain. Nevertheless, as the portents of defeat became clearer, many white and even some black Republicans declared their opposition to the pending bill. Such conversions, made under duress, were derided by many whites as signs of weakness and insincerity, and by resentful blacks as turncoat behavior. The Democrats, of course, capitalized on the discomfiture of the Republicans and were quick to point out that they had betrayed the blacks. Indeed, there seemed no way out of the Republicans' dilemma: any stance designed to conciliate one race merely antagonized the other.[26]

Consequently, the Democrats swept through the state and leveled the Republican party, winning by 54 percent. From the mountains to the seaboard, Republican counties had gone for the state Democratic ticket. A Republican stronghold, Wake County, which included the state capital, Raleigh, had voted Democratic for the first time in fourteen years. The state legislature had shifted from a Republican lead to overwhelming Democratic control in the upper chamber, and from a Democratic majority to complete mastery in the lower. A combined gain of seventy-seven seats had given the Democrats virtually three fourths of the legislature. In fact, the Democracy had polled the heaviest recent vote in the congressional races, greater than the previous presidential turnout, and had won by a solid majority of 21,000. The Democrats had increased their percentage of the statewide congressional vote from 49 in 1872 to 53 in 1874, and in the process gained two congressional seats in the coastal plain and Piedmont regions, capturing seven of eight congressional districts. Republican whites, who held the balance of power in many localities, had either defected or stayed at home. The result was decisive; as Democratic Senator Matt W. Ransom put it: "It gives us the control of our own affairs and hereafter the State is Democratic."[27]

The Democratic triumph in August was widely and minutely analyzed by the northern press, which predicted that fierce opposition to the civil rights bill in the southern and border states would, in the fall, bring more Republican disasters like those in Tennessee and North Carolina. Claiming that the "campaign really turned on 'Niggers,'" the New York *Tribune* summarized the frequently repeated but always powerful arguments against the civil rights bill: "Do you wish to be buried in a nigger grave-yard? Do you wish your daughter to marry a nigger? Are you going to send your boy to a nigger school?" The Democratic Chicago *Times* also saw the compelling force in the election to be racism—"the damnigger." Examining the election statistics, the New York *Herald* professed no surprise at the fact that North Carolina had gone Democratic, though it had not been prepared for the unexpectedly large majorities. Discussion of the civil rights bill, the newspaper maintained, was weakening, if not wrecking, the party everywhere in the South; its declining power was emboldening southern whites and their northern sympathizers. Given the size of the Democratic majorities, the journal believed that because the racial issue was part of the campaign, the Republicans could only hope to carry those southern states with black majorities. The Louisville *Courier-Journal* remarked that the pending civil rights bill had pitted white against black throughout the campaign and had decided the election. And according to the Springfield *Republican*, the pending measure was the "most successful apple of discord that has lately been tossed into American politics."[28]

Southern Democrats gloated over their success, confident that they had at last found the Achilles heel of the Republican party. The August elections, they observed, marked the beginning of the end of Republican rule throughout the South. They presented the voter with only two choices—white rule or black ruin of the southern states. Avoidance of the civil rights bill, which was "revolting to our manhood, to our customs, and our institutions, and our education," could only be assured if there were absolute white control in state and local government.[29]

Southern Republicans also fully recognized that the issue of civil rights had been the cause of their downfall in the elections held thus far. The whites had deserted the party because of it, wrote a North Carolina Republican postmaster; there had been "too much fool-discussions, and bad management with the weapon 'Civil Rights' hammering upon us. It certainly killed us," since many whites who normally voted Republican had been "forced away by this measure." One Raleigh Republican asked why the party persisted in such a suicidal policy: Why should its power be "jeopardized for a bare abstraction—a sounding brass? You gain not a single colored man, and lose nine tenths of your whites. Oh! what fatuity." Another North Carolinian claimed that a political hurricane had swept over the state in reaction to the "hot-house measures of reconstruction." Still another thought that the passage of the pending bill "would be death to the party in North Carolina, if not in every Southern State." The consensus of southern white Republicans was clear: since the civil rights bill would not be enacted or if enacted, not enforced, why make it an issue at all?[30]

By August, northerners of both parties recognized that the racial and reconstruction issues, as well as Democratic resurgence, were not limited to the South. Maine Republican Congressman Eugene Hale, for one, observed that because of the southern election results the Democrats in Maine were gaining in strength and confidence; he thought that the state Republican vote would "sag" in September and that the "civil rights bill as pushed was a cursed folly stirring up all the prejudice of the southern whites and having no chance of getting through." So many victories in such a short time and without a single defeat encouraged the Democrats to hope for even greater success in the fall. As Indiana Democratic Congressman William E. Niblack noted: "the drift both North and South is in our direction now and especially so in the South"; the Democratic Harrisburg *Patriot* believed that the civil rights bill "sits like a nightmare on the Republican party."[31]

The August results gave northern Democrats their cue for the campaign, suggested the skillful strategist Richard Vaux. Since other issues, such as the financial question, were dividing the Democracy, he advised that the campaign be pitched on the race issue everywhere: "My opinion is that here with us in the North the anti-negro is the certain card." The Democratic New York *Sun*, in an assumed show of concern for Republican fortunes, advised the party to abandon any further demonstration of support for the pending civil rights bill, since by and large its constituency would not tolerate it. It was all very well for Republicans to indulge in rhetorical flourishes in regions where there were practically no Negroes, the newspaper allowed, but in the Middle Atlantic, Midwest, and Pacific Coast states, most Republicans objected to the measure, and in the South and the borderland, civil rights would bring bloodshed. Most Republican journals, perhaps whistling in the dark, chose to interpret their defeats in Tennessee and North Carolina as unimportant, accidental, and temporary, resulting mainly from local issues and interests. Banking on past experience, they hoped that electoral blunders would continue as the Democratic stock-in-trade.[32]

During the fall campaign, virtually everywhere in the South and in the borderland, the Democrats continued their provocative talk against civil rights, often accompanying it with violence. Their reason for going out in search of trouble was not only to intimidate the opposition but to exterminate their political enemies: one Tennessee black candidate for the legislature as well as other Tennessee blacks were murdered. Throughout Kentucky, there were brawls and street fights between the races; in tidewater North Carolina, which had a high concentration of Negroes, skirmishes between whites and blacks took place on election day; and at campaign gatherings in south Georgia, the Republicans were terrorized by mobs that created a din with pans and cowbells and cursed the Republicans and the civil rights bill.[33]

Typical of the Republicans' desperate efforts to unload their albatross was Congressman Maynard, who was running for governor of Tennessee in November and who first endorsed the civil rights bill as a party measure, but added that it did not mandate racial mixing in the schools or affect social activity in any way. Once he was nominated, he warmly embraced the bill in its entirety, but then in the course of the campaign he equivocated, and by late September he expressed his disapproval of it as it stood. In West Virginia the situation was handled less ambiguously: a prominent Republican pledged before a Republican congressional convention that the party would go no further than equal suffrage, for civil rights that were social in nature did not concern the party or the government: "Socially he [the black man] must take care of himself. . . . As a party, we wash our hands of Negro-ology." In other states such as Alabama, the Republicans changed their stand according to the audience. To whites in north Alabama, Republican office seekers claimed that there would never be social equality enforced by law, whereas campaigners in middle Alabama promised the blacks a jubilee once the civil rights measure became law. One reporter in Alabama described the situation as "fish to the negro, flesh to the white Republicans, and fowl to everybody else." But despite the Republicans' determined efforts to dissociate themselves from civil rights in order to placate whites, the Democrats' charge that any Republican congressman would vote for the pending bill was more widely believed than the Republicans' disavowal of that view.[34]

As the campaign in the southern and border states continued its violent course toward the November finish, the outcome seemed inevitable. In the minor elections held in October, Georgia and West Virginia fell into line, with large majorities voting for the Democrats.[35] In May, North Carolina Republican Tourgée had predicted that the bill would be "just like a blister-plaster put on a dozing man whom it is desirable to soothe to sleep. . . . For its evil influences it will be vivid and active." Tourgée commented that since the Republicans of the North did not understand the actual condition of blacks in the South or the feelings of southern whites, they lacked a realistic appreciation of the political possibilities in the region; he warned that many southern whites felt genuinely threatened by a partial passage of the bill, convinced that it jeopardized racial separation. Tourgée thus castigated "Sumner's Supplementary": "It is the idea of a visionary quack who prescribes for the disease without having made a diagnosis."[36]

Similarly, reporter Redfield in October ascribed the death of three hundred blacks to the violence aroused by this one burning issue of civil rights. He believed that as a result of the bitter racial antagonism that had been generated, the southern Republican party would surely lose at least ten congressmen in the fall. He lamented the harm done by northern "theorists [who] persist in legislating to enforce their beautiful theory of 'equal rights'" and thus proposed to do away with the customs of hundreds of years by a simple act of Congress. Were the Republicans to lose control of the next Congress, the civil rights bill, in his view, would be to blame. It had also "destroyed the Republican party in the South. And every Southern State lost to the Republicans is lost forever. Nothing short of a second reconstruction can bring them back." Surveying party defeats, a Mississippi Republican found little solace in the high ideals embodied in the Senate bill or in its timing: "There is to me, no recommendation in the fact, that it is Mr. Sumner's dying donation. It is well enough at a funeral to indulge in romance, and even poetic flattery is tolerated. . . . but I have no special desire to be a witness at the burial or part cause of the death of the Republican party either, North or South. I do not think the Republican party bound by the bequest. . . . I appreciate highly their delicate sentimentality. But mere sentiment never governed well, and I apprehend never will." He advised that first political equality be enforced, however much even that would tax the energy and ability of the government. "Beyond that," he wrote, "you launch on an unexplored sea, with sharp rocks some above the surface and some hidden below it."[37]

When fall came, beleaguered Republicans in the South were casting about for help. Acting with their congressional campaign committee, they decided to present their case to the nation at a regional convention, reveal the true condition of the South, and suggest steps to maintain reconstruction, not to mention their unstated objective of rallying northern Republican support. The opposition claimed that the conclave was just one more occasion to unfurl the tattered old bloody shirt and that such a gathering merely advertised the failure of Republican rule in the South. Even the Washington *National Republican* was unenthusiastic about the meeting, complaining that its purpose was vague and indefinite and suggesting that the convention limit itself to southern business alone, to selecting delegates with considerable care and avoiding the presence of federal officeholders.[38]

When the convention of southern Republicans got under way on

227

October 13 in Chattanooga, the representation was uneven and the attendance poor; indeed, of the thousand delegates that had been expected, only two hundred showed up. Some of them were prominent politicians, but many were federal officeholders or office seekers, and no well known northern Republican appeared as a speaker. As for the condition of the hall in which the convention met, it was similar to that of the southern Republican party—only partially constructed; the walls were not finished, and the floor was covered with sawdust, which at first was regarded as picturesque but later really began to reek. The proceedings were generally dull and uninspired, and the speeches were set pieces of party wisdom. The delegates appeared unenthusiastic, seldom breaking into spontaneous applause, and during debate, according to one reporter, they seemed to drift off into a sea of talk, with men bobbing up and down.[39]

Despite all this, the delegates acted discreetly in their final resolutions. They dodged the third-term issue in accordance with rumored instructions from Washington and tabled purely local grievances. The civil rights bill, buried in committee, was neither discussed nor endorsed. To deal with the question of southern outrages, the gathering merely created a committee to investigate reports of violence, stipulating that the findings would be published after the election in an effort to persuade Congress to pass new enforcement measures. Through evasion and procrastination, the convention attempted to create a decorous appearance to enable the regional party to regain its credibility, recruit support within and without the South, limit the damage that the discussion of civil rights had done, and try to check the implacable Democratic advance through the South.[40]

Even before the Chattanooga convention finally met in October, the campaign had accelerated everywhere in the South, its pace matched by a crescendo of violence. Reports had filtered north concerning the sinister nature and savage behavior of the various white terrorists, whose activities had seemed to indicate that a new and energetic spirit of resistance had emerged in many parts of the South. Georgian Amos Akerman had written in his diary: "There is an uprising throughout the South against the Negroes and all who befriend them in politics. It shows itself in acts of violence and in bitterness of language in speakers and newspapers." The wave of insurgency, observed the Cincinnati *Gazette*, had been a "savage proclamation of war against the colored people and all white Republicans." A white woman from North Carolina had also reported that the White League was more prevalent than the public supposed: "it holds a tremendous surveillance over both white and colored. . . . It is a vortex striving to draw everything to itself."[41]

Indeed, it was during the campaign of 1874 that the new white terror, as it was called at the time, had burgeoned. These new organizations, such as the White Leagues, which had been formed to defeat Republicans and demolish reconstruction, were in fact more serious and more menacing than their predecessors, the Klans. Throwing masks and gowns aside, they had acted with a cool calculation directed toward specific political purposes; their tactics had been more comprehensive and determined, and they had been altogether more effective and sustained in their organized intimidation of voters. Their program was a politics of color: by agitating the race issue they had hoped to drive all whites into the Democratic camp while at the same time keeping the blacks from the polls. White supremacy and black subordination had provided the campaign themes, and the blacks had been their targets for rifle practice.[42]

Some northern Democrats had become worried that this upsurge of lawlessness might provoke northern indignation and renewed enforcement activity. As California Democrat Eugene Casserly had written early in September: "every 'outrage' reported from the South, gives me a chill to the very marrow—for it gives new life to Radicalism and all its atrocities." But the Chicago *Times* had disagreed, speculating that the southern Democrats had been acting bolder than usual because northern Republicans' growing indifference to the fate of the Negro was encouraging these Democrats to act with impunity. Suspecting this was indeed the case, a leader of the Mississippi Democrats, James Z. George, asked Congressman Lucius Q. C. Lamar, who was in Washington, whether it was true that "there is a great reaction going on in the Northern mind against negro government in the South? I have concluded that our African friends have so misused the privileges that they have that the Northern people are dying to see the end of all this misrule. . . . Let me know . . . what the North thinks of these things and whether the animosities of the war are dying out." The ultra-Bourbon Mobile *Register* had no doubts about dominant public opinion in the North: "The white people of the North have awakened from their nightmare. The negro is no longer the fashion. . . . The North have come to their senses. The negro has disgraced and ruined the party which pushed him forward, and the oscillating pendulum of public opinion is now swinging over to the side of the Southern white man. . . . The North have found that they could not make a silk purse out of a sow's ear, and have cast Sambo overboard."[43]

Signs of such a change had been thought to be legion. The New York *Tribune* had declared in an editorial that the "sentiment of the North is rapidly turning against them [the southern blacks]." The northern press, many Republican politicians, and most voters had been opposed to the civil rights bill. Also, during 1874 President Grant had not lifted his hand to save southern Republicans from their downfall in Texas during the winter or in Vicksburg, Mississippi, during the summer, and he had cut loose from the radicals at the conclusion of the Arkansas imbroglio in the late spring. Republican rule in the South, and black political participation in particular, had then been the subject of severe criticism; federal election enforcement had been growing more lax because of budgetary starvation and bureaucratic inertia; meanwhile, the federal courts had begun to gnaw away at the reach and power of the enforcement laws—a trend earlier advocated or subsequently endorsed by many northern newspapers. Elections everywhere had been going against the Republicans, possibly indicating that their campaign slogans with regard to the war and reconstruction no longer had the same appeal.[44]

But when reports of violence in the South had grown to epidemic proportions during August and September, and the Republican officials there had deluged Washington with frantic requests for troops, the government had quickly dispatched army units to disturbed districts in Tennessee, Arkansas, South Carolina, Alabama, Georgia, and Louisiana. Southern federal marshals and attorneys, given control of the troops, had been instructed to enforce election laws to the fullest. The attorney general had made a ringing pronouncement that lawlessness would not be tolerated, that the guilty would be punished, that peace would be preserved, and that honest elections would be held, and the president had publicly announced his intention to use all the means in his power to enforce order in the South.

The Democrats, of course, were expected to stridently denounce the use of troops for the cynical purpose of carrying the elections for the Republicans.[45] Indeed, federal election enforcement in 1874 had been yet another case in which both evenhanded justice and partisan expediency coincided. Stationing troops and posting special deputy marshals and election commissioners to prevent persecution and bloodshed where blacks were concentrated had indicated an intelligent anticipation of Democratic terrorism; but the Democrats had been right in asserting that the federal presence in a particular district would promote Republican chances at the polls.

Although most Republicans had maintained that lawlessness must be suppressed, some had wondered whether there was sufficient trustworthy information about the situation in the South to be certain that federal intervention was warranted; moreover, they had remained uneasy about Attorney General Williams' judgment and his ability to handle the unsettled situation without partisan bias. Some journals had conjectured that federal action had to be at least partially political in purpose, judging from the location and distribution of troops by the attorney general, who had dispatched them to some counties where no outrages had yet occurred, but where a good Republican showing was greatly desired. And they had been concerned about the potential for abuse of those officials who could make arrests when violence threatened. As one northerner had sardonically remarked: "the Government is ordering troops into the South again. That is republican reconstruction!" The considerable number of reservations expressed by various Republicans about the latest round of intervention had been symptomatic of their growing desire for disengagement and their numbing sense of futility about the federal government's chances of doing anything to stem the mounting disorder.[46]

Still, the Chicago *Times*, itself a Democratic paper, warned the southerners that they were mistaken in assuming that the Republicans were about to sound a retreat: "They are tired enough of the everlasting negro question, it is true. . . . But they have not altered their resolution that the negro shall be a citizen, and that he shall be protected in the enjoyment and exercise of his human rights." The *Nation* hedged, remarking that the southerners may have "better information than we of a decay in the North of the feeling that, as regards the negro, the South will bear to be watched. Some decay there has been; how much, nobody yet knows." The administration's Washington *National Republican* provided the dominant theme: "if a reign of murder is inaugurated, the white leaders . . . mistake the temper of the North if they suppose it will stand by with folded hands and sanction it."[47]

When the northern Republicans reiterated their steadfast determination to maintain reconstruction, they emphasized in particular the sanctity of the ballot, for the Fifteenth Amendment had made the ballot for blacks a federal trust that the states could not annul. Others argued that although the votes of freedmen might be bargained for, even bought or stolen, their franchise could not be destroyed because of the competition between the parties who needed black voters. This view was shared by all groups in the political spectrum of the North. Thus the New York *Tribune* found Negroes to have become an indispensable and indissoluble part of the body politic. And according to the Democratic *Leslie's Newspaper*, "It would be as easy to wipe out the story of the Rebellion from our history as to destroy that vote," to which the Chicago *Tribune* remarked that, however desirable an educational qualification on black suffrage might be, it was impracticable for at least a generation, for the spirit of the age demanded universal manhood suffrage; the postwar amendments to the Constitution had taken too firm a hold upon the people and were too thoroughly endorsed by both parties to be disturbed at that point.[48]

An English observer, however, dissented, predicting that whatever political equality the southern blacks had had would probably be suspended easily and rapidly with the acquiescence of many, if not most, people in the North. "There will be no difficulty discovering plausible reasons for the formal or practical disfranchisement of constituencies which have proved themselves grossly corrupt and incompetent." It was naive to assume that corruption stemmed solely from the ranks of new voters, and it was certainly inaccurate to lump all blacks together as incompetent or politically ignorant, but it was significant that American journals (with the important exception of some editorials in Negro newspapers) had generally failed to recognize the truth of the Englishman's observation that widespread disfranchisement of blacks could be accomplished easily, and that in many places it had already been done. Overlooking a spreading pattern of Negro disfranchisement and Republican defeat, most northerners, including Republicans, had taken refuge from reality by repeating the optimistic platitude that the right to vote was secure forever.[49]

More revealing than the general statements affirming the Republicans' resoluteness of purpose had been the public reaction to specific events during the campaign. The situation in Alabama provides a case in point. The controversy there had begun when Alabama Republican Representative Charles Hays wrote a letter in early September enumerating specific outrages in his state and charging that a reign of terror existed. Dubious northern newspaper editors had sent correspondents scurrying around Alabama to check Hays's allegations, which had been widely publicized. Reporters from the New York *Tribune* and the New York *Times* found that Hays had invented some incidents and exaggerated others. Acidly commenting on the plentiful supply of outrages, the *Tribune* had noted that so long as there continued to be a profitable market for such sensational stories, they would continue to be manufactured and peddled. Many people had dismissed all reports of southern outrages—not only those in Alabama—as merely Republican efforts to introduce their trump card into the campaign. Thus a lot of northerners had hit upon a tidy solution for absolving themselves of responsibility: combining declarations that they would not tolerate southern lawlessness or efforts to disfranchise the blacks with equally strong assertions that southern lawlessness and disfranchisement hardly existed, they had neatly circumvented any need to act.[50]

Certainly the northerners, with cold skepticism, had quickly quelled any efforts to make much of the Alabama outrages. Yet when the White Leaguers in September had attempted to overthrow the state Republican regime in New Orleans, the North had reacted heatedly, denouncing the audacity of the Democratic revolutionaries and applauding all federal intervention used to put down the rebellion. Although the northerners' response to the coup d'etat in Louisiana had indicated that their ire could still be sparked by events in the South, it had nonetheless been ominous: apparently only a highly visible, dramatic rebellion against a state government could have roused the North from its lethargy in order to muster overwhelming support for a coup de grace.

Republican politicians generally agreed that the Louisiana revolution had occurred at a propitious time. Even its opponents and critics admitted that the Republicans had been lucky once again, with the Louisiana affair turning up just in the nick of time. Instead of the issues of southern policy and reconstruction being shunted aside by most Republicans, as they had been early in the campaign, because of the coup in New Orleans the southern counterrevolution had become a leading issue in the North in the closing weeks of the canvass. Many politicians had begun to predict that the old Republican magic might be somewhat belatedly casting its spell: northern voters, once again repelled and alarmed by southern terror, would resist it by voting Republican. Similarly, the Democratic St. Louis *Republican* had warned southern Democrats that continued violence in the South during the campaign would "re-radicalize the north, give the republican party a new lease of power, defeat the democracy in every northern state, insure the enactment of the civil rights bill, and provoke from Congress a harsher supplement of reconstruction than has yet been witnessed."[51]

The New York *Times* counseled that, by their actions, southerners were only forging chains to continue their own bondage to southern Republican rule. And the Democratic Louisville *Courier-Journal* calculated that every murdered black in the South would produce many additional Republican votes in the North. Current violence, according to the newspaper, had already dashed the Democrats' hopes for a majority in Congress and had supplied Washington with ample pretext to invoke emergency measures, including virtual declaration of martial law. The Utica *Herald* noted that the Republican party had been renewed by the transfusion of fresh blood shed in the

South, and that the party once again, as in other postwar elections, would reap the benefit of the reflexive northern reaction to a rebel howl and a southern outrage. Such sentiment could be measured only by the fall elections in the populous states of the North: it was there that control of Congress would be decided.[52]

10
REFERENDUM ON RECONSTRUCTION
The Congressional Election of 1874

IMMEDIATELY after the Democratic uprising at New Orleans in mid-September, Republican leaders became convinced that once again the North would be receptive to their traditional campaign message. Changing their tactics from those of the previous months, many Republicans again trotted out the specter of Democratic resurgence, namely, that all that had been won on the battlefield and all the laws of reconstruction that Congress had passed would amount to nothing if the Democrats won. A prominent Philadelphia Negro, William D. Forten, asked whether the Republicans would wish to be held responsible by coming generations for all the terrible results that would follow were the Democratic party allowed to return to power. So what the Republican politicians did was to step up the war dance, insisting that the party of treason and slavery had to be defeated.[1]

The Maine election results in mid-September seemed to bear out their reasoning and were a balm to the Republicans, especially when compared to the returns in traditionally Republican Vermont, where elections had been held in early September, before the blowup in Louisiana. In Vermont, the Republicans' weakness had been clearly pointed up in the rejection of stalwart Congressman Luke P. Poland, just as it had been in the state contests in which the Republican majority in the legislature had been drastically reduced as a result of stunning upsets in seats held by Republicans for a generation.[2] But in Maine, despite all expectations, the Democrats failed to gain a single congressional seat and suffered a loss in their percentage of the gubernatorial vote. According to the Cincinnati *Commercial*, that unexpected stroke of luck decidedly checked the Democrats' advances and was directly attributable to the Louisiana insurrection and to the White Leaguers' emphasis on a white man's government.[3]

Soon after, however, the Republican tactics seemed to lose their effectiveness. In the North the sense of outrage over Louisiana subsided within a fortnight, and with it, the momentary support for firm control of southern affairs. Ironically, the chronic chaos in Louisiana was soon to be used as a counterargument to the effect that the Republicans, because of their inability to rule, could not possibly maintain their power much longer, and that continued support of those fragile dependents on the federal government was futile. Actually, such mercurial changes in public opinion indicated that many northern Republicans could not decide whether to continue the attempt to influence events in the South or to give up the struggle. There was also evident distaste for relying once again on the army to prop up Kellogg.

Thus Louisiana had suddenly become yet another Republican handicap, and by late September the party again seemed to be without any viable campaign issue. Naturally, the Republicans were anxious about the fact that public opinion was against them, and their anxiety was reflected in the surprising omission of an outrage report by the Chattanooga convention. As a New York *Tribune* reporter surmised, the "'outrage' business had already been overdone"—an opinion that was apparently shared by a number of Republican politicians. Indeed the Louisville *Courier-Journal*'s Washington correspondent, on October 12, reported that one observer who had just returned from upstate New York's Finger Lakes district, which had nourished the antislavery movement, had discovered that such frequent appeals on the eve of elections had by then "entirely lost their force." On that same day the Chicago *Times* remarked that northern voters were not so foolish as to get excited over the outrage business because they were so accustomed to hearing about southern atrocities at election time. Such views were underscored by similar observations in more independent journals.[4]

The major tests of strength were the congressional contests on October 13 in Indiana, Ohio, Nebraska, and Iowa. They were not only important in themselves but, if the results were decisive, they would affect the outcome in other congressional contests in November. The New York *World*, for example, counted on a bandwagon effect if there were a Democratic victory in Indiana: "each hundred votes of our majority there in October will influence a thousand votes elsewhere in November, encouraging the timid in our own ranks and carrying dismay into the ranks of our adversaries."[5] In the Ohio canvass the controversy over monetary policy was the most publicized issue, but perhaps not the most potent. Like the temperance cause, the currency issue cut several ways in different parts of the state, helping one party in a particular region and doing harm to that same party in another. Reconstruction matters were also prominent and probably more significant. Ohio Republicans were then cautiously avoiding any discussions on the future of the civil rights bill, concentrating instead on the past recalcitrance of southerners and on the current disturbances in the South. When pressed by the Democrats into any mention of civil rights, many leading Ohio Republicans, such as Senator John Sherman, endorsed separate but equal schools in those localities where blacks were numerous. And Republican politicians explained that the defeat of the bill in the House of Representatives was necessary in order to delete certain of its provisions. Yet despite such tacking away from dangerous subjects, the state campaign was, according to one Ohioan, "very hard pulling for the party this fall. . . . I never seen so much dissatisfaction with the People as there is at present . . . to leave the Grand Old Party and go over to the enemy."[6]

If there were defections in the moderate wing of the party, there was exhaustion in its radical ranks. A former member of Congress, George W. Julian, after visiting a cemetery monument to abolitionist Joshua R. Giddings in the Western Reserve of Ohio, wrote in his diary: "The abolition element has almost died out in that old stronghold of radicalism, as it has in so many others throughout the country and the few antislavery pioneers who remain seem to feel lonely and lost." Their momentum had not carried them much beyond the war, he lamented, and they no longer had the heart or strength of mind to wrestle with any new question. Noting the tepidness of those who had been zealous about emancipation, the London *Observer* commented: "people who risked their lives and property for a cause which they believed to be holy so long as it was struggling, now talk dubiously and hesitatingly of the results of emancipation." The cause of the Negro, it remarked, seemed to appeal more to idealism and to people's sense of drama when the blacks were apt to be bought and sold on the slave block than when they were involved in politics and patronage or tainted by their supposed corruption and factional intrigue. At that point, many abolitionists had become "disappointed and chagrined. They did not count upon anarchy and bloodshed and disturbance being the first crop to be reaped on a field which they had tilled so laboriously."[7]

As for the Ohio Democrats, they concentrated their fire upon the Republicans' mismanagement, centralization, and corruption, while deploring both their reconstruction policy and the civil rights bill. Typical was George H. Pendleton, who opposed the increasing power of the federal government for its meddling in the private lives of citizens. He promised that the Democracy would limit and localize power. Harking back to Jefferson, he maintained that the best government governs least.[8]

In pivotal Indiana, the Republicans were also running scared. Much was at stake—control of the state legislature, the federal senatorship, and the congressional seats. Consequently, expediency prevailed at the Republican state convention, with the platform being sufficiently bland and conciliatory on all subjects to avoid offending anyone likely to vote the ticket, an approach that prohibited mention of the civil rights bill. In contrast, the Democrats put forward a state platform with a raw racist appeal, opposing integrated schools, denouncing the pending civil rights bill as forced social equality, and attacking the Republicans as the oppressors of the white people of the South, and, by implication, the oppressors of the white people in the North by way of mischievous centralism and misplaced paternalism.

Clearly, civil rights and racially mixed schools were more than academic questions in Indiana, because the black population could be significant as a voting bloc and thus was a political issue. Indeed, a state court had recently ruled that Negroes could not be excluded from a public school attended by whites. In an attempt to straddle the volatile question, Senator Morton espoused separate but equal education and maintained that the civil rights bill would be complied with if black children merely had equal advantage in separate schools, despite the fact that an amendment proposing just that had been rejected by the Senate on May 22; on the other hand, he did endorse the bill, though it had not been endorsed in the state platform. What the two parties in the state canvass did was put on an old-fashioned show of mutual denunciation: Hoosier voters would have to choose between Republicans who pandered to the sectionalism of the bloody shirt and Democrats who pandered to the racism of the "damnigger."[9]

Early in the canvass some Indiana Democrats conceded that they could not regain the legislature, now divided into gerrymandered districts by the Republicans. Many midwestern Republicans, however, were disturbed by signs of slackening partisan loyalty. The state party chairman reported that at a time when funds were most needed, contributions were lower than usual. After the Louisiana coup, the Republicans did their best to keep indignation alive by disseminating sensationalist stories about conditions in the South; the campaigners were advised to exploit southern outrages to the hilt. But here, as elsewhere, this tactic only worked for a while; by the end of September it began to have less influence.[10]

On election day the state Republican party chairman in Indianapolis telegraphed during the polling: "things are hot here today. The enemy is desperate and have resorted to the foulest of means. Tell our friends to get out every vote." Yet despite all the last-minute efforts, the Republicans were routed across the state. The legislature and the senatorial seat were lost, and control of the state congressional delegation also changed hands, with the Democrats obtaining a large majority by gaining five seats. There were even stunning upsets in traditionally safe Republican districts, where incumbents were cut down like chaff; most of those who escaped defeat won by slim, sometimes infinitesimal, majorities. Of course, many experienced politicians had expected defeat, but they had never dreamed of a Waterloo.[11]

In explaining it, a number of analysts agreed that whatever the reasons for voter disaffection, it was the Republican losses, not the Democratic gains, that had determined the results. The state Republican chairman attributed the defeat to the large number of Republican voters who stayed at home because of their general dissatisfaction with the Grant administration. Republican Congressman John Coburn declared that his own defeat was due as much to party blunders and embarrassing congressional investigations of corruption in Washington as to such local issues as temperance. Democratic Governor Thomas A. Hendricks and Joseph E. McDonald, state Democratic party chairman and future federal senator, agreed. Similarly, the Indianapolis *Journal*, the state Republican organ, interpreted the election as a clear vote of no confidence in the party.[12]

Another view was that of the New York *Times*'s Indiana reporter, who singled out the pending civil rights bill as having caused defeat in the southern part of the state. That judgment was confirmed in Washington, where politicians, according to a Washington dispatch to the *Times*, ascribed defeats to agitation over the civil rights bill, "with which very few politicians privately have any sympathy," and regarded the measure as "certainly causing the loss of Indiana." Several observers also believed that the Republican strategy of stressing southern outrages had been overdone and had boomeranged, especially in those districts in the northern part of the state where Liberal Republicans, who were less likely than the regulars to be impressed by such appeals, were strongest. A further liability for the incumbent party was the continuing depression. And it was indeed for all those reasons that the Republicans in Indiana had, in the words of one Hoosier, received a "grand good thrashing."[13]

In Ohio, where the vote was relatively heavier than in Indiana, the Democrats tripled their increase over the Republicans in the state contest, and in the congressional contests the initial positions of the two parties were precisely reversed: the Democrats now held thirteen seats, leaving the Republicans with the Democrats' previous seven; and in those same contests the Democrats won 51 percent of the statewide congressional vote rather than the previous 48. A Democrat even took the strongly Republican Cleveland district—a drastic change—and Republicans in four other districts were barely elected. Many Republicans had either stayed at home (reports estimated that fifty thousand to eighty thousand of them had not voted) or voted Democratic. Thus the statewide results were the clearest indication so far in 1874 that the Democrats were on the offensive, for it was only the second time in nineteen years that Ohio had gone Democratic.[14]

"We are busted, squelched, scooped!" admitted one Republican newspaper. Some at first claimed that the temperance question had contributed greatly to the results, but as the full returns came in, it was clear that although the question had complicated and confused voting patterns, it had not been a primary cause of defeat, for the independent prohibitionist vote had decreased by 2,000. Moreover, the Democratic majority for the state ticket was 17,202, whereas its statewide congressional majority was 25,542, a fact which disposed of the notion that a local dispute such as prohibition had caused the Republican congressional debacle. The Democrats, too, had differing views on the reasons for their success. The inflationists claimed that it was a victory for inflation, whereas the deflationists declared that hard money had won the day; others stressed that the depression had surely not helped the party in power. Still other Democrats attributed their victory to a demand for retrenchment and reform.[15]

Although insisting that bad nominations were the root cause, the Washington *National Republican* did acknowledge that the defeat would be attributed to "dissatisfaction with the National Administration, to the civil rights bill, the Southern problem, the third term." An Ohio paper noted the widespread "hostility to [the] social fanaticism" regarded as implicit in the civil rights bill. And a Democrat, a former member of Congress, Lewis D. Campbell, regarded the election of a Democratic representative from the previously Republican Dayton district as due to "that sentiment of opposition to this line of legislation [the civil rights bill] that had an immense influence on the vote in the Fourth Ohio District." Similarly, the Democratic victor in the third congressional district, John S. Savage, stated unequivocally the major cause of the Republican downfall: "It is the opposition of the people to what is known as the Civil Rights Bill." Both of those districts had elected Republican congressmen in 1872 but had brought back the Democrats in 1874; both were in southwestern Ohio, where the blacks were concentrated but not numerous enough to offset the whites' dissatisfaction with civil rights legislation. Likewise, in southeastern Ohio, where there was another cluster of blacks, the Democrats had defeated a Republican incumbent in the eleventh congressional district. A New York *Times* reporter believed that the issue of civil rights had importantly influenced a great many Ohio voters, a particularly important fact, since the census revealed that except for Kansas the state had the highest proportion of blacks in the Midwest. Then, of course, there was the observation that southern outrages were no more effective in propelling Republicans to the polls in Ohio than they had been in Indiana.[16]

The returns in the midwestern elections had sounded the depths of the prevailing current. In the nation at large, congressional elections had been held so far in nine states out of thirty-seven; sixty-two congressmen, one fifth of the House, had been selected, with Republicans sustaining a devastating net loss of eleven seats. Despite a considerable number of districts gerrymandered by Republicans, the Democrats had elected thirty-seven congressmen. Many independent observers acknowledged that the result showed the resurgent vitality of the Democratic party and a general disgust with what was regarded as Republican misgovernment in the South.[17]

The southern Democrats were particularly jubilant about the results in the Midwest. In the belief that the Democrats' victory would gradually help the South to escape from reconstruction, the Louisville *Courier-Journal* advised them that the only way to win a national victory in November was to use conciliation and moderation in the remaining campaigns in the North, so that they might recruit moderate Republican voters. Thus southern Democrats should emphasize patience and prudence in the South in order to prevent racial disturbances, hold onto the conservatives and moderates, and not upset the national Democratic applecart. The Memphis *Appeal* declared: "Day is dawning. The era of restoration draws nigh; the hours of the carpet-baggers are numbered."[18]

On October 15 the Washington *National Republican* grudgingly conceded the midwestern elections to have been a serious setback, although most Republican newspapers continued in their efforts to build up morale with talk of victory; indeed, the Philadelphia *Press* quite simply dismissed the defeat: "yesterday's straws were moved by a very feeble wind." Putting forth an ambitious last-ditch effort, the party staged grand rallies and giant parades, full of the excitement of flags flying, drums beating, fireworks sparking, and speeches soaring. Energy and resources were concentrated on the two main battlegrounds, New York and Pennsylvania, in the hope of stemming the tide. Reportedly, the administration was making special provisions for federal employees in Washington who were voters in either state to be returned to the polls at half fare, with fifteen days leave of absence as an added inducement.[19]

In private, however, Republican politicians, southern and northern, were increasingly pessimistic. After canvassing southern Republican delegates at the Chattanooga convention in October, Alabama Senator Spencer had reported that most southern congressional districts were hopelessly Democratic and that there was no chance of salvaging them. Republican Congressman James S. Negley of Pittsburgh didn't mince words: all the forces that had been at work in Ohio and Indiana were also at work in Pennsylvania and would, he thought, produce similar effects. He deplored the "unbearable" apathy or hostility of the Republicans, as well as the low campaign contributions. The party, he remarked, was rowing against wind and tide in this election. Still other Republicans regarded their party's frantic efforts as a futile attempt to sweep back an advancing tidal wave with a mop. Congressman Garfield admitted that he had no expectations of success and, on October 31, wrote that if the Republicans lost elsewhere as they had in Ohio and Indiana, the Democrats would capture the next House of Representatives. Postmaster General Jewell predicted that the Democrats would win control of the House: "we need a little punishment, but we don't want as much as this." And consul William C. Howells found the Republican party quite incapable of braking the momentum of its downhill course.[20]

By the end of October, with the general election just days away, many Republicans became panicky. There was some open backbiting, which suggested that certain candidates were giving up because they anticipated defeat. In need of a scapegoat, some of them claimed that Grantism was on trial, not themselves. Governor Dix, who decided to try to save not only the party in New York but his own candidacy as well, publicly repudiated a third term for Grant. It was a desperate expedient—jettisoning the cargo to lighten the sinking ship. Even Congressman Benjamin F. Butler, increasingly concerned during the closing weeks of the campaign, stepped up his speaking schedule and, by election eve, grew anxious about the size of his majority. On October 31 the Washington *National Republican*, also seeking a scapegoat, placed responsibility for the party's perilous situation on the "Daweses and Garfields," who furnished the Democrats with the knife to cut the party's throat because of their "party treason, cowardice, stupidity, imbecility, ignorance," and their support of congressional investigations of corruption. The paper asked where the old party spirit, the fire and faith of earlier years, had gone, and why it had been replaced by "distrust and dissatisfaction, divided councils and wavering lines, captains with uncertain companies, generals with uncertain battalions."[21]

A note of desperation also crept into a cabinet discussion just before the November election, when some members pressed President Grant to disavow a third term, which had become an embarrassing issue in some of the contests, especially in New York. Grant replied that the whole matter was too unbecoming and too absurd to deserve comment. Other members of the cabinet believed that a president's disavowal on the eve of an election would be taken as a personal confession of serious concern. So with the outrage appeal yielding diminishing returns, the Republicans tried to avoid defeat by frantically pushing the hard-money issue late in the New York and Pennsylvania campaigns, attacking the Democracy as prone to inflation. But above all, the Republicans hoped that the past—their proud record of achievement and the emotions and loyalties of wartime— would see them through.[22]

On election day, November 3, 1874, a Kansan wrote: "I think today will make a great deal of history for this country. I look upon the results of the elections today as second in importance only to that of 1860." From Washington, correspondents noted that there was feverish betting and that the elections completely preoccupied ordinary citizens and politicians alike. Given all the intense excitement, the contest was more in the nature of a presidential race than of an off-year congressional election.[23]

Early returns trickling in stunned the administration, as they revealed the likelihood of a crushing defeat for the Republicans. In contrast, jubilant Democrats quickly organized rallies in the capital. As more of the returns came in, the reactions grew in intensity. One Republican Senate employee remarked that he had never seen so many sad faces in his life. As for President Grant, he reportedly read all the dispatches, then threw them carelessly aside in almost ostentatious disregard; and on the day following the election he refused all visitors and remained in seclusion.[24]

What the October elections had foreshadowed, the November elections fulfilled. When all the results were in, the Republican defeat was clearly the greatest upset in national politics since 1854. It was the first catastrophe in the Republican party's twenty-year history and inaugurated an extraordinary shift in power. "The Republican Party Struck by Lightning," declared the Republican Buffalo *Advertiser*. Politicians had expected reverses, but not of such magnitude. As Congressman Garfield wrote: the "people have gone crazy." The seed of opposition had sprouted more vigorously than could have been supposed, observed the editor of the Springfield *Republican* Samuel Bowles.[25] For the Democrats not only captured the House of Representatives for the first time since the beginning of the war, but transformed a Republican majority of 110 into a Democratic majority of 60, a momentous change indeed. The new House was to be made up of 109 Republicans and 169 Democrats, in contrast to the previous division of 198 Republicans and 88 Democrats, thus increasing the Democrats' strength for two fifths of the House to more than one half. Actually, their strength was even greater than the figures indicated because of the additional support of the independents, who were for the most part sympathetic to the Democracy.[26]

Among the prominent Republicans to be defeated was the party warhorse, Congressman Butler, of whom the New York *Times*, never a supporter of this controversial figure, noted, "happily the severest floods carry away the most offensive matter." Butler's defeat meant not only that a formidable politician and radical leader had been cut down, but that a symbol of radicalism as well as a major exponent of Grantism had been smashed. In addition to ending the lengthy careers of a number of leading Republican congressmen, the Democratic victory had upset, in state after state, political patterns that had prevailed for two decades; as a result, the election restored to the Democrats their traditional antebellum control of the House, which they were to retain, with but momentary incursions, for the next two decades.[27]

The Democrats' congressional increases were national in extent and historic in dimension. They won twenty-six seats in the Northeast, and added twenty-two more in the Midwest and Far West. With the additions of thirty-seven seats out of a possible fifty-four in the South and the borderland, the gain throughout the nation came to eighty-five seats. Indeed, the percentage of the popular vote given to the Democrats in the congressional elections of 1874 was the greatest in an off-year congressional election during the period 1870 to 1882. The same trend was shortly reflected in the state legislative elections for seats in the United States Senate: the incumbent proadministration Republican senators were displaced in most instances either by Democrats or by independent Republicans, thus halving the Republican majority and rendering it tenuous and unstable.

Republicans were also defeated in local races. Of the thirteen undisputed state contests decided on November 3, the Democrats won nine, the Republicans, four. In New York popular Governor Dix went down to defeat, and in previously Republican Massachusetts the governorship was lost for the first time since 1858. Pennsylvania also was lost. And even in the few places that had remained Republican in statewide races (Michigan, Kansas, and South Carolina), the Republican totals drastically declined. Out of the thirty-five states that held elections in 1874, twenty-three went Democratic.

Summing up all the contests of the year, the Democrats had been victorious in nineteen gubernatorial races, winning in all but six states, those being rural Republican strongholds. Similarly, in elections for state legislatures the Democrats won handsomely; and again, when the Republicans managed to retain control of a legislature, they did so by greatly reduced margins. According to one 1873 report, the Republicans had had a majority on a joint ballot of both branches of the legislatures (necessary to elect federal senators) of twenty-six states, including all the northern ones, and the Democrats had kept control of only ten. A later analysis showed that in March of 1876 the Republicans held a majority on a joint ballot in only twelve states, and the Democrats in twenty-one, with the Democrats controlling both the executive and legislative branches of sixteen state governments, and the Republicans, but nine. Of the eleven states in which political control was divided, the Democrats, in every case, secured control of that more recently elected branch. It was a Republican rout throughout the nation, and rarely had the Republicans been able to breast the Democratic wave.[28]

The import of this Democratic upsurge and its possible consequences were widely bandied about. Charles Francis Adams regarded the election as a watershed ending an era of sweeping and irresponsible power "under the shambling incompetency of General Grant." The Louisville *Courier-Journal* declared, "Busted. The Radical Machine Gone to Smash," and observed that the Democratic triumph in the nation and in the North meant that southerners were no longer aliens in their native land; the people of both the North and the South had demonstrated their desire for peace, reconciliation, and justice for Dixie.[29]

Certain southerners celebrated the arrival of a new order for the South in a different way. One Tennessean declared that the upheaval "was not an election—it was the Country *coming to a halt and changing front.* . . . The whole scheme of reconstruction stands before the country today a naked, confessed, stupendous failure, at once the most remarkable and the most inexcusable failure in history." Another Democrat believed that the epoch of reconstruction was drawing to a close as "the lights are going out one by one with smoke and stench and the grotesque revelers will soon be reeling homewards displaying their soiled garments and revolting debauch . . . in the accusing broad daylight of triumphant Democracy. *Dios y Libertad* [God and Liberty]." And the southern Democrats' view of one consequence of their victory was spelled out by the Richmond *Enquirer*, on November 10, in a lead editorial entitled "Call Home Your Troops": "There is no longer the shadow of an excuse for a single soldier in the South." Mississippi Governor Ames predicted, in fear, that the "old rebel spirit will not only revive but will make itself felt." Another Republican, noting the ecstasy of the Democrats, commented that such a change of political fortune would elicit only groans from the blacks.[30]

As for the future of the Republican party itself, many people saw it as utterly ruined. According to the New York politico Thurlow Weed, "We are disastrously overthrown and unhappily I do not see or know the statesmen under whose leadership we can hope to retrieve what is lost." The radical Chicago *Inter-Ocean* viewed the Democratic capture of the House as nothing short of calamity; Secretary of State Fish described the results as "very bad—we are just now, so flat on our backs, that we can only be *looking up*—no other way to look." Naturally, certain Republican congressmen found Grant a convenient scapegoat, pronouncing his second term as a failure. He, in turn, blamed them for indecision and inaction. Although there was some measure of truth in all such recriminations, none of them really or adequately explained the 1874 defeat.[31]

A great many causes had combined to produce the disaster, and all of them had been building up for quite a while. Some Republicans had clearly cast a vote of no confidence in their party. Then, too, there had been a desire for change, and it was widely commented on. The Washington *National Republican* likened the voters' craving for it to a railroad "car of revolution [which] came along all covered over with placards of panaceas for all their ills, and in a moment of excitement they jumped on board to try their luck.... It was the insane act of the intoxicated mob, drunk with the excitement of discontent, to be repented of in moments of sobriety." Even an Ohio farmer reportedly remarked that "the people have got tired of lying on one side so long. I guess they are going to roll over." Although a number of independents and Republicans had voted Democratic, many others had either stayed at home or scratched their party ballots by eliminating some of the candidates. Thus the Republican vote fell off enormously in state after state. This varied, of course, in different areas: occasionally white Republicans, as in Tennessee, turned out for the Democrats, whereas many Republicans in the North did not go to the polls.[32]

Certainly the fact that the Republican party was governing the nation when the depression began intensified people's dissatisfaction with its rule. Another cause was said to be a lack of confidence in the administration's way of dealing with it. Yet the returns were not a mandate for any specific financial program, since both parties were about equally divided on the solutions to economic problems, and both western inflationist and eastern deflationist Democrats had been victorious. President Grant went to the heart of the matter when he reportedly observed that economic questions were not strictly partisan matters. To be sure, the failure of Congress to appropriate money for public works, which would have provided jobs, did not win votes for the Republicans, although this, as an issue, had not figured prominently in the campaign.[33]

According to defeated Governor Dix, "No doubt commercial depression had its influence; but the chief reason is the feeling of deepseated dissatisfaction with General Grant's administration." Although many Republican newspapers, especially the Chicago *Inter-Ocean*, did chalk up defeat to the depression, *Harper's Weekly* blamed it solely on the Republicans' thorough disgust with the mismanagement of their own party. And the results were also regarded as a rebuke to the lively ghost of a third term for Grant; yet, despite the third-term hysteria promoted by a few leading newspapers, the issue did not excite voters in most regions of the country. Complaints of Grant's "Caesarism," of course, took their toll, but more important than those much publicized shibboleths were the concerns about unwise policy and unworthy leadership. One observer remarked that too many officials in the administration lacked both party credentials and political pluck: Grant "does not select the representative men to fill his chief places—that's what's the matter! . . . Has he a Cabinet officer who can carry a county in his own State?"[34]

Despite all the charges, including an extraordinary series of scandals over rampant corruption in the administration, which had helped the Democracy, a certain measure of reaction against Republican rule was doubtless inevitable, as Vermont Republican Senator Justin S. Morrill observed. Although Morrill was another who interpreted the election returns as a snub to Grant's wish to run for a third term—a liability which, he lamented, could have been so easily avoided—he also put defeat into perspective, noting that seldom had a party in power during a war long retained power after a return to peace. Since a government must levy taxes, it is held responsible for the business cycle, even, he added sarcastically, for the eclipses of the moon, making adverse reaction virtually inevitable. Moreover, long occupation of office carries with it the penalties of unpopularity; in the course of time, the list of mistakes grows long and the number of dissatisfied people multiplies. But Morrill also argued that such re-action could have been delayed, possibly averted, or at least diminished, had Grant reformed a fair number of obvious abuses.[35]

Whatever the causes, the consequences of victory were beyond dispute, particularly in the South and in the borderland. According to the London *Saturday Review*, the most immediate and important result would be the southern white population's recovery of their ascendancy. Democratic rule had been restored in both the statehouse and governor's mansion in Arkansas and Alabama, as well as in the Florida legislature, so that, given the previous gains of the Democrats, over a half of the eleven former Confederate states had reverted to Democratic control. Only four remained under Republican influence. November also signaled the destruction of several state Republican parties as well as their reduction in other states to mere skeletons, without much support outside black-belt districts. Even in the states still under Republican control, defeat seemed shortly inevitable, for the Democrats' victory in certain southern states would, in the opinion of many northerners, embolden the Democrats to seize power in others. The Republican defeats also meant that the state-wide influence or local power of the blacks would be curtailed or eliminated and that the Democrats would undoubtedly continue, with increased zeal, their efforts to disfranchise black voters. Indeed, throughout the South and the borderland, Republicanism was in its twilight.[36]

Also, the Democrats' extraordinary gains south of the Mason-Dixon line brought increasing national influence to that regional party. Of the necessary 59 additional seats required for the Democrats to secure an absolute majority in the new House of Representatives (assuming that the Democratic incumbents were safe), southern and border Democrats gained 37 (63 percent), which greatly increased their leverage in the national councils of the Democratic party. Indicative of the composition and spirit of the southern and border delegation in the new House was the fact that, according to one analysis, 80 out of 107 members had served in the Confederate army, and it was estimated that there would be 35 former Confederate generals in the next Congress. The weight of southern influence was also underscored by the presence in new House of almost as many southern and border Democrats as there were Republican representatives from the nation as a whole (89 to 109). Another indication of regional predominance was the fact that only 17 southern and border Republicans were left in the House, whereas their Democratic colleagues now numbered 89. It seemed to promise no less than the sudden ascendancy of a House of Bourbons. With the North divided, it was possible that the southern whites would hold the balance of power in the presidential election in 1876. Thus, by 1874, the South had virtually returned to Democratic control and was gaining unprecedented regional solidarity and strength.[37]

With the House of Representatives about to become Democratic, the Republicans would lose their unqualified power to shape national legislation and their control over appropriations. To be sure, the Senate remained Republican, but it would only be able to prevent the repeal of existing laws and defeat any legislative initiatives. Moreover, with a Democratic House and a Republican Senate, the likely prospect of a protracted deadlock between the chambers signaled a period of paralysis in the governance of the country.

Such a change in the national political balance would not have been possible without a sharp and significant shift in attitude in the North, where the Democrats' success was less blatant than in the South but equally important. The rash gamble of the southern Democrats had paid off, for they had accurately gauged the degree to which northern sentiment had changed. For the first time, the southern Democrats' attacks on Republican reconstruction had not provoked an all-out counterattack by northern Republicans and independents, nor had they elicited the usual sympathy for black freedmen and white unionists in the South. As usual, northern Republican politicians had, as a last resort, pitched their campaigns to elicit such a reaction, but unlike in the elections of 1866, 1868, and 1872, it had been unsuccessful. A growing number of people agreed with the Springfield *Republican*'s view that southern outrages were manufactured or magnified. "Never was sheet-iron more vigorously banged to produce counterfeit thunder," the paper declared, adding, "lying begat incredulity, and incredulity has begotten indifference." But the most damning admission of failure to enlist Republican support came from the staunchly proadministration Washington *National Republican*: the "National Republican party of the North has forgotten and ignored their [southern Republicans'] very existence, or has snubbed and flippantly treated their appeals for aid." Southern Republican Akerman inveighed against the "heartless indifference" of northern Republicans toward the southern party; looking back, he remarked that it was a "great misfortune that the North flinched in 1874." In the last analysis, the Republican case rested not so much on the audacious actions of southern whites as on the way those actions had been perceived by northern whites. Since neither the recognition of new provocations nor the recollection of old passions had inspired them, many northern Republicans voted Democratic or simply refused to vote.[38]

These northern Republicans, during the campaign and more frequently after the election, had begun to openly advocate restoration of home rule and to reject reconstruction outright. The Republican New York *Times*, although denying that it had forsaken party principles or changed its reconstruction policy during the campaign, declared after the election: "there is much to do, and much to undo," suggesting that the state governments in the South no longer be maintained by federal force, that the federal government cease all direct or indirect interference in the affairs of southern local governments, and that the Grant government fire not only obnoxious and unrepresentative federal officials in Dixie but even Attorney General Williams, because of his fondness for intervention. In this connection General Sherman observed: "The troops in the South were sent at the instance of the Attorney General Williams who doubtless supposed them necessary to prevent conflict and bloodshed. He may have been right but politically he has brought on a catastrophe which will give infinite trouble. The late elections show how common people regard these things. Coercion by the military has ever been pregnant with danger."[39]

In fact, governance of the South had become a local matter and no longer a national problem. The Republican Boston *Advertiser*, for example, professed no interest in which party controlled the South because the purported alternatives were either injustice to the blacks on the part of the whites or flagrant corruption on the part of the blacks; it also contended that the price of peace was oppression, and the price of humanitarian progress and Republican power was public robbery and economic ruin. Although not indifferent to the fate of the blacks, Postmaster General Jewell sadly and fatalistically came to the same conclusion in December, 1874: "it does look as if the South had gone away from us entirely, and I very much fear we shall hardly get an electoral vote there in '76. The Democrats, secessionists and White Leagues are behaving very badly. They seem determined to crowd out the poor colored people." The radicals viewed the loss of the House as an unmitigated calamity for a reconstructed South. Although exhorting the Republican party to stand firm, they seemed at a loss as to how this could be done, and few were listening to their warnings.[40]

The Democrats, in contrast, were full of plans for the future. Some of them proposed a review of the assorted reconstruction legislation; others called for an investigation of the executive branch by the new Democratic House; still others wished to pressure the president into reshuffling his cabinet; and a few suggested that he be impeached. Nevertheless, at Democratic conclaves following the election, the Democrats, on the whole, were moderate in tone and temper. They did not ask that the results of the war be repudiated or that the reconstruction amendments be repealed. However, they said nothing about the central reconstruction guarantees—suffrage and civil equality—or about the federal laws governing election enforcement. When the New York *World* dismissed the notion of repealing the reconstruction amendments, especially the Fifteenth, it did so primarily because it regarded repeal as impossible, not undesirable. Moreover, prominent war or unionist Democrats were not always invited to celebration rallies, and conspicuous among honored speakers and guests were well known former Confederates or their wartime northern sympathizers.[41]

There was also a curious ambivalence in some Democratic editorials. Although pledging to enforce equal rights, they clearly expressed disbelief in both the principle and the practice of equality. The Troy, New York, *Press*, for instance, declared: "We despise 'universal suffrage,' but it is the law of the land, and every law must be enforced." And the Mobile *Register* commented: "Whatever we may think of the duplicity of the 14th. Amendment and of the impolicy of the 15th. Amendment, it is no more possible to blot out the results of these Amendments than it would be to repeal the 13th. Amendment itself." The Republican *Harper's Weekly* viewed such professions with skepticism, alluding to the Democratic record: "while it [the Democracy] preaches the golden rule and brotherly love, it sees the negro hunted and harried without protest." The Providence *Journal* observed that northern Democrats were fond of speaking of all the questions that had grown out of the war and reconstruction as dead issues, but warned that they were not dead to the southern Democrats. Indeed, noted the New York *Times*, the Democrats were "trying to allay natural apprehensions in the North by the assurance that the war questions will never be disturbed while they are courting in every way the support of that portion of the Southern people which is bound by interest and prejudice to reawaken those questions." Although the New York *World* also claimed that the Democratic party's intention was not to make war on the reconstruction amendments, it went on to observe that the Democracy did oppose the unconstitutional, unnecessary, unjust laws on the books, which were purportedly enacted under the pretext of enforcing the amendments. The paper pledged that the Democrats would execute the constitutional amendments "honestly, impartially, and fearlessly," but at the same time declared: "We shall not tolerate laws that elevate the black man above the white; or laws that create offences which the amendments never intended should be a subject of Federal cognizance; or laws that will enable Federal officers to exercise a dangerous control over State elections." It seemed doubtful that, in such a spirit, even the letter of the law could survive intact.[42]

Although the amendments could not be repealed, the Democrats could paralyze the laws that had been framed to enforce them. And to attack those laws was to attack the amendments themselves: "if the former go down the latter must follow," remarked the Chicago *Inter-Ocean*. Perhaps indirection and inaction would suffice. Election enforcement was already collapsing, and the new House, with the power of the purse, could easily curtail the program by imposing a stringent economy, decreasing the size of the army, and attempting to restrict the use of troops; it could also conduct investigations to uncover damaging evidence concerning the administration's governance of the South, so as to further discredit Grant and his party.[43]

The congressional election had been a referendum not only on reconstruction but also on civil rights, and not only in the South and in the borderland, where the civil rights measure had been the major cause of the Republican debacle, but also in many northern districts as well, where the issue of the pending bill had frequently elicited interest, even passionate concern. In the lower North it had helped the Democrats greatly, especially in the states that had both a black population and school segregation—New Jersey, Ohio, Pennsylvania, Indiana, and Illinois. A man from northern Illinois wrote that Americans were fed up with "undue efforts to force civil rights at the expense of *all rights*." What the people wanted was "*rest*, stability, prosperity, and the *greatest individual liberty possible*." President Grant apparently agreed that the issue of civil rights had proved to be a grave liability; he reportedly told friends after the election that he was firmly convinced that the civil rights bill had more to do with the defeat of the party than all the other causes combined, because its features embracing social equality were distasteful to almost all whites.[44]

Even the once staunchly radical Republican Benjamin F. Wade commented in an interview that passage of the civil rights bill in the Senate had provoked the electorate in the southern, border, and midwestern states to such a degree that they voted against the Republican party for fear of mixed schools. Wade did not doubt that the bill was right in principle, but he was also certain that it was impossible to put into practice at the time: "a thing may be right in the abstract, and yet not be expedient, because public sentiment will not tolerate or accept the full application of the principle." Postmaster General Jewell similarly observed that the Republican party "never gained by it [the civil rights bill], but lost all the time. It was a Pandora's Box left us by Sumner." Washburne bitterly agreed: "if his [Sumner's] object could have been, in thrusting it forward, to destroy the Republican party, he would have been gratified at his success, had he lived." Defeated New Jersey Republican Representative William W. Phelps's view was that "if there was any one issue on which we went to the country it was this. . . . And upon this issue the two great parties went to judgment. And the people last fall declared their judgment, and with a thunder that shook one hundred members out of these seats."[45]

Democrat Richard Vaux saw the civil rights question as having caused a huge rift in the Republican ranks when the moderates, in revolt against the radical minority, forsook the party. To him the popular Democratic congressional majority in Pennsylvania "plainly shows the intent and meaning of the voter, and strikes at the Civil rights bill . . . the negro, southern outrages by radicals for power . . . and the policy of the Radicals in the Legislation in Congress." The Louisville *Courier-Journal* and the Baltimore *Sun*, among other Democratic newspapers, agreed that the Republican defeat had been due largely to moderate Republicans putting a check on what was regarded as ultra radicalism.[46]

The election seemed to confirm, at least in part, the fact that the Negro had become too closely and exclusively identified with the Republican party in the eyes of many white Republicans. Two years earlier, Ohioan Jacob Cox had advised that the Republicans not adopt civil rights as a party test but limit their position to defending the status quo. However, he contended that party leaders had refused to take this advice, and, instead, by insisting that the party could be kept together "on the negro question alone, they have made it irrevocably the 'negro party' and must 'fight it out on that line.' It will die, as a national party, whenever voters enough drop off in consequence of these ultraisms to leave us in the minority." After the 1874 elections, Cox observed that emancipation, the Republican party cause, had long "degenerated into an exploiting of everything pertaining to the negro, with a deliberate purpose of making capital out of it." He attacked those radical Republicans who "did not care a coffer for Civil Rights or 'outrages,' real or sham, but used all these things to keep up the cry of radical progress and hold together the well-meaning people whose votes kept them in power."[47]

Unfortunately, there was much truth in the bigoted *Brownson's Quarterly Review*'s harsh judgment that "the forced enthusiasm for the negro is dying out." As Dr. Wells Brown, a Boston Negro, had publicly declared earlier in September: "There is a feeling all over this country that the negro has got about as much as he ought to have." Indeed, by 1874, most white Americans believed that the black man had been cossetted enough; for them he had become the party pet and the national pest. Stories that put the blacks in a bad light were increasingly seized upon and more widely believed. The northerners, stated one American consul in January, 1875, had reached the point at which they wished the "'nigger,' 'everlasting nigger,' was in—— or Africa!" And in point of fact, increasing opposition to federal enforcement and intervention in the South and a distaste for reconstruction rights were all symptoms of a deeper racist reaction.[48]

But this gradual though decisive change in feeling toward reconstruction and the Negro would not have created such a dramatic difference in the election results of 1874 had it not been for the Senate civil rights bill, which served as the catalyst that greatly hastened the reaction against reconstruction. As journalist Charles Nordhoff chided the Republicans, they had only themselves to blame for giving such ammunition to their opponents. Indeed, it was a political bomb that blew apart the southern Republican party and the congressional party. Thus the more visible counterrevolution in the South during 1874, achieved by bullets as well as ballots, was attended by a calmer but very damaging counterrevolution in the North.[49] The election signified that the era of reconstruction was rapidly coming to an end, and that, along with it, the legacy of the war would soon pass from politics into history.[50]

11

INSIGNIFICANT VICTORY

The Civil Rights Act of 1875

WHEN members of the Forty-third Congress met in early December under the shadow of the November elections, most of them had little expectation of accomplishing much in that lame-duck session. Many Republicans had predicted that their thunderous defeat at the polls would impose caution. If they were to regain lost ground so they could retain the presidency in 1876, the party's congressmen had necessarily to adjust to the country's conservative trend by avoiding unpopular legislation. Democratic congressmen could not afford to blunder either. Since they were powerless until the new Congress convened at the end of 1875, they intended to talk little and proceed slowly, but nonetheless guard against any last-minute Republican schemes. Determined to do nothing that might hinder their pursuit of the presidency in 1876, they planned to confine their efforts to the investigation of corruption and to retrenchment in federal spending.[1]

In the short final session (only fifty-six working days) Congress, according to Samuel Bowles, would do no more than enact "half-way measures, neutral policies, the doing of nothing." Indeed, the last meeting of the outgoing Congress was expected to serve as the occasion for a funeral of the majority party, its mournful representatives assembling to put in an appearance at the wake. Thus the pending civil rights bill appeared to be dead, not only at that point but thereafter, given the fact that a Democratic House would soon be in charge. If support for such a law had been shaky before the election, what else could one believe after it had been rejected at the polls?[2]

But all such prophesies of a dull, uneventful session were premature. The Republicans, stubborn and desperate, and refusing to retire quietly, gambled with a belated, perhaps last, opportunity to rescue their party. To reverse the Democratic trend, they—especially the radical contingent—began to develop a number of plans: the enactment of a civil rights law to retain the loyalty of southern blacks; additional federal election enforcement legislation—the so-called "force bill"—to counter disfranchisement of southern blacks; changes in the electoral college by constitutional amendment to improve the Republican candidate's chances of election in the event of a dispute in the 1876 presidential contest; the strengthening of southern Republican regimes by overturning the Democratic rule of Governor Augustus H. Garland in Arkansas and seating Louisiana's senatorial claimant, Pinckney B. S. Pinchback, and, possibly, by installing provisional military or territorial governments elsewhere in the South if conditions warranted it; the admission of new Republican states (Colorado and New Mexico) to gain additional electoral votes and to help hold onto their control of the Senate; two-year appropriations for the army and the Department of Justice, to ensure their continuing operation, especially in such matters as election enforcement and pacification, even if the future Democratic House of Representatives refused to authorize funds; and finally, the launching of congressional investigations of southern states to provide justification for such a program and to supply issues for the forthcoming presidential campaign.[3]

Perversely, the election results and the nature of the campaign were what gave the seemingly defunct civil rights bill new life. Even then, some Democrats uneasily noted that without an election close at hand the reason for the House not having acted on a civil rights bill in 1874 no longer existed.[4]

In the opinion of some Republicans, the need for such legislation had increased as a result of the wholesale violation of civil rights that had accompanied the recent elections. As a Maine Republican commented, it was "manifest that after our *shock* of last fall there is a reaction going on and sober men are asking if we are again to go under the yoke of secessionists or rebels—in fact, I am often asked— are we to fight the old battles over again? I think much depends upon the action of the present Congress on the civil rights bill. Do all you possibly can, constitutionally, to protect and secure *every* American citizen against local attempts to crush him to the earth. This is to be the great issue." New York Republican John Binny noted that blacks "expect a measure to be passed while we have the power," but he cautioned: "it requires time to prepare for such changes. . . . Do what you can by skillful policy to gain the southern votes but use no arbitrary and violent measures as they will react terribly against us."[5]

Thus once again expediency and idealism were brought forth with new variations on old themes. Pragmatic Republicans argued that action on the measure could still help enlist black support in a future bid to regain power in the South. After all, there had been too many Negro defections and abstentions there in the recent election; the only way to rally and reunite that bloc of voters—in order to keep the power and electoral votes of the few southern states that still remained in the Republican camp—was to make civil rights the law of the land, thereby renewing the Negro voter's loyalty to the party. Even if the issue had lost the white voter in the South, contended the Boston *Journal*, the party would be foolish to abandon it now and lose the black voter as well. And indeed, one Mississippian reported that not only was the patience of blacks there nearing its end, but that they expected Republicans in Congress to heed their requests for a civil rights law. As a New Yorker pointedly remarked, "the men who carry with them the colored vote will prevail in '76."[6]

Some Republicans, Congressman Benjamin F. Butler, for example, who was a frequent advocate of radical legislation and the floor manager of the civil rights bill, wished to put into law one last noble expression of Republicanism. Other Republicans, having apparently learned nothing from the last election, continued to hope that advocacy of the bill as a party measure might somehow reanimate some of the old fervor in the ranks of northern white Republicans. Such reasoning was dismissed by their opponents as a foolish and outmoded faith in the power of moral principles to sustain the waning fortunes of the politicians who for years had exploited the issue of the Negro for party gain. Still other supporters, more fatalistic than idealistic, contended that regardless of what happened to the measure, the Democrats would make civil rights an issue in

1876: "we have this thing to fight—either way: so let us Put Civil Right Through," declared a Maryland Republican. After all, the bill had already done the party so much damage in the fall elections that were it to pass, the Republican Congress would reap rewards for its courage and impartial justice, whereas the Democrats, implacable in their hostility to blacks, would be seen in an embarrassing reactionary light. Still others were not sure that the bill would ever be an asset to the Republicans, but believed that it nonetheless ought to be passed in order to dispose of it permanently and prevent it from continuing as an unsettled issue in the presidential campaign.[7]

Radical Republicans hoped the party would redeem its reputation by building a bulwark for the protection of black citizens. The Chicago *Inter-Ocean* reasoned that failure to enact the measure would be proof of timidity and prejudice and would permanently mar the party's record. The bill was the culmination of the policy of reconstruction, and if the party were really "on the decline, and approaching a speedy dissolution," the radical newspaper suggested that "its last days be signalized by a sublime effort for the right." A further incentive to proponents of the bill was the Indiana supreme court's ruling which upheld a law of that state excluding blacks from white public schools. Several journals then regarded federal civil rights legislation as even more urgently needed to counteract such adverse state court decisions in the North. Moreover, there was discussion in Washington about establishing a fund from the sale of federal land for support of public schools in proportion to the rate of a state's illiteracy—which, in effect, meant a federal subsidy for southern and border-state schools, where illiteracy of both blacks and whites was higher—as a sweetener to secure passage of a civil rights bill and to broaden its popular support.[8]

The members of the House judiciary committee discussed the legislative possibilities of the civil rights bill throughout December. Most of them wanted a measure to be enacted, and they intended to drive it through Congress and get it approved by the president. Casting about for a way to ensure its passage, a number of proposals were considered. One suggestion, made by a subcommittee (consisting entirely of lame ducks, including Butler), went so far as to suggest equal but separate facilities for all accommodations for blacks, an alternative altogether contrary to the elimination of the caste system. It was defeated, however, by the full committee, which, on the other hand, also refused to accept the Senate bill in its original form, in the belief that it had no chance of being approved by the House or of being signed by the president because of its provisions for mixed schools and shared cemeteries. Finally, the committee agreed to scrap these two troublesome clauses, thus making the bill more palatable to the public as well as to Grant, who, it was assumed, would not veto the revised form. As an added compromise, the amended version, which was approved by the committee on December 16, explicitly accepted the maintenance of separate schools by race, but required equal educational advantages in all other respects.[9]

The reaction of Republican newspapers was generally favorable. According to the Washington *National Republican*, there could be no serious objection to the legislation now that the school clause mandating racial mixing had been eliminated. Similarly, the Boston *Advertiser* believed that the compromise would greatly strengthen support for the bill. There was, however, some criticism in moderate circles. Although an editorial in the Springfield *Republican* characterized the altered measure as good politics as well as common sense, its editor, Samuel Bowles, in a special report from Washington warned that such a bill would perhaps be "so emasculated in details as to leave little but a declaration of the principle."[10]

Most of the criticism came from old abolitionist stalwarts and from blacks. Wendell Phillips, for example, considered the new House version a dangerous concession to the South and a great injury to the quality of public education everywhere; he also denounced the provision for legally sanctioning the principle of caste and the policy of maintaining racially segregated schools. Other antislavery veterans contended that acceptance of the so-called separate but equal formula was dangerous as a legal precedent, and that once such discrimination was established in law it could be extended to cover all privileges of citizenship. Abolitionist Elizur Wright complained bitterly that "even the foremost 'republican' politicians [were] going back on the Civil Rights Bill written in crocodile tears for Sumner yet moist on their handkerchiefs." And though, as *Harper's Weekly* contended, Congress might not be able to banish racial prejudice by law, it certainly ought not strengthen it by perpetuating inequality before the law.[11]

Among the blacks who protested that the new House version was unjust and insulting, one Kentucky Negro denounced the Republicans in Congress as cringing, vacillating, and temporizing in the deletion of equal educational opportunity; the secretary of the Pennsylvania Equal Rights League, William Forten, described the bill in its new form as inconsistent, incomplete, and ineffectual; and the San Francisco *Elevator*, a black newspaper, decried the proposed measure as a pretense for a civil rights bill, since its most important feature had been omitted, its general enforcement provision weakened, and its penalties for noncompliance reduced from five thousand to five hundred dollars in some instances. Without integrated education, it concluded, the measure was a mockery. Similarly, a Boston Negro wrote that without a provision for mixed schools in the bill, "no intelligent high minded colored man would give a straw for it. . . . If the Republican party is to die *let it die game!* "[12]

When it reconvened after the holiday recess, Congress, in January, 1875, was confronted with a new crisis in Louisiana which swept all other considerations aside. The army had marched into the Louisiana legislature to oust some of its Democratic members, and so party heat was rising and the tempers of congressmen were exploding more violently every day. When a Democrat would denounce illegal interference in a state government, a Republican would often defend or rationalize the action, and the protracted debate drew party lines so tight that members rarely strayed across them. The acrimonious discussion over Louisiana eventually carried over to other measures, especially to civil rights.

The Democrats, who fought any consideration of the measure and thereby any attempts to introduce the committee's modifications, launched a determined and resourceful filibuster which was partly intended to demonstrate to southern whites that they meant business. As it happened, the Democracy found itself in the enviable position of benefiting from its posture regardless of the outcome: a firm stand against civil rights would endear the party to virtually all southern whites and a great many whites elsewhere; and if the bill were passed despite their opposition, they would still have the advantage, because Republican espousal of it would likely cost them the support of the whites.

Such strong partisan action on the part of the Democrats generated a similar reaction from the Republicans. As the Democrats stalled with one tedious motion after another and with repeated roll calls, each of them consuming forty minutes, the Republicans responded with increasing anger and determination. And since every parliamentary maneuver and every vote became yet another test of party strength, more and more congressmen fell in with their party's position. As a result, there were far more Republican votes for the bill than if action had been taken earlier in the session.

Similarly, throughout the country the issue had become an increasingly partisan matter. The Democrats praised their party's vigilance and courage in the cause of free government and civil liberty against an arrogant majority and rejoiced over the renewed fighting spirit of their party in Congress. As the independent Springfield *Republican* noted, if the Democrats had been so many bulls and the civil rights bill the brightest red rag, the Democrats could not have attacked it more ferociously. On the Republican side, the position of the bellwether Washington *National Republican*, which had considered civil rights a matter of secondary importance to be dealt with swiftly in order to take up more pressing matters, began to shift toward the end of January. Although still hoping to get to other legislative business in the session, the newspaper now described the bill as a "great Republican measure" and declared that human rights and human life depended upon it.[13]

Anger at the Democrats had brought some Republicans solidly behind the bill, but their motives and intentions varied. Many of them were still doubtful about the civil rights bill and did not expect it ever to become a law. Even if the bill passed in the House, which was by no means sure at that point, they anticipated that the House measure would be defeated in the more radical Senate, where, because the amended House version was weaker than the Senate's original, it would drown in debate during the limited time that remained before adjournment. For some, their purpose was not to pass the bill but rather to create the impression of supporting it. As Representative Eugene Hale stated in the party caucus, even if the bill failed, the struggle would show that the Republicans in Congress were earnestly trying to pass it.[14]

Several commentators even acknowledged that if the Democrats were to defeat the bill, that would better serve the party than if it were passed. The Washington correspondent of the Republican Cincinnati *Gazette* remarked that the urgent advocacy of civil rights by some congressmen was more "apparent than real, and that parliamentary means will be found to let it escape becoming a law." Similarly, a Washingtonian asked Butler: "How would it affect the Republican Party, after the gallant fight it has made, on the Civil Rights Bill, to *manage* to be beaten? I believe that a large number of that party are hostile to the Bill. *As a Democrat, I* would manage after a hard fight to be beaten; and *as a Republican I* would do the same. My opinion is that the side that wins will be beaten before the Country." And according to a reporter of the Democratic New York *World*: "after all the hue and cry in the Republican party about a Civil Rights bill, it is quite apparent that they intend to deceive the country by a stroke of parliamentary tactics, and not pass any measure at all." Thus symbolic politicking also entered into the fray.[15]

By January 23, however, the House Republican caucus, unwilling to tolerate further delay by the Democrats, sought to pass a new rule designed to end the filibuster and ensure parliamentary control by the majority. Its adoption would change House procedure, so that a majority vote—rather than the existing requirement of two thirds—would be sufficient to suspend the rules in order to take a vote. Having secured this revision, the short-lived Republican majority could then readily pass the rights bill and other desired legislation. In response, many newspapers, notably the New York *Tribune* and the Washington *National Republican*, argued that civil rights served only as a plausible pretext to strengthen the hand of the party by introducing a new rule to allow more important measures, such as election enforcement, to be rammed through. The explanation, however, seems too pat, for, after all, House Republicans did finally take up civil rights first and fight it out on that front. Subsequent measures received secondary consideration.[16]

Nevertheless, when the House attempted to adopt the new rule on

January 25, some Republicans joined with the Democrats to defeat it: either by nays or by absences, a number of prominent Republicans, mainly northern moderates, objected to the broad and loose framing of the rules change, which they feared would invite mischievous political legislation as well as encourage ill-considered passage of public subsidies and private schemes during the closing hours of the session. Also going down to defeat on the same day was the civil rights bill. The radicals, of course, were furious at the Republican defectors and absentees who had caused the double defeat. But the reasons for the Republicans' opposition on the two questions were not necessarily the same: twelve border and southern Republicans, along with two from the North, had joined the Democrats in killing consideration of civil rights legislation, whereas another eighteen Republicans, mainly northerners (all but two of this group had voted to take up civil rights), had opposed an overall change in the House rules. Thus because of disagreements within the party on the two questions at issue, there was mutual recrimination among Republicans and the threat of an open rupture.[17]

With only twenty-three working days of the session to go, the House was still at an impasse. Trying to break the deadlock in another test of party strength and endurance, the House Republican caucus on January 26 decided to sit in continuous session, regardless of how many nights and days it took. In that way they hoped to wear down the Democrats physically and to pressure the Republican dissidents into supporting a revision of the rules. If they succeeded, they could then push through other measures.

So on January 27 the battle began. The House sat without recess for two days and two nights, during which time the roll was called on procedural motions seventy-five times. The Republicans pressed for a showdown—a vote to change the rules so that the civil rights bill could go through. The Democrats stalled, deadlocking proceedings by repeating the same monotonous routines over and over. Since the House chamber had become the temporary home of the representatives, it soon began to resemble a disheveled campground. Chairs and tables were in disarray, and the unswept carpet was strewn with scraps of newspapers and notes, as if members had fought sleep during the long nights by tearing up bits of paper. Other members spent the weary hours smoking, spitting, reading, writing, or eating. Stale cigar smoke hung in the stagnant, reeking air. Some fortified themselves with liquor just to endure. Still others, unable to keep awake any longer, slept hunched up or sprawled in their seats, emitting occasional mumbles and yawns. More fortunate members stole naps on sofas, while others resorted to sleeping on the floors and tables of adjoining committee rooms. A few attempted to sneak away to their homes—one of them by leaping through a glass window. But those who did get home were roused from their beds by zealous employees of Congress. Consequently, members of both sides grew exasperated as time wore on and fatigue set in.[18]

Then, both Democratic and Republican congressmen, whose only wish was release, slowly began to yield their positions. The Democrats declared it futile to prolong the fight, since they could not prevent a vote indefinitely. On the other side of the aisle, many halfhearted Republicans were, according to the Washington correspondent of the Cincinnati *Commercial*, "complaining that they are fighting to pass a bill that will do no good to anybody in the universe when it becomes a law." Once the Republicans' resolve had worn thin, a motion for adjournment finally went through and the parliamentary marathon ended on January 29.[19]

As no action had been taken it was a momentary victory for the Democrats, but the fight was to be renewed within a day and it seemed likely that the Republicans would be able to round up more votes in the next skirmish. For one thing, reluctant Republicans were growing weaker in their opposition to a new rule, being mollified in part by the House leaders' new proposal to add safeguards to ensure no change in the procedures for enacting private and money bills. Moreover, as a result of the exhausting, abortive wrangle, partisan blood was at an even higher boil. As a former member of Congress observed, the filibustering of the Democrats had "compacted the Republicans." Consequently, party considerations received the highest priority, at least for the time being—a situation that had not existed for years.[20]

When they reconvened on February 1, House Republicans again attempted to impose an amended new rule, against which the Democrats voted en masse each time it was brought up. Despite great efforts on the part of its proponents, the proposal repeatedly failed to pass by a couple of votes because just enough Republicans, although in Washington at the time, were absent for those particular roll calls. Gradually tempers grew frayed, until both sides became fiercely belligerent; according to a New York *Herald* editorial, the "reciprocation of invective accusations kept the House at a white heat and caused it to glow like a furnace." Some of the representatives were spoiling for a fight on the House floor. The Democrats denounced Speaker Blaine, and Butler attacked him as well. Then, for good measure, Butler exchanged verbal, almost physical, blows with the Democrats, singling out the southerners for his greatest ire. He and many southern Republicans favored the drastic caucus rule that would empower the majority to push through legislation virtually without any notice, any discussion, or any deliberation. The more moderate northern Republicans continued to steer a course between their party's radicals and the Democratic reactionaries. The moderates supported a modification of the House rules, restricting the minority but also placing certain limits on the actions of the majority.[21]

The siege ended on February 3 when the Republicans adopted the form of the new rule favored by the moderates. Under this new House procedure, the Democratic minority would no longer be able to block the business of the House by filibuster; however, it granted the minority the right of legislative deliberation, with reasonable time for debate. Moreover, under the rule, money matters were excluded. Thus, once again, as so often happened during the legislative history of reconstruction, the moderates had prevailed over the radicals by restraining rash action and blocking recourse to extreme expedients. The Democrats, not surprisingly, predicted that with the adoption of the amended rule, hasty, tyrannical legislation would be forced through Congress, but they failed to note that it was their own obstruction that had caused the unprecedented resort to a change.

The day following passage of the new rule, the civil rights bill was again called up for discussion, and throughout the following two days of debate all the standard arguments for and against civil rights were repeated yet again. Then, as previously arranged by the floor manager, the House had the opportunity to vote on the various amendments concerning the measure offered by the judiciary committee.

On February 5, 1875, it took up and rejected the radical proposal to amend the bill by virtually substituting the words of the more comprehensive measure passed by the Senate. The House also rejected, but by a narrower margin (only 22 votes), the proposition of some southern Republicans to extend the separate but equal facilities rule to cover everything in the bill, including not only schools, but segregated accommodations in streetcars and hotels. Then, by an unexpectedly large margin, with substantial bipartisan support and without a roll call, the House accepted the amendment to strike out all reference to schools. The compromise to rid the bill of the school question in any form had received wide support both from those who had wished to make the bill more radical (requiring mixed schools) and from those who had wanted to make it more conservative (mandating segregated schools).

Next, in a surprise move, House Republicans, over the vociferous objections of some Democrats, added as a preamble to the bill the plank from the Democratic national platform of 1872, which pledged equal rights to all men before the law. In voting on this addition, most Democrats grudgingly assented without entering into any embarrassing debate. Although one Democrat confessed that the only reason his party had adopted the plank in 1872 was to cement its alliance with the Liberal Republicans, Democratic representatives could hardly have resisted the plank at that point. The New York *Herald* described its inclusion as "sublime satire," and many Republicans in the House enjoyed the poetic justice of the irony, as well as the opportunity to deal their adversaries a parting blow.[22]

The final House version, then, which at last passed on February 5 against the combined opposition of the Democrats and twelve regular Republicans, affirmed equal rights in travel, accommodation, amusement, and jury duty, but not in the sensitive matters of education or burial. This was a drastic modification of Frelinghuysen's sweeping bill, which had been passed by the Senate and had included public schools, colleges, benevolent institutions, and cemeteries. Thus, not only was the House revision more limited in coverage and guarded in approach but it was also less exacting in penalties for violation. Consequently, out of a week of struggle and turmoil, commented one Washington correspondent, "a child is born, with one eye punched out, in the shape of the civil rights bill shorn of its mixed school clause." And the *Nation* commented on the inconsistency of the bill's passage—the House having delayed action until the country had decided against the entire bill and then having proceeded to approve part of it.[23]

But the Republican representatives had not acted to spite the people, as the *Nation* implied. They had had a number of reasons for passing the amended bill, including their interest in ensuring their party's future by strengthening the loyalty of the blacks, their rage at the Democrats' tactics, and, not least, an assurance that the final bill was innocuous. Indeed, the widely understood assumption that the measure would never operate effectively was the reason the bill had passed. It would not provoke lasting resentment among the whites and, at the same time, the Negroes would be grateful to the party. Thus the House bill had political and psychological importance out of all proportion to its actual significance, for its Republican supporters had created little more than the illusion of achievement.

The greatly altered measure then returned to the Senate, where its passage seemed doubtful. It was generally assumed that the legislation would first be shunned by the radicals as too weak and then be obstructed by the Democrats, who could mount a filibuster until the close of the session. The Senate Republicans were thus confronted with the choice of passing the House version, however unsatisfactory it was to many of them, or of passing no bill at all, for there wasn't time to alter the measure and then return it to the House for approval.

Although the Democratic senators opposed even the diluted House bill, they did not object as strenuously as their colleagues had in the House, for they were reportedly more concerned with blocking the House election enforcement legislation, which was soon to be sent them. Thus it did not seem likely that they would obstruct the bill if the Republican senators were in earnest. Were the Democrats to try, the Republicans might be goaded into attempting a change in the Senate rules to speed up floor action, which they had the votes to do and which would make it possible to pass both the civil rights and the enforcement bills. In other words, the Senate Democrats had to make a judicious choice between two evils. Some of them considered this form of the civil rights measure, if enacted, as lacking any immediate practical consequence. After all, they reasoned, a few southern Republican states already had equivalent statutes, which were generally ignored with impunity. In addition, they confidently expected that such a federal law would be declared unconstitutional in the next couple of years and also that its passage would lose even more votes for the Republicans, thereby helping their own side in 1876. Perhaps unaware of those motives, or disagreeing with them, the Democratic representatives and the newspapers roundly criticized the "senatorial surrender," as they termed it, and exhorted Senate Democrats to form a firm front and talk the bill to death. Ohio Senator Allen G. Thurman, in particular, was singled out for attack because he had taken upon himself the task of defeating the bill and had then deserted.[24]

But even though the Democrats put up almost no resistance, the Republicans did not avidly seize the opportunity to push the bill through, for they could not agree on the value of the House version. The Republican Philadelphia *Press*, among other papers, advised Republican senators to drop the measure, since its passage would make a present of the South to the Democrats in 1876. At the same time, there was counterpressure for passage, with the arguments that enactment would be proof of Republican resolution and that in striving for equality, half a loaf, even without the staple of mixed schools, was better than none—a point on which the Republican caucus agreed. This controversy caused the Senate to fritter away two days in idle debate.[25]

Then, in an abrupt change of face on February 27, the Republicans beat down all suggested amendments and accepted the House bill without change. Only three northern regular Republican senators, in addition to three Liberal Republicans (from the South, the borderland, and the Midwest, respectively) joined with the Democrats in opposing it. So the House bill now had only to await presidential action.[26]

President Grant signed the bill on March 1, 1875. The revisions in the legislation itself, and the Democrats' intransigence both in the House of Representatives and in the Louisiana legislature, had combined to change the president's attitude toward the measure. In marked contrast to the outpouring of sentiment and optimism in his proclamation of March, 1870, when the Fifteenth Amendment had been ratified at the bright beginning of his administration, he issued no statement to mark the signing of the civil rights bill. And that silence was yet another example of how, in the short span of six years, all the spirit and much of the substance had gone out of reconstruction. The civil rights statute, though superficially the most progressive federal law enacted during reconstruction, turned out to be the most meaningless piece of postwar legislation.[27]

The nation's press did not give the new law much praise. To be sure, a small band of Republican newspapers lauded it. The Albany *Journal*, for example, claimed that by passing that act, the Republican party had carried out its great principle of equal rights for all. However, when the comments descended from generalities to specifics, they were more guarded. Although the Boston *Advertiser* regretted the House's drastic pruning of the Senate version, it did admit that the bill would not have passed otherwise, concluding that social prejudice was reprehensible, but had nevertheless to be taken into account. At the same time, the lukewarm supporters of the statute gave it qualified approval as the best possible solution, implying that at least the courts and the country would not be plagued by the enforcement of mandatory mixed schools.[28]

On the whole, however, the reaction was unfavorable. Opposing camps generally regarded the compromise as either too extreme or too mild. According to the Philadelphia *Press*, passage had been a mistake, for "a measure which offends equally the colored people of the North and the White Leaguers of the South, which satisfies neither the Conservative Republican element North nor the Radical Republican element South, is surely not statemanship." The law's constitutionality was also attacked; indeed even the *Golden Age*, which had once been strongly abolitionist, complained that the act, even in its amended form, was impolitic because it represented a policy of coercion rather than conciliation and would harm rather than help the blacks because it would turn southern whites against them. Similarly, the New York *Times* commented, "It will certainly be of far less advantage to them [the southern Negroes] than would be the existence of a strong, growing, healthy Southern Republican Party." And it was precisely that wing of the party that the new law would weaken even more: "It makes any considerable reinforcement of the Republican party from among the whites of the South a moral impossibility. . . . The passage of the bill, therefore, can at best only retain strength, which will not prevent defeat, and cut off strength that is essential to victory."[29]

Particularly strong in their opposition were southerners of both parties. A few Republicans in the South resigned from the party when the bill was enacted, and most were convinced that the law would cause them even more trouble in the future than it had already. Naturally the most savage attacks came from white Democrats, who labeled the act the crowning horror of a wicked era and an obnoxious attempt to give the Negro legal claims to unwarranted social status. The Dallas *Herald* decried the passage of "the Civil Rights Wrong"; the Mobile *Register* described it as infamous, tyrannical, malicious, insolent, and unconstitutional. Yet, for all that, the southern Democratic newspapers cautioned the Democrats to avoid flagrant violence and open violation of the new law, which might precipitate federal intervention; instead they should wait for the Supreme Court to cut it down.[30]

Democrats from both the South and the North also assailed the motives of the Republicans in Congress, claiming that the bill was passed only to promote the vilest of political interests. Stressing the difference between the old doctrinaire radicals and the new cynical radicals, the Baltimore *Sun* acknowledged that, however blundering and sentimental, the Sumnerian version had at least been honest fanaticism, whereas the House version represented " 'buncombe,' pure and simple" and was merely a transparent device to catch black voters. The Boston *Post* agreed: "it is a shallow trick to make the blacks of the South believe the Administration party its best friend, while actually doing nothing for them which is more than a nominal service."[31]

If many people found that the bill went too far, a few thought it did not go far enough. A scattering of northern journals, such as the Newark *Advertiser*, remarked that the quality of education a person received was more important than whether he was admitted to the best seats in a theatre or given the best room in a hotel. The Republican Philadelphia *Press* pointed out the worthlessness of an act that opened the doors of the opera house and the parlor car to blacks but shut them out of the schoolhouse, finding such a solution replete with all the weaknesses of compromise, but none of the strengths of even temporary gains. Denouncing the pretense of the statute, the *Independent* of New York went on to condemn the hypocrisy of granting the lesser, not the greater, right. *Harper' Weekly* angrily declared that the law actually struck "at the principle of the whole Republican policy of reconstruction," because without the school provision, it indirectly sanctioned the very prejudice it was intended to combat.[32]

There was only one point on which all sides agreed: the new legislation would make no significant difference from a practical point of view. Butler, the House manager of the bill, acknowledged that the blacks would not make much use of the law. The Democratic Chicago *Times*, the Republican New York *Times*, and sundry others argued that the majority of them were too poor to afford the luxuries that had been granted them and so had gained nothing. The Atlanta *Constitution* declared that the law was as full of false promises to blacks as of imaginary terrors for whites. More importantly, almost no one then believed that the law could be enforced. Typical of the opinion of most of the Democratic, and much of the Republican, press was the Democratic New York *World*'s pronouncement of the law as futile, for prejudice was a very volatile thing, hard to define, harder to pin down, and even harder to punish. The Washington *National Republican* itself dismissed the act as a "piece of legislative sentimentalism, the passage of which would not change the condition of affairs in the slightest."[33]

No matter how it was received, the new statute did open up some limited opportunities to the blacks, some of whom took tentative steps in exercising their new rights, provoking a variety of reactions from the whites. That a minority of the blacks had misunderstood what they had been granted was typified by one Washington Negro who said that under the civil rights law all blacks were now to get a free ride, then reportedly boarded a streetcar, refused to pay his fare, and was unceremoniously thrown out.[34]

Although a few whites dwelled on such occasional incidents, the way in which the blacks made use of the law depended more upon the established custom of a community and the diverse reactions of white proprietors than upon the provisions of the statute. In the North, for example, the acceptance of blacks was uneven. Some of them did succeed in breaking the color line in public places, but many more of them did not. There were theatre managers who continued to refuse them choice seats, hotel proprietors who went right on insisting that their rooms and dining halls be segregated, and still others who resorted to "no vacancy" signs.[35]

In the borderland and in the South, there was substantial opposition, but also isolated cases of grudging admission. The railroads differed greatly in their practice of segregation, but even when the blacks were permitted to enter first-class cars, the white passengers occasionally made that a dubious privilege. Indeed, in Georgia one black was actually spat upon. As for restaurants and bars, the Negroes in Richmond were refused service and reminded that there were separate places for them elsewhere. In Texas, equality was extended to blacks at bars but not in dining rooms; in North Carolina, they were generally refused any service whatever, which resulted in numerous disputes; in one Virginia establishment Negroes were admitted, only to be charged five dollars a drink; and whereas in Memphis they were allowed to occupy the best seats in a theatre, in Louisville it depended on the whim of the establishment. Hotel owners in several southern cities circumvented the law by converting their establishments into private boarding houses that were not open to the general public. To make things even more difficult, the state legislatures of West Virginia, Tennessee, Virginia, Alabama, and Texas entertained proposals to end state licensing of hotels, to enact public nuisance statutes aimed at those who complained about accommodations, and to grant proprietors complete control over whom they would admit; in Delaware the legislature required racial segregation. There also were tragic incidents resulting from efforts to integrate. In Augusta, Georgia, for example, a black barber who had demanded his rights in a saloon went into a state of depression and shot himself in the heart when his self-assertion caused his business to decline, and in Waverly, Missouri, a barkeeper who was unwilling to serve a black customer killed another Negro who had come to the intruder's aid.[36]

In general, however, the blacks did not really insist upon exercising their rights, either in the North or in the South. Nevertheless, whenever and wherever they did, they often came up against resistance, mostly in cities and towns with a proportionately large black population, and precisely where life was most segregated. The opposition was just as flagrant in Cincinnati, Chicago, and New York, as in Baltimore, Louisville, and Richmond, for the caste system was ingrained and far more effective than the law.[37]

Federal enforcement thus became essential, not only to secure the rights of those blacks who had tried and failed, but also to encourage others who, fearing rebuff, had not even attempted to make use of their opportunities. However, the fact that white opposition was so strong and federal authority so weak lessened the law's chances of success. An east Texan told a reporter that "such a law will be of no force and effect in Texas. The whites are against it to a man. I do not think the attempt will be made to enforce it here. In truth, there is nobody to enforce it. Therein is our security." According to the Republican Hartford *Courant*, even if there were court challenges, any judges who were disinclined to uphold a statute they considered unpalatable to them and their neighbors could always find valid points against it in the law. In fact, only six days after the bill had passed, the New York *Herald* pronounced final judgment upon it, proclaiming the revolution proposed by Charles Sumner a ridiculous sham.[38]

To compound the difficulties, there were numerous specific legal defects in the new law. Imprecise phrasing of some of its terms caused no end of confusion and controversy. The definition of "inn," for example, was sufficiently vague as to raise the question of whether that clause covered restaurants and saloons. Also, the wording of the statute did not make it absolutely clear whether barbershops were included. Moreover, the jury provision was extremely weak, for states could eliminate blacks from the jury box by simply demanding literacy or educational qualifications. And since the law left the initiation of specific complaints to the blacks, few of whom could afford lawsuits, there was not much concern about legal action.[39]

Moreover, the federal government had neither men nor money to invest in enforcing the law and showed little interest in it to boot. The Department of Justice was exceedingly slow in providing copies of it to local federal officials. Attorneys general made no public pronouncements of its importance, nor did they prod the district attorneys, who were not even given proper instruction or guidance in reply to their questions about the law's meaning. Later, there were contradictory rulings by federal judges on the act's constitutionality and scope, yet the Supreme Court repeatedly delayed its decision on it, causing further confusion and uncertainty and discouraging prosecution and enforcement even more. Although it was generally assumed that the Court would rule within two years of the law's passage, and it had an opportunity to do so in 1876, in fact it waited seven years, until October, 1883, to declare the act unconstitutional.

There were several ways in which the Civil Rights Act of 1875 marked the end of reconstruction. As the New York *Tribune* had commented even before it was passed: "in the probable event of its becoming law, the era of conscientious experiment, based upon convictions of genuine democracy . . . may be considered closed." In a formal sense it was the valedictory statement of reconstruction legislation, for that law was the last major federal legal reform made in the interest of equal civil rights during the postwar decade. But even more important was the fact that both the existence of the bill as an issue and the turmoil that preceded its passage had helped bring into power the enemies of reconstruction.[40]

Of course, the problems and weaknesses inherent in the law were the same as those inherent in the rest of the reconstruction program. For as with so many other measures, its framing was slipshod; the "frantic law-making," as the *Nation* described it, only gave the government and the courts further administrative and constitutional problems.[41] Also, at a time when the right of southern blacks to vote was in greater jeopardy day by day, when even the right to live was periodically mocked by the savage murders of blacks—when those fundamental rights were being denied—new rights were being pressed. Granted, the law made more sense for the blacks in the North, whose political rights were generally secure; but there, too, the civil rights law was frequently flouted and seldom enforced.

Naturally, the aspirations of the blacks for full equality were no less sacred than those of the whites; having been granted some rights, the blacks wished to claim all the rest of them. But since there were obvious limits to how far most white Americans wanted such legislation to go, congressmen often shirked the regrettable but necessary task of determining priorities and defining vital interests when they legislated public policy.

The Republicans, then, had once again indulged in empty ritualism, the results of which were more often negative than constructive. The law thus represented the bankruptcy of legislative sentimentalism and reconstruction rhetoric, which demeaned noble ideals and undercut vital interests. For many disillusioned radicals the act was the expiring flash of a now obsolete philanthropy. For most other Republicans, it was an unwelcome intrusion and an unnecessary initiative. Had great results followed, the cost would have been justified in some measure. But the statute had reaped the whirlwind of racist reaction and had served only to weaken the Republican party, to disappoint the blacks, and to further discredit the integrity of the law. It was the "deadest of dead letters."[42]

12
SYMBOLIC DEFEAT

*The "Force" Bill in Congress and Election
Enforcement in the Supreme Court*

WITH THE battle for civil rights over, and having adopted the new procedure, the House of Representatives turned to consideration of a possible additional election enforcement measure. Their purpose would be to help ensure Republican national victory in 1876—retention of the presidency by virtue of southern electoral votes as well as continuing control of the United States Senate, and the recapture of both the national House of Representatives and many southern legislatures. "We must put on a bold face and be more radical than ever before if we want to triumph," advised one radical Republican in an interview in the Springfield *Republican*. To counter the relentless Bourbon attack against reconstruction, Draconian measures had to be taken, including possible suspension of the writ of habeas corpus until after the elections. The members of Congress who favored such a renewal of vigorous federal activity in the South were those who belonged to the administration's wing of the party, most southern Republicans, and many northern radicals.[1]

However, according to the Springfield *Republican*, the prevailing view of most of the influential journals was that although the same old question still remained unresolved—that is, would maximum or minimum federal interference best serve to rehabilitate the southern states?—it would be unwise to fail yet again: "We have tried . . . constant partisan intermeddling from Washington and bayonets *ad lib*. The malady does not yield to the treatment. Let us now try . . . a little vigorous letting alone." Given that general reluctance toward the expansion of reconstruction, there was concern among both Republicans and Democrats that the radical lame ducks in Congress might try to ram through last-minute legislation of a drastic sort. Democratic Senator Thomas F. Bayard noted with misgivings that the temper of the Republican majority was "very bad"; not only he but others were convinced that the Republicans had been led to desperation by their recent defeat. Some Republicans also feared the plans of the radical faction, and a number of them, including even a few disillusioned radicals, decided to go along with the Democrats and to counter any efforts to pass further federal intervention.[2]

Preparing to promote the case for new legislation, various investigating committees surveyed conditions in several southern states and in their reports emphasized the necessity of remedial legislation. Further bolstering the radical position, President Grant himself favored a new enforcement law. At this juncture Grant had been assuming a hard line in his southern policies and had recently weathered stormy crises in Arkansas and Louisiana. As a result, he was anxious to obtain legal sanction to cover all possible contingencies and to provide himself with extraordinary powers to meet any sort of emergency. He had first suggested the need for new enforcement statutes in his annual message of December, 1874, in which he had expressed his strong disapproval of the southern disturbances and had promised to suppress them. Later he repeated his distaste for such disorders in his addresses concerning Mississippi, Louisiana, and Arkansas respectively, in December, 1874, January and February, 1875. Stating Grant's position more explicitly, the Washington *National Republican* declared on February 13 that no man in the country would rejoice more than the president should a new enforcement measure become law. Similarly, the Boston *Globe*'s Washington correspondent on February 14 reported that Grant was already beginning to lobby, for he had told House members that such a bill was of vital importance to the country and the party.[3]

Pushing hardest for new enforcement legislation were southern Republican representatives, some of whom complained that their needs had been ignored for too long. Republicans in Alabama, according to one of the state's legislators, had "no hope in the future except . . . in such laws as Congress may pass before the fourth of

March next." Moreover, the Republicans pointed out that reinvigorated federal activity was important to the national party as a whole, since the death of its southern arm would jeopardize the entire body to the point of endangering the Republicans' hold on the presidency.[4]

In response, conservatives and moderates, both Republican and Democratic, began to voice their desire for a final adjournment. Liberal Republican Senator Carl Schurz was concerned about the possibility of "another law still strengthening the military grip upon the South." Senator Bayard, among the opponents who counted on delay, wrote that "with the lapse of each day I feel relief. The want of time will be the only thing to save us." On February 14 he commented: "If we can only get through this coming week . . . we can prevent the passage of the violent measures proposed." By that time, the southern Democrats were so worried about the radical offensive that they issued an address to their constituents on February 18, advising them not to cause disturbances that might bring down the wrath of the country and Congress upon them in the form of a force bill.[5]

The Democrats in Congress had good reason to be concerned about the activities of their members at home. The recent crises in Vicksburg and New Orleans had again roused the country against southern terrorism and hardened party lines in Congress. Those crises, combined with the recent fight over civil rights, could well rekindle the sort of partisanship that might help muster wayward Republicans to the radical cause. The party moderates, who were ambivalent about the new spirit in Congress, were pleased with the change from the prevailing indifference toward reconstruction, yet concerned about the irresponsibility that might result from unreasoning and feverish emotions within the party. Uneasy about the situation, Congressman Henry Dawes wrote to editor Samuel Bowles: "you have no idea of the real feeling here. Party lines in both Houses have straightened up wonderfully since this Louisiana fight, and both parties have resolved to stand or die in their old attitude towards the South. Party intensity seems higher than at any time since the war," and no one seemed willing to step out of line.[6]

Meanwhile, the radicals, sensing their advantage and spurred on by the fact that time was running out, made haste to get a bill formulated and supported. On February 3, 1875, a caucus of both the Senate and House Republicans authorized the creation of a joint committee to frame an election enforcement proposal. Since the Republican senators were by and large indifferent to the idea, the House Republican caucus took the initiative and met night after night to discuss proposed legislation. Because of disagreement among its members, no concrete proposals were made, but all the frantic activity and the unusual number of meetings soon provoked comment. The Washington reporter of the Chicago *Times*, for example, was not impressed by what he termed a new era of Republican caucuses, noting that there hadn't been that many of them for fifteen years. Those "star-chamber seances," he acidly remarked, amounted to no more than "random suggestions and bewildered gabble, and ending with a resolve to meet again in a day or two, and then do something terrible and decisive." Indeed, the Democrats and many Republicans grew hopeful that the lack of time would rescue them from a force bill. The Washington *National Republican*, however, criticized the obvious absence of progress and warned that failure to enact protective laws would cause the party to suffer irreparable damage, enforcement legislation being far more important than civil rights, which was still monopolizing the attention of the House.[7]

Finally, after days of being deadlocked, the joint committee managed to reach an agreement because of the numerous absences and abstentions of the moderates, who had reservations about any new far-reaching legislation. The proposed bill was in many respects unprecedented, with such vague and wide-ranging purposes as to protect voters at the polls, to prevent fraud at elections, to provide security against invasion in any state, and to prevent the overthrow of state authority. In order to accomplish those ends, the proposed measure empowered the president to suspend the writ of habeas corpus if he deemed it necessary to suppress disorder (reenactment of section four of the Klan Act, which had expired), gave to federal deputy marshals and election supervisors the new power to arrest persons engaged in intimidation, specified new and more severe penalties for the commission of election irregularities, set the time and place for counting the vote, provided for full registration of voters, prohibited excessive poll taxes, forbade the carrying of firearms on election day, and extended to all federal marshals in rural areas several of the greater powers already granted them in cities.

When the proposal was presented to the House Republican caucus, it was greeted with strong objections. Several members openly declared that they would not be bound by the machinations of a rump caucus of southern radicals and would vote as they pleased if the bill came before the House. Their grounds for opposition were numerous. Particularly stormy dissension was provoked by the clause that allowed the president to suspend the writ of habeas corpus. Some opponents contended that the bill ought not confer the power to interfere with the actions of individuals, but ought to be confined only to the acts of terrorist organizations. Others claimed that the proper sphere of a federal law encompassed only offenses against national authority, and they thus were against those provisions dealing with offenses against state government; also in the belief that the federal system must be preserved, that group disliked the opportunity the law would provide for Washington to tamper with state election requirements and registration. Nevertheless, the House caucus, with most of the supporters of the force bill present and a number of its opponents—either exhausted or apathetic—absent, approved the provision by a majority vote. Thus on February 12 the force bill was adopted as a party measure that was soon to be brought to the floor for debate and a vote. It was referred to by some as "the force bill of 1875," by others as "the new reconstruction or protection bill," and by the hostile as "the southern election measure" or "Grant's bayonet bill."[8]

Proponents of the bill then put all their energy into lively lobbying in hopes of persuading or pressuring recalcitrant party members to support it. However, since it was already known that all or some of the provisions were opposed by many prominent moderates such as Speaker Blaine and Congressmen Garfield and Dawes, and with adjournment approaching, passage appeared doubtful. Indeed, Senator Schurz predicted that no dangerous legislation would ever pass: "The Administration men, at least a large number of them, have no heart in this matter. The party is quite staggering along." Democratic Representative Samuel S. Cox of New York was also of the opinion that the Republicans were too divided to pass the bill. And the Washington reporter of the Cincinnati *Commercial* declared on February 13, "The game of the ultra-Administration party has been a desperate one, played with desperate nerve, but it has failed." On the seventeenth the Chicago *Times* joined in the chorus, claiming that Congress was "sick of the outrage bugaboo." Yet the minority opinion expressed by the New York *World* was that the bill would pass in the House but provoke a battle in the Senate—an opinion with which Grant reportedly agreed.[9]

Once the bill was framed, awaiting consideration by the House, the cross fire of editorial debate became one of the heaviest during the last years of reconstruction. Many radical papers argued that the choice before Congress and the country was one of either enforcing the reconstruction amendments or leaving them as a mere discretionary recommendation to the South, which would mean their virtual nullification. Already, they noted, many southern blacks had been disfranchised. "Shall American citizens be protected and their right to vote . . . be secured to them or shall the wrong and outrage go on?" asked the Albany *Journal*. The radical Chicago *Inter-Ocean* wanted a strong measure passed and stringently enforced: "Show these men that there is sure and swift punishment in store for evil doers, and the disturbances . . . will cease." To default on this federal responsibility and partisan opportunity would surely lead to defeat in 1876 and the downfall of reconstruction.[10]

Opponents pronounced the bill dangerous, unnecessary, and subversive as a precedent. Particularly alarming to them was the enormous amount of discretionary power allowed the president. If the bill became law, he would have even greater powers in judging whether an emergency existed and could suspend habeas corpus at will, even without overt insurrection having taken place in the South. They argued that the Constitution provided for suspension of this safeguard only as a remedy for an actual rebellion, not as a precaution against an assumed one. Although acknowledging that the Constitution did allow federal intervention under certain circumstances, the moderate New York *Times* cautioned that it was unwise to invite such occasions. Furthermore, opponents of the clause noted that under the proposed measure, presidential authority would be unrestricted as to time and not limited to any locality. In short, the so-called force bill raised the specter of bayonet rule. Another argument frequently advanced by Republican opponents was the measure's purported inexpediency, for the very existence of such a law would incense southern whites, who would then cause further disturbances. If the response to them were federal intervention, it would cause a self-perpetuating spiral of more violence, which in turn would call for even more federal action.[11]

Many critics also claimed that the real purpose of the bill was not to protect elections but to carry them. The New Orleans *Daily Picayune*, like most other southern Democratic newspapers, warned that Grant's actions in Louisiana and elsewhere—either bypassing the law or in defiance of it—gave some indication of his future actions if he were sanctioned by law. They also argued that the blatantly partisan nature of the bill was obvious in its provisions. For example, suspension of habeas corpus, based on a contrived pretext, might well become a Republican tool for securing the presidency in 1876 and enabling the party to occupy states, to govern them, and to maneuver elections in places that would be apt to decide the contest. Even more useful for such manipulation was the provision that federal deputy marshals could, at the president's discretion, be named the sole counters of election returns. Thus the president and his fellow partisans would become military policemen, election supervisors, and chief custodians in the state capitals.[12]

Although opponents and champions of the bill frequently became submerged in the intricacies of constitutional law and legal precedent, the crux of the debate turned on the future federal policy toward the South. Critics of the bill claimed that no new legislation was needed because there were already too many laws that specifically applied to the South. Besides, in their view, there was already too much federal power exercised in the southern states, with altogether unnecessary interference from Washington influencing elections there.

Even *Harper's Weekly*, with its radical tendencies, questioned the entire Republican policy of reconstruction, a major departure from its usual thinking. Although the policy itself, according to *Harper's*, had been just, generous, and humane, the actual workings of reconstruction had inevitably produced difficulties and dangers. Indeed, it was the reaction to injustice that had reinforced all the eagerness to employ stringent federal measures to suppress disorder in the South. Then, *Harper's* continued, self-serving Republicans had made demands for more federal action, expanded army surveillance, and used all manner of expedients merely in order to stay in power. As a result of both impatient idealism and irresistible opportunism, the handling of southern problems had drifted dangerously close to federal centralization. Were both self-government and federalism to be preserved, warned the journal, the risks of freedom and local rule would have to be taken. And given the social, economic, and political upheavals in the South, there would be a great deal more injustice and disorder for many years to come. The only solution, according to *Harper's*, was the gradual development of goodwill and moral suasion, not a flawed national bureaucracy and a small army; then, in time, the unfortunate southern situation would be ameliorated.[13]

Similarly, a staunch radical Republican congressman, Joseph R. Hawley of Connecticut, also made a startling about-face in February: "there are wrongs there [in the South] that we can never reach in this Hall until we have changed the Constitution of the United States. There is a social, and educational, and moral reconstruction of the South needed that will never come from any legislative halls, State or national; it must be the growth of time, of education, and of Christianity. We cannot perfect that reconstruction through statutes, if we had all the powers of the State Legislature and of Congress combined. We cannot put justice, liberty, and equality into the hearts of a people by statutes alone." That abrupt swing toward the moderate view by a radical who had joined the antislavery cause early on and had enlisted in the army on the first day of the war (later to become a general) was undoubtedly a sincere change of heart. Yet it also indicated Hawley's need as a politician to better reflect the more conservative views of his Connecticut constituency. (He was to run for reelection to the House in the April election.) Thus the debate on the force bill provided an occasion for the expression of a feeling that had been building up for some time—that there had to be a drastic change in postwar domestic policy. And judging from the decisive reversals of opinion, some of the front ranks were being carried along on that powerful wave of retreat from reconstruction.[14]

Although some Republicans stressed the need for restraint in order to save the Constitution and federalism, they also discussed, with great concern, the effect of the bill upon the national party. As the Republican Boston *Advertiser* put it, "The partisan madness that stakes all on such a measure as the caucus force bill is the madness of suicide." Reflecting the majority of moderate Republican opinion, Congressman Garfield, speaking in party caucus, admitted that disorder in the South was probably worse than most people believed and that its existence was largely ignored—a striking contrast to the earlier widespread concern over the outrages committed when Congress authorized the suspension of habeas corpus in 1871 to counter the Klan. Actually, he said, the idea of federal protection of southern blacks was now decidedly unpopular in the North. Garfield and others who had supported the suspension of habeas corpus in 1871, but opposed it in 1875, argued that a new enforcement bill would hurt the party; by going too far to save and to gain black votes, it would lose more voters in the North than could possibly be made up in the South and might well bring about the party's downfall in 1876. Representative John A. Kasson of Iowa added, at that same caucus on February 12, that in attempting to preserve Republican interests in the South, laws that would destroy party support in the North should not be passed.[15]

Also alarmed by the possibility of congressional radicals legislating the party into a permanent minority, Chicago *Tribune* editor Joseph Medill wrote to Speaker Blaine: "Our chances of winning the next Presidential election are *slim* enough Lord knows without willfully decreasing them. If I had the power I should compress the next 18 days into 18 hours and adjourn this Congress sine die." He complained that "some malicious spirit of destructiveness" seemed to possess a number of Republicans, who appeared bent on perpetuating policies that would rob the party of any remaining chance to regain power in 1876. Medill then singled out the force bill, which would "do our party infinite mischief and arm the Democrats with a club to knock out our brains. Such a bill might have been justifiable 8 or 10 years ago but the time has long passed for it. The necessity therefore has gone by and the *power* to enforce it also. It seems to be forgotten that our party is no longer in the majority—that until the people change their minds at some future election we are in a minority and really *out of power* and have no business to be making such oppressive coercive laws."[16]

In charge of the force bill, Congressman John Coburn, an Indiana Republican lame duck and chairman of the Alabama investigating committee, made determined efforts to bring it before the House, but met with stiff resistance from both sides. Although compromises designed to placate Republican opposition had been made, the passage of the measure still seemed doubtful. The Republicans squabbled among themselves over which pending measures ought to receive priority, for the congressional agenda was crowded with unfinished business and the session would be over in less than two weeks. Appropriation bills vied with political bills for consideration, and pet measures for the relief of various cliques in southern states were in competition with action on the enforcement bill. To complicate matters, the Democrats succeeded in obstructing any action by first refusing to consider the measure, then making points of order, and finally, engaging in a twenty-eight-hour filibuster.[17]

Trying to rally the Republicans, outgoing Representative Benjamin Butler exhorted them to fight it out to the limit of their physical endurance. And fight it out they did. Although promoters of the force bill were undermined by considerable Republican absenteeism, faulty floor management, conflict with Speaker Blaine on parliamentary rulings, and, above all, resourceful delay and sabotage by the Democrats, it was those very Democrats who once again accomplished the virtually unattainable by bringing the Republicans together in an acrimonious partisan struggle. Indeed, it was estimated that because the Democrats had made the issue even more of a party affair, the bill had gained twenty Republican votes overnight. At any rate, the Republicans finally agreed at least to consider it, so on February 25 the measure was brought up for action.[18]

When it came before the House, there remained only four working days before final adjournment. Assuming that the Senate would have

289

neither the time nor the opportunity to vote on the bill, the Washington *National Republican* advised Republican congressmen that the real issue was "whether they [the House Republicans] will do tardy justice to suffering constituencies, and whether they will do their part to win back the Southern States from the violent control of White League conspirators," arguing that the "moral effect of its passage by the House will serve to save the lives of hundreds of Republicans." Furthermore, it would not only encourage many Republican voters in the southern states in the belief that they had not been forgotten and altogether abandoned by northern Republicans, but would renew party enthusiasm for the cherished ideals of impartial equality. Therefore any congressman who hesitated to endorse it was virtually repudiating the egalitarian reconstruction amendments. Then, adding a partisan argument, the bellwether administration organ concluded, as did several party members in House debate, that whatever its other merits, the "PASSAGE OF THE BILL IS REQUIRED TO PRESERVE TO THE REPUBLICAN PARTY THE ELECTORAL VOTES OF THE SOUTHERN STATES."[19]

Some Republicans were doubtless swayed by that lofty appeal to party idealism and the more weighty allegiance to partisan expediency. But their certainty that the Senate would not pass the bill and that the congressional party would never be held accountable for an unpopular law was what persuaded a number of skeptical moderates to favor the measure. Indeed, that fact, more than any other, accounted for the increased support for the measure and the decreased resistance to its passage by those who believed it was far too extreme.[20]

To be sure, other circumstances were working to its advantage. The hardworking radical supporters of the measure still sincerely wished it to become law, in hopes not only that it might somehow stabilize the southern situation but that it might chastise the recalcitrant moderates, whom they regarded as cowardly and disloyal traitors because of their refusal to follow the caucus in a matter of such importance to the party. Another circumstance was the supporters' acute exasperation with the Democrats for their exhausting filibuster, an action that had rekindled the partisan fire that was still smoldering after the recent wrangle over civil rights. Thus, with tempers ruffled and with a desire to move on to what they regarded as more pressing business, a number of moderate Republicans opted to get rid of the bill by casting a vote in its favor, which under ordinary circumstances they would not have done. In addition, certain members of the party responded to the sting of the vigorous lash wielded by the party caucus whip, and others wished to please President Grant in order to win favor and get federal patronage in return for their vote.[21]

When the bill reached the floor on February 27, the Democrats put their delaying tactics into effect. Then, on the same day, in order to satisfy many Republicans the House considerably amended its own measure, restricting the power to suspend habeas corpus to four southern states (Alabama, Mississippi, Louisiana, and Arkansas) and limiting the period during which that power of suspension could be exercised to two years (until June, 1877, thus covering the presidential election and the first four months of the new administration). A proposal to strike out the entire habeas corpus clause was narrowly defeated by 9 votes (despite scores of Republicans in favor of it) and another amendment to weaken the bill was rejected by only 7 votes. There were a significant number of Republicans absent that day. Finally, however, enough Republicans supported the bill to pass it by the slim majority of 21 during the early hours of February 28 by a vote of 135 to 114, with many abstentions. Nevertheless, thirty-two regular (not Liberal) Republicans, mostly northerners and many of them prominent party leaders, remained unconvinced that even symbolic acceptance was necessary or desirable and voted against it.[22]

When the House measure was sent to the Senate, House Democratic leader Samuel J. Randall warned Senate Democratic leader Bayard to be on guard for Republican tricks, since "Grant will do anything in the world to secure this law." In fact, it was reported that both Representative Butler and the president actually went to the Senate wing and talked to a number of senators in an effort to force the measure through or at least obtain a vote upon it. Of course, several senators were also determined to pass it; but all the pressure was to no avail. After two readings, the bill was laid over without even a symbolic—much less serious—effort to obtain action on it.

As an explanation, some staunch administration senators claimed that it would have been impossible to have done anything else until all the appropriation bills had been passed. Yet, in fact, the Senate had delayed action on six of the most important appropriation bills until the last hour, possibly as a plausible excuse to bury the enforcement bill. Thus the Republican senators did not disappoint their many colleagues in the House who had fervently hoped for precisely what had come to pass.[23]

Whereas the opponents of the bill rejoiced over their good fortune and the nation's narrow escape from dangerous legislation, its proponents were bitter, placing responsibility for the delay on those senators who acted like Nero while the South was in flames and blaming the loathsome alliance of moderate Republicans and Democrats, which practically encouraged the White Leagues to renew their violence. Other Republican supporters, although disappointed, tried to salvage the party's self-respect by proclaiming the bill's passage in the House a moral triumpth. However, their self-congratulations had a hollow ring, for they were but another example of pro forma declarations, which in recent years had become the Republican stock-in-trade.[24]

Commenting on the passage of civil rights but the failure of election enforcement, a former attorney general, Amos Akerman, chastised Congress for having "faltered in political action. To pass the Civil Rights bill was in my judgment an error. The measure is not required to secure justice to the negroes and will have a contrary effect by inflaming whites against them. What they need is something to protect them in independent suffrage. With this, they can get every other public right that they ought to have. How a Congress which enacted this bill should have a scruple about the 'Force Bill' is surprising." The Newark *Advertiser* was even more dissatisfied, claiming that Congress had wrought only the "still-birth of civil rights" and the "abortion of the force bill."[25]

Yet it was also true that federal election enforcement had never worked well and that the Department of Justice was not using the powers it already had. Thus there was little prospect that, even with a new law granting greater powers, the situation would have changed, for the creaking administrative machinery was not about to be overhauled, especially since a future Democratic House would be bound to set low appropriations. Moreover, Speaker Blaine was said to have argued that even had the bill passed, it would not have rescued the South, most of which was already lost to the Democrats. Furthermore, if the bill had become an unpopular law, it would have caused the defeat of northern Republicans in 1876, so that the northern wing of the party would not have been able to look after southern interests at all. It was preferable, Blaine thought, to forfeit the South and save the North than to try, through such legislation, to save the South and lose the whole country.[26]

What remained of the radical program aside from the civil rights and enforcement measures—all so bravely planned to resurrect reconstruction—met with various fates. One part of the plan, reform of the electoral college, was not acted upon.[27] Statehood was to be granted only to Colorado,[28] and, lacking moderate support, the idea of providing two-year appropriations was abandoned.[29] That those various stratagems, which had been meant to renew the Republicans' influence, had either been defeated or extensively altered was significant. Also symptomatic of political change was former president Andrew Johnson's election to the United States Senate at the end of January, 1875. Politics had now come full circle. One Ohio Democrat wrote to Johnson that there was an " 'eminent fitness of things' in sending you back among the fellows who tried to impeach you." The former Kansas senator who had opposed impeachment gloated over the appropriateness of Johnson's return to the Senate at a time when many of his old enemies had just been defeated. And Johnson's former attorney general, Henry Stanbery, wrote him that events had vindicated his "policy—the policy of peace, constitutional law, and honesty in administration."[30]

There were other indications that the Republican party was rapidly withdrawing to a more cautious position. The recent defeats of the radicals' proposals seriously undercut what little was left of their influence. The refusal of moderate, and even some formerly radical, Republican politicians and editors to embrace what they regarded as ultra measures of a strategy designed to ensure winning the election in 1876 meant that the moderates were seizing the initiative. It was likely that they would exert it forcefully in writing the Republican platform and in selecting its presidential nominee. Although the House had approved the force bill, it had at the same time contradicted and, indeed, repudiated the return to vigorous federal activity in two of the states that were to have been covered by the bill. For one thing, the lower chamber had created a select committee which, by way of informal, unofficial mediation in the spring, had arranged a compromise: they agreed to leave a Republican in the Louisiana governorship in exchange for a return to the statehouse of those Democrats expelled by the army, thus giving the Democrats control of the lower chamber. For another, the House, despite presidential pressure, had refused to intervene in Arkansas to unseat the Democratic government there, by a majority vote much larger than that which had passed the force bill. The House had therefore in effect declared the bill and further federal initiatives to be unnecessary or futile.

Those actions, combined with the fact that the force bill had succeeded in passing the House only because it had been expected to fail in the Senate, indicated that with certain exceptions Republicans in Congress had begun not only to reject the recent activist initiatives taken by Grant but also, though uncertainly, to play the role of mediator and conciliator and to espouse—however unsteadily—nonintervention. For many Republicans it was time to retrench in order to reduce losses and liquidate liabilities. They were anxious to conserve party power, to preserve at least the northern party, and to scale down both federal activity within the South and the northern Republicans' responsibility for southern reconstruction. Soon after, Grant, too, appeared ready to swing away from his recent interventionist course. To begin with, he went along, though reluctantly, with the Wheeler compromise for Louisiana, made no further attempts to unseat the Democrats in Arkansas, and, later in the year, did nothing to stem the widespread Democratic terrorism in Mississippi.[31]

Thus the year 1875 was the decisive turning point for reconstruction. The emasculation of civil rights, the defeat of the force bill, the backdown in Louisiana and Arkansas, the inaction in Mississippi, and the string of Republican defeats in local contests in the South, all were markings along the road to retreat. As the Republican Philadelphia *American and Gazette* proclaimed: "with the close of this Congress the era of reconstruction may be considered closed."[32]

As reconstruction was coming to an end on the political front, a similar fate was to befall it on the judicial front. The first significant case during reconstruction with regard to the legal foundation of voting rights was finally brought before the Supreme Court in order to clarify the meaning of the Fifteenth Amendment, decide the constitutionality of one election enforcement act, and inform federal attorneys how to frame proper indictments under the act. This case, *United States* v. *Reese*, bearing directly and exclusively on the right of blacks to vote under the Fifteenth Amendment, was to be decided in March, 1876—six years after that amendment had been adopted and election enforcement undertaken.

The Reese case originated in the city of Lexington, Kentucky. In a municipal election on January 30, 1873, federal election supervisors had been on hand. Not to be outmaneuvered, the Democratic state legislature had earlier introduced a poll tax as a prerequisite for voting, which the Negroes, most of whom had little money income, could not easily pay. As a result, two thirds of them were disfranchised; but even when they could have paid, their money had been refused, thereby assuring the election of the Democratic candidates.[33] It was over this poll tax that state and federal authority had collided in the third ward. Election judges had not allowed several Negroes to vote because they had not paid the required tax. Subsequently, in 1873, the officials had been indicted in federal circuit court at Louisville for violating the third and fourth sections of the Enforcement Act of May 31, 1870, which prohibited interference with the right to vote. The cases were argued at the end of the year before Judge Bland Ballard and Judge Halmer H. Emmons, who differed on points of law, causing the pivotal Reese case to go before the Supreme Court in 1875.[34]

In its decision the Supreme Court made future enforcement vastly more difficult, and in some cases clearly impossible.[35] Speaking for the majority of the Court, Chief Justice Morrison R. Waite stated that the federal government had merely a negative power to prevent intentional racial discrimination in voting, not any positive power to confer suffrage outright and insure its exercise. Following that line of reasoning, he concluded that the Fifteenth Amendment did not confer the right to vote on anyone; it merely assured that insofar as the right to vote was concerned, no citizen could be discriminated against because of race. It was a fine legal point, but one with immense constitutional significance and fraught with political consequences. It meant that Congress could only legislate on the subject of exemption from discrimination in the exercise of the elective franchise on account of race, but could not exercise plenary power to pass direct and primary legislation to guarantee the right to vote in the broadest, affirmative sense of the term. In other words, the regulation of elections remained primarily a state responsibility. Since Congress had limited powers in the matter, it was to confine its statutes to those powers, for it could not grant protection to the rights the Constitution did not confer. Specifically, the Fifteenth Amendment authorized federal penalties, not for every refusal to accept the vote of a qualified voter at a state election, but only when refusals at such elections were based upon race. Thus it did not cover acts of interference in general.

The question then turned on where and how to draw the line between federal and state power. Scrutinizing the indictments under the third and fourth sections of the enforcement act, the chief justice stated that the general language of the sections and the act as a whole were broad enough to cover every conceivable instance in which Negroes, for whatever reason, were denied the franchise. In fact, the act's grasp could well have been greater than the amendment's reach. The enforcement law was, he reasoned, like a huge net "large enough to catch all possible offenders, and leave it to the courts to step inside and say who could be rightfully detained, and who should be set at large. This would, to some extent, substitute the judicial for the legislative department of the government." But Waite quickly added that the courts were not about to be a substitute for Congress by making new laws in the guise of interpreting existing laws; nor ought Congress to tamper with the Constitution. And what else could it be called but tampering when Congress undermined state control over suffrage regulation, prescribing ground rules (which was the province of the states) merely on the assumption of racial discrimination, and merely because the victim happened to be a Negro, especially when the two sections of the law itself did not make any explicit statement on the prohibition of racial discrimination with regard to registering and voting?

Thus on such grounds of strict construction, broader constitutional grounds, and still broader, although only implied, political grounds, the chief justice declared the two sections of the act as beyond Congress' power to enact appropriate legislation under the Fifteenth Amendment. At the same time in a companion case, *United States* v. *Cruikshank*, bearing not only on the Fifteenth Amendment, but also on the First and Fourteenth amendments, Waite in effect also restricted the scope of federal enforcement under the same act.[36]

Electoral federalism, which had been regarded with reverence in the nineteenth century, was thus saved, but at the price of restricting rather than protecting Negro voting rights. Yet some observers, then and since, believed that the opportunity for doing so had, in part, been provided by the Fifteenth Amendment's first section, phrased in such a way that it was difficult if not impossible to directly enforce the amendment so as to include the actions of individuals. Also, the failure of the Fifteenth Amendment's enforcement clause to specify what was appropriate legislation and of the enforcement act to be explicit enough allowed loopholes. In addition, the Supreme Court had suffered a loss of prestige and influence since the catastrophic Dred Scott decision of 1857 and scarcely seemed in a mood to step out boldly in behalf of unpopular causes and forsaken policies without more specific constitutional authority than that provided by the new and politically inspired reconstruction amendment. And so the Supreme Court held the amendment virtually in abeyance, sometimes giving the impression that it was not even part of the Constitution.[37]

The fact that public opinion was, by and large, perfectly in accord with the Court's conclusions indicated that retreat from reconstruction was very nearly completed. Most Republican spokesmen declared that, regardless of the effect on future election enforcement, whenever government jumped the constitutional tracks there was more danger of encroachment on liberties from the federal government than from the states. According to the Springfield *Republican*, the Supreme Court in the Reese case had indeed driven a coach and six horses through the enforcement legislation, but only because Congress had "made a botch and mess of it." A Republican member of Congress went even further, blaming the Fifteenth Amendment itself, since its framers had regrettably failed to make it "more explicit on the subject of Congress to enforce the guarantees to the enfranchised race." Similarly, the New York *Times* regarded the decision as a sharp warning to Congress as to the hasty passage of loosely worded, widely drawn laws. And the New York *Herald* observed that the reconstruction amendments had been passed at the high-water mark of reconstruction, at a time when the centralizing national forces left over from the war were still operating and had thus allowed Congress to overstep the limits of the Constitution in its enforcement legislation. But now the tide had receded and the time had come to correct this deviation and to operate within constitutional limits. The *Herald*'s editorial also noted that the decision had assuredly marked "the beginning of a new era in the political relations of the negro race in our Southern States." That the ruling was widely praised as sound was not only proof of an increasing lack of support for both reconstruction and the enforcement of the southern blacks' right to vote, but it helped to encourage that reaction.[38]

The remnants of reconstruction, then, were the unenforced federal statutes and the unused constitutional amendments, which, by their very existence, had created as many problems for jurists as they had originally been intended to solve for politicians. After 1876, and notably in 1903, the Supreme Court, through its various decisions and its interpretation of the Fifteenth Amendment, endorsed the retreat from reconstruction—first narrowing, later substantially reversing, and then virtually repudiating postwar public policy. However, such decisions only served to rationalize and legitimize the earlier retreat during the decisive 1870s when unfavorable public opinion, local sabotage, and federal inaction had achieved the overthrow of reconstruction. Actually, the Court preferred order to freedom and, having bowed to political facts, created legal fictions, the results of which led to black disfranchisement. It was the only time in the nation's history that suffrage, which had been universally extended by national mandate, was virtually reversed in fact; indeed, southern Negroes were almost in the same position they would have been in if the legal right to vote had never been bestowed. Meanwhile, Congress, under Democratic control, repealed most of the enforcement laws that were still on the books in 1894; the state legislatures enacted statutes to ensure the disfranchisement of blacks, first de facto, then later virtually de jure. And, with only some notable exceptions, the course that had been set was to continue for seven decades.[39]

13
CENTENNIAL CODA
Patriotic Fervor and Presidential Politics

IN 1876 the nation wanted to celebrate the hundredth anniversary of national independence, and they wanted a celebration that would satisfy the nineteenth century's love of pomp and pageantry, as well as its fascination with expositions; thus centennial mania, as it was called, began with the New Year. Clanging bells, screaming sirens, and booming cannon ushered in the first new year of the nation's second century. Across the land, Americans celebrated with euphoric vigor and unabashed enthusiasm. Cities large and small boasted displays of sound and light. In Cleveland a huge bonfire, to which twenty barrels of crude petroleum were added, shot up into the dark. Elsewhere and everywhere, spread-eagle speeches, fireworks, and parades continued long into the night, and in fact, throughout the year.[1]

With the country about to enter its second century of existence, many believed that a new America was about to be born. Ushering in the new age, the New York *Evening Post* announced: "the great work of the century is finished, and the year which is about to dawn will be the very first one wholly free from the duty of dealing with the old and dangerous subject. Slavery died in this country ten years ago, but not until now have we finished the work of readjusting our national life to the new order of things; not until now have the questions which grew out of slavery been fully and finally settled; not until now have the echoes of the war died out of our politics and our lives."[2]

Most Americans thought that it was time to hasten the reconciliation between the North and the South so that the nation could go forward as a united people into its second century. There was much talk of fraternity and of recognizing the emergence of a new South. Some northerners even welcomed the return of southerners to national politics, in the expectation that they would temper postwar legislative excesses with their innate conservatism. According to the Springfield *Republican*: "We must get rid of the Southern question. There is no chance or hope of healthy politics until *we do* get rid of it. . . . So long as the 'war issues' are capable of being warmed over from year to year and election to election; so long as a large section of the country is disturbed by violence and paralyzed by misgovernment; so long as white is arrayed against black. . . . so long will our politics be feverish with disease."[3]

Even some former abolitionists agreed. Journalist James Redpath, for example, declared in the once radical *Independent* that Negrophilism had to be abandoned: "sentimental abolitionism was well enough in its day; but Mississippi owes its present sad condition as much to sentimental abolitionists as to fiendish Negro-haters. The blacks were ruined as good citizens by the chronic prattle about their rights, and they were never roused to a noble manhood by instructions as their duties. . . . let us empty our minds of cant and sentimental philanthropy, and learn that our black ward is in very truth a barbarian and needs our best efforts to uplift him in the scale of civilization." Also explicit about the critical change in northern public opinion in general, the New York *Times* observed: "Ten years ago the North was nearly united in a feeling of sympathy for the freedmen, and in a determination to defend their rights. Now . . . not a few believe that the rights of the whites have been infringed upon."[4]

However, some Republicans, troubled by the uncritical centennial spirit of reconciliation, warned that conciliatory gestures should not get out of hand. President Grant, replying to the suggestion that he should have called on the former Confederate leader Jefferson Davis when in St. Louis, declared: "we are not prepared . . . to apologize for the past." Even more suspicious of reconciliation talk were such unionists as the Missouri bank president, who, after six years of reconciliation with Confederate sympathizers in Missouri, protested that "no man can be elected in this State for any thing that did not

301

serve in the Rebel army. Now we are sick and tired of Reconciliation. We are now disfranchised." Speaking on the issue of continuing disorder and disfranchisement in Mississippi, staunch radical Senator Oliver P. Morton instructed his colleagues that denying outrages and overlooking lawlessness in order to encourage reconciliation, at a time when the rights of blacks were systematically violated, was sheer hypocrisy: "It will be the cry of 'Peace, peace,' when there is no peace." Similarly, the Washington *National Republican* was concerned about the fact that the "Centennial Gush fever" abroad in the land was permitting southerners to continue unrepentant and unreconstructed under the cloak of fraternal rhetoric. What some optimistically viewed as mutual reconciliation, then, might have actually been a peace settlement on southern terms.[5]

Earlier in the spring, newspaper correspondent Horace Redfield had commented on the disillusionment among blacks regarding their treatment by the Republican party. He declared that he had never seen so much restiveness at the Nashville National Colored Convention; the delegates were "sick of the Republican party . . . it has deceived them, betrayed them, insulted them, suffered them to be massacred by wholesale, stolen their money through the Freedmen's Bank [which had been created by Congress and then had gone bankrupt in 1874], refused their chosen representative admission to the Senate [Pinckney B. S. Pinchback of Louisiana], given them only petty and insignificant offices bearing no proportion to the value of their votes." Similarly, in a plea for federal protection, a petition from Louisiana blacks to President Grant underscored promises and hopes unfulfilled. Complaining of the fact that the whites had both enacted the laws and disobeyed them, the Negro petitioners stated: "we have tried to obey and be governed by the laws that have been made, and we see very little credit for it." Noting that the blacks had voted the Republican ticket while putting up with a reign of terror and that, even under Republican rule, they had been robbed of their lives and their rights, the petitioners pointed out that the "Republican party agreed to compromise with the Democratic party. What good are the compromises doing . . . it gives the Democrat's party more power to steal from us and to whip us and to kill us." Also disenchanted with the empty promises made in the Civil Rights Act of 1875, they claimed that it made no difference: "Same old whipping, murdering."[6]

Although most blacks were not about to defect to the enemy camp of the Democrats they no longer had any illusions about the Republicans. Furthermore, by 1876 the possibility that the Republicans could garner many electoral votes in the southern states seemed so unlikely that the region was reduced to secondary importance in partisan calculations. With the Negro being of limited help and perhaps even a political liability to the party, the Republicans were primarily concerned not with reconstruction but with reelection, and the two efforts seemed no longer complementary.

On other questions as well, the Republicans were taking a new stance. Given the numerous and sensational revelations of corruption in the administration, including as offenders President Grant's private secretary and the secretary of war, a reform candidate was required to ensure that the "Presidential election of 1876 will mark a new and happy departure of the nation's birthday."[7] Thus, when in June the Republican convention became deadlocked, the delegates turned to the moderate Rutherford B. Hayes.[8]

To be sure, the stalemate provided a lucky break for Hayes, but he and his supporters were able to exploit the situation, not only on the convention floor but also before the delegates assembled. He had all the assets of availability as a dark horse without being one, and there was merit in his nomination as well. Hayes was able, honest, and good-natured, a man with solid credentials as a third-term governor. His was the strongest nomination because he divided the party least, and a divided party would be defeated. Considering the antagonisms that had to be reconciled and the interests that had to be recognized, Hayes's nomination as a compromise candidate made sense. Moreover, with the least prominent national record, he was most sheltered from attack when the national party was on the defensive. If Hayes was not a party giant, neither was he a pygmy nor a figurehead. And as one Republican convention delegate, essayist James Russell Lowell, noted: Hayes "was neither unknown nor even unexpected as a probable nominee." In comparison with the other Republican aspirants in 1876, Hayes was the most viable candidate; unlike the others, he had no bitter opponents and no questionable record, being, above all, a man with unique strategic advantages as an Ohioan, former Whig, and as the candidate who appealed both to potentially critical electoral elements, such as independent German voters and former Liberals, and to reformers and regulars, moderates and radicals. His nomination on June 16, 1876, was no mistake; it was a masterstroke.[9]

Reconstruction did not fare well at the party convention, for the platform included a strong note of reconciliation and could easily have been construed as rationalizing retreat.[10] Besides, Hayes's ambiguous, though muted, talk of reconciliation, honest governance, and a just policy for the South[11] was reinforced by his running mate William A. Wheeler, a proponent of a more conciliatory southern policy.[12] In a short, brave speech to the convention, the influential black leader Frederick Douglass frankly and sorrowfully remarked: "You say you have emancipated us. You have: and I thank you for it. You say you have enfranchised us. You have; and I thank you for it. But what is your emancipation?—what is your enfranchisement? What does it all amount to, if the black man, after having been made free by the letter of your law, is unable to exercise that freedom, and, having been freed from the slaveholder's lash, he is to be subject to the slaveholder's shot-gun?" Douglass went on to ask the assembled leaders of the Republican party whether they meant to make good to blacks the promises written into the Constitution, or whether the party could "get along without the vote of the black man of the South." He then answered, "Yes, that may be, possibly," indicating that he doubted it but was nevertheless worried about such an eventuality. Although the delegates may not have listened, the New York *Evening Post* had: "It is to be regretted that Frederick Douglass will not teach the colored people the lesson of self-dependence, instead of always demanding for them fresh guarantees, by proclamation, by statute, and by bayonet, of the rights which they must largely maintain for themselves." Similarly, the Cincinnati *Commercial* declared that the "colored people are free—they have the ballot—and they must learn to protect themselves." The funereal tone of Douglass' speech and the light shrug with which it was generally dismissed indicated just how little life remained in reconstruction.[13]

The Republican nomination of a midwestern reformer meant that the Democrats had to select an even more zealous reformer from the Northeast, one who could take the offensive with the rallying cry of reform. If they could find such a standard-bearer, it was indeed possible that a marginally Republican nation might choose a moderate Democratic president; and they chose the renowned reform governor of New York, Samuel J. Tilden. If Hayes was politically adroit, Tilden was a consummate politician. On June 28 he deftly secured the nomination by organizing the disorganized Democracy, though not seeming to, until the final ballots were counted.[14] Skillful too, was the Democratic platform, hammered out under Tilden's leadership; its reformist tone appealed to the North, whereas its championship of home rule pleased the South.[15]

Although the issue of reform had been expected to dominate the campaign, it was soon neutralized by the similarity of the candidates' views; and because the congressmen of both parties were for the most part unenthusiastic about enacting reform legislation, the question was increasingly regarded as irrelevant. By September even the reform organs conceded the submergence or disappearance of the issue, and many reformers turned to other concerns in their stump speeches.[16] Similarly, economic differences between the parties were expediently blurred or sidestepped in order to bridge intraparty differences on both sides. Thus this issue, except in a few contests, also turned out to be unimportant.[17]

Another unexpected development was the reversal in the anticipated campaign roles of the candidates. To the surprise of many observers, Tilden, clearly the more brilliant man, with more political experience, a superior gubernatorial record, and a better campaign organization and publications, seemed in the course of the campaign to lose ground to Hayes. His acceptance letter was so slow in coming out (he took almost twice as long as Hayes), so lengthy (469 lines to Hayes's 122), so pedantic in tone and obscure in meaning, that it was not at all the inspiring call to arms that had been expected of a great leader and reformer.[18] In contrast, by fulfilling the reformers' hopes for something more definite and emphatic than the Republican platform's treatment of civil service reform and by pledging to serve only a single term as president, Hayes had stolen some of Tilden's reform thunder.[19] For another thing, Tilden, instead of substantially helping to underwrite his campaign, loosened his own purse strings only grudgingly and belatedly, whereas Hayes finessed the issue of party assessments, denouncing them but not ending them.[20] Yet another matter was the way the candidates differed in responding to various campaign charges and issues: Hayes reacted quickly and forcefully; Tilden was hesitant, timid, and, for the most part, ineffective. Also, the prevailing idea that Tilden would be the chief engineer, keeping his eye on all parts of the party machine, was not borne out, for he stayed largely in the background.[21]

If Tilden's passivity was meant to be part of a grand design to avoid anything that might bring out the full northern Republican vote, it was questionable strategy when its objective was to overthrow the party in power.[22] In contrast to Hayes, Tilden seemed to lack the energy and the motivation to lead an aggressive and masterful campaign. Possibly he had exhausted himself in the struggle for nomination and had no reserves left to battle for the election. Even taking into account his tendencies toward introversion and the careful weighing of alternatives, he had clearly never been so hindered by them before. One reasonable explanation for his lackluster campaigning is that Tilden was a sick man, probably suffering from Parkinson's disease.[23] Indeed, his behavior suggested that he was not physically, and perhaps not psychologically, fit to bear the burdens of a reformist presidency in 1877. That was the belief of one of his advisers and confidants, John Bigelow, who noticed that Tilden took an inordinate amount of time to do things, complained childishly, and engaged in petty faultfinding. As Bigelow noted in his diary: "I begin to have some misgivings whether he will prove equal to the labors of the Presidency." The Republicans, of course, sensed all that and tried to use Tilden's failing health as an issue.[24] Moreover, they continued to keep Tilden off balance by diverting people's attention away from reform. In mid-August the independent New York *Herald* observed that the Democrats were waging a weak fight compared to their feisty opponents, and in early September the Democratic Chicago *Times* admitted that, since their conventions, the Democrats had shown themselves at their worst, and the Republicans, at their best.[25]

In midsummer came the bombshell that was to shape the subsequent campaign. It was the Hamburg massacre. On the Fourth of July, centennial day, with peace and brotherhood being proclaimed in Philadelphia, some white citizens of Aiken County in midland South Carolina were about to celebrate in their own way. A Negro militia company, parading in the predominantly black town of Hamburg, was ordered off the road by two young white men in a buggy. The Negro militiamen first refused to step aside, but then opened ranks, permitting the buggy to pass. Nevertheless, the whites brought suit against the militia company captain, charging him with obstructing the public highway. On July 8, the day set for the trial, the black militiamen were forced to take refuge in their armory when they found themselves surrounded by hundreds of whites from South Carolina and nearby Georgia, who demanded that the militia surrender its arms. When the blacks refused, both sides opened fire. One white was shot in the head and died instantly. The rest of them, infuriated, brought a cannon over from the nearby Georgia militia and bombarded the armory. Surrendering under fire, the militia was captured, and several hours later some of its leaders, who were also officeholders in town, were released, only to be shot in the back as they ran. Six blacks were murdered, and the homes of Negroes were looted by whites. In response to a report from Hamburg, the army dispatched an outfit to restore order.[26]

"I cannot help waving the bloody shirt when men are being murdered" just because they are black and vote Republican, exclaimed Benjamin F. Butler, reviving the traditional Republican campaign theme. The Boston *Journal* commented that if bloody shirt implied "that we have deprecated the shooting of the blacks in cold blood, that we have denounced men as traitors who pull down the American flag on a public holiday, that we have showed that the colored voters are deprived of their rights, and that the Democrats have obtained political ascendency by brute force—then we plead guilty." Many northerners agreed that Hamburg had initiated a program to shoot the Republican party into a minority in South Carolina. If whites could murder blacks during a Republican administration, asked the northerners, what would be fate of blacks under the Democrats? Amos Akerman of Georgia, who had no illusions whatever, advised: "do not unchain the tiger before he is tamed."[27]

307

The southern Democrats played the incident down as much as possible, the Louisville *Courier-Journal* dismissing it as Republican exaggeration designed to cause a "species of revival in the Republican camp-meetings over the country," with "their stock in trade as well as their trick in trade." In any case, the Democrats put the blame on the Hamburg Negroes for refusing to surrender their arms. It proved yet again, they pointed out, that the South Carolina government, like all the other southern Republican regimes, was unable to govern. The resulting chaos was certainly reprehensible but completely understandable. Some papers, such as The Augusta *Contitutionalist*, even justified the deed; "when a Satanic host, like the Radical party in the South, sow the wind, it is but natural that they shall reap the whirlwind."[28] And although many southern Democratic newspapers denounced the incident and admitted that such outrages were not sporadic but endemic, the general southern white response to Hamburg indicated an irreconcilable hostility to Republicanism and to political rights for blacks, even as many Republicans were talking of a lasting peace through reconciliation between the races and sections.

The northerners' reaction to Hamburg was a repeat of their initial response to the New Orleans coup during the congressional elections in autumn, 1874—first an expression of outrage and revulsion against the southern Democracy, but then a rationalization for inaction.[29] Most Republicans and even some Democrats at first declared that they would not permit such terrorism to continue and called for a revived effort to prevent fraudulent elections throughout the South. Encouraged by the apparent resurgence of sectional solidarity in the North, a black newspaper in Virginia suggested that the southern Democrats continue their terrorist tactics so that Tilden would lose all the northern electoral votes: "if a 'United South' can afford to make and antagonize a 'United North' let them try it, and Hamburg the elections through in November." Thus northern ballots would teach southern Democrats the folly of their terrorism.[30]

Rather worried, Democratic Congressman Samuel S. Cox of New York City wrote to Tilden: "You will see by the furor of the House yesterday on the Hamburg massacre, how . . . folks of the lyric mind are yet on race, and war etc." Fearing that federal intervention might be a consequence of all the clamor, a Pennsylvania Democrat claimed that "all they [the Republicans] want is to get up two or three such riots to put the military over them [the southerners] and control the Election." Wondering whether reconstruction still had a more potent effect on the people than reform, he commented, "I wish we could keep them [the white southerners] quiet," and proposed that the Democrats take the initiative. The Democratic national chairman Abram S. Hewitt advised one prominent southern Democrat: "I trust there will be no outbreaks in the South no matter how great the provocation may be," for the people in the North will resist "turning over the government to any party which inherits the odor of rebellion; and the republican speakers are making the most of this fear."[31]

In early August, upstate New York Democratic Congressman Scott Lord startled his colleagues by introducing a resolution that endorsed the right to vote, condemned southern terrorism, and urged the punishment of political terrorists. Southern Democrats tried to dodge the question but finally, with some exceptions and substantial abstentions, they voted for Lord's resolution, a clever move probably inspired not only by Lord, who was working for reelection in a Republican district, but also by Tilden himself. Tilden, however, did not publicly denounce the massacre, and the Republicans scoffed at Lord's resolution, considering it eloquent testimony that the issue was in fact hurting Tilden and helping Hayes.[32]

Although the northerners did deplore the events at Hamburg, it was by no means certain that they would tolerate any massive federal intervention to ensure fair elections. As the venerable abolitionist leader William Lloyd Garrison commented, "I wish I could cherish the hope that the North will meet the issues as inexorably and unitedly as the South: in that case there would be no cause for anxiety." Concerned about rumors that martial law was to be imposed in some southern states, the New York *Herald* declared that perhaps the bloody shirt was even bloodier than the northern Republicans had represented it, but "we are not living in Mexico and the Congress of 1875 did not pass the Force Bill." The New York *Evening Post* similarly opposed surrounding southern polling places with federal troops: it was time that the South "get out of the federal nursery, stand upon its feet and take care of itself."[33]

Meanwhile, the South was carefully reading those northern signals. The Democratic Augusta *Constitutionalist*, for one, noted that since the enforcement laws had just recently been rendered nugatory by the Supreme Court, the much touted "bayonet program of the administration" was "a mere scarecrow, a scheme of bombast, full of sound and fury"; southerners ought to take all that for precisely what it was—empty political gesturing. Moreover, as noted in a Democratic pamphlet, the "Administration has not troops enough to enforce its threats."[34]

Although the campaign theme was not meant to resurrect reconstruction, it did serve to advertise that an almost solidly Democratic South was confronting a somewhat less united Republican North—a division which itself became the leading issue. The Republicans, including Hayes, were convinced that reform alone could never win for them and that they could succeed only by pitting northern loyalty against southern disloyalty and stressing the related questions of potential federal support of southern war claims and internal improvements under a Democratic administration.[35] The solid South, with its past record and its political potential, was preoccupying northern Republicans to such a degree that the Republican Cincinnati *Gazette* claimed that "never before was an election so reduced to a single question," a conclusion with which practically everyone agreed by September. "Once more there is a united Democratic South and a divided North; and if the former should prevail in a Presidential election," warned the Boston *Journal*, "the weakness of the Northern Democracy and their destitution of earnest principles and purposes would combine to revive the old subserviency and sycophancy which we once thought had passed out of our politics for good." In the process, then, the contest became one between two sections, two parties, two tendencies, and two traditions.[36]

As a result, the record of each candidate during and after the war was thoroughly scrutinized, and for Tilden this became a controversial and embarrassing issue.[37] Republicans reiterated that, to quote *Harper's Weekly*, there were "questions which the war has left that can not be treated safely and wisely by a party and politicians who neither approved the war nor sympathized with reconstruction," and that a "Democratic restoration, with a candidate who was not even a 'war Democrat,' would be a reaction."[38]

During all that time, Democrats throughout the South were organizing to complete their counterreconstruction. Virtually united in the conviction that the "infernal" Fifteenth Amendment had made a "terrestrial hell" out of the southern states, they intended to "get rid of the negro as a voter," put an end to the remaining Republican regimes, and regain control of state politics.[39]

The first election skirmishes occurred in state contests in Alabama during early August, in Arkansas during early September, and in both Georgia and West Virginia during early October. As a whole, the results were not surprising, for that part of the South was already solidly Democratic; however, the size of the Democratic majorities and the great inroads into what was left of the Republican black-belt strongholds were larger than had been thought possible, notably in Alabama and Georgia, where there now seemed to be nothing left of the Republican party. It also appeared that border and Appalachian whites were continuing to leave the party.

Generally, the campaigns and polling scenes in those states were relatively quiet; there was almost no cause for controversy or even contest in some districts, where apathetic or feuding Republicans did not even run candidates. In other districts which still had substantial black electorates, the Democrats relied more on fraud than on violence to reduce the number of Republican ballots. Democratic officials did not open polls or did not provide enough polling places in Alabama, given its restrictive precinct law, or else, as in Georgia, they limited the electorate by putting the poll tax into effect. Although many blacks were disfranchised and others were disaffected or frightened, a few did willingly vote for the Democrats.[40] Thus those easy victories in the early contests reinforced the conviction that the "colored vote is not so 'reliable' as it was" and encouraged southern Democrats to redouble their efforts.[41]

Concentrating on the three doubtful states that were still controlled by the Republicans (Louisiana, South Carolina, and Florida), they prepared to employ both force and persuasion, terror and conciliation, a white-supremacist appeal and black recruitment, as well as energetic stumping and rampant cheating. At political meetings, particularly in South Carolina, the Democrats heckled or threatened Republican speakers, and when the blacks fled, they turned Republican meetings into Democratic rallies. Horsemen rode in bands, shouting and shooting in order to frighten the Negroes or, failing that, sometimes burning their cabins or crops, or threatening them with eviction and the loss of their jobs, credit, and businesses. Not that beating and killing were entirely abandoned; but there was less of that type of violence than in past contests, at least in certain areas of Louisiana and Florida, since some southern Democrats realized that reports of overt violence would be detrimental to Tilden in the North. Bribery was sometimes resorted to as well, with a vote being worth a pair of shoes or five dollars in cash. Of course, the intimidation was not all on one side: there were instances of black Republicans meting out punishment to defecting blacks. Still, most of the incidents were perpetrated by whites against black Republicans. Indeed, the whites were so determined in their efforts that Attorney General Alphonso Taft, who had replaced Edwards Pierrepont in May of 1876, confided to candidate Hayes that the question ought to be raised as to "whether the 15th Amendment shall be given up." And the situation was serious enough for Republican reformer Benjamin H. Bristow to ask: "are we to have a Government at all?"[42]

At the same time, southern Democrats were doing their best to make a good impression on the North, as they tried to counter the bloody shirt by wrapping themselves in the American flag. For example, throughout the campaign the Democracy dispatched temperate southern speakers pledging loyalty to the Union and appealing for national harmony to northern centennial observances. In an attempt to allay sectional fears, they repeatedly told the North that all the South wanted was justice and equity, purification of the government and pacification of the country—all within the Union. In fact, what was necessary to everyone in every section was precisely the same—peace and prosperity, and neither could be achieved without reform. This was particularly true in the South, for all the problems there resulted from usurpation and persecution by the Republicans.

Had they reasonably upheld reconstruction, the southerners would not have been that strongly Democratic, or so they argued. Furthermore, it was understandable that the weak, oppressed South solidly opposed the Republicans; on the other hand, it was reprehensible that the prosperous, powerful North perpetuated this spirit of the war by "raising mock issues, waving false lights, throwing firebrands into the sections and dust into the people's eyes." Moreover, if "from 1865 to 1876 the Republican party has been doing its best to reconstruct the South on a solid and satisfactory basis, and, by its own showing, had accomplished nothing, what possiblity is there," asked the Democrats, "that it will accomplish anything between 1876 and 1880." According to the Democratic St. Louis *Republican*, "if eleven years of failure does not constitute failure, pray what does?"[43]

White southerners contended that the criticism of the Republicans kept them in a double bind: when the southerners gave assurances that they had accepted the results of the war, they were dismissed as insincere; yet when they did not give them, they were upbraided and simultaneously "deprived of self-control . . . yet denounced for not exercising it. The fruits of good government are demanded of them and bad government is saddled upon them against their protest." The only remedy, then, according to that line of argument, was to place southern governments in the hands of southern Democrats who would assume complete responsibility, as well as having a real interest in maintaining order. Elect Tilden, advised the Democrats, and an instant pacification of the South would follow his inauguration, just as when the Democrats had regained power in formerly disturbed southern states.[44]

Having observed that ploy firsthand, Amos Akerman wrote that "when speaking for effect at the North," the southern Democrats "say much about accepting the results of the war in good faith, and respecting the rights of everybody," but all that was contradicted by their "drastic policy and unguarded utterances" at home. At the same time, southern politicians in the national party councils stayed in the background, encouraging moderation and endorsing resolutions that implied acceptance of the results of reconstruction. Even within the South, less inflammatory speeches were given when northern reporters were known to be present; even party platforms were drafted with the North in mind. One southern Negro declared that the southern Democracy "subscribes to them [constitutional amendments] one day only to violate them the next."[45]

Despite the claims made to northern Democrats that the national campaign had priority and that southern Democrats were willing to do anything to help Tilden's cause, even going so far as to propose that the state campaign be divorced from the national, their true goal was expressed by a prominent South Carolina Democrat: "it is not Tilden we are working for so much as relief from the rule of the robbers here at home." And as a perceptive correspondent described their motives, "if by trading him [Tilden] off to certain defeat they could get control of South Carolina they would cheerfully do it," though "it is hard to say what they would not trade off to get South Carolina under their control once more. All they want is to get it once, knowing very well that they can hold it forever."[46]

Of the three Republican southern states, Florida's parties were the most evenly matched. Although the Democrats had a slight joint majority in the legislature and were successful in electing their candidate to the United States Senate, the Republicans had an able incumbent governor, Marcellus L. Stearns, who had considerable local patronage and thus influence with the election returning boards in the counties and in Tallahassee. He was not always very astute, however, in the way he handled quarreling Florida Republicans. Stearns was pitted against Democrat George F. Drew, a wealthy businessman who intended to retain adherents while capitalizing on the Republican division, which caused frequent defections. On the other hand, in comparison with previous state canvasses, the campaign was no more violent or corrupt than usual, but the intimidation and irregularities were such that doubts were raised as to whether the campaign was free and whether the count would be fair.[47]

In Louisiana, amid the usual Republican bickering and convention disorder, with black disaffection now substantial, the entrenched customhouse crew again prevailed and nominated the tough, shrewd, but highly unpopular federal marshal, Stephen B. Packard, for governor. United and determined, the Democrats worked energetically to construct a grand conservative alliance. Their gubernatorial choice was Francis T. Nicholls, a lawyer who had been an officer in the Confederate army. Nicholls made concerted efforts to woo black supporters, some of whom agreed to vote for the state Democratic ticket because they were disgusted with the Lousiana Republican party. At the same time, those blacks and whites who remained Republican would be prevented from voting, insofar as possible without large-scale violence, which would play into the hands of the Republican returning boards by furnishing them with the justification to throw out the returns. In New Orleans the Republicans attempted to counter Democratic fraud in voter registration by means of vigorous election enforcement, but elsewhere in the state they relied on phony registration. Moreover, though some troops were to be stationed at specific locations, there wasn't enough manpower to ensure order in every parish or in every area of any specific parish. As for the actual canvass, it was for the most part less violent and fraudulent than usual, with the important exception of five parishes, most of them near the Mississippi state line, where the Mississippi plan was put into operation. Intimidation, irregularities, and murders of Republicans there were so prevalent and so publicized that they popularized the word "bulldoze," and the validity of the outcome would of course be highly questionable.[48]

Regardless of future returns, the Republicans assumed that they could rely on the packed state returning board, which was considered by the Democrats as the "crowning invention of carpetbag ingenuity" because it was the sole and final authority on ruling in and ruling out returns from any polling place according to their purported fairness or fraudulence. Recognizing that the army alone could not ensure a fair election, General Philip H. Sheridan wrote President Grant that the question of irregularity should be left primarily to the returning board, "whose duty it is to correct fraud when the returns are brought in." Grant agreed, and on October 31, even before the election, ordered him to protect the board. Still, the Democrats remained confident that, as Congressman Randall L. Gibson put it, "our majority will be so large and won so fairly that the Returning Board even will not attempt to pervert it."[49]

Meanwhile, in South Carolina the Democrats were attempting to oust incumbent Governor Daniel H. Chamberlain. In office since December, 1874, New Englander Chamberlain was perhaps the best southern Republican governor; however, he was isolated within his party. Many state Republicans were embittered because they believed that his reform administration and his insistence on financial retrenchment, as well as his maneuvering to win the approval of white Democrats, had been done at the expense of white and black Republicans.[50] And, despite all the compliments he received from the conservatives, he did not succeed in gaining their support, for most of the whites wanted no part of any coalition that would mean the continuation of Republican rule.

Also intent on capturing the only remaining legislature in the South with a Republican majority in both chambers, the state Democratic party put together a straight ticket, with every candidate a veteran of the Confederate army. The slate was headed by planter Wade Hampton, a former general and by then a moderate conservative who made an appeal for black support, emphasizing that the interests of both races were identical. A paternalistic aristocrat, he believed in white supremacy, yet advocated special consideration for the needs and rights of what he regarded as the subordinate race. Very different indeed were some of his restless followers, whose actions contradicted Hampton's speeches. Such men constituted a party that resembled an army over which Hampton conveniently exercised little control. They had organized almost three hundred rifle clubs, sporting red uniforms that hinted at bloodshed. Making their presence and strength known by means of frequent, large, and well organized public parades, the Red Shirts counted on an overawing display of white strength to frighten the blacks out of their voting majority in the state and to demoralize the ineffective black state militia.[51]

During the campaign the Republicans split into pro- and anti-Chamberlain factions. Overwhelmed by the opposition within and without his party, Chamberlain, compromised by previous overtures to the Democrats and burdened by unpopular Republican running mates, seemed paralyzed and unable to conduct his campaign or to take decisive action against the mounting turmoil. As a result, fights turned into race riots, with the usual slaughter of blacks; perhaps 150 were killed (Ellenton, in the midlands, during mid-September became a prime follow-up of Hamburg). Virtually all the whites saw the campaign as a fervent religious crusade for deliverance or, as they put it, for redemption of the prostrate state.[52]

Receiving little sympathy from northern Republicans in that unequal fight, one South Carolina Republican despairingly asked: "Must we be subjected to . . . this abuse and degradation in order that our republican friends of the North may be able to hold us up to scorn and detestation? . . . we who have borne the brunt of their persecution are not longer willing to be targets for assassins unless the republican party of the North will stand by us, and in such a way as will be of some avail to us."[53]

Such pleas were unavailing, however, for most northern Republicans and independents saw no future for the southern party. Remarking on Chamberlain's dependence on Washington, the New York *Herald* noted that if Hayes were president, Chamberlain would be in trouble, because "Mr. Hayes does not believe in federal interference in the South." Similarly, on election eve the Springfield *Republican*, which was supporting Hayes, declared that should he be elected, he was "bound to represent to the South the northern good-will and the northern disposition to let alone." Horace Redfield, reporting on the campaign in the South, considered it only a question of time until the whites had every southern state under their control: "withdraw the troops, say 'hands off,' and the black government here would fall like a block of cards. It cannot stand alone." In fact, Redfield believed that the outcome would be much the same no matter who became president: "Hayes can not sustain the concern, and Tilden won't. Tilden will let it fall at once, while Hayes will be apt to try to prop it up yet a little longer."[54]

Nevertheless, an election was to take place, and it was clear that without federal intervention the Democrats with their strong-arm tactics would capture South Carolina, perhaps jeopardizing Hayes's chances. Governor Chamberlain requested troops to quell disturbances. Grant responded in characteristic fashion: initial hesitation, then ringing pronouncements, brisk orders, and some belated troop movements in the South, particularly in South Carolina, where squads of soldiers were sprinkled across the state in seventy locations, most of which were polling places. Events had certainly justified army action, but politics had ensured it. In contrast to the

Mississippi crisis of September, 1875, Grant, now in October, 1876, intervened when the fate of the national, not just the state, party was at stake. Whether the federal aid was early and effective enough to ensure free, orderly elections and to encourage Negro voters to get out to the polls was another matter. The size of the force dispatched (about one thousand men) was so small that their use was limited and their coverage restricted. Still, the army action did have a quieting effect upon many, if not all, of the disturbed districts, and it enabled Republicans in the last weeks of the campaign to hold some meetings without being interrupted by the Democrats. The whites offered no resistance, but the good-humored, friendly reception they accorded the troops on arrival was instructive, for in a sense the troops were disarmed and welcomed as protectors rather than as oppressors. What the whites' hospitable attitude reflected was shrewdness as well as satisfaction with what they had already accomplished. But political intimidation by means other than outright violence was not at all deterred: the Red Shirts did not disarm and disperse, nor could the presence of the army dissipate the effect of months of intimidation or remedy the disruption of the Republican campaign.[55]

Neither could the troops do anything about the frequent registration manipulation, which had already been accomplished. Federal election enforcement was meant to counter all that, but with the exception of New Orleans, the negligible expenditures on the southern states in 1876 amounted to a pathetic token effort. Once again, belated enforcement at election time had more political and psychological importance in the North than any real effect in the South, for it was largely an attempt to gather northern Republicans into a "countervailing unity."[56]

Unfortunately, the various fall elections in the North produced a standoff, thus increasing the tension and intensifying the struggle.[57] With the likelihood that the outcome would hinge upon the electoral votes whose returns might be disputed, there began to be serious talk of the possibility of a constitutional crisis over any of those votes that were contested. And since the Constitution made no provision for such a contingency, and Congress itself, divided between a Republican Senate and a Democratic House of Representatives, had failed to provide a solution for such an emergency, each side claimed that in the event of an electoral dispute, the other would flout law and justice and resort to any expedient.[58]

Although in the closing weeks of the campaign uneasy Americans consoled themselves with the thought that there had been narrow escapes before and that an electoral crisis during the centennial year was unthinkable, not to mention unpatriotic, the drift toward precisely that was as inexorable as the progression of a Greek tragedy. Writing from South Carolina on election day, reporter Redfield prayed, "God grant that the American people have chosen a President to-day by so large an electoral vote that there can be no contest." But he added: "I am fearful."[59]

November 7, the day of the presidential election, dawned inauspiciously throughout the nation, with heavy rain and fog in many places, and a raw wind and gray skies in others. Despite the mounting excitement and apprehension in the North, no serious incidents disturbed the voting, with the usual exception of some arrests in New York and Delaware. Precautions had been taken, especially in New York City, where at many polling booths the voter was met by four election inspectors, two polling clerks, two election supervisors, two federal marshals, and two city policemen, all prepared to preserve order and to prevent fraud. In the South there were scattered disturbances in Greenville, Robbins, and Columbia, South Carolina, but none of any great consequence, since the army had a calming effect at all the polling places where it was stationed.[60]

Democratic cheating and irregularities, however, were rampant throughout the South, and the events of the day accurately reflected the present state of reconstruction. In New Orleans, the customhouse, that Republican fortress in the midst of the enemy's camp, had to be occupied by marines day and night for protection. In Hamburg, South Carolina, correspondent Redfield noted that of the men gathered to vote, every white man was armed, but not one black; he also mentioned reports to the effect that in places where no troops were stationed, the blacks were voting heavily Democratic, but that wherever troops were present, they were voting heavily Republican. Meanwhile, in nearby Augusta, Georgia, whites and blacks were assigned to separate ballot boxes at the courthouse; the whites cast

319

their ballots without any need to show proof of having paid their taxes, "but at the black box, in the same building, the case was far different. Every black man was asked from three to a dozen questions" and was also required to present his tax receipt. As a result, about half the blacks—but not a single white man—were turned away, thus giving Tilden a three to one margin. "And this is equal rights!" scoffed Redfield: "the whole thing looks to me very much like a farce."[61]

Early returns on election night in New York City indicated that Governor Tilden had carried New York, New Jersey, Connecticut, and Indiana in the lower North, as well as most, and possibly all, of the South. So the majority of New Yorkers as well as both candidates went to sleep under the impression that Tilden had won. But the results had still not come in from three southern states: South Carolina, Florida, and Louisiana, and from the Pacific Coast states. At that point Tilden would have won with the electoral vote of any one of those three southern states or that of just one Pacific Coast state. But regardless of the national result, the regional strength of the Democrats in the South was already indisputable. Reflecting the southern view toward the desired end of reconstruction and the Democratic recapture of the South, as well as adding an ironic note thirteen years after the Emancipation Proclamation, a wealthy Washington banker wrote to a prominent Virginian: "I congratulate you on the glorious result of yesterday's election, it ought to be called 'Emancipation day' as it virtually emancipates the *South* from the tyranny and oppression under which it has groaned for so many years, and emancipates also the poor deluded negro from the ignorance, as to his best friends, in which he has long been kept by designing demagogues."[62]

For all the uncertainty about who would be the winner of the presidential race, other matters were considerably clarified by the national vote. For one thing, Americans had voted in unprecedented numbers (the greatest proportionate turnout of any presidential election thus far), with an increase of two million voters over 1872, when many people had abstained. And although the Democrats scored the greatest absolute gains, the relative decline in the Republican percentage of the vote was to have been expected, given their easy victory in 1872. Nevertheless, the Democracy had declined in every northern state since 1874, for the Republicans, in 1875 and 1876, had largely succeeded in countering the major offensive that the Democrats had so successfully launched in the off-year congressional elections. Despite the stubbornly continuing depression, the massive corruption, and the widespread dissatisfaction in 1876, the Democratic majorities of 1874 had been reversed or reduced. The Republicans had improved their relative position with a gain of thirty-three seats in the House of Representatives, yet the Democrats narrowly retained control. But Hayes, with a higher percentage of the vote than his congressional party, had squeaked through in a number of northern states where the electoral prizes were up for grabs: he won eighteen of twenty-two northern states in the two-party vote, with a majority of 255,640 (52 percent); that was far less than in 1868 or 1872,[63] but the burden of the Grant administration record did show "what a Devil of a load the Gov[ernor] had to carry."[64]

Hayes's relative success in the North can be accounted for by the adroit tactics of the Republican campaigners, including the candidate himself; for by bringing to the fore the issue of southern unity, supremacy, and influence, with old and new arguments, however important or insignificant, however true or fabricated, the Republicans had successfully touched upon vital interests, tapped deep emotions, and reached the voters through their fears. Just as they had done in 1872, the Republicans had put great stress on the fact that a Democratic victory meant doubt and change, whereas Republican victory meant certainty and stability. With the major exception of four states in the North, just enough voters in the many marginal northern states (such as Illinois, Ohio, Pennsylvania, California, Oregon, and Wisconsin) had, as their overriding consideration, not their disgust with the Grant administration—although that was real enough—but a pervasive distrust of the Democrats and the solid South.[65] The Republicans were able to convert southern Democratic strength into a source of critical Democratic weakness in the North. And despite all their efforts, the Democrats had found, when it came to the issue of reform, that internal unity and strength were often elusive, whereas their attempts to replace the southern issue of the Republicans with others had been rather inconclusive. Thus Tilden had not been altogether successful in conciliating the southern Democrats without alarming the northern voters.

Although the Democrats had done exceedingly well in solidifying the South and capturing an important fragment of the North, they, to their peril, had ignored and therefore lost the vital Pacific Coast states, apparently operating in part under the assumption that Tilden had enough states without bothering to underwrite the Pacific Coast campaign and to develop strong organizations there.[66] As a result, they had given up, by default, electoral votes that might have been theirs and would probably not have been seriously contested after the election.[67]

As for the candidates themselves, Tilden had seemed to many northerners the more dangerous man to have in the White House, given his and his party's past positions as well as his temperamental indecisiveness, his physical disability, and his uninspiring leadership during the campaign. Hayes had appeared safer and sounder on the great issues. He had been faithful to the Union and had given support to the Fifteenth Amendment; he also had shown himself to be more serviceable as a "level-headed, sensible man," who had adroitly led his coalition and steered his campaign for election as ably as Tilden had in his struggle for nomination.[68]

A number of incongruities could be found in the election results. Hayes, because of his letter of acceptance and courtship of the reformers, regained some disgruntled Republicans, independents, and former Liberals who, attracted by Tilden's reformist credentials, might well have been recruited by the Democrats. Hayes also won indispensable Ohio on the strength of the Negro voters, many of whom were later to denounce him as a turncoat. As for Tilden, he might lose the national election because he had lost the Pacific states, even though the politicians and the press had, all along, assumed that he would win certain of them; and Hayes might yet win by securing several southern states that many observers had predicted he would lose and that many considered rightfully Tilden's.

The election of 1876 demonstrated how precarious the balance between the races, parties, and sections had become and how illusory were the pervasive "centennialities" (that is, the commemorative banalities and exaggerated expectations); for the centennial did not fulfill its purported function as a safety valve for the campaign nor did the campaign live up to the hope that it would be the glorious culmination of the centennial. The year itself, which had earlier been regarded as the high point in the nation's history, turned out to be one of its nadirs. Despite the anticipated harmony between the regions, the actual campaign had caused political patterns to become more rigidly divisive and intensely sectional than ever before. Despite the desired fraternity between the races and comity between the parties, the reverse had taken place, and the huge numbers who voted on November 7 revealed how deeply but equally Americans were divided in the country and in Congress. The campaign was also one that mocked the very principles of republican self-government, which had been extolled everywhere that year, even as such new expressions as "bulldozing" and "solid South" were gaining prominence.[69] Although espousing such issues as comprehensive reform and honest governance, what both parties succeeded in doing was to demonstrate the limits and deficiencies of the democratic process by perpetrating frauds and irregularities, which were to culminate in a national scandal and an unprecedented dispute over the election's outcome. Scarcely anything was left to be salvaged from that centennial wreck—the presidential election of 1876.[70]

The forebodings of the presidential canvass had been justified: who the next president was to be remained undecided on election day. The Democrats, who at first were just one electoral vote short of a majority, with Hayes apparently trailing by nineteen, had expected the full returns to provide a small majority, since Tilden could spare two southern states and still win. But then the Republicans claimed victory in the three southern states still under their control and maintained that the official count would certify Hayes as the winner. Party man William E. Chandler exclaimed with regard to his party and to Hayes: "it seemed as if the dead had been raised."[71]

During the campaign many politicians had expected that if the election returns were close, the results would be contested because of the numerous irregularities and the intimidation involved in the southern canvass. Thus the claim to electoral votes was not just a daring afterthought concocted by politicians and editors in New

York City. The initial reports or claims that might have been sent in by both sides did not really matter. Nor was there any conclusive evidence that the Republicans in Louisiana, Florida, or South Carolina were about to concede. Even if they had, it could have been papered over as a blunder arising from incorrect information. What counted were the official returns and certification of the Republican returning boards. If Hayes obtained all the electoral votes of the three southern states, plus one disputed elector in Oregon, he would have a total of 185 electoral votes to Tilden's 184—that is, just enough to win. Many Republicans counted on the returning boards to do their duty.[72] Northern Republicans in particular implored their southern counterparts to hold the fort, which prompted Amos Akerman to comment about the curious turn of affairs: "The Republicans of the South were abandoned by the Northern wing of the party in the late campaign. Frightened by the Democratic clamor against Southern Republicanism, the managers of the campaign neglected the South and gave all their attention to the North, and yet the South has probably saved the administration, and this by its unassisted labors."[73]

Unhappily for a great many Americans, the contest was to be decided by the electoral votes of three southern states whose postwar political history inspired no confidence in the honesty of their politicians or in the fairness of their elections. The official winner of those electoral votes depended upon the decisions of state returning boards, which were empowered not only to count the votes but to decide which were valid. Such authority was regarded as particularly dangerous in the hands of the Louisiana canvassing board. After all, even Republican Congresses had concluded that the Louisiana returning board had fraudulently manipulated the returns in previous elections. The presidency—then "trembling in the balance"—was to be weighed by boards in which some members were candidates and therefore judges of their own election, and by others who were officeholders counting on future patronage.[74]

The Democrats vowed that they would not submit to such a steal; the ballot must not be prostituted by a fictitious revision of the returns by the corrupt authority of three rotten boroughs. The Elmira *Gazette* saw it as a plot "To claim in advance the election of Hayes and then reverse the majorities for Tilden in the three doubtful Southern States by fraud." Worried in private, they nevertheless publicly proclaimed their side victorious as adamantly as the Republicans were doing.[75]

Commenting on the situation four days after the election, Kentucky Republican John Marshall Harlan wrote that both sides were "claiming a victory with equal confidence and in equal ignorance of the result." While the people alternated in their mood between acute anxiety and a fatalism due to indifference or disgust, the politicians argued passionately, employing whatever rhetoric and assumptions they thought might advance their party's position in the confused and uncertain situation, as rumors of plots and defections burgeoned.[76]

As for President Grant, he promised to maintain order and insisted on fair play.[77] But as before in his southern policy, especially in Louisiana, his actions did not precisely coincide with what he claimed was nonpartisanship, for Grant and his cabinet were in various ways throwing the weight of the administration and the army behind the Republican claims. By instructing the army to prevent interference with the official count, which he had already done for Louisiana even before the election, Grant made sure that the Republicans would continue to control the three southern state capitals. Later, when there were two claimants for the governorship in each of the three states and rival legislatures as well in Louisiana and South Carolina, the soldiers were placed around the statehouses to protect and maintain the Republican regimes while they counted and certified the presidential vote. It was clearly Grant's intention to keep the official electoral votes in the Republican column by continuing to maintain the Republican legislatures until the electoral crisis was over.[78]

Troops were not only dispatched to the South but were also moved from the West to or near Washington, in order to forestall any possible disturbances in the capital during the electoral crisis; but the army was not making any attempt to browbeat the opposition. The timing and location of troop movements, the potential for disorder as conveyed by General Sherman's orders, and the great amount of publicity they received made the president's use of the army as a political instrument very effective. The veiled warning to the disgruntled Democrats was clear: any attempted coup would be crushed, and any disorder around the Capitol intended to intimidate Congress would be dispersed. Thus, Grant helped to limit the crisis and decrease the possibility of unlikely contingencies. Meanwhile, Hayes and Tilden also remained restrained and responsible, although Hayes was to be more accessible, active, and forceful in the coming months. Indeed, given Tilden's procrastination, indecision, irritability, and temper, some Democrats in Congress started to lose confidence in his leadership and judgment.[79]

The four tense days of November were followed by four tumultuous months. During November the main scenes of activity were in the three disputed southern state capitals,[80] where, amid wild maneuvers and rumors of intrigue, the Republican returning boards duly ground out their expected decision for Hayes.[81] Then on December 6, when the Republican Senate and the Democratic House of Representatives refused to agree on a method of counting the disputed electoral votes, the anticipated impasse in Congress was reached. However, the furious controversy was useful as a safety valve for overheated indignation. The repetitious, inflammatory braggadocio began to generate public apathy, and eventually the continued uncertainty caused increasing insecurity and division in the ranks of the congressional parties, which worked to the advantage of bipartisan consultation.[82]

The initially inconsequential procedural move of December 14–18 to create a select committee in each chamber, charged to devise an acceptable way to count the electoral vote, became the central mechanism for a pivotal process of intense negotiation. That action in mid-December was not, however, a victory for compromise but merely an acquiescence to consultation. Both parties supported the resolutions because they doubted that a satisfactory plan could be agreed upon, and both wished to demonstrate the appearance of support for compromise, while attempting to put their opponents at a disadvantage in future jockeying on the committees. But by mid-January the situation was to change; the discussion in the interim shifted from whether there should be a compromise to what kind of compromise could be devised. Congressional consultation had evolved into serious, sustained negotiation, especially because the presidential aspirants themselves offered no acceptable solution. In addition, the public and the business community now demanded a solution so that the nation would have a president on March 4. Finally, the necessity of compromise was underscored by the widespread recognition that neither a constitutional amendment nor a new election would be likely to solve the problem.[83] By January 26, 1877, under the belated but determined leadership of bipartisan moderates in the Senate, who exploited Republican division in that chamber and secured the support of the Democrats in the House (where many Democratic congressmen recognized that only a commission would have the legal authority to reject Hayes's official electoral certificates), and aided by strong public feeling in favor of a peaceful solution, the congressional deadlock was broken, despite the opposition of the two presidential contenders and their staunch partisan supporters.[84]

The decision was to create a board of arbitration, the Electoral Commission, to be composed of members of Congress and the Supreme Court and roughly divided along party lines, leaving each side with the hope, partly justified and partly illusory, of victory, since not all the members who would serve on the commission were known when Congress approved the Electoral Count Act. Some observers speculated that the selection of the odd member from the Supreme Court might cause the outcome to depend on the unrevealed legal thinking or the uncertain political proclivities of that not-yet-chosen justice, but others believed that his selection would be irrelevant because all the justices would be impartial. Many observers thought that Justice David Davis would be selected; however, shortly after the Senate passed the electoral bill, but before the House of Representatives had acted on it, Davis was elected to the United States Senate by a coalition of Illinois Democrats and Greenback party members. Although his election appeared to have made no difference with regard to support for the pending bill, contradictory speculation then centered on whether, if asked, Justice Davis would agree to serve on the Electoral Commission, and, if so, what side he would favor. Clearly, the decision to create the commission was a leap in the dark, for "all was obscurity."[85]

When Davis was indeed asked to serve, he declined. Finally, on January 31, 1877, Associate Justice Joseph P. Bradley of New Jersey, a moderate Republican of sometimes independent views, became the fifth judge. But even the selection of Bradley did not dispel doubt about the outcome. Some Republicans were reassured, whereas others feared that he was more a lawyer than a Republican; conversely, many Democrats worried that he was more a Republican than a lawyer, but were somewhat encouraged by his record of conservative legal decisions.[86]

On February 1 the electoral count began with the Florida dispute. That case turned on whether the Electoral Commission was to go behind the certified count of the Florida returning board as reflected in the official certificate and to inquire whether its returns were accurate and valid. Both sides embarked on a resourceful search for legal reasons to support their own views: the Republicans suddenly became converted to the sacredness of the rights of the states to determine electoral votes; the Democrats were quite willing to forsake their sanctified states' rights position under the circumstances. After due deliberation, the commission, on February 9, voted 8 to 7 to accept the state certificate as official and in proper order, thereby declaring Hayes's electors to be duly elected. That decision greatly narrowed down and simplified the commission's work. Subsequently, by the same strict partisan division, the majority of the commission awarded Hayes with all the disputed electoral votes of the states in question, completing their work on February 27. As far as the Republicans were concerned, the dispute was settled and Governor Hayes was the next president.[87]

The Democrats were furious. One Marylander complained that the Electoral Commission had "refused to do what it was created to do," namely, to consider the dispute itself and decide on its merits, by investigating fraud. Admitting defeat, the St. Louis *Republican* observed that even if the commission had uncovered returning board frauds it would have made no difference, for the certificates of the returning boards covered everything. Associate Justice Stephen J. Field, who served on the Electoral Commission and voted with the Democrats, concluded: "fraud was protected from exposure by a certificate of its authors."[88]

Although the Electoral Commission had all the trappings of disinterested legality and nonbiased authority, the arguments and decisions had been partisan. Given the pressures that were brought to bear, it scarcely could have been otherwise. In addition, there were pressing practical considerations for not going behind the returns in the disputed states. There was simply not enough time to make a detailed analysis of the votes actually cast, or to have a thorough investigation of intimidation or fraud in specific precincts, or to make a careful assessment of the actions of the state canvassing boards in computing and certifying the count. Moreover, as a matter of law, a prima facie case is always very strong, and as the New York *Herald* pointed out, the "presumption is always in favor of the official action of the constituted authorities of a State. Their determination is conclusive and binding until impugned on conclusive evidence." But it would be altogether misleading to suggest that a tribunal could not have reached a different decision. After all, Congress had gone behind a state's official returns before, rejecting the electoral vote of Louisiana in 1873. At the very least, impartial men could have concluded that because a reasonable doubt existed about the correctness of the certificates the electoral vote would not be counted for any candidate, thereby throwing the election into the Democratic House. What the Democrats lacked was not a case but a majority vote. Relieved but realistic, the staunchly Republican Chicago *Inter-Ocean* observed that the "fifth judge, luckily a Republican, has come in to determine the case," but added that the "choice could easily have gone the other way—it is the good fortune of the Republicans, and not their wisdom in consenting to the arbitration, that has won."[89] Perhaps the best that can be said for the decision of the Electoral Commission is that it disposed of the matter in a sanctioned way. For many Americans of independent judgment, the commission's decision made considerable legal and practical sense, but shed no light on the questions raised by moral judgment or common sense with regard to the real disputes, for it did not inquire into whether Hayes was in fact elected or not—only whether he was officially certified as such. The collateral question of form—the regularity of the certificates—had displaced the substantive question of fact, which was the truthfulness of the certificates.

The House Democrats then proceeded to delay the official joint electoral count in Congress, thus raising the possibility that Hayes would not be regularly and duly inaugurated on schedule.[90] Although obstruction was no way to solve the presidential question or to ensure Tilden's inauguration, the tactic was certain to create chaos. If the count were not completed, the whole dispute would be thrown into the next Congress, in which each party would continue to control the same respective chamber, but by such a precarious margin that the possibility of completing the count would be more uncertain. Also, the Republicans might secure the required majority of the states in the next House, thus rendering the Democratic delay pointless if the House alone decided the election according to the constitutionally prescribed procedure when there was no majority in the electoral college. Furthermore, if the intransigence of the Democrats made a new election necessary, what if a number of their northern constituents repudiated them for destroying the electoral compromise, forcing another confrontation, and undermining political and economic stability? In short, the Democrats could gain little from obstructing the count except the questionable benefit of reinforcing their claim of having been cheated, and then they would lose their advantage as the injured party.[91]

However, some dividends could accrue to the Democrats from judicious delay. By allowing Hayes only a few hours between completion of the count and his inauguration, House Democrats could show contempt for him, his title, and his party, and vicariously rid themselves and their constitutents of some pent-up rage. Also, there were southern as well as northern Democrats in Congress who wished to stall the count in order to gain leverage for possible concessions by Hayes on the removal of federal troops in New Orleans[92] —which would mean the collapse of any Republican regime there—whereas still other individuals, mainly journalists, talked enthusiastically about a possible political realignment in the South on the grounds of federal patronage and support for southern internal improvements.[93] With regard to all those possibilities, Hayes, in his personal conversations with southerners and others, as well as in the conversations of his indirect representatives in Washington and elsewhere, was more emphatic and specific about some matters than others. Hayes himself seemed to hope that the army need no longer to be involved in southern affairs,[94] and he definitely wanted a southerner in his cabinet. However, one participant in the various bipartisan discussions in Washington, Democratic Representative E. John Ellis of Louisiana, observed: "Hayes' friends can profess his promises. *He* has promised nothing."[95]

Another reason for delay of the count in the House was Speaker Samuel J. Randall's desire to be reelected Speaker in the next House which meant that he had to mollify that faction of Democratic congressmen who had wanted to obstruct.[96] However, Randall's decision to uphold the commission's conclusion and the fact that many northern and southern Democrats had grudgingly acquiesced to it implied no surrender on the part of Tilden's supporters but rather the realization that Tilden's case had no chance of success after the Electoral Commission had decided for Hayes. Thus the Democrats allowed the count to go on and to be concluded in the early hours of March 2. When Hayes was privately sworn in on March 3 at the Executive Mansion, the electoral crisis ended peaceably.[97]

Clearly, the anomalies of the electoral crisis had been manifold. For several years the probability of a close and disputed election had been foreseen, but no remedy had been provided. Misconceptions about the participants had also been numerous. Tilden had been feared by the Republicans as the supreme manipulator, yet he was neither skillful nor shrewd in the handling of his greatest challenge; Congressman Ellis commented: "The great New York leader has proved himself without a plan or a policy." Hayes, who had been regarded by many Democrats as a nonentity, a mere tool of Washington politicos, had been adroit and successful in advancing his own cause. The Democrats had shown contempt for Grant, but the first angry puff on his cigar had unnerved them, because they feared he might play dictator. In point of fact, they should have taken Grant more seriously for other and more immediate reasons. It was he who had made certain that the count would come out right by keeping three southern state governments Republican in the interim. He had also discouraged any resort to violence by placing troops in Washington and by preventing coups in Columbia and New Orleans; but he had refrained from recognizing any claimant so as not to jeopardize the precarious electoral situation in Congress. He had lobbied for compromise and for passage of the Electoral Count Act, and by making vague assurances to the Louisiana Democrats, he had quieted their fears without undermining the Republican position by actually recognizing the Democrats and removing the federal troops.[98] Above all, it was he who had kept his nerve during the unprecedented crisis.

Moreover, once the Electoral Commission's fifth and deciding judge, Justice Joseph P. Bradley, had been chosen, some of the Democrats had interpreted his previous decisions as sufficiently conservative to guarantee that he would not tolerate any tampering by the state returning boards. As it turned out, his legal thinking had been too conservative to be helpful to them, for he took the view of not tolerating the creation of a national returning board that could tamper with the vote and preferred instead to accept the certificates of the state returning boards. Then there was Speaker Randall, who had been considered a narrow partisan but had in fact insisted on accepting the results by finally ruling out sabotage so as to complete the count. The role of Louisiana, however, was especially anomalous, for its returning board had named William A. Wheeler as vice-president, even though in 1875 he had condemned the board for its frauds. From 1872 to 1875 Louisiana had been recognized by Washington as Republican on the state level but not on the federal level (its presidential vote had been thrown out in 1873 and its Republican senator-elect had been refused a seat); however, by early 1877, Washington had reversed its stand, for Louisiana's electoral votes were indispensable for electing a Republican president, whereas Republican control of the state had now become dispensable. As for the validity of the outcome, Florida had perhaps rightfully been Tilden's, and Hayes had been entitled not only to South Carolina, Louisiana, and Oregon, but also to uncontested and undisputed Mississippi—which would very likely have had a Republican majority had not the black voters been disfranchised—giving Hayes a total of 23 electoral votes and ensuring his election.[99]

The electoral dispute had revealed the limits and defects of both the nation's political machinery and its constitutional framework. It had also shown the inner strength, stability, and flexibility of the people and their politicians. Even though the Republicans had operated with the security conferred by power and the legitimacy bestowed by authority, and though the Democrats had been spurred on by their fear of defeat and an energy inspired by desperation, they had reached an accommodation of sorts and had accepted a solution. By disregarding the objections of the extreme partisans and the presidential claimants, by overcoming their inertia and paralysis, by capitalizing on the internally divided parties, the compromisers had prevailed. In brief, it had been the Republicans' lack of unity in the Senate in January that had made the enactment of arbitration possible, just as it had been the Democrats' lack of unity in the House in February that had made a successful filibuster an impossibility.

The drama and the timing of the disputed election have led many historians to exaggerate the importance of its effect on reconstruction.[100] Actually, the fact that reconstruction was substantially at an end had shaped the outcome of the electoral dispute. Had reconstruction not been all but done for, Tilden would never have gained, in one way or another, almost the entire South and there would not have been a close and disputed election. If the Republican party had still considered the South politically important and had given high priority to the protection of Negro voters, Hayes would not have been the standard-bearer nor would the Republicans have conducted the campaign as they did, especially with regard to the southern canvass. Neither would they have submitted to bipartisan arbitration and bisectional discussions; the stakes simply would have been too high. No matter who occupied the Executive Mansion, the troops at the two southern statehouses would have been withdrawn and the Democrats would have taken possession,[101] for the southern Republican party was practically defunct. Hayes had known that and had been ready to accept the inevitable all along. Indeed, even before his various discussions of the question, Grant had positively and publicly indicated that he had no intention whatever of recognizing the Republican Packard government in New Orleans. The Republicans had not abandoned the Negro to gain the presidency, since the Negro's cause had been, in large part, given up prior to 1876–1877. Similarly, the southern Democrats had not given up Tilden's cause for their own, since his case had already been lost by the vote of the Electoral Commission.

In the perspective of retreat from reconstruction during the preceding decade, the electoral crisis was insignificant and, in many ways, expected—perhaps even inevitable. The Republicans' defeat in the South and the withdrawal of troops from a statehouse had occurred before, and frequently. Indeed, the latest dispute had conformed to the pattern of the past decade, during which actual power had been limited to the precariously held statehouses and the conveniently controlled returning boards, both of which had functioned for a time under the protection of federal troops. But the federal government had found the price too high, the army too small for the entire South, northern support too tenuous, and the results altogether unrewarding. So the troops were withdrawn, leaving one state after another to be engulfed by the relentless Democratic movement to regain control. Southern whites wanted above all to regain local power, regardless of the national outcome. Of course, southern localism had dominated attitudes and actions during the rebellion and throughout reconstruction, so that the electoral crisis merely dramatized and confirmed that fact. Actually, the events that took place during the disputed election were but another symptom of the dislocation of American politics brought about by rebellion and reconstruction. The recurrent disorder in political campaigns, the resort to the use of the army to maintain order, and the dissension over elections by returning boards were all too familiar. Northerners of both parties were almost as anxious as southern Democrats for it all to end. Americans were yearning for peace, prosperity, constitutional order, civil government without army interference, a return to federalism, and national unity. They wanted not only returning boards and the electoral disputes, but reconstruction itself, to come to an end.[102] In the playing out of a decade of reconstruction, the electoral dispute of 1876–1877 had been no more than the sensational drum roll of the finale.

14

PEACE WITHOUT JUSTICE

Hayes's Southern Policy

THE PRESIDENCY had finally been settled by March 2, 1877, but the president's policy appeared to be far from settled. Just before Hayes had left Columbus for Washington, he had reminisced about another departure sixteen years earlier, when he and his fellow Ohioans had marched off to war; after speaking of the successful outcome of that struggle, he only alluded obliquely to his new approach, commenting that not all questions could be solved by force. An end to the "ugly legacy," as a Louisiana Republican termed it, had been strongly suggested in many of the numerous conversations and conferences held during the electoral crisis in Washington, yet no one but the new president could devise the precise methods by which the two governors and two legislatures vying for power in South Carolina and Louisiana could be reduced to a single government in each state.[1]

During the frantic thirty-six hours in Washington before the public inauguration, Hayes was besieged with callers and bombarded with advice. One of his visitors was Thomas J. Robertson, the outgoing Republican senator from South Carolina, who, according to reporter Horace Redfield, was on hand to enlighten Hayes about the state of affairs as he saw it. "I don't think he got much satisfaction," Redfield reported, "for he came out with a troubled look upon his massive brow. I heard a man say to him, by way of consolation, 'You can't expect us in the North to allow our party to be torn into shreds in an attempt to uphold and defend the sort of government you have in South Carolina.'" The *Independent*'s Washington correspondent remarked that since the South was already in the hands of former rebels, the North just had to make the best of it—an opinion that was echoed by the press in general. A New York Republican, formerly a resident of South Carolina, agreed and wrote to Hayes: "I think you will have to accept things *as they are* not as you *would have them*, and build up a new party south—you can't fight the *hopeless battles of minorities*."[2]

Hayes, who was a realist, understood that those Republican regimes unable to exercise their authority a hundred feet from the statehouses would not last unless they were propped up by the army. Yet given the fact that army intervention was extremely unpopular and that he himself was predisposed toward moral suasion rather than compulsion, he thought that the withdrawal of the troops was nevertheless sensible and, above all, necessary. An optimist as well as an opportunist, he also envisioned the alluring possibility of gaining support. By doing what was inevitable with magnanimity and extending an additional peace offering of patronage, he, along with many of his advisers, believed they could attract moderate white southerners—especially those who had been prewar Whigs and Douglas Democrats—into the Republican camp in an alliance with the northern moderate and conservative Republicans. If it were successful, such an alliance would pay large dividends: national unity, pacification of the South, the reascendency of the Republicans in the House of Representatives and much of the South, and an assured place in history for Hayes as the Great Pacificator—indeed, perhaps a place equal to Lincoln's as the Great Emancipator. A majority of the Republican newspapers sounded giddy, even euphoric, when they announced the beginning of an era of peace and prosperity under Hayes. But the heart of the matter, for the southern Democrats, was grasped by Mississippi Senator Lucius Q. C. Lamar, who remarked, Hayes "is full of the idea of being a great Pacificator, and this makes his policy more favorable to us than Grant's."[3]

The strong likelihood of his putting that pacification policy into effect provoked dissent. Many southern Republicans maintained that Hayes was legally and morally bound to recognize and sustain the remaining Republican governments, for otherwise he would "crush the very men who elected him to office." They argued that if Republican gubernatorial claimants Stephen B. Packard and Daniel H. Chamberlain had not been elected, then neither had Hayes; this was especially true in Packard's case, for he had received more votes than the president. Furthermore, in their view, if federal assistance were to be withdrawn, it would encourage the southern Democrats to resort again to revolution, and the Civil War would thus turn out to be a "failure and Reconstruction worse than folly." It would mean, stated Chamberlain in his inaugural address in Columbia, that the "peace of political servitude is better than the abuses and disquiet which newly-acquired freedom has brought." The Democrats kept a wary eye on the Republicans' infighting, for there was no way they could feel safe until Hayes had turned his friendly words into actions.[4]

Hayes's inaugural address on March 5 gave weight to the general conviction that he would not support the two remaining southern Republican governments. Although indirectly acknowledging the difficulties of reconciling states' rights with citizens' rights, he was nonetheless convinced that local autonomy ought to be restored to the southern states. The press, both Democratic and Republican, generally went along with him, but many Republican politicians, especially the radicals, clearly did not. Their lack of enthusiasm and, in many cases, the cold reception they gave the new policy indicated that even the mere possibility of a policy designed to split the Democratic South might already be dividing the Republican party.[5]

If all the talk about pacification stirred up strong feelings, the announcement of Hayes's cabinet unleased a storm. To begin with, he had broken a cardinal rule—that of consulting with the powerful party members in Congress, who were not only surprised but, in large part, unpleasantly so. His selection of a former attorney general of the Johnson administration, William M. Evarts, as secretary of state, the Liberal leader Carl Schurz as secretary of the interior, and the former southern Democratic senator and Confederate officer David M. Key as postmaster general smacked of treason to staunch Republicans, for they considered most members of this new cabinet their traditional enemies. As party preacher Robert G. Ingersoll quipped: "What party do I belong to now?!" And Wisconsin Senator Timothy O. Howe observed: "Greeley adopted the Democratic party four years ago. . . . that he might be made President. Hayes is President and yet I guess he means to adopt the Democratic party."[6] His choices did indicate not only that he was attempting to build a moderate-conservative coalition in the nation and in Congress,[7] but also that he intended to make good his promises to nonpartisan, antiorganization reformers who wanted independents and Liberals to be appointed. With the notable exception of Secretary of the Treasury John Sherman, Hayes's cabinet was composed of honest, respectable men, but men who were political outsiders with no experience and no influence in the national party or in the politics of their states. Indeed, according to one Republican, the "whole cabinet is a gathering of icebergs or men with blood no hotter than that of a toad."[8]

The Democrats were naturally delighted with what they regarded as an "eminently conservative" administration; they were also relieved to see some concrete evidence of what had been promised as a new departure. When a number of Republican senators threatened to oppose the confirmation of some of the cabinet designees, a group of southern Democrats declared that they were prepared to give their support. At the same time, they used that opportunity to press Hayes once again to withdraw the troops from the two statehouses. Obviously, they were still bargaining, still trying to make a trade. And when the Republican senators forsook the idea of mutiny, realizing that the cabinet would be confirmed no matter what they did, Hayes, as a gesture to them as well as an opening ploy to secure the support of black leaders and probably also as a way of softening future blows, appointed the prominent Negro, Frederick Douglass, United States marshal of the District of Columbia, a position that carried with it both prestige and patronage.[9]

At the same time, Hayes had been maneuvering to ease out Chamberlain. He had his confidant, Stanley Matthews, write Chamberlain a personal letter on March 4, strongly hinting that he ought to resign as governor for the sake of the new administration as well as the northern wing of the party. The message was reinforced by a postscript from Evarts, and, adding insult to injury, it was delivered to Chamberlain by a state Democratic party member, who was a relative of Democratic gubernatorial claimant Wade Hampton. (Also on

March 4, Hayes met with a prominent Louisiana Democrat.) Three days later, during a conversation with Hamilton Fish, Hayes indicated that he was toying with the idea of appointing Chamberlain to the marshalship of the District of Columbia (this, of course, before the appointment of Douglass), clearly implying that his tenure in South Carolina was to be short.[10]

In Chamberlain's March 7 reply to Matthews, he flung down the gauntlet. Maintaining that personal honor and public duty required his continuance in office, he vowed to stay, unless capitulation was forced upon him "by a power which it would be idle to resist." Simultaneously, Hampton's representatives requested Hayes to withdraw the troops. And at about the same time, Packard, in New Orleans, was being sounded out about resigning by a bank president who was acting on the request of John Sherman. Similar pressure had been applied earlier, in late February, by Stanley Matthews; but like Chamberlain, Packard stood his ground.[11]

Hayes was clearly stalling for time—"looking about to see how the thing can be done without seeming to do it," as the Democratic St. Louis *Republican* phrased it. Possibly, he was hoping that both Republican claimants could be persuaded to slip quietly away; at any rate, they were being forced to reveal their intentions. The delay also gave the president time to get his cabinet confirmed before any action could be taken that might jeopardize Congress' approval. Besides, he did not want the Senate to be in session when he acted, and in addition, the interval would be useful for exploring various ways of withdrawing the troops and for preparing public opinion in advance.[12]

Between March 7 and 11 all that private maneuvering became public knowledge after Chamberlain's supporters in Washington, looking for allies, published Matthews' letter.[13] Actually, the press had picked up signs of an impending change even earlier. The reform-minded Philadelphia *Times*, formerly a harsh critic of Hayes, became convinced he was really in earnest and was now favorably disposed toward him. Even the ultra conservative Mobile *Register*, which previously had shut its eyes to the mounting evidence of a change in policy, had become confident that Hayes would act according to what the paper assumed were his intentions.[14]

Even staunch Republicans, however reluctantly, conceded that since the southern wing had been reduced to a powerless minority, the administration, as a Virginia party man put it, was "compelled to take a new departure." Then, too, given the expectation that the Republicans would henceforth receive no electoral votes and few congressional seats in the Deep South, it was easy to sacrifice the party's southern wing: in the cotton states the party was, according to reporter Redfield, "as dead as a nail in the coffin," whereas "in others it will continue to wiggle along in a feeble way, but without strength to come to power." That loss meant a possible advantage, for, in the opinion of the Republican St. Louis *Globe-Democrat*, the party would be "relieved of a burden which impeded it, discredited it, injured it." Chamberlain recognized that when he wrote in mid-March: "there is little effective opposition to the policy of surrender," for the "North is *tired* of the Southern Question, and wants a settlement, no matter what." Although the pullout of troops and withdrawal of support from the Republican regimes could be done gradually so as to make it look like a compromise, both were inevitable since they were as much the "logic of history as . . . the judgment of President Hayes."[15]

On the other hand, exactly how the pullout would be accomplished remained unclear. Various options were discussed publicly: new elections, a resolution by the legislatures, recognition of the Republican claimants on condition that they would then be on their own, or simply an immediate withdrawal of troops. Hayes privately favored the last alternative: "Withdraw troops and leave events to take care of themselves." However, all the suggestions, especially the first, met with strong opposition from some quarters.[16]

Meanwhile, in Louisiana, tension was increasing yet again. After the black members of the Republican government's militia and the recruiters had been arrested by the rival Democratic government, Packard telegraphed Hayes on March 19 for immediate recognition. The next day Democratic gubernatorial claimant Francis T. Nicholls complained to Congressman Randall L. Gibson (who relayed the message to Hayes) that Packard was trying to provoke a disturbance in order to trigger both federal intervention and presidential recognition. On March 20 and 21 the cabinet discussed the Louisiana problem at considerable length, the majority agreeing with Hayes, who did "not think the wise policy is to decide contested elections in the States, by the use of the National army." That consensus was duly reported to the press. It was also agreed that a special presidential commission should be dispatched to New Orleans to seek a solution. In the interim the army would maintain the status quo.[17]

The plan for a commission temporarily unsettled the supporters of nonintervention. Assuming that Hayes was buckling under pressure from the radical opponents of withdrawal, not only did certain conservatives accuse him of weakness and duplicity, but the southern Democrats, who were particularly disconcerted, interpreted the plan to mean that Hayes's acceptance letter, various indirect assurances during the electoral dispute, his inaugural address, and his near promises to Nicholls' representatives and to others in Washington meant absolutely nothing. Senator Lamar even roused himself from his sickbed to write Hayes: "*do* as you *said* you would do." Some northern Democrats, including Congressman Randall, regarded the commission as a delaying tactic to frighten the southern Democrats into trading the withdrawal of troops for a Republican organization of the new federal House of Representatives. In other words, they believed that the bargaining was starting all over again. Even Hayes's confidants, who had talked with the southerners during the electoral crisis, wondered whether he in fact was changing his mind.[18]

A great many Americans who by then looked upon any sort of commission with cynicism, dreaded the delay, which would allow the anarchy to continue a bit longer, thereby possibly endangering the settlement that had seemed imminent. Louisianians, in particular, remembered all the congressional investigations as well as the Wheeler committee, which had kept Kellogg in office as governor, and distrusted any body of that type, for as one of them wrote, "our people have been nearly 'commissioned' to death."[19] Still, for many Americans, if a commission could solve the problem, then such an approach was acceptable. Even the Washington *National Republican*, which had frequently favored federal intervention in the South during the 1870s, declared that "any settlement is better than an open controversy" and recommended that, if necessary, the disputes be "decided according to the Darwinian theory, 'survival of the fittest.'" This sort of support for a commission showed that a majority in the North were so weary of the whole affair they were demanding "anything for peace."[20]

In fact, all the fretting was needless. Replying to a somewhat frantic telegram from Congressman Charles Foster, Hayes jotted on the telegram: "No change of policy contemplated." On the Democratic side, Governor James D. Porter communicated to his fellow Tennessean, Postmaster General Key, that there was growing dissatisfaction in the South because of Hayes's inaction. But Porter wrote that he had been advising fellow Democrats to keep cool and to patiently await developments, adding: "I have taken the liberty of saying to a number of them, that you assured me that the 'inside view' was encouraging."[21] In fact, Hayes was not really wavering at that point. The commission was merely an instrument for transforming his intentions into action. To begin with, given the strident opposition from the radical ranks, Hayes needed the unanimous support of his cabinet, and he believed that the only way he could get it from Secretary of the Treasury John Sherman, Attorney General Charles Devens, the more acquiescent Secretary of War George W. McCrary, and Secretary of the Navy Richard W. Thompson, was by making a compromise gesture—that of creating a commission. Also, Packard was silenced by that direct announcement of a commission being set up, for it would have been very foolish of him to create a furor in New Orleans just before an ostensible fact-finding delegation was to arrive. Moreover, by maintaining an uneasy peace in New Orleans, Hayes could quickly dispose of the less volatile situation in South Carolina, thereby establishing a powerful precedent for Louisiana.[22]

When the members of the commission and their instructions were made known in early April, Hayes's intentions became clear. Although the commission was seemingly balanced (both parties and both sections were represented), every member of it actually reflected Hayes's own views. Two of them had earlier endorsed his plans for a southern policy, and no radical opponent was asked to take part. In his instructions Hayes assured the members that they had a free hand, but he also impressed upon them the fact that the troops would soon be withdrawn. Their assignment, although tacitly suggested, was clearly understood: Get Packard out. Indeed, Hayes's creation of that commission was, as the Philadelphia *Times* observed, a shrewd way to protect himself by placing the responsibility for the decision upon selected "representative Republicans of the country."[23]

Having avoided a flare-up in Louisiana and while organizing his commission, Hayes turned his attention to South Carolina. Here Hampton had a wide following and there was not the additional complication of a rival state court system as in Louisiana. Thus, with less chance of violence and of conflict of authority in the courts, Hayes could act decisively. Earlier, through intermediaries, he had invited the rival governors to confer with him in Washington. Hampton, bargaining from a position of strength, had refused to come unless personally requested by the president. After a cabinet meeting devoted to the state on March 22, during which a withdrawal of troops from the Columbia statehouse was favored, Hayes personally invited both men to meet with him separately. Again, it was just a brief postponement to save face for the loser and to create the impression of an impartial hearing for each side, a fact that Chamberlain understood. Indeed, even before he reached Washington, his family had arrived with all their possessions. The only question now was whether he would capitulate or lose his office after the troops had withdrawn.[24]

The circumstances attending each claimant's trip to Washington symbolized the end of one era and the beginning of another. Chamberlain, with—as his only travel companion—his carpetbag, rushed off to Washington anonymously, like a ghost from the past. In contrast, Hampton marched on Washington as a modern-day Roman conqueror: huge crowds turned out to cheer him and to strew flowers before him; cannon salutes, firecrackers, and spirited brass bands announced their jubilation. Even at 2:00 A.M. there was a crowd awaiting him. On his whistle-stop tour, he made speech after speech, telling one audience that he would ask for the rights of South Carolinians and would accept nothing less, and declaring elsewhere that he would not submit to any commission or any compromise, as well as demanding that the troops be sent back to their barracks and that the state government be left in the hands of the men "strong enough to sustain it." Actually, Hampton sounded more like he was about to bring off a coup than to hold a conference with the president.[25]

Hayes told Chamberlain, during their meeting, that he did not want anyone to surrender his rights but only wished to adjust the claims to the satisfaction of all. Chamberlain made it clear, directly and indirectly, that he would not abdicate voluntarily, but candidly admitted that he could not possibly maintain himself as governor without federal troops posted in the statehouse. In one last desperate effort, he proposed that a presidential commission similar to the one for Louisiana be created. Hampton, on the other hand, subsequently told Hayes just what he wanted to hear: that peace would be preserved and that the rights of all would be respected after the troops left. The cabinet reaffirmed the withdrawal from Columbia, and Hayes promised Hampton that it would be carried out shortly. On April 3 the president ordered the removal of the troops, and they left the statehouse on April 10. Chamberlain, realizing that his situation was hopeless, instructed an assistant to hand over the keys, and on April 11 the Hampton government occupied the capitol.[26] In short order the Democrats gained control of both chambers of the legislature.[27]

Soon after the emissaries had arrived in New Orleans on April 5, it had become evident that neither side would be willing to make concessions.[28] Hayes's representatives had then begun protracted negotiations that were designed to establish Nicholls' Democratic legislature with undisputed authority so that it, in turn, could recognize Nicholls' governorship and supreme court. When Packard asked Hayes to let the commission decide which was the legally elected government, thereby giving his case a chance, the president had refused.[29] Through pressure, persuasion, and a number of inducements, the commissioners, their agents, and various others had attempted to convince enough men to leave the Packard legislature and to join the Democratic legislature so that a quorum would be obtained.[30] Funds to reward those who cooperated had been secured from New Orleans businessmen[31] as well as from a lottery and the Democratic legislature; in addition some federal patronage had been dispensed.[32] The commissioners had also been useful in keeping the Democrats together, for as one Democrat noted, "only the presence of the overshadowing commission" had kept the numerous factions from squabbling.[33] Hayes's representatives had not only reassured themselves that what could not be avoided would at least be done in some semblance of order, but they had also legitimized the results and delayed withdrawal for a decent interval. Moreover, by diffusing responsibility, the commissioners had served as a breakwater for Hayes against the expected rebukes from staunch Republicans in the state and elsewhere.[34]

When the United States Senate adjourned on April 17, with the radical opponents of Hayes's policy having lost their most influential public forum, the administration could proceed with dispatch to carry out its plans, for the preparatory work had already been done. The following day the commissioners telegraphed Hayes that the Nicholls legislature would soon have a quorum and that the troops could be safely recalled from their position near the statehouse; by April 19 enough Republicans had defected to give the Democratic legislature a quorum. On April 20, with the recommendation of both the commission and the cabinet, Hayes ordered the troops to be withdrawn. In the interim what was left of the Packard legislature dissolved. As the cathedral clock struck noon on April 24, 1877, the detachment of federal soldiers, keeping step to the music of a military band, left their quarters near the statehouse and marched to a wharf on the Mississippi River, where they embarked for their barracks, after which the crowds cheered, cannon were fired, and church bells were rung. The following day the Democrats took control of the statehouse and the state had both a Democratic legislature and a Democratic governor. Packard, as was to be expected, gave up the fight and stated that he was yielding "only to superior force. I am wholly discouraged by the fact that, one by one, the Republican State Governments of the South have been forced to succumb to force, fraud, or policy."[35]

Although the Democrats fervently proclaimed that the South was "free at last," they did not lavish any praise on Hayes. The Memphis *Appeal*, in the belief that Hayes was trying to make a virtue out of necessity, snapped: "What credit, then, belongs to Hayes for doing what the Democrats have compelled him to do?" Other Democratic organs merely announced their next objectives—the repeal of all federal election laws as well as the reduction and the restriction of the army.[36]

On the Republican side, one Ohioan likened the forced abdications of Packard and Chamberlain to "sacrifices, such as we read of in Russia where peasants throw children from sledges to the pursuing pack of wolves in order to save their own lives." To many southern Republicans and their radical northern sympathizers, the pullback was abject surrender. A South Carolina Negro pointed out that elementary justice required Hayes to stand by the blacks as they had stood by him. Another black from the same state commented to Hayes: "I am a unprotected freedman. . . . O God Save the Colored People." Clearly, as many Republicans had foreseen, it was the end of any guarantee of free voting in the South and of any other reconstruction rights that the white southerners might choose to deny; and it represented, in Amos Akerman's words, the peculiar logic of curing "lawlessness by letting the lawless have their own way." The Chicago *Inter-Ocean* observed that "for the first time in the history of this country the doctrine is promulgated that not he who has the most votes, but he who has the strongest battalions, shall be recognized as the legal authority." True, public discord would be brought to an end: there would no longer be any political controversies, because the southern Republican party would soon cease to be anything to contend with. Indeed, according to a Florida Republican, there would not be enough of it left to make a "grease spot." The solid Democratic South was most certainly to become an accomplished, permanent fact.[37]

However, the reaction of most northern Republicans ranged from enthusiastic relief that the issue of the use of troops in the South would no longer intrude into every campaign, to fatalistic acceptance of the necessity of withdrawal. Many of those who had reservations consoled themselves with the idea that though conciliation might not conciliate, the policy was at least worth a try. The South was, in effect, on trial, they told themselves; time would tell how it would treat the blacks. But such reasoning was merely a way to hide the widely recognized fact that with federal withdrawal, an irreversible step had been taken. Any request for troops to quell campaign disturbances and to watch over the polls had to be made by state officials, who were now all Democrats and would hardly ask for any such thing. As former abolitionist James Redpath wrote to a southern black man, to say otherwise "is boy's talk, or worse. How *can* he [Hayes] change his policy after he yields his power?"[38]

Hayes's defenders pointed out that his opponents offered negative objections, never positive alternatives. Moreover, the New York *Herald* and many other newspapers took the view that there was entirely too much fuss being made over what Hayes had done. He had not begun a new policy. He had merely completed in two states "what in the course of years has been done by his predecessor or by Congress in relation to all the Southern States."[39] The press in general found that the withdrawal of troops had ended "a great scandal and a great danger," for "intelligence and property must be allowed to rule, whatever the question of numbers may be,"[40] and that it had signaled a long-awaited return to the "just subordination of the military to the civil authority," which had, during reconstruction, tended "to destroy the sentiment of self-dependence which is the mainspring of a true popular republic."[41]

With the withdrawal of troops, the protracted funeral for reconstruction could be limited to a swift burial. The deathblows had been brutal, if bloodless. Yet even though such incidents had occurred frequently at other southern statehouses—admittedly, with less fanfare and publicity—the end of reconstruction could have been achieved with more finesse. Stanley Matthews' heavy-handed letters to Chamberlain and Packard, recommending a conveniently quiet political suicide, had been both undeserved and unnecessary. Also, instead of the federal government's conniving with the Democrats, particularly in Louisiana, the Republicans might have earned more satisfactory returns with hard bargaining. After all, so long as the troops remained in the capitols, their presence might have been used to make such advantageous arrangements as, perhaps, coalition governments in Columbia and New Orleans or the Republican organization of one chamber of each legislature. But Hayes, acting with amicable stubbornness, had pursued his set goal of appeasing the Democrats in order to secure their political support. Thus he had transformed a defeat into a surrender. Senator Howe had noted in early April: "we can see already quite distinctly what he is giving away. What he is gaining is not yet visible."[42]

In May of 1877, when the South was enjoying unfettered freedom, there was a particularly brutal massacre of white Republicans in Mississippi, and Hayes's silence was as complete as Tilden's had been after the Hamburg massacre of the previous summer. The Republican New York *Tribune* later claimed that whether the populace was law-abiding had nothing to do with troops being present. Even if the people were violent, federal troops did not belong in the South.[43]

The reaction was very different indeed when violence took place between railroad strikers and state militia in July, 1877. Within eight days Hayes had received nine requests for troops to quell the rioting. And now that the northerners were in fear of labor unrest and perhaps even a workers' revolution, no finespun legal distinctions and constitutional theories were applied to states' rights as they had so recently been to decry army action in the South. In fact, the conclusion was inescapable: the vast majority of Americans agreed that the army ought to suppress all labor riots that threatened the property and the peace of mind of northern whites, but not the race riots that endangered the rights and lives of southern blacks. Ulysses S. Grant commented on the situation in August:

During my two terms of office the whole Democratic press, and the morbidly honest and "reformatory" portion of the Republican press, thought it horrible to keep U.S. troops stationed in the Southern States, and when they were called upon to protect the lives of negroes—as much citizens under the Constitution as if their skins were white—the country was scarcely large enough to hold the sound of indignation belched forth by them for some years. Now, however, there is no hesitation about exhausting the whole power of the government to suppress a strike on the slightest intimation that danger threatens.

He also remarked that if the blacks who formed a majority in certain southern states were to intimidate the whites and prevent them from exercising their rights,[44] "there would be no division of sentiment as to the duty of the President."[45]

Although the withdrawal of troops was the more dramatic part of Hayes's program to recruit the southern Democrats, his patronage policy had more devastating long-term results for what remained of the southern Republican party. To be sure, Grant had damaged that wing of it by appointing some inept and a few corrupt Republicans, but Hayes's appointments totally disabled it. His policy—that of appointing many southern Democrats to federal positions even at the expense of able, honest southern Republicans; of choosing unsuitable

Republicans and passing up qualified ones; of preferring native white southerners to northern residents in the South, while at the same time prohibiting any political activity on the part of federal officials—meant that the southern party would be deprived of its workers. Hayes and the civil service reformers either did not understand or chose to ignore the fact that the very existence of the southern party's fragile organization depended on patronage. Only the security of a federal position provided the freedom to be active in the party, since as a reprisal for their party work, Republicans were frequently denied other types of jobs. Former South Carolina congressman Robert B. Elliott, a Negro lawyer, wrote in despair that he was "utterly unable to earn a living owing to the severe ostracism and mean prejudices of my political opponents."[46] Just as Amos Akerman of Georgia had predicted, "with officers who will not work, and private citizens who cannot work, there is a small chance of having much Republican work done."[47]

Thus, the Republican organization in the South was virtually dismantled. Albion Tourgée reported after the 1878 election, "The Republican party of North Carolina is dead—dead beyond hopes of resuscitation or resurrection." According to a member of the Republican national committee, unless the patronage policy in the South changed drastically, by 1880 southern Republicans would be only "disinterested lookers on," with the "greater part of the machinery of the government against them, and with no future prospect to inspire them." Nor were any of these losses compensated for by an increase of political support from white southerners. Having observed the southern conservative response to all of Hayes's concessions, Akerman reported: "They accept his favors, deny his title, revile all the principles that he has professed in the past and the men who have cooperated with him in maintaining them, and laugh at him for being so easily taken in." Benjamin F. Butler agreed: "Mr. Hayes has lost all hold upon the Republican party and has not gained any hold on the Democrats. They love the treason, but despise the traitor." The result was not a "happy compromise but a square and profitless sellout." Noting the lack of gratitude on the Democrats' part, one Hayes man commented, "These people don't seem to appreciate what the President has done for them." As Akerman summed up Hayes's two-part strategy of patronage and troop withdrawal, "It is suicide for the purpose of a glorious resurrection. Such ends do not come from such means."[48]

In the North, Hayes's patronage policy was not quite so disastrous for the party organization, but it nonetheless weakened his support on all sides. By failing to consult politicians out of courtesy and a recognition of their interests, and by precipitating a bitter fight with the Senate over the power of appointment, Hayes antagonized the party leaders whose help he needed. On the other hand, he was often not the nonpartisan reformer he professed to be, for he did use appointments to pay back debts, reward friends, and punish enemies, and he did retreat from his civil service orders because of the exigencies of the campaigns—inconsistencies within his own policy that lost him the enthusiastic support of the civil service reformers. Thus pleasing neither the regulars nor the reformers, Hayes isolated himself, lost in popularity, and weakened both his presidency and his party.[49]

Recognizing the need to win more converts to his policy before the autumn, 1877, elections and the convening of Congress, Hayes decided to make a series of speeches on tours in New England (June and August), in Ohio (September), and in the South (late September and October). Reminiscent of President James Monroe, who had attempted to inaugurate an era of good feeling with a grand tour, he sought to do the same by uniting the country in a "patriotic love feast."[50] On the northern circuit he emphasized that conciliation of the South would bring sectional unity as well as racial and political harmony and brought along a southern convert, Postmaster General Key, as evidence of the new South, introducing him as a man who "has been greatly wrong in the past, but is greatly right now." Hayes also emphasized that his new policy was an experiment whose wisdom would be justified by the results. In his home state he claimed that peace and prosperity would surely follow pacification and spoke of renewed nationalism in a reunited nation.[51]

In the South, he did an about-face, declaring that his southern policy was not experimental, but a fixed, irreversible fact. Buoyed up by the friendly reception he got and warming to his theme of reconciliation, he began, later in his tour, to compare the Civil War with a contest between Greeks, in which only numerical superiority decided the contest: "It is no discredit to you [the South] and no special credit to us [the North] that the war turned out as it did." He spoke to southern whites about the necessity of accepting equal rights and educating both races, and he told black audiences that they were safer when whites practiced fair play than when they were protected by the army. Both races gave Hayes an enthusiastic reception, as they did Wade Hampton, who not only accompanied him but was publicly praised by him.[52]

Hayes returned to Washington pleased with himself and convinced that his southern policy was a success. Although the northern press in general agreed effusively,[53] his critics contended that he had been taken in by appearances and that the premise of his grand tour had been a grand illusion; an Indiana Republican noted: "Sweet talk is good in Sunday school, but it never carried an election yet." Indeed, in Senator Howe's opinion, he was in danger of drowning in a "sea of gush."[54] Like Horace Greeley's speeches in 1872, Hayes's enthusiastic but loose talk of reconciliation, especially in Atlanta, had made his views on the significance of the Civil War sound distorted. Indeed, perhaps not only his speeches but his policy of magnanimity were misplaced. And, as a northerner living in North Carolina remarked, his task was not "to preach but to rule."[55]

Hayes himself interpreted the friendly reception he got in the South as the ground swell of popular support for his policy, which was meant to develop into a Whiggish party realignment and a resurgence of Republicanism. Earlier in the spring he had predicted that his policy would "secure North Carolina, with a fair chance in Maryland, Va Tenn and Ark and am not without hopes of La SC and Fla." He and his associates also expected that the southern Democrats would help the Republicans organize the House of Representatives.[56]

But the politicians of both parties as well as the parties' newspapers were, as the year went on, increasingly uncertain that even a Whig ghost would be found stalking the South, for "the Whig dead slumber unconscious of the prayers for their resurrection." Democratic North Carolina Congressman William M. Robbins wrote to Congressman Randall, "Having killed it [the southern Republican party] and buried it with scorn and execration, it is nonsense to suppose any of us will dig it up and become its allies." Similarly, the Democratic St. Louis *Republican* offered Hayes the gratuitous advice that he ought not "pin too much faith on such an exceedingly flimsy piece of cloth." Others, particularly the southern Republicans, who were anxiously watching for signs of a political renewal, reported that no perceptible conversion of southern whites to Republicanism had taken place. Indeed, as Akerman noted, the era did not even appear to be one of good feeling, for the southern Democrats had refused to give the Republicans positions in the state governments in appreciation of Hayes's favors. Furthermore, the essence of the Whig creed—governmental aid for internal improvements—was unequivocally rejected by Congress and by the North. With the country still in the grip of a severe depression and given the scandals and corruption involving federal subsidies, they were hardly disposed to provide massive federal funds for southern projects. As one of Hayes's friends from Ohio suggested, the North was willing to "trust the negro to the South," but in no way would it "open its purse strings."[57]

When Congress convened in October, 1877, not one southern Democrat voted for a Republican to be Speaker of the House of Representatives, which thus remained in Democratic hands. Another note of disillusionment was voiced by a previously enthusiastic supporter of Hayes's southern policy, the Springfield *Republican*: the "southern democrats at least should have held the pacification of the South worth something more than a tender of old bourbon and of effusive speeches at railroad receptions." However, it was naive to have expected the Democrats to defect, since the Republicans' ace card—the troops—had already been withdrawn from the statehouses. In fact, as soon as that operation had been completed in the spring, the southern Democrats had begun to urge the election of Democrats, ostensibly to support the administration's policy. But it was only logical to work for the election of Democrats to Congress and then to endorse its being organized as Democratic.[58]

The off-year elections of 1877 confirmed the skeptics' view that party realignment was impossible.[59] Indeed, the returns showed that the southern Republican party was shattered. Reviewing the situation in each southern state, the New York *Times* declared that the solid South was not a bugbear but a "stern political reality."[60] Republican strength in the North had materially diminished as well, and the results in Pennsylvania and Ohio were disastrous. Ohio was a particularly crushing defeat for Hayes, because many staunch Republicans in the Western Reserve reportedly stayed at home to protest his southern policy. Consequently the state was altogether under Democratic control for the first time in twenty-four years.[61] After the elections, an Iowa Republican gave warning that the party had to stop being carried away "by this maudlin sentimentalism called 'conciliation.'"[62]

The congressional elections of 1878 were a decisive test of Hayes's southern policy. The nature and the results of the southern campaign made it eminently clear that no Republican renaissance in the South was possible. Not a single Republican governor was elected, and the few congressional seats still held by Republicans were reduced from ten to four (or 4 percent of southern and border districts; the four congressmen elected were white and from the upper South or the borderland). The Republicans' strength in both black and white counties plummeted: the southern whites went on voting Democratic, and the blacks were disfranchised or they merely deserted the party that had already deserted them.[63] Democratic domination of the region was to be confirmed in 1880.[64] It was obvious by 1878 that rather than reforming, the southern white Democrats had resorted to their usual methods in disfranchising many blacks by intimidation in South Carolina and Louisiana. There the canvass had been so fraudulent that the southern Democrats' earlier promises of fair play became a national mockery, for their efforts to solidify the South had been, in the words of the New York *Times*, "shamefully successful." As a result, the black vote had gone down like a "light ship in a heavy sea."[65]

However, in the North, new economic and social issues, notably the tariff, were beginning to displace the traditional concerns that had arisen from the rebellion and reconstruction. And the northern Democrats were somewhat damaged, but not overwhelmingly so, by the Democrats' behavior in the South. As correspondent Redfield reported from South Carolina, the character of the campaign there would, at an earlier time, "have revolutionized the North," but now

353

most northerners believed the blacks could not or should not be the ruling power. A black South Carolinian confided to Redfield that the northern election results were proof that the cause of the southern Negroes had been abandoned: "The North don't care much for the nigger, else they would not fill up Congress with Democrats at the very same time when the colored vote in the South is being suppressed."[66]

The Republicans comforted themselves with the notion that, given the election results, their party might have enough northern electoral votes to hold onto the presidency in 1880, but the hopes many of them in the administration, including Hayes, had of capturing control of Congress were dashed. After the election, Hayes acknowledged that his southern policy had not succeeded: "I am reluctantly forced to admit that the experiment was a failure," and free elections in the South were "an impossibility." The New York *Times* remarked that his policy had done nothing but encourage the southern Democrats to unite even more and to be more reckless in their pursuit of absolute control. Indeed, though many of his contemporaries had written eulogies for that policy at the beginning of Hayes's administration, they were writing its obituaries at midpoint. According to the black New Orleans *Louisianian*, "President Hayes entered the presidential chair under peculiar circumstances and at once inaugurated a peculiar policy, and the consequence is that he finds himself in a peculiar position." And in point of fact, by the end of 1878, Hayes had neither a southern party nor a southern policy.[67]

Sobered by their failure to regain Congress in 1878 and the wholesale proscription of southern Negro voters during that campaign, the Republicans decided to emphasize their traditional postwar stance in preparation for the 1880 presidential contest. As a New York Republican expressed the postelection consensus, "The Republicans have yielded and yielded and yielded, now is the time to stop yielding." In spring, 1879, the Democrats again provoked a quarrel by attempting to prohibit or restrict the use of the army and federal officials in enforcing fair elections by attaching riders to, or imposing drastic reductions in, various appropriation bills. They had hoped to make an issue of the charge that the Republicans used bayonets to carry elections; also, some of them were still concerned about renewed federal enforcement or presidential intervention in the future. The Republicans responded with a spirited verbal counteroffensive. Hayes, shifting ground, now allied himself with his party by vetoing numerous Democratic bills, so that all the quarreling brought about the expected stalemate, with neither party significantly yielding or gaining.[68]

In truth, earlier federal election enforcement had become increasingly ineffective and irrelevant as far as Negro voting in the South was concerned. The Hayes administration itself made no sustained or substantial attempt to use what enforcement statutes were left intact,[69] and it had appointed some southern Democrats or conservatives to the very offices that would supervise election enforcement. But the political condition of the South provided a safe topic for debate and investigation. Since all the other issues divided the Republican party ranks, and with this "the only great question of the day which seems beyond the reach of specific legislation," it was useful as a way to entrap the opposition into some damaging votes or admissions. Also, there was the possibility that it would serve to rekindle a spark of the old war feeling and reunite the northern Republican ranks. The Republicans thus could freely denounce the southern Democrats without having the congressional power to do anything about the southern problem.[70]

The riders that the Democrats attached to certain bills, thundered Ohio Republican Representative William McKinley, were a "bold and wanton attempt to wipe from the law all protection of the ballot-box and surrender its purity to the unholy hand of the hired repeater and its control to the ballot box stuffers of the great cities of the North and the tissue-ballot party of the South." However, the Republicans hastily reassured the country that they had no intention of deploying the army to supervise southern elections. Senator Blaine accused the Democrats of creating a false issue, since the entire South had but 1155 soldiers (one for every seven hundred square miles) to "intimidate, overrun, oppress, and destroy the liberties of fifteen million people!" and rob them of their freedom at the polls. Although Blaine roundly scolded the Democrats, Congressman Garfield noted in his diary that Blaine was more interested in "the glory

of replying to these men than about having the cause of negro enfranchisement defended."[71]

With reconstruction over and done with, its rhetoric, now devoid
of any immediacy when it came to powerful political interests, was
rapidly becoming a political fossil. The Republicans, in a sham political war, continued for the next twelve years to regularly resurrect
at election time the issue of federal protection of the right to vote in
the South, because it still had some value in rallying the northern
vote, though with diminishing returns. Otherwise, the Republican
lip service accomplished nothing, for not a single southern state was
ever rescued by the Republicans. "Believe me," announced the Nation in 1880, "of all the phantoms which now haunt either section,
this—that reconstruction is not closed—is the thinnest and empti-
est. The date of its expiration is known—in April 1877; there is no
prophet bold enough to predict its revival."[72]

In 1889 the Republicans temporarily regained control of both
houses of Congress and the White House, but the defeat of federal
election enforcement (the Lodge bill, which regulated only congressional elections) in 1891 merely carried on the precedent of all the
former defeats of enforcement provisions in 1871, 1872, 1875, and
1876.[73] Finally, in 1894 the Democrats prevailed and managed to repeal most of the election enforcement laws. After 1896, the southern
question all but disappeared from national politics, because, although the Republican party had undisputed federal control and
could have undertaken vigorous election enforcement in the South,
the bloody shirt was no longer either necessary or effective for uniting northern Republicans, and southern Negro votes were no longer
needed. The Republicans then had the power but not the interest,
and so they did not care about enforcing the Constitution and specifically the Fifteenth Amendment in the South.

For several decades all that remained of reconstruction was concentrated within a few isolated islands under local Republican control in the South, in which some black-belt cities and congressional
districts, along with a few white Appalachian counties and districts,
continued to elect a handful of black and white Republican officials
and congressmen. But the control of all state governments and of all
congressional delegations was in the hands of the Democrats. That

development had taken shape during the decisive decade of the 1870s when the Democrats had succeeded in first paralyzing and then destroying southern Republican power, influence, morale, and organization and in neutralizing or virtually disfranchising substantial segments of the southern black electorate. The decades after 1880 would provide the time and the opportunity to rationalize, codify, and legalize Republican defeat and national retreat.

With a Democratic South and a Republican North, there had been a standoff on the national level for twenty years. Between 1874 and 1894 the country had had with only two exceptions, Republican presidents elected by the slimmest of margins, had had a Democratic House of Representatives all but twice, a Republican Senate all but once, and both chambers had been generally controlled by minute margins. No president had governed with a majority of his own party in both houses of Congress for his full term. Divided power had led to a deadlock. There had been no true accommodation between the parties nor any compromise between federal authority and state prerogative. To be sure, the North had let the South govern itself, but largely because the North had lacked both the will and the power to do otherwise. Indifference and inertia had taken their toll.[74]

President Hayes's supporters had given him every benefit of the doubt during his tenure. His presidency has usually been praised for what he did not do rather than for what he did: unlike his predecessor, he had refused to use the army in the South; he had vetoed a number of bills to counter the Democrats' legislation; he had espoused good causes, though he never actually managed to advance them. In particular, his defense of presidential power to retain influence over appropriations and appointments received high praise, but he had done that, after all, to defend his executive responsibilities and choices. He had had no alternative when his selection of officials in his own executive branch was challenged. And he had had to resort to the veto when an opposition Congress had tried to jam the governmental machinery by refusing appropriations. More importantly, however, his actions did not significantly modify the decline of the presidency for the rest of the century; nor did they prevent the collapse of what was left of reconstruction.

357

The evidence suggests that Hayes's presidential performance was essentially negative and that his accomplishments were negligible. His bright promise had quickly faded; his power and influence, which, at their best, had never been great, had rapidly declined and then altogether disintegrated. Some of his defenders have explained that he had simply been a prisoner of circumstances: any president who had taken office after the electoral dispute and had had the liability of a divided government would have had serious difficulties. That view is fitting so far as it goes, but it ignores the fact that a more skilled politician in the White House would have performed considerably better than Hayes.

Other defenders have contended that Hayes was not really a politician, being altogether too worthy a man to ply that trade. But the facts suggest otherwise, for he had devoted a lifetime to a career in politics and had previously been rather successful at it. In his home state he had been proficient in securing nominations and winning elections, and he had adeptly made himself available through his espousal of popular causes. He had also been clever and knowledgeable in securing the presidential nomination, had adroitly handled the presidential campaign, and had been resourceful during the electoral crisis. Indeed, Hayes had proved to be an astute politician before he ever became president, which is why he was seriously considered for the office in the first place.

Why, then, did Hayes perform so poorly as a politician and as a legislative leader during his presidency? To begin with, his political strategy as president had been in conflict with his character. When he entered the White House, his political position was fundamentally reformist and his presidential posture essentially activist; yet, as Charles Eliot Norton observed, Hayes lacked "the energy of an aggressive leader." He was, noted the New York *Tribune*, "a positive man who is not combative." Thus his own style impeded the translation of his objectives into actions.[75]

His change in political style after his inauguration was perhaps partly due to his reaction to the criticism during the campaign that labeled him a nondescript party tool, causing him to resolve to be a "somebody." As he wrote in his diary: "If elected, the firmest adherence to principle against all opposition and temptations is my purpose. I shall show a grit that will astonish those who predict weakness." Indeed, he was so determined not to be a political pawn that he often refused even to play the game.[76] Another abrupt change was his departure from his earlier role as a party regular and his proud characterization of his administration as nonpartisan. Apparently converted to the Liberalism that had previously appealed to him but had not guided his actions, he declared that the best public policy was the wisest party policy—that statesmanship had to be divorced from politics.[77]

In truth, by refusing to serve his party well, he had undercut his own policies, since it was impossible for them to prevail without the power and the votes that only his party could provide.[78] According to Grant in 1878, Hayes's trouble was due to the "Utopian ideas he got, from *reformers*, of running a government without a party. . . . he has been woefully mistaken." In sharp contrast to his efforts to lead the coalition during the presidential campaign, Hayes, once in the White House, had not attempted to placate the strong congressional leaders whose help he could not do without. Yet however much he touted his self-sufficiency, he had sometimes asked his party to support policies that many of its members were against. Thus his dealings with Congress had been singularly unsuccessful, for he had not gotten on with his party and he had not gotten on with the opposition—nor, for that matter, had he gotten on with the press in general or with the public. Indeed, Hayes, in contrast to his previous behavior, seemed to have developed a habit of stroking against the hair, regardless of which group he was dealing with.[79]

To make matters worse, as he grew less popular and influential, he increasingly insulated himself from criticism, seeking mainly the company of his advisers, who agreed with him. Meanwhile, he had continued to proclaim the worth of his policies, no matter what the political cost or consequences, with self-righteous smugness and obstinancy. Moreover, he confused strength with rigidity, to the detriment of both his presidency and his party. Another of his shortcomings was that he chose to govern from a distance, relying on general policy statements and preaching, rather than on bargaining and pressuring. He thus stated his objectives, but never contrived the means to achieve them. There was "too much proclamation in his method," as Congressman Garfield phrased it.[80]

Hayes as president rarely said anything damaging or controversial, yet as a presidential politician he seldom did anything right. Kansas Republican Senator John J. Ingalls reflected the congressional party's view in his characterization of President Hayes as "the most pitiably helpless, feeble, mushy tea-custard executive," and Democrat Eugene Casserly wrote that Hayes seemed "to be their [the Republicans'] white elephant, just now."[81] Hayes's ambition to achieve a strong presidency failed, and his unsuccessful performance was very like that of John Quincy Adams, who had preceded him, and Grover Cleveland, who later followed him into political oblivion.

Hayes's limitations as a presidential politician were especially evident in the formulation, execution, and defense of his southern policy, which was the most important feature of his administration. His heedless pursuit of southern conservative support was a bold and reckless gamble and a surprising development, for his previous career had not indicated that he was foolhardy in any way. Moreover, his anomalous southern policy suggested that he had confused conciliation with capitulation. It was one thing to have withdrawn military support from two southern Republican regimes, but quite another not only to have withdrawn political support from the southern party, but also to have dallied with the southern Democrats. The new administration could have been conciliatory and fair to them without being deliberately hostile and unjust to the southern Republicans. Instead of an attitude of benevolent neutrality toward the southern Democrats, Hayes had formed an active, if informal, alliance with them, which was proof that his unbounded optimism as to the wisdom of this course and his unquestioning faith in the Democratic promises of fair play were both naive and dangerous delusions. He had no doubt been deceived by the Democrats, but only after he had thoroughly deceived himself. Possibly Hayes's elevation to the presidency had been too heady an experience. New Jersey Republican Horace N. Congar obviously thought so, for he remarked "that only the Gods play with loaded dice."[82]

Another matter that showed Hayes's misunderstanding of political realities had been his belief in the viability of a Whig alliance. The Whig party had been dead for a generation and a great many of its supporters had died or long ago defected; then, too, the war and reconstruction had instilled in most white southerners a deep-seated hatred of a Republican party that had suppressed their rebellion, emancipated all their slaves, imposed reconstruction, and enfranchised blacks. Amos Akerman, who had had some firsthand experience with that animosity, observed that "Hayes made a great mistake if he believed that he could remove it by coaxing." At the same time, by cultivating the southern conservatives Hayes estranged the northern Republicans. Although many northern Republicans had been willing to give up on reconstruction, they were not, by 1878, willing to see the Republican president employ an obviously Democratic strategy when dealing with the South. Before Hayes had become president, he had been something of an idealist, but had had few illusions; as president, he pursued what was called "Hayesism"—his own sort of realpolitik, which involved grand illusions.[83]

Hayes's appeasement and the Democrats' counterrevolution had produced their consequences, especially on the white and black Republicans of the South. Hayes, who in 1867 had denounced "an oligarchy of race, and the sovereignty of States" was, by 1877, to accept both in some measure, in his blind pursuit of peace at any price. As Akerman ironically remarked, "To have espoused here [in the South], under very unfavorable circumstances, the doctrines that he [Hayes], under very favorable circumstances, espoused in Ohio, seems to have been a fault in his eyes." For southern Republicans there was only the peace of despair. "'The Policy' . . . will grind to powder every man in the South who has stood by the Government in the past. Every one who had fought for the country's integrity or favored the policy of reconstruction will have reason to curse," lamented Tourgée. For southern blacks, Horace Redfield predicted a dismal future in South Carolina: "They have the numbers, but the other side have the brute force, the money, the land, the intelligence. These will win."[84]

In many respects, Hayes's southern policy was in marked contrast to his predecessor's. Grant, for example, had employed various tactics in his dealings with the South—at times physical control and at other times political bargaining—but he never had had an overall strategy. He had played for time or had improvised for short-term gains because he had perhaps believed that the best policy was *not* to employ any specific strategy. Grant, then, was sometimes the clever tactician but always a defective strategist. Hayes, for his part, relished the grand design and consistently followed his preconceived, deductive plan in hopes of achieving his well-defined objectives. But his strategy was flawed and his methods were ineffectual. Whereas Grant's leadership had been erratic, Hayes's was inflexible and negligent. On the whole, Hayes's strategy may be likened to Andrew Johnson's, with his attempt at one-sided conciliation by means of policy and patronage. But Johnson's attempts had been reversed by his opponents, whereas Hayes had had no effective political opposition for the first two critical years of his administration. The country had unfortunately been willing to accept peace without justice.

RECONSTRUCTION IN RETROSPECT

RECONSTRUCTION, which had at once stirred up such great hopes and such fear, was virtually over almost as soon as it had begun. Just as it had never been a unified effort, neither was its line of retreat, for some scattered positions continued to be maintained against the assaults of the Democrats and the conservatives. Reconstruction was also crippled by administrative inefficiency, constitutional conservatism, and racism.

To begin with, in the field of administration, federal resources were not equal to the nation's responsibilities. The federal bureaucracy, faced with unprecedented tasks of governance, was too small to cope, for it was scarcely larger in 1871 than it had been in 1861. It lacked money and imagination and was poorly organized and ineffectually managed. Furthermore, the army was too small and too scattered about to have been capable of preserving order. The structure of the government itself was handicapped by the federal system with its separation of powers, diffusion of responsibility, and lack of an adequate mechanism to formulate a coherent policy or to execute it consistently. Therefore very little legislation had been executed uniformly and firmly in the states. Above all, President Grant's confusing policy and contradictory performance, together with Congress' indecision and division, resulted in a lack of direction and fitful governmental intervention.

In the second place, reconstruction was weakened because of a constitutional tradition that was grounded in antebellum decentralization and local autonomy. Many American politicians—especially, although not exclusively, the conservatives and moderates—frequently read the Constitution in the most restrictive sense. Instead of concentrating on what had to be done, they looked to the Constitution to discover what was explicitly permitted, for they believed it more important that the government be restrained from mischief than empowered to do good. And since the laws of reconstruction reflected an awkward and frequently unsuccessful attempt to reconcile postwar changes with prewar habits, public order with the liberty of individuals, paternalistic rule with a preference for a laissez-faire policy, and military might with the principle of the supremacy of civil law, there was a headlong collision of nationalism and federalism at such sensitive points of intersection as the regulation of elections and the governance of the southern states.

For reconstruction to have been effective and enduring, its laws had to correspond to the current political order and to anticipate any future one. Yet those laws and the constitutional amendments had been passed without enough attention being paid to the fact that they had to be accepted by the people. Therefore when yesterday's orthodoxy became the new day's heresy, the laws were either ignored or repudiated. Looking back on reconstruction in 1901, former governor Daniel H. Chamberlain observed: "Rights, to be secure, must, in the last resort, rest on stronger supports than constitutions, statutes, or enrolled parchments."[1] For a law to endure, it had to reflect an enduring consensus.

In truth, a weary North had relied heavily on law as a panacea, expecting, as Vermont Senator Justin S. Morrill phrased it, that the reconstruction amendments, "yet in the gristle, may harden into the very bones of the Constitution." Indeed, many northerners were convinced that with an altered Constitution permanent change would follow automatically. Once national politics were imbued with northern democratic ideals and the Republican creed was incorporated into the law of the land, both had to be and would be transplanted to the alien backwoods of the South in order that, according to a man from Michigan, the former rebels would become "our sort of folks down there."[2]

The notion that all problems could be solved merely by enacting laws meant that many obstacles were overlooked and many legal solutions erroneously applied to political problems. Although reconstruction could hardly have been accomplished within one generation, the leaders throughout the postwar period had repeatedly stated that the job had to be swiftly completed: indeed the people demanded it. That attitude was reflected in the 1874 platform plank of the New Hampshire Republican party requesting that the remaining work of reconstruction be both "speedy and thorough."[3] After each constitutional amendment had been ratified and every major federal statute had become law, the president, the politicians, the press, and the people proclaimed the imminent completion of reconstruction as a whole, with civil wrongs being remedied by successive doses of civil rights, and the practical enfranchisement of blacks being achieved by the passage of yet another federal election enforcement act.

Living too frequently in a paper world of ideal proposals and proclamations of principle, as well as rhetorical posturing and symbolic victories, congressmen, with the support of their constituents, preferred to write new laws rather than to oversee the proper enforcement of existing laws; they also chose to pass noble resolutions and undertake lengthy investigations rather than impose certain duties and fulfill their responsibilities. As Albion W. Tourgée trenchantly commented: "the idea which underlay all this legislation, was that if the freedmen were clothed with the same powers as the whites, had the same privileges and immunities, nothing more need be done in their behalf."[4] So what had been but a modest beginning in securing the legal foundations of political equality for the blacks was viewed by most Americans as a spectacular ending.

When the flimsiness of all the statutory words was confronted with political opposition, deep-seated prejudice, and physical force, the designated programs made little headway and their minor accomplishments did not endure. Given the inadequacies of the laws themselves, not to mention the ease with which they were ignored, it is hardly surprising that federal law during reconstruction proved by and large to be ineffective and unauthoritative, and that faith in the equity of the judicial process, in established law, and in the legitimacy of public authority was seriously undermined. And it did not take long for the courts to deliver the coup de grace to what remained of the illusion that law was a panacea for postwar ills.

Another contribution to the failure of reconstruction was prevalent racism. From the start, reform had been a difficult—even a precarious—experiment, since it was often regarded in negative or ambivalent ways. During the war many northerners had finally though reluctantly espoused emancipation because they thought it essential for the war effort, not because they regarded it as desirable for its own sake.[5] And many white northerners were not only antislavery but antiblack. The only reason they opposed slavery was because it threatened them, not because it debased the blacks. And when the emancipation became a fact, it was praised by many northerners not so much because it freed the blacks as because it promised the whites an end to a recurrent, vexatious public question that had plagued the country for half a century. With slavery out of the way, they presumed that sectionalism would end, that nationalism would triumph, and that there would be no further contention over the status of the southern freedman. Indeed, as one Ohioan wrote, it then would be possible to "get the nigger out of politics."[6]

Similarly, when the Negro was granted citizenship and legal equality, the northern whites insisted that he could—indeed, must—take care of himself. And again, when enfranchisement of the southern Negro became a necessity in order to maintain Republican hegemony in the nation, in Congress, and in the South, a double standard prevailed: enfranchisement was required of the powerless South, but not of the unwilling North—a situation that lasted for three years. Moreover, the option of black voting was consistently and decisively rejected by white voters in all referendums in those northern states that had a potentially significant black voting bloc. Finally, spurred on by the need for more Republican votes in the North, the party secured "national"—that is, northern and border—enfranchisement of the Negro by means of the Fifteenth Amendment. The white northerners' characteristic response to its ratification was one of relief: the issue of black suffrage had once and for all come to an end, and the Negro question was eliminated from national politics.[7]

Thus the essential elements of retreat from reconstruction were to be found in the very achievement of reconstruction reform, with the postwar years in some ways paralleling the antebellum and wartime years. Just as a great many free-soilers, emancipationists, and unionists had once been racist or separatist, most northerners during reconstruction were not pro-Negro but pro-Republican. Indeed, the hatred and fear of the Negro were only temporarily mitigated and subordinated by a greater fear: that of the Democrats' success and southern supremacy. During reconstruction, equal rights were mentioned in party platforms, laws, constitutions, and declarations of principle, but they hardly existed in fact. Racist or separatist customs remained stronger than so-called color-blind laws. And Republicans readily reassured whites that the "imaginary horrors of social equality" were merely Democratic propaganda, for as the Washington *National Republican* explained, the party wanted only "equality before the law, nor more nor less." Such changes as existed were concerned more with the forms, even the fictions, of freedom than with its sources and uses. As a consequence, reconstruction was sometimes paternal, but almost never brotherly.[8]

When it did not produce all the results that had been intended—the conversion overnight of recently freed slaves into established citizens, the elimination of prejudice and violence, the establishment of peace, fair play, and good government—defection began. High morale and firm belief gave way precipitously to defeatism, cynicism, and laissez-faire, which only indicated how formidable, indeed intractable, were the obstacles that had to be grappled with and how ephemeral those idealistic impulses had been.

By 1874, as the call for retreat became more insistent, the cry of racism became more strident, and sectional prejudices more divisive. The northerners and their politicians charged the southern Republicans—most particularly the blacks and to a lesser degree the whites—with causing all the trouble and, according to Amos Akerman, interpreted their appeals to the northern Republicans as an attempt to "cloak their own corruption by an affectation of party zeal, and to maintain themselves here [in the South] by Northern support in places which they ought not to hold."[9] Thus the southern Republicans became the scapegoats, and their unsavory reputation helped assuage consciences and made withdrawal from reconstruction credible.

Consequently, there was a shift in the sympathies of many northern whites, who had previously been antisouthern, but were beginning to feel more kindly toward the white southerners. Suggestive of this change was the statement in the conservative *Leslie's Newspaper*: "the white North cannot avoid sympathizing with the white South." As the concern with the plight of southern blacks subsided, the "old disposition to regard the 'irrepressible nigger' as a nuisance" was reasserting itself.[10] Even among reformers, the question of what the whites ought to do *for* the blacks changed to what the whites ought to do *with* the blacks, as well as what the blacks ought do for themselves. First idealized by some as freedmen metamorphosed by emancipation into noble citizens, or defended as loyalists who had earned the franchise by fighting for the Union, the blacks were then denigrated by most everyone as an ignoble race and a mere party tool. Although some northerners continued to deplore their lot, they did little or nothing to improve it. In 1876 the New York *Evening Post* doubted "whether a much more difficult question ever has demanded to be settled in any land or in any age."[11] And since, as many whites reasoned, the former panaceas had failed, perhaps the achievement of equality between the races was indeed hopeless.

Once that assumption had gained supremacy, retreat gathered momentum and from 1874–1876 it turned into a rout. Many people, including the reformers, argued that political rights ought to follow, not precede, moral, educational, and economic advancement. The elevation of the black race, they pointed out, was the indispensable requisite for any future political equality between the races.[12] Thus the emphasis shifted from governmental action to private philanthropy. Education in particular was to become the new panacea, replacing enfranchisement. But however sincere, the shift amounted to a curtailment of the politically progressive agenda of reconstruction. As a result, goals were abandoned and allies forsaken.

For the ever-growing number of critics of reconstruction, such reservations and racial ambivalence on the part of the Republicans, and even the reformers, were interpreted as ample proof of the impossibility of the entire enterprise. The lack of any visible progress among Negroes merely confirmed the initial view of those who had opposed reconstruction: the experiment had been doomed to failure because of the inherent inferiority of the black race. Many others, too, who had been dubious about reform but not altogether opposed to it, now considered their original doubts justified. White supremacy, the political slogan of southern conservatives, was reasserted as the prevailing belief of the majority of northern whites, whose view was that "the races are presumed to be equal—only they are not. There are two races—an inferior race and a superior race—and the superior race is not willing to accord to the inferior race exact justice"—not even, one might add, a fair chance.[13] During the 1870s, commentators more and more frequently emphasized the importance of racial inheritance, a notion supported by the increasingly fashionable ideas of Charles Darwin and Herbert Spencer, which provided supposedly scientific proof of that popular prejudice.[14]

With the collapse of reconstruction there was another upsurge of interest in black emigration. Some suggested that the blacks were better off on their own, living apart from the whites. Others went so far as to believe that the only solution was a Negro colonization of Africa, Latin America, or some federal territory. Besides, declared the Chicago *Times*, the "removal of a large proportion of the blacks would have a tendency to remove the negro question from politics."[15] It soon became clear that the distinction between eliminating the Negro question from politics and keeping Negroes out of politics was not all that great.

Although the problems mentioned above played an important part, political problems brought about the final downfall of reconstruction. Just as its origins had been largely political in nature, so too was the retreat. In 1867, having realized that partisan interests corresponded with national, northern, and Negro interests, the Republican politicians had been purposeful and well enough organized to launch reconstruction: partisanship and nationalism had prevailed in a generally symbiotic alliance and had provided the motive and the muscle. But the Republican party was soon unable and finally unwilling to carry out reconstruction. For one thing, it was not long before the Republican coalition was having a hard time reconciling its differences. Diverse motives—patriotic, partisan, and philanthropic—made it difficult to create and sustain a coherent program. The prime example of the coalition's problems in establishing priorities and in defining policies was the framing of the Fifteenth Amendment, which involved numerous intraparty disagreements over whether and how to curb the disfranchisement of blacks in the South and whether to accept or displace state control in regulating suffrage, all of which undercut Republican power in that region. Similarly, the labored birth of the civil rights bill as well as election enforcement legislation rent the party and sapped its strength.

Then, too, almost from the very start many Republicans had had second thoughts about the enterprise itself, even though they continued to draft additional legislation. Thus the Republican politicians grew hesitant about using the army and enforcing the law to impose its political terms upon the South. When the party and the government did on occasion stand firm and insist on enforcing a particular policy—as, for example, the crushing of the Klan in South Carolina—their resolve lasted so short a time that, in the end, whatever action was taken turned out to be merely a transitory gain which was soon reversed intentionally or by default because it lacked the support of an impatient, unsympathetic northern electorate. Moreover, since they were seldom convinced of the desirability or feasibility of what they professed to be seeking, they made success highly unlikely by failing to provide adequate means. Similarly, they often shrank from using what tools and allies they had.

A major division in the Republican coalition was between the moderates and the radicals, who themselves varied from practical idealists to doctrinaire visionaries. Of course, the radicals were not all that politically powerful or influential, and although they were the staunchest supporters of reconstruction in theory, they did not always give it the practical help it needed while it was actually evolving. As an embattled minority coming of age and struggling against an entrenched prewar Democratic establishment, the radicals seemed not to grow, either temperamentally or politically, beyond that experience. And they may have turned their vision of reform into a zealous crusade, but being given more to preaching than persuasion, they were seldom able to carry their own legislative measures or to convince the electorate. Characteristically impatient with institutional restraints, constitutional bounds, and volatile public opinion, reckless on occasion, and frequently abrasive, they too often ignored what was politically possible. Their support of the wholesale proscription of many prewar southern leaders and their effort to impeach Andrew Johnson when he had less than a year left in the presidency were not only counterproductive but self-destructive; and their championship of such extremely unpopular reform measures as integrated classrooms in 1874 merely caused them to lose much of the political support they needed for all the reconstruction policies they so wanted to expand and strengthen.

As for the moderate Republicans, who were adept at politics and more influential in Congress, the party, and the country, they nonetheless did little better than the radicals when it came to furthering the cause of reconstruction; for whereas the radicals tended to make substantive compromises too seldom or too late, the moderates were apt to make them too often and too soon. Because of their willingness to see all sides of all questions and to make allowances for the delays or the occasional dysfunction of the political process, and because of their indecision, combined with their ever-present constitutional conservatism and racial ambivalence, they were less purposeful than the radicals. In other words, reconstruction's fate was partially due to a combination of the radicals' and the moderates' most serious flaws—an idealism that had gone sour and a pragmatism that had grown fruitless.

An even more important development in the disintegration of the Republican support of reconstruction, however, was the regional polarization within the party itself. The moderate northern Republican politicians, an influential group within the faction-ridden party of the 1870s, who had earlier joined the reconstruction movement with reservations, began to drift away from it as their northern strategy— the notion that the North, not the South, had the highest political priority—first displaced, and then wholly replaced, their southern strategy. And though southern party interests had, all along, been considered secondary and had been generally subordinated, by the early '70s they were increasingly ignored and northern interests prevailed.

Initially, the northern and southern wings of the party, bound together by a mutual need to stay in power, had toned down or ignored intraparty conflicts of sectional interest. But for all the semblance of unity, the northern party had dictated reconstruction policy from the very beginning. For example, northern fears that the freedman in the South would move to the North influenced northern Republicans to support passage of the Civil Rights Act and the Freedman's Bureau Act during 1866. Similarly, the Fourteenth Amendment, which Congress framed in June, 1866, was in effect an attempt to protect the North by disqualifying former rebels from holding public office, thereby delaying the readmission of southern Democrats to Congress, which might otherwise have jeopardized Republican control. Moreover, the amendment did not substantially protect southern blacks against the onslaughts of southern whites, for it did not grant southern blacks suffrage. Not until almost a year later did the Republicans in Congress, who were in need of southern votes, impose black suffrage upon the South in the First Reconstruction Act of March, 1867.

However, doubts about the Republicans' dependence on the southern black electorate surfaced as early as 1868. Realizing that southern black voters were easily intimidated and readily bribed, the northern Republicans in 1869 sought out the votes of northern and border-state Negroes by framing and subsequently ratifying the Fifteenth Amendment, which included no specific provisions to prevent the disfranchisement of southern blacks. It was becoming increasingly clear to northern Republican politicians that the political war against the Democrats could not be won indefinitely in the South and could very well be lost in the North unless something was done soon in Washington. Similarly, in the federal election enforcement effort, the Grant government spent the greater part of federal allocations on regulations in the North so as to curb cheating in the northern Democratic cities with large immigrant electorates, but gave insufficient aid to check disfranchisement of the blacks in the South. Thus white Democratic terrorism was condemned but not curbed, publicized but not punished.

By 1872 it was widely agreed that the North had to remain the Republican bastion. Although in the midst of the 1872 presidential campaign the generally moderate Republican New York *Times* sounded anxious about the outcome of southern elections, it remained primarily concerned over the electoral vote in the North:

We may easily place too much reliance on the strength of the Republican Party in the Southern States. . . . while we must neglect no opportunity offered us in the South, our main reliance must be on the stanch Union party of the Northern States. The men who saved the Union in war must now allow no tampering with the results of the war. In every Northern State the campaign must be carried out from this moment to the night of election with the utmost possible energy. It is in these States that the moral strength of the party lies. In these States its objects are most intelligently understood; its principles most deeply rooted; its spirit most fervently shared. . . . But we would make sure, and doubly sure, that if, unfortunately, it turns out that the Union men of the South are not in the majority, the Union party shall still hold the reins of power in the whole country.[16]

In 1874 during the congressional campaign, the chairman of the Republican election committee, Zachariah Chandler, also stressed his party's regional priorities: "However unsettled and chaotic the affairs in the South may be, the North is strong sound and sensible." And the New York *Times* stated even more explicitly two years later in 1876, "that the vote of the Southern States has constituted since the close of the war a very important element in the strength of the Republican party is a very familiar fact; but that this element of strength has been constantly declining" had become the fundamental fact.[17] Indeed, by that time even radical papers had joined in the moderate Republican refrain, agreeing that the real battleground was in the North, not the South. The *Inter-Ocean* noted: "It remains clear, however, that the successful battle against treason, disguised under the name of Democracy, must be fought here at the North. Here, where ballots are free; here, where the hosts of the Union sallied forth to meet rebellion in '61; here, where the untrammeled exercise of suffrage is regarded as the groundwork of free government— must the fight be made and won, if it shall be won at all." Emphasizing expediency for reasons of economic self-interest and sectional supremacy, not "mere sentiment," the paper made its appeal sharp and explicit:

Business men of Chicago, farmers of the Northwest, taxpayers of the whole Union, this is *your* fight, this is a matter that concerns *you*, and concerns you vitally. The risk which you assume by inactivity and indifference is a great one. You may care little for individuals, but you ought, nay you must, be interested about results. If there is a man so selfish as to look with indifference on the effort now making to . . . destroy substantially the fruits of the war for the Union, let anxiety for his own weal and his own welfare rouse him from his carelessness and induce him to look at the danger which now threatens. To hesitate, is suicidal.

The *Nation* agreed, declaring, "The Republican party, if saved at all, is to be saved in the North."[18]

Thus out of political necessity, the North—which was regarded by the vast majority of white Republicans who resided there as more familiar, loyal, and important than the South—needed to be made as solidly Republican as the South was becoming solidly Democratic. The South provided some powerful campaign arguments, but they were advanced more in hopes of keeping northern voters Republican than in the expectation of holding the South. Faced with the risk of losing the North by continuing to support unpopular southern Republican regimes, the northern Republican politicians chose to save the northern party and themselves by sacrificing reconstruction. Fully aware that the northerners were "becoming tired of the discussion of abstract questions in which the overwhelming majority have no direct interest," an increasing number of Republican politicians warned their southern party allies and the southern black voters that they could no longer depend on federal assistance.[19] And without the support of the Republicans in Washington and the North, reconstruction and southern Republicanism could not possibly survive for long.

By 1874–1875 the northern priority was clear. When the voters repudiated southern policies, the civil rights bill, and the party's exploitation of outrages in the election of 1874, the party began in earnest to retreat from reconstruction. By 1875, it was the Republicans' fear of voters' reprisals which in large part persuaded them to kill that section of the pending civil rights bill mandating mixed schools. Similarly, the so-called force bill of 1875, designed to extend enforcement, was never enacted because of the North's growing disinterest in chronic southern violence. Its dislike of federal intervention also meant the death sentence for various southern Republican state parties, for Congress, during the spring of 1875, arranged a compromise in Louisiana and failed to overturn the Democratic regime in Arkansas. Later, in the fall of 1875, faced with the choice of possibly saving Mississippi by intervention or possibly losing Ohio because the voters were so strongly opposed to such federal interference, Mississippi was sacrificed to Ohio, the third most important electoral state in the North.

It also became clear during the electoral dispute that what mattered most was not who would rule over South Carolina and Louisiana after 1876, but that there be a Republican president. By 1877, when President Hayes ordered the withdrawal of troops from the state capitols in Columbia and New Orleans, the logic of the withdrawal and its precedent was well established: the end, which had been clearly envisioned since 1874 and vaguely outlined even before then, had arrived. And it was not only expected, but welcomed. The New York *Times* reflected the dominant northern Republican view: "The loss is not wholly unmitigated. The South has been quite as much of a hindrance as a help to Republicans at the North."[20] According to that keen analyst of American politics, the Englishman Edward Dicey, "If I read the signs of the times aright, there is a growing feeling in the North that the South should be governed according to Southern ideas, and that the negroes should be left to shift for themselves."[21]

A number of consequences resulted from that change in public opinion. The northerners convinced themselves that if the Republican regimes in the South could be so easily subverted, the reconstruction regimen had probably never been appropriate to begin with. Indeed, many northerners came to believe that the decision to grant universal suffrage to blacks had probably been a mistake and was therefore not worth upholding. Forced to conclude that the "ballot was a Pandora's Box, when it was given the negro," the Mississippi Republican party chairman admitted that southern elections "have become but a medley of comedy tragedy and farce."[22] And according to Secretary of State Fish, President Grant, at a meeting of the cabinet in January, 1877, "says he is opposed to the XV Amendment and thinks it was a mistake, that it had done the negro no good, and had been a hindrance to the South, and by no means a political advantage to the North."[23] With such convictions, it was easy to disavow all national involvement with black voters in the South, as well as any responsibility for their protection. A Kansan was pessimistic about any presidential action: "no presidential policy could preserve the republican ascendency in any of the southern states. The 'Mississippi plan' had so far succeeded as to be beyond national control by any means within national legal authority."[24] Thus the notion of bringing the freedmen into the mainstream of American life, which had been considered indispensable by many Republican leaders, was soon largely regarded as wholly dispensable. In the process, the southern Republicans, white and black, became pawns who had been sacrificed for the greater stakes of the northern party's needs. The northern Republicans, who during the 1860s had fused political power and reformist principles in launching reconstruction, were forced by the events of the 1870s to recognize the dangerous realities and thus decided to keep their own power and to scuttle reconstruction.

If both the Republicans and the reformers were guilty of backing away from their earlier brave stands, it was the Democrats, many of whom resolutely refused to be democratic, as well as the racist reactionaries, in their refusal to obey the law and practice fair play, who manned the sustained assault on reconstruction. Unreconciled to the consequences of defeat and nursing animosities against the North and the Negro, most white southerners intended to win the peace by repudiating the reconstruction amendments and measures. A Chicagoan commented, "when Rebels and Democrats speak of the people of the South and their rights, they mean the Rebel people. In their eyes there are no other people." Amos Akerman, himself a Georgian, observed that the "science of fraud in elections is better understood by the Democrats of the South than by any other politicians in the country . . . and they put their learning in practice with unbounded audacity," adding, "The North will not fully comprehend the Southern question until it learns that where the negro, the Northerner, or the United States government is concerned, very many men of character and influence of the South are governed by a . . . code wholly different from that which they observe in ordinary life. The stratagems of war are deemed legitimate."[25]

Akerman acknowledged that the southern white man was friendly to the Negro in many ways, but "he hates the negro as a force in politics, and he hates the party which has entitled him to be a force in politics. In this feeling lies the real power of the Democratic Party." With their calls for white supremacy, which they used with great success to evoke southern loyalty and rage against the blacks, channeling both into well-disciplined defiance and organized revenge against those whom they regarded as their enemies, the southern Democrats continued to maintain a propaganda campaign that was more effective and more durable than the northern Republicans' bloody shirt.[26] It was no exaggeration when Judge Hugh L. Bond, a Marylander who presided over some of the federal trials of the Ku Klux Klan, remarked that the South's animosity toward the North was boundless. So too was its audacity. One Virginia Republican pointed out that few northerners truly understood the depth of southern feeling or what the southerners were prepared to do: "You never have lived in the South nor seen what I have of the bitterness, proscription and meanness of the democratic leaders of the South." Concerned about the fact that northerners were often misled by the apparent mildness of southerners and their protestations of good faith, he gave warning that they could "smile, and smile and murder while they smile."[27] White southerners, convinced that if they could rid themselves of all vestiges of reconstruction they could restore conservative hegemony, created a solid Democratic South. In so doing, many southern Democrats behaved abominably, whereas others turned their backs as the weak and the innocent were crushed by the bold and the brutal.

Only a few years after the northerners had left the battlefield they had found themselves involved in another sort of battle with southerners far more obstinate and resourceful than they. Having expended rivers of blood and oceans of money to suppress the rebellion, most northerners had been willing to acquiesce when the white southerners ended reconstruction and when the federal government proved incapable of protecting its own citizens in their right to vote. This need not have been so: there was a solution, but the northerners, in contrast to their wartime resolve, did not put it into effect. As Massachusetts Senator George S. Boutwell accurately observed, "The southern whites respect power and they have but little for anything else."[28] Thus the failure of reconstruction was partly due to the federal government's failure to suppress disorder, with force if necessary.

When the army of the Union had been strong and the direction and determination of the North had been clearer, the dismantling of the Confederate regimen and the slavery system had been accepted more peaceably and more rapidly than had been thought possible, though, to be sure, not without some disorder and repression. "Let us admit," suggested the Republican St. Louis *Globe-Democrat* in March, 1877, that the "untiring hate of the Southerners has worn out our endurance, and that though we staked everything for freedom under the spur of the rebellion, we have not enough of principle about us to uphold the freedom, so dearly bought, against the persistent and effective opposition of the unrepentant and unchanged rebels."[29] It had been easier to win a war than it was to impose and maintain peace.

What was left at the close of reconstruction was mainly the settlement of certain issues that military victory had resolved in 1865. The North had intended that in the peace treaty ending the war, the terms of which were to be gradually spelled out during the postwar years, universal amnesty and universal suffrage at least would be achieved. In the end, however, the South could boast of white amnesty but had rejected black suffrage.[30] The irony was not merely that the South had lost the war and won the peace by nullifying reconstruction, but that it was actually rewarded through congressional apportionment, when the southern states gained more congressional seats and more electoral votes, by having counted the entire free black population, yet prevented the blacks from voting. The blacks in the South were formally represented but generally not represented in fact. "The Republicans curse themselves for the folly of reconstruction which has so augmented the power of southern whites by reason of their physical ability to turn the increased representation against those who granted it, and against those for whose use and benefit it was granted," remarked newspaperman Horace V. Redfield in 1878. "As it is, the Republicans since the war have frittered away all the political advantages they had as the victors in the conquest of arms."[31] The victories of peace were no less significant than those of war.

For the southern Negro, the end of reconstruction meant nothing but defeat, for the southern whites, who became finally reconciled to the end of slavery, decided to treat the blacks as peasants instead.[32] As a result, the Negro was subordinated politically, economically, educationally, and socially. The failure to protect him and his franchise meant that the freedman was not truly free. Having believed that they would enjoy power, prosperity, educational opportunity, protection, equality, and patronage, the blacks found that they were still impotent, poor, ignorant, intimidated, segregated, and largely forgotten.

The South, then, had never been truly reconstructed or reformed, and in most respects it had not been fundamentally changed. Despite all the apparent alterations wrought by a civil war and national reconstruction, the South was more attached to, than severed from, the past. As one newspaper correspondent wrote in March, 1877: "Status quo ante bellum or things as they were before Lincoln, slavery excepted: such is the tendency everywhere."[33] The very term "reconstruction" would suggest that the molders of a postwar future had chosen a model from the past in their efforts to patch up a country that had been rent asunder. The term also, and equivocally, implies the notions of both progressive reform and conservative continuity, of an attempt at both reorganization and reunion, and of a striving for renewal as well as restoration.

Because of the needs of war and reconstruction, the president's power had increased, but it then became more limited as Congress and the courts reasserted themselves. As for the army and the bureaucracy, they had expanded for a time but were then cut back; efficiency decreased as their organization and management began to decay. And although the forces of nationalism had prevailed over those of sectionalism, federalism remained and states' rights and home rule were vigorously pressed. In the end the nation was reunited, but there had been no national settlement, merely a sectional and partisan stalemate, with each side still viewing the other with prejudice and suspicion in a continuation of bitter partisanship, smoldering sectionalism, and combustible race relations.

Both the rebellion and reconstruction had elicited an uneven response in the North. At first—on the part of the whites, the Republicans, and federal officials—there had been concern, efforts, promises and proclamations, programs and panaceas, all of which had been followed by disappointment and frustration at the intractability of the problems and at the degree of sacrifice required. Then interest and optimism ebbed only to be replaced by resentment at, and rejection of, the dream that for most white Americans had become a nightmare.

That such a reversal was so quickly and so successfully brought about is ample proof that reconstruction had been fragmentary and fragile. From the very beginning, reconstruction had had no more than tenuous support and had been racked by chronic crises, marred by profound uncertainties, unsettled because of inner tensions, riddled through with unsolved ambiguities involving race relations and public policy, and blighted by the latent contradictions in the Republicans' attitudes and actions. Moreover, all those problems had been compounded by necessary compromises and incessant change, both of which are inherent in the democratic process itself. Clearly, the American people, their presidents, and their government had not been persevering or resourceful enough to see reconstruction through; and since the Republican governments in the South, with their numerous and supreme crises, had been unable or would not govern, their regimes were inevitably and inexorably replaced by those of the Democrats, who did govern, but in accordance with their own rules.

Thus reconstruction—which had been neglected, discredited, and deserted by many of its friends—fell an easy prey to its enemies. Overwhelmed, its ragged brigades could do no more than sound the retreat.

NOTES

PREFACE

1. William B. Hesseltine, *Ulysses S. Grant, Politician* (New York: Dodd, Mead, 1935); Allan Nevins, *Hamilton Fish: The Inner History of the Grant Administration* (New York: Dodd, Mead, 1936).

2. William A. Dunning, *Reconstruction: Political and Economic, 1865–1877* (New York: Harper, 1907); James Ford Rhodes, *History of the United States from the Compromise of 1850 to the McKinley-Bryan Campaign of 1896* (8 vols.; New York: Macmillan, 1904–1920), V–VIII.

3. David M. Potter, *Division and the Stresses of Reunion, 1845–1876* (Glenview, Ill.: Scott, Foresman, 1973), 187.

CHAPTER 1

1. Abraham Lincoln to Horace Greeley, August 22, 1862, Abraham Lincoln Letter, Wadsworth Atheneum, Hartford, Conn.

2. Draft, May 2, 1876, in Simon Cameron Papers, Library of Congress (LC); *Harper's Weekly* (New York, N.Y.), February 12, 1870.

3. William T. Sherman to Mrs. A. A. Draper, January 15, 1865, in A. A. Draper Papers, United States Military Academy, West Point, N.Y.

4. Charles D. Cleveland to Schuyler Colfax, November 22, 1865, in Schuyler Colfax Papers, LC; Henry L. Dawes to Electa Dawes, February 22, 1866, in Henry L. Dawes Papers, LC; Jacob D. Cox to Lewis D. Campbell, April 28, 1866, in Lewis D. Campbell Papers, Ohio Historical Society, Columbus. Congress overrode both presidential vetoes: the civil rights bill on April 9, 1866, and the Freedmen's Bureau bill on July 16, 1866.

5. John D. Van Buren to Francis P. Blair, Sr., September 21, 1866, in Blair Family Papers, LC; F. Ball to Salmon P. Chase, September 19, 1866, in Salmon P. Chase Papers, LC.

6. Sylvester Robins to Marcus L. Ward, November 7, 1866, Frederick T. Frelinghuysen to Ward, December 6, 1866, both in Marcus L. Ward Papers, New Jersey Historical Society, Newark; New York *Herald*, November 14, 21, 1866.

7. New York *Herald*, December 7, 1870; John Binny to John A. Andrew, September 23, 1867, in John A. Andrew Papers, Massachusetts Historical Society, Boston; Henry Winter Davis, quoted in New York *Times*, July 9, 1865.

8. New York *World*, October 14, 1867; *Nation* (New York, N.Y.), November 15, 1866; New York *Times*, February 17, 1874.

9. New York *World*, September 27, 1867.

10. Benjamin R. Cowen to Ward, June 5, 1867, in Ward Papers; Jacob D. Cox to Charles F. Cox, September 13, 1867, in Jacob D. Cox Papers, Oberlin College Archives, Oberlin, Ohio; Elias Nigh to John Sherman, September 2, 1867, in John Sherman Papers, LC.

11. Burke A. Hinsdale to James A. Garfield, August 19, 1867, in James A. Garfield Papers, LC; James Buchanan to Augustus Schell, November 9, 1867, in James Buchanan Papers, Historical Society of Pennsylvania, Philadelphia.

12. Rutherford B. Hayes to James G. Blaine, June 16, 1875, in James G. Blaine Papers, LC.

13. New York *World*, October 12, 1867; Cleveland *Leader*, October 12, 1867.

14. *Independent* (New York, N.Y.), November 14, 1867; Frelinghuysen to Horace N. Congar, November 12, 1867, in Frelinghuysen Family Papers, New Jersey Historical Society, Newark.

15. *Independent*, October 17, 1867; New York *Times*, October 15, 1867; Jacob D. Cox to Charles F. Cox, October 16, 1867, in Cox Papers.

16. New York *World*, October 12, 1867; New York *Herald*, October 10, 19, 1867. On Democratic strategy, see George B. McClellan to Samuel L. M. Barlow, November, 1867, in Samuel L. M. Barlow Papers, Huntington Library, San Marino, Calif.

17. New York *Times*, November 7, 1867; *Nation*, December 26, 1867; New York *Tribune*, October 14, November 6, 1867.

18. Hinsdale to Garfield, October 22, 1867, in Garfield Papers, LC; Binny to Colfax, November 2, 1867, in William P. Fessenden Papers, LC.

19. John W. Read to Ward, October 11, 1867, in Ward Papers.

20. H. S. Bundy to Colfax, October 19, 1867, in Schuyler Colfax Papers, Rutherford B. Hayes Library, Fremont, Ohio.

21. Ulysses S. Grant to Joseph R. Hawley, May 29, 1868, photostat in Ulysses S. Grant Papers, New York Historical Society, New York; James G. Blaine, *Twenty Years of Congress: From Lincoln to Garfield* (2 vols.; Norwich, Conn.: Henry Bill, 1886), II, 391.

22. New York *Herald*, May 22, 1868; New York *World*, May 25, 1868.

23. *Leslie's Newspaper* (New York, N.Y.), April 4, 1874; Michael C. Kerr to Manton Marble, November 8, 1868, in Manton Marble Papers, LC; Samuel Ward to Barlow, July 14, 20, 1868, Horatio Seymour to Barlow, July 23, 1868, all in Barlow Papers.

24. New York *World*, July 3, July 22, August 7, September 26, October 22, November 5, 1868; New York *Times*, October 20, 1868.

25. Chase to John Paul, October 1, 1868, in Chase Papers; J. T. Smith to Jacob D. Cox, October 2, 1868, in Cox Papers.

26. Volney Spalding to William E. Chandler, September 5, 1868, John Sherman to Chandler, October 4, 1868, both in William E. Chandler Papers, LC; Josiah Gorgas Diary, October 21, 1868, in University of North Carolina Library, Chapel Hill.

27. New York *World*, October 15–22, 1868.

28. David Schenck Diary, November 21, 1868, in University of North Carolina Library, Chapel Hill; Littleton D. Q. Washington to Robert M. T. Hunter, September 25, 1868, in Robert M. T. Hunter Papers, University of Virginia Library, Charlottesville.

29. *Times* of London, November 5, 1868.

30. William P. Hubbard to Chandler, September 7, 1868, J. M. Tomeny to Chandler, December 27, 1868, Spalding to Chandler, September 1, 1868, all in W. E. Chandler Papers; E. Stanley to Cornelius Cole, November 23, 1868, in Cornelius Cole Papers, University of California Library, Los Angeles.

31. John W. Forney to Henry C. Carey, May 25, 1870, in Edward C. Gardiner Papers, Historical Society of Pennsylvania, Philadelphia; James Whitall to Hugh L.

Bond, November 7, 1866, in Hugh L. Bond Papers, Maryland Historical Society, Baltimore.

32. Wendell Phillips, quoted in *National Anti-Slavery Standard* (New York, N.Y.), May 30, 1868.

33. *Ibid.*, June 26, 1869; Washington *New National Era*, February 24, 1870; on the Fifteenth Amendment, see Bibliographical Essay.

34. For an example of mixed motivation, see William Claflin to Charles Sumner, December 25, 1868, in Charles Sumner Papers, Harvard University Library, Cambridge, Mass.

35. William D. Kelley, quoted in *National Anti-Slavery Standard*, November 14, 1868; The Reverend John Peck of Pittsburgh, quoted in Minutes of the Executive Board of the Pennsylvania State Equal Rights League, [August 18], 1869, in Leon Gardiner Collection of Negro History, Historical Society of Pennsylvania, Philadelphia.

36. James D. Richardson (comp.), *A Compilation of the Messages and Papers of the Presidents, 1789–1897* (10 vols.; Washington, D.C.: Government Printing Office, 1897), VII, 6; Mary S. Logan, *Reminiscences of a Soldier's Wife: An Autobiography* (New York: Charles Scribner's, 1913), 189; New York *Times*, New York *Herald*, New York *World*, Springfield (Mass.) *Republican*, Washington *Star*, March 3–8, 1869.

37. *Independent*, March 11, 1869, March 20, 1873; Raymonde in Cincinnati *Commercial*, February 19, 1877; New York *Times*, March 5, 1869.

38. George W. Curtis to Charles E. Norton, March 13, 1869, in George W. Curtis Papers, Harvard University Library, Cambridge, Mass.

39. New York *World*, March 3, 8, 1869.

40. William Johnston to Hayes, November, 1869, in Rutherford B. Hayes Papers, Rutherford B. Hayes Library, Fremont, Ohio.

41. Richardson (comp.), *Messages of the Presidents*, VII, 56; speech of Frederick Douglass at Rochester, April 5, 1870, in Collection on the American Negro, Columbia University Library, New York; New York *Herald*, April 1, 1870; Washington *National Republican*, April 16, 1870; Washington *New National Era*, April 7, 1870.

42. Philadelphia *Press*, quoted in Washington *New National Era*, April 7, 1870; Wendell Phillips, quoted in *National Anti-Slavery Standard*, March 20, 1869.

43. New York *Sun*, January 29, 1870; New York *World*, April 21, 1870. For the ambivalent Democratic attitude toward Negro voters, especially northern ones, and Democratic attempts at recruitment, see William Gillette, *The Right to Vote: Politics and the Passage of the Fifteenth Amendment* (Baltimore: Johns Hopkins University Press, 1969), 39, 89, 94–95, 110–12, 116–17, 121, 130, 134–35, 148–49, 160, and for the 1880s, 188–89.

44. New York *Tribune*, March 31, 1870; *National Anti-Slavery Standard*, April 16, 1870.

45. New York *Herald*, October 19, 1867; William T. Sherman to David F. Boyd, April 24, 1870, in David F. Boyd Papers, Louisiana State University Library, Baton Rouge.

CHAPTER 2

1. Richardson (comp.), *Messages of the Presidents*, VII, 55, 96, 112, 134; U.S. Statutes at Large, XVI, 140, 254, 433, XVII, 13, 348, XVIII, 318.

2. Nashville *Union and American*, November 6, 1874; Charleston *News and Courier*, October 14, 19, 1871.

3. *Congressional Globe*, 41st Cong., 2nd Sess., 3661, 42nd Cong., 1st Sess., 364; Gideon Welles to Montgomery Blair, November 18, 1872, in Blair Family Papers.

4. New York *Tribune*, July 11, 1874; *Harper's Weekly*, April 1, 1871.

5. Amos T. Akerman Diary (MS in possession of Laura Akerman, Augusta, Ga.), April 9, 1874; Hugh L. Bond to Anna Bond, September 20, 1871, in Bond Papers;

Harper's Weekly, April 29, August 5, 1871; Allen W. Trelease, *White Terror: The Ku Klux Klan Conspiracy and Southern Reconstruction* (New York: Harper and Row, 1971).

6. W. Spence to Attorney General, September 3, 1874, Middle District of Tennessee, Source Chronological Files: Selected Record Relating to Reconstruction, 1871–1884, in Record Group 60, "Records of the Department of Justice," National Archives.

7. L. B. Eaton to Attorney General, August 12, 1874, Western District of Tennessee, *ibid*.

8. W. W. Murray to Attorney General, April 26, 1875, *ibid*.

9. G. Wiley Wells to Attorney General, January 16, 1872, Northern District of Mississippi, *ibid*.

10. W. A. Meriwether to Benjamin H. Bristow, November 8, 1871, in Benjamin H. Bristow Papers, LC; Allen P. Huggins to Attorney General, June 28, 1871, Northern District of Mississippi, Amos Morrill to Attorney General, December 6, 1872, Eastern District of Texas, J. R. Beckwith to Attorney General, October 17, 1874, District of Louisiana, all in Source Chronological Files, RG 60, NA; H. L. Wilson to William E. Chandler, September 6, 1872, in W. E. Chandler Papers; William T. Sherman to John Sherman, March 21, 1871, in William T. Sherman Papers, LC.

11. William Story to Attorney General, June 7, 1871, Western District of Arkansas, Eli H. Murray to G. C. Wharton, September 10, 1873, District of Kentucky, both in Source Chronological Files, Amos T. Akerman to John A. Minnis, July 7, 1871, in Letters Sent by the Department of Justice: Instructions to United States Attorneys and Marshals, 1867–1904, hereinafter cited as Instruction Book, all in RG 60, NA.

12. *Nation*, March 23, 1871; Akerman to Minnis, September 8, 1871, George H. Williams to R. M. Wallace, August 27, 1872, both in Instruction Book, A. J. Evans to Attorney General, August 23, 1875, Western District of Texas, Source Chronological Files, all in RG 60, NA.

13. Isaac H. Shields to Attorney General, August 22, 1876, Eastern District of Virginia, Source Chronological Files, in RG 60, NA.

14. L. L. Lewis to A. J. Falls, October 10, 1874, *ibid*.

15. David T. Corbin to Attorney General, District of South Carolina, Source Chronological Files, Edwards Pierrepont to Bernard G. Caulfield, February 25, 1876, Alphonso Taft to Thomas W. Ferry, December 13, 1876, both in Letters Sent by the Department of Justice to Executive Officers and to Members of Congress, 1871–1904, hereinafter cited as Executive-Congressional Letterbook, all in RG 60, NA; New York *Times*, July 19, 1871.

16. Arthur I. Boreman to Edwin D. Morgan, June 14, 1872, in Edwin D. Morgan Papers, New York State Library, Albany; Akerman to E. P. Jackson, August 18, 1871, in Amos T. Akerman Letterbooks, University of Virginia Library, Charlottesville, hereinafter cited as Akerman Letterbooks.

17. Minnis to Attorney General, April 1, 1872, Middle District of Alabama, Source Chronological Files, in RG 60, NA; on the Supreme Court decisions, see Chapter 12.

18. Oregon Republican Senator George H. Williams, the future attorney general, on May 20, 1870, characterized one version of the First Enforcement Act as a "conglomerated mass of incongruities and uncertainties. . . . a sort of moral essay that has been thrown into something like the shape of legislation." *Congressional Globe*, 41st Cong., 2nd Sess., 36568–57, see also 3568–70; for descriptions of the enforcement acts as vague and verbose, see *Nation*, April 20, 1871; New York *World*, May 16, 1871; *Independent*, March 16, 23, 1871; New York *Evening Post*, April 7, 1871, June 24, 1876.

19. Huggins to Attorney General, June 28, 1871, Northern District of Mississippi, Source Chronological Files, in RG 60, NA. Appropriations for the Department of War were reduced from 78 million dollars in 1869 to 35 million in 1872. New York *Tribune*, August 14, 1874.

20. George N. Norley to Thomas F. Bayard, February 18, 1872, in Thomas F. Bayard Papers, LC; William T. Sherman to Alfred H. Terry, December 6, 1870, Letters Received, Main Series, to 1870, in RG 94, "Records of the Office of the Adjutant General," NA.

21. Between 1871 and 1876, seven hundred or less troops were annually stationed in each southern state; the only exceptions were in Texas, Louisiana in 1874, and South Carolina in 1871 and 1872 when about a thousand soldiers were ordered to the upland counties to crush the Klan. In general, only a small number of army posts existed in the South; excluding Texas, there were sixty-five posts throughout the South during 1868, forty-four in 1869, thirty in 1870, thirty-one in 1871 and 1872, forty in 1874, and thirty-eight in 1876. Except for Texas, between 1869 and 1876 no southern state in a single year had more than ten army posts, and each usually had five posts or less. In the nation at large, the total strength of the army in 1869 was about thirty-seven thousand, and from 1871 to 1877 it was only twenty-eight thousand. Given the potential trouble spots in Texas, in the South with the terrorists, in the West with the Indians, and along the Canadian frontier with the Fenians, the army was too small. Indeed, its total strength was only slightly greater than just before the outbreak of the Civil War. *Nation*, December 30, 1875; James E. Sefton, *The United States Army and Reconstruction, 1865–1877* (Baton Rouge: Louisiana State University Press, 1967), 262.

22. O. P. Lincoln to J. E. Carpenter, September 14, 1874, Northern District of Mississippi, extract from a letter of Deputy Marshal Stockton quoted in Stephen B. Packard to Attorney General, November 1, 1874, District of Louisiana, A. W. Stone to Attorney General, October 21, 1872, Southern District of Georgia, all in Source Chronological Files, RG 60, NA.

23. Corbin to Attorney General, November 2, 1872, District of South Carolina, *ibid.*

24. Williams to Virgil Lusk, June 21, 1873, April 25, 1874, Instruction Book, *ibid.*

25. Carl Schurz to Anna E. Dickinson, March 27, 1871, in Anna E. Dickinson Papers, LC; Williams to R. W. Healey and others, September 3, 1874, Williams to Peter Melendy and others, November 30, 1874, Williams to G. Wiley Wells, December 19, 1874, Williams to Wharton, February 25, 1875, all in Instruction Book, RG 60, NA.

26. Mrs. M. C. Mansen to Ulysses S. Grant, August 23, 1874, Middle District of Tennessee, "Colored Citizens of Limestone, Texas," to Grant, July 24, 1875, Western District of Texas, both in Source Chronological Files, RG 60, NA; *Independent*, April 27, 1871.

27. *National Anti-Slavery Standard*, September 18, October 2, December 4, 11, 1869; *Congressional Globe*, 42nd Cong., 1st Sess., 305; Springfield *Republican*, August 3, 1871; Washington *National Republican*, September 11, 1875; New York *Times*, January 13, 1873.

28. *Harper's Weekly*, February 6, 1875; Baltimore *American*, November 5, 1872, November 6, 1878; William C. Pierce to Attorney General, February 11, 1876, District of Georgia, Source Chronological Files, in RG 60, NA.

29. W. H. Smyth to Attorney General, October 27, 1874, Volney Spalding to Attorney General, September 8, 1876, both in District of Georgia, Source Chronological Files, RG 60, NA; *Harper's Weekly*, September 11, 1875; J. R. Hubbard to Chandler, August 28, 1872, in W. E. Chandler Papers; Akerman to James Atkins, November 13, 1871, in Akerman Letterbooks.

30. Wilmington (Del.) *Commercial*, November 8–10, 1870; Akerman to Anthony Higgins, November 8, 1870, telegram in Letterbooks, in Ulysses S. Grant Papers, LC.

31. Wilmington *Commercial*, November 10, 1870; *Delaware Republican* (Wilmington), November 10, 1870.

32. Higgins to Attorney General, October 21, 1872, District of Delaware, Source Chronological Files, Williams to Higgins, July 2, 1872, Instruction Book, both in RG 60, NA.

33. *United States* v. *Given*, 25 Fed. Cases 1324; Higgins to Attorney General, February 15, 1873, District of Delaware, Source Chronological Files, in RG 60, NA; Bayard to Thomas Holcomb, March 7, 1875, Bayard to Archibald Given, March 1, 1875, both in T. F. Bayard Papers.

34. Eli Saulsbury to Bayard, October 29, 1872, in T. F. Bayard Papers.

35. Wilmington *Commercial*, November 9, 1872; *Delaware Gazette* (Wilmington), November 28, 1872.

36. Wilmington *Commercial*, January 7–8, September 3, 1873, October 6, November 2–5, 1874; *Delaware Gazette*, November 7, 1873.

37. New York *World*, March 6, 1871; St. Louis *Globe-Democrat*, March 27, 1877; New York *Times*, October 5, 1872, January 3, 31, 1873, August 5, 1876; William Gillette, "Anatomy of a Failure: Federal Enforcement of the Right to Vote in the Border States During Reconstruction," in Richard O. Curry (ed.), *Radicalism, Racism, and Party Realignment: The Border States During Reconstruction* (Baltimore: Johns Hopkins University Press, 1969), 265–304.

38. J. Birney Work to James A. Garfield, December 16, 1876, in Garfield Papers, LC; C. P. Leslie to Rutherford B. Hayes, February, 1877, in Hayes Papers.

39. It has proved easier to measure statistics than to determine their significance. For example, according to present-day standards, a state prosecuting attorney might consider a conviction rate of 70 percent to be satisfactory. To be sure, certain revisionist historians contend that enforcement was a success between 1870 and 1874. But in 1870, there was a national average of successful prosecution (54 percent), with 61 percent in the border states and 100 percent in the North. However, there were but thrity-two federal convictions in the whole country, with only seventeen convictions secured in the borderland and fifteen in the North. Above all, in the South there was not a single conviction. In 1871, the national average of 43 percent was unsatisfactory. Although the South had more success than the rest of the nation, the performance there was skewed: six southern states lacked a single conviction; in Florida, one conviction was secured. The results were only significant in the Carolinas. In 1872, the record was better nationally (53 percent) and regionally (74 percent in the South), but representation was again poor within the South, with six states lacking a single conviction. There were only five convictions in Alabama, and North Carolina had only one, as compared to forty-nine the year before. Only federal officials in South Carolina and Mississippi were able to achieve a good record that year. In 1873, the record was mediocre, with 36 percent for the nation as a whole and 41 percent in the South. Despite increased federal activity, the regional record of convictions remained meager, except for the Carolinas and Mississippi. There were poor percentages of convictions for both the nation and the South (11 percent for both) in 1874. Only in Mississippi was some action taken, but the number of convictions had been reduced from 184 in 1873 to 57 in 1874. The record in South Carolina had also deteriorated: except for 1875, the years after 1872 were poor, with 3 percent in 1873 and 1877, and no convictions in 1874 and 1876. Elsewhere in the South, either by percentage or by number of convictions or both, the record was abysmal. With few exceptions, matters went from bad to worse between 1874 and 1877, with a southern conviction rate of 7 percent in 1875, 2 percent in 1876, and 5 percent in 1877. Despite rampant disorder, federal election enforcement was virtually nonexistent in seven of the ten southern states. See Bibliographical Essay.

40. Hayes to John Sherman, April 1, 1871, Morgan to Sherman, February 21, 1871, both in J. Sherman Papers; Akerman to J. R. Parott, December 6, 1871, in Akerman Letterbooks.

41. Akerman to Foster Blodgett, November 8, 1871, in Akerman Letterbooks;

comment of George S. Boutwell in Diary, April 2, 1872, in Hamilton Fish Papers, LC; Garfield to James H. Rhodes, April 21, 1871, Garfield to Lyman W. Hall, April 22, 1871, both in Letterbooks, Garfield Papers, LC; *Nation*, March 16, 1871.

42. *Congressional Globe*, 42nd Cong., 1st Sess., Appendix, 179; New York *World*, May 23, 1870.

43. *Congressional Record*, 43rd Cong., 2nd Sess., 370.

44. Pierrepont to Grant, May 19, 1870, in Ulysses S. Grant Papers, Rutherford B. Hayes Library, Fremont, Ohio; New York *Sun*, May 31, 1870; Springfield *Republican*, May 23, 1870; New York *Times*, June 14, 1870; Chicago *Tribune*, February 28, 1871; Diary, October 21, 24, 28, November 1, 1870, in Fish Papers, LC; Akerman to George Sharpe, November 18, 1870 (note also that twenty-four out of twenty-seven communications of the Department of Justice between October 7 and November 7, 1870, were concerned with northern, not southern, election enforcement), in Instruction Book, RG 60, NA; Charles Sumner to Morgan, November 4, 1868, in Morgan Papers.

45. Robert A. Horn, "National Control of Congressional Elections" (Ph.D. dissertation, Princeton University, 1942), 142–364; Albie Burke, "Federal Regulation of Congressional Elections in Northern Cities, 1871–1894" (Ph.D. dissertation, University of Chicago, 1968), 34–220; W. T. Sherman to George G. Meade, October 15, 27, 1870, Letters Received, Main Series, to 1870, in RG 94, NA.

46. Lyman Trumbull to William Jayne, April 9, 1871, in William Jayne Papers, Illinois State Historical Library, Springfield; Akerman to William H. McWharton, November 16, 1871, Akerman to Blodgett, November 8, 1871, both in Akerman Letterbooks; Healey to Willard Warner, March 21, 1871, Northern District of Alabama, Source Chronological Files, Akerman to Minnis, December 26, 1871, Instruction Book, both in RG 60, NA.

47. Frank Morey to Attorney General, November 10, 1874, District of Louisiana, Source Chronological Files, in RG 60, NA.

48. Cornelius Cole to Olive Cole, June 8, 1872, in Cole Papers; Orris S. Ferry to Gideon Welles, May 24, 1872, in Gideon Welles Papers, LC.

49. Garfield to Jacob D. Cox, April 8, 1871, in Cox Papers; *Nation*, March 23, 1871.

50. Garfield to Hinsdale, March 30, 1871, Letterbooks in Garfield Papers, LC.

51. Samuel Shellabarger to James M. Comly, April 10, 1871, in James M. Comly Papers, Ohio Historical Society, Columbus; *Congressional Globe*, 42nd Cong., 1st Sess., Appendix, 116–17, 71.

52. New York *Evening Post*, March 29, 1871, compare February 16, March 28, and April 1, 1871.

53. *Nation*, March 23, 1871, compare May 19, 1870, April 13, 20, 1871.

54. Marshall Jewell to Lucius Fairchild, December 29, 1874, in Lucius Fairchild Papers, State Historical Society of Wisconsin, Madison; *Congressional Globe*, 41st Cong., 2nd Sess., 3613.

55. *Golden Age* (New York, N.Y.), April 1, 1871.

CHAPTER 3

1. William E. Chandler to Elihu B. Washburne, July 19, 1872, in Elihu B. Washburne Papers, LC; Hesseltine, *Grant*, 132–268; Nevins, *Fish*, 105–596.

2. The congressional election of 1870 had indicated restiveness, for the Republicans lost their two-thirds control of Congress for the first time since 1864; the Republican majority in the House of Representatives was slashed from ninety-nine in the Forty-first Congress to twenty-five in the Forty-second Congress, and the national popular majority was drastically reduced. Despite such reverses, the Republicans remained reasonably confident. They still retained control, and with a true

Republican president in office, overriding a presidential veto was no longer critical. Also, there had not been a northern white backlash because of the enfranchisement of northern Negroes; in fact, the recruitment of those new voters was regarded by both parties as a decided asset to the Republicans. *Tribune Almanac and Political Register for 1873* (New York: Tribune Association, 1873), 38–42; New York *Herald*, October 13, November 11, 1870; New York *Times*, October 13, 1870; Newark *Advertiser*, November 9, 1870.

3. Subsequent elections during 1871 reinforced Republican confidence, for the Democrats had only limited and localized successes, since the series of Republican defeats in the South were not duplicated in the North. *Harper's Weekly*, November 11, 18, 1871; New York *World*, November 13, 1870, April 2, 1872.

4. Louisville *Courier-Journal*, August 21, 1874; Michael C. Kerr to Manton Marble, May 30, 1871, in Marble Papers; Marcellus Emery to Horatio Seymour, October 25, 1871, in Horatio Seymour Papers, New York State Library, Albany; Robert B. Roosevelt to John W. Stevenson, March 29, 1873, in Stevenson Family Papers, LC; Littleton D. Q. Washington to Robert M. T. Hunter, October 31, 1869, in Hunter Papers.

5. Wade Hampton to John Mullaly, March 31, 1867, in Hampton Family Papers, University of South Carolina Library, Columbia; Louisville *Courier-Journal*, June 15, 1874; Kerr to Lucius Q. C. Lamar, March 15, 1873, in Lamar-Mayes Papers, Mississippi Department of Archives and History, Jackson; Kerr to Marble, November 8, 1868, in Marble Papers.

6. Richard Vaux to John W. Stevenson, March 8, 1874, in Stevenson Family Papers; Louisville *Courier-Journal*, June 15, 1874.

7. For political developments in Virginia, see Chapter 4.

8. Jacob D. Cox to Horace Greeley, July 17, 1869, Cox to Job E. Stevenson, March 29, 1871, both in Cox Papers; New York *Tribune*, January 10, November 21, 1870.

9. *Harper's Weekly*, April 21, 1866, compare April 22, 29, 1871; G. M. Arnold to Charles Sumner, December 26, 1871, William Lloyd Garrison to Sumner, January 18, 1872, both in Sumner Papers.

10. Richard J. Haldeman to Jeremiah S. Black, April 12, 1872, in Jeremiah S. Black Papers, LC; Daniel Cameron to Cyrus H. McCormick, July 26, August 1, 1872, in Cyrus H. McCormick Papers, State Historical Society of Wisconsin, Madison; James R. Randall to Alexander H. Stephens, November 10, 1872, in Alexander H. Stephens Papers, LC; Samuel Bowles to J. C. Collins, March 22, 1872, in Samuel Bowles Papers, Yale University Library, New Haven, Conn.

11. John G. Sprout, *"The Best Men": Liberal Reformers in the Gilded Age* (New York: Oxford University Press, 1968); David Herbert Donald, *Charles Sumner and the Rights of Man* (New York: Alfred A. Knopf, 1970), 349–544; Ari A. Hoogenboom, *Outlawing the Spoils: A History of the Civil Service Reform Movement, 1865–1883* (Urbana: University of Illinois Press, 1961).

12. New York *Tribune*, April 26, May 1, 1872; Springfield *Republican*, April 23, 1872; Ulysses S. Grant to Washburne, May 26, 1872, in Ulysses S. Grant Papers, Illinois State Historical Library, Springfield; Boston *Advertiser*, quoted in New York *Tribune*, April 26, 1872; Marshall Jewell to William E. Chandler, July 29, 1872, in W. E. Chandler Papers.

13. New York *Tribune*, Springfield *Republican*, Cincinnati *Commercial*, May 2–4, 1872. Why did the Liberal delegates flounder at their convention? Perhaps the answer can be found in the process of selecting delegates, making decisions, and forming judgments. The haphazard procedure in selecting delegates—the failure to rely upon the ordinary political machinery of party caucus and state convention—produced an unusual collection of delegates. Assembled to run the national convention of a party without a real organization, having no real responsibility to a particular constituency, and thus speaking and acting without true authority, many

delegates did not feel constrained to be judicious. They practiced and preached a romantic notion of freedom and an unfettered brand of individualism, and they got carried away by their own rhetoric and zeal. Their ineffective organization made it impossible to give cohesion to the convention, or control to the leadership. The assemblage was too unwieldy to provide order or conduct business. Greeley's nomination was the product of a truly open convention.

14. *Nation*, May 9, 1872; New York *Evening Post*, May 4, 1872; William Cullen Bryant to Lyman Trumbull, May 8, 1872, in William Cullen Bryant Papers, New York Historical Society, New York; S. S. K. Prime to Jacob D. Cox, May 12, 1872, in Cox Papers.

15. Charles Francis Adams Diary, May 4, 1872, in Adams Family Papers, Massachusetts Historical Society, Boston; New York *Times*, November 24, 1871, May 4, July 8, 1872; George Templeton Strong Journal, May 3, 1872, in New York Historical Society, New York; compare New York *Tribune*, May 6, 1872; Springfield *Republican*, July 13, 27, 1872.

16. New York *World*, May 4, 1872; J. Bell Robinson to Thomas F. Bayard, June 14, 1872, in T. F. Bayard Papers; Pittsburgh *Post*, quoted in Chicago *Times*, May 6, 1872.

17. Eugene Casserly to Samuel J. Tilden, June 13, 1872, in Samuel J. Tilden Papers, New York Public Library, New York; George B. McClellan to Jacob D. Cox, July 3, 1872, in Cox Papers; Kerr to Marble, June 13, 1872, in Marble Papers.

18. Louisville *Courier-Journal*, May 17, 1872; Washington to Hunter, May 31, 1871, May 7, 1872, in Hunter Papers; southern editorials quoted in New York *Tribune*, May 8, 1872; Black to William H. Walsh, August 3, 1872, in Black Papers.

19. August Belmont to Bowles, May 7, 1872, Kerr to David A. Wells, June 14, 1872, both in David A. Wells Papers, LC; Hampton to Mullaly, May 19, 1872, in Hampton Family Papers.

20. New York *World*, July 8–11, 1872; Chicago *Times*, July 6, 1872.

21. In contrast, the Liberal organization was a shambles, with incompetent leaders, internal feuding, inadequate funds, and chaotic scheduling. William H. Green to Lyman Trumbull, October 8, 1872, in Lyman Trumbull Papers, LC; Alexander K. McClure to Whitelaw Reid, August 21, 1872, in Whitelaw Reid Papers, LC; William E. Chandler to William Claflin, August 28, 1872, September 29, 1872, in William Claflin Papers, Rutherford B. Hayes Library, Fremont, Ohio.

22. *Nation*, July 4, 1872; New York *Times*, July 8, 1872; compare Kerr to Marble, August 26, 1872, in Marble Papers.

23. Grant to Roscoe Conkling, July 15, 1872, in Roscoe Conkling Papers, LC; Grant, in New York *Herald*, August 16, 1872; Marcus L. Ward to Horace N. Congar, September 23, 1872, in Horace N. Congar Papers, New Jersey Historical Society, Newark. The northern Negro voter was mentioned as an important element in Indiana, Ohio, and Pennsylvania politics: Garland White to Oliver P. Morton, April 30, 1872, in W. E. Chandler Papers; Augustus Schell to McCormick, July 25, 1872, in McCormick Papers; McClure to Reid, September 21, 1872, in Reid Papers.

24. Diary, October 4, 11, November 8, 1872, in Fish Papers, LC. The counterattack against the Liberals was comprehensive. As for the reform of the civil service, President Grant fired some notorious spoilsmen, whereas earlier he had outmaneuvered the reformers by pressuring Congress into creating a commission, by appointing one of the reformers as its chairman, and by promulgating civil service regulations. Congress also had reduced the tariff, eliminated the income tax, and, on May 22, 1872, granted amnesty to former Confederates, who now could hold public office.

25. Hiram Barney to Gideon Welles, June 21, 1872, in Welles Papers; Springfield *Republican*, July 10, August 20, 1872; New York *World*, August 2, 10, September 27, October 19, 1872.

26. New York *Herald*, August 8, 1872; W. D. S. to Marble, August 18, 1872, in

Marble Papers; Levi P. Luckey to Washburne, August 30, 1872, in Washburne Papers; Charles A. Dana to Edwin D. Morgan, August 22, 1872, in Morgan Papers; Chicago *Times*, August 10, 1872. The North Carolina election in August revealed Democratic dissatisfaction with Greeley; the Vermont and Maine elections in early September indicated that Yankee Greeley had failed to break those Republican strongholds. W. A. Avera to Daniel M. Barringer, August 9, 1872, in Daniel M. Barringer Papers, University of North Carolina Library, Chapel Hill; Hannibal Hamlin to Zachariah Chandler, September 23, 1872, in Zachariah Chandler Papers, LC.

27. New York *Times*, September 19–29, 1872.

28. M. Connelly to Greeley, July 19, 1872, in Horace Greeley Papers, New York Public Library, New York; Greeley to Murat Halstead, October 18, 1872, in Murat Halstead Papers, Cinncinnati Historical Society, Cincinnati.

29. Greeley, quoted in New York *Times*, September 20, 25, 26, 1872; New York *Evening Post*, September 23, 1872; *Times* of London, October 3, 1872.

30. Greeley, quoted in New York *Times*, September 22, 1872, and in New York *Tribune*, May 17, 1872; *Times* of London, October 10, 1872; Springfield *Republican*, June 11, 1872; New York *Times*, October 17, 1872.

31. Greeley, quoted in New York *Times*, September 24, 25, 1872; Washington *National Republican*, September 30, 1872; Washington *New National Era*, September 26, 1872.

32. J. H. Warwick to William E. Chandler, September 26, 1872, in W. E. Chandler Papers; Rutherford B. Hayes to Sardis Birchard, September 22, 29, 1872, in Hayes Papers; Diary, September 27, October 11, 1872, in Garfield Papers, LC.

33. New York *Times*, October 1, September 21, 1872; *Atlantic Monthly*, XXX (November, 1872), 640; New York *Evening Post*, September 23, 25, 1872; Chicago *Times*, September 24, 1872; James A. Garfield to William C. Howells, July 11, 1872, in Garfield Papers, LC.

34. Washington to Hunter, October 10, 1872, in Hunter Papers.

35. Luckey to Washburne, July 21, 1872, in Washburne Papers.

36. New York *Evening Post*, August 20, 1872.

37. In the early October elections the Republicans won by a large and surprising majority in Pennsylvania; in Indiana the Republicans captured the legislature, although a Democrat won the governorship. The Chicago *Tribune*, October 10, 1872, estimated that in the Indiana gubernatorial race only 5 percent of the coalition total came from Liberal voters.

38. Greeley carried four border states (Maryland, Kentucky, Tennessee, and Missouri) and two states in the Deep South (Georgia and Texas); except for Missouri and Texas, Greeley carried the other four states by a marginal percentage of the popular vote. However, Grant's sweep of most of the southern states was deceptive; he won most by default because Democrats refused to vote for Greeley. Grant won six border and southern states by a marginal percentage and only four by 55 percent or higher. If the southern Democrats had united, the regional results would have been different.

39. Edwin L. Godkin to Carl Schurz, November 11, 1872, A. R. Cooper to Schurz, November 11, 1872, both in Carl Schurz Papers, LC; Springfield *Republican*, November 7, 1872; Benjamin H. Bristow to John Marshall Harlan, November 26, 1872, in John Marshall Harlan Papers, LC. Liberal contempt for the electorate is expressed in E. Peck to Trumbull, November 11, 1872, in Trumbull Papers; and J. H. Osborne to Wells, November 9, 1872, in Wells Papers. For examples of the Republican repudiation of the elitist Liberal movement, see Joseph R. Hawley to Henry L. Dawes, November 7, 1872, in Dawes Papers; Jewell to W. E. Chandler, July 29, 1872, in W. E. Chandler Papers.

40. Some historians have contended that there was strength in the nomination of Greeley and that Greeley proved himself an excellent campaigner. For example,

Hesseltine, in *Grant*, pp. 275, 308, claims that Grant's vote in 1872 was lower than in 1868; in fact, Grant received 3,013,313 votes in 1868 (52 percent) and 3,597,375 in 1872 (55 percent). Greeley did in fact receive more popular votes (almost 130,000) than had Seymour in 1868, but that was partly because the residents of several southern states had not voted in 1868 but did vote in 1872; however, Grant received almost 600,000 more votes in 1872 than he had in 1868. Seymour won eight states and Greeley, six; Seymour won 80 electoral votes (27 percent of the electoral college), whereas Greeley would have won 66 electoral votes (18 percent) if he had lived until the electoral college voted; Seymour won 47 percent of the popular vote to Greeley's 43 percent. See *Tribune Almanac for 1873*, 45–84; *Harper's Weekly*, January 4, 1873, February 17, 1877; *Times* of London, November 20, 1872; Svend Petersen, *A Statistical History of the American Presidential Elections* (New York: Frederick Ungar, 1963), 42–44; W. Dean Burnham, *Presidential Ballots, 1836–1892* (Baltimore: Johns Hopkins University Press, 1955), 108–18, 246–57.

41. George G. Meade to Spencer Meade, October 17, 1872, in George G. Meade Papers, Historical Society of Pennsylvania, Philadelphia.

42. Washington *National Republican*, January 24, April 4, 1874; Chicago *Inter-Ocean*, May 8, 1875.

43. New York *Times*, September 13, November 12, 15, 1872.

44. Bristow to John Marshall Harlan, December 4, 1872, in Harlan Papers; John C. B. Davis to Washburne, February 21, 1873, in Washburne Papers; New York *Herald*, March 4, 1873.

45. Richardson (comp.), *Messages of the Presidents*, VII, 221; Logan, *Reminiscences*, 241–44; Washington *Star*, March 4, 5, 1873; Springfield *Republican*, March 5, 1873; New York *World*, March 5, 1873.

46. New York *World*, March 5, 1873; Springfield *Republican*, March 7, 1873.

47. Chicago *Times*, March 5, 1873; *Independent*, March 20, 1873; New York *Times*, March 5, 1873; Raymonde in Cincinnati *Commercial*, February 19, 1877.

CHAPTER 4

1. Richardson (comp.), *Messages of the Presidents*, VII, 96, 221, 298–99, 6, 112, 142, 299; New York *World*, April 17, 1871.

2. New York *Tribune*, April 9, 1869; New York *Herald*, July 30, 1874; New York *Times*, January 9, 1875; Springfield *Republican*, March 3, 1877.

3. New York *Times*, June 18, 1871; compare Bruce Catton, *U. S. Grant and the American Military Tradition* (Boston: Little, Brown, 1954), 175, for the view that Grant's course was wholly passive.

4. David Herbert Donald, "The Republican Party, 1864–1876," in Arthur M. Schlesinger, Jr. (ed.), *History of U.S. Political Parties* (New York: Chelsea House, 1973), 1293; see also the southern Democratic pattern in the ratification of the Fifteenth Amendment in Gillette, *The Right To Vote*, 94.

5. Richardson (comp.), *Messages of the Presidents*, VII, 11–15, 29; for the intrastate political background, see Jack P. Maddex, Jr., *The Virginia Conservatives, 1867–1879* (Chapel Hill: University of North Carolina Press, 1970).

6. G. K. Gilmer to Jacob M. Howard, January 28, 1869, in Jacob M. Howard Papers, Detroit Public Library, Detroit; Littleton D. Q. Washington to Robert M. T. Hunter, January 9, 31, February 14, April 12, May 6, June 28, 1869, all in Hunter Papers; J. M. Walker to William Mahone, April 11, 1869, R. F. Walker to Mahone, July 12, 1869, both in William Mahone Papers, Duke University Library, Durham, N.C.; Mahone to James L. Kemper, June 14, 1869, in James L. Kemper Papers, University of Virginia Library, Charlottesville.

7. *National Anti-Slavery Standard*, July 17, 1869; John W. Holtz to Charles Sumner, January 26, 1870, in Sumner Papers.

8. New York *Tribune*, July 7, 1869; New York *Times*, July 8, 1869; New York *World*, July 8–10, 1869.

9. John L. Maryre, Jr., to Mahone, July 26, 1869, in Mahone-Mcgill Papers, University of Virginia Library, Charlottesville; Manton Marble to Samuel L. M. Barlow, August 9, 1869, in Barlow Papers.

10. Kemper to Mahone, June 5, 1869, Maryre to Mahone, July 8, 1869, in Mahone-McGill Papers.

11. Ulysses S. Grant to E. Rockwood Hoar, September 25, 1869, Letterbooks, in Grant Papers, LC; James W. Lewellen to [Mahone], September 10, July 12, 1869, both in Mahone-Mcgill Papers; Washington to Hunter, September 11, 1869, in Hunter Papers; New York *Herald*, September 5, 1869; New York *Times*, September 6, 1869; New York *Tribune*, July 13, 1869; see but compare Hesseltine, *Grant*, 182–83, 186; Nevins, *Fish*, 290.

12. Edward McPherson, *The Political History of the United States of America During the Period of Reconstruction, From April 15, 1865 to July 15, 1870* (Washington, D.C.: Solomons and Chapman, 1875), 572–76; New York *Times*, January 17, 1870; Washington *New National Era*, January 13, 1870; *National Anti-Slavery Standard*, January 15, 22, 1870.

13. Washington *National Republican*, June 12, July 21, October 31, November 7, 1873; Springfield *Republican*, October 31, 1873. Historian Robert R. Jones contends that "there is no persuasive evidence that the election of 1873 marked a significant turn toward increased racism in Conservative campaigning." Yet various journals outside the state had noted at the time and were to comment subsequently about the racist character of that campaign. The question merits a thorough examination. See Robert R. Jones, "James L. Kemper and the Virginia Redeemers Face the Race Question: A Reconsideration," *Journal of Southern History*, XXXVIII (1972), 393–414.

14. New York *Herald*, December 8, 1869; Washington *National Republican*, July 21, 31, 1873.

15. Although Democratic disaffection with Greeley in 1872 was important, perhaps it was not all important. In any event, one Virginian subsequently wrote: "I supported General Grant and canvassed Virginia for him in 1872. General Grant told me that he owed the electoral vote of Virginia to my exertions in his behalf." John S. Mosby to Jesse C. Green, September 25, 1888, in John S. Mosby Papers, University of Virginia Library, Charlottesville.

16. For the intrastate political background, see Elizabeth Studley Nathans, *Losing the Peace: Georgia Republicans and Reconstruction, 1865–1871* (Baton Rouge: Louisiana State University Press, 1968).

17. *Independent*, April 15, 1869; see but compare Hesseltine, *Grant*, 158.

18. Richardson (comp.), *Messages of the Presidents*, VII, 28; A. J. Ricks to Jacob D. Cox, August 14, 1869, in Cox Papers; *National Anti-Slavery Standard*, July 3, 1869; New York *Times*, December 20, 1869.

19. McPherson, *History of Reconstruction*, 609–11; Jesse H. Moore to Richard J. Oglesby, January 2, 1870, in Richard J. Oglesby Papers, Illinois State Historical Library, Springfield.

20. Alfred H. Terry to William T. Sherman, January 19, 1870, Letters Received, Main Series, to 1870, Sherman to Terry, January 12, 1870, Letters Sent, Main Series, both in RG 94, NA; *American Annual Cyclopedia and Register of Important Events of the Year 1870* (New York: D. Appleton, 1871), 331–35; Diary, January 21, 1870, in Fish Papers, LC; New York *Herald*, April 24, 1870; James A. Garfield to Edward Atkinson, May 28, 1870, in Edward Atkinson Papers, Massachusetts Historical Society, Boston.

21. McPherson, *History of Reconstruction*, 611–15; Sherman to Terry, January 16, 17, 1870, Letters Received, Main Series, to 1870, in RG 94, NA; *National Anti-Slavery Standard*, February 12, 1870.

22. Benjamin Conley to Grant, November 24, 1871, in Grant Papers, Hayes Library; Diary, December 1, 1871, in Fish Papers, LC; Amos T. Akerman to J. H. Caldwell, November 10, 1871, in Akerman Letterbooks.

23. Akerman to J. R. Parott, December 6, 1871, in Akerman Letterbooks.

24. Raleigh *Standard*, June 15, 1870; for the intrastate political background, see Horace W. Raper, "William W. Holden: A Political Biography" (Ph.D. dissertation, University of North Carolina, 1951); Trelease, *White Terror*, 189–225.

25. William W. Holden to Pride Jones, March 7, 1870, in William W. Holden Papers, Duke University Library, Durham, N.C.; Royal T. Frank to Adjutant General, July 21, 26, 1870, Letters Received, Main Series, to 1870, in RG 94, NA; William Harris to Daniel M. Barringer, June 13, 1870, in Barringer Papers.

26. Holden to Grant, March 10, July 20, 1870, in Holden Papers, Duke University Library; Holden to Irvin McDowell, May 9, 1870, Letters Received, Main Series, to 1870, in RG 94, NA.

27. Grant to Holden, July 22, 1870, William J. Clarke to Holden, June 18, 1870, Grant to William T. Sherman, June 17, 1870, all in William W. Holden Papers, North Carolina State Archives, Raleigh; Raleigh *Standard*, June 23, 1870; McDowell to Commanding Officer at Raleigh, May 10, 1870, Letters Received, Main Series, to 1870, in RG 94, NA.

28. Holden to Grant, August 7, 1870, William W. Belknap to Holden, August, 1870, both in Holden Papers, North Carolina State Archives.

29. Raleigh *Standard*, August 10, 1870; David Schenck Diary, August, 1870.

30. Springfield *Republican*, July 25, 1870; Cincinnati *Commercial*, August 9, 1870; Raleigh *Sentinel*, August 2, 4, 1870; New York *Times*, August 8, 1870; Washington *Chronicle*, August 4, 8, 1870.

31. Holden to his wife, March 4, 1871, in Holden Papers, North Carolina State Archives.

32. Holden to his wife, March 2, 1871, in Holden Papers, North Carolina State Archives; Holden to his wife, May 15, April 30, 1871, both in Holden Papers, Duke University Library; William H. N. Smith to Edward Conigland, April 29, 1871, in Edward Conigland Papers, University of North Carolina Library, Chapel Hill.

33. Zebulon Vance, quoted in Glenn Tucker, *Zeb Vance: Champion of Personal Freedom* (Indianapolis: Bobbs-Merrill, 1965), 452; Albion W. Tourgée to V. C. Barringer, February 7, 1871, in Albion W. Tourgée Papers, Chautauqua County Historical Society, Westfield, N.Y.; William H. N. Smith to Conigland, May 2, 1871, in Conigland Papers.

34. Holden to L. P. Olds, December 1, 1871, in Holden Papers, Duke University Library.

35. For the intrastate political background, see Walter L. Fleming, *Civil War and Reconstruction in Alabama* (New York: Columbia University Press, 1905), 735–97.

36. W. F. Drum to E. W. Smith, December 3, 1870, S. W. Crawford to Joseph H. Taylor, December 5, 1870, Robert Boxheard to Crawford, December 5, 1870, all in Letters Received, Main Series, to 1870, in RG 94, NA; Mobile *Register*, November 27, 1870; Drum to William Hugh Smith, November 28, 1870, in William Hugh Smith Papers, Alabama Department of Archives and History, Montgomery.

37. Mobile *Register*, December 10, 1870; Montgomery *Daily State Journal*, December 10, 1870.

38. Cincinnati *Commercial*, December 2, 1870; New York *Evening Post*, December 1, 1870.

39. Adjutant General to Robert B. Lindsay, November 30, 1870, Letters Sent, Main Series, in RG 94, NA; Washington *National Republican*, December 1, 1870; Crawford to Taylor, December 5, 1870, Letters Received, Main Series, to 1870, in RG 94, NA; Mobile *Register*, November 30, December 1, 1870.

40. New York *Herald*, November 23, 1872; George E. Spencer to W. E. Chandler, November 30, 1872, telegram from Paul Strobach to Chandler, December 6, 1872,

both in W. E. Chandler Papers; David P. Lewis to T. B. Weir, November 30, 1872, in David P. Lewis Papers, Alabama Department of Archives and History, Montgomery.

41. Chicago *Times*, December 6, 1872; New York *Times*, November 19, 1872.

42. Diary, December 10, 1872, in Fish Papers, LC; Mobile *Register*, December 15, 1872.

43. New York *Herald*, December 13, 1872; compare Washington *Chronicle*, December 11, 14, 1872; Montgomery *Daily State Journal*, December 10, 17, 1872; Lewis E. Parsons to W. E. Chandler, January 29, 1873, in W. E. Chandler Papers.

44. Montgomery *Daily State Journal*, November 4, 1874; Chicago *Times*, February 8, 1875; for the election of 1874, see Chapters 9, 10 herein; for the so-called force bill and the final session of the Forty-third Congress, see Chapter 12.

45. For the intrastate political background, see W. C. Nunn, *Texas Under the Carpetbaggers* (Austin: University of Texas Press, 1962), 13–132; John Pressley Carrier, "A Political History of Texas During the Reconstruction, 1865–1874" (Ph.D. dissertation, Vanderbilt University, 1971), 327–525.

46. *National Anti-Slavery Standard*, April 17, 1869; New York *Herald*, May 20, 1869; Richardson (comp.), *Messages of the Presidents*, VII, 17–18; J. G. Tracy and John W. McDonald to W. E. Chandler, July 14, 1869, in W. E. Chandler Papers.

47. New York *Times*, September 27, 1869.

48. Alvan C. Gillem to Joseph S. Fowler, March 10, 1870, in Joseph S. Fowler Papers, University of North Carolina Library, Chapel Hill; see but compare Hesseltine, *Grant*, 183–84; Nunn, *Texas*, 16–19; William L. Richter, "'We Must Rubb Out and Begin Anew': The Army and the Republican Party in Texas Reconstruction, 1867–1870," *Civil War History*, IXX (1973), 334–52; *Tribune Almanac and Political Register for 1872* (New York: Tribune Association, 1872), 74.

49. Washington *National Republican*, November 13, 1871, July 14, 1873; Springfield *Republican*, October 11, 1871.

50. San Antonio *Express*, January 15, 1874; Dallas *Herald*, January 17, 1874.

51. George H. Williams to Thomas F. Purnell, January 16, 1874, Instruction Book, in RG 60, NA.

52. San Antonio *Express*, January 18, 20–22, 1874; Dallas *Herald*, January 24, 1874.

53. New York *Herald*, January 13, 1874; New York *Sun*, January 14, 1874.

CHAPTER 5

1. New York *Times*, November 16, 1874; New Orleans *Republican*, June 10, 1874; New Orleans *Daily Picayune*, August 10, 1871.

2. George Bancroft to John C. B. Davis, September 18, 1874, in George Bancroft Papers, Massachusetts Historical Society, Boston; New York *Herald*, December 7, 1872; Springfield *Republican*, April 14, 1873.

3. For the intrastate political background, see *American Annual Cyclopedia and Register of Important Events of the Year 1871* (New York: D. Appleton, 1872), 471–74; Ella Lonn, *Reconstruction in Louisiana After 1868* (New York: G. P. Putnam's, 1918), 73–399; Joe Gray Taylor, *Louisiana Reconstructed, 1863–1877* (Baton Rouge: Louisiana State University Press, 1974), 209–313.

4. Stephen B. Packard to Attorney General, July, 1871, Ulysses S. Grant to Amos T. Akerman, August 3, 1871, O. J. Dunn to Grant, July 29, 1871, all in District of Louisiana, Source Chronological Files, Akerman to Packard, August 5, 1871, Instruction Book, all in RG 60, NA; Akerman to Grant, August 5, 1871, in Akerman Letterbooks; Akerman to J. R. West, August 5, 1871, in Henry C. Warmoth Papers, University of North Carolina Library, Chapel Hill.

5. New Orleans *Louisianian*, August 9, 13, 1871; New Orleans *Daily Picayune*,

August 10, 1871; Grant, quoted in New York *Herald*, August 22, 1871; Washington *National Republican*, August 10, 1871; New York *Tribune*, August 10, 1871; John M. Palmer to Warmoth, August 16, 1871, Pinckney B. S. Pinchback to Warmoth, September 5, 1871, H. C. Dibble to Warmoth, August 24, 1871, all in Warmoth Papers.

6. Springfield *Republican*, April 14, 1873.

7. For the intrastate background, see *American Annual Cyclopedia and Register of Important Events of the Year 1872* (New York: D. Appleton, 1873), 471–73; Lonn, *Reconstruction in Louisiana*, 110–37; New Orleans *Republican*, January 24, 1872.

8. New Orleans *Republican*, New Orleans *Daily Picayune*, January 4–24, 1872.

9. Grant to Henry L. Dawes, January 12, 1872, Letterbooks, in Grant Papers, LC; New Orleans *Louisianian*, January 7, 21, 1872; New Orleans *Republican*, January 24, 1872.

10. *American Annual Cyclopedia of the Year 1872*, 474–83; Lonn, *Reconstruction in Louisiana*, 138–220; Edward H. Durell to his sisters, December 22, 1872, March 7, 1873, William P. Kellogg to Durell, May 12, 1875, all in Edward H. Durell Papers, New York Historical Society, New York.

11. *American Annual Cyclopedia of the Year 1872*, 483; George H. Williams to Packard, December 3, 1872, Instruction Book, in RG 60, NA; William P. Kellogg to W. E. Chandler, November 28, December 11, 1872, Chandler to Kellogg, November 27, 29, 1872, all in W. E. Chandler Papers; Frank Morey to Warmoth, December 7, 1872, in Warmoth Papers.

12. Grant, quoted in editorial, New York *Herald*, December 12, 1872. The New York *Herald*, February 27, 1873, declared that Grant's "words amount to nothing when the action is so different."

13. Adjutant General to William H. Emory, December 14, 1872, Letters Sent, Main Series, Emory to Adjutant General, December 15, 1872, Letters Received, Main Series, since 1870, both in RG 94, NA.

14. New York *Herald*, December 12, 1872; Jacob D. Cox to John Lynch, December 24, 1872, in Cox Papers; compare New York *Times*, December 17, 1872; Washington *National Republican*, December 23, 1872; Washington *New National Era*, December 19, 27, 1872.

15. Grant to William W. Belknap, January 5, 1873, Letterbooks, in Grant Papers, LC; Edward McPherson, *A Hand-Book of Politics for 1874* (Washington, D.C.: Solomons and Chapman, 1874), 107–108; New York *Sun*, January 7, 1873; Cincinnati *Commercial*, January 7, 15, 1873; William T. Sherman to David F. Boyd, January 6, 1872, in Boyd Papers.

16. Richardson (comp.), *Messages of the Presidents*, VII, 212–13; Cox to C. C. Starbuck, May 1, 1873, in Cox Papers; William E. Chandler to Kellogg, January 26, 1873, in W. E. Chandler Papers; New York *Herald*, February 4, 1874.

17. Springfield *Republican*, January 27, 31, February 24, 1873; compare New York *Times*, January 16, March 3, 7, 1873; New York *Tribune*, January 14, 1873, February 26, 27, 1872; Washington *New National Era*, March 6, 20, 1873.

18. Grant to Belknap, March 5, 1873, Kellogg to Packard, March 5, 1873, telegram, both in Letters Received, Main Series, since 1870, in RG 94, NA.

19. Nevertheless, the northern press was appalled by the violence. New York *World*, April 20, 1873; New York *Herald*, April 17, 1873; compare Lonn, *Reconstruction in Louisiana*, 243–44.

20. Kellogg to Grant, May 13, 1873, District of Louisiana, Source Chronological Files, in RG 60, NA; Richardson (comp.), *Messages of the Presidents*, VII, 223–24; New York *Tribune*, New York *Herald*, Washington *National Republican*, all May 23, 1873.

21. Kellogg to Oliver P. Morton, November 12, 1873, in Oliver P. Morton Papers, Indiana State Library, Indianapolis.

22. Diary, January 27, 1874, in Fish Papers, LC; Grant, quoted in Washington

dispatch, New York *Herald*, January 29, 1874; W. E. Chandler to Grant, January 22, 1874, draft, in W. E. Chandler Papers.

23. *American Annual Cyclopedia and Register of Important Events of the Year 1874* (New York: D. Appleton, 1875) 476–83; Chicago *Tribune*, July 14, 1874; Kellogg to Grant, August 19, 1874, Kellogg to Williams, August 26, 1874, Packard to Williams, September 15, 1874, telegrams, all in District of Louisiana, Source Chronological Files, in RG 60, NA; Kellogg to Grant, September 14, 1874, telegram, in Grant Papers, LC; for developments in Texas and Arkansas, see Chapters 4 and 6, respectively; for the election of 1874, see Chapters 9, 10.

24. New Orleans *Times* quoted in New York *Evening Post*, September 28, 1874; New Orleans *Daily Picayune*, September 15, 17, 18, 1874; southern editorials quoted in Chicago *Tribune*, September 21, 1874; Louisville *Courier-Journal*, September 17, 18, 1874; Cincinnati *Commercial*, September 17, 1874; New York *Times*, September 17, 1874; Washington *National Republican*, September 17, 18, 1874.

25. Diary, September 15, 1874, in Fish Papers, LC.

26. Diary, September 16, 1874, *ibid.*; Sherman to Boyd, September 21, 1874, in Boyd Papers.

27. Adjutant General to Emory, September 16, 1874, Letters Sent, Main Series, in RG 94, NA; Richardson (comp.), *Messages of the Presidents*, VII, 276–77.

28. Rodgers and Cowan to Orville E. Babcock, September 22, 1874, Adjutant General to Belknap, September 26, 1874, Belknap to Adjutant General, September 28, 1874, all in Letters Received, Main Series, since 1870, in RG 94, NA; Kellogg to Grant, December 9, 1874, telegram, in William W. Belknap Papers, Princeton University Library, Princeton, N.J.; Grant, quoted in *Senate Executive Documents*, 57th Cong., 2nd Sess., No. 209, p. 158; see but compare, Hesseltine, *Grant*, 348; Nevins, *Fish*, 744–45, 748.

29. *Congressional Record*, 43rd Cong., 2nd Sess., 370; Springfield *Republican*, December 28, 1874; Louisville *Courier-Journal*, December 28, 1874; *American Annual Cyclopedia of the Year 1874*, 488–92.

30. Richardson (comp.), *Messages of the Presidents*, VII, 299; Springfield *Republican*, December 8, 1874; New York *Tribune*, December 8, 1874.

31. McPherson, *A Hand-book of Politics for 1876* (Washington, D.C.: Solomons and Chapman, 1876), 27–28; New York *Herald*, December 30, 1874; Louisville *Courier-Journal*, December 30, 1874; Diary, December 29, 1874, in Fish Papers, LC; James G. Taliaferro to his daughter, December 17, 1874, in James G. Taliaferro Papers, Louisiana State University Library, Baton Rouge.

32. New Orleans *Republican*, New Orleans *Daily Picayune*, New York *Times*, New York *Herald*, New York *World*, all January 5, 1875; Cincinnati *Commercial*, January 7, 1875; Emory to Adjutant General, March 27, 1875, Emory to Philippe de Trobriand, January 4, 1875, both in Letters Received, Main Series, since 1870, in RG 94, NA; see but compare Nevins, *Fish*, 749.

33. Philip H. Sheridan to Belknap, January 4, 5, 7, 1875, in Philip H. Sheridan Papers, LC.

34. Belknap to Sheridan, January 6, 1875, two telegrams, in McPherson, *Handbook of Politics for 1876*, 29; D. Cunningham to John A. Bingham, January 15, 1875, in John A. Bingham Papers, microfilm, Ohio Historical Society, Columbus; W. L. Burnett to Benjamin H. Bristow, January 13, 1875, in Bristow Papers.

35. "Friend" to Benjamin F. Butler, February 5, 1875, in Benjamin F. Butler Papers, LC; J. Strong to James Monroe, January 15, 1875, in James Monroe Papers, Oberlin College Archives, Oberlin, Ohio; Wendell Phillips to Belknap, January 9, 1875, in Belknap Papers; G. C. Wharton to Bristow, January 12, 1875, in Bristow Papers; St. Paul (Minn.) *Press* quoted in Washington *National Republican*, January 12, 1875; Chicago *Inter-Ocean*, January 12, 1875; see but compare Lonn, *Reconstruction in Louisiana*, 303.

36. Charles G. Rehlback to Marcus L. Ward, January [11], 1875, in Ward Papers; comment of Henry Wilson quoted in Diary, January 7, 1875, in Garfield Papers, LC; H. Clay Trumbull to Joseph R. Hawley, January 11, 1875, in Joseph R. Hawley Papers, LC; Dawes to Samuel Bowles, January 7, 1875, in Bowles Papers.

37. William M. Evarts quoted in New York *Tribune*, January 12, 1875; Charles Francis Adams to *Herald* Editor, January 11, 1875, Letterbooks, in Adams Family Papers; *Independent*, January 14, 1875; *Harper's Weekly*, January 23, 1875; see but compare Taylor, *Louisiana Reconstructed*, 307; Bristow to John Marshall Harlan, January 11, 1875, in Harlan Papers.

38. Burnett to Bristow, January 13, 1875, in Bristow Papers; New York *World*, January 5, 1875; New Orleans *Daily Picayune*, January 4, 1875; N. Helverson to Samuel J. Randall, January 20, 1875, in Samuel J. Randall Papers, University of Pennsylvania Library, Philadelphia; John M. Bigelow to Samuel J. Tilden, February 10, 1875, in John M. Bigelow Papers, New York Public Library, New York.

39. Dawes to Bowles, January 7, 1875, in Bowles Papers; Diary, January 7, 1875, James A. Garfield to Irvin McDowell, January 8, 1875, Letterbooks, both in Garfield Papers, LC.

40. Dawes to Bowles, January 7, 1875, in Bowles Papers; Lorenzo Danford to "Judge," January, 1875, in Lorenzo Danford Letter, Ohio Historical Society, Columbus; Ward to Rehlback, January [11], 1875, in Ward Papers; New York *Times*, January 7–11, 1875; New York *Herald*, January 10, 1875.

41. Richard Vaux to Randall, January 10, 1875, in Randall Papers; New York *World*, January 13, 1875; New York *Herald*, January 9, 1875.

42. Diary, January 5, 8, 10–12, 22, 1875, in Fish Papers, LC; Richardson (comp.), *Messages of the Presidents*, VII, 305–16; Fred Grant to Sheridan, January 14, 1875, in Sheridan Papers; see but compare Hesseltine, *Grant*, 351–52.

43. McPherson, *Hand-book of Politics for 1876*, 30–32; Chicago *Times*, January 13, 1875; Washington dispatch in New York *Herald*, January 13, 1875; Timothy O. Howe to Grace T. Howe, January 14, 1875, in Timothy O. Howe Papers, State Historical Society of Wisconsin, Madison.

44. E. R. Tinker to Dawes, January 15, 1875, in Dawes Papers; Garfield to Julius O. Converse, January 21, 1875, Letterbooks, in Garfield Papers, LC; New York *Evening Post*, New York *Herald*, Springfield *Republican*, New York *Times*, all January 14, 1875.

45. *Congressional Record*, 44th Cong., Special Senate Sess., 145–46; New York *World*, March 17, 1875; *Independent*, February 17, March 16, 1876; for other congressional developments in the session, see Chapters 11, 12 herein.

46. McPherson, *Hand-book of Politics for 1876*, 36–40, 200–201. President Grant first opposed arbitration but then came around. Diary, February 2, 1875, in Fish Papers, LC; see but compare Hesseltine, *Grant*, 354.

47. William A. Wheeler to Editor, and editorial, New York *Times*, May 10, 1875.

CHAPTER 6

1. William Britton to Attorney General, November 23, 1872, Western District of Arkansas, Source Chronological Files, in RG 60, NA; for the intrastate political background, see Thomas S. Staples, *Reconstruction in Arkansas, 1862–1874* (New York: Columbia University Press, 1923); George H. Thompson, *Arkansas and Reconstruction: The Influence of Geography, Economics, and Personality* (Port Washington, N.Y.: Kennikat Press, 1976).

2. Ulysses S. Grant to William W. Belknap, February 19, 1871, Letterbooks, in Grant Papers, LC; John A. Joyce to Orville E. Babcock, March 14, 1871, Babcock to Joyce, March 25, 1871, in Orville E. Babcock Papers, Newberry Library, Chicago.

3. New York *Times*, December 20, 23, 1872; Cincinnati *Commercial*, May 16,

1874, February 17, 1875; Thompson, *Arkansas and Reconstruction*, 101–105.

4. New York *Sun*, January 15, 1873; New York *Tribune*, May 23, 1873; Washington *National Republican*, May 28, 1873; New York *Times*, May 22, 1873, April 16, 1874; Jesse Turner to his son, May 3, 1874, Rebecca A. Turner to her son, May 23, 1874, both in Jesse Turner Papers, Duke University Library, Durham, N.C.; David Walker to Sam W. Williams, April 22, 1874, in David Walker Papers, University of Arkansas Library, Fayetteville.

5. HVR (Horace V. Redfield) in Cincinnati *Commercial*, May 14, 15, 1874; Little Rock *Arkansas Gazette*, April 16, 23, May 8, 19, 1874; Little Rock *Republican*, April 18, 22, 30, May 16, 18, 23, 29, 1874; McPherson, *Hand-book of Politics for 1874*, 87.

6. Babcock to Belknap, April 16, 1874, Letterbooks, in Grant Papers, LC; McPherson, *Hand-book of Politics for 1874*, 90; Diary, April 17, 21, 1874, in Fish Papers, LC.

7. Washington *National Republican*, April 17, 21, 1874; New York *Times*, April 20, 1874; New York *Sun*, April 23, 1874; Louisville *Courier-Journal*, April 28, 30, 1874.

8. New York *Herald*, April 29, 1874.

9. Washington *National Republican*, April 17, 1874; New York *Times*, April 18, 1874.

10. McPherson, *Hand-book of Politics for 1874*, 90–91; St. Louis *Republican*, April 23, 1874; A. H. Garland to Harris Flanagin, April 30, 1874, in Harris Flanagin Papers, Arkansas History Commission, Little Rock.

11. Diary, May 5, 8, 1874, in Fish Papers, LC; see but compare Staples, *Reconstruction in Arkansas*, 418–20.

12. McPherson, *Hand-book of Politics for 1874*, 92–94.

13. *Ibid.*, 94–97; Diary, May 12, 14, 1874, in Fish Papers, LC; Levi P. Luckey to George H. Williams, May 11, 1874, Letterbooks, in Grant Papers, LC.

14. Washington *National Republican*, May 15, 1874; McPherson, *Hand-book of Politics for 1874*, 97–100; Richardson (comp.), *Messages of the Presidents*, VII, 272–73; HVR in Cincinnati *Commercial*, May 18, 1874; New York *Herald*, New York *Tribune*, New York *Times*, all May 16, 1874.

15. Of 124 elected to the legislature, only 11 were Republicans. Jesse Turner to his son, Jesse Turner to Rebecca Turner, both November 12, 1874, in Turner Papers; Chicago *Tribune*, July 27, August 3, September 8, 1874; for the election of 1874, see Chapters 9, 10 herein.

16. Little Rock *Arkansas Gazette*, November 14–17, 1874; Jesse Turner to Rebecca Turner, November 17, 1874, in Turner Papers; Washington *National Republican*, November 17–21, 1874; Chicago *Times*, November 22, 1874.

17. Washington *National Republican*, September 25, 1874.

18. Diary, November 17, 20, 27, December 3, 1874, in Fish Papers, LC; for congressional developments, see Chapters 11, 12 herein.

19. Augustus H. Garland to Grant, January 13, 1875, telegram, in Grant Papers, LC; Garland to Alexander H. Stephens, February 11, 1875, in Stephens Papers, LC; McPherson, *Hand-book of Politics for 1876*, 19; Jesse Turner to his son, February 1, 1875, in Turner Papers.

20. Richardson (comp.), *Messages of the Presidents*, VII, 319.

21. *Ibid.*; Jesse Turner to his son, February 28, 1875, in Turner Papers; Benjamin H. Bristow to John Marshall Harlan, February 21, 1875, in Harlan Papers.

22. Richmond *Dispatch*, February 12, 1875; New York *Herald*, February 11, 1875; Springfield *Republican*, February 12, 1875; *Independent*, February 18, 1875; Diary, February 11, 1875, in Fish Papers, LC; John Marshall Harlan to Bristow, February 17, 1875, in Bristow Papers; Chicago *Inter-Ocean*, February 11, 1875.

23. All the Democrats present and sixty-five Republicans voted to sustain the report of Representative Luke P. Poland; eighty Republicans opposed it. More than twice

NOTES TO PAGES 149 TO 156

as many Republicans voted against intervention in Arkansas as voted against the so-called force bill. *Congressional Record*, 43rd Cong., 2nd Sess., 2107, 2117, Cincinnati *Commercial*, Cincinnati *Gazette*, March 3, 1875; on the so-called force bill of 1875, see Chapter 12 herein.

24. New York *Tribune*, March 4, 1875.

25. Louisville *Courier-Journal*, March 4, 1875; New York *Herald*, March 4, 1875; James A. Garfield to Burke A. Hinsdale, March 5, 8, 1875, in Garfield Papers, LC; Washington *National Republican*, March 5, 6, 10, 1875.

26. Garland quoted in editorial, New York *Evening Post*, March 9, 1875; New York *Herald*, March 18, 1875; E. H. English to David Walker, March 5, 1875, in Walker Papers.

27. Adelbert Ames to Blanche B. Ames, August 10, 1874, in Ames Family Papers, Smith College Women's History Archive, Northampton, Mass.; McPherson, *Handbook of Politics for 1876*, 40; for the intrastate political background, see James Wilford Garner, *Reconstruction in Mississippi* (New York: Macmillan, 1901); Vernon Lane Wharton, *The Negro in Mississippi, 1865–1900* (Chapel Hill: University of North Carolina Press, 1947); Lucius Q. C. Lamar to E. D. Clark, October 14, 16, 1873, both in Kate F. Clark Papers, Marshall County Historical Society, Holly Springs, Miss.; see Chapters 9–10 herein.

28. Natchez *Democrat and Courier*, August 6, 1874; Benjamin G. Humphreys to Lamar, January 3, 1875, in Lamar-Mayes Papers.

29. Natchez *Democrat and Courier*, December 8, 15, 1874; New York *Tribune*, December 10, 1874; Lamar to Clark, December 21, 1874, February 1, 1875, Samuel J. Randall to Lamar, December 25, 1874, all in Clark Papers. See also p. 452.

30. Copy of message of A. Ames to Mississippi Legislature, December 17, 1874, A. Ames to Grant, December 19, 1874, both in Adelbert Ames Papers, Mississippi Department of Archives and History, Jackson; Richardson (comp.), *Messages of the Presidents*, VII, 322–23; HVR in Cincinnati *Commercial*, January 4, 8, 13, 1875.

31. Chicago *Tribune*, July 23, 1874; New York *Evening Post*, December 17, 1874; New York *Herald*, August 4, 1874; Washington *National Republican*, December 12, 1874.

32. *Independent*, December 31, 1874; New York *Times*, January 19, 1875.

33. Meredian (Miss.) *Mercury*, quoted in Vicksburg *Times*, March 11, 1875; Lamar to Clark, December 23, 1874, Lucius Q. C. Lamar Letter, University of Mississippi Library, University.

34. R. A. Hill to Bristow, March 2, 1875, in Bristow Papers; Lamar to Mrs. Clay, December 26, 1874, Jefferson Davis to Mrs. Clay, January 3, 1875, both in Clement C. Clay Papers, Duke University Library, Durham, N.C.; Natchez *Democrat and Courier*, November 13, 1874.

35. Adelbert Ames to Blanche B. Ames, October 16, 1874, August 3, 1875, in Ames Family Papers; A. Ames to Joshua L. Chamberlain, January 22, 1875, in Joshua L. Chamberlain Papers, LC; copy of message of A. Ames to Mississippi Legislature, January 5, 1875, in A. Ames Papers, Mississippi State Archives.

36. Washington *National Republican*, September 14, 1874; New York *Herald*, August 6, 1875.

37. Cleveland *Leader*, September 15, 1875; Greensboro (N.C.) *New North State*, September 17, 1875; Adelbert Ames to Blanche B. Ames, August 4, 1875, in Ames Family Papers.

38. Adelbert Ames to Blanche B. Ames, September 2, 7, 22, 23, 1875, in Ames Family Papers.

39. New York *Times*, New York *Herald*, both September 8, 1875; Washington *National Republican*, August 31, September 9, 1875; Greensboro *New North State*, September 17, 1875.

40. McPherson, *Hand-book of Politics for 1876*, 40–42; W. W. Dedrick to Edwards

Pierrepont, September 8, 1875, Southern District of Mississippi, Source Chronological Files, Dedrick to Pierrepont, September 10, 1875, Letters Received, both in RG 60, NA; Dedrick to Pierrepont, September 8, 1875, telegram, in Edwards Pierrepont Papers, Yale University Library, New Haven, Conn.; A. W. Allyn to Adjutant General, September 5, 1875, Letters Received, Main Series, since 1870, in RG 94, NA; New York *Tribune*, September 16, 1875. Historians have tended to exaggerate the importance of contradictory reports about conditions in Mississippi sent to Washington by both Republicans and Democrats; in fact, the administration was reliably informed by internal sources. Moreover, reports opposing intervention were probably unimportant, for Attorney General Edwards Pierrepont opposed federal intervention from the beginning. Pierrepont acted on the advice that supported his original intentions. See note 42; Pierrepont to Hamilton Fish, September 10, 1875, Executive-Congressional Letterbook, Pierrepont to Dedrick, September 7, 13, 1875, Instruction Book, both in RG 60, NA; New York *Times*, September 10–13, 1875, September 12, 1876.

41. McPherson, *Hand-book of Politics for 1876*, 41–43. When Pierrepont had been appointed attorney general the press believed that there would be less federal intervention in the South. New York *Evening Post*, New York *Herald*, New York *Times*, all April 29, 1875.

42. Adjutant General to C. C. Augur, September 7, 1875, Letters Received, Main Series, since 1870, in RG 94, NA; Pierrepont to Grant, September 10, 1875, Executive-Congressional Letterbook, in RG 60, NA; Luckey to Pierrepont, September 9, 1875, in Pierrepont Papers. The important differences between the unpublished letter written by Grant on September 13, 1875, and the published letter that quoted Grant and was written by Pierrepont on September 14 have not been generally recognized by historians. See but compare Grant to Pierrepont, September 13, 1875, in Pierrepont Papers; Pierrepont to Grant, September 14, 1875, two communications, Executive-Congressional Letterbook, in RG 60, NA; Pierrepont to A. Ames, September 14, 1875, in A. Ames Papers, Mississippi State Archives.

43. Pierrepont to A. Ames, September 14, 1875, in A. Ames Papers, Mississippi State Archives.

44. *Ibid.*

45. Adelbert Ames to Blanche B. Ames, September 19, 1876, in Ames Family Papers; on Louisiana, see Chapter 5 herein.

46. John R. Lynch, *The Facts of Reconstruction* (New York: Neale, 1913), 150–54; H. R. Ware to Bristow, December 7, 1875, in Bristow Papers; Washington dispatch in New York *Tribune*, October 12, 1875. In a conversation two years later with President Rutherford B. Hayes, Pierrepont's agent in Mississippi, George K. Chase, told Hayes that Pierrepont alone prevented federal intervention in Mississippi during September, 1875, and attributed Hayes's good luck in defeating the Democrats in 1875 for the Ohio governorship to this nonintervention. George K. Chase to Pierrepont, May 4, 1877, in Pierrepont Papers; James Redpath to M. Howard, April 14, 1877, in Hayes Papers; H. V. Boynton in Philadelphia *Weekly Times*, April 3, 1880.

47. New York *Times*, September 10, 13, 16, 1875; New York *Tribune*, September 14, 1875; New York *Herald*, September 14, 1875; *Independent*, September 16, 1875; Greensboro *New North State*, September 24, 1875; Chicago *Tribune*, September 22, 1875; Bristow to John Marshall Harlan, September 10, 1875, in Harlan Papers.

48. Washington *National Republican*, September 15, 17, 18, 21, 1875; Washington *Chronicle*, September 17, 1875; Jackson *Times*, September 17, 20, 1875.

49. Adelbert Ames to Blanche B. Ames, September 12, 1875–October 12, 1875, in Ames Family Papers; A. Ames to Pierrepont, September 27, 1875, Southern District of Mississippi, Source Chronological Files, in RG 60, NA; A. Ames to Grant, September 25, 1875, in Pierrepont Papers.

50. Adelbert Ames to Grant, September 30, 1875, in A. Ames Papers, Mississippi State Archives; A. Ames to Pierrepont, October 16, 1875, in Pierrepont Papers; A.

Ames to Blanche B. Ames, October 14–18, September 30, 1875, in Ames Family Papers; Chicago *Tribune*, September 15, 1875; *Independent*, September 16, 1875; Hill to Bristow, June 22, 1875, in Bristow Papers.

51. Adelbert Ames to Blanche B. Ames, October 20, 1875–November 4, 1875, in Ames Family Papers.

52. *Ibid.*; [?] to A. Warner, October 22, 1875, Yazoo County report in James Redpath Papers, New York Public Library, New York; John B. Raymond to Blanche K. Bruce, November 4, 1875, in Grant Papers, LC; F. H. Little to Bristow, November 6, 1875, in Bristow Papers.

53. Ware to Bristow, December 7, 1875, in Bristow Papers; Jackson *Times*, November 3, 1875. Meanwhile, whites flocked to the polls.

54. HVR in Cincinnati *Commercial*, April 3, March 30, 1876; Natchez *Democrat and Courier*, April 30, 1876; Alexandria (Va.) *People's Advocate*, July 22, 1876; Adelbert Ames to Blanche B. Ames, September 5, October 9, 12, 1875, in Ames Family Papers.

55. Adelbert Ames to Blanche B. Ames, September 19, 9, October 18, 1875, in Ames Family Papers.

56. Adelbert Ames to Blanche B. Ames, September 27, October 18, 12, 1875, *ibid.*

57. Grant to Pierrepont, September 13, 1875, in Pierrepont Papers; G. E. Harris to Grant, November 24, 1875, in T. F. Bayard Papers.

58. John Eaton and Ethel O. Mason, *Grant, Lincoln, and the Freedmen: Reminiscences of the Civil War* (New York: Longman's, Green, 1907), 282; Lynch, *Facts of Reconstruction*, 155.

CHAPTER 7

1. New Orleans *Daily Picayune*, March 25, 1871; Springfield *Republican*, August 6, 1872, February 27, 1875; *Leslie's Newspaper*, January 30, 1875; Augusta (Ga.) *Constitutionalist*, February 13, 1875.

2. James Redpath quoted in *Independent*, August 3, 1876; see the references to certain psychological-political tendencies, the passive-negative and active-negative, in James David Barber, *The Presidential Character: Predicting Performance in the White House* (Englewood Cliffs, N.J.: Prentice-Hall, 1972), 12–13.

3. Mobile *Register*, December 10, 1870.

4. *Congressional Record*, 43rd Cong., 2nd Sess., 369; William T. Sherman to John Sherman, February 3, 1875, in W. T. Sherman Papers.

5. "Home Republican" to [Ulysses S. Grant], enclosed in H. R. Ware to Benjamin H. Bristow, December 7, 1875, in Bristow Papers.

6. Jacob D. Cox to Murat Halstead, June 10, 1870, in Halstead Papers.

7. New York *Times*, July 13, 1870; New York *World*, July 14, 1870.

8. See but compare Henry B. Adams, *The Education of Henry Adams: An Autobiography* (Boston: Houghton, Mifflin, 1918), 262.

9. During the war Grant not only cultivated influential friends in Washington but trimmed his sails to the prevailing winds. Unlike the rigid General George B. McClellan who opposed emancipation, General Grant deftly adjusted to changing circumstances and altered war policy, by accepting emancipation and the enlistment of Negroes, by welcoming fugitive slaves who provided military intelligence and who were put to work in civilian and military support, and by utilizing black troops in combat. Similarly, even though after the war he was in a delicate position as army commander, Grant survived the cataclysmic conflict between President Johnson and Congress. First by circumspect neutrality followed by decisive defection from the Johnson administration with his resignation as acting secretary of war, he gradually moved into the main Republican camp and received the party's presidential nomination. Such maneuvers amply demonstrated his political intelligence. See Chapters 3, 13, and 14.

10. Diary, August 22, 1867, in Welles Papers; Gideon Welles to Montgomery Blair, August 8, 1876, in Blair Family Papers; Jacob D. Cox to E. Rockwood Hoar, September 4, 1872, in Cox Papers; compare Bristow to John Marshall Harlan, October 1, 1871, in Harlan Papers.

11. New York *Herald*, May 20, 1869; Adam Badeau to Charles H. Branscombe, February 21, 1874, in Adam Badeau Letterbook, Rutgers University Library, New Brunswick, N.J.; Grant quoted in New York *Herald*, November 29, 1876; Shirley in Philadelphia *Weekly Times*, March 24, 1877.

12. Grant to Joseph R. Jones, February 8, 1871, in Ulysses S. Grant Papers, Chicago Historical Society, Chicago; *Nation*, January 14, 1875; Grant to Charles W. Ford, May 3, 1871, in Grant Papers, LC.

13. Diary, January 5, 1875, in Fish Papers, LC; Elihu Burritt to Amara Walker, January 16, 1875, in Elihu Burritt Papers, New York Historical Society, New York, N.Y.

14. Burritt to Amara Walker, January 16, 1875, in Burritt Papers.

15. Springfield *Republican*, March 3, 1877; *Nation*, March 1, 1877; New York *Tribune*, January 12, 1874.

16. Diary, January 11, 1875, in Fish Papers, LC; John W. Forney to Charles Sumner, August 3, 1870, in Sumner Papers; Simon Cameron to Wayne MacVeagh, March 14, 1876, in Wayne MacVeagh Papers, Historical Society of Pennsylvania, Philadelphia; Jesse H. Moore to Richard J. Oglesby, January 19, 1870, in Oglesby Papers.

17. Burritt to Amara Walker, January 16, 1875, in Burritt Papers; *Leslie's Newspaper*, June 13, 1874; New York *Herald*, May 19, 20, 1869; William T. Sherman to David F. Boyd, August 17, 1868, in Boyd Papers.

18. New York *Times*, February 21, 1871; William T. Sherman to Boyd, July 1, 1871, in Boyd Papers.

19. James S. Pike, *The Prostrate State: South Carolina Under Negro Government* (New York: D. Appleton, 1874); Charles Nordhoff, *The Cotton States in the Spring and Summer of 1875* (New York: D. Appleton, 1876); Marshall Jewell to Lucius Fairchild, December 29, 1874, in Fairchild Papers; J. Birney Work to James A. Garfield, December 12, 1876, in Garfield Papers, LC.

20. Adelbert Ames to Blanche B. Ames, July 29, 1874, in Ames Family Papers.

21. For an incisive treatment of the southern Republicans and their division, see Carl N. Degler, *The Other South: Southern Dissenters in the Nineteenth Century* (New York: Harper and Row, 1974), 191–270.

22. James Atkins to Garfield, July 7, 1875, in Garfield Papers, LC.

23. Albion W. Tourgée to Thomas Settle, June 24, 1869, in Thomas Settle Papers, II, University of North Carolina Library, Chapel Hill; Washington *National Republican*, August 14, 1874; Springfield *Republican*, August 21, 1874.

24. *Independent*, June 2, 1870; Grant quoted in Washington dispatch, New York *Herald*, January 18, 1874; editorial in New York *Herald*, January 20, 1874.

25. Jason Harlan to William E. Chandler, October 11, 1872, in W. E. Chandler Papers; Washington *National Republican*, September 26, 1876; Washington *New National Era*, August 25, 1870; Chicago *Inter-Ocean*, January 2, 1875.

26. Republican Executive Committee of Virginia to [?], in Grant to Hamilton Fish, August 2, 1875, in Fish Papers, LC; Alfred Morton to Edwin D. Morgan, December 24, 1875, in W. E. Chandler Papers.

27. George E. Spencer to John A. Logan, July 25, 1871, in John A. Logan Papers, LC; Atkins to Garfield, February 1, 1877, in Garfield Papers, LC; Washington *National Republican*, July 30, 1875.

28. Amos T. Akerman to Horace Maynard, November 6, 1874, in Akerman Let-

terbooks; William W. Holden to Louisa Holden, April 30, 1871, in Holden Papers, Duke University Library; Albion W. Tourgée, *A Fool's Errand* (New York: Fords, Howard, and Hulbert, 1879), 216; C (Tourgée) to Editor in Greensboro *New North State*, April 25, 1878.

29. SB (Samuel Bowles), Washington dispatch in Springfield *Republican*, December 22, 1874; Chicago *Inter-Ocean*, January 19, 1875.

30. *North American Review* (Boston), July, 1870.

CHAPTER 8

1. Washington *National Republican*, November 13, 1874; Schuyler Colfax to Mary C. Ames, October 30, 1874, in Mary Clemmer Ames Papers, Rutherford B. Hayes Library, Fremont, Ohio.

2. New York *Times*, November 8, 1873; New York *Evening Post*, November 22, 1873; Cincinnati *Commercial*, October 18, 1873; David A. Houk to William Allen, October 23, 1873, in William Allen Papers, LC; on Virginia and Texas see Chapter 4; for politics in Arkansas see Chapter 6.

3. Henry L. Dawes to Samuel Bowles, February 4, 1874, in Bowles Papers; unidentified lawyer quoted in New York *Tribune*, January 3, 1874, editorial, January 15, 1874.

4. Springfield *Republican*, January 17, 1874; Cincinnati *Commercial*, January 24, 1874; Alexander H. Stephens to Herschel V. Johnson, February 4, 1874, in Herschel V. Johnson Papers, Duke University Library, Durham, N.C.

5. Washington *National Republican*, January 24, 1874.

6. New York *Evening Post*, March 11, 1874.

7. E. P. Walton to Justin S. Morrill, March 7, 1874, in Justin S. Morrill Papers, LC; Elihu B. Washburne to Hamilton Fish, March 4, 1874, in Fish Papers, LC; Richard Vaux to John W. Stevenson, March 17, 28, 1874, in Stevenson Family Papers.

8. Strong Journal, March 11, 1874; Exeter (N. H.) *News-Letter*, March 13, 1874; New York *Tribune*, March 11–14, 1874; Washington *National Republican*, March 14, 1874; Paul T. David, *Party Strength in the United States, 1872–1970* (Charlottesville: University Press of Virginia, 1972), 196–99.

9. Hartford *Courant*, April 7–9, 1874; New York *Tribune*, April 9, 1874; Erastus Collins to Joseph R. Hawley, April 18, 1874, in Hawley Papers.

10. New York *Tribune*, April 8, 1874; Springfield *Republican*, April 11, 1874; New York *Times*, April 7, 1874.

11. New York *Tribune*, April 23, 1874; New York *Herald*, April 23, 1874; Chicago *Times*, April 24, 1874; William E. Chandler to Elihu B. Washburne, May 4, 1874, in Washburne Papers; *Harper's Weekly*, May 2, 1874.

12. New York *Herald*, February 27, 1870; Samuel T. Spear in *Independent*, March 5, 1874, editorial, May 6, 1875; Gideon Welles to Montgomery Blair, January 21, 1871, in Blair Family Papers.

13. William C. Story Diary, July 12, 1869, New York Public Library, New York; New York *Herald*, June 5, 1874; Jacob D. Cox to C. C. Starbuck, May 1, 1873, in Cox Papers; on colonization see J. K. Converse to Justin S. Morrill, January 9, 1871, in Morrill Papers; New York *World*, September 6, 1874; New York *Herald*, June 3, 1873; Washington *New National Era*, July 23, 1874; Nashville *Republican Banner*, September 22, 1874; Washington *National Republican*, June 16, 1876; H. C. Wayne to Fish, May 13, 1874, in Fish Papers, LC.

14. Mary C. R. to her sister, July 17, 1865, in Tod R. Caldwell Papers, University of North Carolina Library, Chapel Hill; Augusta (Ga.) *Chronicle and Sentinel*, 1871, clipping in Thomas N. Norwood Papers, University of North Carolina Library, Chapel

Hill; Mary A. Neely to James A. Garfield, March 14, 1873, in Garfield Papers, LC.

15. Springfield *Republican*, September 10, 1875; William J. R. Brockenbrugh to John W. Stevenson, May 24, 1872, in Stevenson Family Papers.

16. R. W. Johnson to David Davis, June 5, 1875, in David Davis Papers, Chicago Historical Society, Chicago; Schenck Diary, August 4, 1871.

17. New York *World*, March 16, 1867; Springfield *Republican*, June 11, 1872; Washington *New National Era*, August 28, 1873; New York *Tribune*, February 19, 1874; Chicago *Tribune*, March 1, 1875; New York *Times*, March 30, 1877; Frederick Douglass quoted in Gideon, Chicago *Times*, May 29, 1874.

18. By 1874, thirteen states had compulsory segregation in schools; seven states explicitly provided for voluntary racial segregation; eight states had no statute on their books governing the subject; nine states outlawed racial discrimination in public education. Washington *National Republican*, December 5, 1874; New York *World*, July 9, 1877; New York *Times*, December 23, 1874; Roger A. Fischer, *The Segregation Struggle in Louisiana, 1862–1877* (Urbana: University of Illinois Press, 1974), 88–132; James M. McPherson, "Abolitionists and the Civil Rights Act of 1875," *Journal of American History*, LII (1965), 493–510.

19. Case of Henry Johnson, September 29, 1869, in Letters Received by the Secretary of War from the President, Executive Departments, and War Department Bureaus to 1870, in RG 107, "Records of the Office of the Secretary of War," NA; Elihu B. Washburne to Cadwallader C. Washburn, February 5, 1870, in Cadwallader C. Washburn Papers, State Historical Society of Wisconsin, Madison; Diary, November 10, 1870, in Fish Papers, LC; Amos T. Akerman to William E. Walker, September 8, 1871, in Akerman Letterbooks; Frank J. Webb to William Claflin, January 21, 1870, in W. E. Chandler Papers; New Brunswick (N.J.) *Fredonian*, October 14, 1874; Philadelphia *Times*, February 14, 1877; Elon A. Woodward, "The Negro in the Military Service of the United States—A Compilation," 1888, in RG 94, NA.

20. Horace Morris to Benjamin H. Bristow, January, 1875, February 9, 1875, Bristow to Morris, February 1, 1875, in Bristow Papers. Morris rejected Bristow's advice, replying on February 9, 1875: "We believe honestly that the hesitancy, the timidity, afraid to go too far, afraid to probe too deep for fear of hurting rebels a little, has driven thousands more away from the party, than all the radical measures passed in the heroic days."

21. Washington *National Republican*, August 25, 1873; Chicago *Inter-Ocean*, May 26, 1874; Chicago *Times*, December 16, 1874.

22. W. G. Christopher to Editor, New York *Tribune*, August 17, 1874.

23. Louisville *Courier-Journal*, June 1, 1874; New York *World*, July 4, 1874.

24. Washington *New National Era*, May 29, 1873; McPherson, *A Handbook of Politics for 1872* (Washington, D.C.: Solomons and Chapman, 1872), 75: *Congressional Record*, 43rd Cong., 1st Sess., 3451; *Harper's Weekly*, January 10, 1874.

25. Washington *National Republican*, December 9, 1873; Chicago *Tribune*, May 27, 1874; New York *Herald*, May 28, 1874; New York *Times*, May 27, 1874.

26. Donald, *Charles Sumner and the Rights of Man*, 531–33; Ronald B. Jager, "Charles Sumner, the Constitution, and the Civil Rights Act of 1875," *New England Quarterly*, XLII (1969), 350–72; *Harper's Weekly*, October 10, 1874; *Independent*, March 19, 1874; *Nation*, September 17, 1874; New York *Times*, September 22, 1874; Louisville *Courier-Journal*, May 21, 1874.

27. Baltimore *American*, May 25, 1874; *Nation*, February 1, 1872; New York *Times*, February 11, 1871.

28. New York *Herald*, February 20, 1872; *Nation*, February 1, 1872.

29. W. G. Eliot to George F. Hoar, June 2, 1874, in George F. Hoar Papers, Massachusetts Historical Society, Boston; Chicago *Tribune*, August 22, September 25, 1874; Washington *National Republican*, March 31, 1871, July 30, 1873; *Independent*, March 2, 1871, June 4, 1874; Baltimore *American*, May 25, 1874.

30. Washington *New National Era*, April 24, 1873; Samuel Wade to Benjamin F. Butler, March 24, 1872, in Butler Papers; Henry Johnson to Samuel J. Randall, December 4, 1874, in Randall Papers; Springfield *Republican*, April 10, 1871, May 5, 1873, August 25, 1874; New York *Tribune*, January 10, 1874; Chicago *Tribune*, May 27, 1874; New York *Times*, February 11, 1871, September 12, 15, 1874; Washington *National Republican*, August 25, 26, 1873.

31. Chicago *Inter-Ocean*, February 2, 1875, May 30, 1874; *Harper's Weekly*, June 13, 1874; Boston *Journal* quoted in *Republic* (Washington, D.C.), January, 1875.

32. William F. Gaskins quoted in Washington *New National Era*, May 14, 1874; McPherson, *Hand-book of Politics for 1872*, 74–85; Alfred H. Kelly, "The Congressional Controversy Over School Segregation, 1867–1875," *American Historical Review*, LXIV (1959), 537–63; Donald, *Charles Sumner and the Rights of Man*.

33. Chicago *Times*, April 30, 1874; New York *Times*, May 26, 1874; New York *Evening Post*, May 25, 1874; Cincinnati *Gazette*, May 30, 1874; Boston *Globe*, May 12, 1874.

34. St. Louis *Republican*, May 26, 1874; Frederick Douglass to Frederick T. Frelinghuysen, May 23, 1874, in Frederick Douglass Papers, LC; Washington *New National Era*, February 19, April 9, June 4, 1874; San Francisco *Elevator*, January 24, May 16, 1874; William D. Forten to Butler, June 4, 1874, in Butler Papers; New York *Tribune*, January 5, 1874.

35. Washington *National Republican*, January 5, 1874; New Orleans *Louisianian*, May 30, 1874.

36. *Congressional Record*, 43rd Cong., 1st Sess., 3451.

37. *Ibid.*, 3452, 4147, 4082, 4153, Appendix, 305, 359, compare 4116; EJH in Boston *Herald*, May 9, 11, 18, 19, 1874; Washington *National Republican*, September 2, 1874.

38. In the voting there were abstentions and eighteen Republican absentees (thirteen northerners and five southerners). *Congressional Record*, 43rd Cong., 1st Sess., 4176; McPherson, *Hand-book of Politics for 1874*, 207; John J. Ingalls to his wife, May 23, 1874, in John J. Ingalls Papers, Kansas State Historical Society, Topeka; Boston *Globe*, May 12, 22, 25, 26, 1874; Philadelphia *Press*, May 22, 1874; Baltimore *American*, May 29, 1874; St. Louis *Globe-Democrat*, May 10, 1874.

39. Chicago *Times*, December 14, 1874; New York *Times*, January 27, 1875; Chicago *Inter-Ocean*, May 26, June 8, 1874; St. Louis *Republican*, May 27, 1874; Mobile *Register*, June 2, 10, 1874; Boston *Herald*, May 18, 19, 25, 1874.

40. Horace Eaton to John Eaton, June 6, 1874, in John Eaton Papers, University of Tennessee Library, Knoxville.

41. *Congressional Record*, 43rd Cong., 1st Sess., 4242, 4439, 4691, 5329; McPherson, *Hand-book of Politics for 1874*, 207–209.

42. *Congressional Record*, 43rd Cong., 1st Sess., 5329; New York *Tribune*, June 9, 19, July 9, 1874; St. Louis *Republican*, May 26, 1874; Chicago *Inter-Ocean*, November 12, 1874; Washington *National Republican*, June 15, 1874. The black Washington *New National Era*, June 11, 1874, condemned Republican "chuckling" over the defeat of the civil rights bill.

43. New York *Herald*, May 24, 1874; New York *Tribune*, May 11, 1874; New York *World*, May 26, June 1, 1874; Chicago *Times*, June 2, 1874; Chicago *Tribune*, August 22, 1874.

44. D. H. Graves to Butler, June 12, 1874, Eugene B. Drake to Butler, June 2, 1874, both in Butler Papers; Washington dispatch in New York *Herald*, May 26, 1874; Augustus S. Merrimon to David F. Caldwell, April 29, 1874, in David F. Caldwell Papers, University of North Carolina Library, Chapel Hill.

45. Philip Clayton to Stephens, June 2, 1874, in Stephens Papers, LC; Cincinnati *Commercial*, June 8, 1874; Boston *Herald*, May 31, 1874.

46. Washington dispatch in New York *Tribune*, June 9, 1874; Bertram Wyatt-

Brown, "The Civil Rights Act of 1875," *Western Political Quarterly*, XVIII (1965), 763–75.

47. Richardson (comp.), *Messages of the Presidents*, VII, 221, 255; New York *Herald*, November 27, 1872; clipping, December 10, 1872, in Edward White Papers, LC; Charles Sumner to J. B. Smith, January 1, 1874, in Charles Sumner Papers, in possession of Charles M. Segal, Guilderland, N.Y.; Grant's conversation with a friend is mentioned in Clayton to Stephens, May 29, 1874, in Alexander H. Stephens Papers, Duke University Library, Durham, N.C.; Louisville *Courier-Journal*, May 29, 1874; New York *Tribune*, June 12, 1874; Springfield *Republican*, September 16, 1874; Chicago *Tribune*, November 8, 1874.

48. New York *Times*, May 27, 1874; Philadelphia *Inquirer*, May 23, 1874; Chicago *Tribune*, July 17, 1874; Columbus (Ga.) *Enquirer* quoted in New York *Tribune*, June 13, 1874.

49. Springfield *Republican*, June 16, 1874; *Harper's Weekly*, August 1, 1874.

50. Washington *New National Era*, July 2, 1874; Truman Smith to William G. Brownlow, quoted in New York *Tribune*, July 11, 1874; for predictions of probable passage of a civil rights measure at the next session of Congress, see Washington *National Republican*, June 24, 1874; Louisville *Courier-Journal*, July 7, 1874; Greensboro *New North State*, August 12, 1874. Another manifestation of racial and political feeling was the end of local self-government in the District of Columbia by the action of the Republican Congress in mid-May, 1874. New York *World*, July 6, 1874; St. Louis *Republican*, June 28, 1876; HVR in Cincinnati *Commercial*, February 26, 1877, editorial, July 19, 1876; Washington *National Republican*, July 8, 1874.

CHAPTER 9

1. *Independent*, July 9, 1874; Louisville *Courier-Journal*, May 14, 1874; New York *Herald*, June 23, 1874.

2. *Harper's Weekly*, March 14, July 18, October 3, 24, 1874; New York *Times*, May 26, 1874; Washington *National Republican*, July 15, February 22, May 12, 1874; Washington *New National Era*, January 15, April 13, June 4, 1874.

3. New York *Times*, July 16, 1874; J. M. Edmunds to Timothy O. Howe, August 6, 1874, in Howe Papers.

4. New York *Times*, July 16, 1874.

5. New York *Herald*, July 14, September 28, 1874; *Harper's Weekly*, July 18, 1874; *Republic*, August, 1874. Both New York Republicans and Democrats in their platforms, for example, opposed inflation and endorsed a return to payments of United States bonds in gold, whereas both party platforms in Indiana favored the issuance of more paper money and the payment of federal bonds in greenbacks rather than in gold.

6. Henry Watterson to James G. Blaine, August 19, 1874, in Blaine Papers; Louisville *Courier-Journal*, July 28, 1874; Nathaniel B. Meade to James L. Kemper, August 4, July 17, 1874, in Kemper Papers.

7. John M. Bigelow to Whitelaw Reid, September 8, 1874, in Bigelow Papers; New York *Tribune*, September 11, October 29, 1874.

8. Diary, September 19, October 21, 27, 28, 1874, in Fish Papers, LC; Marshall Jewell to Elihu B. Washburne, September 19, 1874, in E. B. Washburne Papers.

9. John A. Dix to N. Capien, September 29, 1874, in Bernard Knollenberg Papers, Yale University Library, New Haven, Conn.

10. Chicago *Times*, August 27, September 9, 1874.

11. *American Annual Cyclopedia of the Year 1874*, 558, 436; Oliver P. Morton quoted in Chicago *Times*, August 1, 1874; Theodore M. Pomeroy and Roscoe Conkling quoted in New York *Times*, September 24, 1874; Isaac H. Bailey quoted in New York *Times*, October 29, 1874.

12. Edwards Pierrepont quoted in New York *Times*, June 25, 1874.

13. New York *World*, July 6, 1874; New York *Times*, June 26, 1874; George F. Hoar quoted in New York *Times*, October 16, 1874.

14. New York *Times*, September 3, October 19, 28, 1874; Washington *National Republican*, August 4, 1874; New York *Herald*, September 4, 10, 11, 1874; New York *Tribune*, July 31, 1874; Louisville *Courier-Journal*, August 27, 1874; *Nation*, September 17, 1874.

15. *Harper's Weekly*, August 29, 1874; Newark *Advertiser*, October 13, 1874.

16. Atlanta *Constitution*, November 7, 1874; Henry Watterson quoted in editorial, Washington *National Republican*, September 2, 1874; Richmond (Ky.) *Register*, quoted in *Independent*, August 13, 1874.

17. Republican politician and Baltimore correspondent, both quoted in Upshur, New York *World*, June 13, 1874; Huntsville newspaper quoted in HVR, Chicago *Times*, August 21, 1874; Benjamin H. Bristow to John Marshall Harlan, March 10, 1872, in Harlan Papers.

18. HVR in Chicago *Times*, August 21, 1874; HVR in Cincinnati *Commercial*, March 4, 1876; New York *Times*, September 1, 3, 7, 9, 12, 24, 1874.

19. A. P. Marble to John Eaton, October 10, 1874, in Eaton Papers; *American Annual Cyclopedia of the Year 1874*, 12–811; *Republic*, September, October, November, 1874; McPherson, *Hand-book of Politics for 1874*, 229–36; Washington *National Republican*, August 28, September 14, 1874; Springfield *Republican*, September 3, October 10, 1874; Nashville *Republican Banner*, August 26, 28, 1874; New York *Times*, September 16, 28, 1874; New York *Tribune*, August 20, 28, December 12, 1874; Philadelphia *Inquirer*, November 9, 1874; Harrisburg *Patriot*, November 7, 1874.

20. Colonel Whitely quoted in Wilmington dispatch, New York *Tribune*, September 24, 1874; William H. H. Stowell to William E. Chandler, October 3, 1874, in W. E. Chandler Papers; Philadelphia *Telegraph*, October 12, 1874, Campaign Scrapbook for 1874, in Edward McPherson Papers, LC; New Brunswick *Fredonian*, October 14, 29, 1874.

21. New York *Tribune*, August 13, 28, October 17, 22, 24, 1874; Jersey City *Journal*, August 28, September 1, 7, 11, 12, 16, 17, 1874.

22. John M. Carmack to Andrew Johnson, May 25, 1874, in Andrew Johnson Papers, LC; L. B. Eaton to Attorney General, August 12, 1874, Western District of Tennessee, Source Chronological Files, in RG 60, NA.

23. Memphis *Appeal* quoted in New York *Tribune*, July 30, 1874; William G. Brownlow to Truman Smith, quoted in New York *Tribune*, September 5, 1874; New York *Tribune*, July 16, 1874; Nashville *Union and American*, August 9, 1874; Chicago *Times*, August 8, 1874; Louisville *Courier-Journal*, June 18, 1874.

24. New York *Tribune*, August 7, 8, 1874; New York *Times*, Chicago *Times*, Louisville *Courier-Journal*, all August 8, 1874; Nashville *Republican Banner*, August 7–15, 1874; Nashville *Union and American*, August 7, 9, 13, 1874; Cincinnati *Commercial*, October 14, 19, 23, 1874. Democrats in the Kentucky statewide contest won 68 percent of the popular vote (in contrast to 58 percent in 1871 and 52 percent in 1872) with a majority of 60,000 in 1874 (in contrast to a majority of 37,000 in 1871 and 11,000 in 1872). *Tribune Almanac and Political Register for 1875* (New York: Tribune Association, 1875), 84–85, 91; Louisville *Courier-Journal*, August 14, 1874.

25. Telegram quoted in editorial, New York *World*, August 13, 1874; Louisville *Courier-Journal*, August 8, 1874; William G. Brownlow quoted in Nashville *Republican Banner*, September 10, 1874; William Cassius Goodloe to John Marshall Harlan, August 25, 1874, in Harlan Papers; New York *Tribune*, May 19, September 30, 1874.

26. New York *Times*, August 8, 1874; Asheville (N.C.) *Pioneer*, June 6, August 15, November 7, 1874; Greensboro *New North State*, July 29, October 24, 1874.

27. Matt W. Ransom to Thomas F. Bayard, August 21, 1874, in T. F. Bayard Papers; *Tribune Almanac for 1875*, 77; David, *Party Strength*, 217. The switch in voting was evident in Wake, Richmond, Beaufort, Davison, and Mitchell counties.

28. New York *Tribune*, August 10, 1874; Chicago *Times*, August 10, 1874; New York *Herald*, August 8, 1874; Louisville *Courier-Journal*, August 8–9, 1874; Springfield *Republican*, August 21, 1874. The Cincinnati *Commerical*, August 8, 1874, commented that the civil rights bill "is regarded as the most important issue in that region in the coming Congressional campaign." Similarly, the Chicago *Tribune*, August 14, 1874, observed: "in North Carolina, as in Kentucky and Tennessee, the Civil Rights bill was a millstone around the necks of the Republicans."

29. Augusta *Chronicle and Sentinel* quoted in New York *Tribune*, August 11, 1874; North Carolinian editorials in Chicago *Tribune*, August 14, 1874; Natchez *Democrat and Courier*, August 8, 1874.

30. Ed. R. Brink to Albion W. Tourgée, August 20, 1874, in Tourgée Papers; a Raleigh Republican quoted in True Blue to Editor, Washington *National Republican*, August 25, 1874; G to Editor, New York *Times*, September 15, 1874; Thomas B. Pace to Editor, New York *Times*, October 24, 1874; Amos T. Akerman to R. H. Whitely, October 1, 1874, Akerman to A. Sloan, September 2, 1874, both in Akerman Letterbooks.

31. Eugene Hale to Blaine, August 9, 1874, in Blaine Papers; William E. Niblack to George S. Houston, August 10, 1874, in George S. Houston Papers, Duke University Library, Durham, N.C.; Harrisburg *Patriot* quoted in New York *Tribune*, August 21, 1874.

32. Richard Vaux to John W. Stevenson, August 11, 1874, in Stevenson Family Papers; New York *Sun*, August 18, 19, 1874; Washington *National Republican*, August 12, 19, 1874; New York *Times*, August 21, 1874; New York *Evening Post*, August 7, 17, 1874; New York *Tribune*, August 8, 1874. At this point in the congressional campaign many editorial writers in independent newspapers believed that the Republicans would retain control of Congress but would lose their two-thirds control of the House of Representatives. The chairman of the Republican congressional campaign committee never anticipated defeat: Zachariah Chandler to Colonel Fitzgerald, July 9, 1874, Chandler to Matt H. Carpenter, August 25, 1874, Chandler to Marsch Giddings, September 18, 1874, Letterbook, all in Z. Chandler Papers.

33. *Republic*, October, November, 1874; enclosure in H. P. Farrow to Attorney General, September 17, 1874, District of Georgia, Source Chronological Files, in RG 60, NA; New York *Tribune*, August 1, 1874-September 30, 1874; for the terrorism in Tennessee, see Chapter 2 herein.

34. Nashville *Republican Banner*, August 12, September 10, 19, 26, 1874; T. B. Swann quoted in West Virginia *Journal*, Campaign Scrapbook for 1874, in McPherson Papers; ZLW (T. B. White), New York *Tribune*, October 12, 1874.

35. In the Georgia legislative election on October 7, 1874, every county went Democratic except three; only eight Republicans were left in the legislature; the turnout of black voters was the lowest since 1867. Given the strong influence of the civil rights issue in the campaign, white Republicans defected. As a result, the outlook appeared bleak for the state congressional contest in November. The Savannah *News*, October 9–10, 1874, predicted the death of the state Republican party. Atlanta *Constituion*, October 17, 1874; HVR in Cincinnati *Commercial*, October 14, 20, 1874. On October 13, 1874, Democrats gained a congressional seat in West Virginia, thus capturing the entire congressional delegation. New York *Times*, October 18, 1874.

36. Tourgée to M. B. Anderson, May 11, 1874, in Tourgée Papers.

37. HVR in Cincinnati *Commercial*, October 14, 23, 1874; A. Burnell to President of Convention of Republicans at Chattanooga, October 10, 1874, filed in Grant Papers, Hayes Library.

38. Washington *National Republican*, October 5, 15, 1874; Chicago *Times*, September 9, October 16, 1874; Zachariah Chandler to S. W. Dorsey, August 31, 1874, Letterbrook, in Z. Chandler Papers.

39. *Republic*, December, 1874; HVR in Cincinnati *Commercial*, October 17, 19, 20, 1874; New York *Times*, October 13–15, 19, 1874; New York *Tribune*, October 14, 15, 21, 1874.

40. New York *Herald*, October 14, 1874; Adelbert Ames to Blanche B. Ames, October 16, 1874, in Ames Family Papers.

41. Chicago *Times*, August 10, 15, 21, 27, 29, September 2, 7, 1874; New York *Times*, October 10, 1874; San Francisco *Elevator*, September 5, 1874; Washington *New National Era*, August 29, 1874; [?] to Henry Wilson, August 23, 1874, in Morton Papers; Akerman Diary, August 29, 1874; Cincinnati *Gazette* quoted in New York *Tribune*, August 21, 1874; Elizabeth Oaksmith to William J. Spence, October 21, 1874, in Appleton Oaksmith Papers, University of North Carolina Library, Chapel Hill.

42. Washington *National Republican*, August 8, September 8, 1874.

43. Eugene Casserly to Bayard, September 10, 1874, in T. F. Bayard Papers; Chicago *Times*, July 25, 1874; James Z. George to Lucius Q. C. Lamar, April 15, 1874, in Lamar-Mayes Papers; Mobile *Register* quoted in *Harper's Weekly*, September 19, 1874; southern editorials in New York *Tribune*, August 22, 1874.

44. New York *Tribune*, August 15, 1874; for developments in Texas, see Chapter 4 herein; for developments in Mississippi and Arkansas, see Chapter 6; for election enforcement, see Chapter 2.

45. New York *Times*, September 5, October 31, 1874; New York *World*, September 11, 1874; New York *Sun*, September 7, 8, 11, 1874; *Leslie's Newspaper*, September 19, 1874.

46. Cyrus Woodman to E. B. Washburne, September 6, 1874, in Washburne Papers; New York *Herald*, September 11, 1874; New York *Evening Post*, September 8, 1874; *Nation*, September 10, 1874. Although some newspapers worried about the potential or actual abuse of federal power, federal officials were in fact concerned with the inadequacy of the federal effort. Farrow to Attorney General, September 17, 1874, District of Georgia, Source Chronological Files, in RG 60, NA; William W. Belknap to George H. Williams, October 7, 1874, Letters Received, Main Series, since 1870, in RG 94, NA.

47. Chicago *Times*, July 25, 1874; *Nation*, August 13, 1874; Washington *National Republican*, August 20, 1874.

48. New York *Tribune*, August 21, 29, 1874; *Leslie's Newspaper*, August 15, 1874; Chicago *Tribune*, October 5, 1874; Akerman Diary, August 29, 1874.

49. London *Saturday Review*, June 20, 1874; Washington *New National Era*, July 23, September 10, 17, 1874.

50. *American Annual Cyclopedia of the Year 1874*, 12–15; HC in New York *Times*, October 24, 26, 29, 1874; ZLW in New York *Tribune*, October 7, 8, 12, 17, 22, 27, 31, November 2, 1874; editorials in New York *Tribune*, October 12, 29, 1874. The subsequent riot at Eufaula, Alabama, on November 3, 1874, election day, and the numerous reports received in Washington by the Department of Justice and the Office of the Adjutant General during the summer and autumn indicated that, whatever the accuracy of the reports by Representative Charles Hays, the situation in certain black-belt counties in Alabama during 1874 justified alarm and federal action. George E. Spencer to W. E. Chandler, July 19, September 17, 1874, in W. E. Chandler Papers; see but compare Fleming, *Reconstruction in Alabama*, 786, 793.

51. Washington *National Republican*, September 21, 26, 1874; St. Louis *Republican* quoted in Chicago *Times*, September 1, 1874; Zachariah Chandler to Marsch Giddings, September 18, 1874, Letterbook, in Z. Chandler Papers; for developments in Louisiana, see Chapter 5 herein.

52. New York *Times*, September 16, 26, 1874; Louisville *Courier-Journal*, August 31, September 1, 3, 11, 15, 1874; Utica (N.Y.) *Herald* quoted in New York *Times*, September 26, 1874.

CHAPTER 10

1. William D. Forten quoted in Philadelphia *Press*, October 30, 1874; New York *Times*, September 15, 18, 24, 26, October 4–6, 22, 28, 1874; Campaign Scrapbook for 1874, in McPherson Papers; *Harper's Weekly*, October 17, 1874.

2. The Republican percentage of the congressional vote in Vermont plummeted from 74 percent to almost 59 percent; an independent Republican surprisingly won in the second congressional district; the Republican majority in the lower house of the legislature dropped from 184 to 110; a Democrat was elected to the legislature from Burlington for the first time since 1853, and another Democrat was elected from Rutland. *Tribune Almanac for 1875*, 49; David, *Party Strength*, 265; Springfield *Republican*, September 3, 1874; Burlington *Free Press and Times*, September 2, 4, 1874; Montpelier *Argus and Patriot*, September 4, 11, 1874.

3. Cincinnati *Commercial*, September 17, 1874; New York *Times*, September 16, 1874; Bangor *Whig and Courier*, September 15–17, 1874. The final figures did not justify Republican jubilation because there was a slight decline in the Republican percentage of the congressional vote, the turnout was smaller, and the Democrats gained ground in the legislature.

4. ZLW in New York *Tribune*, October 21, 1874; Washington dispatch in Louisville *Courier-Journal*, October 12, 1874; Chicago *Times*, October 12, 1874; New York *Herald*, October 3, 7, 9, 1874. William W. Eaton, the future senator from Connecticut, wrote: "My first impressions were that the Louisiana difficulty would have a tendency to decrease our vote in New York and possibly in some of the Western states, but I have changed my opinion . . . and [we] are led to believe that in Kellogg and his government our adversaries have on their hand one *Elephant*." William W. Eaton to Samuel J. Tilden, September 19, 1874, in Tilden Papers.

5. New York *World*, March 20, 1874.

6. New York *Times*, October 15, 1874; John Sherman quoted in Cincinnati *Commercial*, September 3, 1874; Cincinnati *Commercial*, September 23, October 13, 1874; William F. Merriam to James A. Garfield, October 10, 1874, in Garfield Papers, LC; Cincinnati *Gazette*, September 6, 20, 27, October 6, 1874; Cleveland *Leader*, September 22, October 5, 12, 1874.

7. Diary, October 10, 1875, in George W. Julian Papers, Indiana State Library, Indianapolis; London *Observer*, November 8, 1874.

8. George H. Pendleton quoted in Cincinnati *Commercial*, October 13, 1874; Cincinnati *Gazette*, August 27, 1874.

9. Chicago *Times*, August 1, 8, 21, September 17, October 13, 1874; Indianapolis *Journal*, November 2, 1874; Washington *New National Era*, July 23, 1874.

10. Thomas J. Brady to William E. Chandler, September 9, 1874, in W. E. Chandler Papers; Chicago *Times*, September 19, 1874; New York *Times*, September 21, October 9, 1874; Indianapolis *Sentinel*, October 15, 1874.

11. Brady to Daniel D. Pratt, October 13, 1874, telegram in Daniel D. Pratt Papers, Indiana State Library, Indianapolis; Chicago *Times*, October 15, 1874; New York *Times*, October 24, 1874; *Tribune Almanac for 1875*, 78–79; David, *Party Strength*, 136–37.

12. Brady quoted in Chicago *Tribune*, October 17, 1874; Thomas A. Hendricks and Joseph E. McDonald quoted in Chicago *Tribune*, October 19, 1874; John Coburn quoted in Chicago *Times*, October 19, 1874; Indianapolis *Journal* quoted in Chicago *Times*, October 21, 1874.

13. Indiana dispatch in New York *Times*, October 24, 1874; Washington dispatch in New York *Times*, October 15, 1874; Alex. W. Dickson to Benjamin Harrison, November 11, 1874, in Benjamin Harrison Papers, LC; Newark *Advertiser*, October 15, 1874.

14. *Tribune Almanac for 1875*, 74–77; David, *Party Strength*, 225.

15. Cleveland *Herald* quoted in Indianapolis *Journal*, October 16, 1874; New York *Times*, October 13, 19, 26, 31, 1874; Cincinnati *Commercial*, October 17, 25, 1874.

16. Washington *National Republican*, October 15, 1874; Cincinnati *Enquirer* quoted in Chicago *Times*, October 15, 1874; Lewis D. Campbell and John S. Savage quoted in Cincinnati *Commercial*, October 28, 1874; New York *Times*, October 15, 1874; R. M. Stimson to Rutherford B. Hayes, June 29, 1875, in Hayes Papers; Alfred Yapple to William Allen, March 30, 1875, in Allen Papers.

17. The Democrats had gained fifteen seats: one seat in Iowa and in West Virginia (a Liberal Republican is counted as a Democrat), two seats in North Carolina, five seats in Indiana, and six seats in Ohio, without counting the temporarily vacant seat in Vermont. Cincinnati *Commercial*, October 17, 1874; Louisville *Courier-Journal*, November 2, 1874. The New York *Herald*, October 16, 1874, predicted that the Democrats might well capture control of the next House of Representatives. Chicago *Times*, October 15, 16, 31, 1874.

18. Louisville *Courier-Journal*, October 17, 29, 1874; Memphis *Appeal* quoted in Chicago *Times*, October 17, 1874; Nashville *Republican Banner*, October 20, 1874; J. C. Wharton to Benjamin H. Bristow, October 28, 1874, in Bristow Papers.

19. Washington *National Republican*, October 15, 21, 31, 1874; Philadelphia *Press* quoted in New York *Tribune*, October 15, 1874; New York *Times*, October 19, 26, 1874.

20. George E. Spencer to W. E. Chandler, October 15, 1874, James S. Negley to W. E. Chandler, October 19, 1874, both in W. E. Chandler Papers; Garfield to Charles E. Henry, October 31, 1874, in James A. Garfield Papers, Hiram College Archives, Hiram, Ohio; Marshall Jewell to Elihu B. Washburne, October 17, 1874, in E. B. Washburne Papers; William C. Howells to Garfield, October 18, 1874, in Garfield Papers, LC.

21. John A. Dix quoted in New York *Times*, October 27, 1874; Blanche Butler Ames to Adelbert Ames, October 25, November 2–4, 1874, in Ames Family Papers; Washington *National Republican*, October 31, 1874; San Francisco *Elevator*, October 31, 1874.

22. Diary, October 28, 1874, in Fish Papers, LC; New York *Tribune*, October 27–28, November 2, 1874; Chicago *Times*, November 1, 3, 1874; Louisville *Courier-Journal*, November 3, 1874; New York *World*, November 3, 1874; New York *Times*, October 20–23, 29, 1874.

23. David G. Swaim to Garfield, November 3, 1874, Diary, November 3, 4, 1874, both in Garfield Papers, LC; Chicago *Times*, November 3, 5, 1874; Chicago *Tribune*, November 3, 1874; New York *World*, November 4, 5, 1874; New York *Tribune*, November 4, 1874; New York *Evening Post*, November 4, 1874; New York *Times*, November 5, 1874.

24. J. R. McCarthy to Henry L. Dawes, November 11, 1874, in Dawes Papers; Richard Smith to William Henry Smith, November 8, 1874, in William Henry Smith Papers, Indiana Historical Society, Indianapolis.

25. Buffalo *Commercial Advertiser*, November 4, 1874; Garfield to Henry, November 4, 1874, in Garfield Papers, Hiram College Archives; Samuel Bowles to Murat Halstead, November 9, 1874, in Halstead Papers.

26. Because congressional elections were held in different states on different dates, the total number of party members in Congress varied from session to session, and within a session. *Tribune Almanac for 1875*, 44; *Tribune Almanac for 1876*, 32, but note my corrections. The party division was as follows: Forty-third Congress: 198 Republicans, 88 Democrats, 4 Liberal Republicans, 1 Independent Republican, 1 vacancy; Forty-fourth Congress: 109 Republicans, 169 Democrats, 12 Liberal Re-

publicans and Independents, 2 vacancies. The major party division in the Forty-fourth Congress, final session, was 107 Republicans and 181 Democrats. *Tribune Almanac for 1877*, 47.

27. New York *Times*, November 4, 1874.

28. The gains, when compared with the congressional election results of 1872, were impressive. The Democrats increased their national congressional vote from 45.7 percent to 52.2 percent; the Republican congressional vote declined from 50.9 percent to 43.1 percent. The Democratic share in the vote was most dramatic in the southern and border states, for it increased from 47.8 percent in 1872 to 57.9 percent in 1874. Democratic gains were also considerable in the Middle West (49.6 percent instead of the previous 43.9 percent) and in the Northeast (49.9 percent in place of 45.4 percent). In the popular vote for members of the House of Representatives, the Democrats secured a national margin of 374,000 over the Republican total, and the Democratic popular vote marked the greatest in an off-year congressional election between 1870 and 1882. However, it was the unusually low total turnout (affecting outcomes and margins) that was most significant; although the congressional elections of 1874 marked a decline in turnout (by .2 percent) from the last off-year congressional election held in 1870, the 1874 election registered a decided decline from the congressional election held in the presidential election year of 1872 (by 7.8 percent). Roughly 400,000 voters who had voted in 1872 did not turn out in 1874. The Democratic popular gain in 1874 over 1872 was 234,000, but the Republican loss was 683,000. The altered position of the parties was also shown in the legislative elections for the United States Senate. Previously, the Republicans had elected eighteen and the Democrats five for the old Senate, but by March of 1875, of the twenty-five new senators elected to the Forty-fourth Congress, only six were regular Republicans, and five Republicans were elected in opposition to their party caucus nominations with Democratic help. The Democrats elected fourteen. Thus, the regular Republican majority in the Senate was halved, declining from a hefty thirty-two to thirteen. McPherson, *Hand-book of Politics for 1876*, 255; McPherson, *Hand-book of Politics for 1874*, 228; David, *Party Strength*.

29. Charles Francis Adams Diary, November 4, 1874; Louisville *Courier-Journal*, November 4–5, 1874; Chicago *Times*, New York *World*, both November 9, 1874.

30. J. M. Tomeny to Andrew Johnson, February 2, 1875, in A. Johnson Papers; A. Montgomery to John W. Stevenson, January 14, 1875, in Stevenson Family Papers; Richmond *Enquirer*, November 10, 1874; Adelbert Ames to Blanche B. Ames, November 4, 1874, in Ames Family Papers; Knott Marlin to Benjamin F. Butler, November 4, 1874, in Butler Papers.

31. Thurlow Weed to Gerrit Smith, November 13, 1874, in Gerrit Smith Papers, Syracuse University, Syracuse, N.Y.; Chicago *Inter-Ocean*, November 5, 1874; Hamilton Fish to Adam Badeau, November 15, 1874, in Hamilton Fish Papers, New York Historical Society, New York; Washington *National Republican*, November 5, 1874; Chicago *Tribune*, November 8, 1874.

32. Washington *National Republican*, November 6, 1874; Ohio farmer quoted in Garfield to Henry B. Payne, November 6, 1874, Letterbooks, in Garfield Papers, LC; Boston *Advertiser*, November 5, 23, 1874; Harrisburg *Patriot*, November 7, 1874; *Nation*, November 12, 1874; Washington *National Republican*, November 20, 1874.

33. Grant's views reported in Washington dispatch, Chicago *Tribune*, November 8, 1874; Cincinnati *Commercial*, June 24, 1874.

34. Dix to Weed, November 6, 1874, in Thurlow Weed Barnes, *Memoir of Thurlow Weed* (Boston: Houghton, Mifflin, 1884), 506; Chicago *Inter-Ocean*, November 5, 1874; *Harper's Weekly*, February 6, 1875; Rufus Ingalls to W. E. Chandler, November 4, 1874, in W. E. Chandler Papers; Washington *National Republican*, November 9, 1874; New York *Evening Post*, November 4, 1874; St. Louis *Globe-Democrat*, November 5–6, 1874.

35. Justin S. Morrill to Brundige, November 4, 1874, in Morrill Papers.
36. London *Saturday Review*, November 14, 1874; Cleveland *Leader*, October 28, 1874, March 2, 1875; *Tribune Almanac and Political Register for 1876* (New York: Tribune Association, 1876), 32–34. Not a single Republican candidate for Congress was elected in seven southern and border states; the regional Republican party had become extremely weak, particularly in the populous states.
37. Chicago *Inter-Ocean*, February 5, 1875.
38. Springfield *Republican*, November 4, 1874, January 11, 1875; Washington *National Republican*, November 5, 1874; Amos T. Akerman to Edwards Knight, September 20, 1874, in Akerman Letterbooks; Akerman to David Dimond, January 3, 1879, in Amos T. Akerman Letterbooks (MSS in possession of Joe A. Akerman, Jr., Madison, Fla.).
39. New York *Times*, November 25, October 15, November 4, 1874; William T. Sherman to "Colonel," November 13, 1874, in William T. Sherman Letter, Louisiana State University Library, Baton Rouge.
40. Boston *Advertiser* quoted in New York *Tribune*, September 2, 1874; Jewell to Lucius Fairchild, December 29, 1874, in Fairchild Papers; Washington dispatch in New York *Times*, September 26, 1874; Washington *National Republican*, November 6, 10, 30, 1874, January 4, 1875; Chicago *Inter-Ocean* quoted in Cincinnati *Gazette*, November 6, 1874.
41. New York *World*, November 6, 11, 1874; Louisville *Courier-Journal*, November 5, 1874; Chicago *Times*, November 5, 1874; Gideon Welles to Montgomery Blair, November 11, 1874, in Blair Family Papers.
42. Troy (N.Y.) *Press*, quoted in New York *Tribune*, November 10, 1874; Mobile *Register*, November 10, 1874; *Harper's Weekly*, February 27, 1875; Providence (R.I.) *Journal*, November 5, 1874; New York *Times*, February 9, 1875; New York *World*, November 11, 1874.
43. Chicago *Inter-Ocean*, November 7, 1874.
44. Jason Camp to Elihu B. Washburne, November 9, 1874, in E. B. Washburne Papers; Grant's views reported in Washington dispatch, Chicago *Tribune*, November 8, 1874; and in Springfield *Republican*, September 16, 1874; Nashville *Republican Banner*, November 7, 1874; Washington Townsend to George F. Hoar, November 6, 1874, in Hoar Papers; Philadelphia *Press*, November 7, 1874; Harrisburg *Patriot*, November 9, 1874; Michael C. Kerr quoted in New York *World*, November 26, 1874; Alexander H. Stephens quoted in Augusta *Chronicle and Sentinel*, October 16, 1874; New York *Tribune*, December 30, 1874; HVR in Cincinnati *Commercial*, September 22, 29, 1876. The Cincinnati *Enquirer*, March 2, 1875, commented that the civil rights bill "cost the Republican party nearly its entire white vote in the South in 1874, and to some degree that of the North." A man from Savannah declared that the election did not turn "on any national question excepting the civil rights bill." T. F. Johnson to Stephens, November 13, 1874, in Stephens Papers, LC. Subsequently the Republican postmaster of Albany, Georgia, observed that the civil rights bill "ruined us" in 1874. HVR in Cincinnati *Commercial*, September 4, 1876. It was also reported that blacks defected from the Republican party because of the failure to enact the civil rights bill. New York *Times*, November 4, 1874; Trenton (N.J.) *State Gazette*, November 10, 1874; also see note 47.
45. Benjamin F. Wade quoted in "occasional Washington correspondent," New York *Tribune*, December 3, 1874; Jewell to Elihu B. Washburne, December 5, 1874, Washburne to Jewell, December 24, 1874, both in E. B. Washburne Papers; *Congressional Record*, 43rd Cong., 2nd Sess., 1001, 951.
46. Richard Vaux to John W. Stevenson, November 10, 1874, in Stevenson Family Papers; Louisville *Courier-Journal*, November 10, 17, 1874; Baltimore *Sun*, November 14, 1874.
47. Jacob D. Cox to S. N. Pettis, August 13, 1872, in Cox Papers; Jacob D. Cox

to James Monroe, November 21, 1874, in Monroe Papers; *Golden Age*, November 14, 1874; Cumberland (Md.) *Civilian and Telegraph*, November 12, 1874; Boston *Advertiser*, November 10, 1874; New York *Herald*, July 13, August 23, 1875.

48. *Brownson's Quarterly Review* (New York, N.Y.), January, 1874; Wells Brown quoted in editorial, Springfield *Republican*, September 4, 1874; James W. Wilson to Fairchild, January 17, 1875, in Fairchild Papers.

49. Charles Nordhoff in New York *Herald*, July 24, 1875.

50. Philadelphia *Press* quoted in New York *World*, November 9, 1874; Richmond *Dispatch*, November 6, 1874.

CHAPTER 11

1. Chicago *Times*, November 30, 1874; New York *Tribune*, December 5–12, 1874; Cincinnati *Commercial*, New York *Times*, both December 7, 1874.

2. Springfield *Republican*, December 22, 2, November 9, 1874; Chicago *Times*, December 5–7, 1874; New York *Times*, January 28, 1875.

3. Cincinnati *Gazette*, January 29, 1875; *Nation*, February 4, 1875; for developments concerning Louisiana and Arkansas, see Chapters 5 and 6 respectively.

4. New York *Herald*, December 1, 1874, February 3, 6, 1875.

5. Edward Kent to Hannibal Hamlin, February 4, 1875, in Hamlin Family Papers, University of Maine Library, Orono; John Binny to James A. Garfield, February 3, 1875, in Garfield Papers, LC.

6. Boston *Journal* quoted in *Republic*, January, 1875; William E. Walker to Benjamin F. Butler, January 4, 1875, in Butler Papers; John Cochrane to Henry Wilson, February 28, 1875, in Henry Wilson Papers, LC.

7. *Congressional Record*, 43rd Cong., 2nd Sess., 1008; John W. Benson to Butler, December 11, 1874, in Butler Papers.

8. Chicago *Inter-Ocean*, November 12, 1874; *Republic*, December, 1874.

9. Chicago *Times*, December 1, 12, 16, 17, 1874; Louisville *Courier-Journal*, December 2, 4, 11, 1874; New York *World*, December 7, 17, 1874; New York *Tribune*, December 11–12, 16–17, 1874; Washington *National Republican*, December 3, 14, 1874.

10. Washington *National Republican*, December 3, 14, 1874; Boston *Advertiser* quoted in New York *Tribune*, December 7, 1874; editorial in Springfield *Republican*, December 17, 1874; SB in Springfield *Republican*, December 22, 1874; New York *Times*, December 23, 1874; *Independent*, December 24, 1874.

11. Wendell Phillips quoted in New York *Herald*, January 19, 1875; Elizur Wright to Gerrit Smith, December 23, 1874, in Elizur Wright Papers, LC; *Harper's Weekly*, January 9, 1875.

12. A. W. Swope quoted in Cincinnati *Commercial*, February 12, 1875; William D. Forten quoted in Philadelphia *Press*, February 9, 1875; San Francisco *Elevator*, December 26, 1874; Jason M. Trotter to Butler, December 17, 1874, in Butler Papers.

13. B. F. Sloan to Samuel J. Randall, February 1, 1875, in Randall Papers; Springfield *Republican*, February 4, 1875; Washington *National Republican*, January 26, 1875.

14. Eugene Hale mentioned in HVB (Henry Van Ness Boynton), Cincinnati *Gazette*, January 11, 1875.

15. *Ibid.*, January 29, 1875; J. H. Maddox to Butler, January 28, 1875, in Butler Papers; Washington dispatch in New York *World*, February 6, 1875.

16. New York *Tribune*, January 27, 30, February 2, 1875; Washington *National Republican*, January 23, 27, February 1, 1875.

17. *Congressional Record*, 43rd Cong., 2nd Sess., 700, 704; Washington *National Republican*, January 26, 1875; Chicago *Times*, January 27, 1875; Philadelphia *Press*, February 3, 1875.

18. Diary, January 27–30, 1875, in Garfield Papers, LC; Cincinnati *Commercial*, January 28–31, 1875.

19. Cincinnati *Commercial*, January 29, 1875.

20. Jacob H. Ela to Elihu B. Washburne, February 12, 1875, in E. B. Washburne Papers; Springfield *Republican*, February 3, 1875.

21. New York *Herald*, February 3, 1875; *Congressional Record*, 43rd Cong., 2nd Sess., 1008; New York *World*, Chicago *Times*, Baltimore *American*, New York *Herald*, New York *Times*, Cincinnati *Gazette*, all February 1–6, 1875.

22. New York *Herald*, February 6, 1875.

23. *Congressional Record*, 43rd Cong., 2nd Sess., 1010–11; Val in Jacksonville *New South*, February 17, 1875; *Nation*, March 4, 1875; McPherson, *Hand-book of Politics for 1876*, 3–8.

24. C. H. C. Willinghause to Alexander H. Stephens, March 9, 1875, in Stephens Papers, Duke University Library; Baltimore *American*, March 1, 1875.

25. Philadelphia *Press*, February 10, 1875.

26. *Congressional Record*, 43rd Cong., 2nd Sess., 1870. The vote on the civil rights bill was 36 yes, 26 no, and 9 absent.

27. Harrisburg *Patriot*, March 2, 1875; Washington *National Republican*, February 8, 1875; New York *World*, March 3, 1875; see Chapter 1.

28. Albany *Journal*, March 1, 1875; Boston *Advertiser*, February 6, March 4, 1875.

29. Philadelphia *Press*, February 10, 1875; *Golden Age*, March 6, 1875; New York *Times*, January 28, 1875.

30. Greensboro *New North State*, March 5, 1875; Dallas *Herald*, March 6, 1875; Mobile *Register*, February 28, March 3, 1875.

31. Baltimore *Sun*, February 8, 1875; Boston *Post*, February 8, 1875.

32. Newark *Advertiser*, February 9, 23, 1875; Philadelphia *Press*, February 10, 1875; *Independent*, March 11, 1875; *Harper's Weekly*, March 20, 1875; Chicago *Inter-Ocean*, March 5, 1875.

33. Butler quoted in New York *Herald*, March 20, 1875; Chicago *Times*, February 6, 1875; New York *Times*, January 28, 1875; Atlanta *Constitution*, March 2, February 6, 1875; New York *World*, February 6, 1875; Washington *National Republican*, March 6, 1875.

34. Jacksonville *New South*, February 17, 1875.

35. Chicago *Tribune*, March 8, 1875; Cleveland *Leader*, March 4, 1875.

36. Cincinnati *Commercial*, March 7, 1875; Washington *National Republican*, March 9, 1875; New York *Times*, March 3, 7–9, 11, 14, 27, 1875.

37. Springfield *Republican*, March 20, 1875.

38. An East Texan quoted in HVR, Cincinnati *Commercial*, March 4, 1875; Hartford *Courant*, February 4, 1875; New York *Herald*, March 7, 1875.

39. A. J. Evans to Attorney General, August 23, 1875, Western District of Texas, Source Chronological Files, in RG 60, NA.

40. New York *Tribune*, May 25, 1874.

41. *Nation*, February 4, 1875.

42. HVR in Cincinnati *Commercial*, August 10, 1876; New York *Herald*, August 23, 1875; New York *Times*, November 10, 1876.

CHAPTER 12

1. Radical Republican quoted in Van (David W. Bartlett), Springfield *Republican*, February 26, 1875.

2. *Ibid.*, January 11, 1875; Thomas F. Bayard to Manton Marble, February 22, 1875, in Marble Papers.

3. Richardson (comp.), *Messages of the Presidents*, VII, 297, 322, 305, 319; Washington *National Republican*, February 13, 1875; Boston *Globe*, February 15, 1875;

for the crises concerning Louisiana, as well as Arkansas and Mississippi, see Chapters 5 and 6 respectively.

4. D. E. Leoon to Philip H. Sheridan, January 15, 1875, in Sheridan Papers.

5. Carl Schurz to Charles Francis Adams, January 14, 1875, Letters Received, in Adams Family Papers; Thomas F. Bayard to Marble, February 12, 1875, in Marble Papers; Thomas F. Bayard to James A. Bayard, February 14, 1875, in T. F. Bayard Papers; New York *World*, February 19, 1875.

6. Henry L. Dawes to Samuel Bowles, February 2, 1875, in Bowles Papers.

7. Chicago *Times*, January 25, 1875; Washington *National Republican*, February 1, 1875.

8. McPherson, *Hand-book of Politics for 1876*, 13–15; Washington *National Republican*, Cincinnati *Commercial*, Chicago *Times*, New York *World*, New York *Times*, Baltimore *American*, Springfield *Republican*, New York *Herald*, New York *Tribune*, Louisville *Courier-Journal*, Cincinnati *Gazette*, all February 4–17, 1875.

9. Schurz to Whitelaw Reid, February 13, 1875, Samuel S. Cox to Reid, February 18, 1875, both in Reid Papers; Cincinnati *Commercial*, February 14, 1875; Chicago *Times*, February 17, 1875; New York *World*, February 8, 13, 15, 1875; Grant's prediction in New York *Times*, February 17, 1875.

10. Albany *Journal*, February 12, 1875; Chicago *Inter-Ocean*, February 27, 1875; Washington *National Republican*, February 12, 26, 1875.

11. New York *Times*, February 21, 26, March 1–4, 1875.

12. New Orleans *Daily Picayune*, March 1, 1875.

13. *Harper's Weekly*, February 27, March 20, 1875.

14. *Congressional Record*, 43rd Cong., 2nd Sess., 1853.

15. Boston *Advertiser*, February 27, 1875; Washington dispatch in Cincinnati *Commercial*, February 14, 1875.

16. Joseph Medill to James G. Blaine, February 14, 1875, in Blaine Papers.

17. Diary, February 24–28, 1875, in Garfield Papers, LC; Cincinnati *Enquirer*, February 24, 1875.

18. Chicago *Inter-Ocean*, March 4, 1875; Washington *National Republican*, March 4, 1875; Van in Springfield *Republican*, February 26, 1875.

19. Washington *National Republican*, February 26, 1875.

20. James A. Garfield to Burke A. Hinsdale, March 8, 1875, in Garfield Papers, LC; Van in Springfield *Republican*, February 26, 1875; New York *Herald*, February 26, 1875; Baltimore *American*, March 1, 1875.

21. New York *Times*, New York *World*, New York *Tribune*, New York *Herald*, Chicago *Times*, Springfield *Republican*, Richmond *Dispatch*, Cincinnati *Gazette*, Cincinnati *Commercial*, Baltimore *American*, all February 16–March 3, 1875.

22. *Congressional Record*, 43rd Cong., 2nd Sess., 1748, 1929, 1935; McPherson, *Hand-book of Politics for 1876*, 15–18. Of the thirty-two regular Republican opponents, eleven were New Englanders, six were from the Mid-Atlantic region, eight were midwesterners, four were from the border states, and three were from the upper South. Most of the Republicans who voted for the so-called force bill were lame ducks, whereas over half of the Republicans who opposed the bill were not.

23. Samuel J. Randall to Thomas F. Bayard, February 28, 1875, in T. F. Bayard Papers; Richmond *Dispatch*, March 3, 1875; Van in Springfield *Republican*, March 4, 1875; Washington *National Republican*, March 5, 1875; Chicago *Tribune*, March 5, 1875; New York *Times*, New York *World*, both March 1–5, 1875.

24. Atlanta *Constituion*, March 5, 1875; Richmond *Dispatch*, March 5, 1875; Washington *National Republican*, March 1, 5, 1875; Benjamin F. Butler quoted in Boston *Globe*, March 2, 1875; Chicago *Inter-Ocean*, March 4, 1875.

25. Akerman Diary, March 6, 1875; Newark *Advertiser*, March 1, 1875.

26. Lynch, *Facts of Reconstruction*, 131–36; Edward L. Pierce to William Claflin, March 7, 1875, in Claflin Papers. The New York state Republican convention declared

in 1875 that the "welfare of the country requires a just, generous and forbearing National policy in the Southern States, a firm refusal to use military power, except for purposes clearly defined in the Constitution." New York *Tribune*, September 9, 1875; Washington *National Republican*, September 23, 1875; Diary, December 9, 1877, in Hayes Papers.

27. *Congressional Record*, 43rd Cong., 2nd Sess., 1786. Between 1874 and 1875 there was bipartisan concern and widespread anticipation that no candidate would receive an electoral majority in 1876, and thus an electoral crisis in Congress was likely. New York *World*, January 2, 1874; Cincinnati *Commercial*, March 20, 1874; Springfield *Republican*, January 6, 1875; New York *Times*, January 23, 1875; Chicago *Inter-Ocean*, February 16, 1875.

28. McPherson, *Hand-book of Politics for 1876*, 46–47.

29. New York *Tribune*, March 1, 1875; *Leslie's Newspaper*, March 6, 1875.

30. Matthias Martin to Andrew Johnson, January 22, 1875, Edmund G. Ross to Andrew Johnson, January 26, 1875, Henry Stanbery to Andrew Johnson, February 3, 1875, all in A. Johnson Papers; HVR in Cincinnati *Commercial*, January 27, 1875.

31. For developments concerning the South, see Chapters 5, 6.

32. Philadelphia *North American and Gazette*, March 4, 1875. The "negro has been suddenly shuffled out of politics," remarked *Leslie's Newspaper*, December 18, 1875. And later a Tennessean reportedly advised: "'we must eliminate the negro and have two parties there [in the South] again.'" Andrew J. Kellar quoted in William Henry Smith to Rutherford B. Hayes, July 1, 1876, in Hayes Papers.

33. New York *Times*, November 6, 1871, January 31, 1873; Louisville *Courier-Journal*, January 31, February 1, 1872, November 5–6, 1873.

34. A. H. Adams and S. W. Price to Benjamin H. Bristow, March 21, 1873, Bristow to George W. Williams, March 24, 1873, Letterbook, both in Bristow Papers; Bristow to John Marshall Harlan, March 2, 1873, October 15, 1874, both in Harlan Papers; New York *Herald*, March 19, April 23, 1875.

35. New York *Times*, January 14, 1875, March 28, 1876; *United States* v. *Reese*, 92 U.S. 214, and the significant dissent of Justice Ward Hunt, 238; C. Peter Magrath, *Morrison R. Waite: The Triumph of Character* (New York: Macmillan, 1963), 122–29; compare *United States* v. *Raines*, 367 U.S. 17.

36. Sections 3 and 4 of the act of May 31, 1870, penalized inspectors in elections for refusing to receive and count votes and for obstructing any citizen from voting. For Senator John Sherman's anticipation of the Reese decision, see *Congressional Globe*, 41st Cong., 2nd Sess., 3568–70, 3663; see also Chapter 2, note 18. In *United States* v. *Cruikshank*, 92 U.S. 542, Waite invalidated the sixth section of the same enforcement act.

37. Ward E. Y. Elliott, *The Rise of Guardian Democracy: The Supreme Court's Role in Voting Rights Disputes, 1845–1969* (Cambridge: Harvard University Press, 1974), 64–71; Magrath, *Waite*, 129–34.

38. Springfield *Republican*, August 25, 1876, January 18, 1877; New York *Times*, March 28–29, 1876; New York *Herald*, March 29, 1876; Boston *Journal*, March 28, 29, 1876.

39. Although there were some notable exceptions during the 1880s, the Court tended to interpret the Fifteenth Amendment in the narrowest possible fashion for many decades, amounting to judicial emasculation by 1903. *Giles* v. *Harris*, 189 U.S. 475. Indeed one prominent Virginia conservative attorney and self-proclaimed authority on the Fifteenth Amendment, Allen C. Braxton, who was one of the leaders in the 1902 state constitutional convention that succeeded in legally disfranchising most Negroes, looked forward to the day when the Supreme Court would declare the Fifteenth Amendment invalid. See his revealing letter: Allen C. Braxton to Camm Patteson, August 31, 1903, Letterbooks, in Allen Caperton Braxton Papers, University of Virginia Library, Charlottesville.

CHAPTER 13

1. *Annual Register: A Review Of Public Events At Home and Abroad, for the Year 1876* (London: Rivington's, 1877), 315–30.

2. New York *Evening Post*, December 31, 1875.

3. Springfield *Republican* quoted in St. Louis *Republican*, October 16, 1876; Hartford *Courant*, April 30, 1874; New York *Herald*, June 26, 1875.

4. James Redpath in *Independent*, August 31, 1876; New York *Times*, May 8, 1876; Boston *Advertiser*, October 5, 1876.

5. Grant quoted in editorial, New York *Times*, October 1, 1875; John Hancock to Andrew Johnson, January 29, 1875, in A. Johnson Papers; Oliver P. Morton quoted in New York *World*, January 20, 1876; Washington *National Republican*, August 7, 1875.

6. HVR in Cincinnati *Commercial*, April 8, 1876; R. T. Bull to Ulysses S. Grant, May 20, 1875, District of Louisiana, Source Chronological Files, in RG 60, NA.

7. *Leslie's Newspaper*, August 7, 1875; Timothy O. Howe to Grace T. Howe, March 8, 1876, in Howe Papers; HVR in Cincinnati *Commercial*, May 25, 1878.

8. Marcus L. Ward to Horace N. Congar, June 11, 18, 1876, in Congar Papers; Manning F. Force to Rutherford B. Hayes, October 18, 1875, June 16, 1876, Mortimer D. Leggett to Hayes, February 21, 1876, John Sherman to Hayes, May 22, 1876, George W. Jones to Hayes, June 2, 1876, William Henry Smith to Hayes, June 21, 1876, all in Hayes Papers.

9. *Proceedings of the Republican National Convention, Held at Cincinnati, Ohio, Wednesday, Thursday, and Friday, June 14, 15, and 16, 1876* (Concord, N.H.: Republican Press Association, 1876), 83–109; Cleveland *Leader*, June 26, 1876; *Times* of London, July 6, 1876; see but compare, Keith Ian Polakoff, *The Politics of Inertia: The Election of 1876 and the End of Reconstruction* (Baton Rouge: Louisiana State University Press, 1973), 67; James Russell Lowell to Thomas Hughes, July 12, 1876, in Charles Eliot Norton Papers, Harvard University Library, Cambridge, Mass.; New York *Herald*, June 20, 1876; HVR in Cincinnati *Commercial*, June 24, 1876; Thurlow Weed quoted in Columbus *Dispatch*, June 19, 1876; New York *Tribune*, June 20, 1876; New York *Evening Post*, June 16, 1876; AKM (Alexander K. McClure) in Cincinnati *Commercial*, June 17, 1876; Milwaukee *News* quoted in New York *World*, June 20, 1876; St. Louis *Republican*, June 20, 1876.

10. As usual, the platform denounced the sectional, reactionary spirit of the South, while exploiting sectional appeal in the North by waving the bloody shirt. And the platform vaguely pledged complete liberty and exact equality in the exercise of all civil, political, and public rights. It also endorsed permanent pacification of the South, a stand which in fact could be achieved either by enforcing reconstruction or ending it. The platform similarly declared that any just causes of discontent on the part of any class had to be removed, but whether the grievances of both southern blacks and southern whites could be reconciled to the satisfaction of both groups seemed questionable. The general absence of concern about reconstruction in the Republican editorial assessments of the platform was noteworthy. *Proceedings of Republican National Convention, 1876*, 56, 57–63; Cincinnati *Commercial*, June 26, 1876; New York *World*, June 17, 19, 28, 1876; Boston *Post*, June 17, 1876; *Times* of London, June 17, 1876.

11. Hayes's acceptance letter consisted of a double-barreled appeal that weighed the need for traditional Republican support against the need to recruit reformers. He thus pledged continuity by endorsing reconstruction rights in principle, but he also promised change with his plan to allow the southerners more freedom of action to work out their own destiny. Although assuring his adherence to the goal of the pacification of the South, he subtly qualified that assurance with the provision that

there could be no enduring peace unless there was a recognition of the rights of all by all, honest administration of local government, supremacy of law, preservation of order, and an effort to achieve prosperity. He promised that he would cherish the interests of the white and black population alike, as well as those of the North and the South, and would work for peace between the races and reconciliation between the sections. *Proceedings of Republican National Convention, 1876,* 117; Springfield *Republican,* July 17, 1876; Cincinnati *Commercial,* July 10, 19, September 2, 1876.

12. In his acceptance letter, William A. Wheeler quoted from his 1875 letter on Louisiana: progress could "only come through a long course of patient waiting to which no one can now set certain bounds," and would entail a great "deal of unavoidable friction which will call for forbearance." Wheeler's emphatically conciliatory letter also advanced the so-called Whig strategy by hammering in Hayes's wedge, intended to separate southern Whigs from southern Democrats. *Proceedings of Republican National Convention, 1876,* 118, 112; New York *Evening Post,* June 20, 1876; Philadelphia *Times,* New York *Times,* both July 21, 1876; Boston *Globe,* June 21, 1876.

13. Frederick Douglass quoted in *Proceedings of Republican National Convention, 1876,* 26–27; New York *Evening Post,* Cincinnati *Commercial,* both June 15, 1876.

14. *Official Proceedings of the National Democratic Convention, Held in St. Louis, Mo., June 27th, 28th, and 29th, 1876* (St. Louis: Woodward, Tiernan, and Hale, 1876), 121–50; Cincinnati *Commercial,* June 28, 1876; Perry Belmont to Thomas F. Bayard, June 29, 1876, in T. F. Bayard Papers; Boston *Journal,* June 29, 1876. One person in Washington observed that the Democrats in Congress described Tilden's nomination as excellent but "they say it with a *gulp* which reminds me of my *castor-oil* . . . days." J. M. McGrew to James M. Comly, July 3, 1876, in Comly Papers.

15. The Democratic platform promised devotion to the constitutional amendments as "universally accepted as a final settlement of the controversy that engendered the civil war," even professing "equality of all citizens before just laws," and pledging "absolute acquiescence in the will of the majority." Of course the pious planks were drastically at variance with the views and the actions of most of the southern Democrats, but it was sound politics to placate northerners who might still fear that the Democracy in national power would attempt to rescind the amendments; it was also a ploy to blunt the southern issue. This seemingly conciliatory and reformed attitude also indicated confidence that reconstruction no longer posed any real threat to the emerging Democratic supremacy in the South. Then, taking the offensive, the platform condemned Republican incompetence, "corrupt centralism," and the rapacity of "carpetbag" rule; it denounced Republicans who were seeking to "light anew the dying embers of sectional hate," in contrast to the Democratic championship of civil supremacy and republican self-government. *Official Proceedings of National Democratic Convention, 1876,* 94–97; Memphis *Appeal,* June 29, 1876; HVR in Cincinnati *Commercial,* April 2, 1877. Journalist Benjamin Perley Poore, noting the absence of blacks at the Democratic convention, observed: "this is emphatically a white man's convention, with a color line," a fact that the cleverest platform could not disguise. Boston *Journal,* June 28, 1876.

16. Boston *Advertiser,* July 1, 1876; Boston *Globe,* August 8, September 14, 1876; Boston *Transcript,* September 1, 1876; Boston *Journal,* September 14, 1876; St. Louis *Globe-Democrat,* September 18, 1876; *Nation,* September 21, October 26, 1876.

17. *North American Review,* October, 1876; Herschel V. Johnson to Alexander Stephens, August 9, 1876, in Stephens Papers, LC.

18. Tilden's letter was a revised edition of the party platform that had embraced reform. The embarrassing subject of white southern terrorism was avoided to the disappointment of some northern independents who had hoped for a bolder statement. By concentrating instead on Republican misgovernment in the South and on

what he regarded as federal abuses, Tilden clearly intended to strengthen his support in the South while hoping not to weaken it in the North. *Official Proceedings of National Democratic Convention, 1876*, 181–92; New York *Herald*, Boston *Globe*, Cincinnati *Commercial*, Boston *Journal*, New York *Tribune*, all August 5, 1876.

19. *Proceedings of Republican National Convention, 1876*, 115–18; Springfield *Republican*, August 10, 1876; HVR in Cincinnati *Commercial*, July 26, 1876.

20. Abram S. Hewitt to Samuel J. Bayard, October 18, 1876, in Samuel J. Bayard Papers, Princeton University Library, Princeton, N.J.; Hayes to Carl Schurz, September 15, 1876, in Schurz Papers; *Nation*, November 23, 1876. Similarly, in the selection of the Republican party chairman, Hayes studiously and skillfully avoided making enemies of the party regulars and the reformers, while leaving the direction of the campaign safely in the hands of the professionals. His inaction was the most expedient form of action. Ward to Congar, July 9, 1876, in Congar Papers; see but compare Polakoff, *Politics of Inertia*, 98–99, 138–39.

21. Philadelphia *Times*, September 21, 1876; Springfield *Republican*, July 20, 1876; New York *Herald*, August 26, September 8, 1876; *Harper's Weekly*, October 28, 1876. When he did intervene to select the Democratic gubernatorial nominee as his successor, Tilden stumbled for a time until he settled on his fourth choice. New York *Herald*, September 8, 1876; New York *Tribune*, September 16, 19, 1876.

22. New York *Herald*, August 26, 1876; New York *Tribune*, September 19, 1876.

23. Allan Nevins in *Abram S. Hewitt: With Some Account of Peter Cooper* (New York: Harper, 1935), 313, contended that Tilden had suffered a paralytic stroke in February of 1875; Alexander Clarence Flick in *Samuel Jones Tilden: A Study in Political Sagacity* (New York: Dodd, Mead, 1939), 273–74, only referred to rumors of a stroke. Efforts to verify that Tilden suffered a stroke have been unsuccessful. Moreover, Dr. James H. Halsey, Jr., School of Medicine, University of Alabama, Birmingham, reported in a March 29, 1977, letter: "I believe Tilden had Parkinson's disease. Commonly used synonyms which appear in some of the documents you sent me include 'paralysis agitans' and 'shaking palsy.' Its onset is insidious and course gradual, accounting for the absence of any pressing evidence of a sudden onset of physical or intellectual disability like a stroke. Its course is usually slowly progressive. The outstanding hallmarks of the disability include the tremors of the hands, a waxy expressionless face often with a prominent stare, a stooped posture, shuffling gait, and soft, slurred speech. Many of these features recur in the documents. The disorder may begin in and remain more severe on one side, sometimes leading to a mistaken diagnosis of stroke. It is not an unusual experience for me to see cases of Parkinson's disease in consultation—patients who had been told by their physicians that they had suffered a stroke. This same error may have occurred in Tilden's case. It is not rare in such instances that a specific date of onset has been set. I think in most cases it means this was the date significant disability was recognized, with some relief to the people around the afflicted one who now have a 'reasonable explanation' for abnormal behavior or apparently failing powers. Failure of the intellect is not an essential feature of Parkinson's disease, though intellectual decline sometimes occurs. However, I think the progressive physical enfeeblement will progressively constrict the effectiveness of a politician almost as powerfully—maybe more so because the outward *appearance* produced by the dull facial expression and slow speech is one of dumbness." Flick, *Tilden*, 409, 417; Gath (George A. Townsend) in Cincinnati *Enquirer*, January 8, 1877; New York *Herald*, New York *Tribune*, both February 10, 1879.

24. Diary, September 20, 1876, in Bigelow Papers; Chicago *Tribune*, November 3, 1876.

25. New York *Herald*, August 19, 1876; Chicago *Times*, September 4, 1876.

26. New York *Times*, July 14, 1876.

27. Benjamin F. Butler to Reuben Friendly, October 11, 1876, Letterbooks, in Butler Papers; Boston *Journal*, September 11, 1876; Amos T. Akerman to George W. Friendly, August 22, 1876, in Akerman Letterbooks.

28. Louisville *Courier-Journal*, August 30, 1876; Augusta *Constitutionalist*, July 14, 1876.

29. For the New Orleans coup, see Chapter 5; for the northern reaction to the coup, see Chapter 9.

30. Alexandria *People's Advocate*, August 19, 1876.

31. Samuel S. Cox to Samuel J. Tilden, July 15, 1876, in Tilden Papers; John J. C. Harvey to Samuel J. Randall, July 19, 1876, in Randall Papers; Hewitt to Lucius Q. C. Lamar, October 20, 1876, in Lamar-Mayes Papers.

32. Scott Lord to Tilden, July 31, 1876, in Tilden Papers; *Congressional Record*, 44th Cong., 1st Sess., 5419–22; New York *Times*, Boston *Journal*, both August 11, 1876.

33. William Lloyd Garrison to Samuel May, August 1, 1876, in William Lloyd Garrison Papers, Massachusetts Historical Society, Boston; New York *Herald*, September 23, 1876; New York *Evening Post*, August 12, 1876.

34. Augusta *Constitutionalist*, August 22, 1876; pamphlet quoted in editorial, St. Louis *Globe-Democrat*, October 6, 1876.

35. Cincinnati *Commercial*, August 18, 1876; Hayes to William Henry Smith, October 5, 1876, in Hayes Papers; Hayes to Murat Halstead, October 14, 1876, in Halstead Papers; Springfield *Republican*, October 7, 1876. Finally, Tilden dealt with the issue decisively, but only after being pressured to do so. New York *World*, October 25, 26, 1876; Philadelphia *North American and Gazette*, October 28, 1876.

36. Cincinnati *Gazette*, September 19, 1876; Boston *Journal*, June 28, September 6, 1876; Springfield *Republican*, August 28, 1876.

37. During the war Hayes had served in the army and had been wounded in action. Although Tilden's health had precluded military service, he had neither joined the national government nor backed its war policies. Instead, he had been an inarticulate, ineffective, and not entirely convincing supporter of the Union in its supreme crisis, more concerned about the *potential* perils of dictatorship than about *actual* dangers of the dismemberment and destruction of the nation. He had said too much in favor of the activities and causes that had handicapped the war effort, and too little in support of the requirements of Union victory. According to Lincoln's secretary of the navy, Gideon Wells, himself a Democrat in 1876, "Tilden failed his country in a great emergency." The Springfield *Republican* commented on Tilden's damaging war record: "Governor Tilden's course during the war was not one, on the whole, for a patriot to be proud of." Gideon Welles to Montgomery Blair, June 19, 1876, in Blair Family Papers; Springfield *Republican*, September 30, 1876.

38. *Harper's Weekly*, July 22, 1876. Whereas Hayes had supported the efforts to reconstruct the South, Tilden had not and had urged the exploitation of the race issue. Tilden to William Bigler, February 28, 1868, in William Bigler Papers, Historical Society of Pennsylvania, Philadelphia; New York *World*, March 14, 1868, January 13, 1875, October 28, 1877; New York *Tribune*, November 5, 1874.

39. Augusta *Constitutionalist*, September 19, 1876; Mobile *Register* quoted in Boston *Journal*, September 16, 1876.

40. HVR in Cincinnati *Commercial*, August 14, 17, 18, 19, 21, September 2, 4, 9, 1876; Akerman to Clark, July 11, 1876, Akerman to Cilley, August 3, 1876, Akerman to Audan, August 12, 1876, all in Akerman Letterbooks; Savannah *Tribune*, November 4, 1876; Atlanta *Constitution*, October 18, 1876.

41. Springfield *Republican*, August 14, 1876.

42. Alphonso Taft to Hayes, September 12, 1876, in Hayes Papers; Benjamin H.

Bristow quoted in New York *Times*, October 7, 1876; Zachariah Chandler to Edward C. Wade, December 1, 1876, in Z. Chandler Papers; Grant quoted in New York *Herald*, March 5, 1877.

43. Louisville *Courier-Journal*, July 10, 1876; St. Louis *Republican*, September 27, 1876.

44. Thomas F. Bayard to August Belmont, July 18, 1876, in T. F. Bayard Papers.

45. Akerman to John Sherman, June 17, 1876, in Akerman Letterbooks; southern Negro quoted in HVR, Cincinnati *Commercial*, November 13, 1876.

46. Wade Hampton quoted in HVR, Cincinnati *Commercial*, September 12, 15, 1876; Hampton to Tilden, July 17, 1876, in Tilden Papers.

47. John F. Rollins to William E. Chandler, August 9, 1876, in W. E. Chandler Papers; George D. Allen to George W. Lapham, October 26, 1876, in Tilden Papers.

48. HVR in Cincinnati *Commercial*, December 30, 1876, March 3, 1877; J. R. G. Pitkin to Old Whigs, March 1, 1876, J. R. G. Pitkin Letter, Louisiana State University Library, Baton Rouge.

49. New York *Sun*, September 8, 1876; Philip H. Sheridan to Grant, September 15, 1876, in Sheridan Papers; James D. Cameron to Sheridan, October 31, 1876, Letters Sent by the Secretary of War Relating to Military Affairs since 1871, in RG 107, NA; Randall L. Gibson to Samuel J. Randall, October 19, 1876, in Randall Papers; see but compare Hesseltine, *Grant*, 414, for the statement that Grant was unprepared for a contested election.

50. C. P. Leslie to Hayes, February, 1877, in Hayes Papers; Savannah *Tribune*, September 2, 1876.

51. L. Cass Carpenter to James A. Garfield, September 25, 1876, in Garfield Papers, LC; L. Cass Carpenter to Hayes, December 14, 1876, in Hayes Papers; Reminiscences of Loula A. Rockwell, University of North Carolina Library, Chapel Hill.

52. HVR in Cincinnati *Commercial*, August 23, September 11–12, 20–21, 29, October 1, 4, 27, 30, November 1–5, 10, 1876, October 31, 1878.

53. L. Cass Carpenter to W. E. Chandler, August 26, 1876, in W. E. Chandler Papers.

54. New York *Herald*, September 27, 1876; Springfield *Republican*, October 30, 1876; HVR in Cincinnati *Commercial*, September 15, November 6, 1876.

55. Daniel H. Chamberlain to Grant, October 11, 1876, District of South Carolina, Source Chronological Files, in RG 60, NA; Richardson (comp.), *Messages of the Presidents*, VII, 396–97; Cincinnati *Commercial*, October 23, 1876; William T. Sherman to David F. Boyd, October 26, 1876, in Boyd Papers.

56. Memphis *Appeal*, August 12, 1876. Only one fourth of the federal election enforcement expenditures were devoted to the southern and border states during the presidential campaign of 1876.

57. On October 10, 1876, the Democrats in Indiana just barely retained the governorship, by a 5000 majority (49 percent); the Republicans in Ohio won the state secretaryship by a mere 6000 majority (50 percent). *Tribune Almanac and Political Register for 1877* (New York: Tribune Association, 1877), 74–76, 111–13; David, *Party Strength*, 137, 224; Garfield to Harmon Austin, October 15, 1876, in Garfield Papers, LC; Force to Hayes, November 3, 1876, in Hayes Papers.

58. Boston *Globe*, October 30, 1876; Charles Francis Adams Diary, October 12, 19, 1876.

59. HVR in Cincinnati *Commercial*, November 10, 1876, the dispatch was dated November 7.

60. Special American correspondent in *Times* of London, November 29, 1876; Springfield *Republican*, November 8, 1876.

61. Pitkin to S. L. Breese, November 7, 1876, District of Louisiana, Source Chronological Files, in RG 60, NA; HVR in Cincinnati *Commercial*, November 10, 1876.

62. New York *Times*, Chicago *Inter-Ocean*, New York *World*, all November 8, 1876; William W. Corcoran to Alexander H. H. Stuart, November 8, 1876, in Alexander H. H. Stuart Papers, University of Virginia Library, Charlottesville.

63. The northern vote (in the states outside the South and the borderland) is figured by the totals provided by Peterson, *Statistical History of Presidential Elections*, 46; *Tribune Almanac for 1877*, 46, 51; David, *Party Strength*, 103–281, 302; see but compare Burnham, *Presidential Ballots*, 118–27. The New York *Herald*, November 25, 1876, figured the net Republican loss in the northern states in 1876 over 1868 to be 233,000, over 1872, 521,000. Clearly, the Republican vote in 1872 was inflated because of the unusually poor support of Greeley. Counting the southern vote, Tilden had an ostensible national majority of the two-party vote of 251,746 (51½ percent). But Horace V. Redfield concluded that a "fair election in all the Southern States, and Tilden would have been without a majority of the popular vote" of the nation. Cincinnati *Commercial*, March 26, 1877. The results of the congressional elections were mixed: the Democrats narrowly retained the House of Representatives (52 percent), and the Republicans narrowly retained the Senate (51 percent); each party suffered an almost identical loss (10 percent) in the chamber it held in the previous Congress. Thus, Congress was more closely divided after 1876 and the partisan majority in each chamber was precarious.

64. T. W. Davenport to William Henry Smith, November 27, 1876, in W. H. Smith Papers, Indiana Historical Society.

65. HVR in Cincinnati *Commercial*, December 23, August 3, 1876.

66. Charles A. Wetmore to Hayes, September 27, October 21, 29, 1876, W. E. Chandler to Hayes, October 12, 13, 30, 1876, all in Hayes Papers; Henry M. Yerington to D. O. Mills, November 6, 1876, in Henry M. Yerington Papers, University of California Library, Berkeley; Eugene Casserly to Tilden, July 15, August 29, 1876, William M. Gwin to Tilden, August 7, 1876, all in Tilden Papers.

67. There were hints of fraud in San Francisco: New York *World*, December 9, 1876, March 6, 1877; Augusta *Chronicle and Sentinel*, February 28, March 16, 1877; Tilden to Adams, April, 1877, Casserly to Tilden, May 27, 1876, both in Tilden Papers; New York *Times*, March 6, 1877.

68. Ward to Congar, July 9, 1876, in Congar Papers.

69. J. Birney Work to Garfield, December 16, 1876, in Garfield Papers, LC; Cincinnati *Commercial*, August 16, September 4, 1876.

70. The Democratic St. Louis *Republican*, October 12, 1876, declared: "To the Republican party belongs the responsibility of having celebrated the Centennial year by preaching a crusade against half the country—a crusade which makes the Centennial a solemn farce and transforms what might have been the beginning of a new and more blessed union into a fountain of bitterness." But the Democrats in the South had fulminated against both the North and the southern Republicans; if Republican partisans of the North had fought the Civil War over again with ink, the diehard Democrats in the South had done so with shotguns as well.

71. W. E. Chandler to Hayes, November 9, 1876, in Hayes Papers; Raymonde in Cincinnati *Commercial*, November 14, 1876.

72. New York *Tribune*, November 29, 1876; Gath in Philadelphia *Weekly Times*, March 3, 1877. The single electoral vote of Oregon, which Hayes had carried, was contested by the Democrats on a technicality: the Republican elector was ineligible because he was a federal employee.

73. Akerman to his brother, February 19, 1877, in Akerman Letterbooks, in possession of Joe A. Akerman, Jr. A South Carolina Republican newspaper noted the northern Republican neglect of the southern Republican campaign: "the republicans of the North, as a general thing, withdrew their sympathy from their struggling brethren in the South." Columbia *Union-Herald*, November 22, 1876.

74. Garfield to William C. Howells, November 11, 1876, in Garfield Papers, LC;

Nation, November 16, 1876, January 25, 1877; Philadelphia *Times*, November 15, 1876.

75. Elmira *Gazette* quoted in New York *World*, November 14, 1876; New York *Sun*, November 10, 1876; *Leslie's Newspaper*, December 6, 1876.

76. John M. Harlan to David Davis, November 11, 1876, in Davis Papers; Cincinnati *Commercial*, November 11, 1876; *Nation*, November 16, 23, 1876.

77. Diary, November 9, 1876, in Fish Papers, LC; Grant to W. T. Sherman, November 10, 1876, enclosed in Sherman to Sheridan, Letters Sent, Main Series, in RG 94, NA; Memorandum of Abram S. Hewitt, December 3, 1876, in Allan Nevins Papers, Columbia University Library, New York.

78. Grant to James D. Cameron, November 26, 1876, Letterbooks in Grant Papers, LC; Grant to Thomas H. Ruger, December 3–4, 1876, in Grant Papers, Hayes Library; James D. Cameron to Ruger, December 5, 1876, Letters Sent, since 1871, in RG 107, NA; Diary, November 30, December 1, 4–5, 1876, in Fish Papers, LC; Richardson (comp.), *Messages of the Presidents*, VII, 418–21; Grant, interviewed in New York *Herald*, February 27, 1877; Philadelphia *Times*, April 7, 1877.

79. New York *Times*, November 22–26, 1876; New York *World*, November 21, 1876; W. T. Sherman to W. F. Barry, November 16, 1876, W. T. Sherman to R. C. Drum, November 16, 1876, Sherman to Winfield Scott Hancock, November 21, 1876, all in Letters Sent, Main Series, in RG 94, NA; Hilary A. Herbert Reminiscences, University of North Carolina Library, Chapel Hill; Chicago *Tribune*, February 22, 1877; New York *Tribune*, January 13, 1877; Boston *Journal*, February 12–13, 1877; New York *Herald*, February 22, 1877; William R. Morrison to Manton Marble, April 13, 1877, in Marble Papers; Richard Vaux to Thomas F. Bayard, December 8, 1876, in T. F. Bayard Papers.

80. Horace Redfield believed that in a free election Louisiana would certainly have gone for Hayes, and he defended the action of the returning board in going behind the returns; but he thought that in a fair count of the ballots actually cast the result would have favored Tilden. HVR in Cincinnati *Commercial*, November 25, 27, December 2, 4, 30, 1876, February 18, March 6, 1877; compare MPH (Moses P. Handy) in Philadelphia *Times*, November 27, 1876; ZLW in New York *Tribune*, November 28, 29, 1876.

81. Which candidate won on election day and what had actually been done in returning the results will never be fully known. The evidence does suggest that in many places the Democrats had prevented a free election and a full vote; there are also indications of blatant partisanship on the part of the Republican returning boards, for they had rejected valid votes and had accepted fraudulent substitutes. The Democrats had done their dirty work before the election; the Republicans in some cases had done so after the election. In the end, with a measure of poetic justice, some fraudulent Democratic victories were transformed into suspicious Republican victories.

82. New York *Times*, Philadelphia *Times*, both December 7, 1876.

83. *Congressional Record*, 44th Cong., 2nd Sess., 91, 197–98, 258; J. Sherman to W. H. Smith, December 11, 1876, in W. H. Smith Papers, Indiana Historical Society; E. B. Wight to William W. Clapp, December 27, 1876, January 11, 1877, in William W. Clapp Papers, LC; Van in Springfield *Republican*, December 18, 1876, January 11, 15, 1877; Richard Taylor to Samuel L. M. Barlow, January 7, 1877, in Barlow Papers.

84. On January 25, 1877, the Senate approved the electoral count bill by a vote of 47 to 17; all but one of the twenty-six Democrats supported it; a majority of the Republicans, twenty-one, also approved it, but with sixteen Republicans (43 percent) in opposition (eight were northerners and eight were southerners). The following day the bill received the approval of the House of Representatives, 191 to 86; a minority of

the Republicans (thirty-three, with eighteen from the Northeast, twelve from the Midwest, and two from the South) supported the measure, whereas sixty-eight (67 percent of the Republican forces) opposed the bill. On the Democratic side, all of the New England congressmen endorsed the bill; eighteen Democrats (10 percent) opposed the method of compromise, with thirteen opposition votes from the South and five from the Midwest. President Grant, who had strongly supported the bill, signed it into law on January 29, 1877. *Congressional Record*, 44th Cong., 2nd Sess., 913, 1050, 1081; New York *Times*, January 27, 1877. Although a larger margin of Democrats supported the electoral compromise plan than did Republicans, the actual voting record did not accurately reflect all those who were friends or foes of the bill. Some members of both parties finally voted for the bill, however much they disliked it, because they knew it would pass and was popular outside Congress. And some who might have supported the bill opposed it because they did not want to be held responsible if their party lost the presidency. Senator Frelinghuysen, a proponent of the measure, hinted at its opponents' motives: "You may ask why so many Republicans voted against the bill. . . . but can't you see that I might have voted against the bill and yet it would have passed." By casting negative votes, they allowed the compromisers to assume the crushing responsibility if the decision went against them. Frederick T. Frelinghuysen to Congar, January 31, 1877, in Congar Papers. A Louisiana Democratic representative wrote of the electoral compromise bill: "I opposed it, disliked it, distrusted it, and then permitted myself to be cajoled into voting for it as a 'peace measure.'" E. John Ellis to Ezekiel Parke Ellis, February 25, 1877, in Ellis Family Papers, Louisiana State University Library, Baton Rouge; George F. Edmunds to Schurz, December 23, 1876, January 2, 1877, in Schurz Papers; St. Louis *Republican*, January 26, 1877; Chicago *Tribune*, January 22, 1877; Diary, January 18, 1877, in Bigelow Papers; Diary, January 21, 1877, in Hayes Papers.

85. HVR in Cincinnati *Commercial*, February 19, 12, 1877; Boston *Advertiser*, February 1, 1877; Louisville *Courier-Journal*, February 1, 1877; Van in Springfield *Republican*, January 26, 1877; New York *World*, January 25, 26, 1877; New York *Sun*, January 29, 1877; R. Taylor to Barlow, January 18, 1877, in Barlow Papers.

86. Diary, January 28, 1877, in Bigelow Papers; New York *Sun*, January 31, 1877.

87. Hayes received the disputed electoral votes of Florida on February 9, 1877, Louisiana on February 16, Oregon on February 23, and South Carolina on February 27. Chicago *Times*, November 14, 1876; Springfield *Republican*, Boston *Transcript*, both February 19, 1877; *Congressional Record*, 44th Cong., 2nd Sess., Part IV, Vol. V; Joseph P. Bradley to Ward, March 3, 1877, in Ward Papers; Bradley to Congar, July 24, 1877, in Congar Papers; Bradley quoted in Newark *Advertiser*, September 5, 1877.

88. H. H. Mitchell to Samuel J. Randall, February 20, 1877, in Randall Papers; St. Louis *Republican*, February 9, 1877; Stephen J. Field to Matthew P. Deady, April 2, 1877, in Matthew P. Deady Papers, Oregon Historical Society, Portland.

89. New York *Herald*, November 9, 1876; Chicago *Inter-Ocean*, February 24, 1877; Garfield quoted in Fay, Louisville *Courier-Journal*, February 16, 1877; *Nation*, February 15, March 1, 1877; SB in Springfield *Republican*, February 14, 1877; Gath in Cincinnati *Enquirer*, February 10, 1877.

90. Rumors that the Democrats would refuse to submit and would filibuster had begun to circulate after the decision on Florida; such rumors increased after the decision on Louisiana. After the Oregon decision on February 23, the Democrats in the House of Representatives engaged in dilatory maneuvers. HVR in Cincinnati *Commercial*, February 16, 19, 21–22, 27, March 3, 6, 1877; Van in Springfield *Republican*, February 15, 27, 1877; MPH in Philadelphia *Times*, February 17, 1877.

91. St. Louis *Republican*, February 17, 1877; Louisville *Courier-Journal*, February 12, 19, 1877; John R. Tucker to Henry S. Tucker, February 25, 1877, in John

R. Tucker Papers, University of North Carolina Library, Chapel Hill; Wight to Clapp, February 14, 1877, in Clapp Papers; HVR in Cincinnati *Commercial*, February 16, 19, March 2, 6, 1877.

92. Boston *Journal*, February 12, 1877; Wight to Clapp, February 14, 1877, in Clapp Papers; HVR in Cincinnati *Commercial*, February 26, March 2, 1877; Chicago *Tribune*, November 21, 1876; New York *Herald*, December 12, 13, 1876, February 15, 17, 20, 22, 1877; Paul Leland Haworth, *The Hayes-Tilden Disputed Presidential Election of 1876* (Cleveland: Burrows, 1906), 268–83.

93. C. Vann Woodward, *Reunion and Reaction: The Compromise of 1877 and the End of Reconstruction* (Boston: Little, Brown, 1951); compare Polakoff, *Politics of Inertia*, 201–324; for evidence that those with economic objectives had confessed uncertainty as to their influence, information, and control, see Henry V. Boynton to Benjamin H. Bristow, January 21, 1877, in Bristow Papers; H. V. Boynton to [Richard] Smith, February 11, 1877, Charles A. Boynton to William Henry Smith, January 22, 1877, H. V. Boynton to W. H. Smith, February 18, 1877, all in W. H. Smith Papers, Indiana Historical Society; Hayes to W. H. Smith, January 3, 1877, W. H. Smith to Hayes, January 5, 1877, Edward F. Noyes to Hayes, January 2, 1877, all in Hayes Papers. Reporter Redfield observed: "where there is so much talk, and particularly so much confidential talk as there is here, so much said about the old Whigs in the South, Southern Pacific Railroad, Democratic dissatisfaction, new deal, etc., in all this smoke there must be some fire. But it may not burn very much. It may go out like a match with a flash and a bad smell." HVR in Cincinnati *Commercial*, February 26, 1877; New York *Times*, February 26, 1877, August 19, July 21, 1876; New York *World*, August 25, 1876. For a definition of a national compromise, see David M. Potter, *The Impending Crisis, 1848–1861* (New York: Harper and Row, 1976), 113.

94. Diary, December 1, 17, 30, 1876, February 25, 1877, Lamar to Hayes, March 22, 1877, all in Hayes Papers; New York *Evening Post*, December 18, 1876; DWB in *Independent*, January 4, 1877; Philadelphia *Times*, February 21, 1877; HVR in Cincinnati *Commercial*, February 27, March 3, 1877; *Congressional Record*, 44th Cong., 2nd Sess., 1708; Diary, February 26, 1877, Charles Foster to Garfield, March 30, 1877, both in Garfield Papers, LC; telegram from Edward A. Burke to Francis T. Nicholls, February 27, 1877, in W. E. Chandler Papers; New Orleans *Daily Picayune*, February 27, March 1, 1877; New York *Times*, March 26, 1877. One North Carolina Democratic legislator wrote to his wife that if Hayes should become president "he will deal more kindly towards the South than Grant has done. . . . Even with Hayes [as] President every Southern State will be in the hands of the Democrats, including South Carolina and Louisiana," for "he will place no obstacle in the way of the Southern States governing themselves." John S. Henderson to Bessie Henderson, February 6, 1877, in John S. Henderson Papers, University of North Carolina Library, Chapel Hill; New York *Tribune*, February 9, 1877.

95. Diary, January 17, February 2, 1877, Force to Hayes, January 7, 1877, both in Hayes Papers; HVR in Cincinnati *Commercial*, February 26, 1877; E. John Ellis to Ezekiel Parke Ellis, February 25, 1877, in Ellis Family Papers; compare E. J. Ellis to Bayard, February 27, 1877, in T. F. Bayard Papers.

96. Sam Dickson to Randall, February 19, 1877, in Randall Papers; Boston *Journal*, February 20, 1877; New York *Tribune*, New York *Herald*, both February 24, 1877; Cincinnati *Commercial*, February 13, 23, March 3, 1877; Boston *Advertiser*, March 3, 1877.

97. *Congressional Record*, 44th Cong., 2nd Sess., 1905–1907, 2068; Diary, February 24, 1877, in Garfield Papers, LC; New York *Herald*, February 26, March 1–5, 1877; Joseph Frazier Wall, *Henry Watterson: Reconstructed Rebel* (New York: Oxford University Press, 1956), 162; New York *Times*, February 21, 1877; Augusta *Constitutionalist*, March 8, 1877.

98. E. J. Ellis to E. P. Ellis, February 25, 1877, in Ellis Family Papers; Cincinnati

Commercial, February 21, March 2–3, 1877; New York *Herald*, February 27, 1877. It would appear that President Grant in the final days of his administration told the Louisiana Democrats exactly what they wanted to hear, but procrastinated long enough and was vague enough in his actual army orders so as not to pull out the troops at the statehouse in New Orleans before the electoral count was completed and the new Republican president was inaugurated. R. Taylor to Barlow, January 9, 14, 1877, in Barlow Papers. Subsequently, Grant was to make the comment that he regarded the real governments in South Carolina and Louisiana as Democratic, which prompted the Philadelphia *Times*, April 7, 1877, to wonder who would have been president if Grant had enforced his judgment back in November-December 1876. And the *Nation*, August 22, 1878, observed that President Grant's last public act was to notify Packard that he would not recognize him as governor of Louisiana: "In other words, he indicated his intention to do (after his time for doing it had gone by) the very things in respect of the South which have since been done by his successor."

99. George F. Brown to Warner M. Bateman, October 3, 1876, in Warner M. Bateman Papers, Western Reserve Historical Society, Cleveland; Van in Springfield *Republican*, February 16, 1877; HVR in Cincinnati *Commercial*, March 6, 26, 1877.

100. See but compare Haworth, *Presidential Election of 1876*; Woodward, *Reunion and Reaction:The Compromise of 1877 and the End of Reconstruction*; Polakoff, *The Politics of Inertia: The Election of 1876 and The End of Reconstruction*.

101. Some commentators have contended that if Tilden had been elected, he would have moved slowly and, as a Democrat, would have encountered difficulty in withdrawing the troops from the two statehouses; in fact, this view was not shared by contemporaries. Grant in New York *Tribune*, January 1, 1877; EVS in Chicago *Tribune*, January 5, 1877; HVR in Cincinnati *Commercial*, February 18, 1877. As the Charleston *News and Courier*, February 20, 1877, viewed the difference: "With Tilden the South will be safer; but with Hayes . . . South Carolina will be safe."

102. Philadelphia *Weekly Times*, March 24, 1877.

CHAPTER 14

1. New York *Times*, March 2, 1877; Lionel A. Sheldon to James A. Garfield, January 7, 1877, in Garfield Papers, LC. There was no longer any disputed state authority in Florida; the statehouse in Tallahassee fell to the Democrats in early January after its electoral vote had been counted and certified for Hayes, and after the Republicans, reluctantly but peacefully, had accepted the state victory of the Democrats.

2. HVR in Cincinnati *Commercial*, March 6, 1877; DWB in *Independent*, January 18, 1877; C. P. Leslie to Rutherford B. Hayes, February, 1877, in Hayes Papers; Baltimore *American*, March 8, 1877.

3. Diary, February 9, 17, 25, March 14, 16, 1877, in Hayes Papers; Cincinnati *Gazette*, March 6, 1877; Edwin Cowles to Garfield, March 3, 1877, in Garfield Papers, LC; Lucius Q. C. Lamar to E. D. Clark, March 30, 1877, in Clark Papers.

4. HVR in Cincinnati *Commercial*, February 18, 1877; J. C. Winsmith to John Sherman, March 2, 1877, in J. Sherman Papers; Daniel H. Chamberlain quoted in New York *Times*, December 8, 1876; Columbia *Union-Herald*, January 17, 1877; Louisville *Courier-Journal*, March 2, 1877; Memphis *Appeal*, March 4, 1877.

5. Richardson (comp.), *Messages of the Presidents*, VII, 442; New York *Herald*, Boston *Post*, both March 6, 1877. One perceptive correspondent noted how emphatically, earnestly, and strongly Hayes read his address, "as though he had made up his mind; and it was his mind, and he intended to stand by it." Grace Greenwood (Sarah J. Lippincott) in New York *Times*, March 17, 1877.

6. Robert G. Ingersoll quoted in New York *Herald*, March 8, 1877; Timothy O. Howe to Grace T. Howe, March 10, 1877, in Howe Papers.

7. Diary, October 24, 1877, in Hayes Papers; Thomas C. Donaldson Memoirs, November 29, 1877, Indiana Historical Society, Indianapolis. The Republican New York *Tribune*, March 28, 1877, classified the cabinet as four Republicans, two independents, and one Democrat; the Democratic New York *World*, April 6, 1877, found only two regular Republicans; Redfield reported that Liberal Republicans regarded the new regime as a "Liberal administration" and speculated himself that possibly four of the seven members of the cabinet had voted for Greeley in 1872. HVR in Cincinnati *Commercial*, March 16, 1877.

8. Sheldon to Garfield, May 19, 1877, in Garfield Papers, LC; Whitelaw Reid to James M. Comly, October 17, 1877, in Comly Papers.

9. Washington dispatch in New York *Herald*, March 8, 1877; New York *Tribune*, March 8, 20, 1877; HVR in Cincinnati *Commercial*, March 19, 1877; New York *World*, March 18, 1877. For evidence that President Hayes personally gave "assurances, amounting almost to a positive promise" during the special session of the Senate in March of 1877, see Washington dispatch in Philadelphia *Weekly Times*, March 24, 1877; Lamar to Hayes, March 22, 1877, George A. Sheridan to Hayes, April 3, 1877, Diary, March 14, 1877, all in Hayes Papers.

10. Stanley Matthews to Chamberlain, quoted in New York *Times*, March 11, 1877; E. A. Burke to John Sherman, March 4, 1877, in Hayes Papers; Diary, March 7, 1877, in Fish Papers, LC. The New York *World*, March 12, 1877, in an editorial characterized Matthews' letter as an "apology at its head, a compliment at its tail and an insult in its bosom." One friend of Hayes described the letter as lacking finesse. William M. Dickson to Hayes, March 20, 1877, in Hayes Papers.

11. Chamberlain to Matthews, quoted in New York *Times*, March 26, 1877; Matthews to Stephen B. Packard, quoted in New York *Times*, March 15, 1877; New York *Herald*, March 7, 1877; Joseph H. Oglesby to J. Sherman, March 12, 1877, R. Hutcheson to Matthews, April 11, 1877, both in Hayes Papers.

12. St. Louis *Republican*, March 13, 1877; New York *Herald*, March 8, 1877; New York *Tribune*, March 22, 1877.

13. Philadelphia *Press*, March 6, 1877; *Congressional Record*, 45th Cong., Special Sess., Senate, 21. Chamberlain at the time still had hope, although he admitted that "Hayes' apparent policy" was "alarming." Chamberlain to Frank J. Garrison, March 11, 1877, in William Lloyd Garrison Papers, Boston Public Library, Boston.

14. Philadelphia *Times*, March 8, 1877; Mobile *Register*, March 11, 1877; New York *Tribune*, Cincinnati *Commercial*, both March 12, 1877. Many Republican newspapers contended that Hayes's policy was not abandoning Republican principles but only relinquishing ineffective methods to achieve them. Boston *Advertiser*, March 12, 1877; *Independent*, March 15, 1877; Boston *Journal*, March 16, 1877.

15. J. W. Porter to J. Sherman, March 10, 1877, in Hayes Papers; HVR in Cincinnati *Commercial*, May 15, 1877; St. Louis *Globe-Democrat*, April 23, 1877; Chamberlain to F. J. Garrison, March 18, 1877, in Garrison Papers, Boston Public Library; Springfield *Republican*, March 9, 1877; ZLW in New York *Tribune*, March 14, 1877.

16. Diary, March 16, 1877, in Hayes Papers; Washington *National Republican*, March 16, 1877. The futility of holding new elections was widely recognized. New York *World*, New York *Herald*, both March 15, 1877; Springfield *Republican*, March 16, 1877.

17. Packard to Hayes, Hayes to Packard, telegrams of March 19, 1877, telegram from Francis T. Nicholls to Randall L. Gibson, March 20, 1877, Gibson to Hayes, March 20, 1877, Diary, March 14, 20–21, 23, 1877, telegram from George W. McCrary to Packard on telegram of Hayes to Packard, March 26, 1877, all in Hayes Papers; New York *Herald*, March 21, 1877; New York *Tribune*, March 22, 1877.

18. Lamar to Hayes, March 22, 1877, telegram from Charles Foster to Hayes, March 21, 1877, Matthews to Hayes, March 23, 1877, all in Hayes Papers; Washington *National Republican*, March 16, 1877; Samuel J. Randall to Chauncey F. Black, March 22, 1877, in Randall Papers; Josie Ellis to Mary E. Ellis, March 21, 1877, in Ellis Family Papers. The idea of forming a special federal commission to go to the South had been suggested earlier and accepted by Hayes. Carl Schurz to Hayes, February 20, 1877, in Hayes Papers; Cowles to Garfield, March 3, 1877, in Garfield Papers, LC; Andrew J. Kellar to William Henry Smith, March 25, 1877, in W. H. Smith Papers, Indiana Historical Society; New York *Tribune*, March 8, 1877. Attempts at other sorts of bargaining also seemed to go on and on; see, for example, the editorial concerning a railroad, in New York *Times*, June 23, 1877. So much for the argument that the various meetings during the electoral crisis definitively closed all questions in the minds of all participants as to what would happen in the South and in Congress concerning political and economic policies.

19. George Foster to John Marshall Harlan, April 9, 1877, in Harlan Papers; Philadelphia *Times*, March 23, 1877; New Orleans *Daily Picayune*, New York *Herald*, both March 22, 1877. The Democratic Boston *Post*, April 9, 1877, dismissed such a commission, contending that it was unauthorized as a tribunal, was an impertinence as an advisory board, and amounted to an insult as a board of trade.

20. Washington *National Republican*, March 27, 1877; HVR in Cincinnati *Commercial*, March 26, 1877; Boston *Transcript*, Baltimore *American*, both March 22, 1877.

21. Charles Foster to Hayes, March 21, 1877, telegram, in Hayes Papers; James D. Porter to David M. Key, March 29, 1877, in David M. Key Papers, Chattanooga-Hamilton County Public Library, Chattanooga, Tenn. Similarly, Kentucky Senator John W. Stevenson predicted that Hayes would not recognize the Republican governors. John W. Stevenson Diary, March 29, 1877, University of Kentucky Library, Lexington.

22. Diary, March 20, 23, 1877, in Hayes Papers; HVR in Cincinnati *Commercial*, March 26, 1877; Van in Springfield *Republican*, March 29, 1877; New York *Times*, March 23, 1877; New York *Herald*, April 12, 1877.

23. Philadelphia *Times*, March 30, 1877; New York *Evening Post*, Boston *Journal*, both March 29, 1877; *House of Representatives Executive Documents*, 45th Cong., 2nd Sess., No. 97, pp. 2–4.

24. Wade Hampton to T. J. Mackey, March 22, 1877, Hampton to Hayes, March 26, 1877, telegrams in Hayes Papers; William K. Rogers to Hampton and to Chamberlain, quoted in New York *Times*, March 24, 1877; Charleston *News and Courier*, March 22, 1877; New York *Tribune*, March 23, 1877; New York *Herald*, March 24, 1877; Boston *Journal*, March 27, 1877.

25. Hampton quoted in New York *Herald*, March 29, 1877; New York *Times*, March 29, 1877; New York *Tribune*, March 30, 1877; Cincinnati *Commercial*, April 2, 18, 22, 1877.

26. Chamberlain to Hayes, March 31, April, 1877, Hampton to Hayes, March 29, 31, 1877, all in Hayes Papers; New York *Herald*, March 29, April 1–4, 1877; McCrary to William T. Sherman, April 3, 1877, Letters Sent, since 1871, in RG 107, NA; New York *Evening Post*, March 30, 1877; New York *Times*, April 1, 1877; St. Louis *Globe-Democrat*, April 11, 1877.

27. The Republicans still had a majority of one in the upper chamber of the legislature, but the Democrats by the tactic of impeachment were to seize control. Cincinnati *Commercial*, May 9, 1877. The *Nation*, July 5, 19, 1877, reviewing the legislative elections in Charleston and Darlington, in which white Democratic candidates swept formerly Republican bastions, observed that the state Republican party was now "completely broken to pieces."

28. Joseph R. Hawley to his wife, April 11, 1877, in Hawley Papers; George A. Sheridan to Hayes, April 3, 1877, Hutcheson to Matthews, April 11, 1877, both in Hayes Papers.

29. Packard to Hayes, April 5, 16, 1877, in Hayes Papers.

30. Kellar to Key, April 14, 19, 1877, Wayne MacVeagh to Hayes, May 12, 1877, John Marshall Harlan to Hayes, May 25, 1877, all in Hayes Papers; Sheldon to Garfield, April 7, 1877, in Garfield Papers, LC; H. V. Boynton to Benjamin H. Bristow, May 30, December 10, 1877, in Bristow Papers; Matthews to John Marshall Harlan, May 7, 1877, in Harlan Papers.

31. John M. Harlan wrote that money would be secured from New Orleans businessmen to the "point of 'bulldozing' the politicians into a settlement." Harlan to Bristow, April 9, 1877, in Bristow Papers.

32. New York *Sun*, March 28, 1877; Chicago *Tribune*, April 6, 1877; New York *Herald*, April 10, 1877; New York *Tribune*, April 13, 17, 1877.

33. A. M. Gibson to S. J. Randall, April 6, 1877, in Randall Papers.

34. Diary, March 27, 25, 1877, in Fish Papers, LC; HVR in Cincinnati *Commercial*, March 26, 28, 1877; New York *Tribune*, March 22, 29, April 25, 1877; New York *Herald*, March 27–29, April 25, 1877.

35. Packard to Republican legislators, quoted in New York *Times*, April 26, 1877, see also April 20–21, 25, 28, 1877; *House of Representatives Executive Documents*, 45th Cong., 2nd Sess., No. 97, pp. 4–15; Hayes to McCrary, April 20, 1877, MacVeagh to Hayes, April 25, 1877, both in Hayes Papers; McCrary to W. T. Sherman, April 20, 1877, Letters Sent, since 1871, in RG 107, NA; W. T. Sherman to C. C. Augur, April 21, 1877, Letters Sent, Main Series, in RG 94, NA; Columbus (Ohio) *Dispatch*, April 20, 1877; New York *Herald*, April 20, 1877; Philadelphia *Weekly Times*, April 28, 1877; Desmond Fitzgerald to Lizzie, April 24, 1877, Desmond Fitzgerald Letter, Louisiana State University Library, Baton Rouge; see but compare Lonn, *Reconstruction in Louisiana*, 525.

36. Mobile *Register*, April 11, 1877; Memphis *Appeal*, April 18, 1877; New Orleans *Daily Picayune*, April 23, 1877; New York *World*, April 14, 1877; James Atkins to Garfield, May 3, 1877, in Garfield Papers, LC.

37. Joseph A. Howells to Garfield, May 19, 1877, in Garfield Papers, LC; Will H. Thomas to J. Sherman, March 24, 1877, in J. Sherman Papers; [?] to Hayes, April 6, 1877, in Hayes Papers; Amos T. Akerman to Chamberlain, April 16, 1877, in Akerman Letterbooks, in possession of Joe A. Akerman, Jr.; Chicago *Inter-Ocean*, April 23, 1877; D. Montgomery to William E. Chandler, March 25, 1877, in W. E. Chandler Papers; St. Louis *Globe-Democrat*, April 27, 1877; HVR in Cincinnati *Commercial*, March 26, 1877; New York *Times*, April 21, 1877. Although many southerners and northerners lauded the return of self-government, Senator Timothy O. Howe reminded the Senate that self-government is "government not of the strongest but of the greatest number." *Congressional Record*, 45th Cong., 2nd Sess., 2002.

38. James Redpath, A Letter to a Colored Mississippian, April 14, 1877, in Hayes Papers; Cleveland *Leader*, April 4, 1877; Columbus *Dispatch*, April 13, 1877; Cincinnati *Gazette*, April 20, 1877; *Harper's Weekly*, April 21, 1877. Most northern Republican editorials suggested that the removal of troops did not represent an abandonment of reconstruction but a surer way to fulfill it through state autonomy. Boston *Transcript*, April 11, 1877.

39. New York *Herald*, May 1, 1877; H. P. Baldwin to Schurz, April 6, 1877, in Schurz Papers; Chicago *Times* quoted in Washington *National Republican*, April 29, 1877. Horace V. Redfield observed: "surely, a ten years' trial is sufficient, and the people may be pardoned for the belief that the one way was not a success." HVR in Cincinnati *Commercial*, April 30, 1877.

40. New York *Tribune*, Chicago *Tribune*, both April 2, 1877.

41. Philadelphia *Times*, April 2, 1877; *Harper's Weekly*, June 23, 1877.

42. T. O. Howe to G. T. Howe, April 4, 1877, in Howe Papers; Reid to C. M. Walker, November 20, 1877, in Reid Papers; New York *Times*, March 2, 1881.

43. Cincinnati *Commercial*, May 12, June 3, 8, 10, 1877; New York *Tribune*, July 11, 1877; *Harper's Weekly*, June 23, 1877. For a penetrating dissection of the moral and political surrender of Hayes and the North, see Grace Greenwood in New York *Times*, April 7, May 5, 15, 26, June 2, 23, 1877; Akerman to Atkins, August 4, 1877, in Akerman Letterbooks, in possession of Joe A. Akerman, Jr. Although the Hayes administration did attempt to prosecute both election irregularities and political murders in Kemper County, the effort was unsuccessful. Also during the spring of 1877 the army was reorganized with a change of command in the South; the aggressive General Philip H. Sheridan was relieved of all southern responsibilities, which were given to more conservative General Winfield Scott Hancock. W. T. Sherman to McCrary, March 19, 1877, and W. T. Sherman to Augur, May 3, 1877, both in Letters Sent, Main Series, in RG 94, NA.

44. Grant to Daniel Ammen, August 28, 1877, in Daniel Ammen, *The Old Navy and the New* (Philadelphia: J. B. Lippincott, 1891), 537–38; *Harper's Weekly*, August 11, 1877; *Nation*, August 9, 30, 1877; Donaldson Memoirs, September 29, 1877; Cabinet-meeting notes, July 27, 1877, in Hayes Papers. Indeed Hayes defended his southern policy on the ground that he required troops in the North to control the strikers. HVR in Cincinnati *Commercial*, August 2, 1877.

45. Grant to Ammen, August 28, 1877, in Ammen, *The Old Navy and the New*, 538; W. B. Smith to W. E. Chandler, December 6, 1877, in W. E. Chandler Papers; New York *Times*, April 14, 1877.

46. Robert B. Elliott to J. Sherman, June 23, 1879, in J. Sherman Papers; Akerman to Ben, July 12, 1877, July 22, 1878, July 20, 1879, Akerman to James S. Hook, August 31, 1877, all in Akerman Letterbooks, in possession of Joe A. Akerman, Jr.; New York *Times*, April 23, 1877, June 30, 1879; John M. Harlan to Matthews in Matthews to Rogers, May 29, 1877, Diary, April 22, October 18, 24, 1877, copy of Hayes to Guy M. Bryan, March 28, 1880, all in Hayes Papers; J. M. Bynum to Blanche K. Bruce, November 21, 1877, in Blanche K. Bruce Papers, Rutherford B. Hayes Library, Fremont, Ohio; St. Louis *Globe-Democrat*, March 21, 1877; James L. Alcorn to Kenneth Rayner, February 6, 1878, in Kenneth Rayner Papers, University of North Carolina Library, Chapel Hill.

47. Akerman to V. M. Barnes, April 9, 1877, Akerman to Sloan, August 7, 1877, both in Akerman Letterbooks, in possession of Joe A. Akerman, Jr. A Georgia Negro complained that Hayes had only appointed southern blacks to menial positions and concluded: "Grant was more liberal to the Colored people and not quite so generous to democrats." Edwin Belcher to J. Sherman, October 7, 1879, June 29, 1880, L. C. Hook to J. Sherman, August 5, 1879, all in J. Sherman Papers.

48. C (Albion W. Tourgée) to Editor, Greensboro *New North State*, April 25, 1878; George M. Buchanan to J. Sherman, November 17, 1879, in J. Sherman Papers; Akerman to George W. Smith, November 9, 1877, Akerman to Sprague, July 14, 1877, both in Akerman Letterbooks, in possession of Joe A. Akerman, Jr.; Benjamin F. Butler to L. Stiger, March 23, 1878, Letterbooks, in Butler Papers; N. V. Robbins to Garfield, March 30, 1877, in Garfield Papers, LC; HVR in Cincinnati *Commercial*, February 4, 1878. One Georgia Republican noted that the "Democrats feel that they can use him and at the same time despise him as they do!" Helen D. Atkins to Garfield, April 5, 1877, in Garfield Papers, LC. It was estimated that one third of all federal appointments went to Democrats. Donaldson Memoirs, July 10, 1879. Senator Howe observed that if Hayes intended to lure the southern Democrats by patronage he should have done so wholesale. *Congressional Record*, 45th Cong., 2nd Sess., 2005; Philadelphia *Weekly Times*, April 3, 1880.

49. Garfield to Burke A. Hinsdale, September 10, 1877, July 25, 1880, Letterbooks, Samuel S. Sumner to Garfield, June 12, 1877, J. Q. A. Campbell to Garfield, March

15, 1878, Diary, March 1, 1878, all in Garfield Papers, LC; W. H. Mason to Hayes, October 15, 1877, Robert P. Kennedy to Hayes, October 20, 1877, both in Hayes Papers; Reid to Comly, October 17, 1877, in Comly Papers; New York *Times*, February 2, 1879; Hoogenboom, *Outlawing the Spoils*, 166, 176; Hawley to his wife, April 27, 1879, in Hawley Papers.

50. HVR in Cincinnati *Commercial*, September 18, July 4, 1877; New York *Tribune*, September 20, August 24, 1877.

51. Hayes quoted in New York *Tribune*, August 21, 1877.

52. *Ibid.*, September 24, 1877; compare Hayes's northern speeches in Cincinnati *Commercial*, September 8, 1877; and in Washington *National Republican*, September 15, 1877; for southern reaction, see Sue Harper Mims in Atlanta *Constitution*, January 25, 1914.

53. Diary, September, October 4, 1877, in Hayes Papers; Springfield *Republican*, September 20, 26, 1877; New York *Herald*, September 24, 1877; New York *Tribune*, September 26, 1877. One of Hayes's enthusiastic supporters believed that Hayes's tour had killed all opposition to his southern policy for all time. William Henry Smith to Edward F. Noyes, October 6, 1877, Letterbooks, in William Henry Smith Papers, Ohio Historical Society, Columbus.

54. John Coburn to John Marshall Harlan, September 16, 1877, in Harlan Papers; T. O. Howe to G. T. Howe, October 15, 1877, in Howe Papers; New York *Times*, September 17, 1877; Diary, October 26, 1877, in Garfield Papers, LC.

55. J. E. Rue to Garfield, 1877, in Garfield Papers, LC. Chandler later observed that Hayes in his Atlanta speech had "blotted out all distinctions between loyalty and treason, between Union and rebel soldiers, between the torturers of Andersonville and the veterans of the North." William E. Chandler, *Letters of Mr. William E. Chandler Relative to the So-called Southern Policy of President Hayes* (Concord, N.H.: Monitor and Statesman, 1878), 17; Marshall Jewell to Bristow, October 14, 1877, in Bristow Papers; R. B. Avery to Chandler, January 10, 1878, in W. E. Chandler Papers.

56. Hayes to William D. Bickham, May 3, 1877, Diary, November 3, 1877, both in Hayes Papers; New York *Tribune*, September 11, 1877; Donaldson Memoirs, May 19, October 17, 1877; Garfield to Reid, April 10, 1877, in Reid Papers; Jewell to Bristow, May 17, 1877, in Bristow Papers; Richardson (comp.), *Messages of the Presidents*, VII, 459–60; New York *Times*, New York *Herald*, New York *Tribune*, all December 4, 1877.

57. New York *Times*, May 6, 1877; William M. Robbins to S. J. Randall, May 19, 1877, in Randall Papers; St. Louis *Republican*, April 2, Akerman to Celia, June 7, 1877, Akerman to James S. Hook, August 31, September 11, 1877, all in Akerman Letterbooks, in possession of Joe A. Akerman, Jr.; William D. Dickson to Hayes, September, 1877, in Hayes Papers; HVR in Cincinnati *Commercial*, June 13, 24, 1877; St. Louis *Globe-Democrat*, April 30, 1877; EVS in New York *Tribune*, August 23, 1877; Marcus L. Ward to Horace N. Congar, July 17, 1877, in Congar Papers; William L. Garrison to Stacy, May 4, 1877, in Garrison Papers, Boston Public Library; Diary, October 13, 1877, in Garfield Papers, LC.

58. Springfield *Republican*, October 23, 1877; Cincinnati *Commercial*, November 24, 1877; *Nation*, May 3, 1877; Freeman Thorp to Garfield, April [23], 1877, in Garfield Papers, LC.

59. Despite the fact that other issues intruded, the elections were still highly suggestive. The New York *World*, December 10, 1877, estimated that in the fifteen states that held elections during 1877 there was a net Democratic gain of 109,000 votes.

60. New York *Times*, November 16, 1877; New Orleans *Louisianian*, November 3, 1877; Washington *National Republican*, November 7, 1877; Philadelphia *Press*,

November 9, 1877; Akerman to George W. Smith, November 9, 1877, in Akerman Letterbooks, in possession of Joe A. Akerman, Jr.

61. Warner Bateman to J. Sherman, October 11, 1877, in J. Sherman Papers; Kennedy to Hayes, October 20, 1877, in Hayes Papers; Edward Hayes to Garfield, July 23, 1877, Diary, October 8, 10, 1877 both in Garfield Papers, LC; New York *Herald*, October 11, November 7, 1877; New York *World*, October 11, 1877; New York *Times*, October 11, 13, 18, 1877; Charles Francis Adams Diary, October 10, 16, November 7, 1877, in Adams Family Papers; Butler to S. G. Wood, November 27, 1877, Letterbooks, in Butler Papers.

62. S. M. Boling to Garfield, November 18, 1877, in Garfield Papers, LC. Even after the election reverses, President Hayes evidently decided not to change his course. Senator Howe observed of a meeting of congressmen with Hayes; "it seemed pretty evident that the President is very confident he can revolutionize the South, if he can have free scope for his policy, and he is not at all convinced that his policy is not really popular in the North. But as yet he doesn't care to define it. He wants you to understand that his policy is to make Eight Republican States in the South in 1880, and whatever he may do he wants you to applaud, irrespective of what it is, but solely because of the fruits it is to yield in 1880. He is something of a fanatic and is surrounded by Jockeys." T. O. Howe to G. T. Howe, November 16, 1877, in Howe Papers; Diary, October 24, 1877, March 12, 21, April 13, October 1, December 25, 1878, in Hayes Papers; New York *Times*, December 24, 1877; Reid to W. E. Chandler, February 28, 1878, Letterbooks, in Reid Papers; Washington *Post*, January 7, 1878; Greensboro *New North State*, April 25, 1878.

63. Vincent P. De Santis, *Republicans Face the Southern Question—The New Departure Years, 1877–1897* (Baltimore: Johns Hopkins University Press, 1959), 99–101; New Orleans *Louisianian*, December 14, 1878; J. S. Bean to W. E. Chandler, December 31, 1877, in W. E. Chandler Papers. The New York *Times*, November 14, 1878, acknowledged the "indifference of Northern Republicans . . . their abandonment of the colored people" of the South.

64. One Washington correspondent reported that the election returns in 1878 "are uniformly interpreted here as forecasting a solid North against a solid South hereafter." Maxwell in Greensboro *New North State*, November 14, 7, 1878; Chicago *Times*, November 8–9, 1878; De Santis, *Republicans Face the Southern Question*, 101–103, 262. The Republican presidential vote in the South as a percentage of the total Republican presidential vote in the nation declined from 18 percent in 1876 to 15 percent in 1880 and was to fall below 10 percent after 1900. Similarly, the southern Republican presidential vote as a percentage of the total presidential vote of all parties within the South declined from 40 percent in 1876 to 37 percent in 1880—an historic low point. Before Hayes was inaugurated, there were eight southern black members of Congress; when Hayes left office, there were none. Subsequently, some southern Negroes were elected to Congress until 1901.

65. New York *Times*, November 7, 1878, June 30, 1879; HVR in Cincinnati *Commercial*, November 1, October 31, 1878; Washington *National Republican*, October 30, 1877; Springfield *Republican*, November 7, 1878; New York *Tribune*, August 20, November 6, 8, 1878; Henry B. Anthony to Justin S. Morrill, August 31, 1878, in Morrill Papers; Hampton to Lamar, September 12, 1879, in Lamar-Mayes Papers.

66. James G. Blaine to Chandler, September 27, 1878, in W. E. Chandler Papers; HVR in Cincinnati *Commercial*, November 1, May 25, 1878; Diary, November 6, 1878, in Garfield Papers, LC; Akerman to Margaret, November 14, 1878, in Akerman Letterbooks, in possession of Joe A. Akerman, Jr.

67. Hayes quoted in New York *Tribune*, November 13, 1878; New York *Times*, November 14, 1878; New Orleans *Louisianian*, December 1, 1877; Washington *Post*, November 15, 1878; HVR in Cincinnati *Commercial*, November 1, 1878. Despite

Hayes's statement, he contradicted it by his own words and by the continuation of his southern patronage policy. Hayes to Comly, October 29, 1878, in Comly Papers; Diary, October 5, 26, November 6, 12, 1878, compare December 4, 25, 1878, April 11, 1880, in Hayes Papers. Some of Hayes's associates in various ways for various reasons repudiated the southern policy or were themselves politically repudiated. J. Sherman to Bateman, November 16, 1878, in Bateman Papers; *Nation*, August 15, 1878.

68. E. Hinds to Garfield, November 18, 1878, in Garfield Papers, LC. In gingerly fashion Hayes, in his second annual message, alluded to disfranchisement of southern blacks; in his third annual message in 1879 he called for renewed federal election enforcement. Richardson (comp.), *Messages of the Presidents*, VII, 493–94, 560–61, 602, 523–47; New York *Times*, December 3, 1878; Diary, March 9–July 3, 1879, in Hayes Papers; *Nation*, February 13, April 3, 1879.

69. In the early years of the Hayes administration, federal election prosecution in the South, with certain exceptions, was not pressed. Such inaction prompted some Republicans to criticize the record. Garfield declared that the "policy of the President has turned out to be a giveaway"; Hayes "has nolled suits, discontinued prosecution" while southern Democrats were "whetting their knives for any Republican they could find." Garfield to Sheldon, February 12, 1878, Sheldon to Garfield, November 21, 1878, in Garfield Papers, LC; Hugh L. Bond to Morrison R. Waite, April 25, 1877, in Morrison R. Waite Papers, LC; Cincinnati *Commercial*, December 30, 1878; Lucius C. Northrop to Attorney General, April 23, 1879, District of South Carolina, Source Chronological Files, in RG 60, NA. The overall federal election enforcement effort between 1877 and 1880 was, as before, inadequately organized, supervised, staffed, and funded; the actual record of indictments and convictions in the southern states was poor, and federal prosecutions after 1878 in Alabama, Louisiana, and South Carolina were unsuccessful. Despite federal expenditures for marshals in some southern and border states, there was no discernible improvement in the conduct of elections. Robert M. Goldman, " 'A Free Ballot and a Fair Count': The Department of Justice and the Enforcement of Voting Rights in the South, 1877–1893" (Ph.D. dissertation, Michigan State University, 1976), 80–130. If President Hayes was serious about enforcement in the South, his thought of possibly appointing a Virginia conservative as attorney general did not suggest it. However, vital federal interest in, and major expenditures for, election enforcement in northern cities continued, as President Hayes acknowledged. Diary, December 4, 1878, March 31, April 7, 1879, in Hayes Papers.

70. *Nation*, March 6, 1879.

71. *Congressional Record*, 46th Cong., 1st Sess., 548, 415; Diary, January 23, 1879, Garfield to Hinsdale, December 20, 1878, Hinsdale to Garfield, December 17, 1878, May 7, 1881, all in Garfield Papers, LC. The party line was later summed up, with considerable truth, by Republican Senator Joseph R. Hawley when he characterized the Democratic party as a "motley compound of all the don'ts, won'ts, shan'ts, hates, prejudices . . . of the times." Hawley to George W. Curtis, March 3, 1884, in George W. Curtis Papers, Rutherford B. Hayes Library, Fremont, Ohio.

72. *Nation*, September 2, 1880, May 8, 1879. Historian H. Wayne Morgan, in *From Hayes to McKinley: National Party Politics, 1877–1896* (Syracuse, N.Y.: Syracuse University Press, 1969), 537–38, persuasively contends that some historians have overemphasized the political importance of, and popular concern with, reconstruction rights during the 1880s.

73. Democratic Senator Wade Hampton observed that the object of the Republicans was to "provoke sectional debates." Hampton to Theodore G. Barker, January 29, 1891, in Hampton Family Papers. But one Massachusetts man was prophetic when he wrote: "I thank God for the 15th Amendment. It cannot be annulled *always*. The power is vested and will sooner or later be fully exercised." Erastus B. Williamson

to George F. Hoar, March 20, 1890, in Hoar Papers. Similarly, Amos T. Akerman of Georgia believed that some day a future generation would have to resolve the contradiction "that denies practically rights which are recognized theoretically." Akerman to Charles N. Bell, April 23, 1879, in Akerman Letterbooks, in possession of Joe A. Akerman, Jr.

74. The Democrats won control of the House of Representatives in 1874, lost it in 1880, won it again in 1882, lost it in 1888, and regained it in 1890; the Republicans lost their hold on the Senate only once, between 1879 and 1881, but their usual majority between 1876 and 1890 was small. New York *Times*, April 21, 1877.

75. Charles Eliot Norton to James Russell Lowell, August 4, 1878, in Norton Papers; New York *Tribune*, December 4, 1877. Hayes was indeed a paradox; he could be both activist and passive, both forceful, frank, and direct, and evasive, cautious, indirect; he was so friendly, convivial, accessible, yet so cool, reticent, private. He was for his time both unconventional and conventional, liberal and conservative, generous and firm, infinitely flexible and very stubborn, utterly idealistic at one moment and ruthlessly pragmatic and single-minded in another. He was both sincere and devious, saintlike and Machiavellian. Philadelphia *Weekly Times*, March 24, 1877; Boston *Herald*, March 11, 1877; for references to certain psychological-political tendencies, the passive-positive and the active-negative, see Barber, *The Presidential Character*, 12–13.

76. Diary, September 24, 1876, in Hayes Papers; New York *Tribune*, March 3, 1877; New York *Times*, January 5, 1878. Congressman Garfield observed that Hayes "has that worst infirmity, the fear of being influenced by men of his own party who are larger than he. The result is that he shuts himself up, and does not avail himself of the help which every President needs." Garfield to Harmon A. Austin, March 3, 1878, in Garfield Papers, LC; Diary, October, 24, 1877, March 12, 1878, in Hayes Papers; New York *Times*, April 8, 1878.

77. Diary, March 12, 1878, in Hayes Papers; for Hayes's aphorism, "he serves his party best who serves the country best," see Richardson (comp.), *Messages of the Presidents*, VII, 445; W. H. McDevitt to Key, March 13, 1877, in Key Papers; Donaldson Memoirs, May 1, 1879.

78. President Hayes in embracing Liberal and British notions of party assumed that overriding principles and paramount questions of policy were supposed to define party and enable it to develop along such lines. Thus Hayes assumed a party to be plastic and malleable, so that a president could mold it as he pleased, and the party could be easily manufactured with majorities made and coalitions formed. New York *Times*, April 8, 1877; E. B. Wight to William W. Clapp, March 26, 1877, in Clapp Papers. The Philadelphia *Times*, April 27, 1877, shared this view when it declared that Hayes would divide Congress "by the lines of its integrity and statesmanship rather than by the lines of power" and existing parties. When party realignment appeared increasingly unlikely the Philadelphia *Times*, June 29, 1877, stated its view that Hayes's strength "lies with the people, not with the politicians." The contrary view was stated by the New York *Times*, October 29, 1877, when it noted that Hayes hugged the "delusion that parties no longer represent the people." Senator Roscoe Conkling added: "Administrations do not make parties. Parties make administrations, go before administrations and live after them." Roscoe Conkling quoted in New York *Times*, September 27, 1877. And a disgruntled Alabama Republican wrote to Hayes: " 'He who serves his country best serves his party best.' " J. T. Harris to Hayes, April 6, 1877, in Hayes Papers.

79. Grant to Ammen, March 25, 1878, in Ammen, *The Old Navy and the New*, 541; Grant to Hamilton Fish, September 9, 1877, in Fish Papers, LC; New York *Herald*, December 31, 1877; HVR in Cincinnati *Commercial*, February 18, 1878.

80. Garfield to Hinsdale, September 10, 1877, in Garfield Papers, LC; New York *Times*, February 2, 1879.

81. John J. Ingalls to Elias T. Ingalls, December 16, [1879], in Ingalls Papers; Eugene Casserly to Thomas F. Bayard, October 22, 1877, in T. F. Bayard Papers; Conkling to Hawley, August 27, 1877, in Conkling Papers.

82. Congar to Hayes, October 19, 1877, in Hayes Papers; Akerman to George W. Smith, November 9, 1877, in Akerman Letterbooks, in possession of Joe A. Akerman, Jr.; John Shackleford to Garfield, February 25, 1878, in Garfield Papers, LC.

83. Akerman to Margaret, November 14, 1878, in Akerman Letterbooks, in possession of Joe A. Akerman, Jr.; Baltimore *Gazette* quoted in New York *World*, March 14, 1877; Diary, March 27, 1877, in Garfield Papers, LC.

84. Hayes quoted in New York *Times*, August 9, 1867; for his reluctant admission that the supremacy of the "States, and an oligarchy of race" existed in the South, see Hayes quoted in New York *Tribune*, September 18, 1879; Akerman to Ben, May 26, 1878, in Akerman Letterbooks, in possession of Joe A. Akerman, Jr.; Chicago *Inter-Ocean*, April 4, 1877; Albion W. Tourgée to Dr. Sutherland, April 15, 1877, in Tourgée Papers; HVR in Cincinnati *Commercial*, May 10, 1877; St. Louis *Globe-Democrat*, March 31, 1877; Samuel B. McLin to Noyes in Noyes to Hayes, May 7, 1877, and compare copy of Hayes to W. A. Short, January 9, 1868, both in Hayes Papers.

CHAPTER 15

1. *Atlantic Monthly*, LXXXVII (April, 1901), 484.

2. Justin S. Morrill to Charles Sumner, September, 1870, in Morrill Papers; S. M. Freeland to Charles Sumner, March 21, 1871, in Sumner Papers; William T. Sherman to David F. Boyd, July 1, 1871, in Boyd Papers.

3. New York *Tribune*, January 8, 1874.

4. Albion W. Tourgée, "Root, Hog, or Die," [1875], Scrapbook, in Tourgée Papers; W. T. Sherman to Boyd, April 21, 1871, in Boyd Papers.

5. Frederick Douglass observed: "Liberty came to them [freedmen], not in mercy, but in wrath; not by moral choice, but by military necessity; not by the people among whom the Freedmen were to live and whose good will was essential to the success of the measure; but by a people regarded as strangers and foreigners, invaders and trespassers, aliens and enemies. The very manner of their emancipation naturally invited to the head of the Freedmen the bitterest hostility. They were hated because they were free, and hated because of those who had freed them." Speech of Frederick Douglass at Elmira, August 1, 1880, in Douglass Papers.

6. Elias Nigh to John Sherman, September 2, 1867, in J. Sherman Papers.

7. The negative emphasis continued to the end of reconstruction. Before the troops were withdrawn from the last two southern statehouses, *Nation*, April 5, 1877, declared: "The negro will disappear from the field of national politics. Henceforth the nation, as a nation, will have nothing more to do with him."

8. Washington *National Republican*, September 7, 1876. General Sherman observed: "You hear of negro equality here, a negro senator etc., but I feel no social change." W. T. Sherman to Boyd, April 24, 1870, in Boyd Papers.

9. Amos T. Akerman to J. Sherman, June 17, 1876, in Akerman Letterbooks.

10. *Leslie's Newspaper*, January 30, 1875; Edward Dicey in London *Fortnightly Review*, December, 1874.

11. New York *Evening Post*, August 3, 1876; *Nation*, May 24, 1877.

12. *Nation*, September 6, 1877, commented that it was a "hideous mistake to suppose that anything but social progress can give him political value."

13. HVR in Cincinnati *Commercial*, March 31, 1876, March 26, 1877.

14. Richmond *Dispatch*, December 21, 1876; New York *Evening Post*, March 21, 1877. The Democratic St. Louis *Republican*, March 22, 1877, observed that "all the laws in the world cannot repeal the edicts of nature." The independent Republican

Springfield *Republican*, March 19, 1877, observed that "federal protection of the negro is a delusion. . . . no remedy whatever exists against moral intimidation and caste prejudices." One New Yorker granted that the freedman needed guardianship "but the U. S. Government cannot undertake the job," and he continued: "Concede the very worst, that the blacks are about to descend into political servitude. What of it? I say that every community develops its ruling caste." Thomas K. Beecher to James G. Blaine, April 9, 1877, in Blaine Papers.

15. Chicago *Times*, October 13, 1876; Philadelphia *Weekly Times*, August 4, 1877; Benjamin F. Butler to Joseph Hallowell, April 6, 1877, Letterbooks, in Butler Papers.

16. New York *Times*, August 6, 1872.

17. Zachariah Chandler to Benj. Leas, September 14, 1874, Letterbook, in Z. Chandler Papers; New York *Times*, January 26, 1876.

18. Chicago *Inter-Ocean*, September 13, 1876; *Nation*, April 26, 1877. Suggestive of the northern priority was the statement of one prominent New Yorker: "One of the most cherished of our party principles is justice to the black man of the South. Your speech formulates the still more incisive principle of justice to the white man of the North." John Cochrane to Blaine, December 17, 1878, in Blaine Papers.

19. Washington *National Republican*, January 24, 1874.

20. New York *Times*, April 21, 1877. Indeed the loss could be turned to advantage, for, according to the Republican St. Louis *Globe-Democrat*, April 23, 1877, instead of losing strength, the northern party "merely parted with a source of weakness, erased a blot on its record, bettered its condition in every way." And an Illinois Republican pointed out to President Hayes: "If we can carry the day [win control of Congress] without the aid of the Southern States it will be far better for the party. I have always thought those States were in a bad state of affairs and they have no honor in politics whatever and by weeding them out and securing by the Educated and enlightened masses in the North our party will be in a more healthy condition a stronger and surer basis. The *North* needs looking after and the party builded up more than the South." W. H. Mason to Rutherford B. Hayes, December 11, 1877, in Hayes Papers.

21. Edward Dicey in London *Fortnightly Review*, December, 1874; Tourgée, *A Fool's Errand*, 151–54.

22. H. R. Ware to Hayes, November 30, 1876 in Hayes Papers. Depressed by the outcome in South Carolina and the South, Governor Chamberlain noted: "I see no present hope for the colored race here. It would have been better if they had never had the ballot." Daniel H. Chamberlain to Frank J. Garrison, April 8, 1877, in Garrison Papers, Boston Public Library.

23. Grant's views summarized in Diary, January 17, 1877, in Fish Papers, LC. The Democratic St. Louis *Republican*, March 22, 1877, observed: "The Fifteenth amendment was made the pivot upon which reconstruction turned. . . . The pivot of reconstruction broke off at the first trial." The Springfield *Republican*, March 19, 1877, believed that blacks were "unfit in general for the wise exercise of the ballot, blind to the just demands of a manly citizenship." The same newspaper, April 14, 1877, later sounded an even deeper note of disillusionment: "When one recalls the glowing prophecies of a decade ago as to what wonders the ballot was to work for the freedman, and then reflects upon the actual results, it is natural that there should be bitter disappointment and gloomy foreboding. . . . The simple fact is, that we expected the impossible. The whole reconstruction policy was full of absurdities that seem now so plain the only wonder is we could not have seen them ten years ago."

24. D. P. Lowe to Warner M. Bateman, October 5, 1877, in Bateman Papers. The Republican Philadelphia *Press*, March 28, 1877, declared that the nation was "weary of sectional agitations and sectional issues."

25. John H. Hammond to Philip H. Sheridan, January 7, 1875, John H. Hammond

Letter, Louisiana State University Library, Baton Rouge; Akerman to his brother, February 19, 1877, Akerman to Sprague, February 7, 1877, Akerman to Mrs. H. Felton, December 21, 1878, all in Akerman Letterbooks, in possession of Joe A. Akerman, Jr. Another Georgian Republican observed: "there is no such thing as good faith among the baffled, desperate leaders of the Southern Democrats. One will make a promise with the distinct understanding that his associates are to break it, and allow him to outwardly condemn them for so doing, without any loss of standing among such associates. No conciliation is possible; it must be *conquer or be conquered.*" James Atkins to James A. Garfield, February 12, 1878, in Garfield Papers, LC.

26. Akerman quoted in New York *Times*, June 30, 1879. Akerman observed that "when speaking in obscure places, in the absence of reporters, the gentlemen who made Democratic speeches in the South often let out their sentiments more freely than in places where their utterances are more likely to get into print. . . . nothing but the fear of damaging their party at the North prevents them from expressing every where the sentiments." Akerman to S. N. Clark, August 11, 1879, in Akerman Letterbooks, in possession of Joe A. Akerman, Jr.

27. Hugh L. Bond to Anna Bond, October 16, 1872, in Bond Papers; J. Birney Work to Garfield, December 16, 1876, in Garfield Papers, LC.

28. George S. Boutwell to Whitelaw Reid, August 19, 1876, in Reid Papers; Charles Whittlesey to Garfield, March 13, 1877, in Garfield Papers, LC; HVR in Cincinnati *Commercial*, November 5, 1878. Akerman also noted that the South "yields to fear but not to persuasion." Akerman to Margaret, November 14, 1878, in Akerman Letterbooks, in possession of Joe A. Akerman, Jr. For mention of the earlier alternative approaches to reconstruction, see C (Tourgée) to Editor, Greensboro *New North State*, April 28, 1878.

29. St. Louis *Globe-Democrat*, March 31, 1877; Akerman to William B. Woods, July 30, 1878, in Akerman Letterbooks, in possession of Joe A. Akerman, Jr. The New York *Times*, April 21, 1877, noted that the controversy over reconstruction had been "so long continued that the public are tired of it. They are glad to be rid of it in almost any way." For the southern Democrats' objective, see Robert M. T. Hunter to James M. Mason, February 14, 1871, in Hunter Papers.

30. The New York *Times*, April 21, 1877, commented that the essentials of the reconstruction measures were left "at the mercy of the enemies of reconstruction." The St. Louis *Globe-Democrat*, April 27, 1877, observed that the southern Negro now had "no rights except such as the white people of the South choose to allow him."

31. HVR in Cincinnati *Commercial*, March 4, 1878. Estimates varied as to the increased number of southern congressional seats and electoral votes, depending on whether both the southern and the border states were counted together. The New York *Times*, November 8, 1878, estimated at least twenty-three. Senator James G. Blaine figured thirty-five. *Congressional Record*, 45th Cong., 3rd Sess., 84. Horace V. Redfield calculated about forty. HVR in Cincinnati *Commercial*, November 15, 1877; Augusta *Chronicle and Sentinel*, April 19, 1877. Redfield wrote that the Democratic control of the House of Representatives was a "shot-gun, rifle and red-shirt majority." HVR in Cincinnati *Commercial*, November 14, 1878.

32. Joseph R. Hawley to George W. Curtis, March 3, 1884, in Curtis Papers, Hayes Library.

33. Gath in Philadelphia *Weekly Times*, March 24, 1877; Boston *Transcript*, April 13, 1877. To be sure, the abolition of slavery, the Confederate regime, and its debt, as well as the beginning of significant industrialization, urbanization, and public education did indeed mark major new departments for the South. And if the South did gain mastery over race relations and regional governance, the North secured control of the federal government and national economic policy.

BIBLIOGRAPHICAL ESSAY

MANUSCRIPT collections vary enormously in quantity, quality, chronological concentration, and subject matter; and many important figures left no single significant collection of manuscripts to aid the historian in assessing public policy and party politics. That was particularly true of Ulysses S. Grant, and the dearth of Grant manuscripts is all the more disappointing in that President Grant did write pungent political letters, yet was a puzzle to his contemporaries and has remained so to political historians.

Manuscript and archival research was undertaken for twelve years in forty states within 130 repositories in which 500 collections were examined; 187 collections from 58 repositories in twenty-seven states are cited in the notes. The manuscript collections I found most valuable were the Records of the Department of Justice, Record Group 60 (National Archives), the James A. Garfield Papers (Library of Congress), the Rutherford B. Hayes Papers (Rutherford B. Hayes Library, Fremont, Ohio), the William E. Chandler Papers (Library of Congress), and the Amos T. Akerman Letterbooks (in the possession of Joe A. Akerman, Jr., Madison, Florida).

Two very useful collections on Republican politics in the postwar period up until 1870 were the Chandler Papers and the Marcus L. Ward Papers (New Jersey Historical Society, Newark). The archives of the Department of Justice were the foundation for the study of federal election enforcement, but I also found the Akerman Letterbooks (University of Virginia Library, Charlottesville), the Thomas F. Bayard Papers (Library of Congress), and the Garfield Papers most fruitful. The latter collection is also the most illuminating on the presidential election of 1872. For charting President Grant's southern policy, the Records of the Office of the Adjutant General, Record Group 94, and those of the Department of Justice (both in the National Archives), as well as the Garfield Papers, the Hamilton Fish Papers, the Benjamin H. Bristow Papers, and the Ulysses S. Grant Papers (all in the Library of Congress) were invaluable. For an understanding of political developments concerning certain southern states during the 1870s, I was helped greatly by the following collections: on Virginia, the McGill Family Papers (University of Virginia Library); on North Carolina, the William W. Holden Papers (Duke University Library, Durham, North Carolina); on Louisiana, the Chandler Papers and the Philip H. Sheridan Papers (Library of Congress); and on Mississippi, the Ames Family Papers (Smith College Women's History Archive, Northampton, Massachusetts), the Adelbert Ames Papers (Mississippi State Archives, Jackson), and the Edwards Pierrepont Papers (Yale University Library, New Haven, Connecticut).

On the struggle over civil rights and the congressional election of 1874, the Elihu B. Washburne Papers, the Garfield Papers, and the Stevenson Family Papers (all in the Library of Congress) shed the most light; the Benjamin F. Butler Papers (Library of Congress) were most helpful on the passage of the Civil Rights Act of 1875. The fight in Congress over the so-called "force" bill during 1875 was clarified by the Bayard Papers and the Manton Marble Papers (Library of Congress). The most fruitful collections for the presidential election of 1876 and the electoral crisis were the Hayes Papers and the Samuel J. Randall Papers (University of Pennsylvania Library, Philadelphia). The most outstanding group of manuscripts concerning the southern policy of President Hayes are the Hayes Papers, the Garfield Papers, and the Akerman Letterbooks (owned by Joe A. Akerman, Jr.), but also important were the Timothy O. Howe Papers (Wisconsin State Historical Society, Madison), the John Sherman Papers (Library of Congress), and the Chandler Papers.

About two hundred newspapers and periodicals were also examined; one hundred of them from thirty states and Great Britain are cited in the notes. I found that newspapers and periodicals between the years 1866 and 1879 were significant sources, for they contain a wealth of information and interpretation. Although many of them were wholly partisan and mediocre, numerous others proved to be perceptive in their reports and judgments. It also needs to be noted that both editorial views and political positions of diverse correspondents varied considerably not only in independent and somewhat independent publications but also in partisan journals. Given that fact, it frequently would be misleading to typecast a newspaper at a particular time. And, in addition, highly suggestive of shifting attitudes was the general change in opinion in a single source over a period of time. Furthermore, many reporters managed to obtain invaluable interviews, and the correspondents in Washington and in various trouble spots were frequently well informed. Of particular value to me were those reports written by E. Hudson of the Boston *Herald*, Benjamin Perley Poore of the Boston *Journal*, Horace V. Redfield and "Raymonde" of the Cincinnati *Commercial*, George A. Townsend of the Cincinnati *Enquirer*, Henry Van Ness Boynton of the Cincinnati *Gazette*, Mary Clemmer Ames and "DWB" of the *Independent* (New York, N.Y.), Charles Nordhoff of the New York *Herald*, Sarah J. Lippincott of the New York *Times*, Eugene V. Smalley and T. B. White of the New York *Tribune*, Moses P. Handy and "Shirley" of the Philadelphia *Times*, and David W. Bartlett and Samuel Bowles of the Springfield *Republican*.

The two newspapers that proved to be of prime importance for this study were the New York *Times* and the Cincinnati *Commercial*, but also valuable were the New York *Herald*, the New York *Tribune*, the Washington *National Republican*, the Springfield *Republican*, the New York *World*, the Chicago

Times, the *Nation* (New York, N.Y.), *Harper's Weekly* (New York, N.Y.), the Louisville *Courier-Journal*, the New York *Evening Post*, the Chicago *Inter-Ocean*, and the *Independent*. Other useful publications included the St. Louis *Republican*, the Philadelphia *Times*, the *National Anti-Slavery Standard* (New York, N.Y.), and the Washington *New National Era*. Such sources are essential for an understanding of political history, despite all the frustrating duplication and the arduous, time-consuming nature of newspaper research.

My notes constitute a guide to the greater variety of my sources, but in the cause of brevity, I had not only to condense but to make a representative selection of both primary and secondary sources. For those readers who wish to consult the secondary accounts of the postwar period in all its aspects, see the best guide to the vast literature—the comprehensive, critical, and incisive bibliography in J. G. Randall's and David Herbert Donald's, *The Civil War and Reconstruction* (2nd ed. rev., Lexington, Mass.: D.C. Heath, 1969), 703–834. For wartime reconstruction, see Herman Belz, *Reconstructing the Union: Theory and Policy During the Civil War* (Ithaca: Cornell University Press, 1969). Recently published works that cover various facets of the early postwar period are: David Herbert Donald, *The Politics of Reconstruction, 1863–1867* (Baton Rouge: Louisiana State University Press, 1965); John Hope Franklin, *Reconstruction: After the Civil War* (Chicago: University of Chicago Press, 1961); Rembert W. Patrick, *The Reconstruction of the Nation* (New York: Oxford University Press, 1967); Kenneth M. Stampp, *The Era of Reconstruction, 1865–1877* (New York: Alfred A. Knopf, 1965); Hans L. Trefousse, *The Radical Republicans: Lincoln's Vanguard for Racial Justice* (New York: Alfred A. Knopf, 1969); Hans L. Trefousse, *Impeachment of a President: Andrew Johnson, the Blacks, and Reconstruction* (Knoxville: University of Tennessee Press, 1975); Ward E. Y. Elliott, *The Rise of Guardian Democracy: The Supreme Court's Role in Voting Rights Disputes, 1845–1969* (Cambridge: Harvard University Press, 1974); Charles Fairman, *Reconstruction and Reunion, 1864–1888: Part One* (New York: Macmillan, 1971); Harold M. Hyman, *A More Perfect Union: The Impact of the Civil War and Reconstruction on the Constitution* (New York: Alfred A. Knopf, 1973); Stanley I. Kutler, *Judicial Power and Reconstruction Politics* (Chicago: University of Chicago Press, 1968); as well as George M. Fredrickson, *The Black Image in the White Mind: The Debate on Afro-American Character and Destiny, 1817–1914* (New York: Harper & Row, 1971); James M. McPherson, *The Struggle for Equality: Abolitionists and the Negro in the Civil War and Reconstruction* (Princeton: Princeton University Press, 1964); C. Vann Woodward, *The Burden of Southern History* (Baton Rouge: Louisiana State University Press, 1968); and C. Vann Woodward, *American Counterpoint: Slavery and Racism in the North-South Dialogue* (Boston: Little, Brown, 1971).

The following are valuable recent studies of political reconstruction between 1865 and 1868: Michael Les Benedict, *A Compromise of Principle: Congressional Republicans and Reconstruction, 1865–1869* (New York: W. W. Norton, 1974); W. R. Brock, *An American Crisis: Congress and Reconstruction, 1865–1867* (London: Macmillan, 1963); La Wanda Cox and John H. Cox, *Politics, Principle, and Prejudice, 1865–1866: Dilemma of Reconstruction America* (New York: Free Press, 1963); Eric L. McKitrick, *Andrew Johnson and Reconstruction* (Chicago: University of Chicago Press, 1960); and Michael Perman, *Reunion Without Compromise: The South and Reconstruction, 1865–1868* (Cambridge, England: Cambridge University Press, 1973). Modern works that first emphasized the importance of the off-year elections of 1867 are Richard Nelson Current, *Old Thad Stevens, A Story of Ambition* (Madison: University of Wisconsin Press, 1942); and Selden Henry, "Radical Republican Policy Toward the Negro During Reconstruction, 1862–1872" (Ph.D. dissertation, Yale University, 1963). In this selective bibliographical essay I have commented only upon secondary accounts that have a direct and significant bearing on the course of, and the reasons for, retreat from reconstruction during the 1870s.

Although restricted in subject matter and chronology, the only detailed, historical analysis of the framing of the Fifteenth Amendment and the political undercurrents of the national enfranchisement of the Negro is given in William Gillette's *The Right to Vote: Politics and the Passage of the Fifteenth Amendment* (Rev. and expanded ed.; Baltimore: Johns Hopkins University Press, 1969). For a critical appraisal of this work, see La Wanda Cox and John H. Cox, "Negro Suffrage and Republican Politics: The Problem of Motivation in Reconstruction Historiography," *Journal of Southern History*, XXXIII (1967), 303–30. Specifically, an investigation of the motives and purposes of the framers and ratifiers of the Fifteenth Amendment must necessarily focus on matters that *they thought* to be important, regardless of whether the assumed political gains were realistic or exaggerated by the politicians in 1869, regardless of whether such gains were achieved or not. Moreover, the intent of the proposed amendment may be found in the congressional records, but the *understanding* of the proposed amendment and of that intent is revealed equally in the state legislatures that acted on the amendment. Also, studies published since 1967 cast the gravest doubt on the primacy of the idealistic motivation of northern Republican politicians; specifically, the contention that the risk of a white, anti-Republican backlash was so great that only sheer idealistic determination could have induced the Republicans to support the Fifteenth Amendment is just too speculative and runs counter to historical evidence. Finally, political expedience as a force in the framing of the Fifteenth Amendment was essential, for had there been no motivation to gain power and to increase it, and had black suffrage not been identified with partisan advantage as well as the preservation of the party, there would have been no Fifteenth Amendment at all. And since it was the politicians who were responsible for framing and securing the suffrage amendment, it would seem eminently clear that political motives and methods were largely responsible for having shaped both the process and the outcome. And for my detailed rejoinder, see the 1969 edition of *The Right to Vote*, 166–90.

The best and most thorough work on the early neutralization of Negro voting in the South is Allen W. Trelease's *White Terror: The Ku Klux Klan Conspiracy and Southern Reconstruction* (New York: Harper and Row, 1971); however, Trelease ends the story of political terrorism in the South during the early 1870s, before terrorism in fact burgeoned—that is, after 1872. A scholarly account of the army's role in the enforcement effort is given in a single-chapter treatment of James E. Sefton's *The United States Army and Reconstruction, 1865–1877* (Baton Rouge: Louisiana State University Press, 1967), 213–35. But since Sefton concentrates only on the late 1860s, there is need for a detailed analysis of the army in the South during the 1870s.

Five studies of federal election enforcement exist, and each is helpful in one way or another. However, not one of them attempts to show the federal enforcement effort against the larger background of national reconstruction and northern politics. One of them is William W. Davis' "The Federal Enforcement Acts," in James W. Garner (ed.), *Studies in Southern History and Politics Inscribed to William Archibald Dunning . . . by His Former Pupils the Authors* (New York: Columbia University Press, 1914), 205–28, an essay that is limited in scope, outmoded in outlook, and inadequately researched, but valuable in its assessment of the various difficulties that beset enforcement. Indeed, its findings are similar to the conclusions that have been drawn in a more recent survey of those difficulties by Everette Swinney in his "Enforcing the Fifteenth Amendment, 1870–1877," *Journal of Southern History*, XXVIII (1962), 202–18. As a counterpoise to Davis' Dunningite interpretation, revisionist Swinney's article is useful, compact, and enriched by archival research. However, the essay is marred by a singular lack of analysis, and by the author's claim that the enforcement effort was relatively successful in the early 1870s, whereas he in fact concentrates on the failures of enforcement; his essay also attempts to show that the enforcement acts were soundly and correctly drafted, despite the fact that there was little substantiation of that opinion at that time; indeed, it was not even held by a majority of the Supreme Court. In fact, enforcement was neither dictatorial as the Dunningites maintain nor as effective as some revisionists contend. Another essay on enforcement may be found in Homer Cummings and Carl McFarland's *Federal Justice: Chapters in the History of Justice and the Federal Executive* (New York: Macmillan, 1937), 230–49, which is a pioneering work, given the authors' use of Department of Justice communications to its officials in the field; however, the chapter does not include any commentary on the politics of enforcement.

Broader in scope and more penetrating in analysis is Robert A. Horn's "National Control of Congressional Elections" (Ph.D. dissertation, Princeton University, 1942), which sheds light on the political importance of the North concerning federal election enforcement. However, Horn's dissertation fails to recognize the significance of black enfranchisement in the North by the Fifteenth Amendment. A more recent study by Albie Burke, "Federal Regulation of Congressional Elections in Northern Cities, 1871–1894" (Ph.D. dissertation, University of Chicago, 1968), substantiates Horn's earlier thesis and at the same time supplements his research with a detailed archival investigation of federal enforcement in the North. However, Burke's dissertation does identify preventive regulatory legislation exclusively with northern city elections, which was not the case, and considers preventive legislation solely in relation to the third enforcement act, when in fact it was evident in other enforcement acts. His work is also misleading in its assumption that the problems and issues of reconstruction were exclusively limited to the South; he thus neglects the national and northern political dimensions of

443

reconstruction that helped to shape its outcome in the South. Clearly, a detailed study of administration in the Department of Justice during the 1870s is sorely needed, as are biographies of three attorneys general: Amos T. Akerman, George H. Williams, and Edwards Pierrepont.

On the political history of Ulysses S. Grant's administration, quantity exceeds quality. The accounts of James Ford Rhodes, *History of the United States from the Compromise of 1850 to the McKinley-Bryan Campaign of 1896* (8 vols.; New York: Macmillan, 1904–1920), and Ellis Paxson Oberholtzer, *A History of the United States Since the Civil War* (5 vols.; New York: Macmillan, 1917–1937) are dated and biased. In addition, three books, all in the same biographical series, must be taken into account: William B. Hesseltine's *Ulysses S. Grant, Politician* (New York: Dodd, Mead, 1935); Allan Nevins' *Hamilton Fish: The Inner History of the Grant Administration* (New York: Dodd, Mead, 1936); and Leon Burr Richardson's *William E. Chandler, Republican* (New York: Dodd, Mead, 1940). All of them are solid, competent biographies, though they do not have especially penetrating analyses, are frequently superficial in research and treatment, and are somewhat dated. One recent contribution to the subject is David Herbert Donald's incisive essay "The Republican Party, 1864–1876," in Arthur M. Schlesinger, Jr. (ed.), *History of U.S. Political Parties* (New York: Chelsea House, 1973), 1281–94. On the whole, studies of President Grant seem to run to extremes, being either undercritical or overcritical, so that a detailed, balanced political biography of Grant as president would be extremely welcome. So, indeed, would a comprehensive work on Congress during the 1870s. There is also a dearth of modern biographies of such figures as James G. Blaine, Samuel Bowles, Joseph P. Bradley, Benjamin F. Butler (in the postwar years), Salmon P. Chase, Jacob D. Cox, Henry L. Dawes, Oliver P. Morton, and John Sherman.

Historians have long neglected the Democratic party during the 1870s, and biographies are generally thin. Thus there is a call for competent studies of the party during the period and biographies of Samuel J. Randall and Michael C. Kerr, among others. However, two major, recent works on the party during the 1870s are Keith I. Polakoff's "The Disorganized Democracy: An Institutional Study of the Democratic Party, 1872–1880" (Ph.D. dissertation, Northwestern University, 1968), and Lawrence Grossman's "The Democratic Party and the Negro: A Study in Northern and National Politics, 1868–1892" (Ph.D. dissertation, City University of New York, 1973). Both are comprehensive studies, resourceful in research and useful in detailed description; but both dissertations skirt important developments, for example, the character of Greeley's campaigning in 1872 and the nature of the 1874 elections. Grossman's study has a narrower focus of interest but covers a longer period of time, and its analysis is penetrating; however, his thesis of the increasing moderation of the Democracy during the 1870s is oversimplified and overemphasized. In Grossman's subsequent book, *The Democratic Party and the Negro: Northern and National Politics, 1868–1892* (Urbana: University of Illinois Press, 1976), he so reduced the coverage of the 1870s that his dissertation actually has greater value than his book on that period.

On the Liberals, the works are extensive and of high quality. For a general background two excellent studies are Ari A. Hoogenboom's *Outlawing the*

Spoils: A History of the Civil Service Reform Movement, 1865–1883 (Urbana: University of Illinois Press, 1961), and David Herbert Donald's *Charles Sumner and the Rights of Man* (New York: Alfred A. Knopf, 1970). On the Liberal reform movement, the most important early work is Earle Dudley Ross's *The Liberal Republican Movement* (New York: Henry Holt, 1919), but it is outmoded, uncritical, and narrow in approach. On the origins of reform, with emphasis on the role of the intelligentsia prior to 1872, see Matthew T. Downey's "The Rebirth of Reform: A Study of Liberal Reform Movements, 1865–1872" (Ph.D. dissertation, Princeton University, 1963). Comprehensive in scope and critical in interpretation is John G. Sproat's *"The Best Men": Liberal Reformers in the Gilded Age* (New York: Oxford University Press, 1968), which traces the Liberals and their activities between the 1860s and the 1890s; and despite some problems in organization, Sproat does a fine job of dissecting the Liberals. Yet another thorough and critical work, this one concentrating on the politics of the Liberal movement, is Jacqueline B. Tusa's "Power, Priorities, and Political Insurgency: The Liberal Republican Movement, 1869–1872" (Ph.D. dissertation, Pennsylvania State University, 1970).

Two worthy accounts of the Liberal convention at Cincinnati are Matthew T. Downey's "Horace Greeley and the Politicians: The Liberal Republican Convention in 1872," *Journal of American History*, LIII (1967), 727–50, which effectively demolishes the stereotyped argument that Greeley's nomination was due to the success of conspiring professional politicians in undercutting reformers (the article unfortunately goes on to defend the delegates and the wisdom of their final choice); and James G. Smart's "Whitelaw Reid and the Nomination of Horace Greeley," *Mid-America*, XLIX (1967), 227–43, which fruitfully focuses on the competence of Greeley's managers but overstates its thesis: the confused balloting was what clinched the nomination, not managerial manipulation and firm control. The best available biography of the Liberal nominee is Glyndon G. Van Deusen's *Horace Greeley: Nineteenth-Century Crusader* (Philadelphia: University of Pennsylvania Press, 1953), but his study is wholly inadequate in its description and analysis of the presidential campaign of 1872 and in its appraisal of Greeley as a campaigner. A probing psychological study of Greeley would be a welcome addition to the literature, as would a trenchant analysis of Carl Schurz. Overall, some historians tend to overemphasize the importance of the Liberals as a political force and as the decisive influence in causing national retreat from reconstruction. After all, the reform causes of the Liberal movement had little to do with either the actual canvass of the Liberal party in 1872 or with Horace Greeley's presidential strategy and campaign. Some historians also overstress the significance of the Liberal articulation of reconciliation, given the fact that the Liberals were not particularly effective in converting the northern electorate in 1872 or in changing the collective mind of the North afterward. The Liberals simply did not monopolize the reconciliation theme, as Ulysses S. Grant had demonstrated in 1868–1869. Similarly, the Liberals were not alone in voicing their dissatisfaction with reconstruction and in desiring northern escape from the southern problem, for northerners in general had been doing both all along, notably since 1867. On the Liberals in particular and on the canvass in general, see William Gillette's "Election of 1872," in

Arthur M. Schlesinger, Jr., and Fred L. Israel (eds.), *History of American Presidential Elections, 1789–1968* (New York: Chelsea House, 1971), 1303–30.

The long-neglected field of state studies is also improving. On the border states, see the one major survey: Richard O. Curry (ed.), *Radicalism, Racism, and Party Realignment: The Border States During Reconstruction* (Baltimore: Johns Hopkins University Press, 1969). On the North, there are a number of outstanding recent state histories: James C. Mohr (ed.), *Radical Republicans in the North: State Politics During Reconstruction* (Baltimore: Johns Hopkins University Press, 1976); James C. Mohr, *The Radical Republicans and Reform in New York During Reconstruction* (Ithaca: Cornell University Press, 1973); Frank B. Evans, *Pennsylvania Politics, 1872–1877: A Study in Leadership* (Harrisburg: Pennsylvania History and Museum Commission, 1966); Felice A. Bonadio, *North of Reconstruction: Ohio Politics, 1865–1870* (New York: New York University Press, 1970); Emma L. Thornbrough, *The Negro in Indiana: A Study of a Minority* (Indianapolis: Indiana Historical Bureau, 1957); Emma L. Thornbrough, *Indiana in the Civil War Era, 1850–1880* (Indianapolis: Indiana Historical Bureau and Indiana Historical Society, 1965); Richard N. Current, *The History of Wisconsin: The Civil War Era, 1848–1873* (Madison: State Historical Society of Wisconsin, 1976), among others. There is still a need, however, for book-length political analyses of such bellwether states as New York, Ohio, New Jersey, and Connecticut during the 1870s, as well as of the Negro in the North. A study of the Far West during reconstruction is being written by Eugene Berwanger.

Despite its importance, Grant's southern policy has been neglected by historians. The only study previous to this is Edwin C. Woolley's "Grant's Southern Policy." in James W. Garner (ed.), *Studies in Southern History and Politics Inscribed to William Archibald Dunning . . . by His Former Pupils the Authors* (New York: Columbia University Press, 1914), 179–201. Often taking Grant's words for his actions, the essay also confuses the problem of federal election enforcement with that of presidential intervention in a southern state. Three further studies exist, which in various ways are concerned with some aspects of Grant's southern policy. One is the only scholarly biography of Grant as president, William B. Hesseltine's unsatisfactory *Ulysses S. Grant*, which not only treats southern policy briefly and episodically, but also accepts many, though not all, of the Dunningite assumptions with regard to reconstruction. Add to that, simplistic, conspiratorial economic notions combined with inadequate research and the result is, for the most part, a superficial political analysis. Allan Nevins' authoritative biography on the secretary of state, *Hamilton Fish*, concentrates appropriately on diplomatic developments. Thanks to Nevins' effective, though by no means exhaustive, use of Fish's manuscripts, he provides the foundation for a larger view of the Grant administration. On the other hand, Nevins' treatment of southern policy, while brief and superficial, is also frequently misleading or erroneous, though it is nevertheless a bit more satisfactory than the same subject as dealt with in Hesseltine's biography. Finally, a recent and short treatment of Grant's southern policy is given in John A. Carpenter's *Ulysses S. Grant* (New York: Twayne, 1970), a work in which fifteen pages are devoted to it, but the nature of Grant's southern policy as well as the political and personal considerations that guided it and its consequences are not analyzed.

Two accounts filled with insights into the problems of southern Republicans are Richard N. Current's *Three Carpetbag Governors* (Baton Rouge: Louisiana State University Press, 1967), and Carl N. Degler's *The Other South: Southern Dissenters in the Nineteenth Century* (New York: Harper & Row, 1974); also useful is Otis A. Singletary's *Negro Militia and Reconstruction* (Austin: University of Texas Press, 1957). But there is a serious need for discerning biographies of such southern Republicans as Adelbert Ames, Rufus B. Bullock, Daniel H. Chamberlain, John M. Harlan, William W. Holden, and John L. Lynch.

On local political backgrounds, the histories of the southern states are invaluable. All but the most recent are evaluated in Randall and Donald's *Civil War and Reconstruction*, 817–26; I will only mention below those works that provide significant intrastate backgrounds relevant to my study. A helpful but dated history is Walter L. Fleming's *Civil War and Reconstruction in Alabama* (New York: Columbia University Press, 1905); however, a detailed revisionist study of state politics before 1875 would be welcome. On Arkansas, the two best works are Thomas S. Staples' *Reconstruction in Arkansas, 1862–1874* (New York: Columbia University Press, 1923), and George H. Thompson's *Arkansas and Reconstruction: The Influence of Geography, Economics, and Personality* (Port Washington, N. Y.: Kennikat, 1976); but a thorough revisionist history has yet to be written. With regard to Florida, there are two excellent studies: Joe M. Richardson's *The Negro in the Reconstruction of Florida, 1865–1877* (Tallahassee: Florida State University Press, 1974), and Jerrell H. Shofner's *Nor Is It Over Yet: Florida in the Era of Reconstruction, 1863–1877* (Gainesville: University Presses of Florida, 1974). Similarly, on Georgia there are two fine studies: Alan Conway's *The Reconstruction of Georgia* (Minneapolis: University of Minnesota Press, 1966), and Elizabeth Studley Nathans' *Losing the Peace: Georgia Republicans and Reconstruction, 1865–1871* (Baton Rouge: Louisiana State University Press, 1968).

For the two standard works on Louisiana, see Ella Lonn, *Reconstruction in Louisiana After 1868* (New York: G. P. Putnam's, 1918), a Dunning-school monograph, and Joe Gray Taylor, *Louisiana Reconstructed, 1863–1877* (Baton Rouge: Louisiana State University Press, 1974), a sweepingly revisionist corrective of that view. The value of Lonn's study lies in the details of a complicated political story, but the monograph is weak in interpretation, inadequate in its treatment of Grant's policy, and frequently erroneous in its characterization of northern public opinion. Taylor's book is a richer, more comprehensive study, including nonpolitical developments, but it lacks a detailed account of the state's political history; in other words, both Taylor's work and Conway's study of Georgia have the same strong points, but also the limitations of a sweepingly revisionist approach. On the problem of school segregation in Louisiana, see Louis R. Harlan, "Desegregation in New Orleans Public Schools During Reconstruction," *American Historical Review*, LXVII (1962), 663–75, and Roger A. Fischer's penetrating work *The Segregation Struggle in Louisiana, 1862–1877* (Urbana: University of Illinois

Press, 1974). The developments in Mississippi are covered by James Wilford Garner in *Reconstruction in Mississippi* (New York: Macmillan, 1901), and by Vernon Lane Wharton in *The Negro in Mississippi, 1865–1900* (Chapel Hill: University of North Carolina Press, 1947). See also p. 452.

Although there is still a call for a balanced revisionist history of North Carolina politics during the 1870s, as well as an authoritative biography of Zebulon B. Vance, three works cast light on the broader developments in the state: Trelease's *White Terror*; Otto H. Olsen's *Carpetbagger's Crusade: The Life of Albion Winegar Tourgée* (Baltimore: Johns Hopkins University Press, 1965), the standard biography; and Horace W. Raper's "William W. Holden: A Political Biography" (Ph.D. dissertation, University of North Carolina, 1951). Several historians have made distinguished contributions to the history of South Carolina during reconstruction; among the state studies, the two outstanding political accounts of the period 1869–1877 are: the pioneering work by Francis Butler Simkins and Robert Hilliard Woody, *South Carolina During Reconstruction* (Chapel Hill: University of North Carolina Press, 1932), and Joel Williamson's perceptive and equally pioneering *After Slavery: The Negro in South Carolina During Reconstruction, 1861–1877* (Chapel Hill: University of North Carolina Press, 1965). As for Texas, although a comprehensive revisionist history during reconstruction has yet to be written, two studies are: W. C. Nunn's *Texas Under the Carpetbaggers* (Austin: University of Texas Press, 1962), and John Pressley Carrier's "A Political History of Texas During the Reconstruction, 1865–1874" (Ph.D. dissertation, Vanderbilt University, 1971). For two excellent works on Virginia, see Jack P. Maddex, Jr., *The Virginia Conservatives, 1867–1879* (Chapel Hill: University of North Carolina Press, 1970), which somewhat overemphasizes the Virginia conservatives' tendency to be paternalistic; and Richard G. Lowe, "Republicans, Rebellion, and Reconstruction: The Republican Party in Virginia, 1856–1870" (Ph.D. dissertation, University of Virginia, 1968). But there is still a call for a history of the state Republican party in Virginia during the 1870s, and for a comprehensive study of southern blacks during reconstruction.

Heretofore, no extensive treatment of the critical congressional election of 1874 has existed, despite its evident importance, given the Democratic recapture of the House of Representatives. When briefly alluding to that election, historians have generally leaned toward an undiscriminating eclectic interpretation of the causes of Republican defeat and have frequently downgraded or dismissed the significance of the issues of civil rights and reconstruction. On the other hand, the Civil Rights Act of 1875 has received considerable attention, particularly in recent years. But only one work is noteworthy for its detailed elucidation of the legislative history—Alfred H. Kelly's "The Congressional Controversy Over School Segregation, 1867–1875," *American Historical Review*, LXIV (1959), 537–63, which is more successful and more persuasive in its description of the measure's fate during 1872 than in its revival during the years 1874–1875. Although the so-called "force bill" of 1875 is alluded to in several secondary accounts, the subject has not been covered in detail.

Despite numerous descriptions of the centennial celebration, some lengthy and others brief, a first-rate story of it has yet to be told. As for the presidential campaign of 1876, there is only one extensive account of it based on primary sources, Keith Ian Polakoff's *The Politics of Inertia: The Election of 1876 and the End of Reconstruction* (Baton Rouge: Louisiana State University Press, 1973), 13–200, which is strong on organizational matters relating to the canvass but does not place the presidential contest in the broader context of reconstruction developments; moreover, the author's bias against Hayes affects his judgment of the campaign, and the newspaper research is deficient. Alexander Clarence Flick's work on the Democratic nominee, *Samuel Jones Tilden: A Study in Political Sagacity* (New York: Dodd, Mead, 1939), is detailed and thorough, but the author is uncritical of Tilden as a politician and unaware of the various dimensions of reconstruction; thus there is still no incisive interpretation of Tilden as a politician. The same generalization holds true for Rutherford B. Hayes, who has been the subject of several biographies, none of them brilliant.

On the electoral dispute, extensive work has been done and six accounts of it are noteworthy. The first major study, Paul Leland Haworth's *The Hayes-Tilden Disputed Presidential Election of 1876* (Cleveland: Burrows, 1906), recounts the political and legal story. Although narrow in approach, deficient in research, and overly dependent on the published official record, the book is still sound and useful in some respects. C. Vann Woodward's pioneering *Reunion and Reaction: The Compromise of 1877 and the End of Reconstruction* (Boston: Little, Brown, 1951), is a seminal study, with a provocative thesis that downgrades the importance of the narrowly political discussions during the electoral crisis emphasized by Haworth and instead sees broader political-economic forces at work. Thanks to Woodward's resourceful and prodigious research, he uncovered many of the intrigues that characterized those frantic months. The best available but nevertheless disappointing biography of Hayes, Harry Barnard's *Rutherford B. Hayes and His America* (Indianapolis: Bobbs-Merrill, 1954), contains a great deal of information but is weak in its interpretation of the electoral dispute. Recent critiques that raise important questions regarding Woodward's thesis are Joseph Frazier Wall's *Henry Watterson: Reconstructed Rebel* (New York: Oxford University Press, 1956), and Allan Peskin's "Was There a Compromise?" *Journal of American History*, LX (1973), 63–75, to which Woodward added a rejoinder "Yes, There Was a Compromise of 1877," *Journal of American History*, LX (1973), 215–23. Moreover, Polakoff in his *Politics of Inertia*, despite interpretative gaps and meager newspaper research, makes the most detailed case for the primacy of political considerations. In particular, both Peskin and Polakoff question whether the parties to the alleged compromise of 1877 were in fact in control of events, whether the economic portions of the so-called agreement were as significant as Woodward maintains, whether the effects of the purported deal lasted as long as has been contended, and whether Woodward has not mistaken one part of the picture for the whole. These are all, in any case, complex matters that raise fundamental questions. It would be helpful if an historian did a statistical analysis of congressional voting in chronological sequence with regional patterns, if there are any, but the problems of the beliefs and the motivations of the participants still remain. It is to Professor Woodward's credit to have formulated a provocative thesis that continues to stimulate interest and further investigation. One matter, however, needs to be kept in mind: most of the writers mentioned above tend, in varying degrees, to overstate the electoral dispute's effect on the outcome of reconstruction. Since that electoral crisis was unique and dramatic, the historical significance of the dispute and its resolution have been exaggerated.

Hayes's presidency has been treated extensively and, in contrast to Grant's, has more often been given every benefit of the doubt; but Hayes's overall performance in the White House deserves a probing examination rather than the usual sentimental apology. The only extensive analytical treatment of Hayes's southern policy is in Vincent P. De Santis' *Republicans Face the Southern Question—The New Departure Years, 1877–1897* (Baltimore: Johns Hopkins University Press, 1959), 9–132; and the most detailed coverage of Republican southern policy between 1879 and 1897 was done by Stanley P. Hirshson in his *Farewell to the Bloody Shirt: Northern Republicans and the Southern Negro, 1877–1893* (Bloomington: Indiana University Press, 1962). Both books, however, must be supplemented by the major political studies of the postreconstruction period so as to place the southern question in the larger political context.

In a recent work, James M. McPherson's *The Abolitionist Legacy: From Reconstruction to the NAACP* (Princeton: Princeton University Press, 1975), the author devotes his first part to the 1870s. The study is based on prodigious research regarding a number of abolitionists and their descendents who are extensively quoted on their reactions to political events, but McPherson made almost no attempt to analyze the events in themselves, or to explain how and why the abolitionists' objectives and methods proved unsuccessful. Then, because he stressed the efforts of some of them in the realm of philanthropy and education, he glossed over the more significant fact that many of them defected from progressive politics during the 1870s; moreover, the ambivalence of many white reformers in general and of many abolitionists in particular is not emphasized enough. As a result, the author dealt with the central political retreat from reconstruction peripherally and relegated it to the background.

Finally, although substantial progress has been made in the field of reconstruction history, with the recent literature on the subject having gained in coverage, depth, and excellence, important gaps remain and need to be filled. In completing this task I believe that the postrevisionist approach is the most fruitful one. Postrevisionism does not reject revisionism; it is certainly not reactionary in the sense of returning to the undeserved abuse and prejudicial condemnation that characterized the views of the Dunningite historians. However, postrevisionism does seek to replace the tendency of certain neorevisionist historians to overestimate the accomplishments of reconstruction and provide apologies for its shortcomings; thus the postrevisionist approach attempts to provide a fresh view with which to analyze the limits of legislation and the manifest failures of reconstruction.

ACKNOWLEDGMENTS

THIS BOOK would not have been possible but for two leaves of absence and the financial support I have received from the Social Science Research Council and the Research Council and Faculty Academic Study Program of Rutgers—the State University of New Jersey—as well as research grants from the Research Council of Rutgers University, the Penrose Fund of the American Philosophical Society, the Social Science Research Council, the Graduate Center of the City University of New York, and Ohio State University.

I wish to thank Johns Hopkins University Press and Chelsea House Publishers for permission to use material drawn from my studies of federal election enforcement in the borderland and the presidential election of 1872, versions of which originally appeared in Richard O. Curry (ed.), *Radicalism, Racism, and Party Realignment: The Border States During Reconstruction* (Baltimore, 1969), 265–304; and in Arthur M. Schlesinger, Jr., and Fred L. Israel (eds.), *History of American Presidential Elections, 1789–1968* (New York, 1971), II, pp. 1303–30, respectively.

I also wish to thank everyone who has helped me in the course of research and writing and to acknowledge in particular the aid I have received in various ways from the following individuals: Julius Abeson, Mary Addy, Laura Akerman, Anne Brugh, Howard Burr, the late Samuel Caplain, Barbara Coburn, Lois DeJulio, Karl Easton, Bob Gillette, Martin Haas, Jodith Janes, Louise Janes, John Little, William L. McGill, James K. Martin, Richard Mendales, Mary Northrop, Pauline Ames Plimpton, Horace Raper, Margaret Samartino, Charles Segal, Heidi Seitz, Thelma Tate, Ross Webb, Harry Winner, and Leonard Levy.

The staffs of certain research libraries deserve special commendation, notably that of the Rutherford B. Hayes Library, under the able direction of Watt Marchman and with the great help of its manuscripts librarian Thomas Smith, the extremely efficient and hospitable Ohio Historical Society, the Library of Congress, where Oliver Orr, among others, has been especially helpful, as has Ferris Stovel at the National Archives. Also extremely helpful was Joe Akerman, who so kindly lent me the letterbook of Amos T. Akerman.

ACKNOWLEDGMENTS

I completed a draft of the manuscript on March 2, 1978. Twenty-seven days later my father, Samuel Gillette, died after a long illness. I will always be grateful to him and to my mother, Lillian Gillette, for encouraging my interest in history and geography and for providing support for my undergraduate education.

In the latter stage of research, a former student of mine, Eleanor Wyckoff, volunteered to serve as my unpaid assistant; she helped immeasurably as researcher, copyreader, and critic.

To my friends, former students, and colleagues, I have a special debt. I thank William C. Harris, who furnished parts of two chapters of his new book, *The Day of the Carpetbagger: Republican Reconstruction in Mississippi* (Baton Rouge: Louisiana State University Press, 1979). Certain individuals, Eugene Berwanger, James Brennan, Susan Buzby Denitzio, Thomas Denitzio, Charles Fairman, Howard Glickstein, William C. Harris, Sidney Hook, Milton Janes, Jonathan Lurie, Gerald Pomper, Stephen Salmore, William Van Alstyne, and Margaret Wyszomirski read a part of or an entire chapter; Herman Belz, Fred Nicklason, and Allan Peskin read several chapters; Richard N. Current, David Herbert Donald, Elisabeth Gillette, June Guicharnaud, James Halsey, Sylvia Hutchinson, Graham Knight, David Miller, Sidney Ratner, Fred Russell, Claire Simon, Hans Trefousse, Eleanor Wyckoff, and Mary Young read the entire work at various stages in the preparation of the manuscript. I thank immensely all of them for their thoughtful suggestions and helpful criticisms. Of course, I remain solely responsible for all faults of organization and interpretation as well as errors in research and proofreading.

It was my good fortune to have the support and help of three fine editors at the Louisiana State University Press: Beverly Jarrett, Martha Hall, and Mary Jane Di Piero.

My wife, Elisabeth L. Gillette, as resourceful researcher, diligent typist, and penetrating critic, all while overseeing exuberant son Scott and beguiling daughter Wendy, as well as completing her library training, made the greatest contribution. I dedicate this book to Elisa.

INDEX

Abolitionists: support Negro suffrage, 6, 17–19, 23, 24, 64, 309; on federal southern policy, 82, 124, 346; on civil rights, 263; approach questioned, 191, 237–39, 287, 301

Adams, Charles Francis, Sr., 62, 126, 248

Adams, Henry, 185

Adams, John Quincy, 360

Akerman, Amos T.: on southern judges, 33; on Klan issue, 46, 47; on election enforcement, 50; on Republican employees, 50; on Ga. election, 90; on northern neglect, 90, 183; advises N.C. authorities, 92; replaced as attorney general, 97; advises on La., 107; ignores racial discrimination, 195; on southern Democratic purposes and tactics, 228–29, 307, 313, 346, 349, 352, 376–77; on northern flinching (1874), 253; criticizes Congress's priorities (1875), 292; on northern Republicans' changing needs (1876–1877), 324; on Hayes's policy, 349–50, 361; on southern Republicans, 367; on unexercised rights, 435

Alabama: politics (1870), 94–96, 166; politics (1872), 96–99, 103, 166, 168; election (1874), 98, 99, 103, 153, 218–19, 226, 230, 233, 251, 289, 409; mentioned, 33, 42, 43, 50, 80, 166, 183, 244, 276, 281–82, 291, 311, 386, 434–35

Albany (N.Y.) *Journal*, 273, 285

Alcorn, James L., 204

Ames, Adelbert, 150–64, 181, 248

Amnesty, 13, 60, 61, 66, 69, 72, 80, 81, 99, 378, 389

Arkansas: Brooks-Baxter dispute, 118, 136–45, 166, 168, 230, 398; politics (1875), 145–50, 166, 168, 173, 175, 260, 281, 374–75, 398–99; mentioned, 42, 166, 187, 218, 230, 251, 291, 311, 351

Army; southern occupation, 6, 11, 13; U.S. Military Academy, 12, 73, 100; and election enforcement, 25, 33–37, 49, 230–31, 253, 255, 260, 309–10, 317–19, 351, 354–56, 370; distribution in South, 35, 36, 363, 378–79, 385, 431; president's use of in South, 79, 80, 170–74, 177, 182, 248, 333, 347–48, 370; in Ga., 88, 230; N.C., 91, 94, 168; Ala., 95–98, 230; Texas, 99, 100, 385; La., 105–35, 140, 147, 158, 169, 171–72, 230, 237, 264, 272, 286, 294, 315, 325, 385; Ark., 136, 139–40, 143–44, 230; Miss., 151–52, 155–64, 172; S.C., 168, 230, 307, 317–19, 325, 385; appropriations, 260, 293, 354–57, 384; and electoral dispute, 325, 331; removal from statehouses, 330–33, 336–47, 352, 360, 375, 427–28, 430; use in labor union riots, 348, 431

Arthur, William E., 27

Atkins, Helen D., 431

Atkins, James, 438

Atlanta, Ga., 88, 90, 351, 432

Atlanta *Constitution*, 217, 275

Atlantic Monthly, 68, 69

Augusta, Ga., 276, 319

Augusta *Constitutionalist*, 308, 310

Newark *Advertiser*, 216, 274, 292
New Hampshire, 189, 365
New Jersey, 5, 9, 66, 70, 119, 156, 194–97, 220, 256, 320, 327, 360, 413
New Mexico Territory, 260
New Orleans, La., 104–23, 127–30, 133, 168–69, 184, 195, 234, 236, 282, 308, 315, 318–19, 330–33, 339, 341–42, 344–45, 347, 375, 427, 430
New Orleans *Daily Picayune*, 126–27, 166, 286
New Orleans *Louisianian*, 354
New Orleans *Times*, 118
New York, mentioned, 6, 9, 11, 14, 48, 49, 126, 132, 186–87, 194, 196, 214–15, 237, 244–49, 261, 275, 284, 305, 309, 319–20, 336, 406, 410, 416, 420, 437
New York City, 7, 13, 48, 49, 57, 70, 126, 128, 193–94, 214, 277, 308, 319–20, 323–24
New York *Evening Post*: on election enforcement, 53, 54; elections, 67, 69, 70, 189, 300, 309–10; federal southern policy, 95, 96, 151–52; Negro rights, 304, 368
New York *Herald*: on elections, 6, 10, 13, 223, 306, 309, 317; federal southern policy, 98, 102, 107, 112, 122, 140, 147, 149, 152, 155, 159, 182, 298, 347, 395; Grant, 176; civil rights, 191, 200, 269–70, 277; electoral crisis, 329
New York *Sun*, 73, 140, 225
New York *Times*: elections, 10, 68, 72, 211–12, 215, 233–34, 241, 243, 246, 253, 255, 301, 372–73, 435; inaugural ball (1869), 21; federal southern policy, 84, 93, 97, 119, 140, 152, 159, 180, 285, 352–54, 433, 438; civil rights, 199, 205, 208, 209, 273–75; election enforcement law, 298; priority of the North, 372–73, 375
New York *Tribune*: on elections, 24, 159, 190, 223, 230, 232–33, 237; federal southern policy, 159, 348; Cushing, 187; civil rights, 203, 208, 266, 278; Hayes, 358; mentioned, 2, 62
New York *World*: on elections, 7, 14, 62, 63, 215, 238, 254–55; Grant, 22, 77; election enforcement, 42, 47, 48; inaugural ball (1873), 74; federal southern policy, 126, 285, 428; civil rights, 266, 275
Niblack, William E., 224

Nicholls, Francis T., 314–15, 340–41, 344–45
Nordhoff, Charles, 180, 258
North Carolina: Holden's tenure, 90–94, 103, 166–67; election (1874), 220–26, 229, 408, 411; mentioned, 3, 15, 32, 35, 36, 38, 42, 54, 145, 166, 176, 182, 192, 207, 276, 349, 351, 386, 390, 426
Norton, Charles Eliot, 358

Ohio: election (1867), 7, 8; election (1874), 219, 237–38, 241–44, 249, 256, 411; election (1875), 158–59, 163–64, 168; mentioned, 11–15, 22, 46, 47, 53, 66, 68, 127, 186, 194, 257, 272, 293, 300, 304, 321–22, 335, 345, 350, 352–53, 355, 358, 361, 366, 375, 389, 400, 422
Oregon, 321–24, 332, 384, 423, 425

Packard, Stephen B., 106–108, 111, 115, 314, 333, 337–47, 427, 429
Pardons, 4, 5, 36, 45
Pease, Henry R., 204
Pendleton, George H., 14, 239
Penn, David B., 117–20
Pennsylvania: 9, 16, 64, 66, 194, 219, 244–47, 256–57, 309, 321, 353, 389–90
Phelps, William W., 256–57
Philadelphia, Pa., 11, 41, 49, 59, 193–94, 203, 236, 307
Philadelphia *American and Gazette*, 294–95
Philadelphia *Inquirer*, 209
Philadelphia *Press*, 243, 272–75, 437
Philadelphia *Times*, 339, 343, 435
Phillips, Wendell, 18, 23, 124, 263
Pierrepont, Edwards, 156–64, 215, 312, 400
Pike, James S., 180
Pinchback, Pinckney B. S., 111, 131, 260, 302, 332
Pine Bluff, Ark., 141, 145
Pittsburgh, Pa., 19, 67, 244
Pittsburgh *Post*, 63
Poland, Luke P., 146–49, 236
Poll tax, 18, 29, 38, 41, 42, 46, 283, 295, 311, 320
Pomeroy, Theodore M., 214–15
Pool, John, 54
Poore, Benjamin Perley, 419
Porter, James D., 342
Pratt, Daniel D., 204